INTERNATIONAL MARKETING STRATEGY

Titles of Related Interest

ALLEN
Sales and Distribution Guide to Malaysia

BUBNOV
Foreign Trade with the USSR: A Manager's Guide to Recent Reforms

CAMPBELL
A Strategic Guide to Equity Joint Ventures in China

CAMPBELL & ADLINGTON
China Business Strategies

DAVIS
Managing and Organizing Multinational Corporations

DOZ
Strategic Management in Multinational Companies

RENARD
Sales and Distribution Guide to Thailand

SASAKI
Management and Industrial Structure in Japan, 2nd Edition

Related Journals*

Ecotass

Long Range Planning

Omega

Scandinavian Journal of Management

* Free specimen copy available on request.

INTERNATIONAL MARKETING STRATEGY

THIRD EDITION

Edited by

HANS B. THORELLI
S . TAMER CAVUSGIL

PERGAMON PRESS
Member of Maxwell Macmillan Pergamon Publishing Corporation
OXFORD · NEW YORK · BEIJING · FRANKFURT
SÃO PAULO · SYDNEY · TOKYO · TORONTO

U.K.	Pergamon Press plc, Headington Hill Hall, Oxford OX3 0BW, England.
U.S.A.	Pergamon Press, Inc., Maxwell House, Fairview Park, Elmsford, New York 10523, U.S.A.
PEOPLE'S REPUBLIC OF CHINA	Pergamon Press, Room 4037, Qianmen Hotel, Beijing, People's Republic of China
FEDERAL REPUBLIC OF GERMANY	Pergamon Press GmbH, Hammerweg 6, D-6242 Kronberg, Federal Republic of Germany
BRAZIL	Pergamon Editora Ltda, Rua Eça de Queiros, 346, CEP 04011, Paraiso, São Paulo, Brazil
AUSTRALIA	Pergamon Press Australia Pty Ltd., P.O. Box 544, Potts Point, N.S.W. 2011, Australia
JAPAN	Pergamon Press, 5th Floor, Matsuoka Central Building, 1-7-1 Nishishinjuku, Shinjuku-ku, Tokyo 160, Japan
CANADA	Pergamon Press Canada Ltd., Suite No. 271, 253 College Street, Toronto, Ontario, Canada M5T 1R5

First edition 1973

Second (revised) edition 1980

Third edition 1990

Library of Congress Cataloging in Publication Data
International marketing strategy/edited by Hans B. Thorelli, S. Tamer Cavusgil. — 3rd ed.
p. cm.
Includes bibliographical references.
1. Export marketing. 2. Marketing. 3. International business enterprises—Management. I. Thorelli, Hans Birger, 1921— II. Cavusgil, S. Tamer.
HF1416.I64 1990   658.8'48—dc20   90—7123.

British Library Cataloguing in Publication Data
International marketing strategy.—3rd. ed.
1. International marketing
I. Thorelli, Hans B. (Hans Birger) *1921* — II. Cavusgil, S. Tamer
658.848

ISBN 0—08—036285—0 (Hard cover)
ISBN 0—08—036284—2 (Flexicover)

Printed in Great Britain by BPCC Wheatons Ltd, Exeter

Contents

PREFACE   1

INTRODUCTION   3

Part I Conceptual Foundations

1. International Marketing: An Ecological View
   HANS B. THORELLI   13

2. The Gains from Trade
   The Economist   31

3. Some New Competitive Factors in International Marketing
   RICHARD D. ROBINSON   39

4. Becoming a Triad Power: The New Global Corporation
   KENICHI OHMAE   57

5. Networks: The Gay Nineties in International Marketing
   HANS B. THORELLI   73

6. International Marketing and Purchasing of Industrial Goods:
   An Interaction Approach
   HÅKAN HÅKANSSON   87

7. Export Trading Companies in World Markets: A Conceptual
   View
   LYN S. AMINE   103

8. Assessment of Company Readiness to Export
   S. TAMER CAVUSGIL AND ROBERT W. NASON   129

Further Reading — Part I   141

Part II Internationalization of the Firm

9. On the Internationalization Process of Firms
S. TAMER CAVUSGIL   147

10. Japan's Kao Enters U.S. Cautiously with Jergens Co.
JEREMY MARK AND MASAYOSHI KANABAYASHI   161

11. Wilkinson's New Edge
JOACHIM SCHYPEK   165

12. Selling Swedish Style
JUDY STEED   173

13. Western Ways: How a German Firm Joined with Soviets to
Make Good Shoes
THOMAS F. O'BOYLE   179

14. Selling to Japan: We Did it Their Way
FRED REINSTEIN   185

Further Reading — Part II   195

Part III Global Markets

15. A Market-Oriented Clustering of Countries
S. TAMER CAVUSGIL   201

16. The Promise and Challenges of Europe 1992
Business International   213

17. The New Powers of Asia
LOUIS KRAAR   221

18. Marketing Environment in the Middle East and North
Africa: The Forces behind Market Homogenization
LYN S. AMINE AND S. TAMER CAVUSGIL   229

19. What can Third World Countries Learn from China?
HANS B. THORELLI   249

20. Marketing to the Third World Countries
OSMAN ATAC AND S. TAMER CAVUSGIL   261

Further Reading — Part III   277

Part IV Researching, Understanding, and Negotiating for Global Market Opportunities

21. Guidelines for Export Market Research
   S. TAMER CAVUSGIL   283

22. Market Research the Japanese Way
   JOHNY K. JOHANSSON AND IKUJIRO NONAKA   297

23. Demand Estimation in a Developing Country Environment: Difficulties, Techniques and Examples
   LYN S. AMINE AND S. TAMER CAVUSGIL   305

24. Customer Analysis for Strategy Development in Industrial Markets
   N. C. G. CAMPBELL AND M. T. CUNNINGHAM   327

25. The Information Seekers: Multinational Strategy Target
   HANS B. THORELLI   341

26. Guidelines for International Business Negotiations
   PERVEZ N. GHAURI   353

Further Reading — Part IV   367

Part V Market Entry Strategies

27. International Market Entry and Expansion via Independent or Integrated Channels of Distribution
   ERIN ANDERSON AND ANNE T. COUGHLAN   373

28. Diffusion of Franchise System Use in International Operations
   LAWRENCE S. WELCH   383

29. The Bright Future of Service Exports
   RICHARD I. KIRKLAND, JR.   397

30. Marketing to China: Still the Silk Road
   HANS B. THORELLI AND JOSEPH Y. BATTAT   403

31. How Caterpillar China Coped with Key Obstacles in Major Licensing Deal
Business International   415

32. MicroAge Targets Japan's Small Businesses in Franchising Venture
Business International   419

33. How Japan Won a Contract to Build Turkey a Bridge
LAWRENCE INGRASSIA   423

34. Strategic Alliances – Guidelines for Success
GODFREY DEVLIN AND MARK BLEACKLEY   431

35. International Barter and Countertrade
SANDRA HUSZAGH AND FREDRICK HUSZAGH   439

36. Countertrade Suits Metallgesellschaft Fine
GEORGE MELLOAN   449

Further Reading — Part V   453

Part VI Developing, Implementing, and Controlling the International Marketing Mix

37. Marketing-Mix Standardization: An Integrated Approach in Global Marketing
RALF T. KREUTZER   459

38. International Product Positioning
JOHNY K. JOHANSSON AND HANS B. THORELLI   471

39. Distributors — Finding and Keeping the Good Ones
GUNNAR BEETH   487

40. Black & Decker's Turnaround Strategy
Business International   495

41. 3M's Global Marketing Plan: How a New Package Helped its Worldwide Reorganization
Business International   499

42. Unravelling the Mystique of Export Pricing
    S. TAMER CAVUSGIL   503

43. Price Escalation in International Marketing
    HELMUT BECKER   523

44. Taking Advantage of Trade Fairs for Maximum Sales
    Impact
    Business International   527

45. How Multinationals Can Counter Gray Market Imports
    S. TAMER CAVUSGIL AND ED SIKORA   531

Further Reading — Part VI   551

Part VII Integrated Marketing Planning and Action

46. Strategic Planning in International Marketing
    HANS B. THORELLI AND HELMUT BECKER   557

47. Strategic Planning for a Global Business ec, ppll, stra
    BALAJI S. CHAKRAVARTHY AND HOWARD V. PERLMUTTER   569

48. Japanese Export Marketing: Structures, Strategies and
    Counterstrategies sukima/suprise
    JOHNY K. JOHANSSON AND IKUJIRO NONAKA   585

49. Kodak's Matrix System Focuses on Product Business Units
    Business International   601

50. Performance Audits: The MNC Through the Glasses of the
    LDC
    HANS B. THORELLI   605

Further Reading Part VII   619

GENERAL READINGS IN INTERNATIONAL MARKETING   621

GLOSSARY   623

COUNTRY INDEX   625

COMPANY INDEX 627

NAME INDEX 629

SUBJECT INDEX 631

APPENDIX: NEW TECHNIQUES FOR EXECUTIVE DEVELOPMENT AND
TRAINING IN INTERNATIONAL BUSINESS/MARKETING 637

ABOUT THE EDITORS 639

Preface

You are looking at the third edition of a book on international marketing strategy. The first edition (1973) and the second, revised edition (1980) were both sold out within a few years of their publication. The rapidly changing world marketing environment as well as the availability of excellent new writing on the subject prompted this third edition.

In preparing this book of readings, original editor Hans B. Thorelli has been joined by Professor S. Tamer Cavusgil as co-editor. Our theme, strategic thinking and action in international marketing, is carried forward from the earlier editions. In most specifics the contents are changed, however, on the basis of extensive search, sifting, and editing. We can say with confidence that within this compact volume each contribution covers an important topic and each principal article is written by an outstanding expert. With the exception of a few articles which withstood the test of relevance over time, all of the readings are new to this edition.

The third edition of *International Marketing Strategy* puts a premium on managerial applications. There are also several readings which are case studies of actual successes or failures in international marketing, each illustrating the prime points made in the main articles. Many of these, too, are interspersed with concrete examples.

The third edition also features a "global" orientation, discussing frequently industries or companies outside of North America. Selections come from a large number of worldwide publications. Several contributions are original. Each article has been carefully edited and, in most cases, abridged in order to eliminate redundancy. Continuity in the book is maintained by a short introduction preceding each of the seven parts.

Previous users of *International Marketing Strategy* indicated that they have found the indices and listings of further readings quite useful. Therefore, we maintained these features in the third edition. Each part offers additional "further reading." There is also a general reading list at the end of the book. There are four separate indices — country, company, name, and subject. Finally the Appendix provides

1

information about the new version of the international business computer simulation, INTOPIA.

We expect the book to be equally well adapted to executives and students, for reasons detailed in the introduction. It will also be useful to public policymakers who wish to understand the operations and motivations of the companies they deal with in performing their administrative duties. Above all, we expect that readers from all corners of the globe will find ideas and counsel of value to them. We all need to learn from each other — and we all benefit in the process.

Introduction

The Blooming Importance of International Marketing

International business is blooming as well as important. The value of world exports in 1988 was about 2.6 trillion (2,694 billion or 2,694,000 million) U.S. dollars. Export trade has grown at an annual rate of approximately 12% over the past decade. Of course, export trade is only a part of the total international business activity. When one considers foreign direct investment and the local subsidiary sales of multinational companies abroad, the figures are even more impressive.

Many countries are vitally dependent on international commerce. Belgium and Holland derive more than 50% of their gross national products from world trade. South Korea exports 46% of its output. For most industrial nations the figure is over 20%. Traditionally, among Western industrialized countries, the U.S.A. has been least dependent on international trade, which accounts for only about 7% of GNP. Nonetheless, due to the magnitude of the American economy, this modest share is sufficient to make the U.S.A. one of the largest trading partners of the world.

West Germany, U.S.A. and Japan are the largest traders of the world. For the past three decades, the U.S. share of the world market has been declining for two reasons. First, with more rapid economic development in many other countries it is only natural that the trade of those countries has increased more rapidly than that of the U.S.A. Second, the rest of the industrial world has been catching up with American technology, managerial knowhow, and financial prowess. These have been the prime sources of U.S. competitive strength. Paradoxically, American management — the originator of modern marketing concepts and wonderfully adept at implementing these concepts at home — has often been woefully inept in applying them abroad. In view of future U.S. international economic dependence, American business clearly faces an enormous challenge in international marketing.

Clearly, in years ahead international marketing will be even more pervasive than it is today. Indeed, most business will be either globetrotters or globewatchers. Globetrotters, an increasing proportion of all firms, are those who engage in export, import, or production

3

abroad; this group is likely to set the pace in most economies of the world. Those who elect to stay at home will have to be globewatchers; that is, they will have to face up to ever-increasing competition with overseas firms in their own home market. Even such a trite local venture as the village barbershop will have to follow international fashions on hair colors and hairdos, or face the prospect (hair-raising as it may be) of extinction. Indeed, globewatching in general has great merit: *by observing marketing in other cultures, the executive (or the student) frequently gains a better understanding of marketing in his own.*

With the Reader in Mind

This being a book on marketing, we have attempted to keep the customer in mind. We envisage two groups of readers: seasoned executives and university students of business. The manager should find the book integrated and comprehensive to hold its own, whether he personally is a globetrotter or a domestic executive sizing up the international scene. The book also caters to the business student looking for a single concentrated source on international operations. In academic curricula focused on marketing or international business, this collection of readings should find its prime use as a fairly rich supplement to any textbook.

It should be evident, then, that we are assuming some practical or theoretical familiarity with marketing management and at least the rudiments of international trade policy and theory. While the book does specialize on international marketing our selections have been made in full awareness of the fact that in international operations, more than elsewhere, marketing is inextricably intertwined with other management functions. Let it not be forgotten: in nine cases out of ten international business begins with export or import and the lifeblood of the international firm is marketing abroad.

The treatment here differs from most other books of readings in international marketing. This collection has an integrative framework to both guide and stimulate the reader — and to ensure a useful selection of readings. In contrast to other books of readings which deal with differences in domestic operating conditions (comparative marketing), this collection focuses on *international marketing*. It is more analytical then descriptive — we feel that descriptive material, in these fast-moving times, ages rapidly. To promote integration of materials we have edited and abbreviated a great many selections. In this manner, too, it has been possible to include a greater number and range of contributions. We have also minimized incest by overlap — too many articles are making the rounds of the readings books. By digging further, we are able to present here many valuable contributions not elsewhere reprinted. Finally, in an unorthodox twist, we have resorted to excerpts from books and monographs when no suitable articles were at hand — or have tailor-made readings ourselves.

The level of generalization aimed at is that of the practically oriented and analytically interested executive, as well as of the university student contemplating a career in international marketing at home or abroad. We are avoiding the extreme of generality as found in some background writings on cultural anthropology and international economics as well as the opposite extreme of specificity as encountered in the export-manual type of discussion of bills of lading and letters of credit. The watchword is managerial pragmatism based on sound theory.

Our purpose, then, is to provide an analytical framework in international marketing rather than specific answers for the concrete situation. The objective is to help the reader define the problems he is likely to encounter in international marketing, bearing in mind that defining the problem is the most important prerequisite to solving it. The executive and the student have a characteristic in common: they are looking for impulses to stimulate their own thinking rather than for a set of patent medicines allegedly curing all maladies. The present collection is intended to meet this need. It should enable the reader to make his own diagnosis of differences and similarities in marketing structures around the world, and it provides guidelines for the planning of appropriate marketing strategies.

The book should be equally relevant whether the reader (or his company) be European, Asian, or American, a national of an industrialized or of an industrializing country. We have tried to avoid items looking at the world as a kind of enlarged Yankee playground.

Success Formula: Harmonizing Structure and Strategy

Ultimately, the whole field of marketing revolves around a single key question: how to adapt marketing strategy to the prevailing market conditions (i.e., the market structure). Whoever has the answer to this question carries the key to success. In domestic marketing it takes no great discerning skills to see that the marketing of ladies' fashion goods differs from that of cigarettes, which in turn differs from the marketing of petro-chemicals or construction equipment. But to note such gross differences is not enough. They are of little interest to a hosiery manufacturer trying to find a niche next to twenty other hosiery manufacturers all catering to the same general market. The rise and fall of firms and brands about which we read daily in the financial pages shows that even subtle variations in strategy may spell the differences between failure and success in the marketplace.

The principal distinction between domestic and international marketing is that as you move from the former to the latter the problem of harmonizing (or "matching") strategy and structure takes on two *additional* dimensions. One set of complications is encountered in the interface between nations: tariffs, quotas and invisible trade barriers, xenophobia, currency problems, embargoes, and other manifestations of nationalism and international politics. The second array of complications stems from the very fact that one deals with two or more markets on the international scene. Market structures for a given product may vary appreciably from one country to the next due to such factors as differences in values, lifestyles, economic development, government regulation of business, and political stability. The scale of operations apart, a soft drink can be successfully marketed in almost the same way in New York and Bombay, but this clearly is not the case with beef hamburgers. The free automarkets of Europe differ drastically from the rigidly regimented ones in most Latin American countries. Superciliously, an economist may tell you that the differences between domestic and international operations are only a matter of degree. Remind him that so is a difference between normal body temperature and one five degrees above (or below).

The Plan of the Book

This collection of readings is somewhat unique in the number of contributions included in a compact volume, as suggested above. To bring this bounty together, all the while minimizing overlaps, it was necessary to excerpt and edit several items. Such an approach was possible only due to the outstanding cooperation of participating authors.

Beyond seeking coverage for relevant areas of subject matter, the selection of readings in central parts of the book has been guided by two principal concerns. We have tried to provide an integrated mix of survey-type, conceptually oriented articles with quite specific contributions oriented to particular markets or firms. We have also tried to have a balance of articles covering industrialized nations, emerging industrial countries, developing countries, and East Bloc nations.

The general scheme is as follows:

Part I identifies harmonization of market structure and marketing strategy as the key to success in international operations and provides an analytical framework for the parts to follow. Various thoughtful essays in this section provide the conceptual foundations of contemporary international marketing practices.

Part II highlights the internationalization process of the firm. Short case stories illustrate the process and common patterns in "going international." The company examples lead to interesting observations and conclusions about the internationalization process.

Part III exposes world markets for the reader. The thesis of the first reading — that markets require in-depth attention by the international marketer — is explored by the remaining selections in this part.

Part IV deals with the analytical techniques for assessing market opportunities. Selections address the international customer analysis as well as the differential availability of market data, and other aspects of marketing infrastructure. Negotiations in the international context are also discussed.

Part V is concerned with market entry strategies. Entry modes from franchising to strategic alliances and countertrade are illustrated with company examples.

Part VI is focused on the harmonization of marketing strategy and market structure. Product, pricing, promotion, and distribution strategies in different environments are given special emphasis.

Part VII pulls the threads of the book together. The marketing plan is viewed as the practical means by which market structure and strategy may be harmonized. What is involved in international marketing planning is analyzed both at the conceptual level and in down-to-earth, checklist fashion.

The reader will note that each Part concludes with a "Further Reading" list to complement and reinforce our selections.

Acknowledgment

The co-editors were assisted by several individuals in the preparation of this book. Tiger Li, a doctoral candidate in International Business at Michigan State University, was instrumental in the process of editing each selected article and preparing the various indices. Our administrative support staff at Michigan State and Indiana provided cheerful assistance. Finally, Senior Editor Sammye Haigh and others at Pergamon Press are owed credit for bringing this product into fruition.

I
Conceptual Foundations

Introduction to Part I

From the production-oriented idea and the customer-directed philosophy to the ecologic view, the concepts of international marketing have experienced a gradual evolution over the last three decades. The purpose of Part I is to acquaint readers with different concepts and views in international marketing. Familiarity with those concepts will not only provide marketing scholars with guidance in their research but also allow practitioners to design successful marketing strategies.

The first reading by Thorelli evaluates the traditional views of marketing and introduces the ecologic perspective which sees the firm, the marketing strategy, and marketing environment as an open interacting system. This ecological view provides the main theme of the book — it stresses the fact that the environment is in a constant flux and the firm has to continually react, interact, and proact for the sake of survival.

Robinson in the third reading challenges the "global homogenization of markets" proposition advanced by Levitt. The author argues that the world markets are more likely to become increasingly fractured by culturally and environmentally based preferences. Robinson also discusses how to use "value added chain" as a useful tool for assessing a company's international competitive strategies.

In recent years, the Triad (Japan, Western Europe and the United States) have emerged as the most important strategic battlefield for any company operating on a global scale. Ohmae in the fourth reading points out that old strategies and organizational frameworks designed to reach 200 million customers at most have become insufficient in the Triad's new and dynamic markets of 600 million people. The author examines the steps some companies have already taken toward becoming a Triad power.

Whether a company is ready to export is a question that puzzles many businessmen. In the last reading of Part I Cavusgil and Nason introduce a computerized decision support system for assessment of company readiness to export. The system, called CORE (COmpany Readiness to Export), employs artificial intelligence methodology to help entrepreneurs to assess and develop the internal readiness for export operations.

1

International Marketing: An Ecologic View*

HANS B. THORELLI

At least three dramatically different views of marketing are being applied today. The oldest of the current marketing concepts is producer and seller oriented. It is based on the standard that "we sell what we make". This beautifully simple notion derives directly from the industrial revolution: the economies of scale realized in mass production were so great that consumers were more than glad to accept the offering as specified by the producer. This philosophy is still prevalent in many firms dominated by engineering minds, or by the type of sales management which feels that there is something amiss with customers who fail to see the beauty of its product. A variant of the same theme is practiced in the socialist world: "planners know better what is good for the people than consumers themselves."

In affluent and "post-industrial" society with hectic competition between products as well as brands and inhabited by increasingly finicky consumers, the production-oriented idea of marketing has obvious shortcomings. In the fifties, the customer-oriented marketing concept was developed in the United States. In this view, the needs of the customer rather than those of the factory should define the offering (product, price, image, service, etc.) of the firm in the marketplace. The standard is now, "we make what we sell". Customer orientation has since been adopted as the keynote of business policy to varying degrees in most industrialized Western countries.

Certainly, the customer-oriented philosophy of business has great merit. It has called attention to the fact that ultimately firms exist not for their own aggrandizement but to serve the public. It has led to a

*Revised from *International Marketing Strategy*, Revised Edition (Elmsford, NY: Pergamon Press, 1980).

virtual explosion of marketing research in both theory and practice, such research being the prime vehicle of identifying consumer needs. It has also stimulated much-needed integration of product planning, sales, pricing, advertising, market research, service, and other marketing-related activities in thousands of firms. Without doubt, consumers as well as businesses have been—and are—beneficiaries of this process.

Railroads at Bay

Yet this concept of marketing has at least one major shortcoming. This may be illustrated by one of the examples often quoted in the discussion of producer- versus customer-oriented marketing, i.e., the ailing railroad industry in America. It has been said that the prime reason for the demise of railroad companies has been their producer orientation: they saw themselves only in the business of running trains. Had they but been customer-oriented, so the argument runs, they would have seen their business as that of meeting the transportation needs of the population. Ergo, when buses, trucks, and planes emerged on the scene the railroads should have rushed into these new forms of transport. Superficially, the argument is plausible indeed. But it completely neglects one critical question of entrepreneurship: what are the things we are very good at, and what are the things we are not very good at? Now, there is nothing that prompts us to believe that railroad managers are particularly good at running airlines or trucking companies. Indeed, sociological studies suggest that most railroad executives would lack the flexibility and flair that would be required. Nor is there much evidence that the great physical resources (fixed assets) of the railroads would become much better utilized by the addition of, say, airline operations.

The logic of the situation suggests an entirely different tack. Faced with a long-term decline in the demand for their services, alert railroad managers might more reasonably have asked themselves the question: are there any customer wants we might be good at satisfying besides the need for railroad transport? This would have led them to recall that between 1830 and 1900 American railroads received grants of federal and state lands aggregating the land mass of France to stimulate expansion of the iron roads. These vast domains in large part are still owned by the railroads. What could be more natural than investigating, stimulating, and exploiting the needs of an expanding and affluent population for community developments, recreational facilities, and industrial parks on these lands? The prospect should be especially attractive in that a by-product of these activities would be the generation of additional railroad traffic. And, let it not be forgotten, real estate development is something railroad management *has* to be good at. Until recent years, however, what had been done by the railroads to develop outlying territories owned by them was unimpressive, with a few notable exceptions.

We have developed the railroad case in some detail because it also illustrates the emerging third approach to marketing: what we prefer to call the ecologic view of marketing. Under this view the marketer's standard becomes "we market what customers need *and* we are good at". By taking into account both clients needs and own resources the ecologic marketing concept in effect combines the producer-oriented and the customer-oriented points of view in a way that yields more meaningful conclusions than those which might be reached by either of the older approaches. Hence the notion of real estate development as a natural extension of American railroads.

Marketing is an Interactive Process

The ecologic view of marketing provides the theme and outline of this book. It is also an approach to theory by which we can improve our understanding of international marketing. Most importantly, it provides a framework of analysis of direct utility to practical decision-makers. In view of its treble significance, the approach will be developed in some detail.

In common with biological organisms every human being and every company is dependent on its environment for survival. Neither nature nor human civilization are in the end eleemosynary institutions. No one is self-sufficient. The interdependence of the company and its setting stems from the incessant drive towards specilization, or division of labor as the prime means of survival in a world of scarce resources. In effect, what happens in the process of interaction is that the company is obtaining the support of the environment by disposing of some of its differential advantage—or conversely, procuring resources from other organizations where they enjoy a differential advantage. The process of *exchange* is manifested by a perennial stream of *transactions*. Indeed, marketing may be defined as the generation, effectuation (and evaluation) of transactions. Without marketing there could be no division of labor.

The environment consists essentially of a series of input and output markets (for labor, capital, productive equipment, raw materials, end products, etc.) in which the company must transact. For long-term survival the customer market is of paramount significance, as in the end satisfying customer needs is the *only* reason for the environment to

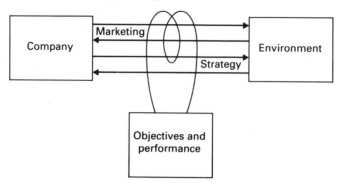

FIG. 1.1. Ecologic View of Marketing.

provide the wherewithall (sales revenue) on which company existence depends. This observation is often made to establish the importance of marketing. What is far less clearly realized is that it also establishes that increasing *customer satisfaction* automatically becomes a key objective of any company with the will to grow.

An ecologic model of the company interacting with its environment is displayed in Figure 1.1. There are four critical and interdependent parts in the system: the company, the environment, the marketing strategy governing the interplay between the two, and the objectives at which the strategy is aimed (or, the other side of the coin, the performance actually achieved). Each part actually represents a set of factors or variables distinguishing one marketing situation from another.

The ecology approach to marketing postulates in effect that a company trying to meet its objectives in a certain environment (market structure) should expect to find some marketing strategies a lot more workable than others. As we are not claiming that there is a single best solution for every situation, it should not be surprising to find several strategies coexisting in a given market environment.[1] This is still a far cry from saying that any random strategy might work. And the more we are able to specify the variables composing each of the four parts of the system, and their likely impact in a given situation, the more adept we shall become in zeroing in on superior strategies. This analytical job is that of the practitioner as much as of the theorist. A point of departure is provided by Figure 1.2, which displays a representative selection of variables for each part of the model.

In passing we mention as an example of early ecologic thought in marketing the product life cycle idea, directly derived from biological ecology on the growth and decline of populations.

Company
Aggregate size
Size of operation by country
Resource profile
Headquarter relations
Local domain:
   product span
   territorial extension
   mode of operations
   customer groups served
Organization structure
Leadership

Marketing strategy
Product
Intelligence and promotion
Channels of distribution
Price
Service, before and after sale
Trust

Objectives (Performance)
Survival
Growth
Customer satisfaction
Profitability
Market share
Sales volume
Differential advantage
Data feedback
Productivity
Local vs. global

Environment
Layers:
1. Market structure
2. Local marketing environment
3. International environment
See text for further specification

FIG. 1.2. International Marketing Ecology: Representative Variables.

Company Characteristics

Our discussion of details in the model is confined to variables of general significance to the planning of international marketing strategy. Clearly, in a given case some variables will be more important than others and some factors not even mentioned here may be of special relevance. Too, different dimensions of a given variable may be significant in different situations. In considering the role of the *aggregate size* of an international company, for instance, one might have in mind available export capacity in the mother country in thinking about International Nickel, or the ability of the concern to absorb losses in a new venture abroad during a build-up period (Toyota automobiles in Germany), or the strengths and weaknesses of being a large multinational corporation (Unilever, Siemens) versus a small specialty outfit (a maker of paint sprayers, let us say) interacting with the environment in an LDC such as Peru.

That the *size of the local operation* in a given country is a strong determinant of what strategies may be pursued is beyond doubt. This is also true of the *resource profile*, notably the proportion of fixed to total assets and of investment to sales, cost structure, manpower skills, patent position, degree of liquidity, and other sources of competitive advantage or disadvantage. In listing *headquarter relations* we are primarily thinking of the degree of centralization of decision-making about marketing strategy. As an illustration: a few years ago a large American drug maker required that any local price changes be approved by the New York office. When the Venezuelan government invited bids on behalf of public hospitals the company lost out to a nimbler German competitor whose local management was permitted to make price concessions on the spot.

We come next to the *local domain*. This is an extremely important part of company characteristics. Indeed, together with the set of objectives, the domain defines the mission of the local operation (Thorelli 1972, p. 290). Every company, every organization may be defined in terms of the four domain dimensions: *product* span, *territorial* extension, *mode* of operations, and *customer* groups served. Note that the "product" marketed may be a service (dry-cleaning). Territory covered may be confined to a few cities in an LDC, while being nationwide in Britain. The local mode of operations may range all the way from the most modest (marketing a few units through an export agent in the mother country) to the most ambitious (a fully integrated production-marketing operation supplying both the local market and exporting to other countries). Customer groups served may be distributors, industrial buyers, or end consumers, or specialized subgroups of these. Each clientele will require a more or less unique strategy.

The local domain may be viewed as the niche which the company has carved out of the total environment of a given country. The niche may be quite specifically defined (Ford Escort in America) or it may cover an entire spectrum of products and activities (Nestlé in France). Any domain is likely to change over time, if for no other reason than that the environment is in an incessant flux. In planning for company growth, eco-man (the ecologically-oriented manager) will seek to obtain common economies—or, more fashionably, *synergy*—between old operations and new. Can any of our existing resources (managerial skills, plant facilities, etc.) be utilized? Does the new product logically supplement the existing assortment? Can the existing sales organization handle the new product? Can we promote it to our existing customers? To capitalize on common economies is especially important in the development of small and medium-sized operations, the paradoxical circumstance notwithstanding that it may be more difficult to find synergistic opportunities in small operations than large.

Organization structure is another critical company characteristic. Of prime significance here is the structuring approach—does the organization setup emphasize product, territory, functions or customer categories? In other words, which dimension of the domain is given priority in shaping the organization? Frequently of equal importance is the allocation of decision-making authority, in other words, the degree of decentralization within the local operation. MNCs have tended to favor territory, product and function (in that chronological order); as customer segments become increasingly transnational or even global organization by customer groups is likely to become more common.

Our last company variable is *leadership*. More than in domestic operations, leadership in international marketing tends to call for skills in perceiving and interpreting environmental signals. For instance, entrepreneurial decisions are typically required more often. The international executive needs the ability to see what the salient similarities and differences are between various parts of the world. He should be able to see when the situation calls for adaptation of his operations and when for the strategy of a change agent. He has to motivate people of a different cultural background than his own and build relationships with them based on mutual respect. Wherever he may find himself in a multinational organization he needs the ability to "think upstream" in global terms rather than with the blinders of local suboptimization. Yet he must have a profound understanding of the tensions inherent in local vs. global perspectives and be ready to strike a workable balance between the two.

The company characteristics discussed here are of special relevance to company strategy. Taken together, they define a profile of the company which largely determines the types of strategies it is capable of pursuing in the short run. In the long run, environmental change will reflect itself in adjustments in strategy which ultimately result in changes in company characteristics. If there is no adaptation, the organization will not survive. Conversely, in the pursuit of company objectives aggressive management may deliberately change company profile and/or strategy in order to affect, or capitalize upon, desirable changes in the environment.

Objectives

The domain defines the nature of a local operation, but says nothing specific about its intended objectives or actual performance (results). Every firm has a set or a hierarchy of goals, more or less clearly perceived. The goal set of an ecologically-oriented marketer would include the objectives listed in Figure 1.2. Any two objectives may be partially overlapping, partially conflicting. Clearly, too, the relative priorities of individual goals will change from time to time.

Of the objectives, *survival* and *growth* would seem self-explanatory. *Customer satisfaction* occupies a key place in ecologic management, as such satisfaction provides the ultimate rationale for the existence of the business. In the ecologic view of the market economy *profitability* can no longer aspire to be the end-all of business activity. It becomes an objective among others, though still critically important as the vehicle of ensuring survival and growth. As we have said elsewhere, the modern corporation is not in business to earn profits but earns profits to stay in business (Thorelli 1965, p. 250). *Sales volume* is an important gauge of viability and growth. An unequivocal finding of PIMS is that *market share*, once attained, is strongly related to profitability. It is also clear that increases in market share are often bought at the expense of short-term profitability.

Relative to competition any firm has a set of *differential advantages* (and disadvantages), deriving from its resource profile, niche, and objectives. This differential advantage in the ability to meet customer needs may take any number of forms, such as cost leadership, specialization on a certain clientele or function, high quality, reliable delivery, outstanding service. Like a capital asset, differential advantage is subject to constant change: at any given time the firm is either adding to it or is in the process of using it up. If nothing else, environmental developments inevitably will cause shifts in the differential advantages and disadvantages of competing firms. To identify and maximize differential advantage (while trying to reduce attendant disadvantages) is a major entrepreneurial challenge.

Ecologic marketing requires a great deal of *data feedback* to establish customer needs, to measure their satisfaction, to keep track of competition, and to forecast changes in the market and in the marketing environment. To ascertain that the company is in tune with its environment, the maintenance of an orderly information flow becomes a natural strategic objective among others. This environmental intelligence operation may take the shape of a Management Information System or simply of personal contacts, analysis of sales data, and other less formal means. In a going concern, marketing research and feedback from distributors and salesmen should provide key elements of feedback, whatever other ingredients may be. *Productivity* is viewed here as a measure of saleable output relative to the total input of resources, i.e., as an expression of internal efficiency. It is almost tautological to say that increased productivity is an objective of all economic organizations.

In international business operations it becomes necessary to make a distinction between *local* and *overall* (global) objectives of the company. In most international concerns top management makes a deliberate effort to harmonize these objectives. Due to such factors as nationalism among governments and a tendency of local managers to overemphasize the significance of their particular operations, one must expect to find varying degrees of suboptimization in international marketing. Suboptimization simply means that some of the achievements of a local operation occur at the expense of overall achievement of the concern, such as an increase in sales in country A of high-cost goods made in an inefficient local plant rather than of low-cost goods imported from efficient facilities at headquarters. While perhaps worth striving for, complete synchronization of local and global goals is hardly a realistic proposition.

The spelling out and periodic redefinition of objectives is a critical part of international marketing planning.

Strategy and Structure Defined

Since the key challenge in marketing is to adapt the marketing strategy of the firm to the market structure in which it operates, it is necessary to define these concepts. *Market structure* refers to all relevant characteristics of the marketplace surrounding the firm, notably consumers, middlemen, competitors, and the product (offering) with which the market is identified. Important consumer characteristics include their number, income distribution, and geographical dispersion as well as the values and attitudes determining their needs and behavior. The same variables apply to distributors and dealers in addition to their classification by size and functions performed. Competing firms may be analyzed in similar terms with market share, and trend therein, as important additions. Also, their profiles of differential advantage and disadvantage are of special interest. So are their strategies; from the viewpoint of firm A the strategies pursued by competitors B to Z constitute a part of market structure, at least in so far as the strategies of B to Z are beyond the immediate influence of A.

Several characteristics of the product (offering) itself are among the determinants of market structure. Physical size and weight of the product may place territorial limits on the market. High unit price may preclude its distribution through such channels as supermarkets, drugstores, and kiosks. A custom-made product faces a different market from a highly standardized one. A complex product, or one requiring special service, will typically have specialized or even exclusive distribution. The markets for industrial products are different from consumer markets, and consumer durable goods markets have little in common with those of foods or household supplies. In many markets the product life cycle represents an important structural feature (Levitt 1965 and Thorelli 1967). These illustrations could be extended further.

Marketing strategy on the other hand is the approach, or the stance, that the firm adopts in order to cope in the market structure. Ecologically, strategy is the means of harmonizing corporate resources, domain, and objectives with environmental opportunity at acceptable levels of risk. In starkly simplified language market structure may be likened to an arena, while marketing strategy would be the play staged by the home team. Properly conceived, marketing strategy capitalizes on the differential advantages of the firm, while protecting it from unwholesome effects of its differential disadvantages. As strategy refers to the *principal* means of reaching key objectives, it is often long-range in nature. Hence the current interest in Strategic Planning, a topic with which this book is largely concerned.

The marketing strategy of the firm is reflected in the so-called marketing mix, that is, the particular combination the firm makes of the marketing instruments, notably product, intelligence and promotion, distribution, price, service, and trust (Figure 1.2). Note that marketing strategy is a concept going far beyond the marketing mix. Marketing strategy is what makes the elements of the mix work in a coordinated fashion, as a whole rather than as disparate parts. We may say that *marketing strategy = marketing mix + synergy* among the instruments in the mix. Strategy is a qualitative concept, related to the idea of intermesh and the German notion of Gestalt. To build a house we need a materials mix of bricks and boards, mortar and nails. But without a strategy for putting them together we would more likely wind up with a big pile of rubble than with a house.

Thus, strategy is a scheme or a recipe for applying the means to reach the end in view. Classical marketing strategies include high price-high quality (Rolls Royce autos), low price-mass volume (Ford's old Model T), multi-channel distribution of a standard product with globally homogenized promotion (Coca-Cola). Clearly, the high price and the high quality of Rolls Royce cars fit like hand in glove; the marketing instruments reinforce each other. We may, however, also observe that these instruments to a fair—but always limited—extent may substitute for each other. Rather than to introduce an improved model of our product we may prefer to increase our advertising or to cut price. Yet as time goes by an increasing number of customers will generally switch to the improved models introduced by competition no matter how much we increase promotion or cut price.

The marketing instruments constituting integral parts of Marketing Strategy in Figure 1.2 are generally well-known from domestic marketing and do not need redefinition here. Their international implications are developed in some detail in later readings, and especially in Part VI. Only three points need emphasis here. In the context of strategy "product" refers to the specific variant or offering of a firm (Coca-Cola) rather than the generic product characteristics of interest in discussing the market structure in which it is being sold (soft drinks). Commercial intelligence—arranging for data feedback about market structure and broader aspects of the environment—is of special significance in international marketing.

"*Trust*" has been included for several reasons. In consumer markets it builds store and brand loyalty—especially in the LDCs. The fact that faith in the integrity and reliability of the other party is often a prerequisite to transactions in industrial marketing is familiar to every supplier and purchasing agent. Due to intercultural differences, time lags in communicating, inability to control the other party, and lack of personal contact, trust is a critical ingredient in international marketing strategy. Networking is the key means of building trust (Reading 5). None have realized this more clearly than the Japanese, who have made a heroic and immensely profitable effort to transform prewar international distrust into a strong faith in the quality of their wares and the seriousness of purpose in their commercial dealings.

Environmental Structure

Three layers of environment of interest to the international marketer were identified in Figure 1.2. These environmental layers reappear in diagram form in Figure 1.3. A firm engaged only in domestic marketing may largely confine its attention to the domestic market structure. The international environment is largely irrelevant (at least short-term) and managers generally have acquired an ingrained sense of the local marketing environment as part of growing up in it. The situation is drastically different—and more complex—in international operations. Not only must differences and similarities in two or more market structures be recognized: the international marketer must also be aware of the local marketing environment abroad and of salient aspects of the interface between his own country and those others in which his company wishes to operate. Indeed, his ability to see the strategic implications of developments in these two broader layers of

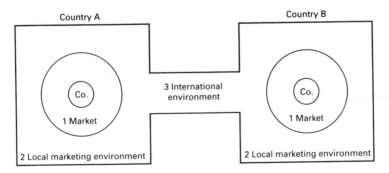

FIG. 1.3. Layers of Environment in International Marketing.

1 Market structure
Consumers
Distributors
Competitors
Product
   (for details, see "Strategy and structure defined" section)

2 Local marketing environment
Government stability
Predictability of public policy
Economic development, stability, and development policy
Government controls:
   competitive practices
   price controls
   state marketing bodies
   health and safety, environmental controls
   product labeling, standardization
Local business culture
Marketing infrastructure:
   data availability
   market research agencies
   advertising media, agencies
   transportation facilities

3 International environment
Relations between countries A and B
Tariffs
Non-tariff barriers
Currency controls
Transportation costs

FIG. 1.4. Market Structure and Environment: Representative Variables.

the environment will frequently spell the difference between success and failure in multinational marketing. Once again, the ecological view of the field points to the importance of commercial intelligence and environmental scanning in international operations.

Representative variables in the different layers of the total environment are listed in Figure 1.4. Market structure has been discussed earlier. The figure also gives a sample of typically important variables in the broader environments. Their relative significance will differ from case to case, and frequently other variables than those mentioned here will be of even greater importance. The identification of relevant factors and the evaluation of their likely relative impact is an important challenge to the international marketer. The successful accomplishment of this task is a logical prerequisite to the design of strategy. In the *local marketing environment* lack of government stability and predictability of public policy—and attendant so-called *political risk*—is generally of less immediate concern in Western democracies than in the LDCs. Degree of economic development is an important determinant of market potential. Economic instability—engendered, for example, by excessive dependence on one or a few commodities in export trade or high rate of local inflation—often means extra risk. Aspects of development policy of key interest include government outlook on the role of marketing and consumer products in general, import substitution policy, local ownership, and minimum local value-added tax regulations. In the same league are inducements to or restrictions on entry into certain trades.

Government rule-making for domestic marketing is critical in any country. The role and nature of antitrust, consumer protection, and unfair trade practices legislation, as of health, safety, labeling, and standardization requirements and of the direct government engagement in marketing activities (food distribution, agricultural export boards, etc.) varies enormously and somewhat unpredictably around the world. So do public procurement practices. It is a sobering reflection that in most countries at least some products are subject to some form of price control. Such control may not always be governmentally administered—prices may be set by local cartels too powerful to overcome. Other aspects of the local business culture set the tone of competition and cooperation between firms, define the level of business ethics, the outlook on corruption, and so on. A small operator will often have to take the local culture as given. To the large international concern a major challenge in defining strategy is to decide what aspects of local business customs to emulate and in what respects to be the nonconformist.

Marketing infrastructure refers to the relative existence of data and facilitating agencies needed in the course of marketing management activity. Industrialized Western countries generally have a rich and reliable data base maintained by government statistical offices, but the LDCs as a rule are not equally well endowed. Corresponding conditions typically prevail with regard to market research agencies, advertising media and agencies, transportation facilities, mail and telephone systems, etc.

Beyond the local marketing milieu is the *international environment*, certainly no less important than any other part of the three-tiered setting surrounding the international marketer. The significance of political arrangements and relations between nations are illustrated by the European Economic Community and other regional associations and by the special challenges surrounding East-West trade. While the General Agreement on Tariffs and Trade (GATT) and later rounds of tariff reductions between the major trading nations of the world have lessened the obstructions placed on international economic intercourse by customs duties, the fact remains that tariffs still are far from eliminated and that even highly industrialized nations such as E.E.C., Japan and the U.S. will reach for import surcharges, "voluntary restraints" on foreign exporters, and other pseudo-tariff devices when in a balance-of-payments pinch. Meanwhile, the role of non-tariff barriers has been rapidly increasing, both relative to tariffs and absolutely speaking. Not without justice these obstacles are sometimes called invisible trade barriers: their existence and/or significance often is not clear (occasionally not even *made* clear) to the international marketer until he has already made contractual commitments on the assumption that they did not exist (or would be of but little significance). Neglecting to examine the likely impact of non-tariff barriers on a proposed international marketing venture is simply indefensible. Less likely to be forgotten in pre-transaction planning are the transportation costs and related risks (war risks, dock and maritime strikes, and so on) in international commerce.

A vital aspect of the global environment is exchange rate fluctuations and currency controls. Whether as buyer, seller or investor, most MNCs are directly affected by changes in currency values, reflected in the form of realized or unrealized gain or loss on financial statements. Typically these effects are short-term, and, at least in part, they may even be avoidable by hedging and similar techniques. Many executives too easily forgot the more serious part: Currency fluctuations manifest themselves in corresponding changes in *competitiveness* of the firm, *at home* as well as abroad. Currency controls may extend all the way from restrictions on the repatriation of profits to sales between subsidiaries and other day-to-day transactions.

Interactive Marketing Strategy

Rather widely different strategies may be viable in a given market structure. The ecologic concept of marketing does imply, however, that the superior strategies are those truly interactive. These are strategies based on the fullest possible utilization of differential advantage and/or common economies of the firm in satisfying a well-defined (narrow or broad) set of consumer needs.

In nature, the survival of plants and animals is dictated by the environment. It is crucial to realize that human ecology implies no such simple environmental determinism. *What distinguishes us from plants and animals is our ability to plan and hence, to impact our environment much as we are impacted by it*—indeed within broad limits we even have the ability to move from one market environment to another! We will conclude our somewhat abstract discussion of the ecologic approach by a few specific examples of interactive strategy.

Synergy: American Railroads

Relating to the analysis of American railroads at the beginning of this essay, let us restate that one clear cut application of the ecologic concept of marketing in this case involves the diversification into natural resource and community developments, recreational and industrial parks, and similar large-scale projects based on strong contemporary customer needs and prevailing on the common economies (synergy) derivable from the vast land holdings of the railroads as well as their already existing cadre of real estate oriented management.

Synergy: Multinational Life Cycles

A number of complex products have first been developed in highly industrialized nations and then gradually been diffused around the world, somewhat in tune with local economic development. Growth companies pursuing ecologic marketing strategies will prevail on the scale as well as common economies to be derived from hot pursuit of the international life cycles of these products. A typical example is Ericsson Telephone Corporation of Sweden. While that country has the second highest telephone density in the world, it is obvious that Ericsson would have to be satisfied with modest growth indeed if confined to a market of eight million people. Before the last world war, the company's major thrust of expansion was south and eastwards in Europe—in tune with the natural growth of local telephone demand. After the war the greatest rate (although not always dollar value) of expansion has been in the LDCs. Scale economies occur when export is possible from the Stockholm factories as well as some other West European plants. Common economies occur when the technical, financial, and marketing skills of the company are applied in the LDCs.

Nichemanship: Volkswagen in North America and Brazil

Nichemanship—or market concentration—is our term for the successful application of a strategy of highly selective market segmentation or selectivity. Perhaps the single most outstanding example of nichemanship in history is Volkswagen's strategy in the United States from 1955 to 1965. Instead of striving to get 10% of the U.S. car market model for model (which would be a catastrophic proposition for a European auto maker) Volkswagen said, in effect, "let us get 100% of 10% of the U.S. market". This was the niche of the "beetle," the standard VW economy model of which several million units were sold in the period—long before the onslaught of other European, Japanese, and American economy cars (inspired by VW success). Indeed, Volkswagen even had the stamina to withold from the American market for years its fastback and four-door models, precisely in order not to clutter its nichemanship image.

In the mid-seventies, when the long-lasting beetle had had its heyday, VW nearly went bankrupt by adopting a broad-scale diversification strategy both in Europe and the U.S. As part of the process of getting its house in order the company successfully repeated its nichemanship strategy in Brazil 10–20 years later than in North America. This is also an example of pursuing the product life cycle around the world. On the other hand, when the new Rabbit was introduced in the U.S. the ecologic niche established by the beetle was already crowded with competitors.

Cost and Service Leadership: Hong Kong Tailors

In the 1960s and 1970s the tailors of Hong Kong made great inroads in the woollen clothing market among male sophisticates around the world. Their simple but effective strategy was based on two elements. Low price (based on low labor cost) without compromising quality of materials was the first element. Personal—custom-tailored is indeed the word—and speedy service was the other. The differential advantage of a rich supply of skilled labor willing to work hard at low wages was utilized to the hilt.

Massive Resources and Homogenization of Demand: Boeing Jets

The differential advantage of Boeing in the jet aircraft market was almost the opposite of the Hong Kong tailors. What counted in the Boeing case was the ability to marshall and manage massive professional manpower, technical resources, and financial strength and then to make maximum use of this type of differential advantage by a strategy of homogenization of carrier demand for jet planes. Only towards the end of the seventies was this strategy being challenged by Airbus Industrie and other planemakers.

We may note in passing that airline deregulation in the States and elsewhere has greatly sharpened the distinction between trunk and feeder lines—a natural ecologic phenomenon. This development has created a major niche for smaller planes for the feeder lines. For example, in 1989 SAAB of Sweden got an order from American Airlines for its feeder subsidiaries worth well over a billion dollars if all options are taken up by the buyer.

Low Profile: The Differential Advantage of Small Business

Many a small businessman is psychologically overwhelmed by the complexity and risks of international operations, and thus is confined to the domestic market. Small firms which do venture abroad soon discover that they have a natural differential advantage in their low profile. They do not invite aspersions of imperialism, exploitation, or undue influence in local politics. While a large foreign concern is typically expected—or even required—to operate with considerably higher standards than those practiced by domestic enterprise, the small firm typically can avoid this kind of discrimination. The small operation also is a flexible operation. Thus, if it brings a new product, technique or strategy to the market the small international business often has an enviable package of advantages.

The Multinational Corporation as a Change Agent: Sears in Latin America

In contrast to the small overseas venture, the multinational corporation does not have to take all or most aspects of the local environment as given. It will be able to effectuate changes in the host culture. Indeed, only by a judicious blend of adapting to local conditions and effectuating change in them will the multinational corporation render its most effective contribution to local development. In this manner, too, it is most likely to ensure its own long-term acceptability in that environment. An excellent example of what we are talking about is Sears, Roebuck's operations in Latin America; another is Unilever's operations in Sub-Saharan Africa.

Summing Up

The ecologic approach to marketing views strategy as the means of satisfying specific consumer wants for which the resources, talents, and differential advantages of the firm are (or can be made to be) especially suited. Harmonizing structure and strategy is difficult in domestic marketing—even though the international tier of the environment usually will not present insuperable problems and the local marketing environment is familiar and predictable. The special challenge in international marketing is that strategy must take into account all three layers of the environment: market structure, local marketing environment abroad, and the internation interface. Indeed, merely identifying all the environmental factors of relevance and their relative importance in a given business is in itself a task of entrepreneurial rank.

Complications are many and risks tend to be great in international marketing. But the compensation may be greater than average return on investment and an immeasurable sense of satisfaction from contributing to local growth and development.

Note

1. It would lead off the path to discuss in detail the reason why several strategies may be viable in a given case. They include the fact that different marketing instruments may serve in either a substitute or complementary relationship to each other, time lags in the interaction process, and the existence of "slack" and "random events" in both company and environment.

References

Ansoff, H. I., *Corporate Strategy*, (McGraw-Hill, 1965).

Thorelli, H. B., "The Political Economy of the Firm—Basis for a New Theory of Competition," *Schweizerische Zeitschrift für Volkswirtschaft und Statistik*, (September 1965), pp. 248–62.

————, "Concepts of Marketing: A Review, Preview and Paradigm," in *The Marketing Concept: Perspectives and Viewpoints*, P. Varadarajan (ed.), American Marketing Association Workshop, Texas A&M University (February 1983), pp. 2–37.

———— (ed.), *Strategy + Structure = Performance*, (Bloomington: Indiana University Press, 1972). Especially essays by Thorelli and Preston.

Wells, L. T., Jr., "A Product Life Cycle for International Trade?" *Journal of Marketing* (July 1968), pp. 1–6.

2

The Gains from Trade*

THE ECONOMIST

Macroeconomic stability is a prerequisite for rapid development. Although the policies necessary to achieve it may be difficult to bring about, there is no mystery about what those policies are: non-inflationary monetary policy and its fiscal counterpart, tight control of public finance. What might be less obvious, however, is that sound macro-policy is not enough. The evidence shows conclusively that for most countries an open approach to trade is also indispensable. This survey reviews that evidence, and then tries to account for it.

First, what does it mean to talk of an outward-looking approach to trade? It means that the government's economic policies, taken together, do not discourage exports. To sharpen the contrast between the outward-looking approach and the import-substitution approach, some economists talk of export promotion. That term has misled a lot of non-economists. The outward-looking approach requires nothing more than neutrality (intended or otherwise), not the deliberate promotion of one sector of the economy over another. Whereas the import-substitution approach discourages imports (and hence inadvertently discourages exports), the outward-looking approach does not. That's all.

It is easier to be more precise with the help of a yardstick called the effective rate of protection. This measures the protection given to the value added in domestic production, rather than to the finished good. It thereby reveals the true effect on incentives for domestic producers.

Suppose a producer makes raincoats, paying $60 for inputs (cloth and buttons), and then sells them in the domestic market for $100. The value added is $40. If the government puts a tariff of 10% on raincoats, the nominal rate of protection is 10%. But the effective rate

---

* Reprinted from *The Economist*, September 23, 1989, pp. 25–27, with permission.

of protection is higher. If the whole of the tariff is passed on to consumers, so that the price rises to $110, the effective rate of protection is $50 (the value added in domestic prices) less $40 dollars (the value added in world prices) divided by $40 (the value added in world prices)—that is, $10 divided by $40, or 25%.

Now suppose that the government puts a 10% tariff on cloth and buttons as well. The task of manufacturing raincoats enjoys less protection than before. The effective rate of protection will fall, because value added in domestic prices will be $6 lower thanks to the 10% rise in the cost of inputs. The effective rate of protection will be $44 (the value added in domestic prices) less $40 (the value added in world prices) divided again by $40—that is, 10%.

That is why under a single tariff applied to all imports, the effective rate of protection is the same as the nominal rate. By the same token, a pattern of highly variable tariffs is likely to conceal an extremely distorting pattern of effective rates. In many developing countries, effective rates of protection of more than 1,000% have been common. In some such cases the value added in world prices may actually be negative. Protection gives producers their profit even though at undistorted prices they are buying in raw materials and intermediate goods and, by working on them, reducing their value.

Degrees of Bias

Return for a moment to the raincoat producer. As things stand he is being discouraged from selling his goods abroad. If he did he would get only $100 a coat instead of $110—and, as we now know, that difference understates the wedge that the tariff has driven between the returns to be gained from the two markets. By altering the relative price of exports and imports, the government has in effect put a tax on exports.

The government might choose, however, to offset this by protecting raincoats for export as well as raincoats to be sold at home. It could do that by paying a subsidy tied to the quantity of raincoats sold abroad. As with protection in the domestic market, the effective rate of export protection will generally differ from the nominal rate of export protection (that is, the rate of export subsidy).

The picture is further complicated by the fact that straightforward tariffs and subsidies are not the only ways to provide protection either to importers or exporters. Import-licensing rules and other quantitative restrictions, subsidies on inputs, exchange-rate policy—all can increase the effective rate of protection.

Once all these factors have been taken into account, effective rates of protection can be calculated for both imports and exports. The overall

TABLE 2.1. Government Approaches to Trade

Strongly outward-oriented
Trade controls are either nonexistent or very low in the sense that any disincentives to export resulting from import barriers are more or less counterbalanced by export incentives. There is little or no use of direct controls and licensing arrangements, and the effective exchange rates for imports and exports are roughly equal.

Moderately outward-oriented
Incentives favor production for domestic rather than export markets. But the average rate of effective protection for the home markets is relatively low and the range of effective protection rates relatively narrow. The use of direct controls and licensing arrangements is limited. The effective exchange rate is higher for imports than for exports, but only slightly.

Moderately inward-oriented
Incentives clearly favor production for the domestic market. The average rate of effective protection for home markets is fairly high and the range of effective protection rates relatively wide. Direct import controls are extensive. The exchange rate is somewhat overvalued.

Strongly inward-oriented
Incentives strongly favor production for the domestic market. The average rate of effective protection for home markets is high and the range of effective protection rates wide. Direct controls and licensing disincentives to the traditional export sector are pervasive, positive incentives to non-traditional exports are few or non-existing, and the exchange rate is substantially overvalued.

Source: World Bank

bias in the trade regime is then simply the ratio of import protection to export protection. If this ratio is one or thereabouts, the trade regime is neutral or, as most economists would say "outward-oriented." If it is a lot more than one, the regime favors domestic producers of import-substitutes over producers of exports, and is "inward-oriented." If the ratio is less than one, the regime favors exporters over producers for the home market; it is "export-biased."

Note that the ratio can be roughly one—that is, the regime can be outward-looking—either because trade is completely free, with no protection for imports or for exports, or because protection for the two sectors is roughly equal. So an outward-looking regime need not practise laissez-faire. Indeed it might be highly interventionist, with high rates of protection for both exports and imports, which then cancel out overall.

Measuring Up

For its "World Development Report" in 1987, the World Bank used these methods to classify 41 developing countries according to their trade orientation during 1963–73 and 1973–85. It then plotted the

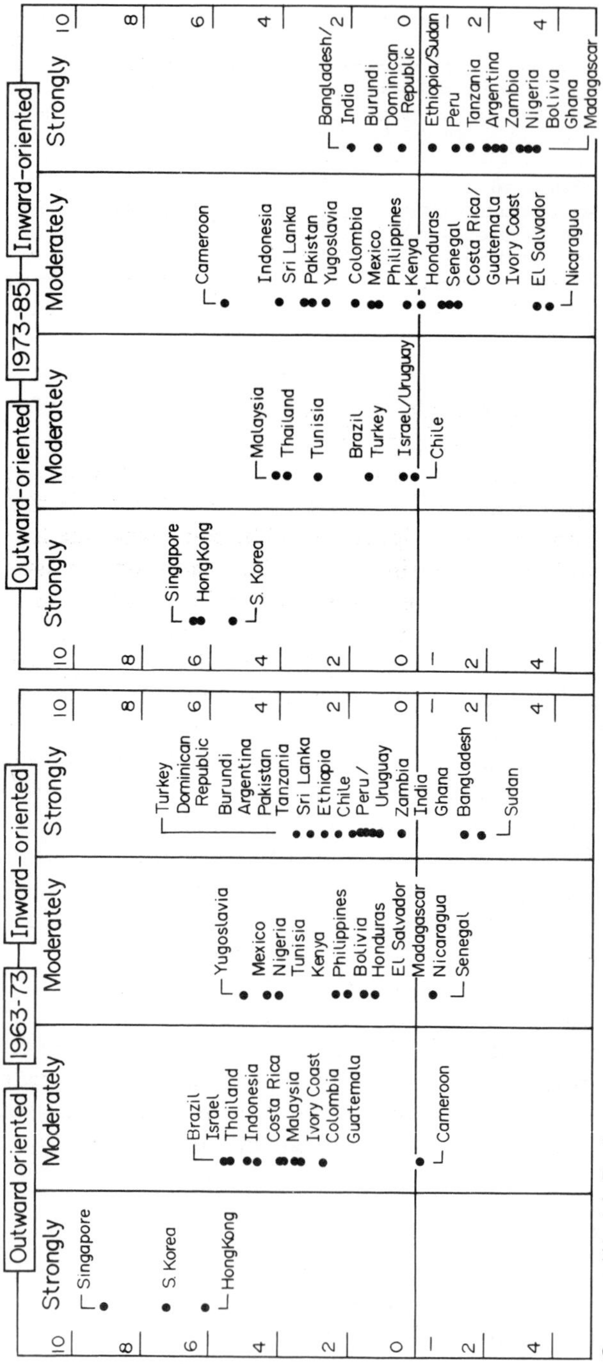

FIG. 2.1. Trade Regimes and Growth:
Real GNP Per Person, Average Annual % Change

Source: World Bank

TABLE 2.2. Looking Outward is Good for You

Trade strategy	Growth of real GDP, % per year 1963–73	1973–85	Growth of manufacturing real value added, % per year 1963–73	1973–85	Incremental output-capital ratio, %, annual averages 1963–73	1973–85
Strongly outward-oriented	9.5	7.7	15.6	10.0	40	22
Moderately outward-oriented	7.6	4.4	9.4	4.0	40	20
Moderately inward-oriented	6.8	4.7	9.6	5.1	30	16
Strongly inward–oriented	4.1	2.5	5.3	3.1	19	11

Source: World Bank

groups against a variety of economic indicators. The most important of these indicators is real income per head.

During both periods, growth in income per head was highest in the strongly outward-looking economies and lowest in the strongly inward-looking ones (see Figure 2.1). The same was true for growth in total GDP and manufacturing value added, and for the usual measure of the efficiency of investment (see Table 2.2). On all these criteria, the strongly inward-looking were also bettered by the moderately outward-looking, though naturally by a smaller margin. The failure of strong inward-orientation to promote domestic manufacturing—not just exports of manufactures—is particularly striking, because the whole point of looking inward for the countries that did so most enthusiastically was to industrialize faster.

Overall, the moderate outward-lookers have the edge over the moderate inward-lookers, but the balance here is finer. GDP and income per head grew faster in the moderately outward-looking countries in 1963–73, but fractionally slower in 1973–85. The moderate inward-lookers have also seen faster growth in manufacturing output. But it is interesting that, despite this, the moderately outward-oriented have seen a faster rise in employment in manufacturing. This points to a bias against labour-intensive methods of production in the inward-looking countries. That fits well with the notion that trade allows a country to exploit its comparative advantage: the comparative advantage of developing countries is cheap and abundant labor.

The Dragons

The three strongly outward-oriented countries in Figure 2.1 are Hongkong, Singapore and South Korea. Taiwan would have been the fourth if it had been in the sample, and would only have reinforced the message. The four dragons, however, have been more diverse in their

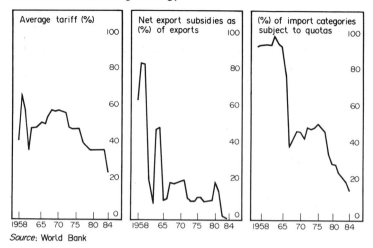

Source: World Bank

FIG. 2.2. South Korea's Trade Incentives

policies than is usually assumed. Hongkong's outward-orientation is due to unalloyed free trade. The other three—to varying degrees—have been interventionist, using various export incentives to offset the export-discouraging effects of domestic protection.

South Korea, on some measures the most interventionist dragon, is sometimes cited as proof that intelligent dirigisme, rather than a broadly outward-looking trade policy, is the key to rapid development. This raises issues that go beyond trade. But often the judgment is in any case based on a false premise—the idea that South Korea has protected its domestic producers as much as (if not more than) the inward lookers have protected theirs, with the difference that it has then piled on top a lot of incentives for exporters.

Not so. South Korea has not countered an unusually high degree of domestic protection with an unusually high degree of export promotion; it has countered a moderate and declining degree of domestic protection with just enough export promotion to achieve broad neutrality.

South Korea's surge of growth began in the mid-1960s. Policy began to change in the late 1950s. At that time almost all imports were subject to quantitative restrictions of some sort, but these did not bind as tightly as in many other developing countries. The government began to provide export incentives to offset its protection for producers of import-substitutes. At first this failed to work, perhaps because the exchange rate was still over-valued, which left too much of a bias against exports. In the early 1960s the government dismantled its multiple exchange-rate system, devalued the currency and (since that helped exporters) reduced its export subsidies. These liberalizing reforms were the turning point. Exports began to grow rapidly.

In 1967 the government reformed its import-control system, greatly reducing the number of imports subject to quotas. It then began to reduce its tariffs (see Figure 2.2). So the background to the miracle in the late 1960s and 1970s was not just outward-orientation (domestic protection offset by export promotion) but a low average level of domestic protection, and moreover with relatively little variation in the rates of protection industry by industry. Later, towards the end of the 1970s, South Korea did increase its support for heavy industry. The economy began to run into trouble. Policymakers acknowledged their mistake and moved back towards liberalization.

3

Some New Competitive Factors in International Marketing*

RICHARD D. ROBINSON

Introduction

In a published interview, Theodore Levitt, the popular Harvard-based marketing pundit, is quoted as having said,

> All over the world, markets are becoming more and more alike, primarily because people everywhere are being exposed to similar things. Within the last twenty years, communication, travel, and transport have been proletarianized [a nonword for reduced price and, hence, availability to ordinary people] . . . This exposure has resulted in a demand, on the part of these isolated populations, for precisely those things which are in demand in the most advanced nations. [For "advanced," read "relatively industrialized and materially rich."]

He goes on:

> Certain historically standardized global commodities such as grain and cotton—and even science and technology products—have been traded around the world for years and submitted to a kind of common commercial language. Even in undeveloped countries [read "poor countries in a material sense"], there are expressed wants for high-tech, for steel mills, for national airlines, for computers, for chemical plants, and for other artifacts of science and technology.

He writes further:

> Now, the same thing has happened to high-touch products [read "consumer products"]. We have Coca Cola everywhere, McDonald's everywhere, Revlon everywhere, Sony everywhere, rock music, jazz, Dallas, 007 . . . You name it. Pizza, Chinese food, Greek salad, and pita bread are all now global products. To call them ethnic is a mistake. They're ethnic only in that they came from one place. They are no longer the exclusive possession of their place of origin (HBS Bulletin 1983).

Professor Levitt then goes on to make a distinction between the multinational corporation and the global corporation. The first, the *multinational*, he claims, operates separately and distinctly in each nation, "customizing what it does to the presumed distinctive needs

---

* Slightly abbreviated from *Advances in International Marketing*, Vol. I, pp. 1–20, with permission.

and requirements of each nation." As a result, it incurs relatively high costs, which arise out of the great variation in product features, packaging, marketing, etc. and out of the management and control of plants which must necessarily operate at an uneconomically low scale. On the other hand, the *global corporation* produces globally standardized products and, by marketing them in the same way to all people everywhere, achieves enormous economies of scale. Obviously, such corporations will sooner or later push the multinationals out of the picture.

He concludes by saying:

> The primary underlying reason for this is the multinational corporation's typical marketing strategy, which says "Give people precisely what they want." This approach is outdated, although not because the concept itself is necessarily bad but because of a failure to see that what people want is increasingly very different from what they *say* they want.
>
> People will sacrifice certain features and certain preferences in the areas of appearance, function, and distinctiveness of product if other versions of those products are offered to them at substantially lower prices. When the price differences are as substantial as those the global corporation is in a position to offer, then the global corporation will clearly win.

Economies of Scale and Global Markets

The question in my mind after reading all of this was why it left me so uneasy. Then I realized that I for one did not really like the sort of world being projected—essentially a one-culture world in which tastes and preferences have been homogenized. How dull. And then I realized further that I deeply resented the notion that large, all encompassing corporations would decide that what I want is quite different from what I think and say I want. In other words, some marketing expert in some organization located someplace will decide what I want, even though it may be at odds with what I think I want, whether culturally or individually determined. What arrogance! What a denial of consumer sovereignty! What nonsense!

Let me point out, however, that Professor Levitt's logic is irrefutable if—and these are very large ifs—

- Competitive economies of scale can only be achieved in plants of world-scale size.
- Underlying differences in tastes and preferences can be eliminated by the price differentials which result.

First, let us admit that certain basic technologies have induced global commonalities in preference up to a point. This commonality rests, I suggest, on three main factors:

1. The satisfaction of certain psychological needs of human beings which are widely shared, that is, the need to communicate, move, eat, shelter and protect themselves, illuminate the night, and so on.

2. The easing of the burden of unpleasant manual work, which leads to a general preference for electrical and mechanical power to facilitate manual effort.
3. The easing of pain and lengthening of life, which leads to universal demand for certain drugs and pharmaceuticals, certain foods, and medical technology.

But merely because x million people in a world of some 4 billion have developed a certain overlap of demand does not lead to one world in marketing terms. On average, how much of the total world product is spent on globally standardized consumer goods and services? Surely not more than 20%. There is no real reason to expect that this percentage will continue to rise indefinitely. Indeed, the 20% is heavily concentrated in what we call the Western world and certain client or satellite populations. And there is some evidence that the *rate* at which goods are being increasingly standardized across national markets is decreasing, not increasing. Even the ubiquitous computer is being constantly redesigned so as to have a better cultural fit.

One should point out that there are a number of environmental and cultural differences which simply will not go away and which can impact heavily on product design and choice. I mention only a few:

1. Aesthetic differences in that there are no absolute measures of relative aesthetic merit; it depends on what constitutes attractiveness in the eyes, mouth, ears, taste, and feel of the beholders. (No matter how long I am exposed to traditional Chinese opera or Japanese kabuki, I doubt that I shall *really* enjoy either. Yet, witnessing the enthusiasm of audiences, I doubt that for them nontraditional forms will ever give the same pleasure.) The same goes for color, form, size, texture, flavors, smells. None is better than any other in some absolute, universal, objective sense. So why should tastes converge?

2. The relative scarcity of space and hence the values associated with space obviously vary enormously from one society to another, which difference is very unlikely to go away in the foreseeable future. [Surely, one reason that the Japanese excel in the miniaturization of products is their very small living space per person. For a major country, the gross national product (GNP) per square foot in Japan is possibly the highest in the world and living space per person among the smallest.]

3. Climatic differences obviously have an enormous impact on the design of thousands of products, likewise topography, soil conditions, availability of water and energy, proximity to the sea, and so on.

4. Perceptions of time vary from people to people and likewise the trade-off between past, present, and future, which trade-off may be closely related to levels of affluence, average life expectancy, sense of

personal security, the demographic structure of a population, and religious belief. Is the demand for a high-price, durable product, or the reverse?

But even for those products with some degree of global common-ality, global standardization makes little sense if substantial savings cannot be realized by that standardization. My more technically quali-fied colleagues tell me that this saving does not necessarily follow, that technology whereby economies of scale can be substantially reduced is at hand. It is not part of any divinely revealed scripture that in order to build low-cost motor vehicles one must manufacture them in runs of 200,000. Indeed, in Alvin Toffler's *The Third Wave*, one reads:

> Everywhere we are seeing a dawning recognition that there are limits to the much-vaunted economies of scale, and that many organizations have exceeded those limits. Corporations are now actively searching for ways to reduce the size of their work units. New technologies and the shift to services both sharply reduce the scale of operation (Toffler 1981, p. 272).

Toffler goes on:

> The essence of Second Wave manufacture was the long run of millions of identical, standardized products. By contrast, the essence of the Third Wave manufacture is the short run of partially or completely customized products (1981, p. 191).

By the "third wave" he refers to the postindustrial era, into which the more industrialized societies are now moving, a movement accom-panied by great unrest and turbulence to which we are all witness. Characteristics of this third wave: small-scale production; greater identity between producer and consumer; decline of heavy industry; shift to renewable energy sources; the fracturing of the nation-state; organization of society into smaller units (regional and/or ethnic); deurbanization; and introduction of new technologies based on elec-tronics and genetic engineering, as well as technologies "intended to provide humane jobs, to avoid pollution, to spare the environment, and to produce for personal or local use rather than for national and global markets alone" (Toffler 1981, p. 164).

John Naisbitt (1984) in his *Megatrends* makes many of the same points. Rather than products and services becoming standardized, consumer options are widening all the while. Even in the United States, the design of buildings is becoming regional, the mass media are being broken up into regional and local media, state and local governments are eclipsing the size and impact of the federal govern-ment in many ways, including regulation of the market place. (Indeed, U.S. statistics relating only to the federal government can be very misleading.)

The result is that one can question both of Professor Levitt's underlying assumptions—that economy of scale (and hence low price) can be achieved only in world-scale plants turning out standardized products and that differences in tastes and preferences can be eliminated by the resulting price differentials (which are likely to be very modest, if they are there at all). What Levitt says may have been true in the recent past, but there are many indications that the Toffler–Naisbitt view of the future is the more accurate one. We can already see the process at work in such a country as the United States. As a reaction to mass production, mass marketing, mass media, and standardization on a mass basis, for many many products and services there is no longer a national market. Rather, there is a bundle of markets differentiated by regional and ethnic tastes that are guarded with increasing jealousy. Apart from a global market, we do not even have a national market into which one can safely throw standardized, undifferentiated products. Market segmentation and product adaptation is the name of the game, the more so as new process technology permits economic production on a smaller and smaller scale. This also suggests the economy of producing many things ever closer to the target market.

We who think about international marketing may have been addressing the wrong question. We have been concerned about how *national* markets vary and what is the best strategy for *national* markets. As international trade barriers are reduced (and in the long run, they *are* coming down, although with periodic backsliding) and as the identity of persons with the state (at least in a cultural sense) tends to erode, we should be thinking more of differentiated subnational markets and their linkages across borders, not so much in terms of *national* markets. For instance, the mass poverty of India should not hide the existence of a large sophisticated, affluent market in India, possibly numbering 100 million, whose tastes and consumption patterns may be quite similar to affluent, elite groups elsewhere—though far from identical, I would hasten to add. But the poverty of India is not going to be eliminated in our lifetime. And poverty, wherever it occurs, has its own distinctive culture. In such a market, the trade–offs between price and durability, price and time saving, capital and labor, price and convenience, the present and the future are very different from those characteristic of more affluent markets, but similar across international borders wherever there is deep poverty. The very concept of *national marketing*, or *international marketing* (if the unit is nations), may be increasingly inappropriate. We should talk, rather, of "intercultural marketing."

Apart from these factors, one must recognize that the affluent elites of many countries travel widely, have much direct contact internationally, and may well develop a certain tendency for taste and preference to converge worldwide among their numbers, thereby creating a global market for certain goods and services—though even *that* convergence should not be exaggerated. Possibly it has already run its course. What we *seem* to be witnessing now is a reaction to such convergence, a reassertion of self-confidence, or renewed loyalty to differentiated traditional cultures, which is reflected in a reemphasis of different tastes and preferences for many goods. And, at the same time, if the cost of adapting goods to those differentiated tastes and preferences is no higher than that achieved by ignoring differences (i.e., by providing standardized goods), one sees a very different vision of future international markets than that postulated by Professor Levitt.

Naisbitt in his *Megatrends* tells us that there are 752 different models of cars and trucks sold in the United States alone (and that's not counting the choice of color or accessories). "In Manhattan, there is a store called Bulbs, which stocks 2,500 types of light bulbs—nothing else. This," he concludes, "is the analog for what is going on in society. Advertisers are forced to direct products to perhaps a million clusters of people who are themselves more individualistic and who have a wide range of choices . . . The multiple-option society is a new ballgame, and advertisers know they must win consumers, market by market (1984, p. 232). And by market is not meant a national market, but one culturally and environmentally determined. In that national borders only delineate systems of politics and law, they are relevant only to the extent that these factors are among important market determinants.

One suspects that as consumers everywhere become more sophisticated they will demand more and more—not less—products which better meet their specific needs and preferences. The firm that markets such products efficiently will win the competitive game. Take the motor vehicle. Granted, a worldwide demand for vehicles has appeared, but as times goes on, demand becomes increasingly differentiated by market, whether on a national basis or a subnational, regional basis. Increasingly, vehicles are being designed for use in different environments. Consider some of the relevant environmental factors:

- Climate and road conditions
- Availability of maintenance facilities
- Relative cost of alternative fuels
- Affluence (i.e., trade-off between price and nonessential features, prestige vs. essentiality)
- Characteristic use (e.g., for family transport, as public carriers, passenger/cargo trade-off).

And in many markets, customers much prefer to buy the chassis and build the body on a custom basis. The market does not belong to the firm which would insist on marketing a line of standardized vehicles worldwide, although subnational markets may be put together, markets which share many if not all of the relevant environmental factors.

Given the fact of increasingly differentiated markets—though not necessarily defined nationally—and reduced economies of scale, there is strong pressure to manufacture close to the center of demand in relatively small plants. There will be a tendency for these to be retained as subsidiaries of foreign-based, or multinational, corporations *only* under two circumstances: (1) if important units or subassemblies of the product can be manufactured more efficiently (i.e., at lower cost) elsewhere (we are talking of parts which can be standardized without jeopardizing important local design features of the final product), and (2) if the parent corporation continues to turn out important technological innovations relating either to the manufacturing process or to the product itself. In that intermediates and technology often can be transferred more cheaply between parent and subsidiary than between two completely independent enterprises, there may be a cost advantage for the multinational in maintaining ownership. That is, there may be a cost advantage for the firm transferring intermediate products and technology *internally*, from itself to subsidiaries. Where internal transaction costs are lower than market-intermediated transactions, firms will try to maintain equity-based control in many situations. The real question is, then, in which situation is it cheaper for the firm to externalize product or process? That brings us to the concept of the value-added chain.

The Value-Added Chain

Unless a firm enjoys the protection of an unknowable trade secret or an unbreakable patent, which enables it to enter international markets with a significantly different or better product than competitors *and* for which there is a continuing demand until the next equally well-protected product can be introduced (a highly unusual set of circumstances, one must admit), it would do well to look at its specific advantages in regard to specific inputs. That is, it should analyze its value-added chain, which collectively constitutes a product. Of course, the point is that a product is nothing other than a bundle of services linked together, but often divisable, from initial information gathering and sorting, through research and development, production and financing, to servicing the final consumer. And a plant, the production part of the value-added chain, simply a bundle of processes, some of which can possibly be performed in separate facilities (Figure 3.1).

One should find that, by concentrating on that which the firm does best, the firm's competitive position in international trade is the strongest, i.e., the most profitable.

It has taken the insistence of Eastern Europe, China, and now many less developed countries on barter, offset, and countertrade and

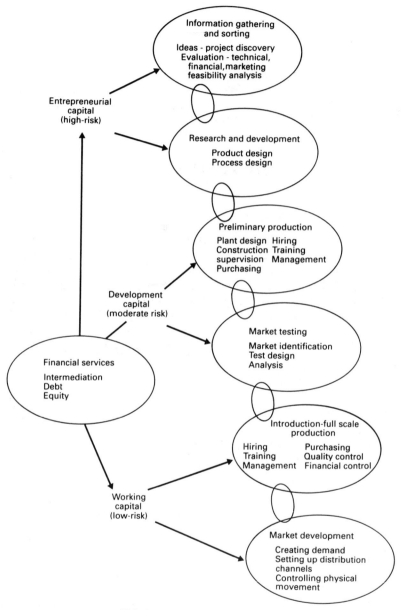

FIG. 3.1. The Value-Added Chain

various types of coproduction to convince many of the North American and Western European firms that they indeed have products other than hard goods to sell internationally. One can sell entrepreneurial services, R&D (research and development) services, engineering services, training services, purchasing and hiring services, marketing and distribution services, financial services, as well as sell parts or partially manufactured hard goods for local finishing. These are all alternative to marketing a final, hard good.

Some of these links in the value-added chain are obvious in terms of international marketing, but some may not be. For example, how does one market entrepreneurial services? Here are a few ways: information gathering and sorting becomes project discovery and analysis (i.e., technical, financial, and marketing feasibility analyses); R&D (i.e., product and process design); preliminary production (which may include plant design, construction supervision, some purchasing, hiring, training, and management); market testing (i.e., market identification, test design, and analysis); introduction of full-scale production (which includes hiring, training, managing, purchasing, quality control, financial control); and finally market development (i.e., selection of distribution channels, creation of consumer demand, physical movement).

All of these services may be the subject of an international transaction under contract, including financial services. These last may take the form of providing (1) financial intermediation (i.e., access) with respect to foreign financial markets with or without the guarantee of the intermediate, (2) risk-bearing of equity finance redeemable after commercial success (either in part or entirely), or (3) straight debt financing—or some combination of these. In all cases payment may be made in the form of goods and services rather than in financial obligation.

This analysis is complicated by a further consideration. We all know that there can be real cost advantages in maintaining the *linkages* in the value-added chain *internal* to the firm. Indeed, the firm exists because of these advantages. Otherwise, we would all operate as independent contractors selling our services to one another on an arm's length basis. Consider some of the savings inherent in internal transactions as compared to external, market-mediated transactions:

1. There is less negotiating time and associated legal expenses; the whole transaction is speeded up.
2. People at both ends of the transaction speak the same language organizationally and technologically; they may even move from one function to another in order to make the communication more complete (e.g., an engineer from research to development to manufacturing to facilitate the introduction of a new technology).
3. There is little or no risk of nonpayment due to commercial failure (e.g., bankruptcy or lack of integrity).
4. There is little risk of nonperformance; hence, no performance bond or guarantee is required.

5. Continuing repetition of transactions (or functions) reduces cost through a learning effect (e.g., in the case of international technology transfer).

So, all other things being equal, *internal* transactions—the linkages between value-added elements—should be more efficient than external, market-mediated transactions. But all else may not be equal, particularly in the international case: some firms specializing in providing functions in the value-added chain via contract may, by offering these functions at reduced cost, overcome the inherently higher cost associated with external transactions. Possible reasons for a reduced cost are as follows:

1. International economies of scale and scope by reason of the ability to employ more fully either highly skilled people and/or information and distribution networks.
2. The development of greater expertise, in part a function of accumulated experience via repetition, as well as the ability to keep high-level manpower more fully employed.
3. The reduction of risk by reason of greater expertise and the ability to diversify function geographically via international information and distribution networks.
4. Access to lower-cost resources (financial and other) by reason of established reliability and integrity, and government intervention.
5. Greater access to customers for similar reasons.
6. Access to local resources at lower cost by reason of the firm's nationality and/or location, possibly by reason of government intervention.

Hence, a firm must evaluate each link in its value-added chain by measuring the cost and benefit of internalization vs. the cost and benefit of externalization. In each case, there is a trade-off. In some situations, the savings to be realized by internalizing a transaction between functions will be such as to outweigh the savings to be realized by contracting with another firm to perform one of the linked functions. In other situations, the reverse may be true.

In any case, the choice is between internalizing each link in the firm's value-added chain and externalizing such links. And the choice, if one is involved substantially in *international* operations, may be quite different from the purely domestic case. It boils down to the question of which value-added links are most likely to enjoy international economies (perhaps the result of government intervention) if performed by external specialist firms, economies which may swamp any benefits derived from the internalization of transaction.

I suggest that it is precisely those firms most sensitive to this dimension, both analytically and strategically, that tend to be most successful in international markets. When to externalize functions—*that* is the question. And, one might add, if a firm has had a long record of success in a continental domestic market without externalizing functions, the decision to externalize part of its value-added chain when it enters international markets may come hard.

Note that if a firm can establish an intimate and long-standing relationship with those firms providing it with externalized functions, then it may capture the benefits of both externalized functions and internalized transactions. Indeed, over time, the external relationships may assume all of the characteristics of internal transactions. The six advantages inherent to internal transactions listed previously may all be satisfied. Long-standing contractual relations as subcontractor, financer, processor, or distributor may be of this nature. International consortia of cooperating firms may become quite common.

To carry the argument one step further, bear in mind the distinct possibility of two major developments:

1. Many firms competing internationally, regardless of their sector, may have achieved maximum economy of scale in respect to internalized function and, thereby, minimum cost due to scale—*a scale which may be undergoing reduction in several sectors by reason of new process technology (e.g., flexible production machinery).*
2. The *commercialization* of radically new technology has probably, for a number of reasons, slowed significantly over the past decade.

If these two developments are in fact occurring, firms in many sectors can be expected to compete less and less on the basis of either superior scale or significantly new technology. Rather, competitive advantage will lie with those firms selectively externalizing functions *and* with those moving most rapidly down their respective learning or experience curves. What sort of firms are likely to do the latter? Obviously, those firms best able to capture their learning most effectively. And who does that? The firm with a relatively low turnover rate and open internal channels of communication, horizontally and vertically and in all directions—that is, the firm which can create an internal environment which (1) best encourages those with the experience (those actually engaged in production on the plant floor or at the office desk or laboratory bench) to analyze what they are doing and suggest improvements to those concerned and (2) is most conducive to a listening attitude by supervisors and managers. (One suspects that a key managerial skill is to encourage initiative on the part of subordinates and to listen rather than to initiate decisions and issue orders.) The other side of the same coin is a low turnover rate. A firm cannot afford to lose those employees in whose skills and insights are embodied the experience and learning that will translate into lower unit cost.

One suspects that the ingredients of the sort of internal organizational environment that enables a firm to capture its own experience is one in which there is a high level of mutual respect among employees of all levels, a high degree of loyalty running from employee to firm and *from firm to employee* (via employment and upgrading training commitment), a high level of trust based on the expectation of all employees that both gains and losses will be shared equitably, and a minimum social-economic distance within the firm between employees of different function and rank (from the "top" to the "bottom"). A hierarchical, autocratic, rule-bound, top-down organization in which pay differentials are high and those at the bottom run the greatest risk is very likely to lose out competitively precisely because it cannot capture its experience effectively and hence fails to move down its learning curve as rapidly as others. Even if employees in such an organization are so intimidated or insecure that they dare not leave the firm's employment, they are unlikely to spend much time analyzing what they are doing and passing along their insights. The assumption is that they would not benefit by doing so. Indeed, in such an organization it is unlikely that supervisors or managers would listen anyway. Movement down the experience curve is thus very slow.

The very complexity of modern technology magnifies the advantage of this more participate sort of shared management, whether in board room, office, or laboratory, or on the factory floor. No one can know enough at a managerial or supervisory level to act wisely without consulting those actually producing the goods or providing the services, as the case may be. The division between manager, supervisor, and production worker becomes necessarily very blurred. Here the term "worker" in the proletarian sense no longer really applies; "technician" or "associate" may be more appropriate.

This argument becomes relevant when it is noted that a firm's position on the experience curve may vary with product or function, depending to a substantial degree on the style of management exercised in various parts of the firm. The differences may well determine wherein the international competitive advantage of a firm's services, *within its value-added chain*, lies and thus relate to the internal–external choice.

One very quickly senses the relevance of the social-political environment in which the firm is embedded for some societies facilitate the sort of internal relationships described above and others make them difficult. To a degree, a firm's culture is a function of the surrounding external culture. Some societies provide structurally incompatible (i.e., high-cost) environments by reason of such factors as the following:

1. The highly valued modes of personal behavior (such as exaggerated individualism, aggressiveness, and intense interpersonal competition).
2. The manner of resolving conflicts (expensive and time-consuming litigation rather than less costly and more rapid alternative modes of conflict resolution).
3. The time horizon of decision making (personal and otherwise).
4. The level of security of person and property.
5. The ability to shift physical and human resources with least cost as markets internationalize and comparative advantages shift.
6. The degree to which society feels compelled to an active role in the affairs of other states, i.e., the level of military investment and generation of a military mentality.

Elements of environmental incompatibility may show up in a firm's competitive position in international markets in the form of costs inherent in employment turnover, repeated entry-level training, brittle management—labor relations, slowed introduction of new technology, work stoppages, litigation, legal expenses, investment in maintaining security, insurance premiums, and taxes. If the firm's international competitors take advantage of less costly environments (those more compatible with maintaining an internal environment conducive to maximum retention of experience), the firm's competitive edge will be dulled. Rather than locking its own assets into foreign and possibly little-known environments, it may make better sense for the firm to externalize those functions peculiarly vulnerable to such social-political costs by contracting with a firm or firms already operating within these environments.

Organizational Implications

There are organizational implications to these arguments quite apart from managerial style. Note that there are essentially four general modes in which international businesses may be conducted (see Figure 3.2). On the one hand, one may trade in essentially finished goods *or* more in the factors of production (e.g., finance, proprietary intangibles, technology or "soft-ware," labor, capital equipment or "embodied technology"). On the other hand, one may conduct transactions either internally *or* largely through the market. (Internal transactions, as already noted, refer to transactions within a single organization, division to division or subsidiary to subsidiary.) *Internal trade* in goods, toward the finished end of the spectrum, is identified with the trading company. *Market-mediated* trade in such goods tends to be undertaken by commodity traders. Of course, both types of trade

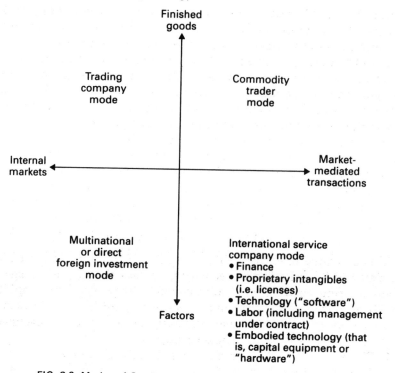

FIG. 3.2. Modes of Conducting International Business Transactions
(I am indebted to Professor Donald Lessard, my colleague at the Sloan School
of Management, for suggesting this analysis.)

may be combined in a single organization, such as in the large, general trading companies of Japan. The *internal* transfer of the various factors of production is represented by direct foreign investment, the vehicle characteristic of the multinational corporation (which is technically defined as an internationally integrated production system over which equity-based control is exercised by a parent corporation that is owned and managed preeminently by the nationals of the country in which it is domiciled). Foreign direct investment is essentially a *package* of factors transferred internationally within a single organization (i.e., internally). The international transfer of these factors *through the market* means that they are "unbundled" and traded separately, and hence we get into the domain of the international service company.

One could write a book about the underlying dynamics of the international trading system with respect to those organizational types which are growing and those which are declining. Suffice it to say here that it would appear that the *trading companies* are becoming more involved in services to complement existing business and to stimulate greater flows of goods; the *commodity traders* are probably likewise moving in the direction of service contracts so as to assure themselves of sources of goods. And the direct foreign investor may be moving both in the direction of pure trading and/or greater involvement in international service transactions—that is, in the unbundling of the foreign direct investment package—by reason of (1) the heightened risk inherent in a strategy of direct foreign investment and (2) reduced competitive advantage the internal transfer of factors provides the firm. Consider these dynamic factors:

1. The degree of centralized control implicit in the multinational corporation tends to give rise to increased political intervention by both host and parent governments, often of an unanticipated nature.

2. The stability of the legal/political climates in many countries leads to heightened political risk for the local plants and personnel of multinationals.

3. The floating of exchange rates and their volatility, often seeming unrelated to "purchasing power parity," means that the advantage of manufacturing goods in particular countries may shift quite rapidly. (In effect, one does not want to get locked into owning fixed assets in particular locations. Hence subcontracting and contract manufacturing may prove less costly in the longer run.)

4. There is increased competition for the multinationals from international financial institutions (for financial resources), from the international service companies (which increasingly sell specific factors at competitive price, whether it be technology, skills, management, etc.), and from the trading companies which offer access to international channels of distributing and supporting services, not to mention organizations specializing in research and development on order.

5. The demand for greater employee participation in decision making generates greater pressure for local control, making central control (the hallmark of the multinational) more costly, if not impossible.

6. There is a rise in various forms of counter trade, which the large trading companies are peculiarly well suited to handle but the multinationals are not—unless they are part of a large multi product conglomerate or international consortium.

7. Finally, the reduction of economies of scale renders the world-scale plant an anachronism.

The result is that it would appear that the most rapidly growing international business organizations of the past 10 years or so have been the trading companies and international service organizations. Even the commodity traders have found it to their advantage to tie in suppliers with various forms of service contracts. Therefore, it is useful for any firm involved in international business to remain alert to the economies and diseconomies of operating in the diverse modes we have outlined. Flexibility (i.e., maintaining open options) is characteristic of the winners.

Underlying these developments, and perhaps a major reason for them, is the possible slowing in the commercialization of significantly new technology; that is, an increasing portion of the technology in use is mature. I shall merely list a few of the arguments made to support this belief:

1. Much of the new technology is really of a marginal nature.

2. That which is radically new is too revolutionary for society to accept, given present knowledge, values, and institutions. (Examples range from nuclear energy to genetic engineering.)

3. Given the enormous stock of industrial assets in place worldwide, the introduction of radically new technology is prohibitively costly. (One needs to wait for the stock to depreciate.)

4. Investment in research and development of a commercially relevant nature is slowing due to (a) the shortened time horizon for investment (a function of political uncertainties, economic unpredictability, inflation), (b) increased uncertainty of outcome (a function of the complexity of new technology and the possibility of government intervention), and (c) inability to protect proprietary rights to new technology (owing to breakdown of patent protection).

5. There is enormous diversion of technical manpower and capital to military technology (with only limited commercial application).

If all this is true, one would expect a slowdown in direct foreign investment (i.e., a decline in the growth of multinationals relative to other forms of international business organization), an increasing tendency to unbundle the foreign direct-investment package into its components (of technology, skills, finance, marketing services, etc.), a rise of the more specialized service and trading companies trafficking in the components of the unbundled foreign investment package, and a shift of manufacturing to certain of the less developed countries (i.e., those with relatively well-developed infra-, or support, structures and some degree of political/legal stability)—all of which, in fact, seems to be happening.

The fact that international trade and investment statistics do not provide unambiguous support for these shifts should come as no surprise, given the multiple deficiencies in such tabulations (but see Oman 1984). Among these are the following:

1. The size of the underground, off-the-books economy worldwide is large and growing. In the United States it is estimated to be about 25%, and rising as the do-it-yourself sector grows, thereby moving an increasing amount of production out of the marketplace, a character-

istic of the Third Wave society described by Toffler. In international trade, we are referring to smuggling, which, let no one deny, is taking place on a grand scale.

2. Barter trade, which is large and growing by all accounts, creates reporting problems because the goods and services involved are not necessarily reported at market prices.

3. Much international trade—possibly 20–30%—is between related firms (parents and subsidiaries, subsidiary to subsidiary), and prices placed on the traded goods and services are necessarily arbitrary (and many services, in fact, move at zero prices).

4. International trade in services is notoriously under reported statistically, if included at all.

5. The international movement of labor—or all skilled people, in fact—is not included in most statistics relating to international trade. (If an Indian doctor emigrates to the United States, the value of his/ her medical service does not show up in trade statistics. Yet something of value has moved.)

6. Likewise not included are the flows of valuable services performed for clients or consumers who move internationally, such as a foreign student, foreign patient, or a foreign client of a domestic law or consulting firm. All of these transactions represent valuable transnational flows but are not reported.

These inadequacies in international trade statistics lead me to suspect a much more massive shift away from trade in hardware to trade in software than is suggested by trade statistics. This trend is very likely to be accelerated, given the fracturing of national markets into differentiated segments and the reduction in economies of scale in production.

Conclusion

The message is relatively simple. Rather than standardized, mass-produced goods taking over a culturally homogenized world market, markets are more likely to become increasingly fractured by culturally and/or environmentally based preference, though not necessarily organized on a national basis. Given a technology that permits *economic* production of widely diversified products on an ever smaller scale, more of the production of final consumer goods is likely to be tailor-made to fit these diverse preferences.

Those firms which will emerge the winners will be those that concentrate on selling that which they do best. Here the value-added chain analysis is a useful device. One clue in identifying those links which a firm forges most economically—and hence can sell internationally most profitably—is its capacity to capture and learn from its experience.

References

Levitt, Theodore, quoted in *HBS Bulletin*, (December 1983), pp. 8–10.
Oman, Charles, *New Forms of International Investment in Developing Countries*, (Paris: Organization for Economic Development and Cooperation, 1984).
Naisbitt, John, *Megatrends*, (London: Macdonald, 1984).
Toffler, Alvin, *The Third Wave*, (London: Pan Books, 1981).

4

Becoming a Triad Power: The New Global Corporation*

KENICHI OHMAE

Three great market regions—Japan, Europe and the United States—dominate the world of multinational business today. The combined gross national products of Japan and the United States now account for 30% of the free world's total. Add in the GNP of the four biggest Western European nations—the United Kingdom, West Germany, France and Italy—and the figure reaches 45%. Customers in the Japan-Europe-U.S. Triad buy over 85% of all computers and consumer electronics products. Japan, the United States and West Germany alone comprise 70% of the global market for numerically controlled machine tools.

The Triad countries all have similar problems: mature economies, escalating social costs, aging populations, a growing scarcity of skilled jobs, dynamic technologies and escalating R&D costs. Triad markets, too, are increasingly similar. Capital equipment until recently reflected its country of origin. Now the best-selling factory machines have become almost identical not only in appearance but in the skills required to operate them. There are 600 million consumers in the Triad with converging needs and preferences. Gucci bags, Sony Walkmans and McDonald's golden arches are seen on the streets of Tokyo, London, Paris and New York. Companies like Seiko, Sony, Canon, Matsushita, Casio and Honda are now routinely developing products for a world market, with minor modifications depending on local tastes.

All this has far-reaching consequences for multinational business. Quite simply, global enterprises organized for doing business in the 1960s are out of date.

---

*Slightly abbreviated from *International Marketing Review*, (Autumn 1986), with special permission.

Following World War II, American multinationals enjoyed a virtually insurmountable technological and competitive edge and could straddle Latin America, Asia and Europe. From 1945 to 1965 some 2,800 U.S. businesses had stakes in 10,000 direct investments abroad, aimed in most cases at exploiting a technological advantage (IBM, Texas Instruments, Xerox), a unique product (Gillette, Kellogg), or a leading position in U.S. industry (General Motors, International Telephone & Telegraph). Most of these subsidiaries were clones, so to speak, of the parent organization, each with its miniature version of corporate headquarters.

Many of today's leading world enterprises are still structured along traditional lines. Yet the world around them has changed dramatically. Consider:

● Siting production facilities in low-labor-cost locations—the "global enterprise" model—is still the fashion. Yet the economic advantages of doing so are likely to be short-lived. Most competitive Japanese companies, for instance, are today pulling out of South-east Asia and investing in capital-intensive robots and machines.

● A strategy favored by American MNCs has been to develop a proprietary technology and exploit it first domestically and then abroad. Today, they don't have time leisurely to market new and probably much more expensive technological developments; many competitors possess comparable technological skills, making it almost impossible to sustain a technological monopoly; and the global diffusion of the new technology had become a matter of months, not years.

● In the Triad markets, a new breed of consumers is emerging, similar in education, income, life style and aspirations. These 600 millions customers exhibit the same basic demand patterns and can be treated for marketing purposes as a single species. They all want the best products at the best price, regardless of origin.

● At the same time, protectionist pressures in each of the OECD countries are mounting, and economic nationalism is fuelling a global trend toward bloc economies.

These interrelated forces have momentous implications.

Capital-Intensive Operations

Automation, robots, machining centers and numerical controls have vastly increased productivity in the past decade. They have halved the labor content of traditional assembly operations, facilitated quick changeovers in manufacturing processes and made possible greater flexibility in plant siting. Microprocessors have swiftly driven down the cost of computer power. Computer-aided design and manufacturing (CAD/CAM) are begetting a manufacturing revolution.

The competitive repercussions of this shift from labor to capital in production are already evident in the automobile industry. To produce over 13 million vehicles a year, the entire Japanese automobile industry (automakers, component suppliers and automobile contractors) employs only 670,000 people—slightly fewer than the global workforce of the single largest U.S. automaker.

During the past decade, Toyota, while increasing its output $3\frac{1}{2}$ times—to 3.3 million units a year—has, by reducing production manhours, managed to maintain its workforce at about 45,000. The productivity of Toyota's rival Nissan is likewise about twice that of its global competitors. These companies have changed the traditionally labor-intensive auto industry into a capital-intensive business.

The story is the same in electronics. During the past five years, the workforce required to assemble a given consumer electronics product has been halved, and direct labor costs have been driven down to an average 5% of the costs. Likewise, the semiconductor industry has become a fixed-cost, capital-intensive game, as opposed to the variable-cost, "learning"-intensive business of only five years ago.

The trend is even more prevalent in continuous processing industries like chemicals, textiles and steel, where automated control systems enhance productivity and competitiveness. In two of Japan's leading steel mills, Nippon Steel and Nippon Kokan KK, the labor tab hovers around 10% of total costs.

This shift from labor to capital intensity shatters the mirage of low-cost labor in developing countries. Companies used to locate their operations in low-labor-cost countries so as to bring down variable costs. Third World labor costs still average only a third of those in developed nations—but when direct labor content accounts for less than 10% of total manufacturing costs, the costs of transport and insurance can more than offset the advantages of cheap labor. For example, the typical cost of transporting a color television set from Southeast Asia to California, including duties and insurance, is 13% of free on board (FOB), totally out-weighing the 10% savings in labor cost.

Changed Economics

Typically, therefore, the economic tradeoff will favor siting a production facility either where the product will be sold or where important component parts are available. The same logic applies in industries where product life cycles are short: constant changes in molds, jigs, tools and components make production locations remote from the core engineering group very inconvenient.

Together with the lack of qualified workers and local managers, these factors have reduced the attractiveness of siting production facilities in developing countries. The Japanese chip-makers have been the latest to learn first hand what the color television (CTV) and textile industries discovered earlier: cheap, inexperienced labor must be trained and, once trained and experienced, does not stay cheap very long.

Managers in automated industries who fail to recognize the implications of this shift from labor to capital will find their profit margins severely squeezed. Automated operations are better equipped to fight inflation, since the ratio of labor cost to total manufacturing is bound to increase when sales are declining or wages rising. Automated operations also resist recession. Highly automated Japanese facilities such as Yamazaki (machine tools) and Fujitsu Fanuc (numerical controls) are said to break even at 10% of capacity. Other manufacturers like Toyota claim that they can operate at 70% and still not lose money.

But this shift from labor- to capital-intensive production has a further consequence. To achieve the economies of scale needed to defray the heavy initial investment and the outlays for continuing production process innovation, deep and immediate market penetration becomes necessary. In the semi-conductor and machine tool industries, even domestic markets as large as Japan or the United States have proved too small to support global-class automated plants.

Costs of Development

The interaction between scientific disciplines, between industries, and between industries and services is blurring existing economic power patterns. So rapid has the pace of technological innovation and its commercialization become in the high-tech industries that a technological advantage can be eroded virtually overnight.

Five vanguard high-technology industries (electronics, data processing, telecommunications, fine chemicals and pharmaceuticals), accounting today for just over 6% of GNP in the OECD nations, contributed no less than 16% of their economic growth between 1975 and 1980. The same high-technology group averaged 1.49 times the sales growth, 2.8 times the labor productivity growth, and 2.75 times the profit growth of six medium-technology industries—iron and steel, automobiles, organic chemicals, textiles, nonferrous metals, and pulp and paper. As can be seen from Figure 4.1, which compares the two

Net profit/sales ratio*

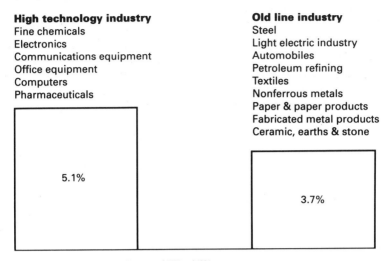

High technology industry
Fine chemicals
Electronics
Communications equipment
Office equipment
Computers
Pharmaceuticals

Old line industry
Steel
Light electric industry
Automobiles
Petroleum refining
Textiles
Nonferrous metals
Paper & paper products
Fabricated metal products
Ceramic, earths & stone

5.1%

3.7%

*World leading companies: weighted average of 1980 and 1981.
Source: *Economic Analysis of World Enterprise – International Comparison*, MITI, 1982.

Fig. 4.1. High Profits from High Technology.

groups in terms of the net profit on sales, it has become very difficult to make money in old-line industries that have become "engineered commodities."

The industries critical to wealth generation in the 1980s are all concentrated in Japan, Europe and the United States. More than 80% of global production and consumption, and 85% of patent registrations, are also taking place in the Triad.

As the costs of developing and commercializing new technologies keep rising, companies are moving in three directions to gain the benefits of integration and cross-fertilization: (1) downstream, to control the interface with the customer, (2) upstream, to acquire new technologies or protect sources of expensive raw materials, and (3) horizontally, to share complementary technologies with the object of creating or exploiting new market opportunities.

The first two moves are obvious. As global competition intensifies, the management of fixed costs, particularly in R&D and distribution, becomes critical for creating wealth. The fixed cost of R&D, especially the cost of developing breakthrough technologies, is becoming so high that their global potential must be quickly exploited to the fullest. But this demands the ability to penetrate deeply into all critical markets.

Few corporations—apart, possibly, from the IBMs, Xeroxes and Kodaks of this world—command a distribution network capable of establishing a share of foreign markets comparable to their established domestic positions. For example, Toyota and Nissan, with domestic market shares of 38% and 28% respectively, have a combined share of only 5% of the European Community (EC) and 12% of the U.S. markets. Even Sony has only an 8% market share in the U.S. consumer television market, as against a 19% share at home.

A natural strategic move, therefore, is to concentrate on strengthening R&D and domestic distribution. Once a corporation develops a unique technology, it can cross-license it to foreign counterparts in the other two regions of the Triad. Beside achieving high penetration and reducing marketing risks in difficult foreign markets, it can thereby gain attractive new technologies in return to be exploited in its own home markets. Such cross-licensing typically doubles or triples the potential of a technology, and maximizes the contribution to the fixed costs of domestic distribution through the handling of products and technologies of foreign origin.

Co-operative Initiatives

The third type of crossover is horizontal. In today's high-technology industries, no single company can control all the critical technological elements, ranging from memory microchips, image sensors and laser emitters to modems, optical transmission devices and the time division multiplex technique for the simultaneous transmission of voice and data over the same phone line.

As a result, any company that wants to compete in office automation, robotics, or consumer electronics markets must concentrate on a few critical internal R&D projects and develop a supersensitive control-tower function to constantly scan and monitor externally available technologies. In order to avoid the risk of losing out totally in a new game, a corporation may very well cross-fertilize with a complementary company, domestic or foreign, across a wide spectrum of the business system, from procurement, design and manufacturing to sales and servicing.

The signposts of structural shifts on a cross-national basis are all there. Companies vying for a piece of the potentially lucrative computer and communications pie are coming from all directions.

One example is the technological patent exchange between the two leviathans in telecommunications and computers, respectively—Japan's Nippon Telegraph and Telephone (NTT) and America's IBM. In Europe, American Telephone and Telegraph (AT&T) is invading IBM's turf with a computer, with help from Philips and Olivetti. American contenders in the Japanese office automation equipment market today include all the traditional and plug-compatible computer competitors, entrants from traditional "office equipment" makers (such as Xerox and Hewlett-Packard), a host of word-processor entrants led by Wang, and even a personal computer manufacturer or two.

Several of Japan's office automation leaders are arming themselves for the coming global battle for dominance through international alliances with competitors. Burroughs, which is trying to latch on to Hitachi's technological edge, is already packaging Fujitsu's high-speed facsimiles and is manufacturing Nippon Electric Company's (NEC's) optical character reading techniques under a royalty license. Toshiba's high-speed facsimiles are being distributed in the United States by Pitney Bowes and Telautograph, a subsidiary of the Arden Group, and by International Telephone & Telegraph (ITT) in Europe.

Accelerating Time Frames

The rapid rate of technological dispersal is a distinct and important phenomenon of its own. The basic research on the transistor, developed at Bell Laboratories in 1947, took over a decade. It was commercially introduced four years later, and another six years passed before it was incorporated into the computer. The integrated circuit, developed by Texas Instruments in 1958, took three years to become a viable product.

Now consider the accelerated time frame for major developments in the semiconductor during the past decade. It took two years in the United States for the chip to move from 4K– to 16K-bit random access memory (RAM). Less than eight months later the Japanese caught up with the United States. It took two years for the United States to move from 16K to 32K chips, less than three months for Japan to catch up. Then, in 1978, Japan's Fujitsu leap-frogged U.S. suppliers and introduced the 64K microchip with a 3-month lead. In 1983, the Japanese started sample shipment of the 256K N-MOS dynamic RAM, and early in 1984 they started its commercial production. American firms are lagging behind by about a year on average.

The strategic implications are threefold. First, technologically advanced companies cannot rest on their laurels. Second, challengers with me-too products may nevertheless have the clout to erode the leader's market share. Third, it costs so much to develop a technologically advanced and differentiated product that the producer must be able to sell to the entire world simultaneously in order to amortize the heavy front-end investment. Companies that choose to develop domestic markets first before going overseas may find themselves totally blocked out by well entrenched competitors set to invade their own home markets.

Universal Users

Whether it produces capital equipment or consumer goods, a company that ignores the universal market potential of the Triad does so at its peril. Not too long ago, capital equipment exhibited clear cultural distinctions: West German machines reflected that nation's penchant for craftsmanship, American equipment was often extravagent in its use of raw materials, and so on. Today, the best-selling factory machines have lost these distinguishing "art" elements. They have become alike in appearance and in the level of skills they require.

Even more conspicuously, consumers in the Triad have become increasingly alike. In his dark blue suit, Regal shoes and Céline necktie, carrying a Casio packet calculator in his Mark Cross wallet, frequenting a nearby *sushi* bar for lunch, and commuting in a Celica, the typical New York businessman would not draw a second glance on the streets of Düsseldorf or Tokyo. Youngsters in Denmark, Germany, Japan and California are all growing up with ketchup, jeans and guitars and worshipping the universal "now" gods—ABBA, Levi's and Arpège. Within the Triad countries, in fact, age-group differences—the so-called generation gap— are more pronounced than differences of taste across national boundaries.

A prime force behind the similarities and commonalities in the demand and life patterns of Triad consumers is purchasing power. In terms of per capita discretionary income, the purchasing power of Triad residents is more than ten times that of dwellers in the less-developed countries (LDCs) and newly-industrialized countries (NICs). More than 94% of households in Triad countries have television sets, as compared to about 60% for the NICs and less than 20% for the LDCs. One-third of both Japanese and American consumers have a high-school education or better, as compared with 15% of the population in NICs, and even fewer in the LDCs. Their purchasing power, their educational level, and what they read and see unite the Triadians and distinguish them from the rest of the world.

Once these commonalities are recognized, universal products can be designed. The increasing commonality of life styles in Triad countries means that the company that comes up first with a universal product has the best chance of winning the global race for consumer acceptance. Companies like Seiko, Sony, Canon, Matsushita, Casio and Honda now routinely develop products against a global perspective. Their product designers spend as much as half their time abroad talking directly with their customers and dealers. When they return, they design and synthesize their global product based directly on their personal impressions.

This concentration of consumer and capital goods users within Japan, Europe and the United States is probably the primary trigger of global high-technology competition. The Triad is where the main action is.

Neo-Protectionism

Most Free World economies were in a severe slump in the early 1980s. High unemployment reduced purchasing power, leading to slowdowns in the automobile, consumer goods and construction industries, and in dependent businesses such as steel and component parts. These economic dislocations made it very difficult for national governments to resist political pressures for short-term remedies in the form of trade barriers. Some countries put up quotas and duties against all imports, others against imports of specific products coming from particular countries.

In consequence, if a company is not a recognized "insider" in a country important to its share growth, it may find the doors to that market tightly closed. The outsider's trade base is always fragile, whereas the insider's position is secure. For instance, Sony, which has a sizeable plant in San Diego, escaped the quota and surcharge litigations and much of the ill-will directed against other Japanese color television producers during the uproar over Japanese color televisions in the United States.

Of course, governmental regulations and media headlines don't necessarily reflect the attitude of the public at large. The Japanese government may take a tough negotiating stance with the United States on beef and orange quotas, but that doesn't mean that Japanese consumers are any less keen to buy American oranges or beef. And, despite quotas, the American people clearly like Japanese color televisions and automobiles.

Quite simply, customers everywhere want the best product for the price from anywhere in the world. That is the reason behind the increase in transnational trade, and hence in trade friction and artificial obstacles to the transnational flow of goods. That is why it is so important for a global corporation-to-be to establish a *de facto* insider position.

Paradoxically, this fragmentation of developed markets is taking place (and seemingly even intensifying) at a time when the residents of the Triad are emerging as a nearly homogeneous buying group. To respond to these two contrary phenomena, pragmatic business strategists must simultaneously develop a Triad perspective and accelerate their companies' "insiderization" in key markets.

Triadic Strategies

As we have seen, the Japan-Europe-U.S. Triad is where the major markets are. It is where the competitive threat comes from. It is where new technologies will originate. And, as competition becomes keener, it is where preventive action against protectionism will be needed most. Thus, in order to take advantage of the Triad's markets and emerging technologies and to prepare for new competitors, every multinational corporation must seek to become a true insider in all three regions.

Xerox's pre-eminence in Japan helped it anticipate and respond to low-end technology being introduced by the Japanese plain paper copier manufacturers. Texas Instruments was able to produce 64K memory chips in Japan quickly, while other U.S. companies were fighting off the intrusion of Japanese semiconductor houses in the United States. Each of these companies was able to adapt quickly to an emerging competitive situation by virtue of its insider position.

A company that can ensure it has equal penetration and exploitation capabilities in each of the Triad regions—and no blind spots—stands a good chance of becoming an effective Triad power. The first condition will ensure that it recovers its investment in unique and diversified products; the second, that it avoids surprises from foreign competitors, or from domestic competitors forming alliances with foreign companies. Failure to satisfy these two conditions allows a company to slip into a vicious cycle of decline: giving up its main market segments, concentrating on relatively peaceful niches, confining its activities to the domestic market, repeating the "cost reduction and removal of overhead" cycle, and ultimately losing its position as a major contender in the global marketplace.

With mighty salesforces in each of the three Triad regions, either their own or a partner's, companies can strike into the market in a relatively short time, preempting both local and other global competitors and realizing high returns on their initial investment. With this profit, they can reinvest in more sophisticated and complex facilities and/or R&D, redoubling their competitive muscle. Should any local company come up with a high-potential new product, the Triad power can swiftly copy it and preempt the local competitors' opportunities in the other two Triad markets. With the profit thus generated, it can then comfortably engage in a head-to-head battle with the originating company on its own turf. That company must generate funds to fight back, although its profits from domestic sales may be hardly enough to recover its developments and launching costs.

The advantages of knowing the Triad customers and competitors as a true insider are so clear that the issue is not whether a company should become a Triad power, but how.

The Road to Triad Power

Three vehicles can be used, alone or in combination, to become an effective Triad insider: wholly-owned subsidiaries, joint ventures, and consortia.

The Wholly-Owned Subsidiary

This, the traditional MNC vehicle, needs no detailed discussion, but for successful implementation in the Triad context three points should be borne in mind: first, a "regional" rather than country-level structure should be established to share common resources; second, headquarters should play the role of strategic lubricator across key regions of the Triad rather than acting primarily as a controller; and finally, equal "citizenship" should be given to each of the Triad regions—and to any region outside the Triad where the company operates on a major scale (we could call this a "tetrahedral" model).

For example, the German chemical giant BASF, which reorganized in 1981, preserves the regional grouping of its nonstrategic areas, but treats the key strategic countries completely separately. The head of BASF's U.S., Japanese and Brazilian subsidiaries (Brazil is an important "hinterland" for the company) each report directly to a member of the executive board. Tailor-made policies are worked out for each of the three areas. This kind of organization is one realistic model for a multinational enterprise.

Despite Japan's critical strategic difference from other Asian countries, too many multinationals consign it to the Far East Department or the Pacific Basin Division of the International Business Sector, with the head of Japanese operations five levels below the CEO—literally, in some cases, below the level of a sales manager in Denver. Japanese companies make the same mistake when they send a deputy general manager from Production Planning to head up their U.S. operations. This is the quickest way for a multinational corporation to undermine its prospects of succeeding as a Triad power.

The Joint Venture

Joint ventures are normally designed to take advantage of the strong functions of the partners and supplement their weak functions, be they management, research, or marketing. The recent announcement of a joint-venture plan in small business computers between Matsushita and IBM is a good example of resource sharing, with each company supplementing the other's functional strengths. This joint venture also testifies that even the biggest companies in two regions of the Triad cannot fight and win the electronics war single-handed.

Yamatake-Honeywell, in which Honeywell owns 50%, the Yasuda group about 16.5%, with the rest traded on the Tokyo Stock Exchange, has grown to be No. 2 in the Japanese process control and instrumentation field. Honeywell has been able to inject needed technologies, and the Japanese partner has supplied a stable management team.

Philips has a long and successful history of joint ventures with Matsushita in electronic components. Similarly, Caterpillar's joint venture with Mitsubishi Heavy Industries has given it real staying power in the rather conservative earth-moving equipment market of Japan. High Voltage Industries (HVI), a 50:50 joint venture between GE and Hitachi in gas switch gear in Philadelphia, uses GE's mighty pooled salesforce for utility customers and Hitachi's advanced gas diffusion technology.

Too often, however, joint ventures fail because of differences between the partners. Since a joint venture is a legal entity with equity sharing, the partners must decide formally how to share profit (or loss) and where and how to reinvest for the future. Unless their management philosophies are compatible, disputes over investments or resource allocation can frustrate common goals. All concerned need to understand at the outset that making a success of a joint venture involves at least as much pain and effort as building a new greenfield plant. Like a marriage, it will demand a lot of effort by both parties over a long period that may bring changes in the environment, in the aspirations of the partners, and in their relative strengths.

Unlike a marriage, though, a joint venture is constrained by numerous legal contracts and forms of capital participation. Instead of talking out their frustrations and differences, the partners are frequently all too quick to point out each other's violations of these legal contracts. Often, critical matters tend to be decided by vote, based on the partners' respective proportions of equity holding.

In my observation, majority voting seldom represents good business judgment and rarely favors entrepreneurial decisions. Indeed, if a voting process is needed to decide on critical matters, the chances are the joint venture has already failed. To put it another way, if your company needs the world's best lawyers to spell out all the possible details and countermeasures in potential disputes, you lack a sound basis for the joint venture. Two companies with "natural" fit are a rarity. Extremely careful planning, and a lot of giving, will be needed before the partners can begin thinking about jointly harvesting the fruits.

Companies that choose the joint venture route to becoming a Triad power will be wise to follow a few simple guidelines:

● Make sure there is at least one key top management sponsor on each side of the venture, each firmly convinced that the undertaking is meaningful and will be good for his company.

● Keep these sponsors responsible for the joint venture for a decade at least.

● Ensure active cross-fertilization and frequent mutual face-to-face communications at the top management, operations management and workforce levels.

● Above all, communicate rather than control.

The Consortium

Traditional multinationals tried to do everything on their own as they entered each market. Today, the skills and resources required to compete worldwide have increased so enormously that they can no longer "go it alone." All but a very few must rely for success on their ability to develop and enhance company-to-company relationships, particularly across national and cultural boundaries.

Given the difficulties a company faces in penetrating the major Triad markets on its own, or in adapting its established corporate culture to establish an insider position in the other regions of the Triad, the strategic benefits of forming a consortium of true insiders in the respective key regions are obvious. Such a consortium can enable each member company to enjoy almost instant access to a vast number of potential customers, and gain vital insight into the purchasing, manufacturing, marketing, distribution, personnel and financing aspects of operating everywhere in the tough but lucrative Triad markets.

The trend of recent consortia is toward sharing resources and swapping products to avert development risk. Instead of geographically close competitors joining forces, distant competitors are merging and sharing functions such as R&D and production: British Leyland produces a medium-sized Honda in the United Kingdom, while Nissan produces Volkswagen's Santana model in Japan.

Many examples of emerging loose consortia can be seen today in such key industries as automobiles, semiconductors and steel. The rationale is to seek partners in other Triad regions to supplement functional shortcomings in order to survive and even expand in home regions. Typically, these consortia are formed to share or trade certain upstream functions such as R&D, production and technology, and to stay abreast of the leading-edge competitors. Sometimes they involve swapping certain product categories in order to take advantage of synergies made possible by sharing critical functions. Rarely does a partner give up an entire function.

Consortium alliances between competitors in the same Triad region should be avoided, however. Distant foes can be real friends, while close cousins can be enemies. Most of the European transnational mergers of the 1960s, involving links between similar companies, failed. Because they were too close, they could not work as partners and ended up at loggerheads.

The most useful ground rule in forming a consortium is to maximize the contribution to critical fixed costs. If R&D becomes expensive, make sure the resulting products are sold all over the world by licensing them to consortium allies, even though you may have some selling capabilities of your own in certain regions. If you have a costly, state-of-the-art production facility that could operate at low cost if fully utilized, then you should think about selling your products through any company with strong distribution capabilities, to original equipment manufacturers or under your own brand name. If you have a well-developed salesforce and/or distribution channel, but your laboratories cannot pump out enough new products, then think about importing attractive products made by other companies. Most product lines acquire a larger value-added increment during distribution than in production.

All these measures aim at maximizing the product's contribution to fixed costs by drawing on a global range of options. The message is: Enlarge your search for sources and potential contributors beyond your traditional neighborhood "shopping areas." Go global for the hunt. If your traditional rival is going global, then your only option is to do the same—but do it better.

The organizational implications of international consortia are complex. Collaborative arrangements with traditional competitors are seldom welcomed by middle managers, whose interest is to show top management that they are as capable as anyone else.

One essential step, therefore, is to conduct a good internal communications campaign to explain the intent of the consortium. Building executive relationships on several levels between the partners, and positioning a strong liaison officer at the top, are also vitally important. Too many consortia have been launched on a great wave of enthusiasm, only to fail subsequently for lack of any built-in means of sustaining it.

Most companies, while generously forgiving themselves their own mistakes, have a terrible habit of recriminating over their trading partner's errors. Maturity and diplomacy are required in a consortium to sustain constructive intercompany relationships.

Any corporation entering into consortium arrangements will need to keep two points in mind:

- Instead of cautious, suspicious and distant alliances of convenience, it will need to allow positive, proactive and strategic interlinkages—ultimately, if not at the outset—among all the participating partners.
- It must be prepared to gradually adjust its business system and terminology in order to minimize fraction among the consortium members in communicating and agreeing on critical matters. Smooth communication among the partners at all times and at all levels of management is vital to the long-term success of a Triad consortium.

Marks of a Triad Power

Whether it has achieved "insider" status through wholly-owned subsidiaries, joint-venture entities or loose consortium alliances, a true Triad power can be identified by a few distinctive characteristics:

1) Well established management systems in each of the Triad regions.
2) A full set of functions (possibly supplemented by headquarters or other regions where that makes strategic sense), fully responsive to local conditions.
3) Managers who are wholly familiar with local and regional customers and competitors.
4) Continuity of management, mostly with home-grown, overseas-trained personnel.
5) Swift, autonomous decision making, fully synchronized with the rest of the corporation. (Corporate headquarters, though fully informed, seldom interferes with regional management.)
6) Strong "staying power" in the key markets during periods of difficulty, and the capacity to come up with creative solutions to problems of market change.
7) Constant active communications—by telephone, personal visits and long-term exchange of people—within the corporation, at the interfaces with affiliated companies, and with headquarters.
8) Intolerance of the customary "it's out of my control" excuses for shortcomings and mistakes.
9) Significant presence and weight in the communities where its operations are located.

10) A corporate headquarters that functions simultaneously in three roles: as resource mobilizer, as interface lubricator and as strategic sensitiser.

The "resource mobilizer" role is self-evident in the case of wholly-owned subsidiaries. But even if a company takes the joint-venture or consortium route to Triad "insider" status, it must be prepared to allocate substantial funds and human resources to the venture with its partners. These alternatives to the on-your-own approach reduce the necessary commitment of management resources, but they must not be used to choke off the allocation of resources. Even a technical tie-up will not bear fruit unless both parties are willing to exchange people and experiment together, and prepared for plenty of "nice tries."

By the same token, corporate headquarters should take every opportunity to act to facilitate and lubricate the implementation strategies of consortia and/or joint ventures, rather than sit and wait for results to come in from the four corners of the world.

The final critical headquarters role is that of strategic sensitizer. If you are in the office automation industry, you had better be in California or Japan so that you can feel the "breathing" of the business. If you are a semiconductor manufacturer you need to visit Hamilton-Avnet, a large microchip distributor in the United States, or Kyushu, Japan's "silicon island," to feel the vibrations of the industry. These are the sensitive zones where trends can be detected first and where insiders can pick up market signals far ahead of competitors based elsewhere. Triad insiders in Japan were the first to pick up such subtle signals as the entry of Japanese sewing machine companies into the electronic typewriter business, or that of Sumitomo and Furukawa Copper Wire Works into fiber optics.

A true Triad insider can extract the strategic essence from these "sensitive zones" on behalf of the Triad partners. In its role as strategic sensitizer, headquarters will act to maximize corporate wealth by finding opportunities and eliminating blind spots over the entire Triad and its submarkets. It will pick up critical information in one region and pre-empt the opportunities of competitors in other regions. It will be alert to signals of structural change in consumers' desires, so that the company can come up with new product and/or service concepts. It will be able to identify and link up with dynamic new partners, catching its domestic and global competitors off guard.

5

Networks:
The Gay Nineties in International
Marketing

HANS B. THORELLI

Networking is Long-Term Strategic Cooperation

The two driving forces in free societies—and in world markets—are
competition and cooperation. The balancing act between them is age-
old and is likely to remain perennial. In recent years cooperation has
received a boost from the growing emphasis on standing contracts and
long-term relationships. This trend is likely to become a key characteristic of international marketing (IM) in the 1990s. *"Networks" is the
term applied here to arrangements promoting long-term strategic
cooperation.*

Such arrangements may take many forms, including standing
contracts, strategic alliances (Reading 34), trade associations, cartels,
patent pools, franchising and joint ventures (Reading 28) as well as
general and export trading companies and their precursors, the traditional European international trading houses.

Networks exist in consumer as well as industrial, and in domestic as
well as international marketing. Speaking relatively, they are, however,
of special importance in industrial, services and international
marketing due to the pivotal role of *trust* in these areas of business.
The burgeoning interest in networking has several roots. Due to the
increasing complexity of modern technology, of markets and of
government-business relationships the efficient solution to problems
ever more often calls for resources greater than those at the command
of any single firm. The greater prominence of professional approaches
to management with their emphasis on strategic planning and analytical techniques—both with a voracious appetite for information—is
another root. So is the ever-growing importance of what may be

labeled software relative to hardware in market transactions. If the product is thought of as hardware, software is the entire battery of "intangibles" that surrounds it, such as service delivery, quality maintenance, parts, applications engineering, ability to innovate, to provide better user information and to handle enquiries and complaints in a way deliberately calculated to suit the customer. Standardization agreements, systems selling and turnkey projects provide many good examples.

It follows that to be strategic a cooperative arrangement must be seen by participant management as a means of reaching key goals, that is, as an important and deliberate part of planning. A certain intensity of communication is also required before a business relationship can really qualify as strategic networking.

Networking may involve a variety of parties, such as

sellers
buyers
individual buyers and sellers
entire distribution channel systems
public and private organizations

The last two varieties are perhaps most typical of IM; networks between public and private organizations are especially prevalent in the LDCs.

Strategic Areas of Network Application

Important examples of networking applications include the following:

- *Marketing Channels and Franchising.* This may well be the single most important area. The clear trend is towards *tighter* networks here, to more governance of the systems (whether the "channel captain" is the manufacturer, wholesaler, or retailer), and to more programs than *ad hoc* actions and isolated strategies of individual members. Local dealer networks of auto manufacturers illustrate international channel systems, while the networks of Christian Dior U.S.A. (which handles 50% of the sales of the French mother company) with 26 U.S. manufacturers represents international franchising.

- *Vertical Integration (VI).* The VI issue is manifested in the make-or-buy decision so common in business. Simply put, the issue is do-it-yourself (or more fancifully, "internalization") vs. contracting out.

  Networking is a means of tighter integration than old-fashioned subcontracting on a spot basis, thus providing the valuable alternative of semi-integration. Kan-ban inventory management implies networking, as does the trend from many suppliers to few and from split to unified buying (sourcing).

- *Patents.* Many MNCs prefer not to license patents to others (in line with the internalization theory of IM), rather holding on to the differential advantage the patents may provide. Characteristic of the age, however, is the fact that MNCs increasingly engage in bilateral or pooled patent licensing; the rationale clearly being that it is rapidly becoming more difficult to keep on top of all relevant technologies, and that, in addition, in a relatively short time many patents will be circumvented by alternate technologies anyway.

  Such cross-licensing has been a part of a time-honored relationship between Bell Labs of the U.S.A. and Ericsson Telephone Corporation of Sweden, for example.

- *Turnkey Contracts and Systems Selling.* These types of transactions by their very nature often cannot be handled by an individual firm. Typically the buyer as well as the sellers stand to gain by close networking. Turnkey contracts are especially associated with technology transfer to the LDCs. Several hotels built by the Swiss and American firms in the PRC are good examples. Systems selling is illustrated by Dutch Philips and Swedish Ericsson teaming up to provide Saudi Arabia with a common telephone system.

- *Barter and Countertrade (Reciprocal Trading).* Here buyer and seller change roles in what is at least conceptually two separate sets of transactions. This often calls for the intimate, continuous kind of cooperation we associate with networking (Readings 35 and 36). Most, though far from all, countertrade involves an MNC and an LDC (or an LDC firm).

  Fairly recent and surely significant is the emergence of *counterdistribution*, typically involving companies from different industrialized nations. In this case company A in country X obliges itself to import a product (line) from company B in country Y, and company B takes on a similar obligation. The net effect can be a win-win situation typical of networking: both companies are able to broaden their product lines at a fairly low level of risk. A good example is the standing agreement between the largest U.S. beer brewer Anheuser-Busch and Denmark's Carlsberg. As a result, the tourist in Tivoli Gardens can have a Budweiser and the writer can obtain his Carlsberg in Bloomington, Indiana.

- *Transactions Between Subsidiaries.* Relations between domestic subsidiaries of the same company are often more distant than between buyers and sellers in the open market. Internal networking and internal marketing are frequently needed as much as networking with outside parties. Indeed in a General Electric Company study some time ago it was found that relations between internal units were often more troublesome and expensive to handle than corresponding transactions with outsiders.

Intra-company transfer tends to be a special challenge to the MNC. The marketing of goods and services between company units can be an extremely important means of global coordination. Yet many national subsidiaries tend to think first of their own aggrandizement. Tax and currency exposure implications must also be considered. So must global scale economies and the intensity of competition in local markets.

● *Joint Ventures (JV) and Acquisitions.* JVs are becoming increasingly popular in IM. Indeed in a country like the PRC a JV is frequently the only permissible form of foreign direct investment. Empirical studies reveal that unless JVs are operated like *tight* networks they are not likely to last more than three to five years, and sometimes even less. They will either be dissolved or one partner will buy out the other one.

Acquisition is often viewed as a means of gaining rapid entry abroad. However, if the prime concern is the human resources (management, skilled employees) acquisitions should be both preceded and accompanied by active networking to make sure that the human talent sought is motivated to stay on and remain productive. Too often in the past this important factor has not been taken into full account.

● *Internationalization.* The process of internationalizing company operations may well be the single most important area of networking applications. It may span across all the above-mentioned subjects, as illustrated below.

Complex International Networks Illustrated

Before going into some of the characteristics and dynamics of networking, a set of empirical illustrations of complex international networks will be provided.

Figure 5.1 presents a view of networking in the international automobile engine business by 1982–83. While individual relationships may be difficult to single out due to the mass of information, it is abundantly clear that most auto engine manufacturers of the world were involved in one or several networks with other such manufacturers. Since that time few networks have been disbanded, but others have been added, e.g., between Ford and Mazda and between Volvo and GM (truck engines). The diagram does not include "networking by ownership," such as GM's 20 + % ownership in Isuzu. Perhaps due to its size and a self-perceived ability to go it alone, GM was at least until recently involved in surprisingly few networking arrangements.

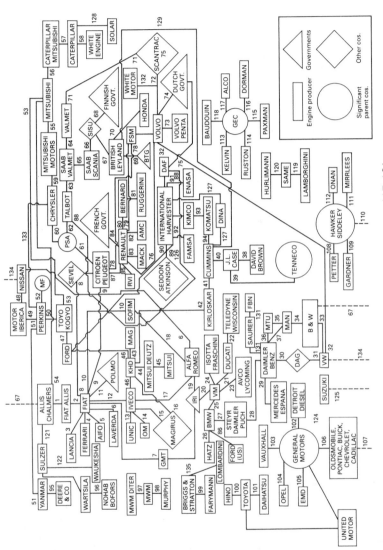

Source: World Engine Digest 1984 (London: John Martin, 1984), pp. 117–121.

Fig. 5.1. Networking in the International Auto Engine Business.

Philips, the Dutch electronics giant, is involved in well over 90 networking arrangements with companies making similar products, e.g., lighting (Matsushita), consumer electronics (Grundig of Germany, STET of Italy, Sony), technology (Siemens, Control Data) appliances (Whirlpool of U.S.A.), defense (Bendix), telecommunications (ATT, Ericsson, Siemens, Alcatel, etc.) and other hi-tech markets (Thorn EMI of U.K., Siemens, ATT, Bull, Nixdorf, Olivetti, etc.). Philips must be in at least an equal number of networks with vendors and distributors. While the U.S. antitrust laws place some obstacles (at least currently modest ones) in the way of networking among competitors we have reason to believe that Philips' involvements of this type are fairly typical of large hi-tech MNCs.

A Scandinavian networking example is provided by SCANCEM—the two joint ventures established by Norwegian Aker Norcem and Swedish Buroc to vastly expand the internationalization of the parent companies. Among the joint acquisitions in the last few years are cement factories in the U.S.A., the U.K. and the Congo.

Networking Objectives: Net Profit and Beyond

Most managers see greater profits as the objective they are ultimately striving for. But on the way to long-term profit (and often *beyond* short-term profit increases), there are other objectives or prerequisites, many of which lend themselves to networking:

- *Risk Reduction.* The General Electric-SNECMA (France) jet engine networking arrangement greatly reduces the risk and also pools the resources of both companies. Risk reduction was also a key idea behind the Anglo-French Concorde project.
- *Division of Labor and Functions.* Division of labor manifests itself primarily in the division of functions performed by various firms. Division of functions can be both *horizontal* (doing your own advertising or marketing research vs. contracting out these activities to ad agencies or marketing research firms) and *vertical* (a manufacturer distributing his own products vs. selling through wholesalers, for example).

  The division of functions in effect defines the firm's position in the so-called Value Added Chain from mine to consumer.
- *Diversification and Assortment.* Networking may help the firm to gain so-called *economies of scope* by diversification or broadening its assortment. Counter-distribution may be cited as an example.
- *Synergy.* Synergy refers to situations where the whole has greater effect than its parts. A good example of synergy is *common economies*, as when a firm can use a standard strategy in both the domestic market and the export market.

- *Innovation.* Several *R&D* projects sponsored by the European Community in areas such as space and electronics make extensive use of networking between both governments and firms in many different countries. In the U.S.A. there are at least two major networks of computer and electronics firms devoted to the joint development of new semiconductor technology. In Japan, MITI—the Ministry for International Trade and Industry—coordinates networks of firms for joint development of a variety of technologies.

- *Decision Support Systems.* Management can become more "scientific" and more professional only when and if the requisite *information* is on hand. Such networks as trade association data banks have found an important mission here.

- *Economies of Scale.* A good example of economies of scale is the manufacturer who, by intense networking with a few suppliers rather than spot buying from a lot of sources, obtained very significant scale economies in the purchase of the components he needed. In the last few years Whirlpool has achieved similar economies by reducing the number of steel suppliers to its appliance business by about one-half.

- *Monopolistic Power.* Cartel-type networks tend to create entrance barriers for outside firms, and to make use of the monopolistic power of the cartel to derive extra profits.

- *Market Share.* Even when not after monopoly power networks may be interested in building market share. The Norwegian suppliers of components to Volvo have a vested interest in Volvo's ability to increase its market share, as their own growth is directly related to it.

  Again, in the U.S.A., nine non-IBM producers of personal computers have gone together to standardize a new way of managing internal data flow in the PC in a different way than the IBM Microbus Channel Architecture introduced in 1987. They are doing this in the hope of collectively gaining market share from IBM.

- *Technology Transfer.* The LDC in general, and the PRC in particular, are often extremely keen on entering into networks with foreign firms involving the transfer of technology to these countries. This, of course also happens in industrialized nations. A case in point is the British Pilkington Group's activity in Japan. As is known, foreign companies trying to break into Japanese markets have to learn to take the long-term view and to build the personal contacts and links which make them acceptable members of the local "family." Pilkingtons are suppliers of the glass going into two-thirds of all Japanese-made sun glasses. According to the local marketing planning manager Pilkington's formula has been "to tie itself closely to the intricate network of sub-contractors which do the cutting, edging, hardening and polishing of the glass before it reaches the sunglass maker.... It is important for us to show a company at each point of the chain that they can rely on us to help them, if necessary."

Differential Advantages and Disadvantages in Networks

We have talked about networks as a whole and their overall objectives. It is time to adopt the perspective of *individual participants* in the network. The position of a firm in the net is largely determined by its relative *power*. There are at least five interrelated but distinct sources of power of a network participant: economic base, technology, expertise, trust, and legitimacy.

A participant's power is manifested by the *differential advantage* in one or several of these areas. Some indicators of economic power in an international marketing network are market share and absolute size of seller, his share of the buyer's purchases, and the centrality of the seller's product to the buyer's core activity. Selling paper as office supply is probably of peripheral interest to a buyer, but if you are selling newsprint paper that is certainly of central concern to the newspaper buying it. The buyer's position is strengthened the greater the number of alternate sources of supply, the less the transactions costs involved in switching to another supplier, and the greater his share of the vendor's total sales. Other important aspects of the economic power base of participants are their relative liquidity, ability to extend credit and ability to integrate vertically.

Superior technology as a source of power is demonstrated in such areas as product and process innovation, marketing skills, quality maintenance, flexibility, logistics management, spare parts availability, and ability to produce to the specifications of the buyer. Cost leadership in production may be viewed as a source of either technological or economic power.

The Greeks, 2000 years ago, coined the phrase, "knowledge is power." *Expertise* as a source of power shows up in such matters as personnel and equipment capabilities in R&D, in applications engineering, in pre– and post-sales service, in the economics of the markets where network members are a part, and general awareness of the situation, problems and priorities of other network members. In the 1950s, General Electric failed to sell its jet engines to the commercial airlines until it switched from emphasizing the technical performance characteristics which had impressed the military in World War II to learning more about the economics of airline operation than was known even by most airline executives. A key source of differential advantage in IM, of course, is superior knowledge of *foreign* markets.

Trust may be viewed as confidence in the continuation of a mutually satisfying relationship and in the awareness of other parties of what this requires of their performance as network members. Trust is based on reputation and, more importantly, on past performance. It is also built by personal friendship and social bonds, established in day-to-day interaction. It is manifested by mutual feelings of belonging and interdependence. Especially in Oriental cultures, trust is a vital supplement to contractual arrangements; it may even take their place. In pre-contractual contexts the establishment of trust frequently takes more time and patience than Western executives are used to invest.

Formal *legitimacy* as a source of power may derive from long-term contracts, part ownership of another network member, interlocking directorates, joint-venture arrangements, etc. It may also originate in patent rights or other privileges conferred by government, such as being the "chosen instrument" in the supply of defense equipment, or having an "inside track" in government procurement by simply being a national of the same country. Legitimacy may also be derived just from a fine reputation in the marketplace.

Again, it must be emphasized that *differential advantage* in one or several of these areas is *indispensable* to successful participation in networks. In IM it often happens that the differential advantage is more *perceived* than real, as it may be difficult to get an objective evaluation of a foreign participant in advance. However, if he is not living up to expectations within a short time he may find himself excluded from the network. Indeed, in the long run termination of such a relationship is probably in the best interest of all parties concerned.

We have talked about the role of differential advantage in networks. But everything cannot be sweetness and light, or we would see nothing but networks around us! Economist Oliver Williamson has helped identify possible sources of differential disadvantages of networking:

Asset specificity—members of a network may be induced to spend a heavy part of their resources on assets which have no realistic alternative use (Coca-Cola bottles, say).

Alternative transaction costs—it might be cheaper to internalize (vertically integrate) an operation than having it done by the network.

Opportunism—one party making use of privileged information in its own interest and at the cost of the other party, misrepresentation, unethical use of the other party's trust.

To these we should add at least two other factors:

Uneven distribution of power ("Power corrupts"); and Entropy (the tendency of everything to fall apart unless deliberately maintained).

Network Management and Dynamics: The Indispensability of Trust

The question of maintenance leads to the dynamics of network management. As in any marriage, the long-term stability of a network is based on mutual advantage. That is, the relationship must be a positive–sum game for all partners, what is often called a win-win situation. In effect, we are no longer just buyers and sellers—we are *partners*! Like any marriage, too, network stability also requires an element of trust. The daily activities in the network may be viewed as either building or drawing on differential advantage. All sources of differential advantage are involved. Thus we find links involving economic performance, technology transfer, diffusion of know-how and expertise, the forging or exploitation of trust, and the flow of legitimacy. The profile—or "mix"—of such links in a given network constitutes the essence of the particular *culture* of that network.

Due to the necessity of forging and maintaining differential advantage, building networks involves expenditure of money and executive talent over many periods of time. It follows that resources spent on all aspects of networking other than everyday care are to be regarded as *strategic market investments*. Some of these may be "hardware" investments in customer-specific productive equipment, inventory, and product development. Others are "software" investments in building expertise, trust or long–term contracts.

Generally, strategic software investments are more important in business-to-business relations, and especially in IM. The fact that American business in the last decade or two has seemed much less successful abroad than at home in large part may be due to a lack of "savvy"—that is, sophistication—about linkages going beyond economic and technological performance in cross–cultural contexts, where investment in trust, expertise and other software often plays a crucial role. Indeed, differential advantage and willingness to invest in building a network is not enough to ensure its long-term viability. We also need *bonding* and *communicating*. The term "bonding" refers to the establishment of social and professional contacts as well as personal friendships between the executives and experts of all network member organizations, and at as many levels as possible. Again, Orientals are more well-versed in this area than other peoples. Communications and frequent exchanges of information and opinions are especially vital in IM, in the absence of daily face-to-face contacts.

These days we often hear about the pending demise of middle management, whose tasks are supposed to be taken over by computers, and about flattened organization structures. But the proponents of these views seem to have forgotten about the *external* relations of organizations, which is what the writer calls *network management*. It seems obvious that network management will be a key task of middle managers in the future.

Good and Bad Networks

When all is said and done, are networks good or bad? Of course, it depends on who is talking! My answer is that they are indispensable, but we must be aware that even a basically good thing can be carried too far.

In the strategic planning of a firm the network may be viewed as a powerful *alternative* to both vertical integration and to diversification, and as an instrument for reaching new clienteles and/or additional countries. In effect, it may serve as an engine of *growth* and perhaps even more as an engine of *change*, and of risk reduction.

Network thinking also brings to the fore *a long-term view* in fairly sharp contrast to the hectic instant-profit perspective more characteristic of American businessmen than many others. Directly linked to this is the notion that marketing-related outlays in many instances are to be regarded as investments from a strategic management standpoint. The conventional elements of marketing strategy are product, price, promotion, distribution and service. The network concept draws our attention to at least two other crucial marketing elements, namely, power and trust.

In IM, networking may yield particular benefits. Networking may:

—effectuate the transfer of technology to the less developed countries (LDC);
—implement a division of labor between countries as well as firms;
—strike bridges between businessmen of different nations and cultures; and
—stimulate trade which otherwise might not have taken place at all.

But networking in IM may also have some drawbacks. It may impose unfair barriers to entry (exclusionary behavior) or perpetrate other malpractices on potential or actual competitors or consumers. Diamonds are a girl's best friend, but the de Beer diamond syndicate is not! Price and production cartels have a bad reputation in the U.S.A. and several other countries.

If a network is based on a very unequal distribution of power, it may perpetuate the existing division of labor between nations, which might impede the industrialization of some LDC.

Those of us who care about open markets may ask, What about the future of competition in a world of networking? Between networks and "administered systems" there are many discontinuities and niches where the market is open and the competitive interplay intense. Indeed, the friction in these interfaces is an antidote to the complete bureaucratization of Western economies that otherwise might conceivably occur. Equally important is the *competition between networks*, especially between different vertical distribution systems. We should also be mindful of the pro-competitive impact of what may be termed *networks shocks*. Examples include the removal of internal trade barriers in Europe and the recent deregulation of air and truck transportation as well as telecommunications in the U.S.A. In the remarkably short period of 10 years the world energy market responded to the OPEC "monopoly" dramatically enough to put the cartel in strong competition with outside oil producers in the North Sea and elsewhere, and with other forms of energy. Even the PRC has chosen to introduce a major open market-like sector in its largest industry (agriculture), with sensational effects on productivity and rural standards of living. It would be difficult to find a better example of shock therapy against market bureaucratization run amuck as in the old commune system.

Note, too, that inter-network competition is vastly intensified in the modern economy by inter-product and inter-materials competition as the product, materials and alternate technology spectra increasingly get filled in. It would be difficult to exaggerate the importance of these dimensions of competition.

The relationship between competition and vertical integration is also a fascinating one. Vertical integration has always been a source of potential competition. It is likely to become an even more tangible competitive force in an era of proliferating technologies and increasingly flexible manufacturing systems.

Emergency Exit—Keep It Clear!

Like economic activity in general, IM needs a *balance between cooperation and competition*. Networking is a powerful force of cooperation between participants, and competition with the world outside, and thus provides a bit of both. (Also, we should not overlook that there is almost always some degree of rivalry within networks themselves.) As has been pointed out, there is no need to fear the demise of competition in the world at large. However, some networks may simply get too powerful (especially if enjoying government privileges) and/or engage in anti-social practices. One may predict that by the tenth round of GATT negotiations—by the year 2000 or so—an effort will be made to draft a global antitrust law regulating dysfunctional behavior of networks and multinational corporations.

In the meantime, the best protection against such behavior is for legislators and courts to safeguard the right of network participants to exit freely from networks to which they no longer wish to belong. We have to keep the emergency exit clear!

6

International Marketing and Purchasing of Industrial Goods: An Interaction Approach*

HÅKAN HÅKANSSON

The International Marketing and Purchasing (IMP) Project Group has adopted an approach which challenges the traditional ways of examining industrial marketing and purchasing. This approach can be outlined below. (See also Cavusgil 1989).

Firstly, we challenge the concentration of the industrial buyer behavior literature on a narrow analysis of a single discrete purchase. Instead we emphasize the importance of the *relationship* which exists between buyers and sellers in industrial markets. This relationship is often close. It may also be long term and involve a complex pattern of interaction between the two companies.

Secondly, we challenge the view of industrial marketing as the manipulation of the marketing mix variables in order to achieve a response from a generalized, and by implication passive market. We believe it necessary to examine the *interaction* between individual buying and selling firms where either firm may be taking the more active part in the transaction.

Thirdly, we challenge the view which implies an atomistic structure in industrial markets. This view assumes a large number of buyers and sellers, with ease and speed of change between different suppliers for each buyer and ease of market entry or exit for those suppliers. Instead, we stress the *stability* of industrial market structures, where those present as buyers or sellers know each other well and are aware of any movements in either the buying or selling market.

---

*Adapted from *International Marketing and Purchasing of Industrial Goods: An Interaction Approach*, Håkan Håkansson (ed.), (Chichester: John Wiley and Sons, Ltd., 1982), with permission.

Fourthly, we challenge the separation which has occurred in analyzing either the process of industrial purchasing *or* of industrial marketing. In contrast, we emphasize the similarity of the tasks of buyers and sellers in industrial markets. Both parties may be involved in a search to find a suitable buyer or seller, to prepare specifications of requirements or offerings and to manipulate or attempt to control the transaction process. This means that an understanding of industrial markets can only be achieved by the simultaneous analysis of both the buying and selling sides of relationships.

Outline of the Model

The Interaction Approach is built on a number of factors which our earlier empirical studies indicate are important in industrial markets and which appear to have been largely neglected in previous research:

Firstly, that both buyer and seller are active participants in the market. Each may engage in search to find a suitable buyer or seller, to prepare specifications of requirements or offerings and to manipulate or attempt to control the transaction process.

Secondly, the relationship between buyer and seller is frequently long term, close and involving a complex pattern of interaction between and within each company. The marketers' and buyers' task in this case may have more to do with maintaining these relationships than with making a straightforward sale or purchase.

Thirdly, the links between buyer and seller often become institutionalized into a set of roles that each party expects the other to perform, for example the division of product development responsibility, or the decision as to who should carry inventory and test products. These processes may require significant adaptations in organization or operation by either or both companies. Clearly, these relationships can involve both conflict as well as co-operation.

Fourthly, close relationships are often considered in the context of continuous raw material or component supply. However, we would emphasize the importance of previous purchases, mutual evaluation and the associated relationship between the companies in the case of infrequently purchased products. Further, we are concerned in this research with the nature of the relationship between a buying and selling company which may be built up during the course of a single major transaction.

Our focus is generally on a two party relationship, but the approach can be applied also to a several party relationship. This, indeed, may be necessary to accommodate the study of the simultaneous interactions between several buying and selling companies in a particular

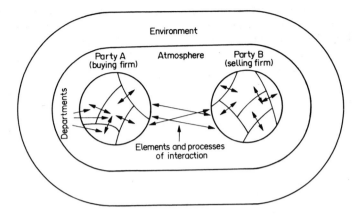

FIG. 6.1. Main Elements of the Interaction Model.

industry. The main components of our approach are illustrated in Figure 6.1.

In the figure we identify four groups of variables that describe and influence the interaction between buying and selling companies:

variables describing the *parties* involved, both as organizations and as individuals;
variables describing the *elements and process of interaction*;
variables describing the *environment* within which the interaction takes place;
variables describing the *atmosphere* affecting and affected by the interaction.

The approach does not only involve an analysis of these groups of variables but it also includes the relations between them.

The Interaction Model

The marketing and purchasing of industrial goods is seen as an interaction process between two parties within a certain environment. Our way of analyzing industrial marketing and purchasing has four basic elements which in turn are sub-divided. These are:

1. The interaction process
2. The participants in the interaction process
3. The environment within which interaction takes place
4. The atmosphere affecting and affected by the interaction.

In this section we will describe each of these four basic elements more extensively. The major focus here is on *description* of buyer–seller relationships and interactions.

The Interaction Process

Relationships between buying and selling companies in industrial markets are frequently long term. Thus, it is important in our analysis to distinguish between the individual "Episodes" in a relationship, e.g. the placing or delivering of a particular order, and the longer-term aspects of that relationship which both affects and may be affected by each episode.

(a) *Episodes*

The episodes which occur in an industrial market relationship involve exchange between two parties. There are four elements which are exchanged:

(i) Product or service exchange
(ii) Information exchange
(iii) Financial exchange
(iv) Social exchange.

(i) *Product or service exchange*. The exchange of product or service is often the core of the exchange. As a result, the characteristics of the product or service involved are likely to have a significant effect on the relationship as a whole. For example, one major aspect of the product or service which seems important is the uncertainty with which they are associated. The exchange process will be quite different depending on whether or not the product is able to fulfil a buyer need that is easy to identify, and for which the characteristics of an appropriate product are easy to specify. It will also be important whether either buyer or seller is uncertain as to the requirements or resources of their opposite number.

(ii) *Information exchange*. Several aspects of information exchange are of interest. The content of information is, of course, important. This can, for example, be characterized by the degree to which technical, economic, or organizational questions dominate the exchange. Furthermore, the width and depth of the information for each of these groups of questions should also be of importance. Information can be transferred between the parties by either personal or impersonal means. Impersonal communication is often used to transfer basic technical and/or commercial data. Personal channels are more likely to be used for the transfer of "soft data" concerning, for example, the use of a product, the conditions of an agreement between the parties, or supportive of general information about either party. Finally, the formality of the information exchange is important. The degree of formality may depend on wider organizational characteristics which can affect the nature of the interaction process and the relationship between the companies as a whole.

(iii) *Financial exchange.* Money is the third element. The quantity of money exchange is an indicator of the economic importance of the relationship. Another important aspect is connected with the need to exchange money from one currency to another and the uncertainties in these exchanges over time.

(iv) *Social exchange.* Social exchange has an important function in reducing uncertainties between the two parties (Håkansson and Östberg 1975). This is particularly significant when there exists spatial or cultural distance between the two parties or where the experience of the two parties is limited. Social exchange episodes may be important in themselves in avoiding short term difficulties between the two parties and in maintaining a relationship in the periods between transactions. However, perhaps the most important function of social exchange is in the long term process by which successive social exchange episodes gradually interlock the two firms with each other. Many aspects of the agreements between the buying and selling firms are not fully formalized nor based on legal criteria. Instead the relationship is based on mutual trust. Building up this trust is a social process which takes time and must be based on personal experience, and on the successful execution of the three other elements of exchange. Furthermore, the need for mutual trust and the requirement of social exchange varies with differences in the elements exchanged in different relationships. Examples are variations in the amount of money exchanged, in the need for large amounts of informational exchange or in the complexity of the product exchanged. However, the development of trust is also dependent upon experience in exchange of the other three elements.

(b) *Relationships*
Social exchange episodes are, as has been described above, critical in the build up of long-term relationships. Exchanges of product and service (which can be in both directions) and of the other elements of money and information can also lead to the build up of long-term relations. The routinization of these exchange episodes over a period of time to clear expectations in both parties of the roles or responsibilities of their opposite numbers. Eventually these expectations become *institutionalized* to such an extent that they may not be questioned by either party and may have more in common with the traditions of an industry or a market than rational decision-making by either of the parties (Ford 1978).

The communication or exchange of information in the episodes successively builds up inter-organizational contact patterns and role relationships. These *contact patterns* can consist of individuals and groups of people filling different roles, operating in different functional departments and transmitting different messages of a technical, commercial, or reputational nature. These patterns can interlock the two parties to a greater or lesser extent and they are therefore an important variable to consider in analyzing buyer–seller relationships. It is important to note that information and social exchange between parties can continue for a considerable time without there being an exchange of product or money. Thus, literature, specification development, and visits between companies can occur before the first order is placed or between widely spaced individual orders.

Another important aspect of the relationship is the *adaptations* which one or other party may make in either the elements exchanged or the process of exchange. Examples of this are adaptations in product, in financial arrangements, in information routines or social relations. These adaptations can occur during the process of a single, major transaction or over the time of a relationship involving many individual transactions. The benefits of these adaptations can be in cost reduction, increased revenue, or differential control over the exchange. Adaptations in specific episodes may also be made in order to modify the overall relationship. Thus one party may make a decision not to offer special products to a customer out of a wish to be more distantly involved with that customer, rather than being closely involved and/or heavily dependent on it.

The manipulation of different aspects of adaptation is of course a critical marketing and purchasing issue. Although adaptations by either party can occur in an unconscious manner as a relationship develops, it is important to emphasize the conscious strategy which is involved in many of these adaptations. Thus, modifications to product, delivery, pricing, information routines and even the organization itself are part of the seller's marketing strategy. Similarly, the buying organization will consider adaptations in its own product requirements, its production methods, the price it is prepared to accept, its information needs and the modification of its own delivery or stocking policies in order to accommodate the selling organization.

The Interacting Parties

The process of interaction and the relationship between the organizations will depend not only on the elements of the interaction but also on the characteristics of the parties involved. This includes both the characteristics of the two organizations and the individuals who represent them. The organization factors include the companies' position in the market as manufacturer, wholesaler, etc. It also includes the products which the selling company offers, the production and application technologies of the two parties and their relative expertise in these areas.

(a) *Technology*. Technology issues are often critical in buyer–seller interaction in industrial markets. The aims of the interaction process can be interpreted as tying the production technology of the seller to the application technology of the buyer. Thus the characteristics of the two technological systems and the differences between them give the basic conditions for the interaction. These basic conditions influence all the dimensions of the interaction processes; for example, the requirements for adaptations, mutual trust and contact patterns. Similarly, if the two organizations are separated by a wide gulf of technical expertise then the relationship between them can be expected to be quite different from a situation where the two companies are close in their level of expertise.

(b) *Organizational size, structure, and strategy*. The size and the power of the parties give them basic positions from which to interact. In general, a large firm with considerable resources has a greater possibility of dominating its customers or suppliers than has a small firm. The structure of each organization and the extent of centralization, specialization and formalization influence the interaction process in several ways; this influence is seen in the number and categories of persons who are involved. It also affects the procedures of the exchange, the communications media used, the formalization of the interaction and the substance of what is exchanged—the nature of product or service and the finance which is involved. In the short term, organizational structures can be considered as the frameworks within which interaction takes place. In the longer term, it is possible that these organizational structures may be modified *by* the emerging interaction process or indeed by individual episodes.

(c) *Organizational experience*. A further factor is the company's experience not only in this relationship but also its experience and activities outside it. This experience may be the result of many other similar relationships and will equip the company with knowledge about the management of these kinds of relationships. It may also affect the level of importance attached to any one relationship, and hence the company's commitment to that relationship.

(d) *Individuals*. At least two individuals, one from each organization, are involved in a relationship. These are usually a buyer and a salesman. More commonly, several individuals from different functional areas, at different levels in the hierarchy and fulfilling different roles become involved in inter-company personal interactions. They exchange information, develop relationships and build up strong social bonds which influence the decisions of each company in the business relationship.

The varied personalities, experience, and motivations of each company's representatives will mean that they will take part in the social exchange differently. Their reactions in individual episodes could condition the ways in which the overall relationship builds up. Further, the role, level, and function of central persons in the interaction may affect the chances of future development occurring in the relationship.

Individual experience may result in preconceptions concerning certain suppliers or customers, for example those in a certain country. These will affect attitudes and behaviour towards those buyers or suppliers. The process of learning from experience on both an individual and corporate level is communicated to and affects detailed "Episodes" in interaction. Additionally, the experience gained in individual episodes aggregates to a total experience. Indeed, the experience of a single episode can radically change attitudes which may then be held over a long period of time.

The Interaction Environment

The interaction between a buying and selling firm cannot be analyzed in solution, but must be considered in a wider context. This wider context has several aspects:

(a) *Market structure*. Firstly, a relationship must be considered as one of a number of similar relationships existing either nationally or internationally within the same market. The structure of this market depends in part on the concentration of both buyers and sellers and the stability or rate of change of the market and its constituent members. It also consists of the extent to which the market can be viewed as strictly national or needs to be thought of in wider international terms. The extent of buyer or seller concentration determines the number of alternatives available to any firm. This has a clear bearing on the pressure to interact with a certain counterpart within the market.

(b) *Dynamism*. The degree of dynamism within a relationship and in the wider market affects the relationship in two ways that are opposite to each other. Firstly, a close relationship increases the knowledge of one party of the likely actions of the other party and hence its ability to make forecasts based on this inside information. Secondly and conversely, in a dynamic environment the opportunity cost of reliance on a single or small number of relationships can be very high when expressed in terms of the developments of other market members.

(c) *Internationalization.* The internationalization of the buying or selling market is of interest as it affects either firm's motivations in developing international relationships. This in turn may affect the company's organization, in needing sales subsidiaries or overseas buying units, the special knowledge it may require, e.g. in languages and international trade and its more general attitudes.

(d) *Position in the manufacturing channel.* A further aspect of the environment which must be brought into consideration is the position of an individual relationship in an extended "channel" stretching from primary producer to final consumer. Thus, for example manufacturer A may sell electric components to manufacture B, who then incorporates these components into actuators that are sold to manufacturer C, who adds them to valves. These valves, with many other products, may form the stock of distributor D and so on. The marketing strategy of A may thus be influenced by and directed at several markets at different stages in the channel. Clearly his relationship with buying company B will be affected by both A's and B's relationship with C and other subsequent organizations.

(c) *The social system.* As well as the effects of both horizontal market and vertical channel influences on a relationship, we must also consider the characteristics of the wider environment surrounding a particular relationship—the social system. This is particularly relevant in the international context where attitudes and perceptions on a generalized level can be important obstacles when trying to establish an exchange process with a certain counterpart. An example of this is nationalistic buying practices or generalized attitudes to the reliability of buyers or customers from a particular country. Other aspects of these general influences concern regulations and constraints on business, for example exchange rates and trade regulations. There are other, more narrow social system variables which will surround a particular industry or market. For example, a supplier who has not previously delivered to a certain type of customer, e.g. in the automobile industry, has to learn both the "language" and the rules before it will be accepted in that industry.

The Atmosphere

The relationships between buying and selling firms are dynamic in being affected by the individual episodes which take place within them. At the same time they have the stability which derives from the length of the relationship, its routinization and the clear expectations which become held by both parties. The relationship is influenced by the characteristics of the parties involved and the nature of the interaction itself. This in turn is a function of the technology involved and the environment within which the interaction takes place. Organizational strategy can also affect both the short-term episodes and the long-term relationship between the parties.

One of the main aspects of the relationship which may be affected by conscious planning is the overall atmosphere of the relationship. This atmosphere can be described in terms of the power–dependence relationship which exists between the companies, the state of conflict or co-operation and overall closeness or distance of the relationship as well as by the companies' mutual expectations. These variables are not measured in a direct way in this study. Instead the atmosphere is considered as a group of intervening variables, defined by various combinations of environmental, company specific, and interaction process characteristics. The atmosphere is a product of the relationship, and it also mediates the influence of the groups of variables. There are reasons for the buying and selling firm to both develop a high degree of closeness with their counterpart as well as to avoid such closeness. There are both advantages and disadvantages connected with different atmospheres. We can analyze the reasons involved with regard to an economic (cost–benefit) dimension and a control dimension.

(a) *The economic dimension.* There are several types of cost that can be reduced for a firm by a closer interaction with a buying or selling firm. One of these costs is that which Williamson (1975) describes as the transaction cost. A closer connection means that it may be possible to handle distribution, negotiations, and administration more efficiently. Another type of cost which may be reduced is the production cost. A close relationship gives opportunities to find a more optimal division of the production process between the supplier and the customer. The supplier and buyer may reallocate some production processes between each other or co-operate in the design so as to make the product easier to produce or for the customer to develop further. There are also increased revenues which can be gained by a closer interaction. Both sides may achieve positive gains by better use of the other's competence, facilities, and other resources. New products can be developed together or old products may be redesigned. Furthermore, the parties can also often give each other valuable technical and commercial information.

(b) *The control dimension.* Another important reason for closer connection with a counterpart can be to reduce the uncertainty associated with that input or output by increasing its control over the other company. Such an increase in control improves the firm's chances of forecasting and determining that part of its environment. The ability to control a relationship is related to the *perceived* power of the two parties. Perceptions of power are likely to be unclear in the early stages of a relationship and one of the key functions of initial exchange episodes will be to enable each party to come to an understanding of each other's power. Even so, perceptions of power may change over the life of a relationship. They will, in turn be related to the resources perceived to be possessed by each party as well as to their relative dependence on this individual relationship. Inter-organizational power will depend on the ability of either party to reward or coerce each other through exchange, or their relative expertise and access to information, as well as on their referent power, i.e., the value which one party places on association with another because of its wish to learn from and act similarly to the other.

The power of organization A over B is directly related to the dependence of B on A. The dependence on any one relationship by an organization is a major element in the wish to restrict interaction. Investment of time and resources in one relationship has an opportunity cost related to the value of those investments in another relationship. Also, the level of dependence on one relationship affects the vulnerability of an organization to the exercise of power by its opposite number. In everyday terms this is exemplified by a selling company which has a large proportion of its sales to one single buying company. It is the management of the closeness of the relationship, with its associated power and dependence which is perhaps a crucial aspect of many industrial marketing and purchasing strategies.

In conclusion, relationships are established and used in order to gain economic benefits, lower costs, higher profits, and/or improving the organization's control of some part of its environment. A critical aspect of the management of these relationships is the extent to which the firm can balance its inter-dependence with others. The firm must seek to balance the advantages of a close relationship, perhaps in terms of cost reduction and ease and speed of interaction, against the opportunity costs of that single relationship and the dependence which it involves.

Conclusion

In Figure 6.2 we have tried to illustrate the different variables which have been presented here. The model shows the short-term and long-term aspects of the "Interaction Process" between buying and selling companies A and B. The short-term "Exchange Episodes" involve product–service, financial, information, and social exchange. These are separated from the longer term processes of "Adaptations" and "Institutionalization".

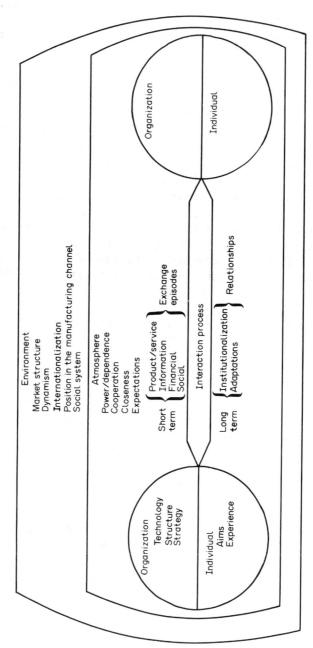

FIG. 6.2. An Illustration of the Interaction Model.

Both the short and long term aspects of the interaction are considered as being influenced by the characteristics of the organizations and individuals involved (circles A and B). Additionally we see the interaction taking place within an "Environment" consisting of the vertical and horizontal market structure and general social influences.

Finally we include "Atmosphere". As the company's relationship develops so the parties' views of their relative power may change. Previous research has shown quite clearly that the interaction between buying and selling companies is conditioned by a clear and commonly held view of the relative power of the parties to the interaction and the areas to which this power extends. At the same time we have noted that conflict can characterize these relationships as well as co-operation. Thus it is quite possible for a company to have one relationship with a particular buyer–seller which is characterized by co-operation. It is also possible for the company to have a relationship with another company which is characterized by co-operation on the *minimum* level, in order for transactions to take place but thereafter is marked by frequent conflict over means and allocations of resources. Thus the detailed interaction process is subject to the perceptions of both parties of the overall state of relations between them—power–dependence and conflict–co-operation.

The figure shows that it is possible to identify and study connections between the variables on different levels. Firstly, at the most general level, one variable group can be related to another, for example it is possible to relate the parties in the exchange process to the interaction environment. Secondly it is possible to investigate the linkage between variables in one variable group, for example between the elements of exchange and the process of exchange. Thirdly, it can be valuable to explore the relation between the variables within a sub-group. An example of this is the connection between the characteristics of the product and the characteristics of the information which is exchanged.

Implications for Management

The practical use of a theoretical model is, of course, that is helps to structure the "world" and thereby the problems. A new model can as a consequence give new opportunities because problems which were neglected earlier may be identified and solved.

Marketing Management

Key issues in marketing according to the marketing mix model are (1) allocation of resources and (2) design of individual competitive means. In the same way we can use the interaction model and identify two groups of important problems. These have been named (1) limitation and (2) handling problems.

Two different kinds of limitation problems can be specified. The first problem concerns the marketing firm's overall limitation of its activities in certain types of relationships. This must be achieved because the demands on its technology, organization, and knowledge, etc., are closely related to the type of relationships. For example, it is very difficult for a seller to have customers with very high demands on the quality and performance of the product *and* customers which just want a standard quality as cheaply as possible. The marketing firm, thus, has to limit itself to be an efficient counterpart in a certain type of relationship and to design its technology, organization, and knowledge in accordance with this.

The second type of limitation problems for the marketing firm are concerned with its individual counterparts. The question is, should customers be treated in a uniform way, or should some customers get special treatment? Normally there is a very clear difference between how those "special" customers are treated when compared with other customers. The special customers—often those who buy most—get special services, extra attention and so on. The customers are in other words often dealt with quite differently and it is therefore necessary for the marketing firm to develop a policy on these questions.

The handling problem concerns both the long-term aspects of the relationships as well as the short-term exchanges of different elements. The long-term problems concern handling the power–dependence and the co-operation–conflict aspects of the relationships. The aim is to have a controlled development of the relationships. This can sometimes mean closer co-operation and sometimes the opposite. The short-term problems are primarily related to attaining an efficient way of handling the elements (the different exchange processes) with individuals as well as groups of customers. One problem area is for example, to design one's own adaptations and to influence the counterpart's adaptations in order to make exchange processes easier. The way of solving the short-term handling problems affect, of course, the long-term problems. Adaptation is an example of one aspect of the power–dependence relationship. This means that the long- and short-term problems in a relationship cannot be divided; they can better be seen as short- and long-term effects of all of the activities which constitute the relationship.

Purchasing Management

The key problems in purchasing that can be identified using the interaction model are (1) to develop an appropriate structure of suppliers and (2) to handle each relationship in an efficient way. The second group of problems are the same as the handling problems for the marketing side and we therefore, can leave them aside and concentrate on the first group.

A supplier can be seen as an external resource by the buying firm. The buyer's aim in relationships is to use these external resources in an efficient way. But in order to be attractive as a counterpart, the purchasing firm also has to have some internal resources. One strategic purchasing question therefore, is to find and maintain a balance between the external and the internal resources. The problem in the short term can be formulated as using these external resources as much as possible given the internal resources of the buying firm.

Another problem is that suppliers can be used in different ways. In some situations the purchasing firm may want to use a supplier's ability to develop and design a special product, while in other situations it may just want to use the supplier's ability to produce a standardized product at low cost. The counterparts are used in different ways and a problem is then to find the right combination of suppliers, i.e. to develop an appropriate external resources structure.

References

Cavusgil, S. Tamer, *Advances in International Marketing*, Volume 3, special volume on "Networks of Relationships in International Industrial Marketing", Lars Hallen and Jan Johanson (eds.), (Greenwich, Connecticut: JAI Press Inc., 1989).

Håkansson, H. and Östberg, C., "Industrial Marketing—An Organizational Problem?" *Industrial Marketing Management*, Vol. 4 (1975), pp. 113–123.

Ford, D. I., "Stability Factors in Industrial Marketing Channels", *Industrial Marketing Management*, Vol. 7 (1978), pp. 410–422.

Williamson, O. E., *Markets and Hierarchies: Analysis and Antitrust Implications*, (New York: Free Press, 1975).

7

Export Trading Companies in World Markets: A Conceptual View*

LYN S. AMINE

Introduction

The purpose of this article is to examine the numerous types of export trading companies (ETCs) and export groups currently operating in world markets, with a view to defining and modeling the ETC concept. Motivating this attempt is a sense of frustration with published research on ETCs, which is largely descriptive and anecdotal. No attempt has yet been made at categorization or model-building.

The approach adopted here is different. It follows an "evolutionary" line of thought, moving dynamically back and forth between phases of description, comparison, analysis, and conceptualization. This approach has the considerable advantage of anchoring the conceptual inputs onto a firm foundation of empirical evidence.

First, a basic categorization of export trading entities is established. The range of variants is identified, along with critical company variables which may explain some of this variation. Next, some examples of ETCs are presented, classified by country of origin, namely Japan, Korea, Brazil, and the United States. Here, environmental and historical factors are examined which have shaped ETC characteristics and performance. These four nations have been the focus of most of the previous research on ETCs, presumably because companies from these countries are currently the most prominent and active in world markets. In order to structure the comparison of the four nations' ETCs, reference will be made to the critical company variables already

---

* Adapted from *Advances in International Marketing*, Vol. 2, pp. 199–238, with permission.

identified. This will demonstrate how these variables have combined to create vastly different types of ETCs in each country.

The next step is to move forward from description and comparison to identify modes of competition between these ETCs and the other export trading entities defined at the beginning of the analysis. Here, a model of "competitive clusters" of ETCs will be presented, all positioned relative to the Japanese ETCs which serve as a baseline for the comparison.

Finally, to complete the analysis, we step back from the definition of current ETC characteristics and activities in order to focus on fundamental aspects of ETC growth and expansion. If a common path for ETC expansion can be identified, similar to the internationalization path assumed to be followed by new exporters (see Cavusgil 1984), this will be a valuable managerial tool for forecasting future ETC growth and performance. It may also indicate which marketing and organizational strategies are appropriate for use by managers during specific phases of ETC development. Thus, this paper offers insights of value to both academics and practitioners.

The analysis and models presented here may have their shortcomings. Nevertheless, the strengths of this research, as well as the weaknesses, should motivate others to continue the challenging task of definition and conceptualization. The analysis is presented in four parts, as follows:

- A typology of ETCs
- Profiles of four nations' ETCs
- A model of competitive clusters of ETCs in world markets
- A generalized model of ETC expansion.

A Typology of ETCs

Attention is drawn to the terms "export trading company" (ETC), "general trading company" (GTC), and "commodity trading company" (CTC). A purist interpretation might state that an ETC is primarily involved in exporting while a GTC both imports and exports, and a CTC trades in specific commodity markets. However, few companies limit their involvement in world markets simply to one type of activity. As will be shown below in the ETC profiles, exporting may lead to importing, domestic sales, offshore trading, foreign direct investment, or even joint ventures.

Trading companies are not a new concept nor are they limited to any one country. In Japan they date back to the nineteenth century, and in West Europe companies can trace back their origins to colonial times. State-owned and state-managed trading companies have existed for many years in Socialist countries. Even in the less developed countries, general trading companies exist today and demonstrate many of the features of their more established counterparts in developed nations or newly-industrializing countries.

These comments highlight a major theoretical problem: how to define an ETC. A loose definition would specify "involvement in export activities" as the principal criterion for classification. A detailed definition might specify official designation or certification as an ETC, conferred on a company by a government agency. Another definition might focus on the type and number of functions performed (such as export financing, assistance in product design, etc.). Yet another approach might focus on the volume of export sales achieved. This approach would eliminate "nominal" or "symbolic" entities involved in only marginal export activities.

Alternatively, attention can be focused on the spread of involvement of the ETC through the distribution function. Involvement may range from that of periodic facilitator of the international flow of goods or services, to a continuing presence in overseas markets as the captain of an international distribution channel. Of course, even these two alternatives are not mutually exclusive.

A further complicating factor in the search for a satisfactory definition is the recognition that companies engaged in exporting may also import, diversify into manufacturing abroad, or have originally been involved in domestic manufacturing. Thus, companies from around the world may, on the surface, appear similar, due to their export interests. However, in reality, they may prove to be radically different commercial entities for whom exporting is either a major or a minor priority.

In order to establish baseline definitions for this analysis, a preliminary classification of export trading companies and groups is presented in Table. 7.1. This typology is necessarily very generalized as each type of ETC may appear in more than one country-context. Moreover, one country may be home for several types of trading companies. One type of trading company is, however, specific to a certain historical and cultural context, the Sogo Sosha of Japan. Their particular characteristics are detailed in a later section. The other types of trading company defined in Table 7.1 are discussed briefly below. Short illustrative examples are presented to establish areas of similarity and difference.

GTCs

Among the first group in Table 7.1 are many long-established, large and diversified general trading companies. Many GTCs remain rela-

TABLE 7.1. Typology of Export Trading Companies

Type	Rationale for Groupings	Some Examples by Country of Origin
I. General trading companies (GTCs)	Historical involvement in generalized import-export activities	Mitsui (Japan), SCOA (France), East Asiatic (Denmark), Jardine Matheson (Hong Kong/Bermuda)
II. Export trading companies (ETCs)	Specific mission to promote growth of exports	Daewoo (S. Korea), Interbras (Brazil), Sears World Trade (U.S.)
III. Federated export marketing groups (FMGs)	Loose collaboration among exporting companies supervised by a third-party and usually market-specific	Fedec (U.K.), SBI Group (Norway), IEB Project Group (Morocco)
IV Trading arms of multinational corporations (MNC-ETCs)	Import-export and trading activities specific to parent company's operations	General Motors (U.S.), Volvo (Sweden)
V. Bank-based or bank-affiliated trading groups (Bank-ETCs)	Extension of traditional banking activities into commercial fields	Mitsubishi (Japan), Cobec (Brazil), A. W. Galadari Holdings (United Arab Emirates)
VI. Commodity trading companies (CTCs)	Long-standing export trading in a specific market, secretive, fast-paced and high-risk activities	Metallgesellschaft (W. Germany), Louis Dreyfus (France), Amtorg Trading Corp. (U.S.S.R.)

tively obscure and unknown to the general public. In some cases, this is due to the nature of their trade, largely among middlemen buyers and sellers. In others, it is due to the dispersion of their activities across scattered market segments, often in developing countries. East Asiatic Company (EAC) of Denmark is diversified with interests ranging from timber to motor scooter manufacturing. With operations in some 50 countries, EAC is one of the largest and oldest trading houses and traces its origins back to early trade with Thailand in 1884.

ETCs and FMGs

The second group of companies includes ETCs which were either (i) specifically created by their respective governments to stimulate national export growth, or (ii) evolved as a result of enabling legislation by the government. ETCs in South Korea and Brazil illustrate the case of government sponsorship, while ETCs in the U.S. are examples of private, public or quasi-public initiatives. Brief profiles of ETCs from these countries are presented in a later section.

In contrast, the federated marketing groups (FMGs) in group three take part in a loose collaboration supervised by a third-party. This initiative is private, not regulated by legislation, and often lasts only as long as the members' interests are being served—for example, until penetration of a specific geographic market is achieved. Thus, federations are market- rather than product-oriented.

In Morocco, the Irish Export Board (IEB), which is well-known for its assistance to developing countries, identified a group of producers who were both interested in and capable of penetrating the North American market. The Moroccan government established the link between the IEB and individual Moroccan businessmen through the national agency, the Export Promotion Centre based in Casablanca.

MNC-ETCs

The FMGs cited above share common features with the more formalized ETCs and GTCs. In each case, the image of a "mother hen and chicks" emerges, with the "mother hen" being either a commercial company, a consultant, or some other agent. In the case of the MNC-ETCs, the set-up is noticeably different with the ETC being merely an extension or "trading arm" of the parent company. For example, Motors Trading Corp. is an ETC subsidiary of General Motors. Volvo International Development Corp. is a trading subsidiary set up to promote sales in all geographic areas outside Volvo's major markets, with special emphasis on LDCs.

Bank-ETCs

This group of ETCs differs from MNC-ETCs by being either bank-based or bank-affiliated. Many of these could be alternately classified as GTCs or ETCs particularly for countries like Japan, Brazil, West Germany, and the United States where legislation has specifically approved such groupings. Indeed, the Japanese trading companies have derived immense benefits from their historical association with banking institutions, the "zaibatsu." Thus, the Sogo Shosha are able to facilitate trade credit, initiate equity investments, and provide direct loans to their suppliers and customers. Bank-based ETCs are important in Latin American countries where, in many instances, the ETC takes its name from the bank. Also, in the Middle East, banks and trading companies are, in many instances, owned by the same family.

CTCs

The last group from Table 7.1 includes the commodity trading companies (CTCs). In some respects, these companies are least similar to the preceding groups of ETCs, partly because of their organization and partly because of their business methods. Most CTCs are privately held and are very secretive about their operations due to the highly competitive and fast-paced nature of their business. Like the Japanese Sogo Shosha, these international traders deal in low-margin, high-volume commodities. Their business is characterized by the high levels of risk associated with owning commodities in an era of increased price volatility, floating currencies, and high interest rates. Two Sogo Shosha, Mitsui and Mitsubishi, and two GTCs, Jardine Matheson and East Asiatic Company are often cross-classified as CTCs, on account of their trading in commodities, along with manufactured goods.

Some of the most powerful and secretive CTCs are the state-run trading organizations in the U.S.S.R. Size, secrecy, and the use of bluff are a powerful combination making the dozens of Soviet trading companies both formidable customers and suppliers. Ironically, the very centralization that makes the Soviet economy inefficient at home increases the clout of the trading companies abroad, as a few key decision-makers strive to manipulate world commodity markets.

From the classification in Table 7.1 and this brief discussion of trading companies and trading groups, it is clear that numerous variants of the ETC format exist. Differences arise with regard to at least fifteen variables. These are listed in Table 7.2. The listing is not exhaustive, since other descriptive and measurement variables could be included to cover areas such as financial and managerial practices. Moreover, no research has yet been performed to establish the respective weights of these variables in determining ETC performance levels. The following will show how these variables have been combined to create vastly different types of ETCs in four selected nations.

Profiles of Four Nations' Export Trading Companies

In this section, brief profiles of Japanese, Korean, Brazilian, and American ETCs are presented. These were selected because of their prominence in world markets. The purpose here is to present a picture of similarities and differences between these four groups of ETCs. To this end, environmental and historical factors, which have shaped these ETCs' characteristics and performance levels, are considered, and current innovations among these companies are identified. In each case, reference is made to the variables defined in Table 7.2. Finally,

TABLE 7.2. Variables Determining the Characteristics of Export Trading Companies

MISSION	PRODUCT TYPE
PLANNING HORIZON	SERVICE TYPE
TYPE OF OWNERSHIP	MARKET FOCUS
SIZE	AGENT OR MERCHANT FUNCTION
AGE	
TYPE OF SPONSOR	QUALITY OF MANAGEMENT
BANK INVOLVEMENT	COMMUNICATIONS CAPABILITY
	GOVERNMENT REGULATION AND SUBSIDIZATION
	PROFITABILITY

in order to structure this four-way comparison, each profile addresses the following issues:

● origins and missions
● performance levels
● types of diversification (functional, product, area)
● types of competitive advantages, and
● current problems and opportunities.

Japanese General Trading Companies: The Sogo Shosha

The Japanese GTCs have a long history of involvement in the accumulation, transportation, and distribution of goods from a multitude of countries. Cho (1984) has documented the early history of the Japanese GTCs, which were modeled after the European trading houses. Mitsui was set up in 1876, Mitsubishi in 1889, and Nichimen in 1892.

Officially, only nine Japanese GTCs qualify for the impressive name of Sogo Shosha in terms of sales volume and revenues. Table 7.3 presents a profile of the top nine Sogo Shosha. Another group of seven very large but less well-known GTCs includes: Chori, Itomen, Kawasho, Kinsho-Mataichi, Nozaki, Okura, and Toshoku. Altogether in Japan there are some 8,600 trading companies but most are small, specializing in only a few products and offering only limited services.

From their distant beginnings, the Sogo Shosha have become highly-complex international business conglomerates. In addition to importing and exporting, current activities include third-country trade and domestic sales.

The Sogo Shosha also direct turnkey projects, act as financial dealmakers, and serve as investment partners.

The Sogo Shosha are credited with being able to trade in anything

TABLE 7.3. Nine Leading Japanese General Trading Companies (Sogo Shosha) (1988)

Company	Revenue ($ millions)	Net Income ($ millions)	Employees (thousands)
Mitsubishi Corp.	96,606	225	13.9
C. Itoh & Co., Ltd	92,356	126	12.0
Mitsui & Co., Ltd.	88,640	95	11.4
Marubeni Corp.	82,871	54	10.1
Sumitomo Corp.	81,709	184	12.2
Nissho Iwai Corp.	75,441	61	7.3
Toyo Menka Kaisha Ltd.	27,631	19	5.0
Nichimen Corp.	23,240	7	3.0
Kanematsu-Gosho Ltd.	21,160	8	3.5

Source: Forbes, The 500 Largest Foreign Companies, July 25, 1988, p. 228.

"from soup to nuts." Product diversification is only one of their strengths. Area diversification or worldwide coverage is achieved through extensive networks of international offices and sophisticated company telecommunications facilities. For example, Mitsubishi has 140 branches and affiliates in 70 countries, Marubeni has 154 offices in 87 countries, and Mitsui has 5 clearing houses in Tokyo, New York, London, Sydney, and Bahrain. Complementary to these two strengths of product and area diversification is a third key factor, functional diversification.

In recent years, the Sogo Shosha have moved in new directions, from reactive to proactive trading, in response to competitive threats. Each of the principal services traditionally supplied by the top nine Sogo Shosha is now competitively supplied by other Japanese business entities. Moreover, direct exporting by other Japanese manufacturers has reduced the role of the Sogo Shosha as intermediaries. As business opportunities for the Sogo Shosha shrink in the home market, over-head expenses continue to increase such as the cost of lifetime employment of skilled manpower. Perhaps most critical to the future of the Sogo Shosha is the fact that they have been by-passed in high growth, high-tech industries, since they were fundamentally "general traders" whose principal products came from Japan's low-growth and declining industries.

At least three new types of activity are emerging among the Sogo Shosha: more third-country trade, increased involvement in "mega" projects, and a move into distribution and after-sales service. Third-country trade may take the form of counterpurchase whereby, for example, a foreign government agrees to buy a given volume of product from Japan on condition that Japan buy a specified amount of another product through the Sogo Shosha. In such cases, the product to be purchased by the Sogo Shosha may lack international competitiveness. It may require the special skills of these traders to locate a prospective buyer.

The Sogo Shosha are increasingly serving as organizers, suppliers, and investors, providing "one-stop shopping" for high-risk international "mega" projects. These projects also open the way to subsequent related offshore deals. In entering the realm of high-tech, the Sogo Shosha face the critical problems of developing appropriate sales, engineering, and after-sales capabilities. Sumitomo is gradually moving toward serving the consumer directly. It has been operating a chain of grocery stores for several years in order to gain experience in retailing.

Thus, there are clear indications that the Sogo Shosha are evolving from the traditional import-export houses into global companies which have heavy commitments in overseas manufacturing, resource extraction, high-tech production and innovative business ventures. These new strategies are important because they allow the Sogo Shosha to exert greater control over their product offerings, all the way from manufacturing to retailing, in increasingly protectionist world markets.

Korean Export Trading Companies

The history of Korean ETCs has been documented by Cho (1984) who points to the Japanese GTCs as a model adopted by Korean Policy makers. Faced with poor levels of national export performance, the Korean government adopted the ETC concept and in 1975 laid down minimum criteria for the creation of an ETC. These effectively positioned the new companies as general export companies, involved in large-scale trading, and diversified with regard to both export products and markets. Functional diversification was not mandated, however.

Subsequently, the minimum criteria were revised six times until 1981, effectively transmuting the original institutionalized ETCs into freewheeling, large trading companies. Wide-ranging subsidies were provided to promote the growth of these fledgling companies. Later, these subsidies were generalized to other large-scale but non-ETC designated exporters.

Table 7.4 lists selected leading Korean ETCs, their date of designation as an ETC, and performance data for 1988. The minimum requirement for designation is the achievement of 2% of total Korean exports. The ten leading Korean ETCs include Samsung, Hyundai, Daewoo, Kukje, Hyosung, Ssangyong, Bando, Sunkyong, Kumho, and Koryo. Korean ETCs have achieved a remarkable rate of growth

TABLE 7.4. Leading Korean Exporters (1988)

Company	Year of Designation as ETC	Revenue ($ millions)	Net Income ($ millions)	Employees (thousands)
Samsung	1975	21,148	250	160.6
Lucky-Gold Star Group	*	14,487	181	88.4
Daewoo Group	1975	13,498	37	94.9
Hyundai Corp.	†	6,387	4	0.9
Hyundai Motor Co.	†	3,972	113	29.8
Sunkyong Group	1976	6,812	91	19.8

Notes: * Lucky-Gold Star Group was not officially designated as an ETC.
   † Hyundai Group, before its reorganization into two separate entities, was designated as an ETC in 1978.
Sources: Forbes, The 500 Largest Foreign Companies, July 25, 1988, p. 222.

and are now huge corporations, particularly in terms of number of employees.

Korean ETCs have tended to emphasize heavy industry exports. They have succeeded in diversifying their export markets away from a dependence on developed markets toward the new markets of the Middle East, Latin America, Oceania and Africa. Korean ETCs' involvement in imports is negligible, quite different from the Japanese GTCs which are responsible for some 55–60% of their country's total imports. New opportunities being pursued by Korean ETCs include joint ventures, vertical integration, and mega projects, as with the Sogo Shosha.

The Lucky-Gold Star Group is family-owned and operated. Its almost $9 billion in annual sales constitute more than 10% of Korea's GNP. Lucky-Gold Star's growth strategy is based on joint ventures, particularly with U.S. firms. Altogether, Lucky has 19 joint ventures and technological cooperation agreements with 50 foreign companies. Advantages of this strategy not only include access to advanced technology and know-how, but also access to U.S. partners' huge world markets.

The Hyundai Group, is one of three companies [along with Daewoo Corp., and KIA Industrial Company,] which the Korean government approved as automobile manufacturers in 1981. This policy of controlled capacity had its roots in the near-collapse of the car industry in 1980. Hyundai is known as a fiercely independent company, which insists on "going it alone" in exporting and servicing its cars in Canada and Britain. As an automaker from a developing country, Hyundai benefits from duty-free status is an importer into Canada. In return, it procures more locally-made automobile parts than all the Japanese importers combined.

In contrast, Daewoo formed a 50—50 joint venture with GM. Daewoo's strategy is less risky than the Hyundai approach, which prefers independence wherever possible. The trade-off affects name recognition abroad. Hyundai cars are already known abroad under the Pony and Stellar names, whereas Daewoo will piggy-back on GM's Pontiac name.

Hyundai is also actively involved in mega projects such as the construction of an Iraqi oil-fired power-station. Korean ETCs are engaged in major projects throughout North Africa and the Middle East and are leading suppliers of manual labor.

These brief examples demonstrate how Korean ETCs are contributing to the growth of their country, as manufacturers of goods which are more sophisticated or have a higher added-value than the steel, ships and textiles, which first brought Korea to international prominence. At the core of the nation's export strategy is a concentrated push toward high technology, intensified production, and lower costs.

Korean ETCs have clearly recognized the need to compete effectively in sophisticated markets for high-tech consumer products. Meeting the challenge of worldwide competition is a major preoccupation, as the Koreans struggle to achieve parity in production, marketing, and distribution skills. Korean ETCs have not yet achieved either the area or functional diversification of the Sogo Shosha. If they are to remain competitive in international markets, they must strengthen such functions as information processing, financing (through trade credits, direct loans, and loan guarantees), and risk-reduction procedures.

Brazilian Export Trading Companies

As with Korean ETCs, Brazilian ETCs came into being as a result of specific legislation regulating their format. The concept of ETCs in Brazil was introduced after a visit to Japan by the former Minister of Finance, Antonio Delfim Netto. He believed that it would be possible to transplant the trading company concept to Brazil, and that trading companies would constitute an essential vehicle for promotion of Brazilian exports. Presidential Decree-Law No. 1298 of November 29, 1972, set up conditions for the registration of new enterprises with CACEX (Banco do Brasil's Foreign Trade Department) and allowed local producers to export by selling to an ETC without losing specific export incentives.

Brazilian ETCs account for some 32% of Brazil's world trading operations. Licensed ETCs now number about 180 and have subsidiaries operating in 42 countries. ETCs are making a substantial contribution to the promotion of Brazilian exports through close imitation of Japanese models, and are successfully involving large numbers of smaller Brazilian companies in international trade activities.

Brazilian ETCs are owned either by the government or by private firms. There are two major government-owned groups, Interbras and Cobec. ETCs owned by private firms are of three broad types:

- Leading Brazilian companies combining to promote their own products or services along with those of other suppliers e.g., Maxitrade, Multitrade, Minas Gerais, Brasil S.A.;
- Export pools formed by producers and even retailers e.g., Unisider, Madebras, Pao de Acucar Trading; and
- ETCs formed specifically to aid small and medium producers in one industry e.g., footwear, lace.

The major advantages of joining an ETC for Brazilian companies are the synergistic effects of combined export effort, economies of scale in export financing and documentation, availability of information, easier access to foreign markets, and availability of support services of various kinds. Brazilian ETCs are heavily involved in a large number of industries through a variety of different organizational formats.

Interbras is of particular interest because of (a) its heavy involvement in services exports, (b) its highly diversified activities, and (c) its role in advising suppliers on marketing problems. Interbras serves as a focus for Brazilian architect-engineering (A–E) services by providing information on foreign market opportunities. Interbras also offers assistance in the commercial administration of exporting, financing, payment, and the execution of countertrade. Barter is a frequent requirement when dealing with customers in LDCs, and the exchange of foreign goods for Brazilian services is not unusual. As a subsidiary of Petrobras, the giant government-owned oil-purchasing company, Interbras' trading operations include primary products, manufactured producer goods, and consumer products.

Brazilian A–E firms demonstrate two types of specific competitive advantage. Many are able to draw on the varied political, cultural, and ethnic traits of their employees to overcome barriers of language, climate, and food encountered by traditional Western firms. In addition, Brazilian firms have promoted the concept of "tropicalization," adapting export technology to the tropical conditions prevalent in their LDC markets. These two characteristics are particularly useful in the area of technology transfer to LDCs.

Brazilian ETCs achieve considerable synergy by collaborative action, not just at the level of the individual ETC, but also through the combination of several very large ETCs. ABECE, the Brazilian Association of Commercial Exporting Companies, exports directly or as an agent for third parties. Privately-owned ETCs demonstrate great diversity. For example, Maxitrade and Multitrade include some of the nation's leading industrial goods suppliers and willingly accept to serve competing suppliers. Brasil S. A. is an important ETC which deals mainly with export financing. It is authorized by the Central Bank to give preferential treatment to ETCs in granting loans. Even states have set up their own ETCs, such as Minas Gerais.

Export pools are formed by producers and even retailers. Each pool specializes in those markets of interest to its members, so greater efficiency and expertise are achieved than would be possible using the general ETCs. Pao de Acucar Supermarkets is the largest retail company in Latin America. Its export subsidiary, Pao de Acucar Trading, handles trade with other Latin American countries as well as Arab and African nations. An important goal of this ETC is to transfer retail technology to rapidly developing markets which do not possess an adequate system of mass distribution.

Two important industries, footwear and handcrafted cotton lace, are also experiencing export growth through the intermediary assistance of ETCs. Brazil is the world's third largest exporter of shoes. ETCs in this industry take several forms such as consortia of small producers and large private general trading companies. Petrobras even has a special staff for tracking international fashions in the shoe industry. ETCs have been formed in the Recife area to promote lace exports to the United States, Canada, and Europe. Being labor-intensive, lace-making is a strategic industry and is being extensively supported by ETCs. For example, assistance is given in the area of fashion and design, and added-value items such as hand-embroidered clothing are being developed for export.

ETCs are contributing significantly to Brazilian export growth. There are some 22,000 Brazilian companies doing business abroad, which is comparable to the United States where about only 10% of the 250,000 manufacturing firms actually engage in any form of inter-national trade. A key organization is responsible for executing Brazil's national trade policy—CACEX (Banco do Brasil's Foreign Trade Department). CACEX controls both import and export activities, and operates according to guidelines set by the Finance Ministry and an interministerial National Foreign Trade Council.

U.S. Export Trading Companies

Passage of the Export Trading Company Act in 1982 in the U.S. created considerable excitement among exporters and nonexporters alike. Seminars, conferences and press editorials were numerous and wide-spread during 1982 and 1983. Yet, in 1984, the *Wall Street Journal* featured a front-page article entitled: "Export Trading Firms

TABLE 7.5. Summary of Six Hypothetical ETC Models

Models	Institutional Participants	Products or Services	Domestic Coverage	Foreign Market	Expected Trade Volume By Fourth Year of Operation
Trade Stream Model	Manufacturer, Freight Forwarder, Bank Holding Company (BHC)	Narrow Product Line	Geographic Region	Single Country	$6.5 Million
Single Product Model	Manufacturers, BHC	Single Product Line	Nationwide	Worldwide	$10 Million
Services Model	Architects & Engineers	Design & Management Services	Geographic Region	Geographic Region	$35 Million
Hub Model	Port Authority, Bankers Bank	Multiple Product Lines	Geographic Region	Geographic Region	$50 Million
Bank Holding Company	BHC, Ocean Shipper, Insurance Company	Multiple Product Lines	Single State	Worldwide	$65 Million
Single Product Area Model	Manufacturers, Venture Capital Institution	Single Product Area Line	Nationwide	Geographic Region	$250 Million

Source: Adapted from *The Export Trading Company Guidebook*, prepared by Price Waterhouse and The Council for Export Trading Companies for the U.S. Department of Commerce International Trade Administration, Washington, D.C. (February 1984), p. 42.

In The U.S. Are Failing To Fulfill Promise." It seems as though the new ETC concept is not after all the panacea for the national "export problem" that it appeared to be in 1982.

When the ETC Act was passed, optimistic forecasts predicted that U.S. exports would increase by $6–11 billion within five years, and that more than 320,000 trade-related jobs would be created by 1985. The Act was expected to help small- and medium-sized firms the most, some 20,000 being considered potential exporters by the Department of Commerce. In reality, major U.S. corporations have demonstrated the strongest response. Ironically, as Czinkota (1984) reports, these MNC-ETC formations would have occurred with or without the ETC legislation. The two major provisions of the 1982 ETC Act (authorization of bank involvement in exporting and prior antitrust protection), apparently have less appeal than expected for current or potential export entities in the U.S.

New ETCs in the U.S.

As a guide for managers interested in forming or joining an ETC, the Department of Commerce developed six hypothetical models which are summarized in Table 7.5. In reality, new ETCs in the U.S. appear to follow one of four patterns which are briefly identified as follows. [See Amine *et al.* (1985), Amine, Cavusgil, and Amine and Cavusgil (1987) for a full discussion.]

1. *ETCs formed by consortia of smaller suppliers*
2. *ETCs formed by service providers* such as banks (bank-ETCs), export management companies (EMC–ETCs), freight forwarders, etc.
3. *ETCs formed by multinational corporations* (MNC–ETCs)
4. *ETCs formed by quasi-public organizations or public entities* such as ports, development councils, state governments, etc.

Groups 3 and 4 above are closest "in spirit" to the Department of Commerce's models ("Single Product" and "Hub"). Most ETC formations have been of the first and third types. Some comments on each type are given below, illustrating the diversity of U.S. ETCs.

   1. Small-Company ETCs. This type of ETC is likely to remain few in number, whether certified or non-certified, due to the psychological barrier of accepting collaborative action.

   2. EMC-ETCs and Bank-ETCs. It is ironic to note that the Director of NEXCO (the National Association of Export Management Companies) considers an "ETC" merely a new name for an "EMC," an export management company. This summarizes the attitude of many export service providers who saw in the ETC Act only a source of threat. Some EMC managers feared that new bank-ETCs would lure away their manufacturer-clients. Others feared that banks would use their knowledge of EMCs' financial operations to gain advantage in their own ETC operations. Many EMCs also consider that they are too small to be concerned by or interested in anti-trust protection. Similar mixed or indifferent attitudes toward the ETC Act persist among other export service providers such as ocean carriers, nonvessel operators, and freight forwarders.

Banks' concerns are of a different nature. Czinkota's (1984) research among 37 U.S. bank holding companies or their subsidiaries found that 41% were interested in investing in an ETC, 32% in forming an ETC, and 27% in using an existing ETC. Bankers anticipated two major problems in this field; organizing for countertrade or barter, and finding qualified trading personnel. They were also concerned about maintaining overseas agents, identifying foreign market potential, and supervising trading personnel. Thus, major obstacles for the banks appear to be emotional, rather than financial.

More recently, Hu and Maskulka (1985) have identified variations in both knowledge about the ETC Act and attitudes toward the legislation among U.S. banks, depending upon the banks' degree of internationalization. This characteristic was measured in terms of bank size, percentage of international business, and number of offices abroad. Small U.S. banks were found to be mostly unfamiliar with the ETC legislation, whereas large- and medium-sized banks are well-informed and favorable toward the legislation. Differences in attitudes also exist among large banks (money-centers) and medium-sized (regional) banks, concerning future participation in ETCs and the relative importance of ETCs in banks' long-term strategic objectives. Among the larger banks, involvement in ETCs may only be a "matter of time," as they explore the opportunities offered by the legislation.

3. MNC-ETCs. The early experiences of MNC-ETCs in the U.S. are proving to be problematic. Virtually none of the U.S. multinational-based ETCs is yet making money. New U.S. MNC-ETCs are finding that it is not enough merely to transfer staff horizontally from domestic units to the trading unit. Genuine trading expertise is a hard-won and expensive skill, as demonstrated by the well-known generous salaries of traders working for commodity firms. Slow growth and preseverance seem to be the keys to success for new MNC-ETCs. Yet, American corporate culture and pressure by shareholders tend to deter managers of MNC-ETCs from taking the long view, so typical of the Sogo Shosha.

4. Public or Quasi-Public ETCs. As in the case of U.S. banks, port authorities have hesitated to get involved in forming ETCs because of

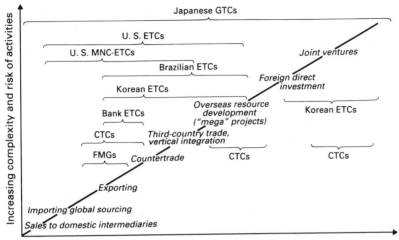

Increasing complexity and risk of activities →

Increasing involvement and commitment

Japanese GTCs

U. S. ETCs

U. S. MNC-ETCs

Joint ventures

Brazilian ETCs

Foreign direct investment

Korean ETCs

Bank ETCs

Overseas resource development ("mega" projects)

Korean ETCs

CTCs

Third-country trade, vertical integration

FMGs Countertrade

CTCs

CTCs

Exporting

Importing global sourcing

Sales to domestic intermediaries

Note: See Table 7.1 for explanation of acronyms.

FIG 7.1. Competitive Clusters of ETCs in World Markets.

possible conflicts of interest in competition between a port and its customers.

From this brief review of U.S. ETCs, we see that many gray areas remain for clarification. Will ETCs eventually accomplish what the government hoped in 1982? Can a balance be maintained between achieving strong, effective ETCs and checking abuses of the antitrust laws? Can U.S. companies, historically so competitive, learn to work together to the degree that an ETC requires, without a clash of "corporate cultures?" Can U.S. managers achieve the skills and mentality of a trader, rather than those of an exporter? Ultimately, it seems that the "people" factor, as opposed to multiple "market" factors, will be critical to the success of U.S. ETCs.

Competitive Clusters of ETCs in World Markets

Presented in Figure 7.1 are several "competitive clusters" which incorporate the six types of trading companies listed in Table 7.1. Given that Japanese GTCs span the full range of market involvement activities, other nations' trading companies and groups have been positioned relative to them. This approach shows which companies compete directly with one another and which ones are focusing on other areas, in order to develop competitive advantages. Again, as in Table 7.1, we must recognize the broad generalizations and simplification which such an approach entails. Nevertheless, one virtue of this approach is to direct attention to specific aspects of competitive clustering among the world's ETCs.

For example, the Japanese Sogo Shosha's option for proactive trading means that they must now compete across the board with other nations' companies. Faced with such broad-scale and varying types of competition, the Sogo Shosha at least enjoy the advantages of being sufficiently massive and resourceful to be able to choose whether to meet the competition, or whether to move into other market segments. The smaller competitors are, in many cases, locked into competition within their segment, with little opportunity to opt out.

This phenomenon of "segment squeeze" can be illustrated by reference to the Korean and Brazilian ETCs. Originally created by their respective governments to promote export growth, both Korean and Brazilian ETCs have recently expanded into resource development in the Middle East. While giants such as Mitsui take on the huge financial burdens and risk of projects such as the Bandar Khomeini petrochemical plant, valued at $3.5 billion, the Koreans and Brazilians serve the specialized niche of supplying construction labor. The Koreans are also beginning to compete directly with Japanese and Western companies to win mega project contracts. Even within this high-risk segment, competition in the Middle East is made more fierce by the appearance of Turkish contracting companies, with their special competitive advantages of geographic proximity to Arab markets and a shared Muslim faith.

In contrast to the Brazilians and Koreans, Japanese GTCs are well established as global competitors. Their major concern is to maintain and even expand their leadership position. At one end of the market spectrum are four low-cost, low-price producers known as the "four tigers," Taiwan, Hong Kong, Singapore, and South Korea. These countries' exports still include such simple consumer items as knit shirts, radios, electric fans, and shoes. But, for all four, the fastest-growing exports have been the more complex electronics products: micro-computer terminals, disk drives, telephone equipment, and semi-conductors. At the other end of the market spectrum, Japanese GTCs are meeting competition head-on from West European and North American multinationals, with their design strengths and technological edge.

One way in which Japanese GTCs have countered the combined threats of globalized competition and market protectionism is through joint ventures with their competitors. It will be noted from Figure 7.1 that "joint ventures" are positioned at a higher level of increasing involvement, commitment, complexity, and risk than "foreign direct investment." Conventional use of the terms would seem to argue in favor of inverting these positions, but from our point of view, the determining factors are degree of control and duration of the activity. Seen in this light, a 20-year joint-venture agreement, signed between two major ETCs of different nationalities, appears infinitely more fraught with risk than might be the relatively straightforward construction and management of a manufacturing plant overseas. Thus, the risk of losing control of a joint venture, for whatever reason, and the often unpredictable outcomes of a joint venture are the principal arguments which support the positioning of this activity on the continuum in Figure 7.1.

As we consider the place of U.S. ETCs in this spectrum of competitive clusters, we discover that U.S. corporations appear to be competing both among themselves and against foreign competitors. For example, some of the large joint venture-type ETCs are challenging both the Sogo Shosha, European multinationals, and other large U.S. corporations in the areas of general trading, third-country trade, and vertical integration. Other U.S. companies, which have not formed ETCs, are expanding their international reach through joint ventures, particularly with the Japanese. Thus, it is entirely feasible that, at some time in the future, a Japanese-U.S. JV will compete against a U.S. ETC. This scenario can be developed even further, since Sogo Shosha such as Mitsui have already expressed their willingness to join U.S. ETCs. Such affiliations may be both reasonable and desirable for U.S. companies, particularly as the U.S. Administration appears to be adopting an increasingly "bilateral" approach to international trade. If this trend continues, the main thrust of world competition would be between giant global conglomerates. The small exporter would then either have to become extremely good at nichemanship, identifying small market segments overlooked or discarded by the big companies, or else simply jump on the bandwagon of the ETCs.

This second option, whereby small companies would be constrained to join an ETC in order to get into export markets, is not without its problems. The intricate relationships between manufacturer-suppliers (M-S) and indirect international marketing vehicles, such as ETCs are susceptible to instability, either because the ETC serves the M-S too well, or not well enough. Thus, if the M-S gets good results from use of an ETC, it may be tempted to "go it alone" and economize on the expense of using the ETC. In the other case, use of the ETC may not produce the results expected by the M-S, if the ETC-parent chooses among its other suppliers for the best deal available.

All the foregoing considerations lead to one question the stability of U.S. ETCs. Will they represent an effective, long term, competitive threat to other nations' ETCs in a particular market or segment? Or will many ETCs be disbanded, because of failure to reach short-term profit objectives? It seems as though the Japanese Sogo Shosha are hedging their bets by offering to join U.S. ETCs and by setting up joint ventures with other U.S. corporations. It will be interesting to see whether U.S. ETCs can survive the initial problems of personnel, management, profit planning, and market development, and succeed in building up sufficient critical mass to become successful viable trading entities.

The Brazilians have avoided much international competition and have developed strong competitive advantages, by focusing on the supply of basic consumer goods to developing markets. They have also strengthened themselves through collaborative action among their own ETCs, tending to avoid the challenges and risks of international joint ventures. In contrast, the Koreans have chosen the joint venture as a means of rapid expansion into high-tech industries. They have also chosen the strategy of market specialization, based on meeting the needs of sophisticated large-volume Western markets. Similarly, federated marketing groups tend to adopt a single-market or geographic focus. In contrast, commodity trading companies have developed specific product or commodity expertise.

U.S. ETCs are remarkable for their wide range of emphases or orientations. Bank-ETCs seem to be opting for functional specialization through the provision of specific export services. The trading-arms of some MNCs specialize in a limited range of products, whereas some manufacturer- or retailer-sponsored ETCs appear to be trying to compete across the board. In so doing, they are of course encountering strong competition from the established and experienced Sogo Shosha, particularly in cases where countertrade is involved.

It will be noted in Figure 7.1 that "countertrade," "third-country trade," "vertical integration," and "overseas resource development" are positioned adjacent to one another. It could be argued that "countertrade" should serve as a global term for all of these activities, and in the case of the Sogo Shosha, this is probably true. However, as seen in the case of some CTCs, bank-ETCs, U.S., Korean and Brazilian ETCs, there still remains some differentiation, and these variations are reflected in the figure. It will also be noted in Figure 7.1 that CTCs are shown to be involved in exporting, mega projects, and joint ventures.

In concluding this discussion of competition, one should not forget the vital material and financial support given to Japanese trading companies by MITI (Ministry of International Trade and Industry), to Korean ETCs by their government through MTI (Ministry of Trade and Industry), and to Brazilian ETCs by CACEX (Bank of Brazil's Foreign Trade Department). No such support system has been initiated in the U.S. This probably explains to a large degree why

U.S. ETCs experienced such extensive "teething troubles." It is unlikely that compensation for this shortfall will soon occur in the United States, since the concept of a uniform "trade policy" supported by extensive government agencies is still at the discussion stage.

A Generalized Model of ETC Expansion

In this final section, information from the foregoing analyses is synthesized. Table 7.6 presents a listing of external factors likely to affect ETC growth, and Table 7.7 presents a similar listing of internal company factors. All the factors listed in Tables 7.6 and 7.7 are incorporated into the generalized model in Figure 7.2. It should be noted, as in the case of Table 7.2, that these listings are not exhaustive. Also, they have not yet been subjected to empirical testing of either their validity or their relative importance in determining the performance of ETCs. These shortcomings are not considered a detriment, but rather a challenge to pursue further research which will validate these conceptualizations.

One of the difficulties in developing the model in Figure 7.2 is to accommodate the multiple types of activities which an ETC may pursue concurrently. Another difficulty is to allow for flexibility in changing a type of activity, either moving into new areas or returning to previous activities. It will be noticed from Figure 7.2 that an ETC may conceivably become an importer at home, and even get involved in domestic manufacturing—as exemplified by the Sogo Shosha and the Korean ETCs.

Another challenge in modeling ETC expansion is to allow for opposing trends among ETCs. For example, the Sogo Shosha have

TABLE 7.6. External Factors Affecting ETC Growth

A. *Country-Specific Factors*

Stage of national economic development
Historical context
Attitudes toward international trade
Status of country's trade balance
Cultural attitudes toward collaborative or group action
Cultural attitudes toward entrepreneurial action
Attitudes toward company organization and operation

B. *Market-Specific Factors*

Source of initiative for creating ETCs
Constraints imposed on ETC performance
Size of domestic market
Level of domestic competition
Sophistication of domestic companies
Availability and type of marketing support services

TABLE 7.7. Internal Company Factors Affecting ETC Growth

A. *ETC Organization*

Type of activity (manufacturing, service provider)
Type of specialization (product, function, area)
Type of sponsor (private, public, semi-public)
Type of ownership (entrepreneurial, collaborative)
Linkages in domestic market
Linkages in international market
Managerial resources

B. *Mission*

Prerequisite characteristics for official designation as ETC
Role in national economic development
Sectoral role and importance
Positioning in domestic market regarding suppliers
Positioning in domestic market regarding competitors
Focus (export, import, general trade, countertrade, offshore trade, mega projects, etc.)
Linkages in domestic market (size and anti-trust issues, affiliations with financial institutions and government, etc.)

C. *Coverage*

Number of markets
Location/type of markets
Size of market segments or niches
Overseas channel power
Linkages in overseas markets (cooperation agreements, exclusive contracts, joint ventures, foreign direct investments

moved away from general trading toward high-risk investment in overseas resource development. Thus, the traditional import-export houses of Japan have evolved into sophisticated global corporations. U.S. companies which have formed ETCs have followed an inverse pattern of expansion, from specialized manufacturing into general trading of their own and related goods. Korean ETCs, in contrast, are pursuing exporting, along with increased stakes in domestic and overseas production.

As will be seen in Figure 7.2, all of these variants are accommodated in the model of the ETC expansion path. Attention is drawn to the fact that the model of ETC expansion is not linear, but allows for the possibility of multiple looping, along with movement forward and backward along the path. These characteristics are essential if all the complexities of the ETC concept are to be effectively represented.

As with any conceptualized model, the question of its value arises. The model has at least four major strengths. First, the model aims to be *comprehensive*. Second, the model is *descriptive*, both in its identification of company and market factors affecting ETCs, and in the presentation of a range of options for ETC growth and diversification. Third, the model is *dynamic* insofar as it allows for change in the

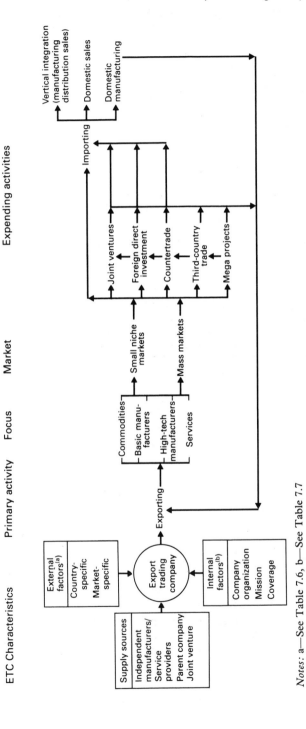

Notes: a—See Table 7.6, b—See Table 7.7

FIG 7.2. A Generalized Model of the Expansion Path for ETCs.

nature of an ETC's activities, and even allows for nonlinear ETC development. Fourth, the model aims to serve as both a *diagnostic and planning tool,* providing answers to the questions, "Where are we now?" and "Where do we want to be?"

These four major features of the model offer clear managerial applications. For example, the model identifies a range of diversification and growth options, which ETC managers may consider when developing their long-range marketing plan. Moreover, when studied together with the competitive cluster framework, this model will lead ETC managers to reflect upon the implications of selecting specific competitive strategies. For example, managers will be led to consider major strategic issues, such as whether to meet the competition head-on; whether to avoid competition by seeking smaller or more specialized demand segments; or even whether to seek a partner-company in order to develop synergy. Other important decisions identified in the model concern the choice of market position, such as specialization in small market niches or mass marketing activities; the role of counter-trade in establishing new markets; the mix of products and services to be traded; and the mix of supply sources for the ETC. Clearly, a range of other issues are also implied or made explicit by the model.

In the case of U.S. ETCs, these questions may prove to be critical. U.S. ETCs appear to be competing both among themselves and against foreign competitors. An objective evaluation of current marketing strategies (by reference to the model in Figure 7.2) would surely help many U.S. ETCs, both large and small, to clarify their market position, and to develop a sharper focus than is evident at the present time. The objective of this research was to go beyond mere description of different nations' ETCs, in order to identify common characteristics of ETCs and incorporate these into conceptualizations. The generalized model of ETC expansion and the analytical framework of competitive clusters of ETCs together represent valuable aids to both managers and academics, in understanding and forecasting future growth patterns for ETCs in world markets. In order to encourage further interest in validation, below is presented a list of major research questions which remain to be addressed:

- What ongoing lessons can be learned from the evolving experience of trading companies in other nations, particularly those of Western Europe and the Newly Industrializing Countries (such as Brazil and South Korea)?
- What factors will prove critical to the success of ETCs in the United States?
- What role will small exporting companies play in the field of international marketing?

- How will multinational corporations react to the trend of cooperative or collaborative exporting?
- What role will the banks play in contributing (or not) to the success of trading companies from different nations?
- How can managers be trained as "effective traders?"

Further study of these issues will contribute greatly to our understanding of the ETC concept and its operationalization in world markets.

References

Amine, Lyn S. and S. Tamer Cavusgil, "Issues to Consider When Creating or Joining an Export Trading Company," *Journal of Business and Industrial Marketing*, (1987).

Amine, Lyn S., S. Tamer Cavusgil and Robert Weinstein, "Japanese Soso Shosha and the U.S. Export Trading Companies," *Journal of the Academy of Marketing Science*, Vol. 14, No. 3 (1986), pp. 21–32.

Amine, Lyn S., S. Tamer Cavusgil, A. Coskun Samli, and John R. Nevin, "Toward a New Export Intermediary: Export Trading Companies in the United States," in *Developments in Marketing Science*, VIII, N. K. Malhotra (ed.), (Miami: Academy of Marketing Science, 1985), pp. 85–89.

Cavusgil, S. Tamer, "Differences Among Exporting Firms Based on Their Degree of Internationalization," *Journal of Business Research*, Vol. 12, No. 2 (1984), pp. 195–208.

Cho, Dong Sung, "The Anatomy of the Korean General Trading Company," *Journal of Business Research*, Vol. 12, No. 2 (1984), pp. 241–256.

Czinkota, Michael R., "The Business Response to the Export Trading Company Act of 1982," *Columbia Journal of World Business*, Vol. 19, No. 3 (Fall 1984), pp. 105–111.

Hu, Michael Y. and James M. Maskulka, "U.S. Bankers' Attitudes and Internationalization: The Case of ETCA," *International Journal of Bank Marketing*, (Fall 1985), pp. 13–21.

8

Assessment of Company Readiness to Export*

S. TAMER CAVUSGIL
ROBERT W. NASON

Two fundamental trends, the shrinking of the economic world and the upsurge of small business starts in the U.S. and around the world, raise the issue of export readiness of entrepreneurial business. This article presents a computerized decision support system for assessment of company readiness to export.

It is clear that the small businesses as a group need to pay more attention to international competitiveness. Typically this involvement will come in the form of exporting and to some degree licensing. At least initially it will not likely be direct investment nor countertrade (a more sophisticated and complicated way of conducting international business). This article will focus on exporting.

In the process of researching, consulting, and working with a large number of firms over the past 15 years we have been able to identify various factors associated with successful exporters, variables that contribute to successful exporting, or those features of entrepreneurs that make the difference in terms of successful international business involvement. This knowledge and experience has been translated into software and stored on a standard floppy which can be used with any IBM or IBM-compatible microcomputer. The name of this software is CORE (Company Readiness to Export). It is designed as a learning tool to aid companies considering exporting as a growth strategy.

Consideration of the desirability and feasibility of exporting is the very first step that most entrepreneurs will have to take when investigating exporting. The CORE decision-support tool is designed to assist the new-to-exporting company in the process of identifying

---

*Adapted, with permission, from *Singapore Marketing Review*, (1990).

TABLE 8.1. Steps in Export Market Development

---

1. Internal Evaluation of Readiness to Export (Audit)
   Organizational Readiness
   Product Readiness
2. Search for Profitable Markets
3. Develop a Business Plan
4. Develop Skills and Resources Needed
5. Implement Export Operations
6. Monitor Export Performance

---

strengths and weaknesses in the context of exporting. CORE does not eliminate the need to work with international business consultants and only focuses on the first step in export market development (see Table 8.1). This is a critical first step and will form the subject of the remainder of this paper. CORE is designed to allow a systematic review of export related capabilities and thus, forms the basis for an internal audit necessary in this first step.

In the context of the initial decision to enter exporting, there are essentially two key characteristics that are relevant. First, is the *organizational readiness* to export. Entrepreneurs and managers need to satisfy themselves that, as an organization, they are ready to take on this challenge. That is, that they have the resources, they are motivated enough, and they are committed to exporting.

The other aspect is *product readiness*. The right products must be available for the right markets. There must be a good fit between the product and the prospective markets. Accordingly, the CORE program develops two scores for each entrepreneur—a score of organizational readiness to export and a separate score of product readiness to export. Research findings on export behavior of firms generally support the notion that these are independent dimensions (see, for example, Bilkey 1978, Cavusgil & Nevin 1981).

Both indicators of export potential are measured by multiple variables; a total of approximately 70 items. These variables were selected from a larger set of characteristics which emerged as significant predictors of export activity in empirical research. They are presented to the user of CORE program either in the form of multiple choice questions or Likert-type statements. User responses are combined with internally-stored weights for each question and response category. These weights were developed as a result of a Delphi process among 35 scholars and seasoned international business executives.

Both organizational and product readiness scores are, then, weighted indices varying between 0 and 100. CORE program presents the user with both numerical scores and an interpretation of them. In addition, each score is classified as High, Moderate, or Low on the basis of

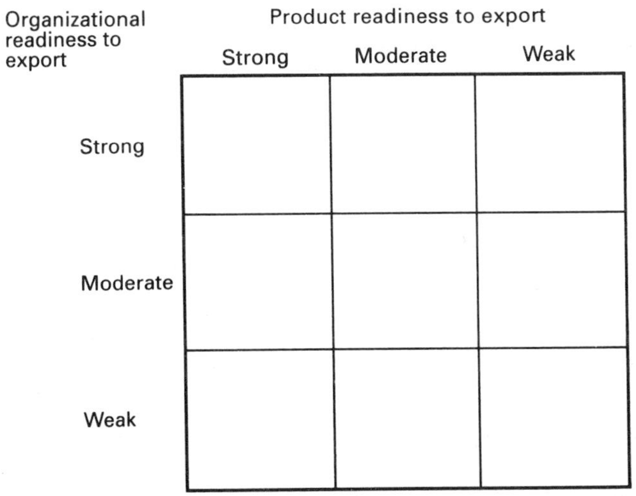

Organizational readiness to export

Product readiness to export

	Strong	Moderate	Weak
Strong			
Moderate			
Weak			

FIG. 8.1 Readiness Classification.

experimentation with a large number of companies. When both variables are cross-classified, a 3 by 3 matrix emerges as in Figure 8.1. This presentation classifies each entrepreneur into one of nine possible scenarios. CORE program provides a unique set of recommendations for each scenario, depending upon the combination of organizational and product readiness. The CORE program also presents a list of major strengths and weaknesses in the context of exporting, based on the response patterns of the particular user. A brief explanation of each strength and weakness is also provided.

Finally, CORE offers an export tutorial section, enabling the user to look up capsulized information about most frequently encountered tasks in exporting. These include terms of payment, researching export markets, price quotations, financing alternatives, distribution methods, and so on.

Technically speaking, CORE is a compiled decision support tool programmed in D-Base III. It comes in the form of a single floppy diskette and it can be used with any IBM compatible personal computer. It is menu driven, requiring only limited typing skills from the user.

CORE software has evolved from an export outreach program designed to identify and assist high-potential exporters. It was conceived as a tool to aid in the process of identifying company strengths and weaknesses in the context of exporting. CORE supplements the relevant human expertise in exporting; it does not substitute it.

Benefits of CORE Analysis

By developing a computerized procedure to drive judgments about an enterprise's readiness to export, we had hoped to accomplish the following objectives.

First, CORE introduces a degree of objectivity as well as efficiency to accomplishing a self-audit of export readiness. The process of eliciting relevant information from the entrepreneur, and then using it to arrive at some conclusion about export initiation, is made more systematic.

Second, since CORE was based upon all relevant research findings on what makes a successful exporter, it served as a bridge between export theory/knowledge and export practice. In essence, CORE serves as a vehicle for impacting successful and sustained export experience by bringing into light pertinent research results. Hence, it has already made a contribution to practice by encouraging export evaluations in an informed and systematic manner.

Third, CORE emerges as a valuable tool for the export advisory personnel who work with entrepreneurs in the assessment of export readiness. It gives the advisors the opportunity to be thorough and systematic in the internal audit process. Perceived credibility of the advice received from the advisory personnel is enhanced because of such a formal procedure.

Fourth, the availability of an export readiness assessment procedure in the form of a computer program stored in a floppy diskette, contributes tremendously to its widespread dissemination. Thus, when used in a self-assessment mode, numerous entrepreneurs can benefit from CORE as it does not require the presence of a human consultant.

Fifth, CORE serves as a useful *screening* tool to those assistance agencies interested in qualifying enterprises for export assistance. When an agency wishes to consider only a select group of "high-potential" enterprises for lending assistance, it can rely upon CORE results for this selection process. CORE scores can be used to identify promising prospective exporters from a larger universe of companies.

General Observations on Export Readiness

Before discussing the steps in export market development in more detail, it is useful to describe five more general observations which emerged from this research. First, exporting is not necessarily for every entrepreneur or company. Even though opportunities exist for the group as a generalization, specific situational and internal variables may make exporting unwise for a particular firm. A company must make sure that it is going to benefit from exporting. Commitment of resources, manpower, management time, production capacity, and salesforce personnel in exporting is not desirable if it is not going to be profitable or lead to competitive strengths. The CORE software is designed to assist in that process of evaluation. If the result is that domestic marketing expansion is likely to be more profitable, that is what should be done as long as a careful eye is kept on competitiveness and international opportunities over time.

Second, companies that have expanded at home before they enter foreign markets are much more likely to be successful than those companies that jumped from being a local company, working with few supplying companies, to being an international marketer. That is, there seems to be some "internationalization" that must take place at home. It does seem to take advantage of attractive domestic market potential before entering overseas markets. The domestic expansion allows organizational development, marketing talent development, and credibility development as a stepping stone to the more complex international environment.

Third, "on again, off again" exporting does not generally work. Exporting must be viewed as a long-term proposition. Patience and perseverance are essential elements of a successful international strategy. It is too costly to move down the learning curve with a short-term focus.

Fourth, passive or "reactive" exporting is not likely to work either. There used to be a time when exporters just simply awaited export business. Unsolicited orders came from foreign customers and distributors. Requests were evaluated when received, with some orders filled with standard products off the shelf. Local bankers took care of the letters of credit and how payments were made. This is reactive or passive exporting. Because of the nature of the competition today, that strategy is no longer feasible in most cases. Successful exporting has become an active and aggressive set of strategies to seek export markets, identify export markets, identify channels (distributors, representatives, and agents in those markets that you can work with over a long period of time), and establish a long term approach to cultivating export markets.

Fifth, systematic exporting is essential. A formal approach to exporting is very important, rather than a haphazard "trial and error" approach to exporting. The same types of management skills, and principles that apply to good domestic business conduct are also applicable to international business transactions. Business plans are essential for the development of export markets. Certain steps must be followed to make sure that opportunities are taken advantage of in a formal and systematic way.

Steps in Export Market Development

The effective cultivation of export opportunities requires a sequence of steps. Six such steps have been identified and emphasis will be placed on the first "readiness" step in keeping with the objectives of this article, but the remaining steps will also be briefly described.

Internal Evaluation of Readiness to Export

Readiness to export is where the CORE, the Company Readiness to Export software is particularly useful. Internal evaluation is focused on organizational strengths and product strengths as has been previously mentioned. Each will be taken in turn.

Organizational strengths or readiness refers to top management commitment, financial resource availability, human resource readiness, and soundness of organizational structure. Unless there is top management commitment on the part of the company to go overseas and to cultivate export markets with a long-term approach, success is doubtful. Senior management is going to be the one that shows determination, makes resources available, and that enables efforts which require time and money to be accomplished.

What are some of the things that can be done to improve organizational readiness to export? Space allows for only the presentation of a few suggestions. Senior and middle management should be involved in exporting forums. Company executives should take part in world trade club meetings, export councils, international site visits, and trade shows, fairs, and overseas trade missions. These are important ways to become knowledgeable and familiar with a variety of opportunities overseas. Exposure to successful exporters in similar circumstances can significantly further this learning process.

A second suggestion is complementary exporting or piggyback exporting. This strategy involves identification of a larger company that is already exporting complementary products which could gain competitive advantage and/or profits by inclusion of a fuller line.

A third suggestion is indirect exporting through trading companies (ETCs) or export management companies (EMCs). These export intermediaries provide functions which substitute for an in-house export department. An experienced, competent export trading company can ease the transition and foster the learning processes necessary for successful exporting. There may be a threshold level of export sale beyond which it would be desirable to develop in-house capabilities, but for the initial period of internationalization, indirect means may be more appropriate.

A fourth suggestion is for concentration geographically and

expanding gradually. That is, don't try to take over the entire world in a year or two. Try to identify the most attractive markets, in your case in your industry, given your particular products. Pick one or two countries, and in each of those countries very carefully pick the right distributors and agents. Then build some experience and expertise. Then move on to the next country. For U.S. companies, for example, Canada, and Europe are the traditional markets. Latin America, Africa, and Asia are more difficult and require more experience and expertise.

A fifth suggestion is to follow up on inquiries and leads from abroad. A lot of companies simply neglect any leads that come from distributors or customers. In some cases it may be possible to *follow domestic customers abroad.* You may find that a customer of yours is exporting or is conducting business, maybe engaged in a technology transfer or a mega project somewhere around the world. You may find that you will be able to sell to them overseas as you would at home.

Participate in catalog and video shows. In case you are not able to participate in international trade fairs and shows, send in your product catalogs and promotional videos. It is likely that such activities are sponsored and perhaps subsidized by your government.

Direct mail is also very helpful. Try the direct mail approach, that is, mailing your brochures to potential customers, especially if you can develop a good, refined mailing list and if you can rely on the postal service in various countries.

Also, exporters must seek assistance. One thing you must do well in the export business is to learn where you can get assistance. There is a host of places that you can turn to for assistance: international trading companies, world trade clubs, and government agencies.

Finally, organizational readiness means that you have a suitable *export organization* or *export structure.* This means that you have to go through either the indirect route and rely on an export trading company or management company, *or* develop the in-house capabilities to take on the functions that are new to your firm, for example, documentation, letters of credit, or shipping overseas. Export transactions can be very mind boggling. It can be very complex, unless you have the people to do it for you. The letters of credit, for example, is a new activity and you need to seek help here from your bankers. The legal, promotional, and communications aspects need to be considered. To maintain a long-term presence in a foreign market and establish long-term relationships with distributors, new ways of doing business will need to be adopted. You must have these capabilities, either in-house, or hired from an independent trading company.

Product readiness to export involves a host of important questions. Consider adaptation of products in terms of redesigning the product, adding and/or eliminating features, refining attributes, and changing specifications or components. Perhaps repositioning the product will also help. You may find that the product's particular attributes which may be appreciated in the home market may not be attractive in the foreign market. You may have to reposition it. You have to, for example, emphasize the nutritional content of your food item in a particular developing country, rather than the taste as a selling point.

It is helpful to place oneself in the position of the foreign customers and attempt to identify what would be desirable from their point of view. What kind of features are important to this product? As a result, you are likely to come up with various ways of improving and enhancing your product appeal. Do take this extra step because you are not going to be able to compete with other exporters unless you adapt your product. Sometimes it may be as simple as package adaptation.

Also, you can try to embellish the product offering by enhancing the product by good customer/after-sales service. This is something we often forget, but, if you are in the business of selling an industrial product, you must have good after-sale service and you must ensure that the service is going to be satisfactory in the foreign market. Delivery can be an important selling point. Also, today, credit and financing terms have become perhaps more important than the prices quoted to your overseas customer. So, do pay attention to credit terms and try to offer favorable financing terms to your customers.

You may also try to ride on your company's reputation. That is another way of avoiding competition on a price basis—which is the last thing that you want to do. You want to emphasize the non-price benefits of your product or service because price competition can be very cutthroat, and you may not be able to make very much money if you offer just the price benefits rather than non-price strengths, such as company reputation and after-sales service. If you happen to have a line of products, do consider all of them for potential candidates for export. If you find that your product does not sell in one particular market, there is no guarantee that it will not do well in another market. So, do consider several markets for the same product in case you have difficulty with one particular market because of non-tariff barriers or because of certain customer characteristics in that market.

Having discussed the first step in exporting, the internal audit, what is the next step?

Search for Profitable Foreign Markets

The next step is to *search for profitable markets* abroad. To simplify this task, an entrepreneur can approach foreign market potential analysis in three stages, as discussed in Reading 20.

Develop a Business Plan

The third step in the systematic export process is to develop a *business plan*. This plan should articulate how you are going to tap an opportunity in the selected market. You must satisfy yourself that demand is sufficiently large, the market is accessible and that you can actually sell into that market. The plan will also propose how you will identify some competent distributors in the market, utilize a particular distribution channel and give certain discounts. All of these principles will be articulated in the business plan.

In the process of developing your business plan, you should be able to answer the basic questions of: What sales growth can I expect for the first five years? What kind of returns am I expecting? At what kind of distribution cost, discounts to trade, and so on? What will happen to my profitability if the exchange rates go up and down in a particular fashion? Add all of this in the context and framework of a budget and a timetable. You must outline your goals and objectives (country specific and product specific) within the framework of a budget and timetable—first year, second year, third year. You should have at least a plan to cultivate that particular export market.

After all, this is how you do business, how you *must* do business in the home market. We are not suggesting anything new, but most exporters, when it comes to selling abroad, are not as systematic. This is a puzzling issue, for they have spent considerable resources on market research in the domestic market, and yet when it comes to exporting they go in by the seat of their pants and fail to be as successful.

Exporting is a serious undertaking. You must have a business plan and follow it through with good execution, which means that you must be careful in terms of quoting, preparing export and bids, and in fulfilling export orders with proper documentation. Documentation is a difficult issue for a small firm that has limited personnel, and there are a number of steps to learn about proper paperwork. Again, you either do it yourself, hire a freight forwarder, or an export management company to do it for you, but do it the right way.

Development of Export Skills and Resources

As a new activity to be adopted by the organization, exporting brings with it new challenges for management. A critical constraint for new-to-export companies is qualified manpower. Personnel with proper training and experience is often limited or non-existent. Therefore, management must develop the requisite staff and resources in anticipation of export involvement. When not available internally, these manpower and financial resources must be secured from outside.

Implementation of Export Operations

In the final analysis, success in exporting will be achieved through smooth export operations. To the extent that export orders are received, processed and completed in an orderly and timely manner, export activities will pay back nicely. A major reason for successful exporting is an excellent working relationship with export intermediaries such as freight forwarders and customs brokers. Ensuring customer satisfaction is also essential in international transactions.

Monitoring Export Performance

So what is the last step? Make sure you *monitor export performance.* Make sure that you compare your actual export performance, with the predicted performance. Make sure that if there are deviations from the plan that you can understand why those deviations have taken place, such as, why you have not performed as well in a particular market and in a particular product category. Make sure that you talk to your distributors or local representatives. Try to understand why certain events took place. If they have not performed well, if they are the ones who failed, make sure that you discuss this with them and put them on the right track. If there is no good solution, make sure that you identify a better distributor. What we are saying here is, do not forget to monitor your results over the long term in that particular export market.

Experience with *CORE* Software

The *CORE* software was developed as a decision support tool for entrepreneurs and managers—to aid in the process of considering exporting as an expansion strategy. As a screening tool, CORE is also helpful to export assistance agencies and export consulting companies. We have also used it in the classroom as a teaching tool to examine the factors which contribute to export success.

Nevertheless, the biggest beneficiaries are individual entrepreneurs or managers who wish to test their readiness to engage in exporting. Over four years of experience with CORE, both nationally and overseas, verifies that it serves as a useful tool for companies that are examining the desirability of exporting. The program instructs the user on key factors which may either hinder or facilitate successful exporting. It provides immediate feedback in terms of how an entrepreneur can go about overcoming any weaknesses his business possesses. A step-by-step guide to exporting is also offered.

Hundreds of copies of CORE have been distributed to individual companies, export consulting/trading companies, export assistance agencies (state departments of commerce or development, U.S. Department of Commerce, etc.), small business assistance centers, world trade clubs, chambers of commerce, trade associations, colleges and universities, and other groups. Internationally, CORE has been adapted for use by several Canadian provinces, the Australian Trade Commission, and the International Trade Center (UNCTAD/ GATT), to name just a few organizations. Given the thousands of U.S. firms which have not yet gone international, the potential impact CORE can make to successful initiation of exports is tremendous.

Current work agenda involves several developmental projects. First, a new version of CORE, CORE II has been developed in the form of an expert system. Second, several variations of CORE are in development for different applications. One application is for "developing country" enterprises. CORE methodology is applied to developing country circumstances to be of assistance in identifying high-potential exporters. Other applications are for specific industries as opposed to the generic nature of CORE. Third, a major project to develop expert systems for international marketers has been initiated at Michigan State University. This multi-year project employs artificial intelligence methodology in developing several decision support modules, including country selection, overseas distributor evaluation, and international pricing applications. As with CORE, the expert systems development effort attempts to represent the state-of-the-art knowledge on international business in a unique and pragmatic manner to improve the quality of international business decisions.

References

Bilkey, Warren, J., "An Attempted Integration of the Literature on the Export Behavior of Firms," *Journal of International Business Studies*, (Spring 1978), pp. 33–46.

Cavusgil, S. Tamer and John R. Nevin, "Internal Determinants of Export Marketing Behavior: An Empirical Investigation," *Journal of Marketing Research*, Vol. 18, No. 1 (1981), pp. 114–119.

Further Reading — Part I

Bartels, Robert, *Global Development and Marketing*, (Columbus, Ohio: Grid, 1981).

Levitt, Theodore, "The Globalization of Markets," *Harvard Business Review*, (May–June 1983), pp. 92–102.

Rugman, Alan M., "A New Theory of the Multinational Enterprise: Internationalization Versus Internalization," *Columbia Journal of World Business*, Vol. 15, No. 1 (Spring 1980), pp. 23–29.

Simmonds, Kenneth, "Global Strategy: Achieving the Geocentric Ideal," *International Marketing Review*, (Spring 1985), pp. 8–17.

Thorelli, Hans B., "Networks: Between Markets and Hierarchies," *Strategic Management Journal*, Vol. 7 (1986), pp. 37–51.

Wind, Yoram and Howard Perlmutter, "On the identification of frontier issues in multinational marketing," *Columbia Journal of World Business*, Vol. 12, No. 4 (Winter 1977), pp. 131–139.

▮▮ Internationalization of the Firm

Introduction to Part II

As domestic markets are continuously shrinking, many companies see internationalization as inevitable and some even consider it the only way for their survival. Part II approaches the issue of internationalization from both a theoretical and an empirical perspective.

Drawing from the findings of various empirical studies conducted in several industrialized countries, Cavusgil in Reading 9 develops a conceptualization of a firm's initial involvement in international marketing activities. Five distinct stages are identified along the internationalization process: domestic marketing, pre-export stage, experimental involvement, active involvement and committed involvement. The determinants of the process and the public policy implications are also discussed.

Reading 11 reviews the development of Wilkinson Sword, the famous international razor producer. The company reached its present international position in three phases. The first was occupied in building up the organization, establishing the name and image of Wilkinson Sword, while concentrating on one product only—the blade. Phase two was a period of consolidation during which new shaving systems were introduced and shaving toiletries were added to the package. The third phase involved diversification in which the company produced "everything that has an edge."

International retailing is an area neglected in the literature. Reading 12 deals with IKEA, a pioneer in international marketing of economical and yet fashionable furniture.

The last reading by Reinstein is a case study of how a small company succeeded in the Japanese marketplace. Essentials for successes are the following: "sell to need; produce a high-quality product not made in Japan; and establish a partnership with a Japanese company."

9

On the Internationalization Process of Firms*

S. TAMER CAVUSGIL

The growing importance of international marketing has created a greater need for conceptual frameworks to guide practice and public policy programs. Despite the greater need, conceptualizations and theory development in international marketing have been scarce. International marketing has been described as an area in which empirical work by practitioners is often more advanced and insightful than academic contributions. It can be argued that marketing academicians have exhibited an ethnocentric behavior in their interests; they have been pre-occupied largely with domestic marketing.

Conceptualizations in international marketing have lagged behind despite the fact that limited but significant empirical research has been conducted in the area. Several aspects of international business activities have been empirically investigated by researchers. Aharoni (1966) and Richardson, for example, have investigated foreign investment decisions; Torneden has studied foreign divestment decisions; Truit researched expropriation decisions; Franko explored joint-venture decisions; and a larger number of investigators have studied export marketing decisions.

The primary objective of this article is to offer and present support for a comprehensive conceptualization of firms' initial involvement process in international marketing. Typically, this involvement is in the form of exporting. Export marketing is usually considered to be a first step in the process of internationalization. Thus, the formulation that is presented attempts to give an account of how firms adopt exporting activity. This formulation is thought to apply to other forms

*Adapted from *European Research*, Vol. 8, No. 6 (November 1980), pp. 273–281, with permission.

of involvement as well. Specifically, the discussion focuses on the following questions: how can the internationalization process be characterized? What are the stages in this process? What are the determinants of this process? What are the implications of the conceptualization for public policy and future research? Hopefully, the discussion will provide a framework by which existing empirical work can be better evaluated and integrated. In addition, it is expected to facilitate hypothesis formulation in future investigations, and help clarify public policy options in the area of export stimulation.

The Internationalization Process: Significant Findings

An examination of the pertinent literature on the initial involvement of firms in international marketing reveals three major conclusions. Perhaps the most important conclusion that can be reached is that such involvement is a gradual process, taking place in incremental stages, and over a relatively long period of time. In their observations of Swedish firms, Johanson and Wiedersheim-Paul noted that the prevailing pattern is a gradual internationalization, rather than large spectacular investments. The authors traced the complete internationalization process for Sandvik, Atlas Copco, Facit and Volvo. Each stage in the process represented successively larger resource commitments and also led to quite different market experiences and information for the firm. In studying Australian firms, Welch and Wiedersheim-Paul also stressed the sequential nature of the export development process. They characterized it as "a multi-stage set of activities, with a high degree of diversity". Firms typically avoided making large commitments to international markets and resource allocation proceeded in an incremental manner.

In a recent article, Johanson and Vahlne (1977) reinforce the belief that the internationalization process represents firms' "gradual acquisition, integration, and use of knowledge about foreign markets and operations, and on its successively increasing commitment to foreign markets". The authors argue that this is the consequence of a process of incremental adjustments to changing conditions of the firm and its environment, rather than the result of deliberate strategy. Absence of prior experience, lack of adequate market information and associated uncertainty in foreign marketing are the causes of the incremental decision-making. Market uncertainty associated with a commitment can be "reduced through increases in interaction and integration with the market environment—steps such as increases in communication with customers, establishment of new service activities or, in the extreme case, the takeover of customers".

Bilkey and Tesar proposed a "staff" model for examining export behavior. The main thrust of their argument is that the export development process of firms occurs in stages. Management is not interested in exporting in Stage One; would fill an unsolicited export order in Stage Two; actively explores feasibility of exporting in Stage Three; and so on. They related each stage empirically to a number of determining characteristics, concluding that the considerations that influence firms' progressions from one stage to the next differed by stage. Independent investigations at the U.S. Department of Commerce also confirm a gradual involvement hypothesis. In particular, firms are thought to progress through an "exporting pipeline". A firm first becomes motivated to export; then decides how and where to export; devotes manpower and resources to marketing efforts, and so on.

The second conclusion that can be reached is that the initial involvement in international marketing can be regarded as an innovation within the closed environment of the firm. In a pioneering study, Simmonds and Smith approached the initiation of exporting in the context of innovations. "Entry into an export market is just as much an innovation as the adoption of a new production process, for example, so there is every reason to suspect that many of the findings concerning other types of innovation will apply to it." The first export order was taken as the evidence of innovation in the nine British firms that were investigated. Their research concentrated on tracing this first order and identifying the situation leading up to it and the characteristics of the persons involved. It was hypothesized, first, that the entry into exporting would be explainable in terms of conditions, persons, or happenings within the firm. This hypothesis was not supported, as the authors found that an external stimulus was responsible for the first export order. Secondly, it was expected that the innovation would be traceable to one innovator who would have distinguishable characteristics. The investigation revealed that the innovators in the firm travelled widely, and possessed an attitude of almost complete unconcern for national boundaries where business was conducted. The authors called this attitude a "Supra-national outlook". The innovating exporters were also found to be aggressive and competitive. They possessed a great degree of risk tolerance, and emphasized expansion and growth.

The third conclusion is that many firms appear to "move ahead" with exporting without much rational analysis or deliberate planning. In an investigation of Nebraska-based small manufacturing firms, Lee and Brasch (1978) found that most new exporters followed a "non-rational decision process". They did not consult with expert authorities or collect much information, and they had only vague justifications for getting themselves involved in exporting. The authors attribute this result to the difficulty of calculating economic benefits of exporting, the naive acceptance of the assertions that "the market is out there" and the lack of sophisticated information, planning and control systems in these small companies. Lee and Brasch also examined whether the export adoption process would be initiated by problem perception or by awareness of the innovation. They concluded that the innovation-oriented adoption process was more common among export adopting firms than problem-oriented adoption process. That is, the initiating force is either precise knowledge of the existence of a market opportunity or gaining technical knowledge of exporting rather than the problems which the firm may be facing.

A Conceptualization of the Internationalization Process

The proposed conceptualization of the initial involvement of firms in international marketing is illustrated in Figure 9.1. This conceptualization is in harmony with the important finding that this involvement is best understood in the context of a process, taking place as a result of

These INTERNAL AND EXTERNAL VARIABLES help explain why a firm may engage in a ...	CRITICAL ACTIVITY which is unique to various ...	STAGES
Inhibiting firm characteristics	Preoccupation with the home market	DOMESTIC MARKETING
External stimuli Unsolicited orders Change agents Internal stimuli Differential advantages and conducive characteristics Decision-maker characteristics International orientation	Deliberate search for information and preliminary evaluation of the feasibility of undertaking international marketing activity	PRE-EXPORT STAGE
Perceptions regarding attractiveness of international marketing activity	Initiation of limited international marketing activity	EXPERIMENTAL INVOLVEMENT
Experience-based expectations Availability of key resources Willingness to commit resources	Systematic exploration of expanding international marketing activity	ACTIVE INVOLVEMENT
Marketing performance Performance in overcoming Barriers	Resource allocation based on international opportunities	COMMITTED INVOLVEMENT

FIG. 9.1. Stages in the Internationalization Process of the Firm.

successive decisions made by management over a period of time, usually over several years. It identifies several distinguishable stages during the process. These stages, as well as the determinants of these stages, can be measured empirically. A brief discussion of the conceptualization will now be offered, followed by its implications for future research and public policy.

Domestic Marketing Stage

For many firms, marketing beyond the domestic market is a distant, sometimes, unheard of, possibility. Indeed, a large proportion of companies are not capable of exporting. A firm producing a bulky product or a component for another firm may not benefit from exporting. Manufacturers of highly specialized products are also less likely to engage in international marketing. Beyond such inhibiting handicaps, however, many firms are not exporting because they are not interested or willing to experiment with exporting. Others are too busy doing other things; considerable preoccupation with day-to-day affairs is also hindering. Unfavorable attitudes or apathy and lack of awareness of foreign marketing opportunities are additional characteristics usually associated with non-exporting firms. Nonexporters undoubtedly make up the majority of the manufacturing sector in many countries. In the United States, for example, it is estimated that approximately 88% of the manufacturing firms are nonexporters.

Pre-Export Stage

Various internal and external stimuli are responsible for arousing initial interest in exporting among decision makers. When sufficiently interested, decision-makers in a firm engage in a deliberate search for relevant information and a subsequent assessment of the feasibility of undertaking exporting activity. External stimuli are often in the form of unsolicited orders from buyers or distributors abroad, or domestic export agents. Banks, trade associations and middlemen also serve as change agents. External stimuli received by firms clearly surpass internal stimuli. In surveying eight separate studies, it was found that external factors made up 54% to 64% of all stimuli.

Three types of internal stimuli can be identified. First, a firm's differential advantages may so serve. Advantages which originate from the firm's products, production processes, resources or markets may provide initial motivation for involvement in international marketing. In other cases, managements are attracted to international marketing alternatives in order to overcome unfavorable circumstances such as saturated markets, growing competitive pressures and spare or obsolete manufacturing capacity. Second, the presence of aggressive, venturesome decision-makers in the firm can be a positive stimulus for export initiation. How highly the managers aspire to profits, growth and market development has been clearly related to exporting activity. Managers who are growth-minded, dynamic and willing to pursue opportunities facilitate initial involvement. Third, the adoption of an international outlook at the top-management level appears to be a critical determinant of initial interest. This orientation, which has been defined as "the extent to which (the decision-maker) perceives and considers as interesting, events occurring outside his own country or perhaps even outside his own local environment", has turned out to be critical in many studies. Furthermore, a favorable attitude toward international marketing can often be correlated with experience gained in living abroad, speaking a foreign language, being young and other characteristics.

The presence of one or more of these stimuli typically motivates the management to engage in a preliminary evaluation of the feasibility of marketing abroad. At this stage, management lacks important basic information. It is not known what costs are involved; how the collection and exchange risks will be handled; how the distribution is to be arranged, and so on. Since the activity is new to the firm, it is likely that the existing staff has no prior experience. Thus, there is frequently a need to seek information outside the firm. This search for information tends to be limited, however, because of the uncertainty associated with anticipated benefits from exporting. It is not unusual to find managements engaging in only a crude cost-benefit analysis at this stage. Decision-making in this phase appears to be based, essentially, on management's diffuse impressions of the attractiveness of exporting.

Experimental Involvement Stage

When the perceptions of management concerning the desirability of exporting are favorable, the firm may progress to the stage of being an experimental exporter. Experimental involvement is usually marginal and intermittent. The proportion of total output exported will not typically exceed 10%. Often, only one or two foreign markets are involved. Many firms will engage in indirect exporting at this stage, shifting some of the marketing tasks to middlemen. Furthermore, short-run profits are likely to be the motivating forces rather than clearly formulated long-term objectives such as firm growth.

There is some evidence that those firms which have moved to the experimental involvement stage tend to be "extra-regional". Investigations of Australian firms revealed that extra-regional expansion—a type of internationalization process within the domestic market— prepares the firm for its export start. Wiedersheim-Paul, Olson and Welch (1978) found that the exporting firms usually expanded inter-state trade well before their first export sale.

There is also considerable evidence that experimental involvement is likely to concentrate on psychologically close countries; that is, the countries that are relatively well-known and similar in business prac-tices. Johanson *et al.* introduced the concept of psychic distance as a variable measuring the degree of uncertainty and the cost of informa-tion in international decisions. Carlson prefers to use the term "cultural distance" as an expression of those factors that create differ-ences in market conditions and difficulties in acquiring information about these differences. Psychic or cultural distance is proposed to be a function of the differences between any two countries in terms of their level of development, the level of education, business and everyday languages, cultural differences and the extent of commercial connec-tions. Empirical investigations carried out at Uppsala University have confirmed that psychic distance is quite helpful in explaining the internationalization patterns of firms. In addition, it was found that firms which produced technology-intensive products and smaller firms were more influenced by cultural distance in their internationalization process.

Active Involvement Stage

In time, some firms may progress to the stage of active involvement in international marketing. Active involvement may come in the form of exporting to new foreign markets, expanding the volume of exports, or exporting directly, if the firm has not been doing so previously. In carrying out any one of these strategies, many tasks—which are new to the firm—will be undertaken. Perhaps the most unique activity at this stage is a systematic exploration of a large number of foreign market opportunities. Prospective markets are screened out and potentials are assessed. In addition, buyer and legal requirements must be estab-lished and dealers will have to be located in international markets. These tasks and the greater need for information place considerable demands on the resources of the firm.

Whether or not these demands will be met—and the firm will progress to the active involvement stage—will depend upon: (1) the favorability of experience-based expectations of management concerning exporting; (2) the availability of key firm resources for undertaking the necessary activities unique to this stage; and (3) the willingness of management to allocate such resources.

A major determinant of active involvement in international marketing is the management's experience-based expectations of the attractiveness of exporting for the firm. There is no longer any need to rely on diffuse impressions. Management now has an information base which has been acquired as a result of its own (experimental) experience in exporting. Johanson and Vahlne (1977) label this element experiential knowledge:

"We believe that this experiential knowledge is the critical kind of knowledge in the present context. It is critical because it cannot be so easily acquired as objective knowledge. In domestic operations, we can to a large extent rely on lifelong basic experiences to which we can add the specific experiences of individuals, organizations and markets. In foreign operations, however, we have no such basic experiential knowledge to start with. It must be gained successively during the operations in the country . . .

"An important aspect of experiential knowledge is that it provides the framework for perceiving and formulating opportunities. On the basis of objective market knowledge it is possible to formulate only theoretical opportunities; experiential knowledge makes it possible to perceive 'concrete' opportunities—to have a 'feeling' about how they fit into the present and future activities".

Thus, the expectations formed and the familiarity gained become significant inputs into further decision making.

The second determinant of the firm's progression into active involvement is the ease of access to key resources necessary for undertaking additional tasks at this stage. The availability of physical, financial, and managerial resources is closely associated with firm size. In addition to limited financial resources, smaller firms do have a number of disadvantages. Absence of trained middle managers, pre-occupation with day-to-day operating problems and lack of time for long-term planning are notable. Thus, smaller firms encounter significant obstacles in progressing to the stage of active involvement.

The third determinant of the active involvement stage is the management's willingness to commit adequate resources to new activities. The existence of a suitable organizational structure within the firm to handle exploration activities is one indicator of the management's willingness to allocate resources for expanded involvement in international marketing. Some firms assign a new department or personnel to such activities while others employ domestic marketing staff. The relative status of the separate organizational unit or personnel within the organization reflects the relative significance attached to foreign marketing. Whether or not direct responsibility for international marketing is placed in the hands of a senior executive who has both the ability and authority to exercise real influence on overall policy matters is critical. Yet another aspect of the allocation process is the emphasis placed on personal visits to overseas markets. Research indicates that executive trips to foreign markets serve as the primary source of information product decisions and assessment of risks and are also helpful in the actual processes of sales negotiations and customer liaison.

Committed Involvement Stage

The next stage in the internationalization process may be characterized as the firm's transition into the position of committed participant in international marketing. In the long run, the management finds itself in a position of constantly making choices in allocating limited resources between domestic and foreign markets. The long-term posture of the firm will be dependent upon how well management performs in terms of planning and executing the marketing mix as well as how well various impediments in international marketing are over-come. In addition, the three determinants of the previous stage will continue to affect the long-term commitment of firms to international marketing.

Competence in managing the elements of the marketing mix is a major determinant of the firm's long-run performance and commit-ment to international marketing. On the whole, entry and survival in foreign markets are more risky and difficult than operating in domestic markets. In the presence of greater uncertainty and stakes, careful manipulation of each aspect of the mix becomes necessary. Empirical research suggests that the following elements are especially critical in international operations: quality and design of the products and pack-aging for foreign markets; development of distribution channels; com-petitive pricing; and extension of credit. Apparently, these tasks are the most bothersome in international marketing—as exemplified by product adaptation, greater control over distribution—and a deliberate effort to enhance customer satisfaction has been found to be as valuable as in domestic marketing. Such an orientation would es-pecially be critical for a committed exporter who is likely to act with an explicit objective of maintaining long-term presence in selected markets rather than an experimental exporter who places greater emphasis on short-term returns on export sales.

The long-run commitment of the firm to international marketing will also be dependent upon how successful management is in over-coming various barriers encountered in international activities. These impediments can be distinguished from those that are confronted by the firm early in the internationalization process. A firm is then concerned primarily with searching, locating and evaluating potential markets, and acquiring experience in how to initiate exporting activities. An experienced exporter, on the other hand, encounters continuing difficulties in maintaining and expanding export involvement. Import/export restrictions, cost and availability of shipping, exchange rate fluctuations, collection of money and expansion of distribution are examples of this type. An extensive survey conducted by the U.S. Department of Commerce also revealed that specific marketing intelligence (sales leads) and opportunities to meet face-to-face with potential foreign customers are specified by exporting firms as primary ongoing needs.

The firm's marketing effectiveness and its success in overcoming various impediments, along with the determinants of the earlier stage, will affect its long-run standing with respect to international activities. If the firm does not perform well in accomplishing its profit, growth, and diversification objectives through its involvement, it may choose to return to an intermittent type of exporting activity, or drop all international marketing activities. If, however, participation of the firm in international marketing has been beneficial, the internationalization process may continue with forms of involvement other than exporting. Many firms continue the process by engaging in licensing arrangements, establishing overseas sales branches and, eventually, building production facilities in foreign markets. Insightful accounts of these latter types of involvement are found elsewhere. Recently, considerable research has focused on the foreign investment process, as involvement in terms of direct investments has shown remarkable growth. Initial involvement in international marketing, however, which usually appears in the form of exporting and licensing, continues to permeate the majority of developed-country firms which participate in international business.

Conclusions and Implications

Marketing of goods and services beyond the home market is a distinct alternative for the firm as a means of accomplishing the organizational goals of growth, profits and market diversification. Admittedly, this avenue is not open to all firms. Some necessary conditions, such as the possession of a unique or competitively priced product, have to be satisfied before a firm can profitably exploit this alternative. Furthermore, risks and uncertainty encountered in international marketing are greater. However, more and more firms are looking into the possibility of utilizing this growth alternative in order to take advantage of attractive marketing opportunities abroad and to relieve themselves from the consequences of unfavorable developments at home, including growing competitive pressures.

The conceptualization offered in this article of firms' initial involvement in international marketing rests on the central assumption that managements approach international marketing decisions in stages. A number of successive phases are identified along the internationalization continuum. The incremental nature of the decision-making process may reflect a cautious attitude on the part of managements towards international marketing. The other explanation is, of course, the greater need for information and "experiential knowledge" in international marketing and the greater costs of obtaining information. Consequently, managements become especially sensitive to the risks involved. Commitments are made gradually, as more information and experience are acquired along the way. Furthermore, international marketing decisions appear to be nonprogrammed. Questions of strategy arise in a highly unstructured form, especially early in the process.

The essentially behavioral nature of the explanatory variables in Figure 9.1 is also notable. The conceptualization attributes the presence and degree of involvement in international marketing to personal evaluations of decision-makers, their subjective expectations and managerial aspirations, among others. The empirical studies clearly suggest that the behavioral variables, along with individual firm characteristics, are especially useful in explaining firm-to-firm variation in export behavior. External variables such as international marketing impediments and macro-level variables such as exchange rates, on the other hand, can be expected to be more useful in explaining aggregate behavior. As such, the conceptualization is in agreement with the behavioral theory of the firm and the empirical investigations of international business decisions. It also represents a clear departure from classical economic theory. The internationalization process does not appear to be a sequence of deliberate, planned steps, beginning with a clearly defined problem and proceeding through a rational analysis of behavioral alternatives. Personal characteristics of the decision-maker's lack of information, perception of risk and presence of uncertainty seem to be especially valuable in understanding firms' involvement in international marketing.

Research Implications

A number of implications for future research can be offered. First, the characterization of the involvement as a process implies that longitudinal investigations of international marketing decision-making may especially be appropriate. Cross-sectional studies of firms cannot delve into the dynamic nature of decision-making. Second, future investigations should take account of the observation that different firms will be at different points along the internationalization process. It is also reasonable to expect that different firms will travel this route at varying paces. Findings promise to be more fruitful and reliable if the investigator attempts to construct his/her sample of firms as homogeneously as possible. The typology sugggested in this paper—domestic marketing, pre-export, experimental involvement, active involvement and committed involvement—may be useful in this respect. The conceptualization lends itself nicely to future validation studies. It identifies specific determinants to be related to each stage of the internationalization process. Suggestions for deriving operational definitions of variables can be found in Cavusgil and Nevin, Bilkey and Tesar or Reffait and Roux. Inferences as to the nature of causal relationships among the determinants can also be found in Cavusgil and Nevin.

Public Policy Implications

The conceptualization of the firm's internationalization process also raises some public policy questions concerning the stimulation of firms in exporting activities:

1. How can the firms in varying stages of involvement be identified? It can be concluded that detailed profiles can be prepared for firms at different stages of involvement. These profiles can be based on organizational and decision-maker characteristics, as well as operational characteristics such as the percent of output exported. One such profiling effort is reported in Cavusgil, Bilkey, Tesar (1979).

2. What types of firms should be targeted for export stimulation and promotion by governmental agencies? The findings of a major study conducted by the U.S. Department of Commerce are helpful for deriving conclusions concerning the United States economy. This study concluded that: (a) smaller, less-experienced firms generally need more help in exporting than large, established exporters; (b) governmental services are better able to meet the needs of smaller firms that cannot afford the higher costs of private-sector services; and (c) larger firms' needs for assistance appear to be well-met by private-sector sources or through their own contacts abroad. It appears that the public-sector assistance should be focused on firms which are in the earlier stages of their internationalization, especially if the intent is to develop a wide exporting base in the economy.

3. What types of programmes would be most appropriate in reaching and serving the particular needs of firms? Needs at each stage of the internationalization process are expected to be different. Since

different firms are at different stages, export assistance programmes should take into account their unique needs at that stage. For a firm which is indifferent to exporting, various motivational programmes may be appropriate. Information on the benefits of exporting or case histories of successful exporters are examples. An experimental exporter typically needs extensive information on how and where to export. Hence, programmes that are designed to inform the firms as to where to go for export assistance; where the best markets are for their products; and who the most promising buyers and distributors are may be valuable. Active exporters, on the other hand, suffer from operational and resource limitations. Specific sales and representation leads for their products abroad and assistance in making successful bids for overseas export contracts may be considered for them. Finally, committed exporters need to struggle with a number of foreign competitive factors and buyer resistance. Creating opportunities for these firms to publicize, advertise and exhibit their products abroad and for meeting directly with foreign buyers and representatives are especially appropriate.

References

Aharoni, Yair, *The Foreign Investment Decision Process*, (Boston: Harvard Graduate School of Business Administration, 1966).

Bilkey, Warren J., "An Attempted Integration of the Literature on the Export Behavior of Firms," *Journal of International Business Studies*, (Spring/Summer 1978), pp.33–46.

Cavusgil, S. Tamer, "Organizational Determinants of Firms' Export Behavior: an Empirical Analysis," unpublished PhD dissertation, University of Wisconsin-Madison, 1976.

Cavusgil, S. Tamer, Warren Bilkey and G. Tesar, "A Note on the Export Behavior of Firms: Exporter Profiles," *Journal of International Business Studies*, Vol. 10 (Spring/Summer 1979). pp. 91–97.

Johanson, J. and J. Vahlne, "The Internationalization Process of the Firm: a Model of Knowledge Development and Increasing Foreign Commitments," *Journal of International Business Studies* (Spring/Summer 1977), pp. 23–32.

Lee, Woo Young and John J. Brasch, "The Adoption of Export as an Innovative Strategy," *Journal of International Business Studies*, (Spring/Summer 1978), pp. 85–104.

Wiedersheim-Paul, Finn, H. E. Olson and L. S. Welch, "Pre-export Activity: the First Steps in Internationalization," *Journal of International Business Studies*, (Spring/Summer 1978), pp. 47–58.

10

Japan's Kao Enters U.S. Cautiously with Jergens Co.*

JEREMY MARK
MASAYOSHI KANABAYASHI

With a combination of financial muscle and scientific know-how, Japan's largest household-products maker is cautiously entering the U.S. market.

Last month, Kao Corp., Japan's largest advertiser and a powerhouse in soaps, toiletries and cosmetics completed the purchase of Cincinnati-based Andrew Jergens Co. from American Brands Inc. But Kao probably won't try to make a big splash in the U.S. soon.

Rather than going head to head with Proctor & Gamble Co. or Colgate-Palmolive Co. in a battle over the massive laundry detergent or soap markets, analysts and Kao executives say the company will focus on skin-care products and cosmetics. They see the takeover as a shrewd way for Kao to make its first foray into the U.S.

"Jergens has a respectable management and more than 100 years of history," says Yosio Maruta, Kao's president. "It also has distribution channels. By combining them with Kao's scientific knowledge or financial assistance, Jergens will be able to serve U.S. consumers [better]."

Both companies have similar images: purveyors of practical, unglamorous, but quality products. In the U.S., Jergens appeals mainly to a Good Housekeeping magazine type of consumer, says Julie Kanagawa, an analyst with Hoare Govett Japan Ltd. "You wouldn't see Jergens ads in Cosmopolitan or Vogue," she says. "That's the tack (Kao) has taken here in Japan."

Says Richard Maynard, a research analyst with Salomon Brothers Inc. in Japan, Kao's image is "fairly staid." The company, which had

---

* Reprinted from *Wall Street Journal*, July 11, 1988, with permission.

sales of $3.77 billion in its year ended March 31, has succeeded by creating innovative products and then by employing "marketing strength to squeeze all the benefits out of them," he says.

Research and development is considered to be Kao's strongest suit. Last year, it put 69 billion yen ($522.7 million) into capital expenditures, up 24% from the previous year. The payoffs from this level of investment were obvious last year with Attack—an "enzymatic," concentrated laundry detergent that took Japan by storm coming out of nowhere to give Kao a 40.5% share of Japan's detergent market, up 7.1 percentage points from the year before.

The focus on R&D is similarly trumpeted with Kao's Biore line of skin creams and its Sofina cosmetics, both of which are expected to be broadly marketed in the U.S. eventually. Ms. Kanagawa says Sofina is marketed with the emphasis on skin care as science.

Whether or not Kao's products actually represent scientific breakthroughs, the company has been able to successfully market them in Japan by sheer weight of advertising dollars. According to Tokyo-based Dentsu Inc., the world's biggest ad agency, Kao spent 35.4 billion yen on advertising in its last fiscal year, putting it ahead of Toyota Motor Corp., Nissan Motor Co., Honda Motor Co. and Lion Corp., Kao's major competitor in some lines.

Last year, Kao's profit was 13.247 billion yen, up 22.5% from 10.811 billion yen a year earlier. That fiscal strength was evident in the Jergens acquisition, which has been estimated at between $250 million and $300 million, substantially higher than competing bids by U.S. companies.

Kao's willingness to pay a premium for Jergens fits the pattern of other recent Japanese acquisitions in the U.S., analysts say. Faced with the choice of building a production-base and distribution network from the ground up, many Japanese companies have opted to buy U.S. companies instead. Fortified by the strong yen, they are even willing to pay prices that U.S. bidders consider too high.

For the moment, Dr. Maruta says, Kao has no plans to market products under its own brand name through Jergens. He said Kao may introduce new products for facial care and hair treatment through Jergens, but it could be several years before Kao becomes visible in U.S. stores. He said Jergens will gradually shift its marketing emphasis to advertising from store promotions and dealer incentives.

Analysts say there is a strong chance that Kao will take advantage of an earlier U.S. acquisition. Last year, it bought High Point, N.C.-based High Point Chemical Corp. for an undisclosed sum. High Point produces raw materials for toiletries and personal-care products.

The analysts also think Kao is pursuing the correct strategy in the U.S., particularly the decision to bide its time. "Kao is a very established, very old and somewhat prudent company. They would not jump into something blindfolded without thorough research," Mr. Maynard says.

11

Wilkinson's New Edge*

JOACHIM SCHYPEK

The frail recovery which the West German economy had registered by the end of 1983 meant improved growth rates for many companies. Anything over 5% was well above average, though, and two-digit improvements produced envy. So did the results reported by Wilkinson Sword Deutschland, the German branch of the Wilkinson group, which has been wholly owned by U.S. Allegheny International since 1981.

The Solingen based subsidiary improved its turnover by 20% in 1983: DM 76.8m against 1982's DM 63.8m, which was itself an increase of 16% on the previous year. Exports accounted for nearly a quarter of the total. Profit growth in real terms has been 12% year on year, and the return on investment before tax averages more than 30%.

Wilkinson Sword has cornered almost a third of the West German market for razor blades, razors and shaving toiletries. The market leader is Gillette Deutschland which holds 55% of the market according to Wilkinson, and 63% on Gillette's own reckoning. Schick, Tondeo and Bic account for the rest. The blades and razors sector in Germany is estimated at more than DM 200m at retail prices. Of the 21 million Germans who shave, about 45% are wet shavers.

Kurt Gruber, managing director of Wilkinson Sword GmbH, attributes his company's success to a combination of good craftsmanship and first class salesmanship. He believes that the growth in turnover reflects the superiority of Wilkinson products and the adoption of the right approach in marketing.

Wilkinson reached its present position in Germany in three phases. The first, from 1962 to 1970, was occupied in building up the

*Reprinted from *Marketing*, May 17, 1984, pp. 29–32, with permission.

organization, establishing the name and image of Wilkinson Sword, while concentrating on one product only—the blade.

Phase two, from 1970 to 1980, was a period of consolidation, during which new shaving systems were introduced and shaving toiletries were added to the package. Since 1980, Wilkinson Germany has embarked on a new phase of diversification, producing "everything that has an edge".

Stainless Blades

Wilkinson first entered the German market early in 1962 when it bought two thirds of the Rudolph Osberghaus company in Solingen, a razor blade manufacturer whose "Fasan" (pheasant) brand represented less than 1% of the market. Production of "Fasan" blades was halted, and they were replaced by the stainless Wilkinson Sword blades, first in North Rhine Westphalia and then progressively in the remainder of the Federal Republic.

The initial launch was carried out by three sales representatives, supported by regional advertising, and the result was that within four months demand exceeded production. "Buyers of hairdressers' supplies and chemists' wholesalers drove into Solingen with lorries and cars, hoping we would not turn them back empty-handed," says Gruber. "It took a lot of diplomacy to send them home without supplies yet not feeling any hostility, and accepting the allocation system that we were obliged to impose temporarily."

What had happened in the market? Clearly, Wilkinson had met a need among the country's wet shavers. While the conventional blade was made to last for up to four shaves, the triple-coated Wilkinson blade promised to last for as many as ten. Also, since it could not corrode, it was easily looked after. The higher price—it cost five pfennigs more than its main competitor—appeared to be justified by the better performance.

However, the blade's performance was not the only factor. The association with aristocracy, symbolized by the company's emblem of crossed swords—attributes of noblement—add a touch of exclusivity. Another element in the company's success has been the "We try harder" approach adopted by all Wilkinson staff in contacts with the trade.

It seems that Gillette, which controlled over 90% of the German blades business before the crossed swords were brandished by Wilkinson, had been fully occupied in the past simply meeting demand. Wilkinson people were curious to see how the market leader would react to their intrusion, and say that for a year or so Gillette simply stood by and showed no sign of fighting back.

TABLE 11.1 Wilkinson's % share of the wet shave market (1962–83)

1962	1965	1969	1971	1973	1975	1977	1978	1979	1980	1981	1982	1983
4.0	12.4	29.4	30.5	31.2	33.7	34.3	33.4	33.7	32.6	31.9	31.4	31.9

Any newcomer in a market may initially enjoy fast growth in share, but, even so, Wilkinson's 4% after ten months in North Rhine Westphalia, and later, in Northern Germany was accepted as an achievement. Within three years—by the end of 1965—this market share had trebled to 12%, and it had more than doubled again, to 29%, by 1969, passing the 30% threshold with the introduction of the T70 single-edge razor in 1971 (see Table 11.1).

A share of 34.3% was reached in 1977, after which the ups were occasionally interrupted by the downs, but the market share has never dropped below 30%. The latest annual report quotes 32%, and first figures available for 1984 indicate that the improvement is continuing.

Bic's bombshell

Gillette introduced its innovatory Tandem twin-edged GII razor in 1972. Then, while Wilkinson technologists were busily working on an answer, a third party, the French disposable razor specialist, Bic, appeared on the scene, causing confusion among the marketing and technology staff of its rivals. Gillette quickly replied to Bic with its disposable Parat, and Wilkinson offered the LSD, the "Low-priced Single-edged Disposable," before introducing its own twin-edged razor to the retail market in 1978.

Gillette kept up the pressure with the swivel-head Contour razor, to which Wilkinson reacted in 1980 with its swivel-head Contact, at the same time introducing a new version of its LSD. Two other disposables were offered by Wilkinson in 1982—a twin-edged version and a swivel-head. The latest in the series of new products has been the Duplo II, a new twin-edge fixed head razor.

Those who had warned against taking throw-away razors too seriously were proved dramatically wrong. Six years ago, the conventional razor blade had 64% of the wet shaving market, with system razors at 33% and disposables at 3%. By the end of 1983, conventional razors had shrunk to 41%, system razors had grown to 49% and throw-aways had risen to 10%. The competition promises to continue putting heavy pressure on prices, and paring margins to zero or less.

It thus became clear that, whether or not Wilkinson could hold on to, or even increase, its market share and earn reasonable profits, substantial growth had to come from other sources. The German wet shaving market as a whole has grown slowly during the past few years.

Expressed in numbers of blades, it sold 340 million in 1978 and 360 million in 1983, a growth of just under 5.9%. Although Wilkinson's share increased from 111.5 million in 1982 to 114.8 million in 1983, this alone could not have produced the record 20% increase in net company turnover. Diversification was required to safeguard Wilkinson Germany's healthy development.

This diversification has taken two main forms. As early as 1970, Wilkinson had started to include shaving toiletries in its sales range by introducing shaving foam. It turned out to be a profitable move, resulting in the present 17% share of the shaving foam market. Shaving cream followed in 1973 and has 10% of its market, while after-shave, launched in the same year, has 2.5% of the after-shave market. Competition among after-shaves is fierce, and Wilkinson Germany is particularly proud of this achievement. Shaving brushes were later added to the range and, today, blades, razors and shaving toiletries together account for 87% of Wilkinson Germany's turnover.

Gruber says that the aim of diversification is "to secure our position and to expand our markets. It is our philosophy that edges are our strength—so edges will provide for our future." The company has consequently tried to ensure that customers will have available—and will be aware of—a Wilkinson product for everything that needs to be cut.

Since 1977, a variety of cutting implements have been introduced. Scissors were the first to be tested. After their acceptance by the market, the company extended the line to include all types of house-hold and hobby scissors, manicure sets and gardening shears. The second step was the Wilkinson Sword knives line, starting with pocket knives in 1980. Kitchen and other household knives were added in 1981.

None of these products required any expansion of the production facilities in Solingen; they are made elsewhere, according to Wilkinson's designs and to Wilkinson's specifications, for example in the U.K., Finland and Italy. In the rare cases where an outside product already has the qualities demanded of a Wilkinson article, the company buys the exclusive distribution rights for the product.

Wilkinson had started by supplying retailers which specialized in shaving articles—chemists and hairdressers. Then there was an upheaval in the German retail trade when the Federal Government abandoned retail price maintenance and about 120,000 outlets disappeared from the market through merger or bankruptcy, leaving about 80,000.

Wilkinson products were then introduced into food retailers, cash and carry outlets, supermarkets, department stores and the like, while cutlery and hardware stores offered knives and scissors.

Sales Training

The initial sales force of three has long since grown to 90. Every new salesman is given a week-long training course before he goes on his first field trip. There are also quarterly regional sales meetings which include refresher sessions.

Wilkinson places great emphasis on offering a personal service to its retail clients. It may even include help in price-labeling Wilkinson products before they are put on the shelves. Wilkinson representatives are also authorized to negotiate tailor-made sales initiatives on the spot—joint advertising, special displays, participation in special projects, etc.

Advertising is an important weapon for the company. The crossed swords have been featured in the company's ads since 1963. The account for the German-language area is in the hands of Düsseldorf based Baums Mang and Zimmermann, which also has Daimler-Benz, Bosch, Kimberly-Clark, Honda and Seiko among its clients. The ad budget, which covers print media, radio and TV, has been fairly constant over the years (see Table 11.2). It was between DM 4m and DM 5m a year into the early 1970s, and has been running at just under DM 5m in the past four years.

The current print campaign, in such high-circulation glossies as *Stern* and *Bunte*, consists mostly of two consecutive black and white right-hand pages. The first features the crossed Wilkinson swords and the copy highlights the 200 years of craftsmanship in precision blades. The second displays the products, crossed like the swords; razor and dispenser, razor and foam container, two razors, etc. All the ads carry the same pay-off line—*"Auf die Klinge kommt es an."* ("It is the edge that counts.") Fifteen-second TV spots open and close with the crossed Wilkinson swords, and, in between, push the products' USP, with slogans like "The only twin-edge razor with triple-coated blades." The universal pay-off again is "It's the edge that counts."

Baums Mang and Zimmermann emphasizes that a brand requires character to be successful and that the Wilkinson Sword brand

TABLE 11.2. Ad spends (DM millions): Wilkinson vs Gillette vs others (1967–83)

	1967	1969	1971	1973	1975	1977	1978	1979	1980	1981	1982	1983
Wilkinson	4.2	4.9	4.5	4.5	3.0	2.5	3.0	3.2	4.7	4.6	3.9	5.0
Gillette	7.0	7.1	8.3	7.1	4.1	4.5	4.6	7.5	8.6	8.3	8.1	7.6
Others	—	—	0.3	1.4	3.2	0.7	0.3	1.0	1.8	—	—	0.2

Note: Figures for Gillette and others are compiled by a commercial agency monitoring media advertising by commercial firms. Figures are for the Federal Republic of Germany, including West Berlin.

Wilkinson's World View

Germany has been one of Wilkinson's star performers in Western Europe in recent years, and together with France and Spain has witnessed high levels of growth. In South America, Brazil has proved a buoyant market. But the achievements in these countries are the result of drastic surgery applied to the group worldwide over the past three years in an attempt to streamline operations.

The labor force has been pared down from 12,000 to 8,000, and ten factories have been closed around the world. Following Allegheny International's acquisition of Wilkinson Sword in 1980, a total restructuring process began, with the aim of placing all business outside the U.S. in a new international trading group. This now houses Rowenta and Sunbeam, as well as Wilkinson's branded goods and its industrial offshoot Graviner. The group is headed by Chris Lewington, and he also sits on the main board as an executive vice president and director.

But the "sexy" bit of the company is that headed by John Bloxcidge, as president and managing director. He was brought in five years ago from Prestige, where he was managing director, to control the company's consumer products group, Wilkinson Sword. "We've had a tremendous purge over the past three years," says Bloxcidge. "But, as a result, we've put productivity up by an immense amount."

Some 80% of Wilkinson's business derives from its operations outside the U.K., spread between South America, Australia, Africa and Western Europe. Its business divides into shaving and toiletries; matches and lighters—it is one of the biggest match manufacturers in the world; housewares and hardware; and packaging.

The U.K. is the major manufacturing base for Wilkinson branded products, and the company claims that its U.K. plant is one of the most modern in the world. Wilkinson has poured substantial investment into its ailing shaving business in the U.K. The main problem was its failure to react to the aggressive tactics of Bic, which launched the first disposable razor in 1977. Bloxcidge now claims to be on Bic's tail with a new disposable product, the Retractor, orders for which have necessitated a doubling of factory capacity to keep pace with demand. The Retractor has not yet been launched in West Germany.

Allegheny International has been Wilkinson Sword's lifeline. The restructuring, streamlining, investment and new management have set the company back on course. It is now going through a period of consolidation and developing a springboard for new product launches.

Gillian Upton

---

distinctly has it. The agency's Peter Zimmermann says: "We have pursued three objectives: to build on the fund of confidence which the brand enjoys; to communicate the performance of the various products to the public; and to achieve a rub-off effect whereby one product benefits from the ads for the others. The crossed swords emblem is the visual constant, lending not only to each product, but also to each ad, its unmistakable identity. Thus the character of the brand became the character of the campaign."

An outsider would ascribe much of the credit for Wilkinson Germany's success to Kurt Gruber, but he modestly emphasizes that it is the quality of the team at the head of the operation that has brought success.

The 53-year-old Gruber read philosophy and economics at university, and then spent five years with Glücksklee, the German branch of

Carnation, before joining the newly formed German subsidiary of Wilkinson Sword.

In Wilkinson, Gruber started as marketing manager in 1962. He became joint managing director for two years before taking sole responsibility in 1978—both for the German company and the European holding company which is responsible for Wilkinson activities in various continental countries.

Many businessmen get so much enjoyment out of some element of their work that they regard them also as a hobby. Sales training has the same effect on Gruber and until recently he conducted seminars and courses, giving them up only in order to devote more time to other duties. Wilkinson's German marketing success provides plenty of valuable lessons.

12

Selling Swedish Style*

JUDY STEED

Who has ever heard of a furniture store that prides itself on ideas? It sounds crazy, even a little corny, but it has caught on in the United States. IKEA, the Swedish-based furniture chain with 77 stores worldwide generating $2.1 billion in fiscal year 1987, recently started its penetration of the American Market. At its cavernous store in the Washington suburb of Dale City, Va., thousands of shoppers lined up during the week of the end of July, 1987 with box-laden carts at a battery of check-out counters, taking advantage of its once-a-year sale. At regular prices, IKEA's unassembled products sell already for at least 30% less than finished furniture of comparable quality. The boxes of all shapes and sizes contain build-it-yourself kits for assembling everything from chairs to cabinets. It may seem an odd way to furnish a house, but not to the throngs of customers who were grabbing, hauling and finally staggering out of the store.

While most Americans have never heard of IKEA, it is the fastest growing furniture chain in the world. IKEA with its blue and yellow reindeer logo has become the watchword for household goods across much of Europe. The company went international for the first time in 1973, opening an outlet in Spreitentach, near Zurich. Now, its operations stretch from Norway to Australia. It came to the North American market in 1976. By 1979, there were a total of eight stores in Canada. Today, IKEA is successfully bringing pizzas and promotion to the U.S. The first shop opened in June 1985 in suburban Philadelphia and the Dale City outlet was opened in the following year. With its two strong footholds in the U.S. so far, IKEA is determined to capture the American market by opening up more outlets in the east coast and expanding to the mid-west, where a big concentration of Swedish decedents can be found.

---

*Adapted from *Report on Business Magazine*, (July/August 1985), pp. 78–81, with permission.

IKEA is the acronym of the company found *I*ngvar *K*amprad who came from the family farm *E*limtaryd near the village of *A*gunnaryd in Sweden. In 1943, the 17 year old Ingvar Kamprad started his first business by selling pencils, seeds and nylon stockings. It was in 1953 when he founded IKEA in Sweden, aiming at providing well-designed, solidly built furniture for working people. Ever since then, Mr. Kamprad began a business career that was to make him the most successful furniture retailer in the world—and something of a guru to his extended industrial family and a renowned Swedish industrial hero. Till today, he maintains the firm grip over the chain, showing no sign of sharing it with anyone else. He is also determined that all the stores keep the Swedish identity.

How Ingvar Kamprad did it—selling Swedish design and good quality at low prices, blending egalitarian socialism and competitive capitalism—is an inspiring tale not without its weak points, a tale that tells us that the real genius of IKEA lies in its ability of having managed to package and export a unique blend of inspirational management, cohesive corporate culture and marketing expertise. It is this blend that stays essentially the same everywhere the company goes.

One of IKEA's keys to success is its unique entry strategy. To test an important target market before entering it eventually a presence is established in a relatively small but similar market to gain experience and to penetrate the larger target market more forcefully later on. German-speaking Switzerland was the test market for West Germany, French-speaking Switzerland was it for France, and Canada was the same for the U.S. market. To keep the expansion within control, IKEA has chosen to franchise its retail concept in certain markets to get the market presence without spreading resources too thin. The company also operates establishment support groups which are highly specialized and experienced in opening new outlets quickly to surprise the market.

Another key to IKEA's success is its outsourcing and mass marketing concept that frees the company from owning factories. IKEA does not produce its merchandise but contracts with furniture and home improvement manufacturers which then custom-make IKEA designs according to IKEA standards for its world market. Construction materials, manufacturing process and finishing technique are all rigidly controlled; once a year, samples are pulled out off each line and sent to Sweden for quality-control tests. With its modern and light style, using mostly natural materials and clear and bright colors and functional designs IKEA became a trend-setter. Usually, there are many designs and several versions of a product for customers to choose from. The furniture comes in easily to assemble knockdown kits that help to keep shelf prices down due to low manufacturing and transportation cost. About 52% of IKEA's merchandise are made in Scandinavia, 21% are from Western Europe, 20% from Eastern Europe and 7% in other countries.

Contracting-out and large production runs have made it possible to achieve economies of scale, thereby, holding down both labor and material costs. An additional cost advantage comes from low shipping costs that are due to the compact packaging of the knockdown kits. As a result, IKEA is able to pass the savings on to its customers which gives IKEA an enormous competitive edge over other furniture dealers in the same region.

Self-assembly of the knockdown kits requires that customers put their kits together at home, using sparely worded but easily understood drawings, a screwdriver and a little hexagonal Allen wrench that IKEA supplies to install the bolts in its furniture. In addition to cutting assembly cost in manufacturing and shipping cost from the factories to the sales outlets knockdown kits also save customers the added costs of delivery since the merchandise can be transported easily in cars, pickup trucks, U-Haul trailers or on roof tops. Selling knockdown kits also keeps IKEA's retail prices down because it allows IKEA to devote most of its floor space to demonstration and floor models while all the flat-boxed goods are neatly stacked back in its warehouse where customers can easily find what they want and pick it up directly from the shelves. This self service reduces the cost for shop personnel. Finally, the devaluation of the Swedish krona has also helped significantly to keep the prices down in North America and most of IKEA's other export markets. The allure of IKEA's unassembled products is that they sell for at least 30% less than finished furniture of comparable quality and design. Through these means the business' central theme that less (in prices) is indeed more (in sales) has been successfully kept.

The IKEA's success is also directly related to other innovative marketing ideas and concepts. Although IKEA's market spans the entire age spectrum main focus is on the baby-boomers, the huge part of the population that is likely to move more often and change relationships more often than its parents did, that is interested in innovative designs and natural fabrics but not in spending a fortune on purchases. Thus, IKEA focuses also on offering convenience to customers while they are shopping. Standard in-store facilities include baby-changing rooms, a supervised play area for children which IKEA calls the ballroom. It is essentially a giant box filled with colorful balls that becomes a delightful diverting wallowing ground. Children may be left there so that the parents can concentrate on what they want to buy, aided by the 196 page catalog, note pad, pencils and measuring tapes supplied by the store.

The in-store cafe is strategically located just off the showroom floor. While savoring Swedish meatballs, open-face sandwiches, or some other Swedish dishes, customers often make their purchasing decisions. The showroom demonstrations give customers some ideas on how to solve such problems as storage in bedrooms and kitchens in ways that are both functional and attractive.

The company uses massive advertising to lure as many customers as possible. Catalogs are IKEA's major marketing tool—45 million copies are distributed in Swedish, Norwegian, Chinese, Japanese, Danish, German, Arabic, Spanish, English, French, and Dutch—accounting for half of the company's marketing budget. Radio and TV are IKEA's other major marketing tools. For the end of July sale 1987 in Dale City, for example, IKEA poured 330 radio and TV commercials to the area besides the double-page ads in the Washington Post. The city buses winked with the company's cryptogram: an eye and a key followed by "ah!" The hoopla brought out 10,000 shoppers on the first day of the sale.

If the IKEA way represents a break with tradition in the marketplace, so does its way with employees. According to the founder, the true spirit of IKEA is based on their enthusiasm, their constant will to review their cost consciousness, their willingness to assume responsibility and to help, their humility and on the simplicity in their manners. This "spirit" translates into some unusual, non-hierarchical practices. Executives do not have fancy titles, offices, wardrobes or perquisites; Authoritarian behavior is out, and "freedom with responsibility" is the motto. There are no first class airline tickets, or deluxe hotels. Employees are encouraged to come up with ideas for new products and new ways of doing things. Everyone has a right to make mistakes, as long as he/she learns from them.

This democratization in the workplace has given IKEA an unusually low employee turnover rate, 50% below even such progressive firms as Hewlett-Packard. At a minimum employees are required to have a 90 minute session on the job that consists of listening to a tape recording and studying a book about how to value their work and deal with irate customers while being nice. As part of IKEA's training program for new employees, Swedish culture is insisted upon—they are told about the government, Swedish holidays, even the climate.

The IKEA style of business still reflects the preoccupation of the company's founder. Stories about Ingvar Kamprad are legion: how he refuses to fly first class, considering it a terrible indulgence his customers would not appreciate; how a chance encounter with Ingvar will motivate an employee for years; how Ingvar met a group of young managers at his Lausanne home and for lunch took them out to the garden to pick vegetables and make a meal. He can spot any item of

IKEA furniture at 100 meters and describe down to the smallest detail how it was made.

For all the strength of its approach and its marketing reputation, IKEA has had its share of problems expanding around the world. From its initial trials in Canada, the company learned some hard lessons about franchising. IKEA opened its first warehouse on the American continent in Halifax in 1976. However, when Bayley, IKEA's North American division manager, arrived in 1979 to take charge, he was greeted by a sorry collection of six ailing franchises run by Canadian owners. Inventory was so low that many of the outlets appeared to be in the business of selling shelves because the stores were under-financed, overexpanded and owed far too much money to IKEA to get stock. To revive such a situation, it was absolutely insisted that orders were delivered, by chartered plane if necessary. Catalog circulation was increased substantially. IKEA's best decorator was brought in from Sweden to train Canadians in techniques of display. At the same time as it filled the shelves and showed off the stock, IKEA lowered prices, increased advertising and added a wider range of furnishings including candles, cutlery, bathmats, towels, picture frames and other home improvements that account for some 30% of the sales. By 1980, IKEA Canada had grown from sales of $29 million to projected sales of $100 million in 1985 from eight wholly owned stores across the country.

Another dilemma is that shoppers are dismayed sometimes by "Sorry Oversold" or "Not in Stock" tags on popular items. This problem arises as the sales have been much greater than anticipated and excess demand must be served from IKEA's warehouses in Sweden. As IKEA expanded so rapidly, managing its growth is now the company's paramount concern. Finally, IKEA would not appear to be an ideal store for a person in a hurry because it offers a lot of choices and customers must do some of the work themselves. They must be prepared to spend a certain amount of time shopping. Another drawback is that American shoppers buying beds at IKEA have to buy sheets there too since IKEA sells beds in European sizes which are different from the American ones.

IKEA, following in the footsteps of Volvo, Electrolux and ASEA, disproved conventional wisdom that a country with a small population (Sweden has only eight million) accustomed to a high standard of living can never achieve the economies of scale necessary to compete in the international market. Specializing in what they do best, namely selling the knockdown kits, the IKEA formula works: IKEA became one of the very few retailers that have succeeded to become international.

13

Western Ways:
How a German Firm Joined with
Soviets to Make Good Shoes*

THOMAS F. O'BOYLE

LENINGRAD—4:30 p.m., and outside a store, in the freezing cold and darkness, customers are waiting patiently for three, four, even five hours.

There are waiting for shoes. Perestroika has finally delivered the goods—and judging from the line, which stretches far down the street and is long even by Soviet standards, you'd think the shoes were being given away. But they are worth the wait, says one fur-capped man who, after two hours, still can't see the door. These are no ordinary shoes.

Although they look much like other Soviet-made footwear, the difference is the quality. "They won't leak, they'll keep your feet warm. They're much better than what you can buy elsewhere in Leningrad," the man explains, stomping his feet to shake off the cold. He hasn't seen the shoes, but his wife, tipped off by friends, told him they are out of this world.

From Another World

Actually, they come from a factory right around the block. In a way, however, they do come from another world. Since last April, the factory has been operated by Lenwest, a joint venture 40% owned by West Germany's Salamander AG and 60%–owned by the Proletarian Victory shoe concern of Leningrad. Every day, the modern, well-lit,

---

*Reprinted from *Wall Street Journal*, February 14, 1989, with permission.

efficient plant churns out 4,200 pairs of basic, utilitarian shoes of a quality previously unknown in the Soviet Union.

The Soviets provide the labor and most of the raw materials. The Germans provide the know-how—plus the machines, the management techniques and the quality control. The Soviets mostly take orders—and watch, listen and perhaps learn. And although Lenwest's output is a mere one million of some 800 million pairs of shoes produced in the Soviet Union last year, they are very important to the Soviets. Besides providing badly needed consumer goods, this joint venture and others like it, the Soviets hope, will help fire up their economy by increasing competition.

"There is no shoe manufacturer in the Soviet Union that compares with Lenwest," says the joint venture's chief bookkeeper, Fyodor Pavlov. Thrusting a Lenwest shoe into a visitor's hands, he asks, "How much would you pay for this?" Then he adds: "You saw how many people want to buy that for 80 rubles, that long line out there in the cold." Even though 80 rubles is slightly more than one week's pay for the average Soviet worker, "the market for this kind of shoe is limitless," Mr. Pavlov says sounding more like an entrepreneur than a state-appointed bookkeeper.

Germany's Big Role

That Soviet citizens want better shoes and that the Soviet Union benefits from this kind of cooperation with Western firms are irrefutable. But what about the Western partners? When Moscow began opening up the Soviet economy by announcing, in January 1987, that it would allow such business ventures, Western companies eagerly lined up for what they saw as lucrative opportunities. The rush continues: Of the 200 or so joint ventures formed in the past two years, nearly half were registered in the past four months. Among Western nations, West Germany leads the pack, with 26 joint ventures already formed and dozens more being negotiated.

Now, many of the companies that got in are asking themselves whether joint ventures here really make sense. For Salamander, a major European manufacturer of good-quality, moderately priced shoes that has more than 1,600 retail outlets in West Germany alone, the answer is yes.

The Stuttgart-based company says that, based on Western accounting standards, Lenwest was profitable in its first year of operation, though Salamander won't disclose any figures. Both parties have agreed to reinvest the profits for at least three more years to double production capacity. Later this year, Lenwest will introduce 16 new models, including a few more stylish women's shoes decorated with bows. Salamander has just opened a second shoemaking joint venture with another Soviet concern near Minsk.

Worth a Repeat

All things considered, says Werner Rost, Salamander's head of export sales in Stuttgart, "If we had to do it all over again, we'd make the same decisions."

Salamander's success stems from various factors, including its patience with the Soviet system, its willingness to reinvest profits during the start-up, its years of experience in the East Bloc and the Soviets' pent-up demand for quality footwear.

But for many companies, joint ventures may be more trouble than they are worth. Lenwest is one of only 20 or so ventures actually operating. Even savvy PepsiCo Inc. needed 15 months to find a suitable site for one of two planned Pizza Hut restaurants; it's still looking for the second.

Says Martin Kallen, the managing director of Monsanto Co.'s European operation: "You don't just walk in there and make a buck. The opportunities are limited, and you have to work hard to reap them." He predicts that the "failure rate of joint ventures is going to be high".

A major problem is the nonconvertibility of the ruble. Because the Soviet currency isn't freely changeable into other monies, Western companies' profits earned here must stay here—although some foreign companies get their profits in barter arrangements that give them Soviet goods that can be sold abroad.

Even more daunting are a raft of operational problems. Until December, when Moscow revised its laws, foreign companies couldn't own more than 49% of a joint venture; so, the Soviets always held the upper hand. In procurement and pricing, Western partners are at the mercy of what can be a capricious Soviet system, under which raw materials are doled out by the government according to the national economic plan and must be requisitioned more than a year in advance. And because prices for many basic goods are controlled, what a manufacturer may charge often doesn't reflect production costs.

"The value of a herbicide to a Western farmer is relatively well established. In the Soviet Union, it isn't," says Mr. Kallen, who tried for several years to negotiate a joint venture to make herbicides. Because food prices are strictly controlled, the price a Soviet farmer pays for a herbicide is also effectively controlled. That, plus the unavailability of raw materials, persuaded Monsanto to give up the project.

"Importing the raw materials would have meant that we had to export more of the final product than we were prepared to consider" to balance a probable deficit of hard currency, he says.

Some Major Advantages

Salamander also had to struggle. But because Lenwest took over a building previously occupied by the Soviet partner, the venture already had perhaps the most precious commodity in the Soviet Union: suitable work space. Luckily, telephones and telex machines were also in place.

Salamander has three employees who live in a nearby hotel and supervise the production. They share one desk in a common office, a ramshackle room with peeling wallpaper and a conference table wedged up against piles of shoe boxes and cartons of files. They travel to Germany every month or so to visit their families, who chose to stay there. They don't speak Russian, and each has a translator during office hours. After work, they're on their own, but that doesn't really matter; they don't have much free time.

To Western businessmen, everything in the Soviet Union seems abnormal. Even routine tasks—from booking a hotel room to changing an airline reservation—can be formidable. "They have a completely different system," says Mr. Rost, Salamander's export chief, who, along with another Salamander executive and three Soviets, sits on Lenwest's supervisory board.

Signs of those differences abound. Just reaching a consensus on what is meant by "profit" isn't easy. Responding to that question, a bewildered Mr. Pavlov at first says: "We don't have that concept here." Then, after huddling with colleagues, he explains that although he thinks he understands the concept, he isn't comfortable with it. "This is a mutual learning process, and we've had to make adjustments to balance our two systems," he says.

Cautious Negotiators

Or consider the negotiations to form Lenwest, which were begun in April 1987 and concluded six months later. The Soviet delegation usually numbered about 20. "They tried to bring as many people as possible so they wouldn't make a mistake," recalls Mr. Rost, one of four who represented Salamander.

One principle on which Salamander insisted helps minimize conflicts. Because the Soviets outnumber Salamander on the board by 3 to 2, all board decisions must, under the venture's bylaws, be unanimous. But that provision hasn't headed off all problems. In filling the job for Lenwest's marketing chief, all five directors voted to hire a man recommended by the Soviets. He was sacked two months later.

"Most of the people who are employed there have no experience at all in the field of marketing," Mr. Rost says. "They've never sold anything. They have distributed goods." The new marketing chief comes from the Soviet foreign-export organization and has had sales experience.

Salamander has won a few battles on the marketing side. It obtained written guarantees from the Soviets allowing the joint venture to sell through its own outlets, such as the one at No. 36 Suvorovsky Prospect in Leningrad.

As many as five more stores may open this year in Leningrad and other cities, including Moscow and Kiev. "The demand is so great that with every new store we open up, there will be a line," Mr. Rost predicts confidently. The outlets give Lenwest a higher profit margin and more control over its shoe sales.

Raw-Material Problems

The biggest problem that it had to overcome was a shortage of first-class raw materials. "Our partners couldn't understand why, if we had the money, we couldn't buy the goods. We said, 'Because we haven't ordered them in advance,' and they said, 'That's nonsense,'" Mr. Pavlov recalls.

What wasn't available through the system had to be trucked 2,420 kilometers (1,450 miles) from Stuttgart—and purchased with precious Western currency. In the first few months, about 35% of the raw materials came from the West; now, all but 5% are Soviet-supplied.

Nevertheless, the Soviet system still frustrates the Germans. "You can't be as flexible here as in the West," says Wolfgang Meiser, a barrel-chested, gray-bearded plant manager. "In Germany, if you have a shoe collection that doesn't sell, you just change to another. You make new models with new material. It's no problem in Germany, but it would be a problem here" because raw materials must be ordered so far in advance.

Fortunately for Lenwest, the shoes have been selling, largely because of Salamander's near-fanatical attention to quality control. Quality is crucial to both partners. For the Soviets, it means goods that would be readily accepted in the West and hence more foreign trade. Although all of the Lenwest production is now sold in the Soviet Union, eventually the partners hope to export as much as 20% of it. Exports are important for Lenwest, too, because the hard-currency income can offset hard-currency spending on the three Germans' salaries (paid in marks), the raw materials purchased in the West, and sales promotions there. And because Salamander is required to buy either shoes or raw materials—soles, for instance—from Lenwest to balance the hard-currency ledger, it, too, wants top-quality production.

Comparable Quality

So far, Lenwest's quality is comparable to the best Western standards. All the machines—even the hand tools—are the same as those used in Salamander's German factories. In addition, each of the 735 Soviet workers got a month of training before starting to work. They also get on-the-job instruction from quality-control specialists from Stuttgart. As incentives, they earn a bonus for higher productivity but are penalized if the quality slips.

"We don't really mean to punish them," says Mr. Meiser, amid the clanking of machines stamping out leather parts. "But they have to learn that quality is absolutely the most important thing to us. We won't accept anything less."

On the whole, the German managers praise the Soviet workers. Although Lenwest has the right to dismiss workers, it hasn't had to. The Germans say that in productivity, entry-level skills, job enthusiasm and motivation, Lenwest workers match or exceed their West German counterparts. "We expected to encounter a lot more troubles in the employment area than we've experienced," says Alfred Hoeh, one of the plant managers.

That may be partly due to Salamander's strict controls. Although its system differs greatly from the typical Soviet factory, some workers here prefer it. One middle-aged woman who once worked at another shoe factory in Leningrad says she likes the more regulated environment.

"If there's a disturbance in the department," she says, "I go get Mr. Meiser, and he deals with the problem immediately. You don't have to tell him twice." She adds: "The workers from other factories envy the workers here."

14

Selling to Japan:
We Did it Their Way*

FRED REINSTEIN

The day is long past when giant foreign companies like IBM or GM can dominate important sectors of Japan's marketplace. The Japanese no longer need these foreign giants, and they will not permit any others to capture a significant market share. They will, however, allow smaller companies, like mine, which compete only in very specialized markets. The only way to re-balance trade between our countries is to have hundreds or thousands of companies like Turbo Tek, each with annual sales to Japan in the tens of millions of dollars range. The way to begin this process for your company is to start thinking like Commodore Perry.

Perry's four-ship flotilla dropped anchor in Yokohama Bay in 1853. He wanted to offer the Japanese some refreshments and conversation, to establish some personal relationships, but none would even speak to him. So he reboarded his ships and sailed away. Eight months later he returned; this time he brought nine ships.

In the meantime Japan's leaders had arrived at a consensus: Open negotiations. At the second meeting a genuine emissary of the Emperor, albeit a lowly one, met with Perry. Perry was invited to eat, drink, and converse. He demonstrated, among many gifts for the Shogun, a mile-long telegraph system and a miniature steam locomotive.

The Japanese had never seen such products and were captivated. They agreed to agree on a treaty which would permit a limited amount of commerce. The details would be painfully negotiated over several

* Slightly abbreviated from *Export Today*, Vol. 3, No. 3 (Sept/Oct 1987), pp. 19–24, with permission.

progressively friendlier meetings, but Perry had won his point. The Japanese would do business.

It's been more than 125 years since then, but things haven't changed all that much in Japan. Despite Japanese protestations to the contrary, most of their markets are still tightly shut against foreigners. In order to do business with Japan, our company employed virtually the same tactics used by Commodore Perry. Here are some of the ways we made our product, Turbo-Wash, a household word in Japan.

Better Mousetraps

No matter what your product is, you haven't a chance of selling it to Japanese domestic consumers unless:

- It's something they need;
- It's something not presently made in Japan;
- It's of the highest quality;
- You can produce it for less than anyone else;
- You're willing and able to defend against patent, trademark, and copyright infringements anywhere in the world;
- You can establish a partnership with a Japanese company.

Partnerships

I started out as a domestic marketer and importer. For many years we were in the fad business. We created a product, got it manufactured in Japan, Taiwan, Hong Kong, or the U.S., and over a short cycle—three or four months was not uncommon—distributed and marketed it. Then we got out. We believed in taking our profits and abandoning the market to the knockoffs which almost inevitably follow successful fad products.

We observed, however, that these knock-offs often stayed on the market for years. We reconsidered our strategy and decided to move beyond fads to quality products. We also decided to tackle Japan.

Since we already had an established relationship with a Japanese exporter, we explored ways to turn that relationship around so that we became exporters instead of importers. At the same time, we hired Japanese firms to conduct market research.

Our product attaches to a garden hose and very efficiently applies a stream of soapy or clear water to small or large areas. In the U.S., most people use Turbo-Wash to clean their cars, but our market research revealed a new, uniquely Japanese usage; Turbo-Wash could be used to clean the finely perforated copper coils used in both public and home baths. These coils tend to become clogged with body oils and hair. Since the product cleaned far more efficiently than traditional brushes, there was an immediate demand for it.

The Japanese Distribution System

Our product retails in the U.S. for between $10 and $20, depending on retail profit margins and customer rebates. In Japan, however, Turbo-Wash retails for Y16,800, or well over $100. This is because of the unique nature of the Japanese distribution system.

Rooted in centuries of tradition, the five-tiered distribution system is an integral component of Japanese society. Japan has no social welfare system comparable to Social Security or its European counterparts. Nor do they have unemployment compensation programs which are in any way equivalent to U.S. plans. Accordingly, near-total employment is a national goal, and until quite recently, Japanese unemployment rarely exceeded 2%, compared to the 6% to 8% which the U.S. has tolerated for decades. One significant reason is that the national product distribution system, with two more layers than usual, provides many service jobs.

Most Japanese retire at age 55, but live to ages older on average than that of almost any other nation. Retirees usually get lump-sum bonuses equal to two or three years' salary. In addition to this money, most retirees have considerable savings; Japan encourages systematic savings with many incentives. Those retirees who cannot find a part-time job with one of their former employer's subsidiaries or suppliers, and who do not have sufficient funds to live out their lives, often invest in tiny, marginally profitable businesses. The net result is that Japan, which has half the U.S. population, has 100,000 more retailers.

The distribution system is tailored to serve these retailers. Home appliance stores, for example, won't buy from the same distributor that serves a department store, even though they sell the same product for virtually the same price. Thus a product, imported or domestic, changes hands from importer to general distributor to special distributor to special subdistributor to retailer to consumer. Sometimes the actual product never changes hands; it's a paperwork exercise. Just as often, however, goods are trucked from one warehouse to another to another, all within the same community.

This creates jobs for salesmen, truck drivers, warehousemen, mechanics, office workers, and managers. The cost of all those extra jobs is borne by the Japanese consumer, who long ago accepted the necessity of keeping every-one working and understands that taking charity is humiliating while working isn't.

Those within the distribution system act in concert in ways that Americans might find collusive. For example, one of the reasons it takes so many meetings between a foreign company and a Japanese company with which partnership negotiations are proceeding is that, while negotiations are going on, the Japanese company is holding other meetings with its distributors. The purpose of these meetings is to eliminate risk, as much as possible, from the whole process.

The Japanese abhor the kinds of risks American businesses routinely take, and they seek to eliminate it from any transaction. Consequently, before they agreed to a partnership to distribute Turbo-Wash, they discussed the product and its marketing at every level of their distribution system. In the end, everybody agreed that they could sell so many units at each level and, when they committed to accepting those units, they also agreed to pay for them whether they ultimately were sold to consumers or not. If for any reason the product had flopped, the risk was spread evenly throughout the system and its impact would have been quite small at any one company.

Superior Quality and Competitive Pricing

We've created a retail price that keeps competition away. Turbo-Wash is made in Anaheim, California. We designed special production equipment to automate the entire process; the only human hands that touch the product before shipping are Quality Assurance hands. While our entire payroll is based on $10/hr.—and no one earns less than $6/hr.—manufacturing is so productive that each payroll slot brings in revenues in excess of $1 million. That's very competitive productivity, and it's proof that American workers and American managers can outproduce foreign competitors if they're willing to invest the requisite capital in facilities and equipment.

Because of our manufacturing capacity, currently in excess of 50,000 units a day, we're far more efficient than our knockoff competitors. These people, chiefly in Taiwan, will start with one machine, which is overtaxed to make 800 units a day, and attempt to slowly grow. But because our manufacturing is so highly automated, they can never match our productivity until they're willing to match our investment, and that's not the way knockoff companies operate.

The Knockoff Problem

The Japanese distribution system doubles as a social welfare mechanism. As a result, firms within it absolutely refuse to cut profit margins. Where a Hong Kong or Taiwanese distributor, for example, will work for a few pennies per unit, Japanese distributors insist on several dollars. That's why the Japanese consumer winds up paying upwards of 10 times what U.S. consumers pay for Turbo-Wash. This also explains why many Americans fail to penetrate the Japanese market: They won't, or can't, price their products to compete with Japanese products.

The most significant effect of this 10-fold price magnification, however, is that it invites unlicensed and often unscrupulous knockoffs.

To protect ourselves against these pirates, Turbo Tek went to the considerable effort of taking patent, trademark, and copyright protection in Japan. In a country which has only about 7500 attorneys, patent registration is costly, extraordinarily complex, and even more time consuming.

Nevertheless, we went to the trouble to load our "anti-infringement" gun with "patent bullets," and we have fired that gun whenever we've been challenged. Some of these challenges have come from our own U.S. customers, who saw in that 10:1 price ratio an opportunity to reap windfall profits at our expense. Because each Turbo-Wash bears identifying marks which enable us to trace its original buyer, we have been able to deal with these predators by cutting off their supplies.

This doesn't end the problem, of course. In fact, our decision to deal with Japan is at the root of our worldwide knockoff problem. If we were not selling many, many units in Japan at the inflated price caused by their distribution system, then knockoff competitors would find little incentive to produce rival products. But many Japanese companies have factories in Taiwan, and many Taiwanese have Japanese partners. Because they can use their distributors' money to leverage the initial purchase of a very small scale production facility, they continue to test our resolve to dominate the marketplace, both in Japan and elsewhere.

Strength of Commitment

The Japanese rebuffed Perry and his predecessors several times before they finally realized that he was committed to his mission and would keep coming back. That holds true today. Japanese companies have dealt with each other for generations; they see no reason to deal with us unless we can demonstrate that we intend to be around for a long, long time.

Our continuing efforts to protect patents, copyrights, and trademarks are symbolic of this commitment. If we did not vigorously defend each and every violation with the best lawyers available, our strength of commitment would be suspect. Our Japanese partners would very likely drop us at the first opportunity.

Our Japanese sales are of the same magnitude as those we make to

U.S. wholesalers in Detroit or in New England. Accordingly, they get the same amount of attention from top management as those large U.S. customers. They're further away and harder to talk to, but we deal with a problem with a Japanese customer just as urgently and expertly as our domestic clients, or perhaps a little more.

The Chosen People

Few people seem willing to say this aloud, but it's true: Many Japanese—perhaps most—don't like foreigners. While they may like Americans more than some other foreigners—Russians or Indonesians, for example—the typical Japanese businessman, like many of his American counterparts, regards his own culture as the world's most nearly perfect. Thus when a foreigner is on Japanese turf, he would do well to learn, respect, and observe as many local customs as possible.

Patience I

To establish any sort of business relationship with the Japanese, long-term patience is an absolute requirement. You must be prepared, like Perry and those who went before him, to attend several meetings which have no apparent result, and to wait years before something favorable happens. You must maintain business contacts with no expectations of immediate success, even with those who have previously rebuffed your overtures. You may have to meet once or twice a year for 10 years before conditions are right. In the end, perhaps, nothing may come of any particular contact, but you will never know for sure. Nevertheless you must continue to talk; often a patiently-nurtured relationship may in time lead to something quite small. The Japanese tend to think of little things growing into bigger things with the passage of time.

Building this aspect of patience into your relationships requires long-term planning. We now routinely look beyond five years for product and relationship issues. The Japanese do the same, but more so. They knew 10 years ago, or more, that the day would come when Japanese labor costs would make their automobile industry uncompetitive, and they began planning to shift production to places like Korea, Taiwan, and Indonesia, where wages are lower. To compete in Japan's domestic marketplace requires that sort of detailed long-range planning.

Patience II

Whenever I schedule a trip to Japan, I leave the entire day prior to departure open. I avoid talking or thinking about business. When I get to Japan, I'm not in a hurry. I'm prepared to spend as much time as needed to conduct the business at hand. When the meeting begins, I'll limit myself to inconsequential conversations, or I may even be silent.

It might take an hour, or two, or more, but eventually someone will announce that it's time to get down to business. That someone will never be me, nor any of my people. Since I am never the first to speak of business, and never the first to put forward any proposal, I always gain a significant advantage: I get information from my negotiating adversary without surrendering any of my own. This is classic Japanese strategy in nearly all business dealings.

Nothing may result from this meeting except an agreement to schedule another meeting. But the time is far from wasted. The Japanese will have learned that while you are interested in doing business, you are not so anxious that you'll make a deal at any cost. And you will have, if only slightly, begun to build the personal relationships the Japanese call "root binding" that are the foundation for future success.

Keeping Secrets—things as they are and as they seem

To a Japanese, every fact about his company has some intrinsic value. They give little away. Just as 133 years ago the existence of the Emperor and of Kyoto, the royal capital, were state secrets, such mundane or trivial information as the name of a company's supplier or the number of people it employs are often company secrets. They tell you nothing without getting something in return, and maybe not even then. So we don't disclose data about our firm unless it will bring some concession, and there are some things we won't disclose at all.

The Japanese have a saying, *tatemae ne honne*, things as they are and things as they seem. *Tatemae* means things the way they should be. *Honne* means the way things really are. Often there's a big gap between the two. Westerners often practice a mild form of this: When you greet someone you know casually you may ask "How are you" and be told "Fine, how are you?" and you reply "Fine". In reality, of course, either or both of you may not be fine at all. You may be suffering from some dread disease, or your spouse has left you, or your mother just died, but you don't burden the other person with this, you just say "Fine."

The Japanese take this concept much further. They rarely tell anyone the *honne*, and they rarely express feelings. So if you were to ask your negotiating counterpart "How do you feel about that?" you'd never get a meaningful answer, because he doesn't know how to express himself in that way. Instead you'd get a platitude or a deft change of subject.

Japanese use the word "hai" to signify yes. They never say *anei*, "no," because that's considered rude. But the Japanese "yes" means only "I've heard what you said." It doesn't mean "I understand and agree." But many an American has come away from a meeting thinking he has an agreement when he has nothing of the sort. At the next meeting he'll be shocked to learn that the Japanese are reneging, but that's because they said "yes" but meant "no."

To avoid this sort of misunderstanding, I use a negotiating checklist. When we're actually talking turkey, I have the senior Japanese present, usually a company director, initial each point to indicate agreement. It takes a lot of hard bargaining to get that set of initials, but once they agree to something they're scrupulous about observing it, and they expect us to be equally so.

The Protocol of Hierarchy

Just as Perry would not speak to anyone of inferior rank, and just as he insisted that only the Emperor's personal emissary could receive President Fillmore's letter, modern Japanese observe strict protocols of rank. Presidents speak only to other presidents. Vice presidents speak only to other vice presidents. There's a rigid pecking order and everyone observes it.

That's one reason they make such a fuss about business cards. When two Japanese meet, they immediately exchange cards. Then they both know who's what and how to proceed. An American in Japan should have a card, in Japanese as well as English, and he should present it to almost everyone to whom he's introduced.

If yours is a smaller company and your emissary to Japan is comparatively junior, consider promoting him to vice president, at least whenever he visits Japan. Like the village cops the Japanese dressed in royal finery to deal with Perry, he will be able to deal with senior Japanese on an equal footing. Just as important, sending a VP proves your company takes its relations with Japanese companies quite seriously. But don't send anyone under 30, regardless of his ability or position. The Japanese respect grey hair far more than we do.

A word about women executives. American women, given the opportunity, have proven themselves as able as American men. But in Japan women are rarely in positions of authority over men. Most Japanese don't quite know how to deal with female executives, and most of them don't want to learn. Japan is a very sexist society. Don't send women executives to deal with Japanese males until your business relationships are very advanced and very secure.

Negotiating from Strength

I came to our first negotiation meeting in Japan with just two people, including myself. Our hosts brought six. We felt outnumbered, surrounded, defensive. So at the next meeting I brought six people, thus demonstrating both commitment to the process and strength of resources. At the following meeting, we made an unspoken agreement to bring four people each, and that's the way it's been ever since.

The necessity of bringing enough people cannot be overestimated. It is true that airfares, hotel rooms, and living expenses mount up rapidly in Japan, but the Japanese accept this as part of doing business. We cannot do any less if we expect to be taken seriously. Accordingly, I always attempt to learn how many people will attend, and I bring an identical number. Usually these "extra bodies" have little, if anything to say during the meeting, but they must be people whose duties are somehow related to our mutual enterprise.

Much of what goes on at meetings is said between members of the respective sides. The Japanese always have English-speaking members present who understand what we are saying amongst ourselves. If you don't have a native Japanese speaker on your team, you operate at a significant disadvantage.

For example, we always have an appropriately qualified Japanese—usually a U.S. resident—on our negotiating team. Frequently we learn that what the other side is saying is actually the opposite of how they feel, based on their side conversations. That allows us to modify our proposal to satisfy their unstated objections. It's a crucial capability.

When we first began to do business with the Japanese, we were the buyers and they the sellers. They refused any discussion of 30- or 60-day billing, demanding instead that we present letters of credit prior to their shipping anything.

When we turned things around and became sellers, this same company demanded 30- or 60-day billing. Had we been negotiating from weakness, we might have conceded.

Instead we insisted they buy F.O.B. our California factory. We wanted their money up front, just as they had gotten ours. They replied that they would never do business that way.

Despite extended negotiations, we walked away. We were prepared to go elsewhere, and we proved it by standing firm. They came right back to us and agreed to our conditions. They didn't like it, but they respected our position.

Honor

Another reason for Japan's routinely long, complex negotiations is that once an agreement is finalized, they will honor it down to the smallest detail. They expect you will do the same. At that point a written contract is really superfluous.

Their word is their bond; yours should be also. That's why it's necessary to iron out all details, no matter how picayune. And it's also why those who want to do business in Japan will not seek to renegotiate a running contract, no matter how badly they miscalculated or how much money it costs to honor the agreement. They might be able to win a few concessions in renegotiating, but generally the Japanese will not do business with them again.

Further Reading — Part II

Cavusgil, S. Tamer, "Differences Among Exporting Firms Based on Their Degree of Internationalization," *Journal of Business Research*, Vol. 12, No. 2 (1984), pp. 195–208.

Mendonsa, Eugene L., "How To Do Business in Latin America," *Purchasing World*, (July 1988), pp. 58–59.

Singh, Karmjit, "Successful Strategies: The Story of Singapore Airlines," *Long Range Planning*, Vol. 17, No. 5 (October 1984), pp. 17–22.

Turner, Rik, "The Third World Aircraft Maker Western Users are Learning to Love," *International Management*, (April 1986), pp. 35–37.

Global Markets

Introduction to Part III

Today the global markets have become more diversified and complex. When companies prepare to enter the international arena they face a number of problems: How can the diverse global markets be analyzed in a meaningful way? What are the features of each market? What should marketers do to successfully enter these markets? Part III intends to provide some of the answers.

To help readers analyze the global markets, Cavusgil in Reading 15 presents a market-oriented clustering approach. Based on factors such as age, education, urbanization and women's status in society, the world markets are divided into five unique clusters: dependent, seeker, climber, luxury and leisure, and rocking chair societies. This approach permits marketers to identify relatively homogeneous cross national clusters, as well as individual market segments.

In the 1990s, much attention is being focused on the European market. Reading 16 from *Business International* analyzes the issue of Europe 1992 and beyond in some detail. The next reading deals with Asia–Pacific developments and their impact on business strategy.

Reading 18 by Amine and Cavusgil analyzes the marketing environment in the Middle East and North Africa. The authors identify five types of clusters in the region: macro-country clusters, attitude clusters, life-style clusters, urban clusters, and shopping behavior clusters. Although many environmental and market factors are unique to certain countries, the authors maintain that diverse market conditions are not necessarily an argument against enlightened use of standardized marketing strategies.

Thorelli in Reading 19 focuses attention to the People's Republic of China, a nation that has taken on the mission of a giant laboratory in political economy. The author describes the recent economic experiments in China, and analyzes current and potential developments as approximating a society of market socialism, a hybrid variety of socio-economic system never truly tested anywhere else. Implications for Western companies interested in doing business in the PRC are also discussed, and further developed in Reading 30 in Part V.

199

15

A Market-Oriented Clustering of Countries

S. TAMER CAVUSGIL

International marketers face a complex task: How can the world's diverse markets be analyzed in a meaningful way? Companies often have difficulty in evaluating the large (some 170) number of countries with varying market potentials. Clustering countries on the basis of common characteristics is one approach to "making sense" out of the diversity. Several approaches to country clustering have been proposed. For example, based primarily on GNP per capita, the World Bank groups countries into five categories: low-income economies, middle-income economies, high-income oil exporters, industrial market economies, and nonreporting nonmember economies.

Business International (BI), on the other hand, offers three indicators of market potential for different geographic regions and individual countries. Designed to provide broad guidance to the international marketer, *BI*'s Market Intensity measures are expressed in three dimensions: Market Size, Market Intensity and Market Growth. Thus each country or region can be evaluated in terms of its relative size (primarily population), the richness or the buying power, and the growth potential.

Table 15.1 provides detailed definitions of the Market Intensity measures and reports these indices for three separate years. Figure 15.1 illustrates the inverse relationship between market intensity and market growth in a graphical manner. This negative relationship between market intensity and market growth is a major dilemma for the international marketer. It implies that the marketer is often faced with a trade-off in assessing country markets.

BI's Market Intensity measures are helpful in ranking regions and countries. They serve as gross indicators of market attractiveness. In-

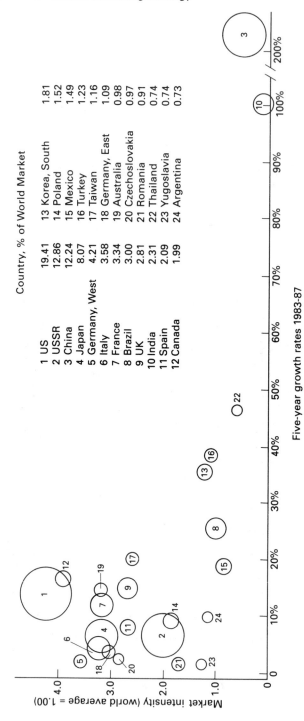

Country, % of World Market

1 US	19.41	13 Korea, South	1.81
2 USSR	12.86	14 Poland	1.52
3 China	12.24	15 Mexico	1.49
4 Japan	8.07	16 Turkey	1.23
5 Germany, West	4.21	17 Taiwan	1.16
6 Italy	3.58	18 Germany, East	1.09
7 France	3.34	19 Australia	0.98
8 Brazil	3.00	20 Czechoslovakia	0.97
9 UK	2.81	21 Romania	0.91
10 India	2.31	22 Thailand	0.74
11 Spain	2.09	23 Yugoslavia	0.74
12 Canada	1.99	24 Argentina	0.73

Five-year growth rates 1983-87

FIG. 15.1. *BI* Market Indexes: Size, growth and intensity of 24 largest markets.

Note: The position of the center of each circle shows the intensity of the market (when measured against the vertical axis) and its cumulative growth over the 1983–87 period (when measured against the horizontal axis). The size of the circles indicates the relative size of the markets as a percentage of the total world market. See text for definitions and methodology.
Source: Business International.

TABLE 15.1. *BI* Market Indexes, 1972, 1982, 1987

	Market Size (% of World Market)			Market Intensity (World = 1.00)			Five-Year Market Growth (%)
	1977	1982	1987	1977	1982	1987	1983–87
Major Regions							
Western Europe	27.62	25.79	22.77	2.81	2.90	2.70	9.15
(EC)	(19.72)	(18.68)	(18.69)	(3.32)	(3.31)	(2.97)	(7.46)
(EFTA)	(3.12)	(2.87)	(2.11)	(3.17)	(3.24)	(3.35)	(15.38)
Eastern Europe	21.83	19.60	18.17	2.24	2.17	2.04	6.56
Middle East	1.66	1.55	1.55	0.53	0.51	0.46	14.86
Africa	1.71	1.98	1.88	0.19	0.20	0.20	25.06
Asia	13.90	20.23	26.55	0.24	0.34	0.46	46.72
Oceania	1.32	1.04	1.15	3.35	2.93	3.11	14.06
North America	25.93	23.46	21.40	4.71	4.50	4.18	14.50
Latin America	6.03	6.35	6.52	0.73	0.77	0.81	21.60
(LAIA)	(5.39)	(5.81)	(6.00)	(0.76)	(0.82)	(0.87)	(22.27)
World	100.00	100.00	100.00	1.00	1.00	1.00	
Major Markets							
United States	23.65	21.39	19.41	4.77	4.56	4.21	14.06
U.S.S.R.	15.21	13.62	12.86	2.19	2.11	1.99	6.71
China	—	4.70	12.24	—	0.19	0.48	232.45
Japan	9.30	9.42	8.07	3.25	3.56	3.17	6.48
West Germany	5.31	4.79	4.21	3.63	3.81	3.56	2.07
Italy	4.25	4.04	3.58	3.19	3.36	3.22	4.42
France	4.00	3.81	3.34	3.21	3.44	3.15	11.95
Brazil	2.17	2.46	3.00	0.79	0.88	1.01	25.62
United Kingdom	3.81	3.23	2.81	2.88	2.78	2.67	15.03
India	1.29	1.49	2.31	0.08	0.09	0.13	100.28
Spain	2.45	2.41	2.09	2.71	2.90	2.65	8.05
Canada	2.29	2.07	1.99	4.18	3.98	3.89	16.47
South Korea	1.01	1.35	1.81	1.02	1.39	1.22	35.62

Notes:
Market Size shows the relative dimensions of each national or regional market as a percentage of the total world market. The percentages for each market are derived by averaging the corresponding data on total population (double-weighted), urban population, private consumption expenditure, steel consumption, cement and electricity production and ownership of telephones, passenger cars and televisions.

Market Intensity measures the richness of the market, or the degree of concentrated purchasing power it represents. Taking the world's market intensity as 1.00, *BI* has calculated the intensity of each country or region as it relates to this base. The intensity figure is derived from an average of per capita ownership, production and consumption indicators. Specifically, it is calculated by averaging per capita figures for cars in use (double-weighted), telephones in use, televisions in use, steel consumption, cement and electricity production, private consumption expenditure (double-weighted), and the percentage of population which is urban (double-weighted).

Market Growth is a five-year average of the growth rates for several indicators: population, steel consumption, cement and electricity production, and ownership of passenger cars, trucks and buses and televisions.

depth evaluations of individual countries are still essential, however, in market entry and expansion decisions.

A Market-Oriented Clustering Approach

The world as we know it is becoming smaller and smaller. We are finally beginning to realize that people from different cultures have unique traits, yet that certain similarities exist between all of us.

This realization has a significant impact on national and especially international marketing. It permits us to identify relatively homogeneous, cross national clusters, as well as individual market segments; i.e., it permits us to follow an "informed" global marketing strategy. This concept represents a significant expansion to the traditional thinking of a homogeneous global world where increasing standardization offers economies of scale. Although clustering and marketing segmentation imply more costly product adaptations, they permit us to reach both new and broader markets in the future.

In this discussion market potential is considered a function of variables such as age, education, urbanization and women's status in society and the world market is divided into five unique clusters: Dependent, Seeker, Climber, Luxury and Leisure, and Rocking Chair societies. The following demographic information is used to delineate homogeneous clusters: population growth, median age, number of children per household, infant mortality, life expectancy and GNP per capital. Commonalities among nations lead to the five country clusters as shown in Table 15.2. The discussion below will highlight the marketing environment in these clusters and draw implications for international marketers.

Dependent Societies: Striving to become self-sufficient

People from dependent societies such as Bangladesh and Ethiopia are probably suffering the most. Dependents' resources for basic necessities including food and housing are inadequate. In addition, these nations' hardships are often worsened by natural catastrophes such as droughts, earthquakes and typhoons. Efforts to survive are dominated by the search for, or exchange of food. Hence, daily life is confined to agricultural, extractive or hunting activities. Economic development is hindered by poor infrastructure and limited access to rural markets. As a result, basic necessities may only be obtained through barter within the immediate, local market area.

In most dependent societies population growth is out of control at higher than 3% per year. Government's primary goal is to satisfy people's basic needs for food, clothing, housing, medical care and education. Demand for medical supplies generally exceeds supply. Even if classrooms exist, chalkboards, desks, textbooks may be missing. In an effort to become self-sufficient most major government investments are related to extractive (agriculture and mining) activities.

The government and state-owned economic enterprises constitute the most significant buying group in these economies. Purchasing for hospitals, schools, etc. makes these buyers, more than any others, rely on company reputation. International marketers must create a desirable company image stressing reliability and long-term commitment.

When selling consumer products, international marketers need to take an educational approach. Most advertising must be information, teaching customers how to safely use products. As literacy rates are low, pictures and product illustrations are critical to effectively communicate the products' benefits and usage. Nestlé, the number one seller of infant formula internationally, neglected to do this in the past and has received negative publicity ever since. In an effort to save costs, mothers in various countries diluted their infant formula, resulting in numerous undernourished children. This needless suffering could have been avoided had Nestlé educated mothers on proper product usage.

Advertising may be further complicated in dependent societies as media such as TV may not exist and radio advertising may be limited by government restrictions. Distribution of pamphlets may be the only effective way to reach these consumers.

As mentioned previously, dependents are largely rural with possibly one or two large cities. People migrate to these cities in hopes of finding jobs. However, overcrowding may result in most people being worse off than before and creating immense problems for local governments.

The use of extremely young children, although outlawed by most countries, may be impossible to prevent in rural areas. Most women are still economically dependent on their families. In addition, they may only be employed in manual labor involving menial tasks. In some of the wealthier and more sophisticated dependents older children take care of their younger siblings while the parents are working.

Seeker Societies: Have been able to produce surplus

The United Nations considers nations in this cluster among the "less developed" but their youthful and progressive economies are no longer hampered by food shortages and severe health problems, and their societies are experiencing a slow transition from an agricultural to

TABLE 15.2. A market oriented clustering of world markets

Cluster	Demographic make-up	Marketing implications
Dependent societies Most countries in Africa, Asia, and a few in South America	Population growth: 3% Median age: 16 Children: 5+ Infant mortality: 100 per 1,000 births Life expectancy: 40 years GNP per capita: less than $300	Demand goods and services related to food, clothing, housing, education, and medical care. Investments related to extractive activities (agriculture and mining) are undertaken. Government/State Economic Enterprises are the major buying groups. Poor infrastructure and access to rural markets are major impediments.
Seekers Most of Latin America; some in Asia, (Indonesia, Thailand, Philippines) and some in Africa, (Morocco, Tunisia, Egypt)	Population growth: 1.5 to 2.5% Median age: 20 Children: 4+ Infant mortality: 50 to 100 per 1,000 births Life expectancy: 60 years GNP per capita: less than $900	Infrastructure-related projects are high priority (construction equipment, machinery, chemicals, etc.) Good opportunities for technology sales and turnkey projects. Independent trading groups and a few large holding companies have much influence. Increased urbanization but a "mass market" does not yet exist.

Climbers
Brazil, Venezuela, Portugal, Mexico, Taiwan, Malaysia, Turkey, South Korea

Population growth: Under 1.5%
Children: 2 to 3
Median age: slightly higher than 20
GNP per capita: Less than $2,000

Industrialization and service sector expenditures assume greater importance.
Private enterprises have become more dominant than the state agencies.
Good opportunities for joint ventures and technology agreements.
Growing mass market.

Luxury and leisure societies
United States, Canada, Japan, United Kingdom, Australia

Zero or very little population growth
Children: 2
Median age: 30+
Reaching maximum longevity
GNP per capita: greater than $8,000

Substantial discretionary income and availability of credit.
Restructuring of economy.
Maturing markets.
Intense competition.
Relocation away from large population centers.

The rocking chairs
West Germany, Switzerland, Luxembourg, The Netherlands

Fertility rates below replacement level
Children: less than 2
Median age: 37
Peak life expectancy
GNP per capita: greater than $10,000

Dominance of service economy and high technology sectors.
Highly segmented markets.
Ideal distribution and communications channels.

an industrial economy and an expansion from local to national markets. In addition, as these nations seek ways to stabilize their domestic economy, they may be becoming outward-looking for the first time.

Governments focus on building their infrastructure. High priority projects involving construction, equipment, machinery and chemicals, and a huge, unemployed labor force, provide opportunities for international companies interested in technology sales and turnkey projects. These opportunities may allow MNCs to enter a highly protected market, especially if the company is experienced in countertrade. (Most Seekers and Dependents have a very limited supply of foreign exchange.) Automakers such as Ford, Fiat, Renault and tire companies have taken advantage of opportunities offered by Seeker nations.

Imported technology and know-how encourages further specialization and division of labor, and results in the emergence of trade specialists, such as wholesalers. Independent trading groups and a few large holding companies, not just governments, start to influence local economies. To protect their emerging local enterprises and to keep national products competitive, governments may become increasingly protective, encouraging residents to buy local goods, placing high tariffs on imports and subjecting international companies to numerous other restrictions.

Although demand for basic necessities is met, demand for consumer goods generally exceeds supply. Barter is replaced as consumers are purchasing excess basic goods. Seekers have not yet developed "mass markets". Advertising must still be in local language and ads must have local context. However, consumers are becoming more educated as the general population is caught up in the transition from an agricultural to an industrial economy. Consumer expectations rise substantially. Through radio, T.V., or other media, people in their late teens or early 20s are exposed to a world their parents never knew existed and they want to be a part of it. Yet, opportunities for continued education are limited, adding to their frustrations and becoming a source of instability in Seeker countries.

Continued migration from rural to urban areas is contributing to a dual economy, as well as overcrowding in the cities. In fact, of the 10 cities predicted to be the largest by the year 2000, more than half are in Seeker nations. Cities, like Manila or Mexico City cannot provide adequate sewer systems, water, electricity and other public services, creating high problematic slum-like conditions.

Women are a large part of the "move to the cities". They find it easier to serve as domestics or caretakers of apartment buildings. In the Philippines, women may support most of their relatives living in the provinces. As "live-ins" they are frequently separated from their husbands and children.

In time, a middle class which is more literate and large enough to qualify as a market segment, starts to emerge in Seeker nations. Customers in this segment are more dynamic and with greater purchasing power even they become more price-quality conscious.

Climber Societies: Fully industrialized Countries

Significant developments which may provide opportunities for joint ventures and technology agreements are taking place in the industrialized nations. The following are noteworthy:

● Greater specialization of production encourages export interests and expansion into international markets;
● A service-based economy is emerging; and
● Private enterprises are becoming more dominant than state agencies.

A growing mass market permits higher rates of consumption. There is a proliferation of products and brands using modern technology. Specifically, sales of products and services such as disposable diapers, convenience foods, labor saving devices, business machines, entertainments, recreation, etc. are on the rise. Although most consumers in these nations have a great deal of ethnic pride, they will be interested in imports as "status symbols". Mercedes and Porsche are among the most popular cars in Hong Kong, Turkey or other climber countries. Climbers may make good markets for specialized products; however, caution is necessary in selling to them. This process is generally facilitated by the availability of increasingly sophisticated market research.

Climber nations undergo significant changes as generation gaps develop between the young and the old. The young are educated, consumer oriented, and interested in acquiring wealth. The older generation is not well-educated and is used to working hard for a living doing without the consumer goods that the young consider essential. In addition younger women want to work outside the home even if they have children while older women consider it their duty to stay at home and take care of the children. The traditional family structure begins to break down. Elderly are used to counting on their children when they grow older and now are not so sure anymore how reliable their children will be.

In the Climber Societies, women are getting an education and entering the labor force as nurses, secretaries, and low-level managers, forcing men to reevaluate their roles.

With the quality of life deteriorating in some of the largest cities, businesses and people look to smaller well-situated cities and decentralization takes place resulting in a boom of secondary cities.

Luxury and Leisure Societies: Mass Consumption

Luxury and leisure societies are most familiar to Western marketers where increased disposable income and credit availability make luxury goods affordable. However, these mature markets are characterized by little or no growth, necessitating taking advantage of growth outside national borders. This explains why countries like the United States are undergoing current economic restructuring, why companies are reevaluating their strategies and why resources are being allocated differently.

Companies compete not only against themselves but against imports from Climbers, Seekers and even Rocking Chairs. The enormous supply of goods and services results in thinner marketing segments. In fact, international marketers need to become more precise, carving out profitable niches. Nevertheless, reaching these sophisticated consumers is no longer difficult as numerous specialized media such as cable T.V. and special interest magazines are widely available.

In these societies international marketers are impacted by the extinction of the traditional family: Singles, either young people who wait longer to marry, or elderly who are left alone, become important market segments. And women, taking advantage of easier access to education, start entering the labor force in large numbers. This trend results in smaller families where teenagers and husbands take care of household chores and shopping while women are more involved in major purchasing decisions.

Another interesting trend involves the continued relocation away from population centers, facilitated by technological advances in communications and transportation. Companies are looking for cost savings and families, at least in the United States, are seeking to recover some of the culture's lost traditional values.

Rocking Chair Societies

Rocking Chair nations have highly developed technology sectors and ideal distribution and communication channels, yet a median population age of 37. This aging population and a stagnant economy result in significantly reduced expenditures for life insurance, new homes, cars, furniture and the like. Hence, international marketers are encouraged to focus on the dominant service economies of these highly segmented markets.

Countries such as West Germany face two economic dilemmas which may have impact on international marketing efforts. First, an ever increasing number of elderly and ever decreasing number of newborn children force Rocking Chair governments to offer various childbirth incentives. And the second concerns a problematic immigrant labor force. Past economic expansion required supplementation of limited national labor supply. Guest workers, foreign nationals from European nations such as Spain, Turkey and Yugoslavia, became essential to local industry.

Conclusion

The approach suggested in this clustering effort has inherent limitations. For example, nations are forever developing and changing. Even in the near future, some of the world's Dependents will be able to become self-sufficient and qualify as Seekers, hence, require adaptation of new marketing techniques. In addition, countries may vary significantly within their own borders and as a result cannot be considered part of any singular cluster. India, for example, exhibits such diversity. While people in cities such as Calcutta and Benares are fighting to survive, New Delhi offers India's middle class (only 15% of the entire population, yet consisting of a sizeable 100 million people) the latest in Western consumer products. Therefore, international marketers must remain alert, flexible, and responsive in using the suggested clustering approach.

In spite of its limitations, this market oriented clustering of world countries, into Dependent, Seeker, Climber, Luxury and Leisure, and Rocking Chair societies, suggests a new and innovative approach to global marketing. By supplementing traditional global, homogeneous market segmentation with targeting world clusters, international marketers can enhance their awareness of new opportunities emerging around the world.

16

The Promise and Challenges of Europe 1992*

BUSINESS INTERNATIONAL

As 1992 draws near, the long-awaited restructuring of the 12 European Community (EC) member states into a unified Internal Market (IM) is moving toward reality. Not only will this have significant political impact for the entire world, the operational impact on companies located both within and outside the EC will be extensive and far-reaching.

The EC Commission's emphasis on achieving the Internal Market by 1992 is essentially a strategem. Companies should view 1992 not so much as a date, but as a shorthand for Europe's institutional response to changes in the global economy. After European economies began reviving in the early 1980s, it quickly became apparent that Europe did not have the competitive environment to sustain the revival. The 1992 program is a shock tactic intended to create that business environment: it is already clear that the program is the most significant development in European commercial policy since 1945.

Dismantling Core Barriers

The ultimate goal of the EC is to restructure European economies into a single market of 320 million people that is equipped to handle increased global competition from the U.S., Japan and the NICs [Newly Industrialized Countries]. To achieve this aim, the EC member states (France, Spain, West Germany, Italy, the U.K., Belgium, the Netherlands, Denmark, Portugal, Greece, Luxembourg, and Ireland) are to have in place a common legislative framework in all areas affecting commercial practice by 1992. This will be no small task

---

* Adapted from *Business International*, June 27, 1988, pp. 193–204, with permission.

considering the diverse nationalities involved and the plethora of member state legislation that will need to be eliminated or amended.

The IM calls for the creation of free EC trade, with the elimination of both nontariff trade barriers and customs duties. The three core barriers that the EC is hoping to dismantle by 1992 are the following:

- *Physical*, i.e. the dismantling of border controls within the Community and the abolition of internal customs duties, together with a corresponding strengthening of the control of external borders;
- *Product and workplace standardization*, with a unification of regulations on product standards and health and safety in the workplace; and
- *Fiscal*, where the harmonization of indirect tax rates is already under way and the harmonization of direct tax rates is still to be tackled by the Commission.

Key Issues to be Resolved

In addition to the dismantling of the above barriers, the Commission's IM brief implies the creation of a wider range of new commercial policies. Many of these are extremely controversial. They involve the deregulation of sectors long accustomed to protection against competition, including the following:

- *Capital markets and financial services.* Many EC member states have already dismantled their exchange control regime, while several others have not, notably Italy and France among the "big five" economies. The IM requires a free capital market by 1992 that will end direct state control of interest rates and lending quotas. A related issue is the European market for financial services, where member states that have already pursued deregulation (like the UK) are well placed to take insurance and investment business away from those member states that have not (like France).
- *Public procurement.* Most member states have not yet fully grasped that the use of public procurement to sustain domestic industries will end with the IM's introduction in 1992. The Commission's requirements for the progressive introduction of "transparent" public procurement practices, under which cases of national favoritism can be overturned in the European Court, is a potent tool for the deregulation of key markets like telecommunications and construction.
- *Antitrust.* The Competition Directorate of the EC Commission is increasingly active in monitoring and managing the level of business' concentration in Europe and in policing member states' attempts to subsidize their domestic industries. In 1987, the

Commission ruled that ECU 747 million [ECU = European Currency Unit] ($1.18: ECU1) of illegal state subsidies to industry had to be returned. The Commission is fighting and gradually winning a battle to establish that the Community institutions, rather than the member states, are the final court on issues raised by European mergers and trade practices.

● *Intellectual property rights*. The Internal Market program has co-incided with the global crisis in the field of protection of intellectual property rights. The Commission has been struggling to create a European policy to deal with the ease with which recorded-material may be illegally copied. This has been an uphill fight, however, in the absence of a clear mandate from industry. As a result, many of the Community's member states are beginning to jump the gun with their own revised versions of intellectual property legislation.

Where the Member States Stand

Despite steady progress, there are still many stumbling blocks. Much of the legislation contained in the Commission's Internal Market White Paper [regulations to be passed before 1992 to bring the Internal Market into place] still needs to be completed. In addition, even when it turned into European "directives," there is no guarantee that those directives will be incorporated into the legislative acts of individual member states by 1992. Member states (particularly the U.K.) have reservations on security grounds about the dismantling of internal border controls, while Germany and Italy are unenthusiastic about the Commission's intervention in competition issues. In addition, Germany has made only notional progress on the deregulation of the telecommunications sector.

Nevertheless, the IM program has built up considerable momentum. It has forced the member states to consider wider issues of economic integration not specifically included in the program, above all the possibility of a unified European monetary policy regulated through a single central bank and the further integration of European currencies.

Reciprocity

External trade policy and reciprocity is also coming under scrutiny. EC Trade Commissioner Willy De Clercq's repeated calls for reciprocity have Washington and the Pacific Basin capitals extremely concerned. Many EC watchers believe that internal EC political reality will require the Community to introduce EC-wide protection if it is to convince national governments to relinquish the protection now granted to national champions and sectors. EC President Jacques Delors labels as "absurd" third-country concerns that the Community's single-market plans will be accompanied by protectionist measures leading to the creation of "fortress Europe." He says, "We are the world's largest trading power and its most open market, and we will remain so." He says it is "extraordinary" that Japan, with the world's most closed market, is worrying about the external impact of 1992. But Delors makes a clear distinction between "areas covered by the GATT and those which are not." In the former area, says Delors, "We will of course bow to our international obligations, but in the latter the principle is simple: reciprocity. This means that in order for third-country companies to benefit from the legislation, their governments must grant the same advantages to European companies."

The Uruguay Factor

It is fortuitous for third countries that the EC's 1992 efforts coincide with the GATT Uruguay Round talks. This will probably be very important not only in keeping the EC in line with its international obligations, but also in providing the forum to negotiate any needed changes or compensation. The EC has already announced that its rollback commitment (whereby any existing barriers to free trade will be abolished on a quid pro quo basis) will be fulfilled by the elimination of Europe's remaining 736 quantitative trade restrictions (QRs). Of course, the Community negotiators have played down the fact that as of 1992, Article 115, which permits member states to maintain controls on intramember state trade, will become inoperable. Therefore, the remaining QRs will be unenforceable, since a member state will have no power to prevent non-EC exporters from routing restricted goods through a second member state. Hence, the EC is giving nothing away. The Commission is asking for no specific concessions in this case, but Community negotiators do "expect other contracting parties to make similar commitments."

A common EC import policy is particularly necessary to prevent member states from introducing quasi-illegal measures to protect sectors that will no longer be protected under Article 115. As one official explains, "the elimination of existing QRs will not eliminate the economic needs for these QRs." In order to prevent a backlash or even disintegration of the Community, major new funding to the less-developed regions and sectors will be required. Without this funding, the single market may be compared with medicine that is so strong it kills the patient. As one official says, "Who really thinks that Greece will allow total freedom of textile imports? Such a policy would mean suicide for its domestic industry without extra help."

Because it is unlikely that the member states will suddenly agree to major new funding for the less-developed areas, the Commission will be forced to increase protectionism aimed at third countries to prevent national objections. The Uruguay Round should prevent the protectionism from getting out of hand. However, without some protection, member states will never be able politically to consent to the economic realities of a single market.

Buying a Local Presence

Whether firms want to develop an insider presence in key member states, secure new low-cost manufacturing bases, integrate OEMs [original equipment manufacturer] or obtain distribution channels, 1992 is triggering a spate of mergers and acquisitions (M&As). Nestlé, the Swiss foods group, has been forced to make its first-ever hostile acquisition bid (against its arch rival Jacob Suchard) to win the Euro and global brands of British chocolate maker Rowntree. Olivetti chief Carlo de Benedetti was only just thwarted in his highly expensive attempt to take over Société Générale in an attempt to create a loosely federated "1992 Holding Company." Two non-EC MNCs, albeit with almost as many assets and customers inside the EC as outside—Sweden's Asea and Switzerland's Brown Boveri—in 1987 executed Europe's mightiest merger (the ABB) and created a pan-European conglomerate 50% bigger than any of its global competitors.

The record year for cross-border M&As in Europe was 1987. Bids from companies based in the U.K., France, and Germany increased from an average of 112 per year during 1983–85 to 169 in 1986 and 266 in 1987, according to Booz, Allen & Hamilton's Paris-based Acquisitions Service. Many traditional views of European M&As are now being challenged. Companies in Germany, once considered impregnable to foreign owners, are being acquired at a faster rate than anywhere else (262 in 1988, compared with 156 in France and 142 in the U.K.). U.K. firms, long regarded as more interested in the English-speaking U.S. than foreign-speaking Europe, are now becoming major Euro-raiders. In the first four months of 1988, U.K. firms made 88 Euro-acquisitions, compared with 117 in the U.S. and just 27 for the same period in 1987. French companies are also starting to develop a taste for non-French firms—97 acquisitions in 1987, vs. 25 in 1986.

Some executives posit that the growth in M&A activity may lead to a two-tiered structure in which firms in the middle are squeezed out; key industries are moving toward domination by a few giants surrounded by small flexible innovators that succeed in niches.

Forging Ties with Competitors

Rather than drain management resources and corporate funds through acquisition, some firms are responding to 1992 by collaborative efforts. Midland Bank (U.K.) and Hong Kong Bank—both oft-quoted takeover candidates—have strengthened their long-term futures through cross-shareholdings. Many companies view 1992 as the chance to pool R&D [research and development] resources. The Commission notes that 46 R&D alliances were established between information technology companies, up from just six in 1983. Interest in other alliances—cross-marketing and distribution agreements, licensing agreements—is also increasing.

The growth in alliances presents a number of challenges for both participants and observers. First, companies not active in the venture game may find themselves frozen out. Second, MNCs developing a strategic network of links need to walk a fine line: It is always possible that today's ally will use the arrangement to become an even more formidable competitor tomorrow. Third, MNCs need to develop the skills to effectively manage the alliances. Managers need to learn much about the selection of partners, negotiation of contracts, protection of intellectual property rights and maintenance of a mutually profitable relationship.

Revamping Organizational Structures

Some MNCs remark that even if a workable "United States of Europe" becomes a reality, differences between EC member states still require a corporate organizational structure that keeps companies close to the pulse of their business—customers spanning 12 distinct national markets. For instance, the Japanese company NEC Electronics believes having a thoroughly European company will significantly boost its ability to increase its share of the European semiconductor market from 5% to 10% by 1992. NEC has created a network of design centers and sales offices close to all major industrial zones in order to provide customized service to over 10,000 individual clients. Each locale feeds market data to a regional coordination centre in Düsseldorf, which runs two high-volume, high-quality factories located in Scotland and Ireland.

A similar attempt to keep close to the customer while reaping economies of manufacturing scale is being made by U.S. agricultural and construction equipment maker, JI Case. The firm is part of the U.S.-based energy and industrial group Tenneco, and it incorporates the old manufacturing facilities of International Harvester and Poclain. It has designated individual European factories in France,

Germany, the U.K. and Spain as specialized, globally competitive sources of key components and assemblies. Such integrated manufacturing facilities clearly offer the potential for substantial economies of scale. At the same time, however JI Case has retained a very decentralized sales network of dealers, distributors, and company-owned stores to cope with the continuing plethora of technical standards and individual market requirements. Local and regional operations are responsible for developing their respective markets and interfacing with the specialist manufacturing plants via a central coordination unit in the U.K. Likewise, ABB, aware that procurement of electricity-generating equipment is likely to remain highly political for some time, has established an organizational structure that retains substantial manufacturing in national markets, but profits from shared R&D and financial resources.

17

The New Powers of Asia*

LOUIS KRAAR

In a flash, it seems, they have gone from scruffy, dependent countries to well-off producers of shoes, clothes, and transistor radios to wealthy powerhouses that appear to turn out the best of everything and threaten the economic well-being of the West. Can this be true? Will the next century really belong to Asia?

Certainly the region, defined here as the countries bordering the Pacific from Japan on the north to New Zealand 5,500 miles to the south, is already a major economic force in the world. Japan's gross national product is more than 50% that of the U.S., and the Japanese economy is growing slightly faster. More important is the rousing growth of the four little tigers—Hong Kong, Singapore, Taiwan, and South Korea. By next year, according to the Organization for Economic Cooperation and Development, their total exports will reach 80% of Japan's.

Thailand is on the verge of becoming a tiger. Malaysia, the Philippines, Indonesia, and the People's Republic of China have great potential if they can solve internal problems. When the 21st century begins, the region may well account for more than 25% of the world's total GNP, vs. less than 30% for North America. The comparable numbers now are 20% vs. 28%.

The Rise of the East does not necessarily ensure the Decline of the West. This does not have to be a zero-sum game, despite what alarmists say. There is opportunity aplenty for the U.S. and Europe in an ever more prosperous Asia. Many Western companies already have plants there that send parts and finished products back home. A bit more than 50% of Singapore's exports to the U.S. are goods turned out by American companies. A wealthier Pacific region is a better

*Reprinted from *Fortune*, March 28, 1988, pp. 126–132, with permission.

market for all kinds of Western products. Says Lee Hsien Loong, Singapore's minister of trade and industry: "As we grow, we don't present a threat to you. We just buy more from you."

Then there is the moral dimension. Which country should we applaud: One like Singapore, where per capita income has risen from $2,810 to $7,673 in the past decade, unemployment is 2.8%, and almost everyone has a roomy, modern apartment? Or Burma, where per capita income is $200 a year and the economy is going backward after years of socialism? And which kind of country should we fear? Political stability flows from prosperity, not poverty.

Yet the doomsayers have some points. The region accounts for more than half the U.S. trade deficit, and the rise of Asia has hardly been a tidy, carefully controlled affair. Japan's brass-knuckles aggressiveness as an exporter is legendary. The insistence of many Japanese that anything Japan makes is superior to American products doesn't help. This view is also wrongheaded.

Taiwan and South Korea have blithely pushed their U.S. trade surpluses to the point of pain. Koreans apparently believed they were doing what the U.S. wanted by earning foreign exchange to pay off the country's huge external debt. Some Korean executives wonder out loud why Americans, who fought a bitter war on their behalf, are not willing to help out now by accepting a lopsided trade balance. The laid-off worker in Ohio or South Carolina who thinks goods from Asia are to blame doesn't see it that way.

Rising Asian exports have triggered fear and anger in Washington and in the Common Market. Washington plans by January 1 to eliminate the tigers' duty-free privileges, which were originally designed to help poor countries. Richard Gephardt, a little-known Democratic Congressman from Missouri, has become a presidential contender largely on the strength of strident attacks on Asian trade policies. He struck a nerve with his contention that Americans would have to pay $48,000 for the modest little Hyundai auto, instead of less than $6,000, if the U.S. applied the same duties and local taxes that South Korea does. (The actual figure is closer to $30,000 and includes heavy taxes the Koreans levy on their own cars.)

The task for the West will be getting beyond the fear that has resulted from some Asian excesses to the very real opportunities that beckon. If the West does sink in the face of the rising East, it will be due more to its own mistakes than to actions of the Pacific countries. One of those mistakes would be failing to participate vigorously in Asian markets.

Viewed as one huge trading bloc, the Pacific indeed looks scary. But this is no homogeneous region, and within its complexity are several trends that ought to be beneficial to the West. Japan has begun to moderate its dependence on exports by stimulating domestic demand. Though the pace is excruciatingly slow, it is bound to quicken even if politicians lose their nerve and try to go back to the old policy. Younger Japanese will keep pushing. With no memories of war or of rebuilding Japan, they are shorter on sacrifice and longer on consumption than their elders.

Increasingly Japan's market is being supplied by other Asian countries. In many cases consumer goods come from Japanese companies that have moved factories offshore in pursuit of lower costs, just as U.S. manufacturers have done in Taiwan and Singapore. But color TVs, VCRs, and microwave ovens are also pouring in from companies in the four tigers and Thailand. The more the tigers sell to Japan, the less they will drive up the blood pressure of Richard Gephardt and his brethren.

The other good news for American business is that ambitious nations like Singapore and South Korea are eager for joint ventures that will help pull them up the technological ladder. To cite one example, government-owned Singapore Technology Corp. invested $5 million in Sierra Semiconductor, a California startup with proprietary technology for custom chips. That led to a $40 million joint venture in Singapore. The numbers may be large, but the pattern is being duplicated again and again.

American companies already have a major presence. Apple, for instance, makes all of its popular IIe computers in a highly automated plant in Singapore, where labor accounts for only 2% to 3% of manufacturing costs. Some parts are made in Singapore, but many others are shipped in from neighboring Asian countries and from suppliers in the U.S. and Europe. General Motors and Ford have joint ventures with Korean automakers to build subcompact cars for the fast-growing local market and for export to America. IBM makes computers for the Japanese market in Japan. But many of its U.S. products contain components from plants in Hong Kong and Taiwan.

Japanese companies invested an estimated $6 billion in various countries in the region last year, up from $2.3 billion the previous year, and the pace is quickening. Aiwa, a consumer electronics company, makes about half its audio products in Singapore and ships 30% to Japan. The rest are sold in the local market and throughout the world. Sony has dispersed production of many consumer products, including compact disc players, among seven Asian nations. Toyota is gearing up in Thailand to make dies and jigs for pressing auto-body panels at 40% of the cost back in Toyota City. Minebea, one of the first Japanese companies to move production offshore, makes 98% of its ball bearings for the world market, including Japan, in Thailand and Singapore.

In Thailand alone, the number of investment applications by Japanese companies has nearly quadrupled since 1986, to 200 projects worth $353 million. Says Nimit Nontapunthawat, chief economist of the Bangkok Bank in Thailand: "It used to be that the Japanese built plants here only so they could avoid tariffs and sell in the local market. Now they build here because it's cost-effective."

Another favorable trend hardly noticed in the U.S. is that the countries Americans often fear most—the four tigers—are taking some helpful steps. When the dollar plunged against the yen, the South Korean won went down pretty much in step. Now, under pressure from Washington, Korea is allowing the won to strengthen, which will make U.S. products more competitive there. The tigers are also cracking open their markets a bit. In Taiwan, 8,000 U.S. cars were sold last year, an eightfold increase over the year before. South Korea (with an average urban family income of $12,000 annually) has the biggest middle class in Asia outside Japan. Both countries should become attractive consumer markets.

Though lumped together in the West, the four tigers are very different places. All they really have in common is their super growth rates, an average of nearly 8% annually for the past five years. Singapore and Hong Kong, both city-states, are probably the only genuine free-traders on earth. They thrive as international manufacturing and banking centers. Korea and Taiwan have concentrated on industrial development, sacrificing domestic consumption and spending on social welfare in the process.

Now Korea and Taiwan are changing. Korean workers called a violent halt to their days of self-denial in a series of strikes last year. The result was pay raises averaging around 20%. The increases hardly strained the system; productivity rose 10% for the year. Political rioting and a tumultuous election late last year have given way to a period of calm under newly elected President Roh Tae-Woo. Korea appears to be successfully carrying out its first peaceful leadership change.

Taiwan ended martial law last July and is starting to invest in pollution control and public transportation. More encouraging was the orderly transfer of power early this year after the death at 77 of President Chiang Ching-kuo, Taiwan's second president and son of the legendary Chiang Kai-Shek.

As rising wages and strengthening currencies push the tigers out of labor-intensive industries, their biggest challenge is finding new things to do. Taiwan is the most vulnerable. Its currency has appreciated 36% against the dollar since September 1986. Warns one cabinet member: "A lot of small businesses will be shut down this year." Manufacturers of shoes and textiles are moving to Thailand and the Philippines.

Simultaneously, Taiwan is getting into more sophisticated industries. Most dramatically, Stan Shih, 43, a charismatic engineer and entrepreneur, exports a full line of personal computer clones and peripherals under his own brand name, Acer. Shih's company, Multitech, has made a deal with Texas Instruments to assemble and service Multitech machines in the U.S. That's quite a role reversal, because Taiwan firms usually produce computers for American companies and put U.S. brand names on them.

South Korean companies have forged similar alliances with American partners. Their primary goal is access to U.S. technology. Goldstar relies on a joint venture with AT&T for semi-conductor research. Daewoo has teamed with a flock of Western companies, including Northern Telecom of Canada and the Sikorsky Aircraft division of United Technologies.

Thailand is on its way to being the next Asian NIC, or newly industrializing country. More politically stable than many of its Southeast Asian neighbors, it has become a magnet for foreign investment, both from the U.S. and Japan. The military-dominated regime of Prime Minister Prem Tinsulanond has been in power for eight years. Despite a few coup attempts by military factions, the Thais are exceptionally unified by a popular monarchy and Buddhism.

An unbroken history of independence has left the Thais free of colonial hang-ups. Perhaps for that reason, Thailand has managed to make the most of the entrepreneurial vigor of the ethnic Chinese by treating them as Thais, not aliens or second-class citizens. Says a Thai corporate executive: "There are obvious political problems in the Philippines, Malaysia is torn by ethnic tensions between its Chinese and Malays, Indonesia has a lousy work ethic and serious corruption, and Singapore has a labor shortage. Where else can investors go?"

Plentiful labor and flexible regulations allow factories to operate around the clock. Says Makoto Ikeda, director of Minebea's operations in Thailand: "Productivity is higher in our plants here than in Japan because the workers are only about 20 years old, much younger than in Japan." Working for wages of under $3 a day, industrious Thais are turning out Nike shoes, Arrow shirts, semiconductors , and toys. The country's only serious drawbacks are a dearth of supporting industries and congestion in Bangkok. The Thai capital has some of the worst traffic jams on earth.

With its tolerant culture that embraces serene Buddhist temples as well as licentious nightspots, Thailand is also a favorite destination of vacationers. It earned over $1.7 billion from tourism last year, almost twice its foreign exchange from rice exports.

From its lush farmland, Thailand gets a cornucopia of agricultural exports. It sells Japan tons of frozen chickens produced by farms that look like assembly lines. Thailand is a major supplier of canned pineapple to the U.S., much of it produced by Dole, the American food processor. The Thais are also the largest suppliers of canned tuna to the U.S., even though most of it is caught far from Thailand.

While foreign investment has been a major factor in Thailand's rise, the country has produced some dynamic enterprises of its own. Dhanin Chearavanont, 49, has quietly built a small family feed business called Charoen Pokphand into an international group with 12,000 employees that operates in 12 countries and had sales last year of $1.7 billion. CP Group runs a high-tech chicken operation that exports to Japan and Europe. Chearavanont plans to mass produce pork, in a joint venture with Oscar Mayer of the U.S., and shrimp, with help from Mitsubishi of Japan. The company also has a joint venture in China with Continental Grain of the U.S.

Thailand's largest exporter of manufactured goods is another local group of companies called Saha-Union, which has diversified from textiles to Nike shoes. Damri Darakananda, 55, started the business in 1961 as a joint venture with YKK of Japan to make zippers, but insisted on using his own brand-name, Venus. He expanded into thread, buttons, and plastic items—then bought out YKK. Saha-Union is an IBM computer dealer as well and holds the Computerland franchise in Thailand. Says Darakananda: "We're thinking ahead. Korea and Taiwan first exported textiles, then moved to electronics and computers. That's the direction we want to go."

Other nations in the region, of course, have much economic potential. Unleashing the energies of over one billion Chinese could create a new industrial powerhouse and a mammoth market. The realities of doing business in the People's Republic, however, can be discouraging. When an Australian investor in the new Ramada Renaissance Hotal in Guilin tried to prevent stealing by workers, the government accused him of violating the employees' human rights. Despite well-publicized reforms, the country has hardly gone capitalist. Almost all prices remain under state control, and party bureaucrats regularly meddle in factory management. Says William Colby, former director of the Central Intelligence Agency who is now an international lawyer: "China will not play a major role in the world economy for the foreseeable future."

Not surprisingly, Asian businessmen, especially ethnic Chinese, are better than Westerners at carving out niches in the People's Republic. Some 30 textile plants in South China are owned by investors in Taiwan in deals funneled through Hong Kong. The Nationalist regime in Taiwan still officially prohibits such investments but has been willing to look the other way. South Korean companies are increasing their trade and investment with China too, by way of Hong Kong.

Three resource-rich Southeast Asian nations—Malaysia, Indonesia, and the Philippines—could become booming economies, but the day seems far off. Malaysia is a leading exporter of rubber and palm oil. The government has tried to expand beyond raw materials into heavy industry with little success. State-owned auto and steel industries have lost heavily. The biggest problem is tension among ethnic Malays, about half the population, and Indians and Chinese, who make up the rest. Prime Minister Mahathir Mohamad has been pushing an affirmative action program that, among other things, is designed to give Malays a 30% stake in all enterprises. Since most Malays lack capital and business experience, the state winds up buying into companies on their behalf.

Indonesia has long relied on revenues from Pertamina, its state-owned oil company, to support the country's 170 million people spread over 6,000 islands. In the process, it acquired some wasteful habits. Over the years, President Suharto has given monopolies to relatives and friends for the import of steel, plastics, cement, and other basic items. The result: unnecessarily high prices for raw materials. A recent survey of U.S. investors conducted by a regional business group gives Indonesia an unfavorable rating compared with other countries in Southeast Asia. To Suharto's credit, he turned over management of the notoriously corrupt customs service to Société Générale de Surveillance, a Swiss survey company.

The Philippines has yet to recover economically from the Marcos years. President Corazón Aquino has been seeking foreign investment and some is trickling in. But Communist insurgents in the countryside, political feuding, and pervasive corruption remain big distractions. Aquino herself has survived at least five coup attempts. Most shocking, the country's sluggish bureaucracy has prevented it from spending a backlog of over $1 billion in foreign aid.

Above all, the top performers of the Pacific are demonstrating that countries can adapt and grow by being part of the international economy. Nothing symbolizes that better than Veitnam, of all places, seeking foreign investors to help reinvigorate its backward economy. As Singapore Prime Minister Lee Kuan Yew puts it, Vietnam won its war, but lost the peace, while the NICs "have succeeded in creating more prosperous and more equal societies." The West should stop being afraid of the Pacific challenge and get down to business in a new frontier.

18

Marketing Environment in the Middle East and North Africa: The Forces behind Market Homogenization*

LYN S. AMINE
S. TAMER CAVUSGIL

Introduction

Interest in North Africa and the Middle East is stimulated by factors such as doubt about the continuing availability of energy resources; changes in political stability and allegiances; religious and cultural upheaval; and, less dramatically, the emergence of important new growth markets for Western exports. The area embraced by the terms *Middle East* and *North Africa* is not a homogeneous bloc of countries. Vast differences exist in terms of climate, natural resources, ethnic and religious background, political tendencies, potential for growth, and desire for modernization.

A potential exporter or direct investor in this region can easily be puzzled and confused by differences which exist within and between the countries of the region. These differences create the impression that each country requires a unique marketing strategy. Yet, as we contend, there are common forces at work which contribute to the homogenization of markets both within individual countries and across the region. Despite significant variation in consumer tastes, preferences, needs, and market institutions, companies can successfully target standardized products and services toward homogeneous clusters of nations or market segments.

*Reprinted in abridged form from *Advances in International Marketing*, Vol. 1, pp. 115–141, with permission.

Recent experience of Japanese companies has shown that understanding commonalities in the region and emphasis on products which are advanced, functionally reliable, and low priced are the keys to marketing success. By standardizing their marketing effort, these companies have been able to benefit from substantial economies of scale in production, distribution, and promotion. In contrast, companies which concentrate on the idiosyncrasies of each market and magnify them risk falling behind competitively.

Our purpose is to identify broad similarities between countries and consumers which together create the characteristic market environment of North Africa and the Middle East. Traveling from Morocco at the western end of the Mediterranean to Turkey at the eastern end, one becomes aware of a certain market "atmosphere" which feels familiar whether one is in Tunisia, Egypt, Saudi Arabia, or Lebanon.

We begin by considering macroenvironmental factors in the region, leading to the identification of *country clusters*. Then we consider qualitative differences among nations and we identify several *attitude clusters*. Our analysis then shifts to the micro level as we identify *lifestyle clusters* which cut across national boundaries. Following this, we address the dichotomy between urban and rural living and focus on the importance of *urban clusters*. Finally, we assess differences in consumer shopping habits and establish two major *shopping behavior clusters*. Thus we present multiple perspectives on the region through five approaches to market clustering. Figure 18.1 summarizes the methodology used in this paper.

Each method of clustering offers advantages and disadvantages to the marketer. Country clustering facilitates costly distribution and promotion decisions such as choice of import agents and dealers, location of warehouses or manufacturing facilities, and selection of regional research or advertising agencies. However, country clustering may result in serious suboptimization of other aspects of the marketing effort. This is particularly true when numerous microsegments are identified which are widely scattered between countries and therefore very expensive to contact. In this case the marketer may not be able to fine-tune those strategy decisions which are affected by consumer lifestyles, preferences, and local fashions.

Attitude clustering resolves in part the problem of qualitative differences among consumers. Indeed it may be possible to direct globalization strategies to homogeneous attitude clusters and thus avoid the cost factors and strategy problems implicit in country clustering. These advantages and opportunities also extend to the three other types of clusters (lifestyle, urban, and shopping), where the focus is on commonalities among actual consumers rather than political or geographic blocs such as "nations" or "countries". The following

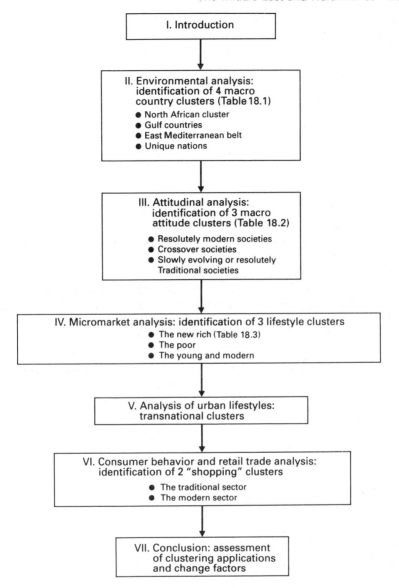

FIG. 18.1. Summary of clustering methodology.

discussion provides a comprehensive understanding of the market environment and recent trends in the Middle East and North Africa. Such an understanding is essential to the marketer who wants to avoid the risk of "not recognizing the forest because of the trees".

TABLE 18.1. Country Clusters

North African cluster:	*East Mediterranean Belt:*
Morocco	Turkey
Algeria	Syria
Tunisia	Lebanon
	Jordan
Gulf countries:	Israel
Saudi Arabia	
Kuwait	
UAE	*Unique nations:*
Bahrain	Egypt
Qatar	Iraq
Oman	Iran
North Yemen	Libya
South Yemen	Sudan

Environment Analysis: Four Macro-Country Clusters

Religious, ethnic, linguistic, geographic, climate, historical, and political differences all apparently argue against the assimilation of various countries into one monolithic market group. It is inaccurate in marketing terms to speak of the "Arab market" in denoting this region. Many groups, such as the Persians, Armenians, Kurds, Turks, and Jews, do not speak Arabic as a mother tongue nor are they of ethnic Arab origin.

It is also incorrect to speak of the "Muslim market" because several religions prevail in the region. However, Muslim Arabs are the predominant group. They share "an unmistakable unity of style. Furthermore the same architecture, the same sense of heritage, and the same passions and temperaments are evident from Baghdad to Marrakesh" (Almaney 1981, p. 10). This similarity is traced back to Bedouin origins, finding expression in such cultural traits as hospitality, pride, honor, and rivalry. The alternating pattern of behavioral extremes is probably one of the factors contributing to the mystique which in Western minds surrounds much of this region, making it a difficult market for Western exporters to evaluate.

Despite this diversity among nations we can identify several homogeneous clusters of nations by focusing on commonalities concerning geography, climate, topography, and political character. Table 18.1 lists four macro-clusters. These are the North African cluster; the Gulf countries; the East Mediterranean Belt; and some "unique nations" which stand apart from the other three clusters and even from one another.

The North African Cluster

This first group of countries has a heritage of Western influence due to former French colonialism. Morocco, Algeria, and Tunisia are regarded by some Arabs as having lost some of their traditional Arab identity and as being engaged in the devopment of a new, more "modern" character. They are associate members of the European Community (EC) and together constitute a separate entity, the Maghreb Economic Community. Future status as EC associated is subject to change because of the entry of Spain and Portugal into the EC. Libya is excluded from this cluster despite geographic proximity to the Maghreb group because of political and ideological differences which are discussed below.

The Gulf Countries

This second cluster of countries is conspicuous by the persistence of the Bedouin tradition, the desert climate, simple cuisine, a very strict adherence to the Islamic faith, and a relatively narrow middle class. In addition, the predominance of absolute monarchy and the unusual degree of political stability are characteristic of this group. Before the exploitation of petroleum, the population of this area was largely dependent on fishing and some limited trade. Although several Gulf nations are currently experiencing a phenomenal rate of change, traditional values and a nomadic lifestyle are still apparent, especially in the rural areas.

Among the economic and political affiliations is OPEC (Organization of Petroleum Exporting Countries), which includes Saudi Arabia, Kuwait, United Arab Emirates (UAE), Oman, Qatar as well as Algeria, Iran, Iraq, Libya, and others. The internal unity of the Gulf region has been strengthened by means of the Gulf Cooperation Council which brings together Saudi Arabia, Kuwait, the UAE, Bahrain, Qatar, Oman, North Yemen, and Iraq. In the Gulf area Saudi Arabia has assumed a leadership role as a result of several factors: charismatic and influential monarchs, oil wealth, population size, and a dominant position in Islam through the location of the two holiest cities, Mecca and Medina, within the country's borders.

The East Mediterranean Belt

The third cluster of countries has always been an arena for opposing ideologies and is therefore the least stable in the entire region. Religious and political differences have long been a source of turmoil in Lebanon, Turkey, Syria, and to some extent in Jordan and Israel. Three of the nations in the East Mediterranean Belt are minority-ruled. Minority Alouites have been ruling the Sunnites in Syria and Christians have been ruling the Muslim majority in Lebanon. King Hussein's regime in Jordan is also a minority rule.

There is an emerging middle class in the East Mediterranean Belt of nations and generally the people have been able to attain higher levels of education than elsewhere. A substantial number of the professional people active in the Middle East, such as bankers, engineers, contractors, teachers, and traders, originate from Lebanon, Syria, Turkey, and Egypt. People of the East Mediterranean Belt demonstrate a more cosmopolitan or Westernized lifestyle than people in other clusters.

Unique Nations

The last cluster includes five countries which differ not only from countries in the earlier clusters but also from one another. For example, Egypt, Iraq, and Iran have made significant strides in industrialization. Iraq and Iran are resource-rich, whereas Egypt is relatively poor despite its geographic size. Both Egypt and Iran have an established middle class which is well educated and familiar with the Western way of life. Iraq, in contrast, is much less cosmopolitan and is a further example of a minority-ruled nation with Sunnites ruling the Shiite majority. All three nations have recently suffered the effects of internal conflict over political ideologies. In addition to the problem of internal disunity, Egypt, Iraq, and Iran stand apart from countries in the other clusters largely as a result of differences relating to the international political scene.

Similarly, Libya and Sudan appear to stand alone. The political regime in Libya has alienated the country from both its "natural" neighbors, the three Maghreb nations and Egypt, and also from its "resource partners", the OPEC countries. Libya's anglophone colonial heritage is an additional factor widening the psychological gap between Libya and francophone North Africa. In contrast, Sudan is moving closer to an affiliation with the Gulf countries despite ethnic and cultural links with sub-Saharan Africa.

Through the identification of these four country clusters, we see how a global corporation might apply a globalized marketing strategy. The following discussion shows how clustering can cut across artificial national boundaries.

Attitudinal Analysis: Three Macro Attitude Clusters

In order to substantiate our clustering approach on the basis of national attitudes, we will discuss several areas of policymaking and choice of national priorities. These include economic development, industrialization, modernization, and attitudes towards the West. Our classification of nations along these attitudinal dimensions is summarized in Table 18.2.

Many of these nations share a common goal of national economic development. However, opportunities for progress vary according to the availability of natural resources and consequent rate of industrialization. Whereas some countries enjoy a flourishing agricultural sector, such as Morocco, Israel, and Turkey, others have only one major option for growth in a barren natural environment—industrialization, as in Kuwait and Saudi Arabia. Yet others, such as Tunisia, Egypt, and Syria, attempt to promote in both areas, not being especially endowed in either.

The huge potential for industrialization is reflected by the fact that North Africa and the Middle East account for about 10% of imports from the free world—second in importance only to the industrialized West. Western industrial companies such as Caterpillar, John Deere, Navistar, and Siemens have established a strong presence in these markets, as have consumer goods companies, petroleum companies, Western banks, and service institutions in the business of office management, sanitary services, electronic mail, and computer services. Global companies looking for new market opportunities have rapidly identified those countries with a growing and increasingly prosperous middle class which offer attractive possibilities for increased sales. Familiar brand-name products of Procter and Gamble, Nestlé, Unilever, Singer, General Motors, Pepsi Cola, Sony, and Nissan are typical purchases throughout the region.

The push to achieve a modern way of life is a common objective among people in many of these countries. Modernism is often equated with the ability to buy and enjoy goods associated with the Westernized way of life, e.g., skateboards and chewing gum in Morocco, televisions and video equipment in Saudi Arabia, Kuwaiti and Egyptian vacation villages, and resort homes on the Mediterranean coast of Turkey.

Several countries are beginning to resist this new "imperialism of values" (Eilts 1982). Muslim fundamentalism in Iran and Egypt, and the determination to preserve the traditional Islamic way of life in Saudi Arabia, have been interpreted as evidence that some nations are

TABLE 18.2. Three Attitude Clusters of North African and Middle Eastern Countries

Resolutely modern societies	Israel, Lebanon
Crossover societies	Morocco, Algeria, Tunisia, Saudi Arabia, Kuwait, UAE, Bahrain, Turkey, Jordan, Egypt
Slowly evolving or resolutely traditional societies	Sudan, Iraq, Iran, Syria, Qatar, Oman, North Yemen, South Yemen

not willing to pay for economic growth at the price of cultural attrition.

A number of historical factors have contributed to the particular "love–hate" relationship existing between some of the Middle Eastern countries and the West. This longstanding antagonism is made worse by the still unresolved problems of peace and justice in the region. Thus any commercial Western "presence" must be evaluated not only in terms of market risk but also political risk, particularly in Iran, Iraq, Syria, Israel, Lebanon, and Libya.

On the basis of this analysis of attitudinal differences, we have made a tentative grouping of countries fully recognizing the inevitable discrepancies and approximations which this procedure may produce. Table 18.2 presents three attitudinal clusters: resolutely modern societies, crossover societies, and slowly evolving or resolutely traditional societies.

The advantages of this attitudinal clustering technique lie in the possibility of concentrating marketing action and achieving synergy in similar markets. Once the consumer market environment in, for example, slowly evolving societies has been thoroughly researched, then the marketing company can achieve economies of scale by developing a uniform set of policies for that particular cluster. Although geographic distance between countries in a cluster may affect distribution costs, these will probably be adequately offset by savings in product development, advertising copy, and media-planning expenses, to name but a few policy areas.

Micromarket Analysis: Three Lifestyle Clusters

We will next examine market characteristics at the micro level. Here we detect additional reasons for the "familiar feel" of the marketplace that is so pervasive throughout North Africa and the Middle East. Lifestyle has been defined as the way that people spend time and money. Important factors in this region include age, education and income levels, urban vs. rural ways of life, and family size and traditions. In the following discussions we review these factors and identify three lifestyle clusters which cross national boundaries and social classes.

The New Rich

The skewedness of income distribution is a common characteristic of the region. For the marketer it means that in virtually every country there exists a small segment, the new rich. Although in some cases this segment is merely embryonic, there is a demand for foreign-made

TABLE 18.3. The "New Rich":
Three Market Segments Deserving Special Attention by Global Marketers

---

Three different target markets for luxury goods can be identified: migrant workers; wealthy local entrepreneurs and professionals; and expatriates. Each group has different sources of income and may buy either at home (paying high levels of import duty for the privilege) or abroad (often benefiting under rules for repatriation of personal effects).

A large number of *migrant workers* (called "guest workers") live in the European Community countries. In West Germany alone there are more than 1 million Turkish workers, most of them semiskilled, working in less desirable jobs. These workers stay in close contact with their homeland, maintaining a steady flow of foreign remittances and returning to visit relatives and friends at least once a year. It is customary to bring home visible signs of success, such as an automobile, stereo or video equipment, TV sets, kitchen appliances, and other "luxuries" which are hard to find in Turkey. Typically, the automobile will be a Mercedes Benz because of its popularity and symbolic value.

Wealthy local entrepreneurs and professionals in the fields of medicine, education, engineering, law, and finance constitute a second target group for luxury items. In Morocco, wealth, education, and social status are almost synonymous with ethnic background, social class, and/or commercial specialization. For example, the people from the region around the city of Fez enjoy a high social status. They accede to positions of responsibility in government and administration, and dominate the wholesale textile sector, the source of much of their wealth. Linguistic particularities and a generally fairer complexion set this group apart from the Moroccan Arab population. Country of origin is an important component of the buying decision and a hierarchy of desirable brand names exist for particular items. Therefore, BMW outranks Mercedes Benz in the automobile market, and Panasonic dominates Blaupunkt for automobile stereo equipment. Such preferences are difficult to explain objectively both with regard to origin and perpetuation.

A third target group for luxury goods and modern marketing is composed of *expatriate managers and experts* located throughout the region. In Saudi Arabia, current success of the supermarket concept and packaged consumer goods is largely attributed to the size and importance of the expatriate segment.

---

luxury items such as expensive automobiles, stereo and video equipment, household appliances, designer apparel, and so on. If not freely available through importation, these items may appear through black markets as in Syria or Morocco.

Table 18.3 presents three examples of new-rich segments across the region. These groups are made up of "guest workers," wealthy local entrepreneurs and professionals, and expatriate managers and experts. Although relatively small, these new-rich segments deserve attention by global marketers on account of their strong buying power, interest in modern consumer goods, and familiarity with mass media communications and modern retailing methods.

The Poor

Throughout North Africa and the Middle East a number of inescapable dualisms exists: the gap between the wealthy and the poor; the gap between urban and rural life; and the gap between the traditional way of life and modern expectations. The social and personal problems created by poverty are widely recognized. They affect health, personal capacities, abilities and skills, motivation, personality, and status achievement.

In many countries rapid population growth is a serious concern for governments, whether it is caused by natural demographic expansion as in Egypt or the inflow of migrant workers as in Saudi Arabia and Libya. Demographic growth results in large numbers of young people coming onto the job market each year, mostly illiterate and untrained, creating enormous problems of both unemployment and under-employment. This factor together with the phenomenon of rural exodus leads to overcrowding in major cities such as Cairo, Istanbul, Baghdad, and Casablanca, putting serious strain on housing, transportation, and utility services.

Young people come to urban centers with expectations of better employment, health care services, educational opportunities, and a better standard of living. When these expectations are not met, frustrations sometimes turn into violence. Surrounding the cities of Istanbul and Ankara, for example, are slum neighborhoods. Primitive shacks, or *gecekondular* (literally "put together overnight"), provide living quarters for tens of thousands of rural migrants.

In contrast, Saudi Arabia is experiencing pressures from the immense numbers of foreign workers who are a necessary part of national growth objectives: 200,000 Syrians and Lebanese, 800,000 Yemenis, 400,000 Filipinos, 250,000 Koreans, 200,000 Pakistanis, 150,000 Indians, and almost 100,000 Thais. The complexity of the problems caused by the presence of these "petro bodies" impinges not only on market behavior but also on culture and politics.

The Young and Modern

Young people, whatever their nationality, are often attracted to new ideas and fashions. The clothes seen in the main streets of big cities such as Casablanca, Tunis, Istanbul, or Cairo make Paris feel much closer than it is in reality. As disposable income increases, access to foreign travel is achieved and local consumers returning home take over the role of opinion leadership that was previously played by Western media. Also, increasing tourist travel by people within the region serves to diffuse new consumption styles. Thus new fashions become local norms rather than being tagged as Western or foreign. We should remember, however, that novelty for young people does not always mean "new" but may mean a rediscovery of the "traditional" as in the case of the Iranian social and political revolution with its return to a strict dress code and rejection of Western values.

Religion not only affects attitudes toward fashion and styles of consumption, but also determines codes of social behavior, particularly for women. Among the Christian and Jewish groups scattered throughout the region, women's lifestyles and opportunities are similar to those in Western nations. Even in those countries in the Gulf where Islamic principles are most strictly observed, change is accelerating due to the enormous presence of expatriates and foreign workers. It is important to recognize here the power of the family, and particularly the father or senior male, in setting the style and tone of behavior for all members of the family.

In conclusion, it appears that the concept of global homogeneity finds a strong application in this context. Globalized or standardized marketing methods could very feasibly be applied within these clusters. The marketing approach and type of offering must be tailored to the individual segments which vary in terms of size, purchasing power, type of demand, and buying behavior.

Analysis of Urban Lifestyles: Transnational Clusters

Urban clusters may be geographically scattered since in many instances only one, two, or three cities per country may be deemed worthwhile market targets in terms of size of potential demand. Yet the concentration of population, relative ease of distribution within the urban centers, and availability of mass media would all compensate for these additional costs of penetrating and supplying several countries. Also relative homogeneity of demand and urban value systems would allow considerable standardization of products, services, advertising imagery, and selling propositions.

Urban households across North Africa and the Middle East demonstrate a striking similarity in consumption patterns and standard of living. This growing homogeneity can be attributed to several factors such as national trade liberalization programs, increased interregional mobility, exposure to mass media, and growing middle-class segments.

Trade Liberalization

For a variety of reasons a number of countries are opening up to international marketers. As countries move from isolationism to an open market system, this usually means exposure to new technology, new products and services, and the creation of new preferences and habits among consumers.

Interregional Mobility

An unprecendented mobility of people across nations in the region has contributed to the "unification" of urban populations. Significantly higher numbers of people have been taking advantage of work or travel opportunities outside their national borders. For example, large contingents of Egyptian teachers work in Saudi Arabia, Turkish workers are employed in Libya, Turkish contractors operate in Kuwait, and Kuwaiti real estate investors are active in Morocco.

Exposure to Mass Media

A third development is the greater exposure of the urban consumer to modern consumption patterns through (1) reception of television broadcasting from neighboring countries, (2) movies brought in from Western nations and played on videotape recorders, and (3) cross-national circulation of media. City life for many people means exposure to advertising. Billboards, radio, television, and newspapers transmit marketing messages which encourage consumption and result in changed personal value system.

Two types of media are used to target consumers in the region: local media (including national and subnational media) and pan-Arab media (including regional editions of worldwide publications). Each nation

TABLE 18.4. A Sample of Local and International Publications in Selected Countries[a]

Local Publications:		
Saudi Arabia	**Kuwait**	**Egypt**
Asharq Al Awsat (A, Daily)	*Al Rai Al Aam* (A, Daily)	*Al Ahram* (A, Daily)
Okaz (A, Daily)	*Al Seyassah* (A, Daily)	*Al Akhbar* (A, Daily)
Arab News (E, Daily)	*Al Anba* (A, Daily)	*October* (A, Weekly)
Saudi Gazette (E, Daily)	*Al Qabas* (A, Daily)	*Akher Saa* (A, Weekly)
Al Majalla (A, Weekly)	*Al Nahda* (A, Weekly)	
Lebanon	**Turkey**	**Morocco**
Al Nahar (A, Daily)	*Milliyet* (T, Daily)	*Le Matin du Sahara* (F, Daily)
	Hurriyet (T, Daily)	*L'Opinion* (F, Daily)
	Cumhuriyet (T, Daily)	*Maroc Soir* (F, Daily)
	Yanki (T, Weekly)	*Al Alam* (A, Daily)
	Nokta (T, Weekly)	*Al Moharrir* (A, Daily)
		Al Mithaq Al Watanai (A, Daily)
Pan-Arab Publications:		
Arabic-Language	**English-Language**	**French-Language**
Al Hawadess	*Middle East Economic Digest*	*L'Express*
Al Mostakbal	*Time* (Middle East)	*Le Point*
Al Watan Al Arabi	*Newsweek* (Middle East)	*Le Nouvel Observateur*
Alam Attijarat	*The Middle East*	*Jeune-Afrique*
Al Mukhtar	*Middle East Travel*	*Paris-Match*

Note: [a]A = Arabic; E = English; F = French; T = Turkish.

has its own particular mix of Arabic and English or French language domestic press, outdoor, radio, and television media. Table 18.4 illustrates the range of local and pan-Arab publications for selected countries.

Standards for advertising creativity vary. On a hypothetical scale of increasing difficulty of acceptance of "Westernized" commercial imagery, one would probably classify Lebanon and Jordan as the easiest countries for which to create commercials. At the other extreme would be Qatar and Kuwait, regarded as the strictest in the region. A form of neutral Arabic has evolved for advertising in most Muslim countries, thus avoiding the intricacies of dubbing many local dialects for each campaign.

All these considerations suggest the need for some localization of promotional strategies within the overall urban clustering strategy. Thus a marketing company which selects urban centers within the "crossover societies" cluster as its market target should seriously consider using local ad agencies to prepare soundtracks appropriate for each country. Flexibility can be built into international promotional strategies by using the "pattern" approach in place of the more restrictive "prototype" approach (see Peebles, Ryans, and Vernon 1978 for a full discussion of these options).

Growth of Middle-Class Segments

Growth of a visible middle class possessing the material symbols of personal success is a characteristic feature of society in Turkey, Lebanon, Egypt, Tunisia, and Morocco. In a wealthy oil-exporting nation such as Kuwait, many young people benefit from education abroad where they experience first-hand the comforts and convenience which modern marketing can provide. Several aspects of urban life contribute to the individual's feeling of emancipation from the traditional lifestyle. For example, middle-class urban households have access to supermarkets in Kuwait, Qatar, Bahrain, and Saudi Arabia; free medical, educational, and social services in Kuwait; and important luxury items such as German automobiles, French furniture, and Italian ceramics at low levels of customs duties in the Gulf countries. In other countries, such imports are prohibited to prevent unnecessary currency outflows. However, consumer demand remains strong there, offering potential opportunities for local production by foreign companies in place of importing finished goods.

These developments have contributed to the emergence of a fairly homogeneous urban population across North Africa and the Middle East. The success of global companies like Sony, Hewlett-Packard, Nissan, Honda, and Toyota is largely due to their ability to identify this substantial market segment and to effectively serve it—with varied but not entirely different marketing programs. Much can be made of cultural differences; however, these differences may represent an over-statement when it comes to comparing urban populations in the region or they may simply be irrelevant to a particular company's marketing efforts.

Consumer Behavior and Retail Trade Analysis: Two "Shopping" Clusters

Here, we identify two major consumer "shopping" clusters: the traditional retail sector and the modern retail sector. International marketing companies should consider carefully the long-term implications of choosing one sector over the other. The modern sector is centered in the capital city and has jet airports, international hotels, new factories, and a small Westernized middle class. Although the traditional sector is only miles away geographically, it is centuries away in terms of producing and consuming. Marketing to consumers in the modern sector may be little different from marketing to middle-class urban households in other world markets. Targeting consumers in the traditional sector, in contrast, may require considerable product modification or simplification and extensive rethinking of promotional policies. Once these changes have been made, traditional market segments in other regions of the world may possibly also be served at little incremental cost. We will first discuss aspects of the traditional sector from both the seller and the buyer points of view and second discuss examples of retail innovation in the modern sector.

Aspects of the Traditional Retail Sector

In many instances, demand for consumer goods far exceeds supply. Local producers very often escape the constraints of quality control, customer service, and even advertising, content in their knowledge that the consumer may have no other choice. This is especially the case in Tunisia, Egypt, Iran, Morocco, and Turkey, where naissant local industries have traditionally been protected from foreign competition through import controls. In such cases concern for "marketing", as opposed to plain selling, and for social issues such as pollution control, recycling of waste materials, employees' health and protection, and consumerism are considered totally irrelevant to everyday business life. Producers and sellers often constitute strong pressure groups, having an unfair advantage over consumers and adding to the many other causes of consumer dissatisfaction. In Egypt and Turkey government regulations, scattered markets, and poor transportation facilities have limited the growth of national wholesalers. By contrast, in Iran religion, politics and economics function as a triumvirate perpetuating the strength of wholesalers or *bazaris*. Two other factors, nepotism and regional/clan affiliations, reinforce the power of this group.

In Morocco the Berbers, an ethnic subgroup from the area around the Atlas Mountains (Soussi), control the retail food sector. These people are efficient tradespeople but their social status is much lower than that of the people of Fez who dominate the wholesale textile sector. The Berbers use their own language as a barrier against would-be newcomers to the sector. In Saudi Arabia an identical role is played by the Yemenis with much of the retail trade coming under their control.

In a marketplace where product choice is limited, companies which entered the market first enjoy a special competitive advantage. In many instances, the brand name becomes assimilated with the generic product itself, particularly when no equivalent word for the product exists in the local language. Examples include Tide (laundry detergent), Dannon (yogurt), Palmolive (dishwashing liquid), Parker and Bic (pens), Kleenex (facial tissue), Frigidaire (refrigerators), and Singer (sewing machines). This habit tends to reinforce brand loyalty even when alternative products come onto the market, since all products are referred to by the name of the original market leader or a composite is created. Thus it is not unusual to hear a consumer ask for a "box of Tide-Ariel" in Morocco.

Haggling or bargaining over prices is a common behavioral pattern. Food products are purchased on a daily basis often during two or three shopping trips per day. Items are bought in small quantities for consumption the same day, not so much due to the danger of spoilage from lack of refrigeration but more importantly for the pleasure and prestige of eating "fresh" food. Indeed it is widely considered an insult to offer guests bread with a meal that has not been bought or baked specially for the occasion.

Grocery stores are small, crammed to capacity with merchandise, and act as focal points for a neighborhood. The use of credit and home delivery service are positive factors in promoting store loyalty in a situation where competing stores may be found on the corner of each block. Negative factors, such as the perceived risk of making a "poor deal" with an unfamiliar retailer and the actual risk of being sold adulterated food, tend to reinforce store loyalty and the value of the "they know me" factor. In the absence of branding, labeling, quality control, and close government regulation of food purity, the shopper cannot buy "off-the-shelf" with the minimal attention typical of supermarket shopping in developed countries. Instead the shopper must rely much more on his or her buying skill.

Shopping behavior follows a complex pattern, with basic purchases of produce, meat, and grocery items being spread over several types of outlets such as corner shops, specialty stores, public markets, and itinerant street peddlers. A middle-class family in Morocco, for example, would typically buy simple toiletries and household products from a tiny neighborhood grocery store, baked goods from a specialized confectionery store, meat and vegetables from the open market, and occasional items such as honey, eggs, and figs from peddlers.

Innovation in the Modern Retail Sector

All these behavioral features of consumer grocery shopping act as a brake on the evolution of retail food marketing. Self-service stores, supermarkets, department stores, and vertical integration require much greater organizational, merchandising, and commercial skills than are the norm in this region. Also much greater investment is required to cover technical services such as refrigeration, inventory control, packaging, price marketing, merchandising, and display. In many cases the supermarket appears out of step with life in this region since it reduces employment possibilities in the retail sector, precludes haggling, limits produce choice, and does not offer the same opportunity for social interaction. Furthermore the basic advantage of supermarket shopping, buying in volume at cheaper prices, is linked to the need for some sort of transportation, either to carry purchases home or simply to reach the new stores. These are often located on the periphery of major cities due to lack of available space or high rents downtown.

Supermarket shopping in Turkey and Israel appeals to the more modern segments of the population. However, these shoppers share a feeling of dissatisfaction regarding product choice, freshness, and price. In Saudi Arabia many of these problems have been solved. Supermarkets practice item addition rather than item substitution. To allow the Saudi customer to inspect, sniff and squeeze the merchandise, vegetables are sold unpacked. Labels list ingredients and directions in Arabic and perishables must be fixed with Arabic expiration dates. Government-set ceilings exist on the prices of many basic food products, so price competition is not a major promotional device. Shopping hours are liberal and accommodate public prayer hours.

Although the original target audience in Saudi Arabia was expatriates, middle-class Saudis have quickly adopted the supermarket innovation. The success or failure of supermarkets here will depend on building loyalty among local people, rather than expatriates who eventually leave and return home. In Kuwait, cooperative supermarkets are flourishing. These *gamiaat* sell both wholesale and retail, and their merchandise offerings reflect the socioeconomic character of the district in which they are located.

Other concepts in the modernization of retailing such as the department store and vertical marketing systems have not made any significant progress in the Middle East and North Africa, probably because inefficiency results in higher rather than lower prices to the consumer. Shopping behavior in North Africa and the Middle East is changing and evolving often in unpredictable ways as witnessed by the success of self-service gas stations and shopping malls in Saudi Arabia.

Conclusion: Assessment of Clustering Applications and Change Factors

In conclusion, we draw attention to three issues which further validate the clustering methods developed here. These issues include first, the growing trend toward globalization throughout world markets; second, sources of change and new influence which may require changes in the clusters which we have established; and third, the marketing opportunities which exist in the region.

Trends Toward Globalization in World Markets

The four clustering approaches to market homogenization are not necessarily restricted to the Middle East and North Africa. A number of worldwide trends are combining to create a "global market".

First, products and their associated technologies are becoming increasingly more standardized. The best examples here are microcomputers, tractors, autos, soft drinks, and even some foods such as pizza, ice-cream, and chocolate.

Second, more and more companies are striving to improve the cost-effectiveness of their business methods through economies of scale in product design, manufacturing, and marketing.

A third relevant factor is the existence of a worldwide network of financial systems which facilitate a global approach to marketing. The relatively stable international monetary system along with instantaneous telecommunications and computerized data-processing systems combine to assist companies in achieving consistent international pricing policies and stable credit and payment arrangements.

Fourth, it is being increasingly recognized that, while certain adaptations to local tastes are sometimes necessary, standardized advertising approaches that are applied persistently are often very effective. Finally, the sheer pressure of competition is forcing companies toward global strategies. A global strategy involves concentration on certain unaltered product lines which are competitively priced, widely distributed, and strongly promoted. This winning combination is currently allowing many companies to excel in a variety of different and far-flung markets.

Sources of Change and New Influence

Our analysis has highlighted commonalities as well as diverse trends and disparities within North Africa and the Middle East. At some time in the future, changes may come about which are sufficiently important to require a reassessment of the clusters which we have established. This is not a detriment. On the contrary, our methodolgy is flexible and broadly based and easily accommodates a reformulation of new clusters.

At least four sources of change can be identified: new local entrepreneurs, national governments, multinational corporations (MNCs), and inter-Arab relations. Each is expected to affect the marketing environment to varying degrees.

1. Local entrepreneurs tend to perpetuate the status quo through decision making based on authoritarianism, traditional nepotism, and the "clan mentality". Innovative retailing entrepreneurs in the developing economies have been generally rare. However, the creation of "new" entrepreneurs may bring about some degree of innovation, as for example in Saudi Arabia where each graduate from vocational training schools is entitled to a government loan for starting his own business. Also the generation of foreign university-trained business graduates returning home to the region will serve as a conduit for innovation and change.

2. Many national governments are characterized by their heavy involvement in market regulation mainly through price and import controls. Unpredictable or unexpected policy revisions may change marketing conditions and opportunities drastically. Unforeseeable changes in market regulation may also come about as a result of abrupt changes in political regime. Such changes affect not only the internal market environment but also disrupt the multimarket activities of multinational corporations.

3. MNCs influence national market environments not only through their financial power and role as large employers, but also through the diffusion of new technologies, new product and service concepts, and new lifestyle images transmitted by global advertising. While governments and the people may resent this invasion of accepted cultural values, many are drawn to accept the fruits of high technology such as hydroponics in Kuwait, solar energy experiments in Morocco, and closed circuit television in Saudi universities.

4. Inter-Arab market relations are flourishing. The vast revenues and limited absorptive capacities of Saudi Arabia, Kuwait, Abu Dhabi, and Qatar give rise to investments in other developing and particularly Arab nations. Kuwaiti investments in Morocco take the form of real estate developments, hotel, and restaurants. Other types of inter-Arab relations include provision of TV soap operas and cultural programs to Morocco by Lebanon and Egypt, exports of citrus fruits from Tunisia to the Gulf states, and the growing tourist trade in Turkey and the Gulf.

Marketing Opportunities

A variety of opportunities exists for companies wishing either to export or to establish a more permanent market presence in North Africa and the Middle East. In analyzing market growth potential, it is necessary to consider the individual character of each nation-state and not merely assume that because various peoples speak Arabic, they all desire similar products and services or even have comparable purchasing power. Yet based on the commonalities other than language identified here, global marketers can develop a meaningful perspective of market potentials. Looking into the future, it is evident that effective environmental analysis and a full understanding of consumer attitudes and behavior in individual countries, country clusters, and the entire region will determine whether foreign marketing companies succeed or fail in meeting the needs of the many growth markets.

References

Almaney, Adnan J., "Cultural Traits of the Arabs," *Management International Review*, Vol. 21, No. 3 (1981), pp. 10–18.

Eilts, Hermann F., "Islamic Resurgence and American Business in the Middle East," in *The International Essays for Business Decision Makers*, VI, Mark B. Winchester (ed.), (Dallas: The Center for International Business, 1982), pp. 241–252.

Peebles, D. M., J. K. Ryans and I. R. Vernon, "Coordinating International Advertising," *Journal of Marketing*, Vol. 11 (1978), pp. 28–34.

19

What can Third World Countries Learn from China?*

HANS B. THORELLI

Ed. Note: The 1989–90 political turmoil in China highlights the interdependence of economics and politics. As autocratic regimes permit—or encourage—aspiration levels in one area to increase (in the P.R.C. economics, in the U.S.S.R. politics) citizens' expectations sooner or later will turn to the other area. When this occurs, governments may react either by repression or further liberalization, as history amply demonstrates. At present no one knows the future of China's economic experiments. This paper, published in 1987, is included here on the optimistic assumption that these reforms will continue and, indeed, be expanded. Meanwhile, it must be admitted that other forecasts are a good deal more pessimistic, particularly in the areas of foreign direct investments (F.D.I.) and joint ventures (J.V.s), predicting that growth in economic intercourse will be confined largely to trade and licensing. Even if the optimistic view is mistaken, it seems that other East Block and Third World countries have a lot to learn from the Chinese experience.

Introduction

The socioeconomic experimentation in the People's Republic of China (P.R.C.) in the last eight years is extraordinarily significant in many respects. It takes place in the most populous country in the world, accounting for some 25% of humanity. It is best interpreted as a unique attempt at combining socialism and liberalism. Returns thus far suggest that the experiments are highly successful in agriculture, at least moderately so in the distribution and service sectors, and promis-

---

*Slightly adapted from *Journal of Global Marketing*, Vol. 1 (Fall/Winter 1987), pp. 69–83.

ing in industry, especially with regard to consumer goods. All this is significant at a time when the classic development gospel practiced in a majority of Third World countries for at least 30 years is manifestly bankrupt. There is a tremendous need for new ideas and new approaches, such as those demonstrated in Japan, Taiwan, South Korea and Singapore in recent years and now, on an almost mind-boggling scale, in the P.R.C.

This article attempts briefly to summarize major implications of the P.R.C. experiments for developing countries (D.C.) interested in learning from them. It is divided into three sections, dealing with accelerating and governing forces, cautions and constraints, and the transferability of the Chinese experience into different settings.

Accelerators and Governors

1. *Motivation is the key for us all as producers and consumers:* Man can be induced to contribute to a joint effort such as socio-economic development in various ways. One is by brute force; the Cultural revolution in the 1966–76 period in the P.R.C. amply demonstrated the shortcomings of this technique. One can also be motivated by social, patriotic, religious, and altruistic appeals, which may be labeled "moral incentives". However, as observed by Xue Muquiao (1981)—famous economist and a guiding spirit in the P.R.C. experiments—"it is essential to provide the working people material as well as moral incentives." There are also sources of personal satisfaction in addition to moral and material ones, such as love and camaraderie, acclaim, power and a certain style of life.

The "mix" of motivating factors emphasized varies considerably between societies. One way of looking at the problem of motivation is from an individual point of view. Among the roles that we all play the two most important are probably those of producer and consumer. Worker or manager, man as producer wants the joy of a good job, companionship, and a pleasant work environment. But a vital part of job satisfaction is material compensation, what one may call *money for value*, the value added to the product by the individual's contribution. While ostensibly taken into account in Marxist theory of labor value, this notion is clearly in contrast with that chronic socialist dogma, "from each according to his ability; to each according to his need." This thesis was incorporated in early P.R.C. constitutions. Of critical importance to the understanding of the recent reforms is that the 1982 constitution of P.R.C. made a dramatic change in the last half of the dictum which now reads, "to each according to his *work*" (emphasis supplied). In the other role we want consumer satisfaction, based on free choice and *value for money*. Here again, a dramatic change in philosophy has taken place. Like other D.C., the P.R.C. before 1978 placed the consumer at the low end of national priorities. If not at the center of the stage, he is now pretty close to it, as will become clearer below. The rationale for this transformation is simple. The present leadership in China realizes that to be motivated as producers, most citizens must also be motivated as consumers.

2. *Open market sector stimulates competition and buyer's markets*: Total planning is typically associated with seller's markets. When a consumer product is in surplus it is generally of a less desirable variety. To move in the direction of the freedom of choice and value for money associated with buyer's markets, China has found it necessary to create a sizeable open market sector. The key characteristics of open markets are decentralized initiative and competition.

3. *Marketing is indispensable as stimulant and allocator*: Classic socialism looks at marketing with a jaundiced eye, seeing a tool of monopolist manipulation and bourgeois profiteering. Socialist doctrine stresses the physical "circulation" of goods produced at the behest of planners and managers presumably knowing better than consumers themselves what is good for them. By contrast, modern China has embraced marketing with considerable enthusiasm, realizing that it plays a dual and important role. In effect, marketing implements the division of labor and specialization without which progress is impossible (Thorelli 1983). It does this by effecting transactions between buyers and sellers. In a competitive context marketing also affects the *future* division of labor as sellers giving better value are rewarded by greater sales.

Of perhaps even greater importance is marketing's role as a stimulant providing freedom of choice and value for money. It is essential to understand that marketing as a motivating force goes far beyond plain materialism. We buy books not for the paper, but for the thoughts. One buys a radio not for a kilo of electronics, but for the music, news, plays,—yes, sometimes even for the advertisements it may bring. Food is bought and consumed not just to fill the stomach, but for the enjoyment of its taste, of local and foreign cultures, and of social life as we break bread together. And the Chinese buys a bicycle not just for transport, but because it sets him free to enjoy nature, see new things, and yes, often to enjoy a degree of privacy difficult to obtain on public buses. In other words, P.R.C. leaders have seen that marketing is indispensable not just to the accumulation of physical goods, but also to deliver individual styles of life in the middle of the mass production society around us.

4. *Public ownership, private property, and diversity in management*: The means of production as well as land are still in public or collective ownership to over 90%, and this may well obtain by 1990 as well.

However, in agriculture, trade and services, and, to a smaller extent, in industry, productive organizations are now run by a diversity of manager types: individual and household entrepreneurs, partnerships, occasional stockholder-owned companies, cooperatives, collectives and municipal, provincial or state government operations. In many markets these various forms of management are competing with each other. Especially interesting is the kind of hybrid enterprise for which the state auctions off the managerial and profit-sharing rights to the highest private bidder or group of bidders, who in effect run the firm on good behavior.

With rising standards of living there is a vast increase in durable consumer goods, including housing in some cases, and in private property in general. The state has encouraged this development, and recently rights of inheritance have been strengthened.

5. *Agriculture comes first*: An outstanding characteristic of the Chinese reforms is the absolute priority given to agriculture in terms of both timing and effort. The essence of agricultural reform was the transformation of this huge sector from status to contract, or what is officially called the *responsibility system*. Under the new dispensation, individuals, households, groups of families, production teams and brigades may contract with collectives, state enterprises and other agencies for a certain minimum output, often more modest than previous quotas. Typically they have considerable freedom in specifying what they want to grow, husband, or produce. They are obliged to turn over their minimum output to the state at fixed prices as before, to pay state taxes, and to contribute to the collective's welfare fund. The contract may also provide for charges for the use of any collective services or means of production. Sizeable increases in the minimum prices paid by the state for farm products have provided a strong practical incentive.

More recent is the emergence of a more modest number of so-called self-managing households, which may own some or all of their means of production short of whatever land they may till. Interestingly, members of some of these contractual units are free to invest money in them in addition to time, occasionally even in lieu of time. We should add that the agricultural reform recognized and included in the contract system "sideline occupations", such as fish-farming and brick-making, and more distantly related activity such as furniture and textile manufacturing or assembly work for urban firms. Designed to increase productivity and retain otherwise surplus labor in rural areas, these side-line occupations now employ an estimated 15% of rural labor.

Crucially significant are the rules governing and disposal of any farm surplus output beyond the agreed minimum. The contractor has three main options: to sell it to the state at a price usually higher than that set for the minimum output, to use it for home consumption (a popular means of providing previously unseen variety in diet), or to sell it in a nearby farmers' market. There are now well over 40,000 markets. As long as prices do not get out of hand they may be set freely. The markets are very popular, and are putting pressure on state food stores to become more customer-oriented.

Clearly, it took stamina to carry out an agricultural reform of these dimensions, albeit that three-fourths of the Chinese population earns its living in agriculture and its sidelines. Although a policy of placing agriculture first is certainly called for in the majority of the Third World it will take even more political courage to launch there. Governments in these countries typically have made themselves dependent on the metropolitan population for support, perpetrating various policies of price control at the farm level and food price subsidies in the metropolitan area. Nevertheless, as food is a crucial concern in the Third World, agriculture *is* the logical place for new approaches to development. From an incentive point of view, farming also has the merit that the relationship between individual effort and output tends to be much more direct than in industry.

6. *Industry: consumer goods, decentralization, incentives*: To ensure that consumer demands are accommodated better, there has been a significant and determined shift in priorities from heavy to light industries. This again is clearly contrary to Soviet-type doctrine as well as the prevailing development orthodoxy. Of even greater potential importance is the application of responsibility system philosophy in ever-larger segments of industry. Thus, "guidance planning" is being substituted for total planning in one branch of industry after the other with the aim that "mandatory planning" ultimately will be confined to defense and a handful of other critical industries.

In many industries obligatory quotas have been abolished altogether, and in others they have been reduced, all in favor of more open markets and decentralized decision-making and entrepreneurship. In return for the self-management and marketing challenges thrown at them, firms have been given a new package of incentives. Earnings after taxes and interest (the cost of money now being explicitly recognized) are at the disposal of the enterprise, subject to overall guidelines which may vary from firm to firm. Typically, minimum shares of after-tax earnings are reserved for the welfare fund of the firm and for "capital accumulation", that is, reinvestment. The remainder is available for bonuses, where a major part is expected to be awarded on an individual basis. In principle, firms are expected to make a profit; managers unable to do so are at risk.

7. *Pricing system driven by cost and market demand*: It is difficult to

imagine an open market sector in which prices are not allowed to move freely. The official view is that China is a country of "socialist planning with supplementary regulation by the market". In many areas, however, China's pricing system is still artificial from the point of view of production costs and/or world market prices. For example, the provision of adequate housing is an enormous challenge, and the government would like to enlist individual entrepreneurs in the effort. Yet it is difficult to attract private initiative in urban areas where for decades rents have been set at levels which have nothing to do with the cost of construction. In rural areas, where pricing is much freer and many farmers personally participate in the building of their houses, residential construction is booming.

Prices have been decontrolled fully or partially in a great number of markets, and the policy is to continue this effort. Yet the fear of inflation and other political sensitivities apply definite brakes on the pace of pricing reform.

8. *Separate government and business—whether business is public or private*: As part of the policy of decentralizing economic activity, the P.R.C. is making a determined effort to separate provincial and municipal government functions from those of business—regardless of type of enterprise management. Especially interesting in this respect is the abolishment of the commune system in favor of local government institutions more similar to those of Western countries. It is proving a bit more difficult to reduce the engagement of urban municipalities in their own businesses or in the activities of "independent" firms within their jurisdictions.

9. *Open door (at least ajar), recognize multinational companies:* The P.R.C. has recognized the value of technology transfer by multinational corporations (M.N.C.), somewhat contrary to socialist nationalism and traditional misgivings about foreign influence. Trade volume has multiplied in recent years, economic zones have been created, well over a thousand joint ventures have been formed, numerous Chinese enterprises are subcontractors to Western firms, and in some instances, M.N.C.s have been granted the privilege of establishing wholly-owned subsidiaries in the P.R.C. China recently applied for membership in G.A.T.T., the very symbol of liberal, international trade philosophy.

To be sure, M.N.C.s would like to see the P.R.C. move a great deal further in opening up her markets and accepting greater managerial discretion from joint ventures and M.N.C. subsidiaries. Her tight restrictions on consumer goods imports are also somewhat contradictory to the notion of freeing up consumer markets for incentive reasons. Nevertheless, the P.R.C. is fast becoming a major international trader.

10. *Balanced development*: In effect, the P.R.C. seems to be pursuing a policy of balanced development. In important respects this policy has been made explicit, as in the case of these dimensions:

light (consumer goods) and heavy (producer goods) industries
rural and urban sectors
short and long term
socialist planning and regulation by the market
buyers and sellers
M.N.C. and host country relations
the role of self-interest and social responsibility in motivation

Not everyone will sympathize with what seems to be the Chinese concept of balance. Too, balance in one dimension may occasionally be obtainable only by sacrificing it in another, and, of course, like life itself, the balance keeps changing. It does, however, appear that in China balanced development is becoming a political philosophy rather than merely the exercising of pragmatic opportunism.

Cautions and Constraints

1. *Inflation and foreign exchange problems*: Any period of rapid development brings in its wake inflationary pressures. This is especially true in a society where prices have long been regimented and in critical markets that have been based on sociopolitical rather than economic considerations. In the sellers' market characteristic of East Block and Third World nations there is also a great amount of pent-up demand and a fair amount of "forced savings" due to the lack of goods and/or choice. As markets open expectations increase faster than the supply of goods. Thus, inflation seems to be an intrinsic phase in the transition from total planning (or other sellers'-market economies) to a greater reliance on open markets. While inflation in the P.R.C. was relatively modest in the first eight years it reached 15–20 + % in the 1987–90 period.

Inflation is a major source of foreign exchange problems. Always interested in technology transfer from industrialized nations (not to speak of consumer goods imports, when allowed), China like other L.D.C. suffers from a chronic actual or, at least, perceived hard currency shortage. Thus, there are strong restrictions on conversion of the yuan, and export of the currency is prohibited. Even so, inflation has generated a series of currency devaluations. Import controls greatly favor technology transfer and productive equipment, discriminating against consumer goods. There is perhaps an undue emphasis on import substitution and export is an obsession—which helps explain why joint ventures are typically obliged to export most of their output.

2. *Inequality in earnings*: The responsibility system and incentive and skills-based compensation systems will inevitably result in an uneven distribution of incomes and, in short order, in property. Chinese leaders have stated that their ambition is for all to get rich, but that for this goal to be met some will necessarily be richer sooner than others. This is indeed contrary to the classic socialist view that poverty is acceptable, as long as it is shared by all! It is natural that after 30 years of innumerable campaigns on the merit of income levelling there are quite a few letters to the editors of China dailies questioning the new philosophy. Meantime, there seems to be no doubt that the new philosophy is holding sway in the country.

Essential social welfare measures for those not able to earn a living wage in this philosophy will be taken by welfare funds of enterprises, by taxation, and by socially responsible individuals (the mutual obligations of family members and good neighbors, for example, are heavily stressed).

3. *Unemployment*: The problem of unemployment is typically associated with capitalist economies. Hidden unemployment is, however, also present in socialist countries. Interestingly, in China hundreds of thousands of city youths "waiting for assignment" have found opportunities for entrepreneurial profit or employment in the burgeoning open market establishments in retail trade and service, previously grossly underdimensioned in the country. The sideline occupations in rural areas have been another important means of avoiding potential unemployment problems. It is not yet clear, however, how China would resolve any structural unemployment problem which may emerge in the future. An inkling of problems yet to be faced was the failure of the Shenyang Explosion-Proof Equipment Factory in August, 1986, the first official bankruptcy in the P.R.C. It is not clear how this and other employment-threatening incidents will be handled in the future. Obviously, unemployment entails special hardship in a country still lacking a modern social security system.

4. *Establishment resistance*: Naturally, China's reforms have met with some resistance from various vested interests, including Maoist hardliners who have seen central and local government powers over the economy being drastically reduced. Vestiges of this resistance are still present. But then, of course, resistance to change is present in all human societies and organizations.

5. *Bribery*: Bribery is also present to varying degrees in all societies. The opportunities for corrupt behavior seem especially prevalent in countries where government and business are closely intertwined. This is still true in the P.R.C., and a number of local and provincial bribery scandals have been reported in the *Beijing Review*. As any other D.C., however, China can ill afford the luxury of bribery, whose

chief characteristic is that it removes the cause-effect relationship between honest effort and results. Constant vigilance is necessary.

6. *Public enterprise to compete on equal terms*: It is exceedingly important that competition between enterprises in the managed and open sectors be conducted *on an equal basis*, notwithstanding the difficulties in maintaining such a state of affairs. If favors are given managed-sector enterprise in the form of location, taxes, governmental purchases, import permits, etc., there is absolutely no way of evaluating the relative contribution of firms in the two sectors. Indeed, the giving of such privileges to public enterprises will merely foster empire building in the managed sector at the cost of flexibility and economic progress.

There are some signs that the significance of this elementary principle is not yet fully appreciated in the P.R.C.

7. *Consumer emancipation*: In most D.C. the consumer is the forgotten man, and consumer rights are typically not enforced, if indeed even recognized. "Let the buyer beware" is the rule in the seller's markets characteristic of these countries. Elsewhere we have developed a program of consumer protection, education, and information policy to enforce consumer rights (Thorelli 1981, 1986). Consumer emancipation is needed not only because consumer rights are elementary *human* rights. Such emancipation is also a *necessary* (if not sufficient) prerequisite for the private sector to work like an open market. Open markets can function only when there is some semblance of equality of status between buyers and sellers.

The P.R.C. has already begun a modest program of formalizing consumer rights. In addition, it is interesting to observe that Chinese middle class consumers apparently have a clearer view of what consumers rights should be than do their counterparts in Thailand (Thorelli 1982).

8. *Nip cartelization and ossification in the bud*: The ultimate rationale for open markets is that they leave ample room for competition—without sacrificing constructive cooperation. Thus freedom of entry (and exit) is important. So is vigilance in counteracting undesirable restraints on competition, such as price cartels, output restricting, or market-sharing agreements. Ubiquitous in many D.C. based on "cryptocapitalism", at least a few such far-reaching attempts at eliminating competition have reared their ugly heads in the P.R.C. Such attempts at tampering with the open market should be quenched at their inception, whether perpetrated by firms in the public or private sectors (or both).

9. *Proceed gradually, but do not lose systems view*: To attain balanced development it is imperative to keep the entire socio-economic system constantly in mind. Yet the P.R.C. experience teaches us that it is

impossible to undertake all reforms at once. Agriculture was given top priority, industry followed and only very recently do we see a transformation in the pricing area. Still, it is true that the overall system has what the Germans would call *Gestalt*, meaning that partial reforms undertaken without regard for the total system may lead to suboptimization and counterproductive inconsistencies.

10. *Interaction of economic freedom with political*: It is our observation that consumer aspiration levels tend to grow (even exponentially) with degrees of economic development. This process may well increase the pressure for economic freedom and open markets, as will freer entry into markets and professions. (The process of freeing up the *labor* market has only really begun in the P.R.C.) If von Hayek was right in his proposition that there is a connection between political and economic freedom, we should expect to find increasing economic freedom to be accompanied by some degree of pressure for greater political freedom. Indeed, it may be that fear of such a connection is what ultimately ended the so-called Liberman experiments in the U.S.S.R. during the 1960s (Thorelli 1965).

Political leaders and development planners are wise to take into account the potential interaction of economic and political freedom. Certainly, for instance, a going back on economic freedoms to which people have become acculturated may be fraught with political danger.

Transferability and the Ecology of Development

Deng Xiao Ping states that China aims to "build socialism with Chinese characteristics". In other words, the P.R.C. wants to adapt socialist ideology to the environment and culture of China, rather than forcing the country to conform to orthodox (notably, Soviet-type) ideology.

Several Marxist-Leninist dogmas have been—or are being—abandoned or modified in the process of transformation from Maoism-Stalinism to Market Socialism:

1. "From each according to his ability, to each according to his need." A revolution in thinking was reflected in the substitution of "work" for "need" in the Constitution of the P.R.C.
2. "State or collective ownership of all means of production." This doctrine is the one *least* affected by the developments discussed here. Nevertheless, many small-scale vendors and craftsmen as well as family-size firms are permitted to own their own equipment. Too, many a farmer can now freely buy his own tractor and agricultural implements. A tiny percentage of productive enterprises are based on share ownership. Nevertheless, state or collective ownership over 90% of the value of all means of production as

well as land is the key socialist element in Market Socialism. The percentage of such ownership may decline, but not likely by many points.

That individual entrepreneurs and a variety of other unorthodox organizations may be granted the *use* of state-owned means of production is, of course, another matter—and directly in line with Market Socialist thought.

3. "One individual employing another constitutes exploitation." This tired doctrine is daily yielding ground as youths and families start up their own firms and find it necessary to add hired hands in order to expand. While it is difficult to establish empirically just how many non-family employees are permitted in a private enterprise, it seems that in most cases it would not be advisable for an individual entrepreneur to expand beyond a dozen or so non-family employees.

4. "Thou shalt not resale for profit." In classic socialist thought, profit is the very symbol of exploitation. Under Market Socialism it is used as a benchmark of performance in both public and private enterprise.

5. "Service and distributive trades are demeaning and parasitical." This doctrine is yielding fast with the realization that marketing generally adds both value and motivation in the development process. Clearly, too, a variety of services are indispensable in modern society. There is nothing demeaning about servicing another human being with professional skill and pride, no matter how modest the service may seem in "occupational prestige".

6. "Competition is wasteful—replace it with total planning." After 30 turbulent years whose only common denominator was the ambition to attain total planning, the P.R.C. by 1978 appears to have learned that there are obvious limitations to such planning in complex modern societies. She also learned the highly significant lesson that it is difficult indeed to practice total planning over an extended period and sustain indispensable levels of popular motivation at the same time. On the other hand, competition clearly served as a motivational spur in many highly developed, or rapidly developing, countries. Thus was born the notion of "guidance planning with supplementary regulation by the market" which is—with the notion of public ownership of the principal means of production—the cornerstone of Market Socialist philosophy.

We are ready to generalize the Deng statement cited at the beginning of this section: each developing country should build a socioeconomic system based on its local culture and environment. Like Deng's own, this is an essentially *ecologic* view of development. Thus, many countries may not wish to follow directly in China's footsteps. Nevertheless, the P.R.C. experience may well have some *universally* applicable characteristics for Third World countries (including those approaching the development challenge from a capitalist rather than socialist basis). These universals may include the following:

- for motivation, man needs personal as well as social, immediate as well as long-term, gratification;
- development calls for a viable open market sector. Viability has three connotations. First, the open sector must be large enough to be able to function reasonably independently of the managed sector and to make cost-and-market based pricing the norm rather than the exception. Second, consumer emancipation is called for, as open markets require a semblance of equality between buyers and sellers. Third, the spirit of enterprise and competition is the very hallmark of open markets; don't-rock-the-boat cryptocapitalism is incompatible with such markets;
- the P.R.C. experience suggests that public ownership of most means of production may not in itself be incompatible with open markets;
- in most D.C. agricultural reform should have priority over industrial;
- real development is balanced development.

We must conclude that P.R.C. reforms initiated in 1978 provide a goldmine of ideas as Third World nations look for badly needed fresh approaches to socioeconomic development.

References

Muquiao, G. S. (ed.), *China's Socialist Economy*, (Beijing: Foreign Language Press, 1981).

Thorelli, Hans B., "Libermanism is not Liberalism", *Business Horizons*, Vol. 8 (Summer 1965).

Thorelli, Hans B., "Consumer Policy for the Third World", *Journal of Consumer Policy*, Vol. 3 (1981), pp. 197–211.

Thorelli, Hans B., "Chinese Middle Class Consumers Look at Marketing Issues", in *Proceedings of the Academy of International Business*, (1982), pp. 743–756.

Thorelli, Hans B., "Concepts of Marketing: A Review and Paradigm", in *The Marketing Concept: Perspectives and Viewpoints*, P. Varadarajan (ed.), American Marketing Association Workshop, Texas A&M University, 1983.

Thorelli, Hans B., "Consumer Emancipation and Economic Development", paper prepared for the International Conference on Marketing and Development, Istanbul, September 1–4, 1986.

20

Marketing to the Third World Countries*

OSMAN ATAC
S. TAMER CAVUSGIL

For various reasons, trade with the Third World can be quite problematic. First, the market potential in each individual country is small, which leads to high selling costs as a proportion of sales. For example, U.S. exports to the Third World exceeded one billion dollars for many countries during 1983, whereas exports to Japan and EEC countries were $22 billion and $42 billion, respectively, in the same year. Most developing countries tend to have unstable markets with very little or no published information available about trends. This discourages western firms that need to plan future sales and production. In addition, most non-commodity type imports to these countries are basically job-order, requiring special planning and custom-made production, thus increasing manufacturing costs.

Furthermore, negotiations with a Third World country usually take more time and require more information, which not only increases the cost of sales but also increases business risks. In addition, most Third World countries do not have stable political regimes. It is not a rare event that a business deal ends up with no agreement because of a change in administration, policies, or personnel. Add to these problems the pain and agony of dealing with a totally different culture, and one no longer wonders why the literature finds the subject unattractive; for it is full of problems for which there may not be any ready solutions.

The fact remains, however, that Third World markets are lucrative markets for most exporters. The purpose of this article is to examine the appropriate marketing strategies, especially for non-commodity

---

* Adapted from *Singapore Marketing Review*, (1990), with permission

industrial goods and projects, for the Third World, especially to the low to medium income countries. A marketing approach for selling to such countries is presented. This discussion is followed by operational recommendations for the international marketer.

Third World as a Market Segment: The Significance of Developing Country Markets in World Trade

While each individual Third World market may be too small to be a target market, with most of them quite poor, their combined wealth is impressive due to the large number of Third World countries. According to World Bank classifications, there are 148 Third World, 6 oil capital-surplus, 20 industrialized, and 12 centrally planned countries.

For example, in 1980, 38% of the total exports of the U.S. were imported by the Third World. The share of world trade accounted for by the Third World is constantly increasing. Exports of manufactured goods from developing countries climbed from $4 billion in 1965 to $39 billion in 1976. Although East Asia alone clearly dominates the export of manufacturers, Latin America, South Asia, the Middle East, and sub-Saharan Africa increased exports as well.

Third World countries are diverse in culture, stage of economic development, and size. However, they possess certain similar economic and marketing characteristics that may be critical for the exporting company. If the Third World is to be targeted as a special market segment, marketing strategies should be based on such similarities. After examining some of these similarities, operational recommendations and a marketing approach will be discussed.

Most U.S. companies are accustomed to marketing in a buyers' market with numerous, diffused buyers and little or no government interference. Markets in the Third World, on the other hand, are characterized by: (1) a sellers' market where individual consumer concerns are not crucial; (2) a concentrated market where most direct selling strategies require modification; and (3) direct and close involvement of government with business.

Although some of the Third World countries such as Turkey, Malaysia, and Chile, who once followed protectionist economic policies, are liberalizing their economies for a variety of reasons, most are still far from becoming open market economies. Even in consumer goods, most Third World markets are still best characterized as sellers' markets.

There are various reasons for this. First domestic markets are small, both in terms of absolute size and purchasing power. This leads to natural monopolies where the production (or imports) of a single entrepreneur becomes more efficient than many. Even with the absence of import restrictions, competition for a share of the domestic market is accompanied by a relatively low return—discouraging new entries. Second, wholesale distribution in most of the Third World is controlled by the manufacturers/importers, thus creating a formidable barrier for entry. A new entrant may soon discover that, although its product is superior to the products of competitors, the existing channel is not willing to distribute it unless excessively compensated. In addition, establishing new channels of distribution is extremely expensive, if not impossible.

Wholesalers tend to control the retailers in terms of their product portfolios and financing agreements. Most wholesalers and traders carry a monopoly on a portfolio of high-margin items that are attractive to the retailers. In the absence of fair trade regulations and antitrust laws, these wholesalers are in a position of dictating the product mix to the retailers. This is especially true in the regional distribution of many products. These market imperfections result in highly controlled markets where the buyer purchases whatever goods are available. The power of the "natural" monopolies in most cases is unchallenged because of their traditional ties with the government and with one another. There is geographical concentration as well. In Turkey, some 60% of the manufacturing is realized in five of the 67 provinces. Of the 40 million people in Egypt, more than one fourth lives in or around Cairo.

Government involvement is more than regulatory. First, the inability of the private sector to accumulate the capital required for investments leads governments to be directly involved in the production of goods and services in the so-called State Economic Enterprises (SEEs). Some of the other reasons for the active economic role played by the governments of the Third World include the maintenance of economic security and the development of externalities, such as creating employment or subsidizing a sector. Although privatization of government controlled enterprises is underway in most Third World and Western European countries, the share of SEEs in most Third World economies is quite substantial. In Brazil, the government still controls more than 75% of postal services, telecommunications, electricity, gas, railway, oil production, coal, and steel industries. In India, in addition to these industries, the shipbuilding industry and the airways are controlled by the State. In Turkey, SEEs control more than 55% of the manufacturing industry—ranging from textiles and ceramics to steel.

Beyond the direct involvement of government in the economy through ownership of economic enterprises, there is also the indirect involvement through centralized economic planning. Government

Phase 1
SCANNING

Market surveillance to
learn about forth-
coming projects

Phase 2
THE APPROACH

Presentation of critical
information to buyer in
order to increase
awareness and to
influence writing of
technical specifications

Phase 3
COMPETITIVE
BIDDING

Preparation and
submission of bid

Phase 4
NEGOTIATIONS

Technical and
economic evaluation of
bids; informal and
formal meetings
concluding in a final
bidding

Phase 5
COMPLETION

Carrying out the
project activity,
typically involving
construction, training
and service

Phase 6
FOLLOW-UP

Monitoring project
performance and
cultivating "spin-off"
sales

FIG 20.1. The Process of Marketing to Developing Countries.

intervention in most cases increases concentration in these economies in the sense that business deals are not made with individual buyers, but with bureaucrats of various government offices. It is common practice for the international marketer to start sales calls with civil servants at the Capitol City instead of the actual buyer. Like the old adage, "All roads lead to Rome," in the case of Third World countries, all deals go to the government at one point or another. The process of marketing to the Third World based on these generalities is illustrated in Figure 20.1.

Phases in the Marketing Process

The marketing process suggested in Figure 20.1 is typical of the experience which would be encountered by a firm in selling to both private and government sectors in the Third World. Most of the experiences are related to cases where a non-commodity type product or a project is offered. Each phase is discussed below in detail.

Phase One: Scanning

Most aggressive firms develop and maintain sophisticated marketing intelligence systems to monitor global sales opportunities. Internal sources are traveling managers, subsidiary managers, and overseas representatives. External sources are the Agency for International Development and corresponding organizations in other industrial countries, World Bank, embassies, international banks, industry organizations, and other firms in the industry. Many publications exist, including *Worldwide Projects* which is a particularly helpful source.

Often it is too late for an exporter to sell to the Third World once the sales opportunity is published/publicized. For that reason, intelligence about sales opportunities must be alert to the early signs, in addition to the aforementioned more traditional sources of information. One such source is the country development plans. Unlike their Western counterparts, most Third World buyers must comply with an annual economic plan and its yearly implementation programs. Development plans differ in detail and direction from country to country. Nevertheless, although they are called "advisory" for political reasons, most plans are sufficiently directive. Understanding the process of plan preparation and familiarity with the plan itself is one of the first steps in successful marketing to the Third World.

A U.S. manufacturer of power plants lost a sizeable market niche in a European country when this country changed its power plant specifications from oil to coal in their five year development plan (see example II below for reasons). The U.S. company was capable of offering both types of power plants. But once the plan was out, competitors were already ahead in establishing contacts. The U.S. company did not have a chance although they had been doing business in that country for almost two decades.

It is through the planning process that most Third World governments announce their import and investment priorities. Industrial-sectoral programs are usually integral parts of development plans. These too, are important documents for market planning for the international marketer. In many countries, plans change with governments. Therefore, the international marketer must also be familiar with the programs of powerful political parties where the policy guidelines for the annual plans can be found.

Sometimes certain sectors may be left outside of the scope of annual plans or the plan may not be directive. In this case the situation is not much different. Given the insufficient capital accumulation in these countries, almost all private and government enterprises are forced to operate with high financial leverage. Most financing originates from: (a) private-state owned banks, and (b) direct/indirect government subsidies. The government subsidies, such as tax rebates and low interest credits, are more directive than the plan in most cases. Without such incentives, it is almost impossible to realize an investment in many of the Third World countries. Therefore, even in the sectors that appear to be not regulated by plans, government interference and control is quite dramatic.

Obviously, the task of following plans, programs, and party policies can be quite cumbersome for the international marketer. This is why international marketers use overseas representatives or agents to stay abreast of sales opportunities. These agents are usually local business people who work on a commission-on-sales basis. As natives, local business people are in a better position to identify sales opportunities and can provide invaluable services during lengthy sales negotiations.

There are two types of representatives, exclusive and non-exclusive. An exclusive representative earns commissions regardless of the role in sales. As the only representative in that country, whether involved with the sales or not, the exclusive representative is compensated. A non-exclusive representative is compensated only when personally making a sale.

Several considerations are relevant to selecting a representative. First, since non-exclusive representatives do not get paid unless a sale is made, they may attempt to represent as many companies as possible to increase revenues. The international marketer should be careful in selecting a representative to avoid a conflict of interest. Second, most representatives essentially run "one-man-show" operations. Even if there is a professional manager running office operations, there always is a majority shareholder, or a family, who is actually known to the locals as the owner. The personal history and reputation of this person is extremely important. A representative's business is a business of reputation and contact. A check on the history and degree of success of the representative with other clients is always advisable. Relevant experience of the representative is also important.

> A U.S. company had supplied power plants to a Near Eastern country successfully for sixteen years and was represented by a very shrewd and capable representative. The country was contemplating changing the specifications from oil to coal under the pressure of increasing oil prices. The representative, however, had no contacts or experience in coal fueled power plants and was known as an oil fueled power plant expert. Therefore, he was neither approached by nor was he informed of the change by the client. When the specifications were finally changed from oil to coal, the U.S. company was not prepared.

Finally, corruption is a reality in most of the Third World. The international marketer, without the help and commitment of an exclusive representative, would be in a very difficult position when confronted with such a situation. Representatives, being familiar with the culture and people, could be beneficial under such circumstances. When a top manager of a Canadian nuclear power plant was negotiating a potential deal a payoff of $100,000 was mentioned. In reality, the actual amount asked was only $25,000.

Phase Two: The Approach

Once the opportunity for a specific project is identified, the marketer must approach the buyer with relevant information and attempt to influence the writing of tender specifications, which usually take the form of a *feasibility report*. A marketer's aim at this stage is to present information and, if possible, monitor the specifications.

> The feasibility reports, like the annual plans, contain information when published that is practically useless to the international marketer. A U.S. company started building its market in Turkey which has traditionally been ordering 150 MegaWatt power plants. Two years prior to bidding, the U.S. corporation working with the middle level technocrats managed to convince the client to order 300 MegaWatt plants. When the feasibility reports were prepared and the bids were invited, the U.S. corporation had no competitors.

Therefore, an important aspect of the marketing effort is to use the *first mover* advantages. A marketer that can beat competitors in supplying relevant information to a buyer will have a head start in the selling process.

These *tie-up strategies* are usually based on: (a) a technical solution to the buyer's problem, (b) social linkages between the buyer and seller, (c) financial linkages in terms of provisions for financing, and (d) other informational linkages. These linkages are illustrated in Figure 20.2. Creation of first mover advantage can be likened to a spinning of a web so that the buyer is enclosed in the net while the competitors are locked out. Growing interdependence between the

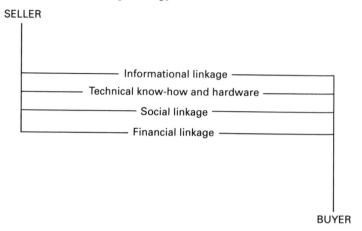

FIG. 20.2. Strengthening Buyer-Seller Linkages

buyer and seller, strengthened through the four types of linkages, should be a facilitating factor in successful bidding. Japanese companies, for example, are known to frequently invite the top managers of the potential overseas partners and buyers to Japan for a tour of their facilities. Efforts of this sort can make the difference between successful and unsuccessful sales in Third world markets.

The local exclusive representatives usually lack necessary technical know-how. In addition, they cannot make commitments on behalf of the foreign vendor. Therefore, when the prospective project idea warrants it, a team from the vendor must be in direct contact with the potential client during the preparation of the feasibility study. One way of accomplishing this to have *ad hoc* project teams for Third World markets. The *ad hoc* project staff must be organized quickly in order to avoid missed sales opportunities.

When feasibility reports are prepared by outside consultants, these consultants must be treated as the client. It is always a good idea to keep a mailing list of technical personnel in private, government, educational, and consulting organizations, establishing regular contacts with them.

For large-scale projects, it is not unlikely to find an international consulting firm to be assigned to the preparation of the feasibility report. In fact, for large scale projects which are financed by the transnational financial markets, a feasibility report prepared by an international consulting company is usually a loan requirement. The use of a consulting firm hardly guarantees a better report. Since most international consultants are unfamiliar with the market, they may overlook major factors or rely on incomplete information. Furthermore, political and business considerations force international consultants to act as mediators in most cases. Rarely, will a consulting firm be willing to make radical suggestions, since in most Third World countries, almost all decisions, especially related to large investment/import projects, result in power struggles and political controversy. In almost all cases, international consultants employ a local company/person as their counterpart. Both the international consultant and their counterparts must be closely monitored during the preparation of the feasibility report.

Phase Three: Competitive Bidding

In most cases, once the feasibility report is written, a tender is published and competitive bids are invited from a list of selected vendors. Needless to say, a company must be on the mailing list to get the tender, which is the job of the local representative. Usually tenders are purchased for a nominal fee. Competitive bidding can be open or closed, with closed being the norm. In open competitive bidding, firms bid down in an auction, whereas in closed bids, firms turn in their offers in sealed envelopes and bids are opened all at the same time. Communication during the open competitive bidding sessions is crucial since time is extremely limited and millions are at stake.

For large-scale projects, the technical terms and conditions will be followed by a so-called "Administrative Terms and Conditions" (ATC). Various legal, financial, and administrative issues are also spelled out and procurement procedures are revealed. Due to its expensive nature, a critical decision at this stage relates to how much time and other resources should be invested in the preparation of the bid.

In most Third World countries, government or SEE buying is regulated by law. This is actually helpful to the vendor since the organizational buying process and the authority and responsibility of each unit is clearly described. The regulations related to government procurements state how the requisitions are to be placed, who will have decision-making authority, and how the decision will be implemented. The international marketer must become familiar with these regulations. Unfortunately, almost all regulations carry an exemption clause. Using this clause, the SEE or the government agency may exempt itself from the regulations, especially as related to the conditions specifying the terms under which the bids are to be awarded. Often these terms award the contract to the lowest bidder, and in many cases bind the buyer to award the contract, even if there are no acceptable offers.

In the case of privately owned concerns in the Third World, there usually are no guidelines related to procurement. Organizational structures of the corporation are usually centralized. Shares of even the largest corporations are controlled by either individuals or families. This is actually helpful to the foreign vendor to identify the decision-makers.

Phase Four: Negotiations

Once the bids are submitted, they are evaluated by the buyer from both a technical and economic perspective. In large scale projects, typically the bids are short listed and a few vendors are invited for further discussions which usually mark the beginning of lengthy negotiations. These meetings provide opportunities for the marketer to present additional explanations and details. As such, they can be crucial in terms of their impact on the selection of a bid.

Finding the right person to negotiate in the government of SEEs, however, may be difficult. International marketers may be surprised to discover that they have to talk to a dozen people from different echelons and divisions of an agency or agencies without knowing the actual decision-maker(s). Some agency personnel will pretend to be the real decision-maker. Inside information from the local representative will provide valuable guidelines in such instances.

Some international marketers concentrate their efforts on the person who appears to be the final decision-maker and neglect or even avoid the others in the process. In Third World countries this strategy is likely to backfire. Bureaucrats in lower levels of the hierarchy are generally intolerant of being bypassed.

A sales opportunity was lost by a U.S. firm because of an oversight. The contract was seen as a sure bet. Corporate executives were told by the Minister of Industry and other top level officials that an $80 million textile machinery renewal project sponsored by the World Bank was going to be awarded and that the U.S. bid was the most attractive. However, at the last minute, an "expert" in the state planning organization claimed "inappropriate technology," and convinced the Ministry of Finance, who was negotiating the financing of the contract, not to award the contract.

The Third World drives a hard bargain in most cases. Through bilateral and multilateral agreements, Third World buyers try to improve their bargaining position. Application of uniform import taxes, pooling of commodity imports, and cartel type agreements are not rare. Pooling of import purchases for commodity production such as fertilizers and tractors from the multinational corporations is one example of such agreements.

More frequently, the bargaining power of Third World buyers will be affected by the military and economic agreement with the governments of the suppliers. Usually, such agreements weaken their bargaining positions. It would be a mistake, however, to use this point as a bargaining strategy. It should be remembered that, unlike the Eastern block, the Western countries do not act as a uniform front, especially on matters of business. Having an alliance with the West does not mean much to a Third World country when it comes to business negotiations. Furthermore, for a Third World buyer it does not make any difference whether the supplier is a Japanese, Canadian, German or American firm. If forced, they may go to another Western supplier and still keep their commitments. Political alliances are best kept out of the business deals.

Most Third World countries lack the necessary financial resources, especially in terms of foreign exchange. For most large scale imports, 100% financing by the seller is now a common practice. Tight international money markets and low credit ratings of many Third World countries force them to look for the best terms of payments. Increasing international competition places the Third World in a position where they can drive a hard bargain. Japanese firms for instance, are quite successful in negotiations because they provide a complete package including low interest financing. Limitations in certain products/processes may be overcome by strengths in financial terms.

Australian and Dutch competitors get 30% to 70% of their overseas marketing costs subsidized through direct government reimbursement known as a bounty. An Australian dredge builder used this 20% bounty to overcome a 10% price disadvantage and won a contract in Africa against a U.S. company.

Balance of payments continue to be a serious problem for most Third World countries. Therefore, an opportunity to improve the importing country's payments enhances the bargaining power of the seller. Even in countries where there is no balance of payments problems, many Third World buyers are not technically, but financially minded.

An Arizona based company manufacturing prefabricated housing units, after spending years in negotiations, failed to capture a niche in the Saudi market. Although the company's products were of much superior quality to those offered by the competition, numerous presentations seemed to have failed in convincing the buyers. A New York based consulting organization suggested a change in the marketing approach. Instead of lengthy technical presentations, the company presented very simple financial analyses to the prospective clients. The results were very successful.

Most Third World countries are trying new channels and suppliers. The increasing aggressiveness of the Eastern Block in international markets provides additional bargaining power for them. Many U.S. firms are at a disadvantage in this respect, especially with regard to supplies, parts, and raw material requirements. U.S. manufacturers often limit the options of buyers, which, in addition to being managerially unattractive to the buyer, also creates psychological resistance.

Many successful bidders include alternative sources for parts and suppliers as a standard document.

> A Turkish company was planning to buy a deep sea fishing vessel. The U.S. bid submitted was superior in quality and was acceptable in price. However, the Soviet bid specified that the parts for the vessel could be obtained from any Soviet Block country or from the West. The U.S. corporation demanded that the parts could only be bought from them. The contract was awarded to the Soviets.

Negotiations can take a long time. The bidder should be prepared for an adequate time and patience allotment. Sometimes the information requested by the buyer may seem endless. There are various reasons for this, in addition to the well publicized cultural differences. At times, the bidders supply the buyers with conflicting information. Thus, the Third World buyer gets confused and keeps demanding more and more information.

> A country which was a large consumer of refined salt decided to become self sufficient in salt. A project based on solar evaporated salt pans was offered. A feasibility study paid by the government stated that evaporating ocean water in boilers is a more attractive alternative, although requiring a much higher initial cost. The government was confused and asked for more information. After more than a year, negotiations were still continuing.

Also, when the buyer is at a disadvantage, the bidder requests certain conditions to guarantee a certain level of profitability. These conditions range from monopoly rights to tax holidays, including a host of other bargaining elements such as a special tariff on competitive imports, duty relief on raw materials, anti-dumping control, currency convertibility, and repatriation privileges. The Third World buyer may demand more information to justify the demands of the seller.

> A surgical dressings manufacturer agreed to invest in a Third World country in exchange for a monopoly equal to 80% of current imports. The government asked the company to justify its position. After a year of negotiations, the government officials were still not convinced.

Distasteful and unethical as it may be, lubrication or grease payments are a way of life in most Third World countries. The international marketer should be prepared to take a position on such issues and make this position known to representative from the outset. In certain countries, one must go through intermediaries who are close to the government. Their commissions, usually about 10%, are paid almost automatically. Although such payment is considered a bribe by U.S. standards and the Foreign Corrupt Practices Act, to them it is payment for services. Local representatives will be in a position to advise the international marketer in such matters.

When technology is relatively simple and available, buyers play one seller against another to get better terms. Some of the alternatives offered may be simple and therefore inexpensive. It is tempting for a buyer to procure such machinery and technology, or play inexpensive offers against more modern and expensive ones. In this case, the seller can point out that simple technology is usually single-purpose, whereas modern technology is flexible. The old adage that one should not put all the eggs in one basket is extremely relevant for the Third World. Hundreds of millions of dollars worth of investments in the Third World are idle or closed because of inflexible manufacturing systems, changing world markets, and economic conditions. Custom made, flexible designs will have a considerable advantage in the bargaining process.

Ability of the supplier to utilize local resources is an additional feature which is attractive to most Third World buyers. Especially in the case of government purchases, the seller who can demonstrate that the offer creates additional jobs and added value will have better bargaining power. The ratio of the cost of the goods imported to the prices of the final product is an important consideration in the bargaining process. In many cases, the share of imports in the total cost of the manufactured or processed goods is considerable. This makes it very difficult for the Third World country to pass it on to the end user, domestic or international.

Buyers who are serving local markets are not seriously concerned about the quality of the final product. For instance, in aluminium die-casting, Italy may be preferred as a source of supply because of its low price. However, the silicon content of such raw material is low and the metal is basically recycled and therefore less durable. Nevertheless, buyers may be willing to sacrifice quality for price. If there is a price disadvantage, emphasizing quality is not likely to increase the bargaining strength of the seller. The seller should try to provide similar quality at lower prices. It should be noted that top quality is not always the best for many Third World countries. Many times inexperienced representatives of sellers express their surprise when told about the prices of competitors. It is only then that they examine the offers and note quality differences, which leads them into an effort to build a case around quality which is usually fruitless. Therefore, the international marketer should be ready to compete against low as well as high quality.

In many cases where the procurement of the developing country is related to export oriented programs, any assistance that can be extended in the distribution of the final product will strengthen the bargaining position of the seller. Often, Third World countries are unable to market what they produce because they cannot penetrate the international channels of distribution. The seller who has some control over such channels or who can secure the cooperation of a trading company or broker will have considerable bargaining power in the negotiation.

Finally, an important element which strengthens the bargaining power of the seller is the managerial expertise and flexibility that can be provided in the post-investment operations.

> A U.S. construction company building a military complex in Saudi Arabia almost failed to meet the deadline if it had not been for the flexibility of the site manager. A change in construction specifications was required due to a mistake on the part of the client represented by a high level military officer. The bomb site selected by this officer covered a historic caravan route that had been in use for centuries. The contract did not cover the expenses of the U.S. firm that would result from the change. The representative of the client did not want the embarrassment of asking for additional funds from the Saudi Government, but did not want to assume the cost. The representative of the company manipulated certain excavation figures and accommodated the Saudi representative by changing the bomb site without incurring any additional expenses. The project was completed on time as well.

Turnkey agreements are no longer attractive to many Third World countries. There are various reasons for this. First, they feel that they do not have the managerial expertise needed to successfully run the investment. Second, even though the operations can be handled, marketing becomes a problem. Third, and most importantly, Third World countries feel they are sold inappropriate or outdated technology. As a solution, *turnkey-plus* operations or Build, Own, and Operate Models, are favored by many Third World countries. In this kind of an agreement the host guarantees to buy all or most of the output of the investment. The seller is asked to provide a turnkey investment and then operate it, also providing the managerial expertise needed. After a specific period, the host guarantees to buy the seller out. This way the buyer tries to put the burden of choosing the right kind of investment on the seller. The risk for the seller is naturally greater with such an agreement, thus strengthening the seller's bargaining power.

Phase Five: Completion

Once a certain supplier is selected, the supplier then delivers, installs, and initiates different components of the project. Typically, a temporary organization is formed to complete the assignment. Most projects in Third World countries involve a combination of construction, training of personnel, project management, and service. Any one of these can be used as bargaining chips during negotiations.

> Many countries offer direct grants to the buyers when equipment is bought from that country. For example, a training grant to China totaling $1.5 million from Holland was very influential in the client's decision to choose a Dutch manufacturer over a U.S. contender.

One of the most critical problems for the exporter can be the financial guarantees in this phase. Once the contract is signed, many Third World countries usually insist that the seller buy insurance from them to protect Third World insurance revenues. The rates can be as much as 200% higher and most policies obtained are quite restrictive. For further protection, sellers can hire a skilled international broker and buy DIC (Differences in Conditions) insurance in New York or London which would become effective if the local policy is inadequate.

Phase Six: Follow-up

Successful completion of a sale usually generates a considerable amount of spin-off sales. Opportunities exist for selling service contracts, parts, peripheral equipment, and software. Of course, it is desirable to maintain contact with the consumer to ensure satisfaction and to learn about developing projects.

TABLE 20.1. Guidelines for Marketing to Third World Countries

1.	Follow the development plans, yearly programs, government programs and programs of political parties closely. These are easily accessible.
2.	Familiarize yourself with the government incentives for investments. These will determine future demand.
3.	Select a good exclusive local representative. Make sure that he does not represent your competitors, that he has an area of specialization and that he is reliable.
4.	Familiarize yourself with the process of preparing a feasibility report.
5.	Provide technical know-how during the preparation of the technical specifications.
6.	Keep in close contact with the domestic and international consulting organizations who may be preparing technical specifications or feasibility reports. Keep in touch with the local technocrats and engineers. They are small in number and easily accessible. They will determine what will be bought.
7.	Establish friendly relations with potential buyers even if they are not buying now. It is an inexpensive but very effective public relations effort.
8.	Familiarize yourself with the regulations related to government and State Economic Enterprise procurements. Note that the governmental agencies do not have to follow such regulations at all times.
9.	Find the "Lion" in each organization. In each organization one or two people will have the "final say." Make sure that you know who they are, but never ignore others who are involved.
10.	Familiarize yourself with the international agreements of the country. Do not use political-military alliances as a part of your sales strategy.
11.	Offer a complete deal. Be ready to finance your own sales.
12.	Certain issues prove efficient in negotiating sales. The ability of your offer to improve the balance of payments, create employment, add value, utilize local resources, countertrade, decrease import dependence, increase the international options of the country both in terms of buying and selling in the future, and improve the flexibility of the operations are examples.
13.	Be ready to deal with bribery. Use your local representative and stay out of it.
14.	Get ready for a turnkey-plus operations agreement.

Conclusion

In the light of the recent pressures to globalize marketing operations, the previously neglected Third World markets gain importance. It is a misconception that Third World markets are unorganized and chaotic. On the contrary, the buying process is usually more formalized in many respects. The fact that Third World markets are more concentrated and that the government is an integral part of most processes provides opportunities for the international marketer. Most buying is done by organizations, either private or government operated. Markets are basically sellers' markets. Most purchases are based on some sort of a feasibility plan compatible with a macro economic country development plan. Marketing plans can be built on these purchasing patterns.

Experience in working with Third World customers has generated a battery of useful principles for the Western business executive. These are summarized in Table 20.1. Although they are by no means rigid rules, these guidelines can assist the executive in successfully cultivating business in the Third World and in managing relationships with Third World customers.

It should be recognized that putting these suggestions to work requires teamwork on the part of the seller. A team that includes managerial and technical expertize will be needed. International selling to the Third World is not solely the job of a sales representative. A mistake, unfortunately, made by many companies, is to send a sales representative and expect that representative to close the sale. Given the competitive nature of global markets, appropriate marketing strategies promise considerable rewards in the Third World market.

Further Reading — Part III

Hill, John S. and Richard R. Still, "Adapting Products to LDC Tastes," *Harvard Business Review*, (March-April 1984), p. 95.

Luqmani, Mushtaq, G. M. Habib and S. Kassem "Marketing to LDC Governments," *International Marketing Review*, (Spring 1988), pp. 56–67.

Reeder, John A., "When West Meets East: Cultural Aspects of Doing Business in Asia," *Business Horizons*, (January-February 1987), pp. 69–74.

Samli, A. C., "Changing Marketing System in East Europe: What Marketers Should Know," *International Marketing Review*, (Winter 1986), pp. 7–12.

Terpstra, Vern and Kenneth David, *The Cultural Environment of International Business*, (Cincinnati: South-Western Publishing, 1985).

Thorelli, Hans B., "Marketing Socialism in the People's Republic of China," *International Marketing Review*, (Summer 1985), pp. 7–14.

IV

Researching, Understanding, and Negotiating for Global Market Opportunities

Introduction to Part IV

The subject of Part IV is researching and understanding global market opportunities. The realities of today's competitive business environment require that foreign markets be sought systematically and continuously. But how to seek and analyze export market opportunities remains baffling to many marketers. The selections in Part IV intend to familiarize the readers with major issues associated with identifying global market opportunities.

The lead article by Cavusgil illustrates how firms can exploit overseas opportunities through a proactive posture in researching overseas markets. A sequential and systematic approach is proposed for searching attractive opportunities. The information gained from such an approach can help managers reduce uncertainty, pinpoint major factors, and design appropriate marketing strategies.

Reading 22 by Johansson and Nonaka introduces the Japanese way of market research. Japanese corporations want accurate and useful information about their markets as much as anybody else does. But they just go about it differently. Japanese-style relies heavily on two kinds of information: "soft data" obtained from visits to dealers and other channel members, and "hard data" about shipments, inventory levels, and retails sales. Japanese managers believe that such data often better reflect the behavior and intentions of their customers than statistics-based survey research.

Campbell and Cunningham in Reading 24 suggest that a company shoulds find its market opportunities through analyzing its existing customers. Their emphasis on supplier/customer relationship derives from the interaction approach to marketing and purchasing strategy.

The reading by Thorelli examines similarities and differences in multinational consumer market segments. Based on research in Europe and the U.S., the author develops a profile of cosmopolitan, elite consumers, called the Information Seekers (IS), whose common attitudes and consumption patterns often supersede national differences found among average consumers. The IS are found in increasing numbers in industrially advanced countries, raising the interesting proposition that cross-cultural similarities between certain market segments in different countries may outweigh in importance differences between segments in the same local markets. Several strategic implications for the multinational marketing strategy are discussed.

21

Guidelines for Export Market Research*

S. TAMER CAVUSGIL

Why and how do companies actually conduct export market research? How do they identify foreign markets potentials? What sources of information do they use? To answer these questions, we conducted personal interviews with executives of 70 companies in Wisconsin and Illinois.

In all cases, the respondent was the executive principally responsible for the international business activities of the firm. The two-hour interviews covered a variety of topics, including the history of the company's international involvement, the nature of current international activities, the scope of export market research in the company, and major company characteristics.

Approximately one-half of the firms in the sample were manufacturers of industrial products, 29% were producers of consumer goods, and the remaining companies were primarily export intermediaries. Annual sales ranged from $200,000 to $3 billion. About one-third of the sample employed less than 100 full-time employees, and 42% had more than 500 employees.

The firms were at various stages in developing international marketing programs. A few had started export operations in just the past several years. The remaining firms had export experience ranging from five to well over 50 years. The sample also varied in the percentage of total company sales exported. Twenty-eight percent of the firms studied had export sales that accounted for up to 9% of their company sales. The remaining firms were divided almost equally among the following exports/total sales ratios: 10–19%; 20–39%; and more than 40%.

---

*Adapted from *Business Horizons* (November/December 1985), with permission.

The Nature of Export Market Research

Few of us know even simple facts about the geography, culture, and economics of countries other than our own. Even fewer people have at their fingertips details that tell whether their goods will sell in a particular market. Therefore, export issues must be carefully researched before the decision is made to enter a foreign market. Of course companies can bypass marketing research if there is little at stake. An example of this is a firm that chooses simply to respond to unsolicited orders from foreign customers. However, when the risks are substantial, it is essential to clarify certain issues before committing greater resources. In some cases, companies know what specific markets they want investigated when they sponsor market research, and they provide sufficient funds to cover field research in each market. But very often they have not decided on particular markets and conduct the research in order to find out which are the most promising. In still other cases, they ask for research on more markets than, given the budget, can be investigated in depth.

Major questions the companies in our study addressed through export market research include:

- In which foreign markets can company products be sold profitably?
- Which countries offer the best prospects?
- What sales volume and margins can be expected in each market?
- Does the foreign market require any modification of the product?
- What distribution channels and arrangements should be employed in selling to a particular country?
- How sensitive is the market demand to product price?
- What should the landed price be? Retail price?
- What performance criteria should be used to monitor company activity in each foreign market?

Perhaps the most important concern of export market research is the identification of attractive foreign markets for company products and the assessment of *sales potentials* in each selected market. The other major purpose of export market research relates to *distribution*—the identification, selection, motivation, and evaluation of foreign distributors and agents. For many firms these two tasks are the most problematic, and many marketers view them as the primary challenge of export marketing. Although substantial resources may be expended for export marketing research, managers note that they have yet to develop a "perfect" procedure for dealing with these two tasks. An approach that appears suitable for one market may not be satisfactory for another.

Frequency of identifying and analyzing new foreign market opportunities was characterized as "infrequent" (40%) or "occasional"

(28%) by the firms we studied. The complexity of foreign market research was characterized as "very simple" (24%) or "simple" (33%). Only about 14% of the respondents employed rigorous techniques, such as regression or econometric forecasting, in analyzing foreign market research data. Similarly, only about one-third of the companies had formalized their research activities with written procedures and clear definition of responsibilities. Research reports prepared by the staff in this regard typically stayed at the middle-management level, suggesting that top management attached little importance to export market research.

Why is export market research generally more subjective and less precise than domestic market research? Executives usually attributed the difference to the limited experience of managers in conducting export market research and the difficulties encountered in gathering relevant, accurate, and timely information. The nature and complexity of export market research is very much a function of a company's international involvement and the risks it encounters. When the amount at stake is marginal, managers prefer to make decisions on the basis of limited research, aided by "judgment calls." This is illustrated well by Nicolet Instruments, a Madison, Wisconsin, producer of sophisticated scientific instruments. One executive puts it this way:

> When we go into a foreign market on an agent basis, we do not engage in any in-depth analysis since our investment is small. It may be a blind decision. If the agent sends someone here for training, we know he is committed and serious. When we make a direct investment in a foreign market, there's more risk involved. We will then engage in an in-depth analysis. Much of our potential in that market is probably established by a representative prior to that move.

The stage of company internationalization is also a significant determinant of the nature and complexity of export market research. The extent of international involvement, which varies from opportunistic to fully-committed exporting, dictates the nature of research and the types of information to be gathered.

Company executives consider export research to be most useful when it is ongoing and systematic. Nevertheless, some companies viewed export market research as an intermittent activity and approached it haphazardly.

Essential questions in conducting export market research so that it is most beneficial to a company include:

- Has management developed an export marketing program with accompanying market research tasks?
- Does management understand that foreign market research is an ongoing activity?
- Have procedures been developed to monitor, evaluate, and correct export marketing performance?

- Has the firm provided means for timely warning of pertinent changes in foreign markets?
- Does the export market research seek the most specific information concerning the firm's products?
- Is mature judgment being applied to the facts developed by the export market research efforts?

Specific export market research tasks should be identified in the framework of an overall export marketing plan. The company should ensure that the necessary information for monitoring, evaluating, and correcting export activity is made available to management through such efforts.

It is also important for management to recognize that export market research is no substitute for judgment. Market researchers should always attempt to understand the reason behind the events and bare facts. In order to understand future developments, they must know not only *what* has happened, but also *why* it happened. They also should investigate the implications of current and past trends on their company and its sales. Furthermore, export market research should always search for the most specific information concerning the company's products. Market demand for a *type* of product, such as medical equipment, should not be confused with the potential demand for a specific brand, say intravenous fluid equipment.

Researching Foreign Market Potentials: A Sequential Approach

In most of the firms we studied, the process of analyzing foreign market opportunities was fairly unstructured. How important managers considered foreign market opportunity analysis depended on how important they considered exporting. That is, if they placed a low emphasis on exporting, they attached a low level of importance to the analysis.

The process usually had evolved from one person's handling the job or a series of exporting "change agents." Many companies employed experienced international marketing people who had a good grasp of the potential for their industry in different countries of the world. Others found it difficult to hire or train individuals for international positions.

Since the number of world markets to be considered by a company is very large, it is neither possible nor advisable to research them all. Thus, a firm's time and money is spent most efficiently and effectively in a sequential screening process. This process eliminates many unsuitable countries from the large number of available alternatives.

Although many of the companies we studied had not developed a formal procedure for analyzing foreign market opportunities, some of the experienced exporters employed an approach that tends to support the value of such a sequential process.

Stage One: Preliminary Screening

The first stage in this sequential screening process for the company is to select the more attractive countries that it wants to investigate in detail. Preliminary screening involves defining the physical, political, economic and cultural environment. Among the factors to be included in each category are the following.

Demographic/Physical Environment:

- Population size, growth, density
- Urban and rural distribution
- Climate and weather variations
- Shipping distance
- Product-significant demographics
- Physical distribution and communication network
- Natural resources

Political Environment:

- System of government
- Political stability and continuity
- Ideological orientation
- Government involvement in business
- Government involvement in communications
- Attitudes toward foreign business (trade restrictions, tariffs, nontariff barriers, bilateral trade agreements)
- National economic and developmental priorities

Economic Environment:

- Overall level of development
- Economic growth: G.N.P., industrial sector
- Role of foreign trade in the economy
- Currency: inflation rate, availability, controls, stability of exchange rate
- Balance of payments
- Per capita income and distribution
- Disposable income and expenditure patterns

Social/Cultural Environment:

- Literacy rate, educational level
- Existence of middle class
- Similarities and differences in relation to home market
- Language and other cultural considerations

The exporter marketer will eliminate some foreign markets from further consideration on the basis of this preliminary screening. An example would be the absence of comparable or linking products and services, a deficiency that would hinder the potential for marketing company products.

Stage Two: Analysis of Industry Market Potential

Once several attractive countries have been selected for further study, the firm is ready for the second stage of the screening process. This stage involves assessing industry market potential for each selected foreign market. At this stage, the company will want to determine the present and future aggregate demand for the industry within the selected markets. Factors to be studied at this stage include market access, product potential, and local distribution and production.

Market Access:

- Limitations on trade: tariff levels, quotas
- Documentation and import regulations
- Local standards, practices, and other nontariff barriers
- Patents and trademarks
- Preferential treaties
- Legal considerations: investment, taxation, repatriation, employment, code of laws

Product Potential:

- Customer needs and desires
- Local production, imports, consumption
- Exposure to and acceptance of product
- Availability of linking products
- Industry-specific key indicators of demand
- Attitudes toward products of foreign origin
- Competitive offerings

Local Distribution and Production:

- Availability of intermediaries

- Regional and local transportation facilities
- Availability of manpower
- Conditions for local manufacture

Indicators of population, income levels, and consumption patterns should be considered. In addition, statistics on local production trends, along with imports and exports of the product category, are helpful for assessing industry market potential. Often, an industry will have a few key indicators or measures that will help them determine the industry strength and demand within a foreign market. A manufacturer of medical equipment, for example, may use the number of hospital beds, the number of surgeries, and public expenditures for health care as indicators to assess the potential for its products.

Stage Three: Analysis of Company Sales Potential

The third stage of the screening process involves assessing company sales potential in those countries that prove promising based upon the earlier analyses. The issues that must be addressed at this stage include forecasting sales volume, landed cost, cost of internal distribution, and other determinants of profitability.

Sales Volume Forecasting:

- Size and concentration of customer segments
- Projected consumption statistics
- Competitive pressures
- Expectations of local distributors/agents

Landed Cost:

- Costing method for exports
- Domestic distribution costs
- International freight and insurance
- Cost of product modification

Cost of Internal Distribution:

- Tariffs and duties
- Value added tax
- Local packaging and assembly
- Margins/commission allowed for the trade
- Local distribution and inventory costs
- Promotional expenditures

Other Determinants of Profitability:

- Going price levels
- Competitive strengths and weaknesses
- Credit practices
- Current and projected exchange rates

Competitive information in the foreign market is often very valuable in determining export prices and, hence, export profitability. To help project sales, factors such as quality, design, sizing, and packaging should also be compared to competitive offerings.

Much of the information needed for the first and second stage of opportunity analysis can be gathered through desk research—for example, documentary sources, international business publications, and so on. In contrast, the third stage, estimating company sales and profitability, often requires field research. Therefore, some type of primary data collection usually will be undertaken in the foreign market, sometimes with the assistance of market research firms. One of the best ways to gather this information is to visit potential foreign end users and distributors. Industry trade shows and fairs are also useful in sizing up the competition and in meeting potential distributors. Advertisements can be placed in trade journals. The firms in our study also value surveys or direct mail campaigns to end users or distributors.

Sources of Information for Export Market Research

Companies can obtain export market research data from a variety of sources. These include the U.S. Department of Commerce (D.O.C.) and other governmental agencies; international organizations such as the Organization for Economic Cooperation and Development (O.E.C.D.), United Nations Food and Agriculture Organization (F.A.O.), United Nations Conference on Trade and Development (U.N.C.T.A.D.), and General Agreement on Tariffs and Trade (G.A.T.T.); service organizations such as banks; export trading companies, trade associations and world trade clubs; as well as a multitude of private research organizations and their publications.[1]

The U.S. D.O.C. assistance programs are varied to suit the needs of companies at different stages of internationalization. These include business counseling, new product information service, agent/distributor services, trade opportunities program, catalog exhibitions, trade missions, and many others. Figure 21.1 identifies various sources based upon the particular type of information sought.

In our interviews, we found that there is *no* lack of data on international markets and marketing. On the contrary, managers may be *overloaded* with information and have difficulty in sorting out what

Type of Information	*U.S. Dept. of Commerce Sources*	*Other Sources*

Foreign market information	Business America
	Foreign Economic Trends
	Overseas Business
	  Reports
	International Economic
	  Indicators
		Business International
		Dun & Bradstreet
		  International
		Chase World Information
		  Corp.
		Stanford Research Institute
		International Trade
		  Reporter
		Accounting firms

Export market research	Country Market Sectoral
	  Surveys
	Global Market Surveys
	International Market
	  Research
		Market research firms
		Advertising agencies
		Publishing companies
		Trade associations

International statistics	Export Statistics Profile Custom Service Statistics	Predicasts U.S. Foreign Trade Reports United Nations International Monetary Fund O.E.C.D., E.E.C., G.A.T.T.

Overseas representatives	Customized Export
	  Mailing List
	World Traders Data
	  Reports
	Agent/Distributor Service
		Banks, chambers of
		  commerce, consulting
		  firms

Sales leads	Trade Opportunities
	  Program
	Strategic and Industrial
	  Product Sales Group
	Major Export Projects
	  Program
	Export Information
	  Reference Room
		Banks, chambers of
		  commerce, consulting
		  firms
		State development agencies

Reference data on foreign firms	World Traders Data
	Reports
		Banks, chambers of
		  commerce, consulting
		  firms
		State development agencies

FIG. 21.1 Sources of Information for Export Market Research

is relevant, useful, timely, and consistent with other sources of the same information. As one executive noted, one has to develop a sense of familiarity and history with a source of information and be cautious about interpreting statistics, especially those prepared by the developing countries.

Even the U.S. D.O.C. information may not be satisfactory. An executive of Nicolet Instruments indicated that, while the firm receives well over half of its information from the U.S. D.O.C. publications, it needs to "filter it out." With these publications, he says, the firm "becomes aware of the trends; you get a number to start with." But he adds, "You still have to interpret it with a critical eye."

Many executives noted that they often travel abroad to support the statistics and to meet foreign customers and distributors. While they may be costly, trips to foreign markets appear to be the preferred way of gathering foreign market information.

U.S. D.O.C. sources of information and assistance are likely to be more satisfactory for smaller firms and those new to exporting. In contrast, the larger and more involved firms tend to have developed their own more sophisticated information bases. These firms also rely to a greater extent on private sector suppliers, such as Business International, Dun and Bradstreet, Predicasts, and the international departments of major banks.

As firms gain more experience with exporting, they may become dissatisfied for various reasons with the quality of available information. Besides their potential errors, data obtained from different sources may be contradictory. How does one know which source is reliable?

Multinational corporations are more likely to depend on private sources of information. For example, S. C. Johnson, of Racine, Wisconsin, uses A. C. Nielsen data collected in each foreign market. Syndicated research data gathered from each market appear to better suit their needs. Secondary sources of information, such as Business International publications or government statistics, provide more general information, such as economic indicators, political stability, and the exchange rate fluctuations.

Data obtained from secondary sources are usually too broad to be useful for predicting company sales potential. In addition, frequent political and economic changes in many foreign markets may limit substantially the usefulness of projections for a country. Because of these problems, companies tend to supplement quantitative data with the subjective judgments of executives.

Practical Approaches to Identifying Foreign Market Opportunities

Academicians have exhorted companies to employ techniques such as input-output analysis, income elasticity measures, econometric fore-casting, and macrosurveys in international market research. In reality, however, companies find little use for these theoretical techniques. Companies apparently develop approaches that suit their own needs for estimating foreign market potential. Five specific approaches are:

- Using existing distributors as a source of information about developing market opportunities;
- Directing promotion to prospective distributors or other customers;
- Participating in overseas trade fairs and shows;
- Following major contractors around the world; and
- Using trade audits for assessing market potential.

Distributors as a Source for Identifying Foreign Market Opportunities

Companies, large and small, experienced and inexperienced, have learned that perhaps the best way of identifying market potentials is to use their foreign distributor/agent contacts. Because of their local market presence, familiarity with customer needs, and contact with governmental agencies, distributors are often the best source of valuable and timely information about market developments. Consequently, the more experienced companies tend to shift much of the opportunity analysis and identification function to capable distributors and representatives.

In addition, they establish fairly formalized communication channels for a free and frequent flow of information from those closest to the market back to headquarters. General Electric Medical Division, in Waukesha, Wisconsin, for example, achieves this through their formalized country planning processes.

Advertising Directed to Prospective Distributors or Other Customers

Many companies have found it useful to generate inquiries and subsequent orders by advertising their products in trade journals, directories, or other publications. Still others engage in direct mail campaigns in order to uncover potentials.

Managers are pleasantly surprised to find that English-language American trade journals often circulate in foreign countries and thus reach prospective customers. Unsolicited inquiries often result from these publications, as well as from favorable word-of-mouth publicity generated by satisfied customers.

Participation in Trade Fairs

A related approach to delineating foreign market opportunities is through attendance at foreign trade fairs and shows. In some cases, thousands of buyers from around the world congregate at international trade fairs for specific industry branches. Companies in our sample generally rated trade fairs high in effectiveness. With the assistance of the U.S. D.O.C., even small companies with limited resources can participate.

According to an executive at Research Products Inc., of Madison, Wisconsin, trade fairs are "probably one way that anyone trying to make assessments of foreign markets can gain a tremendous amount of information."

Following Other Suppliers Around the World

A few of the companies we studied had been able to expand their supplier relationships with some of their domestic customers to overseas markets. These customers typically are large multinationals involved in contract manufacturing, turnkey operations, or foreign production abroad. Thus, it is often desirable to explore the possibility of supplying multinational customers in overseas projects.

For example, Snap-on-Tools, of Kenosha, Wisconsin, regularly identifies large construction projects abroad where American companies are involved. It then contacts these companies with an offer to supply tools.

A similar approach is followed by EduSystems of Fontana, Wisconsin. This small concern sells complete packages of vocational education products to foreign governments. In addition to providing all of the equipment needed for a vocational or technical school, EduSystems plans, designs, purchases, consolidates, ships, and installs the equipment. The company identifies new opportunities by monitoring announcements of new educational projects from funding agencies such as the World Bank and the Agency for International Development, as well as by tracking the announcements of individual countries. Then the company engages in a bidding process to secure a contract.

Trade Audits

A technique that is especially suitable for consumer goods companies is a trade audit. Parker Pen Company of Janesville, Wisconsin, has refined this approach and finds it very useful in its international market research.

With trade audits, a company attempts to size up the market potential from the perspective of the channel members. A senior vice president of Parker Pen describes that company's use of trade audits in the following way:

> With trade audits, it is important to understand that we are viewing the potential from the eyes and the level of the retail trade. No more. We begin by listing the key questions

we want answered, and in some cases it is an omnibus list: First, what accounts are we in, and where aren't we? What is our penetration of the market by distribution channel (e.g., jewelry, stationery, gift shop, pharmacy and other outlets)? Second, how does the trade regard us? What is our company's image in the eyes of the trade concerning quality of our products, discounts, terms, sales calls, deliveries, after-sales service, and other aspects? Third, what is our visibility in the store? How well are our displays (space and technique) versus competition? What is the client's view of our advertising? Most popular and most successful promotions? Best and worst selling products? Fourth, what are the characteristics of the gift market versus personal purchase market? What are the most important factors in buying a gift? Gift box? Price? Clerk? Etc.

We normally conduct trade audits using a team of 10 to 15 people and always include people from the outside so that we assure objectivity. This team will spend one or two weeks combing major trading centers. They are given maps each day and told to cover a certain number of square blocks. Each is equipped with a standard questionnaire. We have called on as few as 300 accounts during an audit and as many as 900.

In addition to providing the company with a realistic profile of how it stands in a particular market (for example, penetration of the market, perception of company products, sales terms, delivery, service), trade audits can help identify competitive strengths and weaknesses. To the extent that a representative portion of the trade is surveyed and objectivity in data collection is assured, trade audits can be reliable in estimating potential demand for company products.

Given the increasing importance of international business opportunities, companies need to be more methodical in their approach to identifying and cultivating export market opportunities. Systematic export market research can facilitate successful international business involvement.

Note

1. Non-U.S. firms should be aware that DOC documents are available to them as well as similar information from their domestic government agencies.

22

Market Research the Japanese Way*

JOHNY K. JOHANSSON
IKUJIRO NONAKA

When Sony researched the market for a lightweight portable cassette player, results showed that consumers wouldn't buy a tape recorder that didn't record. Company chairman Akio Morita decided to introduce the Walkman anyway, and the rest is history. Today it's one of Sony's most successful products.

Morita's disdain for large-scale consumer surveys and other scientific research tools isn't unique in Japan. Matsushita, Toyota, and other well-known Japanese consumer goods companies are just as skeptical about the Western style of market research. Occasionally, the Japanese do conduct consumer attitude surveys, but most executives don't base their marketing decisions on them or on other popular techniques. As the head of Matsushita's videocassette recorder division once said, "Why do Americans do so much marketing research? You can find out what you need by traveling around and visiting the retailers who carry your product."

Hands-on Research

Of course, Japanese corporations want accurate and useful information about their markets as much as U.S. and European companies do. They just go about it differently. Japanese executives put much more faith in information they get directly from wholesalers and retailers in the distribution channels. Moreover, they track what's happening among channel members on a monthly, weekly, and sometimes even daily basis.

---

* Reprinted from *Harvard Business Review*, (May-June 1987), pp. 16–22, with permission.

Japanese-style market research relies heavily on two kinds of information: "soft data" obtained from visitors to dealers and other channel members, and "hard data" about shipments, inventory levels, and retail sales. Japanese managers believe that these data better reflect the behavior and intentions of flesh-and-blood consumers.

Japanese companies want information that is context specific rather than context free—that is data directly relevant to consumer attitudes about the product, or to the way buyers have used or will use specific products, rather than research results that are too remote from actual consumer behavior to be useful. When Japanese companies do conduct surveys, they interview consumers who have actually bought or used a product. They do not scrutinize an undifferentiated mass public to learn about general attitudes and values. When Toyota wanted to learn what Americans preferred in small, imported cars, for example, the company asked owners and others who had driven the car what he liked or disliked about the Volkswagen Beetle.

Soft-Data Gathering

Senior as well as middle-level Japanese managers get involved in gathering soft data because they see the information as critical both for market entry and for maintaining good relationships later. Though impressionistic, such hands-on data give the managers a distinctive feel for the market—something they believe surveys or quantitative research methods can't supply. Talks with dealers yield realistic, context-specific information about competitors' as well as their own market performance.

A good example is Canon's decision on a new U.S. distribution strategy. In the early 1970s, the company's senior management became concerned about U.S. camera sales. Other product lines were doing well, but camera sales had lost ground to the chief competitor, Minolta. Canon finally decided it needed its own sales subsidiary because its distributor, Bell & Howell, wouldn't give additional support for the Canon line. Senior managers didn't use a broad survey of consumers or retailers to make this decision. They sent three managers to the United States to look into the problem and changed strategies based on their observations.

Canon's head of the U.S. team himself spent almost six weeks in 1972 visiting camera stores and other retail outlets across the United States. From talks with store owners, Tatehiro Tsuruta learned that U.S. dealers weren't giving Canon much support because their sales forces were too small. He also found out what kinds of cameras and promotional support would get them excited about the company's line.

This soft-data approach appears to lack the methodological rigor of scientific market research, but it's by no means haphazard or careless. In fact, Tsuruta's results were more meaningful because he actually observed how consumers behaved in the stores and how salespeople responded. On entering a store, Tsuruta would act as if he were just a customer browsing around. He would note how the cameras were displayed and how the store clerks served customers. Then by simply asking "What cameras do you stock?" he could assess whether the dealer was enthusiastic or indifferent about the Canon line. He could also determine how knowledgeable people were about camera features.

Tsuruta would then identify himself and invite the store manager to lunch to discuss cameras and whatever else happened to be on the dealer's mind. The payoff was more than just market research. He was building lasting relationhips with the dealers—an important competitive advantage.

When Tsuruta visited drugstores and other discount outlets that Minolta favored, he could see that these markets wouldn't work for Canon. Customers got poor service—in part because salespeople knew little about the products they were selling. The mass merchandisers' heavy price competition also made it difficult to project a quality image.

Tsuruta's research decided Canon's distribution strategy: sell exclusively through specialty dealers serving an upscale, high-quality niche just below Nikon's targeted segment. The successful introduction of Canon's AE-1 camera in 1976 proved the strategy right.

Canon is by no means unique among Japanese companies in the sales and distribution problems it experienced in the United States or in the means it used to remedy them. A group of managers Honda sent to the United States in 1965 learned to their surprise that few dealers there stocked and serviced motorcycles exclusively. Company executives realized they would have to develop their own dealer network. Sony entered the U.S. radio and TV market in the late 1950s and almost immediately decided to establish its own U.S. distributor so it could be sure to get adequate sales support.

This soft-data approach is popular even after a Japanese company has penetrated the market. Frequent visits to people on the distribution channel help manufacturers resolve problems before they escalate and damage sales or relationships. Isao Makino, president of Toyota's U.S. sales subsidiary from 1975 to 1983—a period of great gains in market share—used to visit every Toyota dealer in the United States at least once a year. "I found," he said, "that out of the ten complaints from each dealer, you could attribute about five or six to simple misunderstandings, another two or three could be solved on the spot, and only one or two needed further work."

Hard-Data Gathering

When Japanese managers want hard data to compare their products to competitors', they look at inventory, sales, and other information that show the items' actual movement through the channels. Then they visit channel members at both the retail and wholesale levels to analyze sales and distribution coverage reports, monthly product movement records (weekly for some key stores), plant-to-wholesaler shipment figures, and syndicated turnover and shipment statistics on competitors.

Japanese managers routinely monitor their markets at home and abroad this way. Consider how Matsushita dealt with the weak performance of its Panasonic line distributor in South Africa. The sales figures he reported were reasonable, but he couldn't produce reliable data on sales and shares for the various types of stores or on inventory levels in the distribution chain.

In early 1982, three managers from the company's household electronics division paid a call on the South African distributor. Then they dropped in on the distributor's retail stores and wholesale facilities. Customarily, after exchanging greetings and presenting a token gift from headquarters, they got right down to business. They asked to see inventory, shipment, and sales records as part of a complete store audit covering Matsushita and competitive products. Six weeks later, after analyzing all the data, they gave the incredulous distributor a complete picture of Panasonic's product movement and market share through the entire South African channel. They also told the distributor what figures he should collect and report to the home office in the future.

Monitoring the Channels

Japanese managers try to track changing customer tastes closely and quickly. Their "one step at a time" management style for decision making also applies to how they approach marketing. After analyzing both hard and soft data on their channels, they make small, incremental changes in product features, packaging, and promotional efforts. Awareness of what's happening in the channels on a weekly or even daily basis gives them a deep and focused understanding of the marketplace and enables them to fine-tune their marketing rapidly—thereby protecting their competitive edge. This skill is especially important in the highly competitive packaged goods and consumer durable goods markets.

Kao Corporation, which dominates the detergent and soap market in Japan, illustrates this tight channel monitoring and incremental changes in marketing strategies. Kao executives analyze point-of-sales data weekly and wholesale inventory and sales statistics monthly.

The company occasionally uses consumer surveys and other quantitative research tools, but executives never base marketing decisions primarily on the information from them. These findings merely trigger more thorough audits of the channels using both soft- and hard-data gathering. If a survey or household panel study, for example, shows a sudden change in brand preferences or in family purchase patterns, Kao will send a high-level management team out to the stores. The group will spend one day at each store just observing customer behavior. The next day the team will talk to the store owner or manager to learn what kinds of support will move the products better. They'll also ask if the dealers needs help stocking shelves or if special promotions would help.

Such tight channel monitoring has paid off handsomely for Kao, among others. When Procter & Gamble introduced disposable diapers in Japan in the mid-1970s, it immediately took 90% of this new growing market. Lured by the big sales and earnings potential, Uni Charm, Kao, and other Japanese manufacturers created their own lines. With tight channel monitoring, the Japanese could quickly change product features to better suit consumer tastes, and by 1984 P&G's market share had plummeted to an anemic 8%.

One factor that frustrates U.S. and other Western corporations' efforts to enter Japanese distribution channels is their lack of knowledge about distributor expectations, which limits their ability to respond to consumer tastes. The handicapped Westerners can't refine their marketing quickly enough in Japan to parry competitors' moves.

Tight channel monitoring also improves operations and cost control. Kao and other Japanese companies would never be caught with the kind of inventory pileups that Warner Communications' Atari subsidiary found itself saddled with in 1983. A six-month lag in reports from retailers led to disastrous inventory levels of TV game cassettes.

Strong Vertical Integration

Japanese companies exert considerably more control over their distribution channels than do most U.S. and European corporations. Toyota has been more successful than Nissan in the Japanese market because of its stronger distribution network. In many cases, this control is nearly absolute because the manufacturer actually owns the distributors or has sufficient market power to dominate the channel. Shiseido, for example, a cosmetics manufacturer, has a strong market presence in Japan. It sells through a network of independent stores that use company-trained salespeople and reserve exclusive shelf space for the company's brands. In Japan, a consumer's choice of store often dictates what brand he or she will buy.

Such strong vertical integration affects the kind and quality of market research information Japanese managers can gather. They can shift some research tasks to the dealers, for example. It's not unusual for store employees to survey Japanese households by mail or phone, interview people when they come into a store, or even visit customers' homes for a talk.

Japanese salespeople change jobs less often than U.S. and European retail employees, so they are in a better position to develop expertise about customers and competitors. Moreover, stores tend to remain in the same locations. When Matsushita wants information on its Japanese customers, it goes to its 4,000 retail stores to find out.

General Managers

Few Japanese managers at all corporate levels have received a formal business education; it is still something of a novelty in Japan. Other than Keio Business School, only a few business institutes exist there, and those offer continuing education programs more often than degree options.

That's one reason why marketing isn't yet a specialized business profession in Japan—and hence one of several reasons why Japanese companies haven't adopted Western-style market research. But even if formal training in marketing did exist, Japanese executives would probably consider the marketing function too important to leave to mid-level specialists.

Honda is a case in point. When it picked Kihachiro Kawashima to head its U.S. sales organization, the company chose a domestic sales expert who knew very little about the United States. Kawashima ascribes his ultimate success in America to three principles: "Be real, be close to the action, and be localized." What made the difference for Honda in the United States was the senior managers' decision to spend up to 50% of their time visiting and talking with distributors and dealers—the people who knew what U.S. customers really wanted. The ultimate goal of this hands-on, close-to-the customer approach is to generate a better understanding of customer desires and behavior. The Japanese don't see marketing as something like engineering or finance that can be taught in school. Sensitivity to customers' desires is learned through hard work and experience.

Consensus Decision Making

In contrast to Western practice, Japanese executives don't give managers sole responsibility for a research area. They conduct research and make decisions by consensus, and they lean toward their intuitive judgment. Rarely do Japanese executives call in an outside professional, and when they do, they often disregard the consultant's report if it goes against their instincts about the best course of action. When Kozo Ohsone, the executive in charge of developing Sony's portable, compact Discman, heard that the company's marketing people were thinking about commissioning a research study, he told them not to waste their money.

Lack of Diversification

Tight channel monitoring is also closely associated with the more specialized nature of Japanese industry. Most Japanese corporations have only one or a few related product lines, so managers and employees at all levels can learn more easily what's needed to succeed in the business. This specialization fosters an inductive, bottom-up approach to business planning and problem solving, whereas U.S. and European managements favor more deductive, top-down planning methods. Many large, diversified American corporations have to depend on Western-style market research because they lack the experience and knowledge to sell effectively in multiple industries. But outside marketing consultants and the battery of survey and other research tools they offer cannot fully substitute for intimate knowledge of distribution channels and customer tastes.

But Will it be Enough?

General Electric's chief, John F. Welch, put it this way, "The Japanese have got the American consumer's number." Hands-on market research has given Japanese companies solid beachheads in the United States and other countries. Especially in mature industries like consumer goods, where customer preferences are so well understood, incremental adjustments in product features or promotional tactics may be all that is needed to have a competitive product.

Japanese-style research is starting to catch on in the United States and in other Western countries. Western executives are trying to get close to the customer and fine-tune product lines and marketing practices after listening carefully to what customers and distributors tell them. But this practice is still the exception in the West.

Ironically, just as some American and European executives are adopting a hands-on approach, a few Japanese companies are asking if their market research style can sustain their competitive edge over the long run—especially in the global marketplace. Some Canon executives, for example, are coming around to the view that surveys and other more scientific methods may be necessary as the company begins to look for ways to diversify.

Why are both sides changing like this? Increasing internationalization of both industries and business practices is doubtless one important reason. Global marketing is leading to a blending of managerial cultures and practices for all countries. Japanese executives are now thinking they may need some Western practices to keep their overseas footholds.

Consider, for example, the problem that Shiseido experienced in the U.S. market. Because it followed the Japanese tradition of sending in executives and managers from the home country, rather than hiring foreign nationals to fill top overseas posts, the company made no headway in the United States for ten years. No one at Shiseido headquarters understood that its cosmetics had to be introduced first into the high-status New York City stores before they could be sold successfully elsewhere. Only after hiring an experienced American cosmetics executive did Shiseido finally get its U.S. marketing effort on the right track.

Japanese corporations' reluctance to hire non-Japanese executives reflects a kind of provincialism that now poses hazards in an era of global markets. Their approach to market research could reinforce this parochialism because it focuses management attention on products and markets that the company already knows well—rather than on potential markets and industries. In their intensive channel monitoring, Japanese business leaders may see only narrow paths and miss the big picture.

Japanese executives today may need a broader perspective than they have taken in the past. Concentration on step-by-step marketing changes may keep them from spotting the social and economic trends that can throw seemingly unshakable industries into upheaval—precisely the changes that large-scale surveys and other Western-style methods uncover very effectively. As bulging surplus cash reserves and global marketing pressures push big Japanese corporations to diversify, more Japanese managers may begin to consider the potential advantages of Western-style market research.

23

Demand Estimation in a Developing Country Environment: Difficulties, Techniques and Examples*

LYN S. AMINE
S. TAMER CAVUSGIL

Introduction

Thus far, scant attention has been paid in the literature to the problem of estimating market demand *from within* a developing country. Multinational companies considering entry into an L.D.C. market often have difficulty in accessing needed information and using rigorous data analysis methods. When one attempts to assess past, present or future marked demand in an L.D.C., improvization may have to be the final resort.

This paper demonstrates that improvization was indeed the only recourse available in estimating market demand for two consumer products in Morocco. The empirical research reported here was conducted under the aegis of the Moroccan national business school (I.S.C.A.E.). First a review of the related literature is presented. A discussion of alternative techniques for demand estimation is provided next. Then a profile of the environmental context of Morocco is offered, followed by the presentation of the two examples. Finally implications for marketing practitioners are identified and the value of these methods in a developing country are assessed.

---

*Reprinted in abridged form from *Journal of the Market Research Society*, Vol. 28, No. 1 (1986), pp. 43–65, with permission.

A Review of the Literature

The literature can be reviewed in three distinct categories: (a) determining market potentials in international marketing, (b) opportunities and problems associated with marketing research in L.D.C.s, and (c) difficulties of cross-national research.

Determining Market Potentials

In a classic article, Moyer (1968) describes techniques appropriate for determining potentials. Brasch (1979) distinguishes the determination of export market potential for a product from the determination of national market potential, which is a separate and recurring task. Lindberg (1982) discusses the use of ratios to express economic activities and/or demand for durable consumer goods, concluding that relative demand is a useful ratio (the proportion of a country's personal consumption expenditure spent on the good being investigated) in potential analysis. Although pertinent to the present case, none of these contributions addresses directly the problem of use of proxy variables in place of unavailable data—a major characteristic of the examples discussed below.

Marketing Research in L.D.C.s

Typically a long, familiar list of unremitting difficulties is encountered when undertaking marketing research in L.D.C.s. For example, the feelings of suspicion and the tendency to exaggerate are common among L.D.C. managers and consumers alike. Major problems include the lack of research organizations. The failure of universities to cooperate with industry, the lack of data availability, restrictions on sample selection, and unpredictable behavior among interviewers and interviewees alike.

In many countries where demand typically exceeds supply, there is little motivation for producers either to study the market or to satisfy consumers. In the context of the Egyptian industry it has been said that "(Companies) have a long way to go to make fair use of marketing research. It is generally regarded as some kind of luxury that can be disposed of. Most companies do not normally think of marketing research except in crisis situations." Some progress in both attitudes and methods is reported in Turkey. Thus, there exists a paradox between the economic imperative demanding more marketing research in developing countries and the empirical evidence reporting just the contrary.

Marketing research conducted by an agent outside the country (e.g.

a multinational corporation or a world development agency) may be more sophisticated due to increased familiarity with methods, more research funds and resources, longer lead time, and/or more "authority" as an outside agent in gaining cooperation. Systems models have been applied to survey findings on consumer behavior in the area of family planning in Kenya. Typically, however, U.S. executives trained in the use of quantitative techniques make less use of them abroad, particularly in L.D.C.s. Unreliability of statistics and slowness in obtaining information are two contributing factors. In the highly individualized markets of Asia, flexibility and creativity are needed for successful research in the region.

In sum, marketing research within L.D.C.s continues to be hampered by well-known practical and conceptual problems which often render sophisticated analysis techniques either inappropriate or worse, inoperable.

Cross-National Research

Even if one escapes the pitfalls of the "self-reference criterion", commonly accepted assumptions, constructs and methodologies may themselves be a source of difficulty when applied to a cross-national context. For example, a five-country study found that the attainment of measure equivalence is seemingly more difficult for attitudinal and perceptual variables than for demographic and other background variables.

Mayer (1978) has taken an integrative approach to multinational marketing research pointing out the many pitfalls that the multinational marketer learns to avoid through experience. Mayer emphasizes the reality that different cultures have different response styles and that not all survey instruments are available in all countries. This is vividly illustrated by a Kuwaiti market research director's sardonic comment: "It is difficult to find people, needless to mention a representative sample, walking on the pavement in the hot sun." The plethora of market research agencies operating out of Athens, Cyprus and London, each with their own area of geographic or functional specialization confirms the need for specialist knowledge of individual market areas within such broad regions as the Middle East and North Africa.

This review highlights those problems to be anticipated when conducting marketing research and market forecasting in an L.D.C. environment, namely:

- inaccessibility or absence of published data.
- lack of research resources (survey funds, agencies, data processing facilities, trained interviewers, etc).

● hostility among local nationals toward survey and interview methods, and/or "halo" effects among actual respondents trying to please the interviewer.

These problems result in three types of sub-optimization in research:

● forced simplification of research methods.
● improvization in the use of proxy data.
● guesstimates to replace missing or unavailable data.

All three were encountered in the examples to be presented after a brief discussion of alternative techniques for demand estimation.

Alternative Techniques for Demand Estimation

Specific techniques for measuring demand for a product in L.D.C. markets can generally be categorized in the following groups:

1. Method of analogy
2. Macro surveys
3. Multiple factor indices
4. Chain ratio method
5. Proxy indicators
6. Trade audits
7. Analysis of production and import trends.

The first three techniques were not suitable for estimating demand in the context of the examples discussed. The other four techniques were used, resulting in varying degrees of precision. All of the above techniques are discussed briefly below. (For more information on these techniques, see Moyer 1968, Samli 1978, Douglas, Craig and Keegan 1982, Cavusgil 1984 and the 1976 special issue of the *Columbia Journal of World Business*.)

1. Method of analogy. Analyzing market potential in itself is a difficult task. If the available data are scarce or inadequate, the task is further complicated. One of the techniques useful in such situations is estimation by analogy. There are two approaches to the application of this method, cross-section comparisons and time-series analyses.

Cross-section comparison entails computing the ratio of a particular economic indicator for two countries for which data are available. This ratio is then used as an estimate of the consumption ratio for the two countries. The economic indicator utilized in computing the ratio may be the G.N.P., per capita income, disposable personal income, or some other gross economic variable. If the demand estimate for one of the two countries is known, then by using the ratio just computed, it is possible to calculate the demand estimate for the second country.

When using time-series analysis to estimate the demand for a product or commodity in one country, we utilize the demand level for the same or a similar product in a second country at a time when it was at the same level of economic development or growth as the first. The underlying assumption behind this approach is that product usage varies with the level of economic development.

Use of either approach will lead to incorrect estimates if:

- the consumption functions are non-linear;
- consumption patterns vary significantly due to cultural differences;
- technological innovations allow use of a product in a country at an earlier stage of economic development; or
- other factors such as competition, pricing, packaging, or trade barriers cause actual sales to be different from the estimate of market potential.

2. Macro survey approach. This technique can be used when market information is either not available or inadequate. The technique is based on an examination of the presence or absence of specialized types of institutions in a community. There are two basic steps for determining market potential. First is the construction of two scales, one indicating the relative stage of community growth, and the second indicating the commercial advancement of the community. The second step is to infer growth and market potential. If the market is not adequately developed in terms of commercial activity, it will not be able to carry the load of distributing goods, whether imported or locally produced. The market potential is inferred by applying both scales to certain absolutes.

3. Multiple factor indices. Multiple factor indices rest basically upon two major aspects of a market, size and quality. In the absence of detailed data and in the presence of unfamiliar market conditions, this method may be used to provide a reasonable approximation of the total market. In most cases population is considered a reasonable measure of market size. Market quality, on the other hand, necessitates an analysis of the internal conditions prevailing in the market. Two aspects of market quality may be considered: the degree of economic development and the quality of life. A series of general indicators with appropriate relative weights are used for this purpose. The degree of economic development is detected by surrogate measures such as the consumption of steel, the amount of electricity produced (kwh), income and employment in manufacturing. Motor vehicle registrations, the number of televisions in use, the number of radios in use, and the number of telephones in use have been employed as useful indicators of the quality of life.

4. Chain ratio method. This method of demand estimation involves multiplying a base number by several "adjusting" percentages. The base, which represents the maximum size of the total market potential, is gradually reduced by applying a series of percentages in order to create a smaller but more realistic magnitude of potential. For example, the potential market for beer drinkers can be better represented by considering the *percentage* of the beer drinking population—say those in the 18 to 60 age category. As long as the initial base is reduced sequentially by considering meaningful dimensions and realistic percentages, the chain-ratio method usually represents a practical approach to demand estimation.

5. *Proxy indicators.* In the absence of any useful information about the product category to be studied, one may resort to using information about another product category whose consumption patterns bear some similarities to those of the first product category. This simple approach may lead to useful results especially if the two products exhibit a complementary demand relationship. For example, a proxy or surrogate indicator of demand for professional hand tools may be the level of construction activity. Surrogate indicators of potential for a particular piece of medical equipment in a market may include total number of hospital beds or total number of surgeries performed. The application of proxy indicators to demand estimation can be defended to the extent that there is a meaningful relationship in the consumption of the two product categories.

6. *Trade audits.* An alternative approach to demand estimation is to survey a portion or all of the present and potential channel members (including importers, wholesalers, distributors, and retailers) for the product category. The major advantage of a trade audit is that the potential is viewed through the eyes of the *trade members* in a market who are the immediate customers for the product. These intermediaries reflect the perspectives of the final users or consumers.

The primary objective of a trade audit is to ascertain product potential by relying on the insights and expertise of channel members. Trade audits direct a series of questions to the respondents ranging from the product's characteristics (price, packaging, distinctiveness, etc.) to the company's image in the eyes of the trade. Other issues which may be explored relate to the channel composition, market penetration by competing companies, advertising and promotion, or price levels. Results of a trade audit may indicate opportunities for new modes of distribution, identify types of alternative outlets, and finally, give insights into company standing relative to the competition.

7. *Analysis of production and import trends.* It is possible to achieve a close approximation of market demand by adding together local

production figures and imports, with adjustments made for exports and current inventory levels. Although international organizations such as the United Nations publish the statistics needed for this kind of analysis, considerable problems may be encountered in the case of L.D.C.s which report late, incomplete or simply inaccurate figures. Underlying a simple method of extrapolation is the assumption that trends of the immediate past will continue and be repeated in the future. This is certainly a risky assumption in L.D.C. environments which are characterized by abrupt economic policy changes, rapid economic growth, or political upheaval.

Having briefly reviewed alternative techniques for demand estimation, we will now present a short profile of the specific L.D.C. environment in which several of these methods were applied when estimating demand for two consumer products.

The Environmental Context

Morocco is the Muslim Arab Kingdom situated at the western end of the Mediterranean. Topographically and politically Morocco is part of North Africa and a member of the "Maghreb" trading group along with Algeria and Tunisia. Recent involvement in the war with Algeria over possession of the Western Sahara has had serious repercussions on the Moroccan economy. Current national problems focus on management of the heavy burden of foreign debt. Long-term development objectives include: maintenance of a free market economy directed by five-year plans; rapid modernization of the way of life (compatible with Islamic traditions); and the general emancipation of the people through education, health services, and equal employment opportunities. However, unemployment, underemployment and illiteracy are major problems among a population of approximately 20 million, 50% of whom are under age 20.

The concept of marketing is steadily gaining significance in the business community. Causing this trend are several factors including: the presence of numerous multinational marketing companies (Nestlé, Unilever, Procter and Gamble, Ford, Navistar—some of which are "Moroccanized" in name, ownership, and management); the existence of a university-level business school in Casablanca (I.S.C.A.E.); the activities of five major advertising agencies (Shem's, Univas, T.O.P., K.L.E.M., Cinemapresse) and one international marketing research agency (M.E.M.R.B.).

Notable characteristics of Moroccan business customs are: a relentless drive to preserve business and administrative secrecy at all levels; a general fascination with novelty and innovation in all its forms; and widespread and rapid imitation of successful new ideas.

Marketing research activities of any type meet with much resistance, being considered an invasion of privacy by business people and consumers alike. However, once successful inroads are made, then "me-too" activities will soon follow. For example, when the leading commercial bank decided to attempt high-street intercept surveys of consumer satisfaction with banking services in Casablanca, within one month all four major competitors had carried out similar surveys with the assistance of business school students.

This overview indicates potential problem areas in evaluating market demand. The two examples illustrate a series of major problems, both practical and conceptual in nature, but in each case, the demand estimation problem is resolved using different techniques.

Evaluation of the Market for Locally Produced Wallpaper

Market Description

Traditionally, homes in Morocco were built to the classic Arab model of single-family homes with two floors built around an open courtyard. Floors and walls are decorated by ceramic tiles, and ceilings are covered with wood carvings or stucco reliefs. Modern homes consist of villas with two floors or two/three-bedroom condominium apartments. These modern homes represent the target market for wallpaper.

Nine importers were the sole source of supply for the local market. Therefore an opportunity for import substitution existed which would benefit from government support grants. A market evaluation study was commissioned by the leading local printer interested in diversification into this industry. The objective was to track past demand patterns with a view to forecasting future demand.

Data Requirements

Initial data requirements specified such items as: historical import data by value and volume; domestic sales records; discretionary income by type of household; income distribution; home construction data; and general lifestyle information. Typically, when researching markets in L.D.C.s, the tendency is to collect significant amounts of general supporting data in order to establish as coherent a picture as possible of markets which often operate under chaotic conditions. Even though a local company was involved here, it was diversifying out of its familiar market and thus faced many types of uncertainty commonly encountered by foreign marketers.

Improvised Use of Available Data

Intensive searching revealed four potentially useful sources of secondary data. However, all suffered from various deficiencies as indicated below.

(1) *Import statistics.* Although available for ten years prior to this research, imports of wallpaper were recorded by weight (kgs) and value (thousands of dirhams). Wallpaper is sold by the roll and different qualities and designs have different weights. Since the number of rolls was not specified, one could not even speculate on the number of "modern" households buying wallpaper over the past ten years.

(2) *Domestic water-heater industry study.* This was completed by the national economic development bank (B.N.D.E.) and offered two types of indirectly useful data, population growth statistics and annual home construction figures. The B.N.D.E.'s objective was to determine the market for large, electric domestic water-heaters. For the purposes of our research, we assumed that if a home featured this important "modern" convenience, then in all probability family life-style (along with home decorations) would also be more modern than for families in traditional homes. Consequently, these modern homes could be considered legitimate members, actual or potential, of the target market for wallpaper sales.

Importers claimed that the expected life of the product was five years. The "ballpark" figure for number of modern households (equal to the proxy market for water-heaters) was therefore divided by five to establish a base number of assumed customer households per year. Population growth statistics of 5% per annum gave some indication of expected expansion rate of the total consumer market, but not specifically of our identified "modern" segment.

(3) *Study of the potential market for locally produced wallpaper.* Although of great apparent relevance, this research by the Office for the Development of Industry (O.D.I.) proved virtually useless. As mentioned, imports were recorded by weight, therefore O.D.I. researchers had calculated future demand per inhabitant also by weight. The study assumed that all consumers, traditional or modern, urban or rural, were potential customers with the result that the final weight per inhabitant was infinitesimal. Clearly, in an L.D.C. such as Morocco such assumptions are invalid.

(4) *Income distribution study.* Again, although of great apparent use, the propagandist nature of this study entitled "Inequality for how long?," published by the local periodical *Liberation* suggested the need for caution in using these statistics. It was asserted that 65.4% of national

TABLE 23.1 Estimating Consumption of Wallpaper for an 11 Year Period using Chain Ratio Method

	Year 1	Year 2	Year 3	Year 4	Year 5	Year 6	Year 7	Year 8	Year 9	Year 10	Year 11
A	14,174	14,529	14,893	15,267	15,692	16,124	16,570	17,025	17,450	17,887	18,334
B = 0.2(A)	2,834.8	2,905.8	2,978.6	3,053.4	3,138.4	3,224.8	3,314	3,405	3,490	3,577.4	3,666.8
C = B/5	566.96	581.16	595.72	610.68	627.68	644.96	662.80	681.0	698.0	715.48	733.36
D = 0.1(C)	56.69	58.11	59.57	61.06	62.76	64.49	66.28	68.1	69.8	71.54	73.33
E = 0.25(D)	14.17	14.52	14.89	15.26	15.69	16.12	16.57	17.02	17.45	17.88	18.33
F = E × 30	425.1	435.6	446.7	457.8	470.7	483.6	497.1	510.6	523.5	536.4	549.9
G	425,100	435,600	446,700	457,800	470,700	483,600	497,100	510,600	523,500	536,400	549,900

Notes:

A—Population of Morocco in 000's (*Annuaires Statistiques du Maroc* 1974–1979).

B—Estimated one-fifth of the population with substantial purchasing power (*Liberation* 1980).

C—Estimate of five persons per household.

D—One-tenth of the population estimated responsible for the largest part of consumer expenditures (*Liberation* 1980).

E—Estimate of potential proportion of wallpaper purchasers (25%).

F—Estimated consumption of 30 rolls per household (000's) (survey data).

G—Total estimated consumption by number of rolls.

income was owned by 20% of the population making up the "class A." Moreover, a mere 10% of class A was responsible for 37% of total consumer expenditure. Many members of class A would clearly be customers for wallpaper along with other luxury and status items. We therefore assumed that the maximum size of the target market (in terms of individuals) included this 20% of the national population. Making the further assumption of five persons per household, it was then possible to estimate the number of households in the target market.

Our own survey of the nine importers using a standardized questionnaire and personal interviews yielded the following lifestyle information:

- Consumers shop for wallpaper as a complementary decoration to fitted carpets (in place of traditional rugs), modern living-room and bedroom sets.
- Generally, the wife makes all decisions regarding quality and style.
- Customers are members of the upper class consisting of professional, technical and commercial leaders and high-ranking administrators.
- Homes are modern and situated in the new or prestigous residential areas in Casablanca.
- Average annual household consumption of wallpaper is about 30 rolls.

All the foregoing assumptions, generalizations and resulting figures are summarized in Tables 23.1 to 23.3. These tables demonstrate the various calculations made on the basis of available data and proxy data. Values from each table are compared in Table 23.4 and a final average

TABLE 23.2 Estimating Consumption of Wallpaper using Proxy Data

	Year 6	Year 7	Year 8	Year 9	Year 10	Year 11
A	6,444	7,546	9,986	11,612	12,462	14,297
B	35,051	35,051	35,051	35,051	35,051	41,495*
C = (A + B)	41,495	42,597	45,037	46,663	47,513	55,792
D = C × 30	1,244,850	1,277,910	1,351,110	1,399,890	1,425,390	1,673,760

Notes:

A—Number of new homes equipped with a water heater (B.N.D.E.).

B—Number of existing homes equipped with a water heater, less an estimated 15% of traditional homes, spread equally over the five-year period (Years 6–11) to reflect assumed demand among established households (*Annuaires Statistiques du Maroc* 1974–1979).

*—Year 11 would be the first year of expected replacement purchases, assuming a product life of five years. Therefore Year 6 A and B values are summed for Year 11.

C—Total number of estimated customer households.

D—Total estimated consumption by number of rolls, assuming 30 per household (survey data).

TABLE 23.3 Estimating Demand for Wallpaper using Import Data

Year	Kilograms	Dirhams (000's)*	Rolls†
1	14,465	182	16,072
2	19,348	283	21,498
3	43,449	463	48,277
4	78,439	707	87,154
5	81,624	670	90,693
6	81,510	680	90,567
7	109,468	1,351	121,631
8	207,579	1,804	230,643
9	265,625	2,176	295,139
10	472,917	3,356	525,463
11	511,255	3,211	568,061

Notes:

*—*Annuaires Statistiques des Importations,* Department of Commerce, Morocco, 1969–1979.
†—Weight per roll varies from 500 gm to 1300 gm, standard quality weight being 500–600 gm and deluxe quality 1200–1300 gm. A mid-point of 900 gm was used as an average weight per roll in order to convert weight of imports into number of rolls.

value (number of rolls purchased per year) is calculated for a five-year period.

Discussion of Results

The comparison of results in Table 23.4 derived from the three different approaches invites several comments. First, we note the wide variation in magnitude of the three sets of estimates. Second, the general tendency is towards market growth. Third, annual percentage growth rates reveal a saw-tooth type of market expansion. This is probably explained by the unpredictable nature of import consignments for this product, the embryonic state of the industry, and perhaps the faltering first steps of a new fashion among modern households. Clearly, the variation between these sets of figures renders any accurate extrapolation a hazardous task. Probably a range of future values would be required, expressed as either "optimistic" or "pessimistic" scenarios.

TABLE 23.4 Comparison of Estimated Values for the Wallpaper Market calculated using Chain Ratios, Proxy Data and Import Statistics

	Year 6	Year 7	Year 8	Year 9	Year 10	Year 11
Table 1	483,600	497,100	510,600	523,500	536,400	549,900
Table 2	1,244,850	1,277,910	1,351,110	1,399,890	1,425,390	1,673,760
Table 3	90,567	121,631	230,643	295,139	525,463	568,061
Average value	606,339	632,213	697,451	739,509	829,084	930,573
Percentage value	—	+4.3%	+10.3%	+6.0%	+12.1%	+12.2%

In examining the magnitude of the values associated with the respective methods of demand estimation, we see that conversion of imports by weight into number of rolls gives the most modest values. In contrast, use of proxy data (water heaters) gives the most ambitious values. A combination of income and population estimates used in the chain ratio method gives a middle range of values. It is interesting to note that results for the chain ratio method and import data analysis tend to converge for years 10 and 11. This finding appears to endorse the value of the chain ratio method when compared with the more conventional analysis of import statistics. In contrast, results from use of proxy data are approximately three times greater than the other two sets of figures for years 10 and 11. This confirms the general principle that the further one strays from use of "hard" data, the greater the margin for variation and, presumably, error.

In the present case, the potential investor had no recourse for verifying actual accuracy of the three sets of values. The research confirmed that a growth market exists and that future demand by number of rolls might be expected to fall within a given range, albeit broad. Although cursory, this knowledge was used as a guideline in planning production capacity. It was expected that the local production unit would quickly reach a position of market dominance, benefiting from protectionist measures to be imposed by the government, namely import surcharges or restrictions placed upon the nine competitors. However, the acceptability of a locally-made wallpaper in relation to the well-known foreign products remained unexplored, invoking the complex marketing task of combating "country of origin" effects.

Evaluation of the Market for Bandaids

Market Description

In Morocco 70% of demand for pharmaceutical items including bandaids is met by local production which is concentrated in Casablanca, the commercial capital and major port. Sixteen manufacturing laboratories produce some 1,800 pharmaceutical items and also market a range of 600 foreign imported items.

The bandaid segment is supplied wholly through imports. This sector is experiencing rapid growth due to several factors including:

● rapid population growth (estimated at 2.5% per annum)
● free hospitalization and medication for the needy
● reimbursement of medical and drug expenses for on-the-job accidents

- reimbursement for government-backed mutual health insurance schemes.

In contrast factors limiting growth of this segment include:

- high fixed production costs resulting from strict government regulations and requirements (e.g., minimum wage and salary levels, high quality control standards, minimum inventory levels, full product-line representation, etc.)
- low levels of need and consumption in poor peasant and working-class areas (estimated to include 70% of the population)
- seasonal fluctuations in demand in tourist areas (e.g., north and south-west coastlines).

An attractive market opportunity was thus identified by the leading local pharmaceutical producer and marketing company for expansion of established activities into the bandaid segment. This move into import substitution would also benefit from generous government support grants. The major obstacle for this company was the lack of statistical data which might indicate the true dimensions of current market demand and allow some estimate of future potential. Although import statistics for the industry are consistently recorded and published, confused nomenclatures made it impossible to isolate the product group of bandaids. Moreover, an active black-market supplied by smugglers operates in the country, bringing in unknown quantities of bandaids from various sources through the Spanish enclaves of Ceuta and Melilla (on the north coast).

Data Requirements

Knowledge about the bandaid segment was superficial and incomplete. Three areas were documented through exploratory interviews with company members, namely consumer behavior, pricing policies, and distribution.

(1) *Consumer buying behavior.* The company's salesforce provided some insights on buying behavior. Consumers are known to be price-sensitive in buying bandaids but they also rely heavily on doctors and pharmacists to prescribe a brand-name product. Mistrust and dissatisfaction are common problems in poorer areas where uninformed consumers may have suffered the effects of harmful or ineffective pirated products.

(2) *Pricing practices.* Public distribution of manufactured or imported pharmaceutical items is regulated by the government which stipulates a "Moroccan Public Price" (P.P.M.). Industry pricing policy for bandaids is therefore as follows:

	%
Retail price	100
Pharmacist's discount	30
Pharmacist's price	70
Wholesaler's discount	10
Importer's price	60

(3) *Distribution channels.* Typical of many L.D.C. markets, distribution channels in Morocco are characterized by much confusion of functions, overlapping trade services, and unpredictable trade relations. The company sponsoring the research has always leaned heavily on sales to wholesalers, using some promotional "push" strategies but little point-of-sales material and no television advertising to consumers.

One of the early research tasks was to track the channels through which bandaids passed from importation to final purchase or use in order to indentify sources of supply and measure sales volume. The three alternative channels in Figure 23.1 were identified by company members and the research team. They illustrate distribution in the public and private sectors and serve to indicate the most appropriate methodology, a trade audit.

The objective for the trade audit was to collect statistical data on actual purchases by channel members at each stage of the channel. These would then be summed to arrive at an estimate of total current market demand for bandaids. This approach was necessary to detect the volume of smuggled brands which, of course, did not figure in

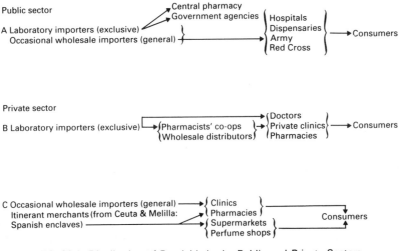

FIG. 23.1. Distribution of Bandaids in the Public and Private Sectors.

TABLE 23.5. Sample Characteristics of the Trade Audit

Channel member	Universe	Sample	Non-respondents
Importers	12	9	3 (2 refusals, 1 ceased trading)
Wholesalers	19	18	1 (refusal)
Pharmacies	360	31	0
Government agencies	Four major agencies and a large number of smaller buyers	4*	0

Note:

* The four agencies surveyed use the central purchasing system and are responsible for the bulk of purchases in the public sector. They are the Ministry of Health (supplying hospitals), the Ministry of Defence (supplying the Army), the Cherifian Phosphate Office (a major national employer), and the Hopital Avicenne in Casablanca (the major teaching hospital).

import statistics. These illegal supplies had reached sufficient proportions to seriously affect any estimate of market demand which might exclude them.

Trade Audit Methodology and Results

Four universes were defined within the distribution system for bandaids. Field surveys were carried out using standardized questionnaires administered during personal interviews. Census interviewing was attempted among importers and wholesalers but, as anticipated, some refusals made this incomplete. Judgmental sampling was carried out in the public sector focusing on the largest customers. Pharmacies were surveyed according to a stratified random sampling plan. The strata were designated as distinct zones within cities (e.g., old and new medinas, industrial areas, city centres, etc.). Final samples in the trade audit are described in Table 23.5.

The risks of incomplete results from survey research were anticipated along with other difficulties of marketing research in L.D.C.s, namely inadequate sampling, guesstimates by respondents, exaggeration and refusals. However, non-response was not expected to affect overall results since non-responding businesses were peripheral to the industry. Results from the trade audit are presented in Tables 23.6 to 23.10. Unit sales are not reported because of the great variety of

TABLE 23.6. Imports of Bandaids by Value (DH) Year 1-Year 5

Year	1	2	3	4	5
Imports (DH)	943,337.87	817,107.80	1,186,364.40	2,083,687.70	1,384,972.40
U.S.($)	188,667.57	163,421.56	237,272.88	416,735.74	276,994.48

Source: Survey of importers.   *Note:* US$1: 5DN.

TABLE 23.7. Public Sector Purchases of Bandaids by Volume and Value (DH)
Year 1-Year 5

Year	1	2	3	4	5
N of rolls	148,583	144,561	122,048	142,523	110,892
DH	842,417	1,075,528.1	1,038,889	1,368,583.9	1,280,043
U.S.$	168,483.4	215,105.62	207,777.8	273,716.78	256,008.6

Source: Survey of public sector institutions.   *Note:* US$1: 5DH.

bandaid sizes, shapes and applications which channel members were largely unable to record accurately.

Discussion of Results

One of the major problems of this trade audit was the lack of corroborative data with which to establish accuracy and reliability. The import figures in Table 23.6 demonstrate an average annual growth rate of about 18%. This parallels the growth rate of 17.1% per annum for total imports of pharmaceutical items. Although one naturally expects a high degree of correlation between the two, this finding tends to confirm the importers' accuracy and honesty in reporting their figures for bandaids. Similarly, the government-reported average annual growth rate for total consumption of pharmaceuticals for the seven-year period preceding this study, calculated at 16.9%, is reasonably close to the figure of 14% for private sector sales of bandaids (see Table 23.8).

Table 23.7 presenting figures for the public sector invites comment on the sawtooth pattern of growth. This is attributed to several factors. The central purchasing process had splintered considerably. For example, the municipality of Casablanca buys in its own name. Small rural services such as the Red Cross and State-run dispensaries even buy supplies from the local pharmacy at retail prices! An incidental factor appears for Year 2 when considerable overstocking took place which was compensated in Year 3. The Army and the Ministry of Health in contrast purchased at a consistent rate of growth over the five years.

Table 23.10 offers several interesting insights. The leading French brand, Peloille, demonstrates a normal pattern of progress through the channel of distribution. It is challenging to speculate whether effective representation at each stage has led to its position as a market leader. Alternatively, brand image and loyalty among pharmacists may be responsible for "pulling" the brand through the channels. It is unlikely that consumers pull the brand through the channel, given the lack of mass media advertising. The only other brands cited at all three

TABLE 23.8. Private Sector Sales of Bandaids by Value (DH) Year 1-Year 5

Year	1	2	3	4	5
A	253,088,000	246,929,000	277,949,000	340,923,000	429,786,000
B = 70/60 × A	295,269,000	288,083,000	324,273,000	397,743,000	501,417,000
C = 0.954% × B	2,816,866.2	2,748,311.8	3,093,564.4	3,794,468.2	4,785,518.1
U.S.$	563,373.24	549,662.36	618,712.88	758,893.64	957,103.62

Source: Survey of pharmacies.
Note: US$1: 5DH.
A—Total value of sales by all pharmacies in Morocco (at wholesale price) (*source*: Institut Marocain de Statistiques).
B—Total value of sales by all pharmacies in Morocco (at retail price).
C—Total value of sales of bandaids (at retail price). Bandaids were calculated to represent an average 0.954% of individual pharmacy sales on the basis of survey data.

TABLE 23.9 Summary Table Demand in Morocco for Bandaids (DH) Year 1-
Year 5

Year	1	2	3	4	5
D	842,417	1,075,528	1,038,889	1,368,584	1,280,043
E	2,816,866.2	2,748,311.8	3,093,564.4	3,794,468.2	4,785,518.1
F	*3,659,283.2*	*3,823,839.8*	*4,132,453.4*	*5,163,152.2*	*6,065,561.1*
U.S.$	731,856.64	764,767.96	826,490.68	1,032,630.4	1,213,112.2

Notes:
D—See Table 24.7 on public sector purchases.
E—See Table 24.8 on private sector sales.
F—Total value of bandaid market.

levels of distribution are the Chinese "Snowflake" and the West German "Beiersdorf." The cases of "Urgo" and "3M" illustrate the existence of some direct sales between exclusive importers and pharmacies (see schema B in Figure 23.1).

Finally, Table 23.9 presents the estimated total value of the bandaid market by summing figures for the public and private sectors. In extrapolating these figures into the future, the question arises as to the validity of the assumption that past economic conditions will continue into the future. In the event, for example, of a limitation or prohibition

TABLE 23.10. Trade Audit

Brands (country of origin)	Importers	Wholesalers	Pharmacies
Peloille (France)	×	×	× (market leader)
Durexport (France)	×	×	
Urgo (France)	×		×
Fisch (France)	×	×	
Beiersdorf (West Germany)	×	×	×
3M (West Germany)	×		×
Blank (West Germany)	×		
Albuplast (East Germany)	×	×	
Intermed (East Germany)	×	×	
Bioplast (Italy)	×	×	
Snow Flake (China)	×	×	×
Elastoplast (U.K.)		×	
E. A. (Japan)		×	
Agatone (Italy)		×	
Salvelox (Spain)		×	×
Malpaplast (not known)		×	×
Lenkoplast (not known)		×	
Malpasteril (Algeria)			×
Vitrofilm (not known)			×
Ankerplast (not known)			×
Sparaplast (not known)			×

Source: Survey data from the three groups of channel members, importers, wholesalers and pharmacists.

of imports, then the market opportunity for the potential investor would become many times greater. Doubtless also the "slack" would increasingly be taken up by the illegal pirated products already evident in the market.

Conclusion

Certainly the approaches to marketing research and market evaluation presented here are unusual. The needs for creativity and flexibility in undertaking marketing research abroad are clear. One wonders how such improvized methods might be viewed by professional researchers in sophisticated global marketing companies. Would they pursue a clear market opportunity such as the wallpaper case or abandon the project for "lack of data"? Could the available data in both the wallpaper and bandaid examples have been located by a researcher not familiar with the country? More seriously, would local market knowledge and cultural understanding be critical factors in successful use of such data? Finally, do the resultant figures inspire any confidence?

From the standpoint of the international marketer, it may be the case that certain research problems can only be solved through creative improvization where local market knowledge is a critical factor. In other cases, the greater resources of international companies allow deployment of considerable funds and effort for the collection of relevant primary data. However, even this approach may not be appropriate in countries where marketing research is viewed with suspicion or the product is too new for opinions and experience to have been established among consumers.

Insofar as our knowledge of marketing in L.D.C.s is concerned, we need to know not just that "doing research is a difficult task," but how the difficulties can be overcome to provide some workable estimates of actual or attempt to show how improvization, as a method, can be usefully applied.

References

Brasch, J. J., "Assessing Market Potential for Exports," *Journal of Small Business Management*, Vol. 17 (April 1979), pp. 13–19.

Cavusgil, S. T., *Researching Export Markets: A Guide to Successful Involvement in Exporting*, (forthcoming).

Columbia Journal of World Business, Special issue on forecasting (Winter 1976).

Douglas, S. P., Craig, C. S. and Keegan, W. J., "Approaches to Assessing International Marketing Opportunities for Small and Medium-Sized Companies," *Columbia Journal of World Business*, (Fall 1982), pp. 26–32.

Lindberg, B. C., "International Comparison of Growth in Demand for a New Durable Consumer Product," *Journal of Market Research*, Vol. 19 (August 1982), pp. 346–371.

Mayer, C. S., "The Lessons of Multinational Marketing Research," *Business Horizons*, Vol. 5 (December 1978), pp. 7–13.

Moyer, R., "International Market Analysis," *Journal of Marketing Research*, Vol. 5 (November 1968), pp. 353–360.
Samli, A. C., "An Approach for Estimating Market Potential in East Europe," *Journal of International Business Studies*, Vol. IX, No. 4 (Winter 1978), pp. 49–53.

24

Customer Analysis for Strategy Development in Industrial Markets*

N. C. G. CAMPBELL
M. T. CUNNINGHAM

Assessment of a company's strategic position must include an analysis of the company's situation in the markets which it serves. Normally, this analysis focuses on the company's products relative to competitors with questions such as: what are the sales trends, profits and market shares of different products in different market segments?

To do this analysis business planners have available an array of tools such as the well-known product portfolio matrix (Henderson 1970), the product-positioning matrix and the product/performance matrix (Wind 1982). Such tools neglect trends in purchases by individual customers, and profits and market shares by customer. This may be a weakness, particularly in concentrated industrial markets which have a small number of key customers.

This paper suggests that in many industrial markets, a company should develop its strategy from an analysis of existing customers. The analysis should highlight the current allocation of resources to different customers and customer groups and identify the company's position with key customers relative to competition in different market segments. The purpose of the analysis is to improve the allocation of scarce technical and marketing resources between different customers to achieve the supplier's strategic objectives. It leads to a reappraisal of a supplier's competitive strength with different customers, and it also ensures that relationships with key customers are managed more effectively.

*Slightly abbreviated from *Strategic Management Journal*, Vol. 4 (1983), pp. 369–380, with permission.

In contrast to Porter (1980) who lays stress on the need to counter-act buyers' bargaining power, this paper emphasizes the scope for developing relationships of mutual interdependent and shared objectives. This approach has its origin in a major research study which is briefly described in the next section.

Methodology

The new approach to industrial marketing and purchasing which underpins this paper is based on a continuing effort by the I.M.P. research group (Hakansson 1982) to understand the nature of buyer/seller relationships in industrial marketing. The major part of the I.M.P. project was an international cross-sectional study with companies selected to represent different types of products and different production technologies in a 3 by 3 matrix as below:

		Buyer's production technology		
		Unit production	Batch or mass production	Process manufacture
Sellers' product technology	Raw materials			
	Components and parts			
	Capital equipment			

This matrix enabled the research group to investigate the influence on supplier/customer relationships of the nature of the supplier's product and the nature of the customer's production process. Product complexity, product essentiality, frequency of purchase, consequences of product failure, and extent of adaptations by each partner, were among the factors investigated.

Some 300 companies drawn from 15 different industries in five countries were involved in the research. Interviews were conducted with marketing and purchasing managers, who were directly involved in, or knew about, particular relationships.

The ideas presented here came from further research carried out to complement the previous I.M.P. project. An intensive study over a two year period was conducted in the packaging industry in one European country. The research, using a "direct" approach, focused on the marketing strategy of a leading company through a detailed analysis of its relationships with 63 customers. Information about customer relationships was obtained from company records (sales and profit histories, age of relationships, resource allocation) and from semi-structured interviews with the 27 senior managers who had contact with customers. Several managers were interviewed more than once. Wherever possible each relationship was considered in the context of trading relations between other suppliers and customers in the same market segment. Altogether data were collected from the supplier for 167 trading relationships in 10 market segments. In addition, a cross-section of customers and non-customers was interviewed which generated additional information about their supplier relationships. In several cases, interviews were conducted with the buyer and seller on both sides of the same relationship.

The "interaction" approach to marketing and purchasing strategy which emerged from this research emphasizes the active role of both buyer and seller. Their interaction can lead to co-operation or conflict, and the implications of this approach for marketing and purchasing strategy are reported by different members of the I.M.P. group in Hakansson (1982).

The Need for Customer Analysis

That there is a need for customer analysis may seem self-evident. In fact there are a number of particular reasons why a customer analysis, in addition to a market and product analysis, is particularly relevant to industrial markets.

In industrial markets, a company's customers are often its greatest assets. Corey (1976 p. 5) says that "the development of strong, multi-dimensional and constructive working relationships with one's customers is the key to industrial marketing success". In addition, researchers beginning with Wind (1982) and Hakansson (1982) have testified to the importance of source loyalty and long-term relationships. One consequence is that, particularly in mature markets, it is difficult to break into new customers. This means that the supplier should avoid any erosion of loyalty by his existing customers. He must maintain his competitive strength with key customers on a regular basis.

Industrial concentration is high and probably increasing. Sawyer (1981) reports figures for the five firm concentration ratios derived from the British Census of Production for 1975. For 118 industries, at the 3 digit S.I.C. level, the largest 5 firms produced, on average, 50.6% of the net output. A similar high concentration is found in American industry and in the European Community and, although slight, there seems to be a continuing upward trend. With the largest 4 or 5 firms accounting for such a high proportion of activity in many industries, an emphasis on customer analysis seems greatly overdue.

Empirical evidence shows that suppliers tend to follow the growth and development of customers often by adding new products, and even new technologies, to continue to serve the needs of that customer. Indeed, Parkinson (1980) states that close cooperation between suppliers and customers enhances technical innovation, and Achiadelis *et al* (1971) have proposed that a thorough knowledge of customers' needs increases the probability of successful marketing of new products.

Although the argument above has concentrated on industrial markets, it also applies to many consumer markets, where manufacturers develop or sell "retailer branded" or "own label" products to a few large retailers and distributors. With the need for a customer analysis established, the next section describes the three steps proposed.

The Three Steps Proposed

Step 1: Life Cycle Classification of Customer Relationships

Despite its limitations the product life cycle is a useful concept. Why not apply the same idea to customers? Porter (1980) points out that, as an industry matures, customers tend to become more price sensitive. Their own margins are squeezed and they become more expert purchasers. To counteract this tendency the supplier must either develop new substitute products, or find ways to lower his production costs. He must allocate his resources appropriately to different customer groups. Table 24.1 suggests a simple classification of customers to each category.

Management should have all the information available except possibly customer profitability and the use of strategic resources. The

TABLE 24.1. Life Cycle Classification of Customer Relationships

Criteria for Classification of Customers	Customer Categories			
	Tomorrow's Customers	Today's Special Customer	Today's Regular Customers	Yesterday's Customers
Sales Volume	Low	High	Average	Low
Use of Strategic Resources†	High	High	Average	Low
Age of Relationship	New	Old	Average	Old
Supplier's Share of Customer's Purchases	Low	High	Average	Low
Profitability of Customer to Supplier	Low	High	Average	Low

Note †The technical, marketing and production resources devoted to developing future business rather than maintaining existing business concept of strategic resources is the same as that used by Hofer and Schendel. It includes the financial, technical, marketing and production resources, which are devoted to developing future business, rather than maintaining existing business. The classification of customer relationships is derived from the work of Cunningham and Homse and it owes a debt to Drucker, who proposed a similar analysis for products. Before describing each customer category it is necessary to emphasize that only customers for one product or one relatively homogeneous product group should be included in the same table. Where a company manufactures several different products, separate tables are needed. Thus, a company which is a regular customer for product A may appear as tomorrow's customer for a new product B.

Tomorrow's Customers. These are the customers that the company is trying to gain, or regain, at home or abroad. They may be customers in a new market area, opened up as a result of technical developments, or they may be vital "reference point" customers in an export market. Sales to these customers are low, but strategic resources are allocated to improve the current sales position and to develop the relationship.

Today's Special Customers. These customers usually purchase large quantities; they are old established and the company is continually engaged in development work with them. Frequently a supplier and its special customers have adapted to each other in various ways, mutual trust and commitment are at a high level and many people from each side are in regular contact. For example, such relationships exist between British Leyland and Lucas, between British Steel and Davy Engineering; Black and Decker and Marks and Spencer have policies of developing such special relationships with suppliers, and reports from Japan suggest that this structure is favored there (Campbell 1982).

Today's Regular Customers. These customers also purchase large quantities and the relationships are old established, but the exchanges are less intimate, the customers are less loyal and more price sensitive; development work tends to be intermittent.

Yesterday's Customers. These customers are often numerous, but, although the relationships are old established, each contributes only small sales volume and they receive little or no technical development work. Customers in this category are those in market segments now abandoned, or those whose requirements are now more like "commodities". The company continues to serve them, but without any great enthusiasm. However, they provide useful additional volume for little effort.

The number of customers and the proportion of sales in each category will differ from company to company. In the packaging company studied the proportions were as in Table 24.2. This company

TABLE 24.2. A Packaging Company's Customer Analysis

Category of Customer	Number of Customers	% of Sales	% of Technical Development Expenditure
Tomorrow's Customers	7	1	39
Today's Special Customers	2	43	38
Today's Customers	38	44	23
Yesterday's Customers	175	12	—
Total:	222	100	100

pursues an innovation strategy so that considerable resources are devoted to developing tomorrow's customers. The company also has two very special and important customers with whom relationships are especially close.

In any one year the number of customer companies and the proportion of sales in each category is not, by itself, very significant. The value comes from carrying out the exercise regularly and from monitoring the progress of tomorrow's customers. To justify the development expenses committed to them they must move to become either special or regular customers. The length of time before such a move takes place will vary depending on the industry. The time also varies depending on the circumstances under which the customer took on the new supplier. Contrast the following two situations. In the first, the customer's demand for the product is expanding; he is seeking additional sources of supply, and so he approaches the supplier. If the supplier is familiar with what is required, he will be able to meet the specification quickly, and the time from the start of the relationship to regular supplies may last only a matter of months. By contrast, assume that the second situation involves a proposal from the customer for the development of a substitute product which will save him money. If the application is outside the supplier's current knowledge, he must learn the requirements, and devote research and development time to establishing whether his technology will provide a solution. This process may take years.

To summarize, this classification provides management with a useful overview of its customers. It shows how the strategic resources, which will ensure the future health of the business, are allocated among customers. Management can ask whether the resources devoted are sufficient and, by following their progress, verify that prospects yield a reasonable return. The existence of special relationships with some customers is highlighted as well as the customer's dependence on them. Is the loyalty of such customers in danger of being eroded?

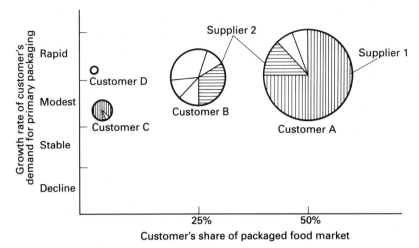

Note: Size of circle is size of customer's purchases of primary packaging and "pie slice" is size of each competitors share.

FIG. 24.1. Customer/competitor Analysis: Primary Packaging for a Range of Packaged Foods.

What can be done to strengthen the relationships? Or, are market conditions such that management should try to disengage from such customers, whose position in their own markets is weakening?

Step 2: Customer/Competitor Analysis by Market Segment

The life cycle classification of customers provides a general overview. The allocation of critical resources is highlighted and management can take decisions to retain or modify the amount. The next stage is to introduce competition and this is done by the use of a customer/ competitor chart for each market segment. A typical chart is presented in Figure 24.1 for one of the food markets in which the packaging company operates.

The horizontal axis simply measures the customer's share in his market. Thus in Figure 24.1 customer A has about 50% of the market, customer B has 25%, and there are two smaller companies. The vertical axis is a measure of the growth rate in the customer's demand for the product. This is not the same as the customer's sales growth, as it also reflects changes that may occur in usage of the product, owing to design changes at the customer or, because of penetration of the market by substitutes.

The size of each circle is a measure of the volume of the supplier's product purchased by each customer and the size of the "pie slice" represents the share of each competitor. Detailed market share information of this kind is not easy to obtain. Buyers are often reluctant to divulge the split of their business between suppliers. To get round this reluctance, the supplier needs to seek information from several sources—from technical and production staff of the customer, from other non-competitive suppliers, from other more open customers, and so on. In this way, suppliers can build up a reasonably accurate picture. In Figure 24.1, customer B purchases about half as much as customer A; supplier 1 has a dominant position with customers A and C, but does not sell to B; supplier 2, on the other hand, has a strong position with customer B, but a weaker one with A and C. The explanation for this pattern is bound up with the historical development of the trading relationships of each company.

To be useful, management should procure a customer/competitor chart for one product or one homogeneous product group. The product should serve the same customer function and be manufactured by the same basic technology for all customers on the chart. Thus, in Figure 24.1 the function is the primary packaging of a food product and the competitors all use the same technology. In other words, the chart does not mix different types of packaging (glass, plastic bags, cartons, etc.). Although Figure 24.1 is for a homogeneous product range it still masks differences between individual members of the range. Management can prepare separate charts where the additional analyses would yield greater insights.

The customer/competitor chart must also have a geographical boundary. Should it include only domestic customers and competitors, leaving out overseas companies? The choice depends on what is relevant and what is practically available in the way of data. It is best to make the geographical spread as wide as possible.

The value of the customer/competitor chart is to assess opportunities and threats. In Figure 24.1 supplier 1 has no sales to customer B. Should supplier 1 attack this customer? If it did, would supplier 2 retaliate and attack its large market share with customer A? Such questions are highlighted by the customer/competitor chart, as it enables management to see the strength of its position compared to competitors. Charts prepared over a number of years will indicate whether competitors are increasing their penetration.

In carrying out the customer/competitor analysis management may find it helpful to think broadly about the type of buyer/seller relationships which operate in their market segments. Buyer/seller relationships can take a wide variety of forms, but three general categories can be distinguished, as shown in Figure 24.2 and Table 24.3.

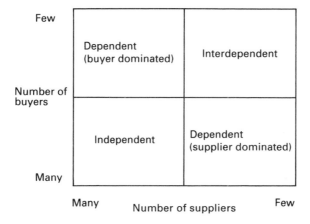

FIG. 24.2. Power Balance in Buyer/Seller Relationships.

Relationships are characterized by dependence when either the buyer or the supplier dominates. Relationships are buyer dominated when there are many suppliers and a few buyers; when the share the buyer takes of the supplier output is high; and when the buyer has a low need for the supplier's skills, but the buyer's requirements are specialized, so that suppliers must make an investment (in special facilities or knowledge). There are many examples of such buyer dominated relationships between the automotive companies and their smaller suppliers. Interdependent relationships arise when there are few suppliers and few customers; when each party is dependent on the other; and when the buyer needs the supplier's skills, because the

TABLE 24.3. Power Balance in Buyer/Seller Relationships

Criteria for classifying Buyer/Seller Relationships	Categories of Buyer/Seller Relationships			
	Dependent			
	(Buyer dominated)	(Supplier dominated)	Inter-dependent	Independent
Number of suppliers	Many	Few	Few	Many
Number of customers	Few	Many	Few	Many
Share of supplier's output taken by the buyer	High	Low	High	Low
Share of buyer's requirements purchased from the supplier	Low	High	High	Low
Buyer's need for supplier's skills	Low	High	High	Low
Buyer's need for a customized product	High	Low	High	Low

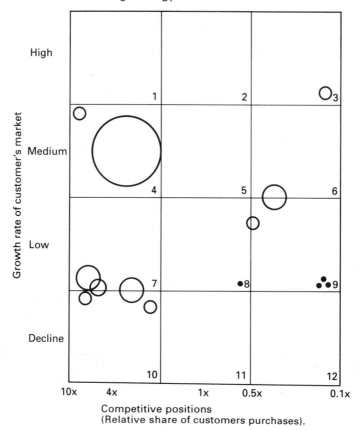

Note: Size of circles represents sales volume to each customer.

FIG. 24.3. Portfolio of Key Customers.

purchase is customized in some way. The supplier dominated and independent categories have opposite characteristics to those identified above for buyer dominated and interdependent relationships.

This type of analysis can also help management in the third and final step of the analysis.

Step 3: Portfolio Analysis of Key Customers

This final step involves the analysis of key customers. Management can choose which customers to include. Key customers are likely to be existing large customers plus those on which strategic resources are expended. First, the key customers are analyzed together, and then the most important ones analyzed individually. The customer portfolio in

Figure 24.3 is an analysis of the key customers of the packaging supplier using a variation of the familiar growth share matrix. The coordinates are the competitive position of the company with the customer on the horizontal axis, and the growth rate of the customer's market on the vertical axis. Competitive position is measured by the share the supplier holds of the customer's purchases relative to the share held by the largest competitor. The positions are plotted on a log scale to accommodate the wide variations. Within the matrix the size of the circles represents the sales volume of each customer. Thus, Figure 24.3 shows that the company has one key customer in cell 4 whose business is growing steadily and where the company's share of purchases is very high. The company also holds a very high share of the purchases of customers on the border line between cells 7 and 10. However, the markets in which these companies operate are not growing. On the right hand side of Figure 24.3, the company has a weak competitive position because of its low share of the customer's purchases.

The main purpose of Figure 24.3 is to show the position of the largest customers, but it can also be used to indicate the position of tomorrow's future prospects. These are represented by dots rather than circles as sales are negligible at present. There are three dots in cell 9, one in cell 8 and only one in cell 1. Thus, the supplier is devoting some of its strategic resources to developing sales with customers whose markets are not growing. The supplier justified this because its objective was to develop a substitute, which, if successful, would lead to substantial business. Nevertheless, the company would have preferred more prospects in the top left hand corner of the portfolio. The management implications of Figure 24.2 are discussed in the conclusions.

Although Figure 24.3 gives useful information about key customers, clearly, this is not sufficient where the largest customer itself represents 45% of sales, as in the case of the packaging company studied. A more detailed breakdown is needed as shown in Figure 24.4 where the customer is split up into a series of subcustomers. Figure 24.4 shows that the largest customer really consists of four separate businesses which have been classified on the horizontal axis using the life cycle categories. The vertical scale shows, as before, the real growth in the customer's purchases. The size of the circle is drawn to represent the size of the customers' purchases. A "pie slice" can be added to represent the share held by the supplier company.

For the life cycle classification and for the customer/competitor chart only customers who bought products with similar usages manufactured by the same technology were included together; for the analysis of key customers the reverse is true. The chart should display

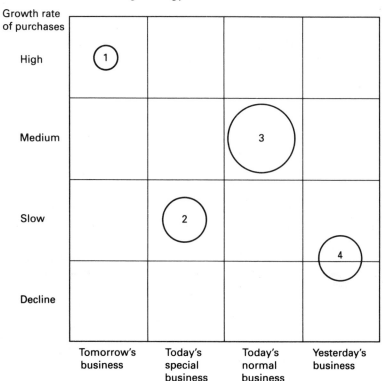

Note: Size of circles represents the volume of customer's purchases. Numbers refer to the different products of the suplier company sold to the customer.

FIG. 24.4. Analysis of a Key Customer.

all the different products sold to that customer. Figure 24.4 shows that there is a small but developing business for product 1; a slow growing, but specialized business for product 2; a large and steadily growing, standard business for product 3; and an average, slightly declining, business for product 4.

With the aid of these two analyses management can obtain a clear picture of its strategic position with key customers.

Conclusion

This paper has put forward proposals to help managers in industrial companies analyze their customers in a way which will highlight critical issues. The analysis concentrates on customers rather than products because of the small number of key customers in so many markets. The emphasis on customers is compatible with the way forward thinking management intuitively carry out their activities, but not in the way in which company planning is undertaken. The presentation here makes explicit and logical what is latent and uncoordinated practice in many firms.

References

Achiadelis, B., Jarvis, P. and Robertson, B., "Project Sappho: A Study of Success and Failure in Industrial Innovations," *Report to the Science Policy Research Council*, (University of Sussex, Brighton: Science Policy Research Unit, 1971).

Campbell, N. C. G., "Organizational Buying Behaviour: An Interaction Approach," Organizational Buying Behaviour Workshop, EIASM, Brussels, December, 1982.

Corey, E. R., *Industrial Marketing: Cases and Concepts, 2nd Edition*, (Engelwood Cliffs: Prentice Hall, 1976).

Hakansson, H. (ed.), *International Marketing and Purchasing of Industrial Goods: An Interaction Approach*, (Chichester: Wiley, 1982).

Parkinson, S. T., "User-Supplier Interaction in New Product Development," Ph.D. Dissertation, University of Strathclyde, Glasgow, 1980.

Porter, M. E., *Competitive Strategy*, (New York: The Free Press, 1980).

Sawyer, H. C., *The Economics of Industries and Firms*, (London: Croom Helm, 1981).

Wind, Y., *Product Policy: Concepts, Methods and Strategy*, (Reading, Mass: Addison-Wesley, 1982).

25

The Information Seekers: Multinational Strategy Target*

HANS B. THORELLI

International Market Segmentation—A Challenge

No one can be everything to everybody. This is true even of General Motors. Whether by design or accident, every seller is confined to a part of a broader market (served market vs. potential). When the concentration to a certain sector or sectors is part of a strategic plan we shall call it market segmentation. A viable market segmentation strategy is based on at least four assumptions: the segment is readily identifiable; it calls for a different marketing strategy than the market as a whole; it is large enough to provide a profitable opportunity, alone or with another segment; it can be reached in an economical manner.

Segmentation is practiced in both industrial and consumer markets, but here the attention is confined to end consumers. Segmentation may be based on geographic, demographic, or psychographic variables, or typically, some combination of them such as career-oriented young women in U.S. metro areas.

A key issue in international business is whether to use a strategy of homogenization (standardization) or heterogenization (adaptation, differentiation) when expanding to another country. Clearly standardization is attractive by offering economies of scale in production, marketing, and management time. Homogenization calls for similarity in values and demographics. This is readily achieved in the case of a low-unit-price good catering to a universal drive. The classic example is Coca-Cola. The more expensive, complex, or status-oriented the product, the less likely it is that a unified strategy will reach the mass market in widely different cultures. In these cases management may be

* Revised from *International Marketing Strategy* Revised Edition, (Elmsford, NY: Pergamon Press, 1980), pp. 133–142.

faced with a tradeoff situation between possible cost savings in reaching a limited new clientele with the standard strategy and possible cost increases in reaching a broader new market with an adaptation strategy. The equation is complicated by the fact that it is sometimes feasible—though never costless—to convert local tastes by the strategy of a change agent.

Our research has established an important way in which consumers may be segmented across national borders in the industrialized countries of the West: the search behavior of consumers. It turns out that the Information Seekers of these countries constitute a truly cosmopolitan market, while the average consumers are the prime exponents of variation in local culture. The use of search behavior as a basis of market segmentation strategy is essentially a new concept.

Consumer Information Gap and the Information Seekers

In most consumer markets a gap exists between the product information readily available and the data needed not just by the perfectly savvy economic man of classical economies but even by ordinary mortals bent on semi-rational purchasing. Somewhat paradoxically, the prime reason for the consumer information gap is the very richness of our markets, with product and brand proliferation, increasing complexity of the average product, and rapid change. Too, nonmetro areas, due to the narrow selections of local stores, are removed from much of this richness, as much information is lost when the actual product is not at hand. Mass production calls for mass distribution and mass communication, resulting in the growing depersonalization of individual transactions. In addition, commercial information is sometimes misleading. At the same time consumer expectations regarding product performance seem to grow exponentially with the level of affluence. No doubt, a yawning consumer information gap is there—and it is growing.

The average consumer (AC) copes with the gap of adopting an essentially passive strategy; he makes a fairly superficial search limited to the most readily available alternatives. Many AC do indeed perceive themselves as well-informed buyers, while others are aware that continued search might well have resulted in a better buy. They are not willing, however, to spend the time and nervous energy required—or make that sacrifice in the face of the risk that they might not find a better buy after all. Typically, students tend to buy gas and snack foods from outlets closest to campus, often those that charge the highest prices in town.

By contrast, a small but influential group of consumers do their best to bridge the CI gap. These Information Seekers (IS) are distinct from the majority of AC in at least five important respects pertaining to search:

1. IS are more conscious about information than AC. IS will rank availability of information as a much more important buying criterion (next to performance, price, etc.) than will AC.
2. IS are knowledgeable about more information sources than AC.
3. IS consult a greater diversity of information sources than AC.
4. IS consult more systematic and complex sources of information (such as *Consumer Reports*) than AC.
5. IS make use of a broader range of media, especially with regard to printed matter in various forms.

The IS we have in mind is a *generalist*, that is, he is interested in indepth information about a broad range of products. Frequently he wants to know about new products or models even though not contemplating immediate purchase. Demographically, he (or she) tends to be highly educated, have a professional or managerial job, be in the middle or upper middle income group, and 25–45 years of age. There are as yet no hard data as to the size of this segment. We estimate that it comprises 5 to 20% of the adult consumer population in the industrial countries. Southern European countries tend to be at the lower end of the range, France, Switzerland, and Austria in the middle, Benelux, Britain, and Germany in a higher tier, and the Scandinavians at the upper end of the range. Canada and the United States are probably in between Scandinavia and Britain-Germany.

The IS group may seem to be a modest one, although their number is in the millions in all larger Western nations. Three major factors lend additional interest to information-seeking as a basis for market segmentation strategy. First, the number of IS is growing in all these countries as the level of eduction in general (and consumer education in particular) keeps rising, accompanied by greater affluence. Second, it turns out that a great many AC engage in intense information search for a single good (in the U.S. most often autos) or a narrow set of products of special interest to them. When acting in this capacity AC may be labeled Speciality Searchers. Taking the IS and Specialty Searchers together one might speculate that the population of information-conscious is twice as great among camera buyers as among vacuum cleaner buyers, and that even among the latter there is a Specialty Searcher for every IS.

The third factor may well be the most important. It appears that the IS play a role in the marketplace much greater than their numbers (and income) would indicate. At least they perceive themselves as opinion leaders, frequently asked for advice by their AC friends. (The IS are not always early adopters, however, preferring to have reliable information before they plunge.) As opinion leaders they seem in some ways to be acting as proxy purchasing agents for many AC with whom they may never have been in personal contact. While we do not have data permitting us to isolate the Specialty Searchers it seems plausible that in the markets of special interest to them they act much like the IS do in general.

Before a marketer takes off in hot pursuit of the IS he should be reminded that these consumer professionals are also the vigilantes of the marketplace. They have high expectations and they have the clout and mind to give vent to dissatisfaction. Data demonstrate that they complain a lot more often than AC about shoddy or defective merchandise, misleading advertising, out-of-stock conditions, and any other shortcomings they encounter. More than others, IS take on the often thankless task of blowing the whistle, of filing a complaint, of battling public and private bureaucracy in the perennial struggle to ensure consumer sovereignty.

German and American Consumers: Comparative Research

Before discussing the strategic implications of the IS (and AC) segments for multinational corporations we shall briefly touch on the research on German and American consumers, in which the existence of the cosmopolitan IS group was discovered. The research is reported in agonizing detail elsewhere (Thorelli, Becker, and Engledow, 1975).

The researcher needs tighter and less ambiguous definitions than the marketing practitioner is perforce willing to live with. We defined IS operationally as subscribers to consumer product testing magazines, i.e., *Consumer Reports* in the U.S. and *test* and *DM* in Germany. Operational definitions provide a practical and unambiguous vehicle for research, but rarely correspond on a one-to-one basis with the underlying concept under study. Clearly, one can be an IS as previously defined without being a test magazine subscriber. (There are many other information sources; one may borrow a test magazine copy from the library or a friend.) One may also be a subscriber without being an IS. (The subscription was an unwelcome Christmas gift from my mother-in-law.) Figure 25.1 schematically shows the relationship between subscribers and IS, and how these groups fit into the social structure. The figure makes no pretense of being drawn to scale. Our data show that the vast majority of subscribers *are* indeed IS—the three "spillover" triangles are small. About 3% of U.S. households are subscribers to *Consumer Reports*, and it may well be

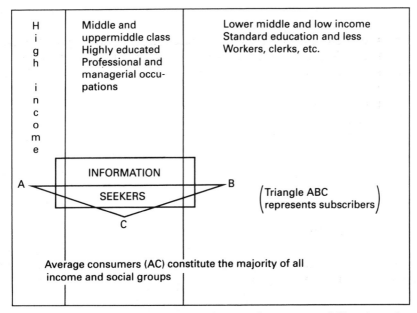

FIG. 25.1. The Information Seekers, Average Consumers and Test Journal
Subscribers: Demographic Characteristics.

that as many as 7–9% of the adult consumer population read it. This is
just over one half of our gross estimate of the number of IS in the
country.

Our study used large representative interview samples of subscribers and, separately, of non-subscribers in metropolitan areas in
both countries, supplemented for control purposes with national mail
subscriber samples. A methodological finesse is worth recounting: our
colleague Jack Engledow added another interview sample of nonsub-
scribers matching the subscribers on demographic variables as well as
location and type of dwelling. Not unexpectedly, the great majority of
this matched sample were in the AC group.

A general overview of hundreds of detailed findings is presented in
Figure 25.2. The figure reflects the basic research carried out in 1970.
A selective update in 1976 showed nearly identical results regarding
demographics and media use as well as self-perceived planfulness and
opinion leadership. There was some change in other attitudes,
reflecting the decline of confidence in all institutions, and notably
government, business, advertising, and, to some extent, product
testing agencies themselves. Interestingly, there was also some further
convergence of German and American IS characteristics. The
discussion below ties in with the 1970 data, which demonstrated its
robustness by our research update.

American Comparisons
Subscribers vs. Average Consumers

		Subscribers High	*Neutral**	*Subscribers Low*
German Comparisons *Subscribers vs. Average Consumers*	*Subscribers High*	A. Universal "Highs" Demographics: Income Education Social Class Attitudes Planfulness Business Opinion Leader Newspaper and Magazine Readership Shopping Concern: Available Information Information Source: Product Testing Consumer Activity by Government Ownership of Selected Durables	B. German High-American Neutral Demographic: Age Information Source: Other newspaper or magazine Shopping Concern: Styling	C. German High-American Low Attitude: Increased Government Control of Business Satisfaction Measures: All, including satisfaction with product and shopping activity and available information
	Neutral*	D. American High-German Neutral Attitude: General Liberalism Shopping Concern: Brand Reputation Increased Consumerist Activities	E. No Significant Difference From Average Consumer Most other variables not listed elsewhere fell into this category.	F. American Low-German Neutral Attitudes: Advertising Student Power Shopping Concerns: Product Availability Economy of Operation Credit Information Source: Personal Observation
	Subscribers Low	G. American High-German None	H. German Low-American Neutral Attitude: Welfare	I. Universal "Lows" Television Viewing Radio Listening

Note: *No significant difference between Subscribers and Average Consumers

FIG. 25.2. Within and Between Country Comparisons of Subscribers (IS) and

Figure 25.2 actually presents two levels of comparison: between subscribers and AC in both countries separately and inter-country comparison between these two groups. To achieve this, the information in the cells directly reports on subscribers only. AC are "opposite" to IS, except in the "neutral" case, when there is no statistically significant difference between the two groups. Thus, the least interesting cell is that labeled E.

The most interesting cells are A and I, which in effect profile the cosmopolitan subscriber and, we claim, the cosmopolitan Information Seeker. We have already discussed income and social class, where the IS (as represented by subscribers) tend to be members of the occupational elite. In both cultures over 40% of IS were college graduates (as opposed to 11% of the total population in the U.S. and 5% in Germany), and less than 7% had completed grade school only (as opposed to 28% of all Americans and 32% of all Germans). Little wonder that we find major differences between IS and AC in media use. IS are multi-media types, while AC are lookers and listeners. Though IS indeed do some TV viewing and radio listening, their focus is on reading. It comes as no surprise that IS rank high on ownership of consumer durables; that in itself adds to their store of consumer information.

In the attitude area, we already know that IS consider themselves as planful and opinion-leading consumers. Perhaps surprising to some, a greater proportion of them than of AC have an overall favorable opinion of business as an institution. This does not stop them, however, from being more critical than AC of a variety of specific business practices. IS in both countries wanted more government activity in the consumer affairs area—notably with respect to consumer information and education.

We now come to some relatively modest differences between IS in Germany and the United States, as indicated by cells B, D, F, and H. In these cases IS in one of the countries differed strongly from the local AC while there was no significant difference between IS and AC in the other nation. German IS were significantly older than local AC, and they quoted nontest magazines and newspapers as an information source in their latest purchase of a major durable good more often than did AC, while this difference was not observed in the U.S. Relatively minor differences were also found in shopping concerns (buying criteria) in the latest purchase of a major durable good. Relative to local AC, German IS were more concerned with styling than American, while the latter were relatively more concerned with brand reputation than the former. Among the dozen buying criteria respondents were asked to rank in importance, American IS ranked immediate availability of the product in the store, economy of operation, and availability of credit significantly lower than local AC. Apart from the strong concern for availability of information both American and German IS ranked performance and durability high as buying criteria across the broad range of durables covered by the survey. Although the IS-AC difference as regards these two criteria was not statistically significant, there is some reason to believe IS are better judges of these characteristics than fellow consumers.

American IS were significantly more critical of advertising than AC, while, as shown by cell F, there was no such difference between German IS and AC. However, German attitudes toward advertising were uniformly lower than American. Thus IS in the two countries were actually much closer together in their views than American and German AC.

In only two areas did German and American IS have *opposite* views when compared to AC in the respective countries. German IS were more in favor of increased government control of business than German AC, while in the U.S. these views were reversed. It would carry us too far to philosophize about the underlying reasons for this discrepancy. More immediately relevant here is the fact that while American IS were less positive in all areas of consumer satisfaction—with the product itself, with the shopping experience, with overall availability of information in the marketplace—than American AC, German IS were more satisfied on all scores than the local AC. We do not believe that these differences are due to better products, distribution, or information in Germany, but rather to a longer legacy of affluence and consumerism in the United States. There is reason to believe the German IS will move closer to the American: our observation from consumer research in some 20 nations around the world is that expectations among consumer sophisticates are highly correlated with affluence. Thus it is that the most affluent countries also have the strongest consumerist movements.

As the research summarized here represents somewhat of a new departure, a number of the findings must be regarded as tentative. In many specifics, however, our results are corroborated by researchers in Britain, Holland, Belgium, France, Norway, Sweden, and Canada. We are quite confident that a sizeable segment of IS exists in the industrialized nations of the West, and that it is cosmopolitan in the sense that in demographics, media use, and, in some respects, even in style of life the IS in one of these countries are more like IS in other countries than they are like average consumers in their "home" country.

Strategic Implications for the MNC

There are a number of strategic guideposts for the multinational corporation bent on catering to the cosmopolitan IS and deriving the economic benefits of a homogeneous market strategy through the industrialized West.

1. *Communications.* The key role in singling out and reaching a market segment is played by communications. Being voracious users of personal and commercial as well as independent media, the IS can easily be reached in the same manner as consumers in general. However, the IS may be reached more cheaply and more effectively by special tailoring of both media and message. IS read a lot more than AC. Many highbrow periodicals have heavy IS readership. Magazines of general consumer interest, such as *Good Housekeeping* in the U.S., Britain, and Canada reach many AC as well as IS. A number of auto and hobby magazines will have a concentration of IS as well as Specialty Searchers. Most product testing magazines will not accept advertising. The way to impress readers of *Consumer Reports* and corresponding publications abroad is to have products good enough to come up with consistently favorable ratings.

Superior information will be an important business strategy in the future as a means of gaining differential advantage in the marketplace. The IS much more than AC are interested in "hard" rather than "soft" information, in fact rather than fancy (though not constitutionally averse to subjective appeals), and in multi-faceted, systematic information rather than simplistic approaches. Point-of-purchase information in the form of labels, educational brochures, and sensible owner's manuals (made available *before* the transaction) are good illustrations. Comparative ads covering an array of product characteristics, including some where the advertiser's rank is *not* outstanding, is another.

2. *Product mix.* IS indicate a concern for what may be termed "quiet quality," as reflected in such product characteristics as performance and durability in cars, appliances, and other durables. It is difficult to generalize beyond this point. As noted, German IS were relatively more interested in styling than American, while the latter were more concerned with brand reputation (possibly as a proxy for incomplete information) than the former. There is, indeed, no reason to assume that IS should have homogeneous preferences regarding all characteristics of all products—even inside any given country. Speaking generally, it seems clear that IS more than AC everywhere are concerned with getting "value for money," but, of course, value in some respects is a subjective matter.

Though the IS often are not in the group of early adopters, they follow hard on its heels. For this reason, and because they tend to be pace-setters, it is advisable to reach them early on in the product life cycle.

3. *Pricing.* Price is no isolated or dominant concern of the IS. They are bent on value, whether the car they are looking for is a Cadillac or

Chevette. Although many IS take stock in brand reputation, most IS are too savvy to accept blindly the easy decision rule that "you get what you pay for" used by many AC.

4. *Distribution.* Although not unimportant, dealer reputation and location and immediate product availability do not rank as major buying criteria among the IS. Credit ranked last of all IS shopping concerns. But service aspects in a major purchase loom high on the list of priorities of the IS. We dare say this is why foreign automobile manufacturers have placed such an emphasis on trying to build good service networks in the United States. They may not have realized that at least until the early 1970s the IS were their prime customers, but certainly it was those IS who put the pressure on for good service and availability of parts. Best of all in international marketing, of course, is if the product can be designed in such a way as to require only a minimum of service.

Conclusion

We have seen that the cosmopolitan Information Seekers constitute a readily identifiable and reachable market segment extending across the industrialized West. Taking the cosmopolitan view, the segment is a large and affluent one, and must offer many golden business opportunities. Basically, each such opportunity may be exploited by a standard strategy (local competition, marketing infrastructure, and government regulations may call for some variation). The attractiveness of this segment is enhanced by the IS' tendency to be opinion leaders and "proxy purchasing agents" for fellow consumers. Incidentally, this fact should serve as a warning against adopting a strategy which might disappoint them.

For the foreseeable future the IS in any given country will continue to be a relatively small, though highly articulate market next to the majority of average consumers. These AC are the prime bearers of local culture and local values. The MNC interested in reaching the AC market must generally be prepared to make significant local adaptations in strategy.

On a selective basis, our discussion may be applied *within* any single nation as well as in international marketing. A Dutch producer aiming only at the local IS market might find it big enough at least for starters. If he wanted to expand he would have the tantalizing choice of refocusing on Dutch AC, most likely by a different communications mix, or of pursuing the IS segment in other countries. We must, however, warn against extrapolating the argument to either the communist bloc or to the less developed countries. In these cases the local market systems are sufficiently different from those of the industrialized West to make most of our propositions inoperable.

Reference

Thorelli, Hans B., Helmut Becker and Jack Engledow, *The Information Seekers—An international study of consumer information and advertising image*, (Cambridge, Mass.: Ballinger, 1975).

26

Guidelines for International Business Negotiations*

PERVEZ N. GHAURI

Business relationships between firms from different countries have expanded substantially during the past two decades. Today there is no country which is not involved in international business.

Moreover, international business is no longer a matter of just two actors, as it was in the postwar decade. During the period of 1955–70, the political impact of host and home governments has greatly increased in international business transactions. In the 1980s, a multi-actor era has emerged, where a variety of international organizations and interest groups become involved in international business.

Despite the increased importance and complexity of international business, little research has been done on international business negotiations. Many of the conflicts between firms from different countries have been studied, but little attention has been devoted to the process whereby these conflicts can be resolved (Ghauri 1983). Only a few studies have appeared which provide an insight into these negotiation processes.

In the past, the ability to negotiate was considered innate or instinctive, but it is now regarded as a technique which can be learned. Experimental studies, empirical observations and experience have made it possible to grasp the art of negotiation. Based on this belief, this paper endeavors to provide some guidelines for these negotiations. It deals with business negotiations which result in some kind of long-term relationship between the parties, and covers such topics as:

● What are the different stages in the negotiation process, and what is discussed in these stages?

---

*Slightly abbreviated from *International Marketing Review*, (Autumn 1986), pp. 72–82, with permission.

- How should firms prepare for these negotiations?
- Who within the firm should negotiate?
- What is a good outcome of negotiating?
- What makes a good negotiator?

Stages of the Negotiation Process

The process of international business negotiations can be divided into five different stages: 1) The offer 2) Informal Meetings 3) Strategy formulation 4) Negotiations (face-to-face) and 5) Implementation (Ghauri 1983). These stages are described below with the help of a strategic planning model for international business negotiations (see Figure 26.1).

The process of international business negotiations is influenced by two groups of variables:

(1) Background factors, which influence the parties' objectives, often categorized as common, conflicting, or complementary. Other aspects include third parties involved, the position of market (seller's vs. buyer's market), and finally, the skills and experience of the negotiators.
(2) Atmosphere is the perceived "milieu". Perceived cooperation/conflict, power/dependence, distance and expectations, as well as the parties perceptions of the process and one another's behavior.

Stage I—Offer. The Offer stage begins with the first contact between the parties concerning a particular venture, and ends when the vendor has submitted a final offer.

In between, negotiations take place and counter offers are made, often resulting in revision of the vendor's offer. Already, at this early stage of the process, the dynamism of negotiation can be observed. It is in this first stage that the parties begin to try to understand one another's needs. It is important that the parties (especially the vendor) realize that in submitting an offer, he is committing himself to his end of the deal. As far as his demands are concerned, it may be necessary to make some concessions on many issues.

The offer stage is heavily influenced by the previously mentioned background factors and the atmosphere. These variables often convey an awareness of the power/dependence relationship, or the relative power which exists or is perceived to exist between the parties.

To gain this relative power, parties should gather relevant information on each other and the operating environment, particularly on such factors as third parties involved, influencers, competitors and the infrastructure. The parties need to be aware, however, that their

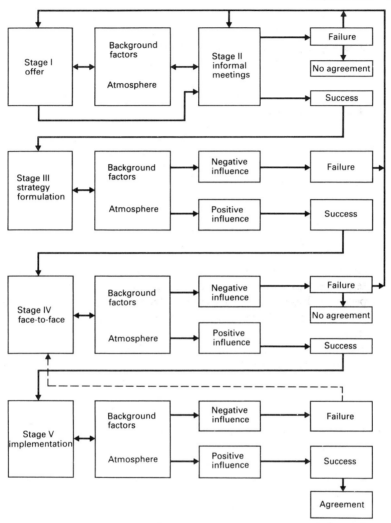

FIG. 26.1. A Strategic Planning Model for International Business Negotiations.

relative power relationship can be altered at any time by such events as positioning of competitors or movement in exchange rates. Obviously, negotiators must realize and appreciate the volatility of the environment to maintain their bargaining integrity.

Stage II—Informal Meetings. After the buyer has received the offer, the parties meet to discuss the terms and to get acquainted.

Informal negotiations take place as the parties examine each other's position. As in the offer stage, the informal meetings are influenced by the background factors and the atmosphere. Negotiators perceive cooperation or conflict, power or dependence and the degree of distance. If excessive conflict or distance is sensed or if there is little perception of successful dealings or a future relationship, the process often ends in failure. This can entail no agreement (end of the process), or the parties can start anew and go back to Stage I. On the other hand, if the parties perceive cooperation and high expectations for the future, the stage is a success and the process moves on. This success is heavily dependent upon communication and on each side's perceived behavior and expectations.

In some parts of the world (Asia and the Middle East), informal meetings are often more important than formal negotiations. A social, informal relationship developed between negotiators at this stage can be of great help. Contacts gained from these relationships not only increase the chances of agreement, but also decrease the distance (especially psychic distance) between the parties.

One method of establishing such contacts is to invite individuals from the buyer's side to visit the seller's factory, in an attempt to develop trust between the parties. If the firms have done business before, it is easier to develop the relationship. It is also often beneficial to utilize a consultant and/or agent in the particular country to initiate contacts in establishing an informal relationship.

Stage III—Strategy Formulation. If Stage II has ended in success and the parties decide to continue the process, each side turns to the task of formulating its strategy for formal negotiations.

The parties try to build their relative power. The buyer compares the offers submitted by different vendors, makes checklists and assigns pro and con arguments/competitive advantages to all competing vendors. The seller decides on what points concession is most likely, and to what extent his firm can concede.

As stressed in the discussion of Stage I, a volatile environment can severely upset established relative power positions. In this third stage, it is essential that negotiators attempt to foresee and predict events to protect their power position.

However, this is not always the case. For example, a small U.S. supplier quoted a large European electric company the terms of their deal in the European currency. He was asked in negotiations to accept payment in dollars, which he did with alacrity. What the U.S. supplier did not know was that the European company had information on currency fluctuation projections which indicated that over the period between agreement and payment, there would be a considerable weakening of the dollar relative to the European currency. Clearly, any relative power the U.S. supplier might have had was diminished by his lack of knowledge of affecting factors.

In Stage III, the parties must also foresee and protect against unpredictable events. For instance, in negotiations between a Swedish firm and an African buyer, the employ of expatriates was a major problem in the final negotiations. The buyer could not guarantee that the supplier's engineers would be granted permission to work in the country of interest. Remittance of funds, taxes and import duties, and work permits are just a few examples of unpredictable and uncontrollable rules and regulations in the particular country that must be researched in this stage.

An understanding of the infrastucture of the country or company is critical at this point. In some countries, especially when the public sector is the buyer, the buying organizations issue a "letter of award" (also called letter of intent/acceptance) after offers have been received. This document states that the order for the project has been awarded to company ABC, and ABC is called for formal negotiations.

The vendors from Western countries often perceive this letter of award as grant of contract, so that all that remains is the formal signing of the contract. This is an incorrect assumption, as it is possible that one or two other competitors have received the same kind of letter. The letter merely suggests that after receiving the final offer, the buyer intends to negotiate further.

If the buyer is a government organization, the selling firm should realize that the buyer has differing objectives, from a business firm, in making a deal (job opportunities, an increase in the capacity of the industry, balance of payments or other matters of policy). This was precisely the situation which existed in the negotiation process for paper and pulp plant where a big state-owned Swedish company, ASSI, was the buyer. In this deal, the right to reject the seller's subcontractors was reserved. The aim was to accept the offer which utilized local subcontractors, thereby solving regional unemployment problems.

Stage IV–Face-to-Face Negotiations. The negotiation process is now controlled by the party who arranges the agenda, since he can accentuate his own strong points and the other party's weaknesses.

Observations reveal that it is always the party having the relative power which arranges the agenda. Some negotiators prefer to start by discussing and agreeing on the principles of the deal. After determining the principles, the conflicts can be resolved with a broader perspective, and trading off is done in relation to overall performance.

Another way to handle this stage is to negotiate/discuss the contract step by step—discussing both conflicting issues and those of common interest. Discussions on common interests can hopefully create an atmosphere of cooperation between the parties.

Alternative strategies used in the negotiations have been widely discussed. For example a "tough strategy" is one in which a party starts with a high initial offer and avoids making concessions. A "soft strategy" is one in which the granting of concessions enhances trust and facilitates negotiations. To obtain a concession, one must first make a concession. In a "fair strategy", the negotiators appreciate that a certain settlement would be fair to both parties (50/50 split) and as soon as one of them suggests such a settlement the other party agrees, rather than holding out to obtain more concessions.

The choice or strategy depends upon the customer or supplier one is involved with. Therefore, it is helpful to understand the strategy of the other party as early as possible and then choose a strategy to match/complement it. In this case there is a risk that both parties, by applying a tough strategy, may lead the negotiation process to a deadlock. But, sometimes deadlocks are necessary to convince the other party to change its strategy if the negotiations are to continue. It is hoped that in such cases, both parties would resort to a fair or soft strategy.

It is also in Stage IV that both parties take the initiative by asking questions about the other party, the offer, price, quality, delivery and credit possibilities. All these questions would disclose the negotiation range, or the gap between the minimum point of one side and the acceptable point of the other.

If one of the parties realizes that there is a considerable overlap between its position vis-a-vis the other party, the negotiator should not at once agree to a settlement. By prolonging the negotiation process, he may obtain further concessions. Moreover, most business people like to see themselves as strong negotiators. It is therefore desirable that both parties feel that they had to work hard for the contract. Negotiators who make an immediate final offer can only be at a disadvantage.

Consideration of international negotiations almost invariably involves discussion of environmental differences, especially in view of the culture and business traditions prevailing in different countries. It is very difficult for the parties to comprehend or adjust to each other's culture or traditions, but it is important to be aware of these differences. We cannot expect others to act or react as we do. In certain countries such as Asia and the Middle East, the social contacts developed between the parties are far more significant than the technical specifications and the price. In other cultures like China and Japan, pride and honor are of great importance. Negotiators from these countries take their time and are very careful not to offend or use strong words, and expect the other party to follow suit.

A balance between strength and credibility is essential in all kinds of negotiations. It is essential to give and take signals of preparedness to move from the initial stage, without in fact making a concession. Negotiators having previous experience can easily send and receive signals, but it is very difficult for those who are meeting for the first time.

The timing of making a move is also crucial. The attitude (behavior) of both sides can be a decisive factor for these movements. A negotiator can be firm, but with a courteous or problem-solving attitude, he can develop an atmosphere of ambience. Frequently however, negotiators from Western countries adopt a tough attitude in negotiations, which is perceived as "big brother", and is very offensive to the other party.

Negotiators often send conditional signals such as, "We cannot accept your offer as it stands," or "We appreciate that your equipment is quite suitable for us, but not at the price you mentioned." The seller might say, "I understand, but you know that this is the last price I can offer, otherwise I will have to call my head office and discuss the price with them". This kind of communication is used to test each side's commitment, as well as the resolution of the offer. It is also common that the party who perceives greater relative power makes fewer concessions, while the weaker party yields more often to create a better atmosphere.

The maintenance of flexibility of parties and issues is of great importance in Stage IV. The flexibility is particularly important on issues such as terms of payment, delivery time, and of course, price. It is often necessary to trade off (give and take). This usually occurs after both sides have tested the commitment, and have sent and received signals to move on. For example, price can often be reduced if the party offers better terms of payment. There are other elements which can be traded off but which cannot be evaluated in accounting terms. Obtaining a reference project or the entry into a huge market are frequently more important than a large profit on the present deal.

Finally, there comes a point when the negotiators have to make the final move. For example, in the Swedish/Indian pulp plant deal, the customer announced: "The order is yours if you reduce the price by seven per cent." The seller replied: "That is something beyond my authority, I cannot give that big a reduction." The buyer then said, "It is up to you," indicating he had made his final move. In order to test further, the seller still insisted that he could not make that kind of reduction, and finally called his head office to preserve his credibility.

It is usually poor strategy to announce that the negotiators do not have the final authority to conclude the contract. When it is used as a tactic to check the final move of the buyer however, it is quite effective.

Stage V—Implementation. Finally, all the terms have been agreed upon.

The contract only remains to be signed, and is being drawn up. Experience shows that the writing of a contract and the language used is a negotiation process in itself. In the two cases mentioned above (Swedish/Indian and Swedish/Nigerian), the language and the writing of previously agreed issues took a considerable amount of time. If the influence of the background factors and the atmosphere has been negative, this stage can lead to face-to-face negotiations once again (see strategic model, Figure 26.1).

To avoid this delay in the process, after the negotiations, the discussions should first be summarized. The concessions exchanged, the discussions held, and the terms finally agreed upon should be read aloud for each side. This is facilitated by keeping minutes of meetings which can be summarized and compiled. This will help to test the understanding of the contract, as the parties may have perceived issues or discussions differently. This is helpful not only in the writing and signing of the contract, but also in its implementation.

If the parties reach an agreement without attention to the details, there is sure to be trouble later on in the implementation of the contract. The best way to solve this problem is to be sure before leaving the negotiating table that both sides thoroughly understand what they have agreed upon. A skilled negotiator should summarize and test the understanding by asking "Do I understand that if we agree to the credit being repaid in equal installments, accept a four week longer delivery period, and agree to the supply of your standard discharge mechanism, you will reduce the contract price by $15,000?" (McCall and Warrington 1984, p. 42).

How Should Firms Prepare for Negotiations?

Having discussed the different stages of the negotiation process, we can now consider the best way to prepare for these negotiations.

Identifying the Contents of the Deal. The first point to consider covers such issues as implications of the deal, the concepts at stake, the "fit" of the deal with organizational objectives, and possible economic, political or other restrictions between the countries.

Parties should simultaneously gather information that will be useful in understanding the effect the above issues will have on one another. What will each gain and/or lose and how important is the deal for them? What alternatives does either side have?

These issues must be considered monetarily, as well as in terms of motives. Failure to understand motives can lead to misconceptions, as happened in the following example. A British manufacturer received an inquiry from Pakistan for special filtration equipment, to which he responded with an offer and subsequent visit, in the hope of finalizing the deal. He was quite surprised, therefore, to learn that the real motive for the requested offer was to establish whether an offer from an Eastern European country for the same equipment was reasonable.

Create Alternatives. This point is particularly applicable to buyers, who should investigate available market alternatives and numbers of suppliers, their relative positions and technology levels.

The buyers should gather offers from at least three competing suppliers, even if they have already decided to buy from one in particular. After receiving the offers from a number of suppliers, the pros and cons of each proposal should be considered. Each offer should be judged on characteristics such as the level of technology, long-term relationship possibilities, position in the industry, service possibilities, and finally, the people who comprise the organization. This is also the proper time to rank and categorize those issues which have some flexibility and those which cannot be conceded.

Put Yourselves in Their Shoes. One very important factor in successful negotiations is understanding the other party's position, and foreseeing his reactions to our arguments.

Anticipating his rational reactions to our arguments allows us to formulate new arguments/alternatives. This stimulates flexibility on different issues through the development of a number of alternatives for issues where conflict exists. The harder one party tries to show that they understand the opposing viewpoint, the more open the opposition will be to alternative solutions.

Appropriateness of the Message. The information we exchange should be tailored to the other parties to the deal.

For example, technical specificiations and other material should be provided in the local language. This will not only facilitate effective communication, but will also demonstrate respect for the local language and environment.

Americans and Westerners normally find if difficult to "read" business-people from other cultures. This problem of perception and the language barriers often hinder the process of negotiation. Even if the other negotiating team speaks English, it is sometimes difficult to tell when they are angry, embarrassed or agreeable. For example, Arabs speak loudly, giving an impression that they are angry, and Japanese never say no, even if they mean no. This is frustrating and places an added burden on all involved in the negotiating process.

Barriers to communication arise from actual or perceived differences in expectations, which create conflict instead of cooperation between the parties. In cross-cultural negotiations, non-verbal communication is sometimes more important than the spoken language. This is particularly true in the expression of emotion and attitude towards the opposition. Negotiators will often continue to hold out, not because the proposal is unacceptable, but because they want to avoid the feeling of surrender. Sometimes a simple rephrasing of the proposal or a different approach to presentation can alleviate the problem.

Who within the Firm should Negotiate?

Whenever a deal is to be negotiated in a new market, the difficult question arises of who should conduct the negotiations. Who is the most appropriate person to hammer out a particular deal? Management should be wary of "volunteers," if negotiations are to be held in Hawaii or Las Vegas. Those same "volunteers" might not be so eager to travel to Tripoli or Kiev.

Moreover, the persons involved in international business negotiations can in fact do more harm than good if they lack integrated knowledge of their own firm, and how the deal at hand would affect different departments. Since we are discussing long-term relationships, it is of prime importance that whoever is selected for the negotiations have a good grasp of the implications of the deal.

One way to minimize this risk is to appoint a negotiation team, the members of which are selected from different departments, particularly those which are expected to be affected the most. The management should give team selection important consideration, since from here on out, negotiators are on their own.

The possibilities of external help should also be seriously considered. If the firm is entering a new market in which it has no experience/knowledge, it is perhaps better to take advice/help from outside consultants. The consultants need not act as negotiators for the firm, but they can offer assistance in formulating a strategy or providing necessary information on different environmental factors. In addition, it is advisable to seek the help of a lawyer who has some expertise on law in the particular market. This may become necessary, since most deals involve the application of local law in the contract.

The consequences of signing a contract which entails principles of which the firm has no knowledge are quite obvious. It is very important for management to realize that person(s) selected should be "expendable" in case replacement is necessary to escape from a deadlock without creating organizational problems. Often, negotiations end in an impasse, and must start anew with new players. It can also happen that the selected negotiators and those from the other side can not reach a so-called "meeting of minds," or the "personal chemistry" does not work. In such situations, it becomes necessary to change negotiators.

This discussion gives rise to another problem—what level executives should be chosen for the negotiations? In some countries, the parties expect to negotiate with an organizational equal. If the managing director from the buyer's side is negotiating the deal, he will expect to negotiate with his counterpart. It is advisable that the firms attempt to match negotiators.

What is a Good Outcome?

A good agreement is one which leads to successful implementation. A good outcome is a deal which benefits both parties, and neither feels that it has a less advantageous contract.

It is not a question of win or lose, it is a problem-solving approach. The main purpose of the contract is to avoid misunderstanding and trouble in the future, and thus we define business negotiations as a process through which two or more parties interact to reach an agreement which provides terms and conditions for the future behavior of the parties involved (Ghauri 1983).

The agreement should foster the development of the relationship and be flexible to deal with expected or unexpected changes which can occur in the future. In addition, the language and the terminology used in the contract should be simple and clear. It should not be necessary to seek legal help every time the contract must be read.

Who is a Good Negotiator

There are a number of studies available which discuss the different characteristics of a good negotiator. Iklé defined a good negotiator as having a "quick mind but unlimited patience, one that knows how to dissemble without being a liar, inspire trust without trusting others, be modest but assertive, charm others without succumbing to their charm, and possess plenty of money and a beautiful wife while remaining indifferent to all temptations of riches and women" (Iklé 1964, p. 263).

Respect for different perspectives and environments is of utmost importance. It is not necessary to adapt or change oneself to local environments—it is more important to be aware of these differences and to show them due respect or acceptance. Asians and Arabs for example, attribute great importance to social contacts and informal relations with the other party. In Arab countries, the seller's personality and his social behavior is at least equally important. Their decision in favor of a deal is often based upon the personality of the salesman and not on the quality of the product.

It is also essential to know the exact authority of the negotiators. In Eastern Europe, a team negotiates one day, followed by a fresh team the next day. The process is repeated a number of times and it becomes very difficult for the Western firms to ascertain which team is most important, or which has the final authority.

Finally, a good negotiator is not just a person who can conclude a good contract for the company, or who can arrive at a contract in a short time. A good negotiator is one whose agreements lead to successful implementation.

Conclusion

Having surveyed the different stages of the process, the strategic planning model and examples from different negotiations, it is not difficult to conclude that in international business negotiations, it is very important to have a problem-solving orientation. It must not be a game-oriented negotiation, where the main purpose is to win or to decrease the benefits of the other party.

We can also conclude that negotiation is a skill or knowledge which can be learned and improved. It is not an instinct, as most business-people believe. Careful planning before the start of the negotiation process can be of great benefit to both parties and to their future relationship. Yet there is obviously a great need for some sort of standard conditions, especially for issues such as price adjustment due to inflation.

Choosing the law to regulate the contract and arbitration is a crucial problem in the negotiation process, and requires an entity like the International Chamber of Commerce (ICC) to act as an arbitrator in all international deals.

Sometimes a third country law is acceptable. In the case of the Swedish Defibrator negotiating with India's HPC, after much argument, the seller was told that the Indian law was in fact very similar to English law, and the seller agreed to the deal.

Finally, the negotiators should have an integrative approach to the negotiation—not only to the process as a whole, but also to the implications of the deal for their firm/organization and for the other party. This approach would help in arriving at a better strategy and tactics.

References

Ghauri, P. N., *Negotiating International Package Deals: Swedish Firms and Developing Countries,* (Stockholm: Almqvist & Wiksell, 1983).

Heiba, Farouk I., "International Business Negotiations: A Strategic Planning Model," *International Marketing Review*, Vol. 4, No. 1 (Autumn/Winter 1984), pp. 5–16.

Ilké, F. C., *How Nations Negotiate*, (New York: Praeger, 1964).

McCall, J. B. and Warrington, M. B., *Marketing by Agreement—A Cross-Cultural Approach to Business Negotiations*, (Chichester: Wiley, 1984).

Further Reading — Part IV

Cavusgil, S. Tamer and Pervez N. Ghauri, *Doing Business In the Third World: Entry and Negotiations Strategies,* (London: Routledge, 1990).

Douglas, Susan P. and C. Samuel Craig, *International Marketing Research,* (Englewood Cliffs, N.J.: Prentice-Hall, 1983).

Graham, John L. and Roy A. Herberger Jr., "Negotiators Abroad—Don't Shoot from the Hip," *Harvard Business Review,* (July–August 1983), pp. 160–168.

Green, Robert T. and Arthur W. Allaway, "Identification of Export Opportunities," *Journal of Marketing,* Vol. 49 (Winter 1985), pp. 83–88.

Kushner, J.M., "Market Research in a Non-Western Context: the Asian Example," *Journal of the Market Research Society,* Vol. 26 (1982), No. 2, pp. 116–122.

"Locating U.S. Foreign Trade Data," *Business America,* (October 1985), pp. 5–7.

Pye, Lucian W., "The China Trade: Making the Deal," *Harvard Business Review,* (July–August 1986), pp. 74–80.

V
Market Entry Strategies

Introduction to Part V

Whether a company is approaching a foreign market for the first time or has been operating in it for years, periodic reviews of the entry strategies used are necessary to maintain the company's competitiveness. While a number of entry modes, ranging from direct exports and licensing to joint-ventures and multinational production, are available for marketers, it is no easy job to find the most appropriate strategy to match the company's strengths and objectives as well as the foreign market requirements. Part V introduces issues related to entry modes and discusses how to select the optimal strategies.

Should the product be marketed primarily by company sales force or by independent intermediaries? Reading 27 by Anderson and Coughlan explores the issue through an empirical investigation of distribution channel choice in foreign markets. Based on interviews, the authors build a model of the factors affecting the nature of distribution arrangements in foreign markets.

Welch examines the franchise system used in Australia. One of the major recipient countries of the franchise system, Australia, has moved rapidly through a process of adoption and imitation of the U.S. franchise systems in the 1970s and 1980s. Having applied the franchise system in domestic operations, a number of Australian companies have now begun to develop an international thrust.

The important area of international services marketing is the subject of Reading 29 by Kirkland.

International strategic alliances among companies from distant parts of the world have flourished in recent years. Reading 34 by Devlin and Bleackley expresses concern that a growing number of firms are forming too many "bandwagon" alliances in a vacuum of strategic consideration and, as a consequence, are placing their organizations at a competitive disadvantage. According to the authors, because of implementation problems associated with differing management styles, cultures, operational practices and degrees of control, not too many firms can point to having positively capitalized on the potential advantages. The authors believe it is time to put alliances into a strategic context and urge senior management to consider this business route with guidelines for success.

Barter and countertrade have been significant tools for market entry. To familiarize the readers with these tools Huszagh and Huszagh describe key forms of barter and countertrade, products typically traded, markets served, and objectives advanced by each form. The authors also explore the utilities of these transactions to international marketing strategies.

27

International Market Entry and Expansion via Independent or Integrated Channels of Distribution*

ERIN ANDERSON
ANNE T. COUGHLAN

Once a domestic manufacturer decides to introduce an industrial product to a foreign market, a difficult question must be resolved. Should the new product be distributed via a company-owned distribution channel, or is it more efficient to contract distribution to an independent organization? To an economist, this is a question of vertical integration, in which the choice is between primarily captive agents (company salesforce and company distribution division) or primarily independent intermediaries (outside sales agents and distributors). The former option is an integrated channel, which generally affords the manufacturer more control than the latter, which is a non-integrated channel.

To a manager, this is the "make or buy" issue, the company system being the "make" option and the independent channel the "buy" alternative. Robinson calls these make-or-buy issues "one of the most debated and critical areas in international business". The reason is that ownership gives the entrant control over its international distribution channel, its link to the industrial customer. However, ownership also brings responsibility, commitment, and attendant risks. Channel choices, once made, are often difficult to change. Hence, the question of whether to integrate foreign distribution can have a large and lasting impact on the success of a firm's international operations.

---

*Adapted from *Journal of Marketing*, Vol. 51 (Jan. 1987), pp. 71–82, with permission.

We explore the intertwined issues of ownership and control through an empirical investigation of distribution in foreign markets by U.S. companies in the semiconductor industry. The products we study first were commercialized in the U.S. between 1955 and 1975 and were immediately or subsequently sold in major overseas market areas. We use the marketing, international management, and economics literatures to generate a list of factors affecting the organizational forms (integrated or independent) chosen by these firms in various foreign markets. Specifically, we model this choice as a function of both production and transaction cost considerations.

In our data analysis we use detailed proprietary information gathered by field interviews about distribution decisions for 94 product introductions in foreign markets. From this information we develop scales to measure critical variables. We then employ the scales to estimate, by logistic regression, the probability that a new product will be introduced via an integrated (rather than independent) channel of distribution.

Our approach is a significant departure from most of the empirical international management literature, which tends toward intensive case studies, or, alternatively, analyses of single-proxy indicators gleaned from published sources. Further, we explicitly model the impact of a number of factors taken together. In contrast, empirical research to date generally has considered only one or two factors per study, ignoring or holding constant a broad variety of influences on organizational form. In most of the international marketing and management literature the researchers do not even ask why the channel assumes a particular form. Instead, the form is taken as given and other issues are examined, such as conflict within the independent channel.

In the next section we use analytical and empirical literature to postulate a model of distribution channel choice. We then describe the data base and how psychometric procedures were used to build scales measuring the variables of interest. Next the model estimation results are reported and discussed. We conclude with discussion and managerial implications.

A Model of Integrating Distribution in Foreign Markets

The choice between an integrated or independent distribution channel to serve a foreign market is complex and poorly understood. We cannot capture all the factors that contribute to a particular integration decision, but attempt to describe major, generalizable forces influencing channel selection.

We begin by framing the problem according to transaction cost analysis (Williamson 1981), which posits that *a priori* the entrant is better off choosing an independent channel. This choice enables the entrant to tap the benefits of a distribution specialist in the foreign market. These benefits include the economies of scale and scope that the independent obtains by pooling the demand for distribution services of several manufacturers. Further, by avoiding integration, the entrant avoids some of the disabilities of bureaucratic governance structures (Williamson 1979), in particular, organizational politics. Market contracting is thought to work well when the market for distribution services is competitive, because a distributor who fails to perform can be replaced. Indeed, it is argued that the threat of replacement alone is sufficient to keep an independent distribution system running well.

The presumption of the superiority of market contracting is based on the manufacturer's ability to replace nonperforming distributors. When this ability is diminished, for whatever reason, the impetus to integrate is increased. A proposition derived from transaction cost analysis is that integrated channels are more likely to be used when substantial "transaction-specific assets" accumulate. These assets are specialized knowledge and working relationships built up over time by the agents (either employees or independents) distributing the brand in question (Williamson 1979). These experience-based assets are specialized to the task of distributing the brand. Hence, the manufacturer will face difficulty in replacing the current agent, because any replacement agent must duplicate the experience needed to acquire the assets. In short, the current agent, by virtue of experience, can become highly valuable to the firm. Hence, the firm will be reluctant to terminate the agent, even if the agent is abusing his/her agreement with the firm ("opportunism").

Williamson (1981) proposes that firms can better monitor and motivate their difficult-to-replace distribution agents (i.e. dampen opportunism) if the agents are employees rather than outsiders. Hence, where task-specialized knowledge and relationships are important, we expect firms to select integrated distribution channels. In support of this proposition, Anderson (1985) finds the selling function tends to be integrated when two transaction-specific kinds of knowledge are important: brand knowledge and confidential inside information. However, she finds no influence due to several other forms of asset specificity.

The product category's age also influences channel selection. It is reasonable to expect that older product categories are more likely than newer product categories to be distributed through independent channels, because the older categories are more established and well known. Manufacturers therefore should be able to find a large number of qualified (knowledgeable) independent distribution agents to replace nonperforming agents. This fact in turn tends to encourage good performance on the part of any agent. In accordance with this reasoning, the channel choice decision by *Fortune 500* firms in the U.S. was studied and a tendency to use independent channels for mature product categories was found.

Davidson (1982) adds another reason to use independent agents for mature products in foreign markets. In many countries, governments pressure multinational firms to use local agents whenever they are available. Where they are plentiful, as for a well-diffused product, a foreign firm may have difficulty persuading the host government that it needs to set up its own distribution branch.

Service requirements can affect channel selection. Where the firm's marketing strategy calls for a high level of service (before or after sale), integrating the channel helps ensure that service will be performed. Though performing service can be specified in contracts with independent entities, ascertaining whether the independent adheres to the contract can be difficult and costly because there are few readily available indicators of service performance unless the firm integrates the channel. Giving the distributor employee status grants the firm the legitimate authority needed to monitor an agent's behavior and adjust rewards subjectively.

Hence, we would expect integrated channels to be used more commonly than independent channels for products with high service requirements. Some limited empirical support is provided by Anderson (1985), who found that employee salespeople are used more commonly than contract independent salespeople for service-intensive products. Though the selling function is only one part of distribution and the sample was confined to U.S. sales, Anderson's findings may generalize to international distribution activities.

Product differentiation also may influence channel choice. McGuire and Staelin (1983) develop an analytical model of retail channel choice in a duopoly wherein retailers carry only one manufacturer's product. They conclude that integration (company store) is more profitable for the manufacturer than non-integration (independent retail store) when consumers perceive the two manufacturers' products to be highly differentiated (not substitutable). In their analytical model, the reason is that such products do not compete directly. In contrast, nondifferentiated products do compete directly, creating price wars that drain the manufacturers' profits in integrated channels. If such products are sold through middlemen, however, the manufacturers' ability to respond to price changes (wage price wars) is inhibited, thereby protecting the manufacturers' profits. Coughlan (1985) tested this theory using 62 industrial (not retail) distribution choices by 26 electronics firms. The findings support the proposition that highly differentiated products are more likely to be sold through integrated channels.

Legal restrictions on foreign direct investment can have a major impact on whether the channel selected to carry a product in a foreign market is integrated or independent. Another important influence is the presence of established distribution arrangements. If the firm has an integrated channel in place, the new product may be added to the line carried by this channel to utilize fixed assets (e.g., salaried personnel) more fully. Conversely, if an independent channel is already in place, adding the new product may be less costly than installing an integrated channel. In short, firms are likely to introduce a new product through their existing channel.

Integrating distribution is especially likely if the new product is closely (rather than peripherally) related to the firm's principal business. For such "core" products, the entrant may be more willing to commit resources to distribution to ensure direct contact with customers and greater control over decision-making. For peripheral products, however, management may not view the product as important enough or synergistic enough to merit a major resource commitment (Davidson 1982).

The strength of the firm's patent may have an impact on channel choice, though the direction is difficult to specify. A firm with a strong patent is protected and may not worry about information leaking via independent channels to actual or potential competitors. However, patent protection is never ironclad (Davidson 1982). A product sufficiently innovative to warrant an inclusive patent may need further protection in the form of closely guarding *all* information about the product, as well as access to it (so-called "trade secret" protection). This protection is accomplished best in an integrated channel, where the manufacturer can control distribution activities (including information dissemination) relatively closely.

Competitive behavior may influence an entrant as well. If firms already established in the market have integrated channels, the entrant may wish to have one also. In this way, entrants signal to customers that they, too, are committed to serving that market and are willing to dedicate resources (e.g., personnel) to do so. A game theoretic interpretation of this behavior is that oligopolistic competitors "exchange threats" by imitating the establishment of subsidiaries in each other's markets.

The choice of an integrated or independent channel may be influenced by the country being entered (Thorelli, Reading 1 in this volume). In particular, managing an integrated channel may be more difficult in countries culturally dissimilar to the U.S. because U.S. management techniques may not transfer readily to the foreign environment (Davidson 1982).

In sum, the literature suggests a model of overseas distribution channel choice depending on many factors. In this model, integration of the distribution channel function is more likely

- the greater the level of transaction-specific assets in the salesforce,
- the less mature the product category,
- the higher the service level associated with the product,
- the more differentiated the products in the product class,
- the less prevalent the legal restrictions constraining direct foreign investment,
- when an integrated distribution channel is already in place (the converse is true for the case of a non-integrated channel),
- the more closely related the product to the company's core business,
- the more important the trade secrets relative to patents in protecting the technology,
- the more competitors have integrated distribution channels in the foreign market, and
- the more similar to the U.S. the culture of the country being entered.

Existing Distribution Arrangements

Given any existing distribution channel, a firm makes a marginal cost-benefit calculation when choosing a channel through which to sell a new product: will the added return of using an integrated channel for the new product justify the marginal cost? Because establishing an integrated channel involves significant fixed setup costs, use of an integrated channel is much more likely when one is already in place (so that the fixed setup costs are sunk) than in the case of either *de novo* market entry or a previously established non-integrated channel (when the fixed costs have yet to be incurred and are thus not yet sunk). Similarly, when a non-integrated channel is already in place in the foreign market, the incremental cost of selling a new product through the existing channel is lower than that of selling through an integrated channel.

The setting of this study is the international semiconductor industry. A National Science Foundation study undertaken in 1978–1980 yielded extensive original interview information on 94 overseas distribution operations that were started between 1955 and 1975. These operations were carried out by 36 U.S. based firms. The interviews, consisting of both scaled response and open-ended questions, were conducted with a senior executive, knowledgeable about the market entry in question. For more complex technology transfers, more than one executive was interviewed and their responses were cross-checked in order to obtain a consistent picture.

Integrating Distribution: Discussion and Managerial Implications

The results lend support to several complementary approaches to the choice of distribution channels for products introduced in foreign markets. The neoclassical economic approach emphasizes achieving scale economies and fully utilizing lumpy indivisible inputs. Consistent with this rationale, in instances of market expansion we find manufacturers tending to add their new products to their established channels (if any), thereby more fully utilizing the relationships they have developed with independent organizations or the distribution branches they have installed in the host country. Interestingly, these scale effects override whether the product is related to the firm's principal business or to its periphery.

Our results indicate that entrants tend to pyramid their products within a channel, thereby cementing their current arrangements and raising exit barriers. The "inertia" entrants display in adding to existing arrangements underscores the importance of selecting the appropriate channel in the first place. Should this choice prove inferior, the entrant becomes vulnerable to new competition, which can elect the more appropriate channel for the product class without incurring switching costs. Interestingly, extensive research on how managers actually make these critical strategic decisions indicates that the decision making process is often nonsystematic and based on little information. One of the primary reasons is that managers operating outside the familiar domestic settings have few guidelines to use.

Consistent with transaction cost analysis is the finding that entrants use integrated channels for products whose distribution entails asset specificity. These products have a common profile: they require the distribution agent to undergo considerable training to learn about the product. This finding is consonant with Lilien's (1979) that complex technical products tend to be distributed through integrated channels.

Though we did not measure the importance of relationships, we speculate that complex products also require the development, deepening, and specialization of working relationships in order to be distributed effectively. The specialized learning and these relationships constitute transaction-specific assets, which figure prominently in Williamson's explanation of why organizations choose to perform a function internally (make) rather than contract with outsiders (buy).

Our results indicate that where these assets arise in international distribution, entrants elect to use the distribution agent rather than write a contract with an independent party. Presumably, they do so because employee status facilitates the monitoring of these difficult-to-replace agents. Further, entrants then can use legitimate authority and a broad range of subtle incentives to influence their agents' behavior.

The results also support the widespread belief that firms are somewhat hesitant to manage integrated operations in cultures that are very foreign to the managers of the multinational firm. Such caution appears warranted. The successful, efficient operation of an integrated distribution channel demands significant managerial and financial resources and capabilities even in the domestic setting that management knows. In settings unknown to management, successfully managing an integrated distribution channel is even more demanding.

What do the findings mean for managers? One important managerial implication is that there are high costs to making an incorrect initial channel decision when entering a foreign market. Our evidence indicates that once such a decision is made (whether right or wrong), it tends to be reinforced over time as new products are sold through established channels. If the "wrong" channel form is set up upon initial market entry, high costs of changing the channel face the firm. This possibility emphasizes the importance of taking a long-run, dynamic view of marketing channel choice rather than settling on an alternative that meets transient criteria (such as convenience or availability). The empirical evidence only reinforces the long-held institutional view that marketing channel choice is a significant investment that should not be made lightly (Thorelli, Reading 1 in this volume). We also find support for McGuire and Staelin's (1983) proposition that differentiated products are more likely to be integrated. Their model is developed under a variety of restrictions, leading the authors to caution that "to confront our models to empirical data would be premature". Our results suggest otherwise.

Further research is needed to develop knowledge of what drives a firm's methods of introducing its products to foreign markets. One approach would be to include other explanations for international channel choice, such as the firm's expectations and level of risk aversion and the availability of qualified distribution agents. Another would be to study joint ventures as an alternative to either integrated or independent channels.

Clearly, our work is exploratory and subject to limitations. Nonetheless, note the extreme difficulty of obtaining *any* data about a firm's international operations, particularly at the division or product level. Our data, though somewhat crude, do afford some insight about launching a product in a foreign market—an important strategic issue in international management. In particular, we find indications that entrants tend to

- reinforce channel choices by adding new products to their current channels,
- erect a protective, restrictive governance structure around the distribution of complex, sophisticated products that require an investment in learning,
- integrate the distribution of products whose differentiation protects them from price competition,
- distribute substitutable products through independent middlemen, who bear the brunt of the price competition common to such products, and
- use middlemen when introducing products to non-Western markets.

Lilien (1979) argues that modeling the decisions of recognized, established firms (as we do here) can provide a useful benchmark for future decision-making. If so, our findings may be of considerable value to managers faced with the complex task of selecting an international channel of distribution for a new product.

References

Anderson, Erin, "The Salesperson as Outside Agent or Employee: A Transaction Cost Analysis," *Marketing Science*, Vol. 4 (Summer 1985), pp. 234–254.

Coughlan, Anne T., "Competition and Cooperation in Marketing Channel Choice: Theory and Application," *Marketing Science*, Vol. 4, No. 2 (1985), pp. 110–129.

Davidson, William H., *Global Strategic Management*, (1982).

Lilien, Gary L., "Advisor 2: Modeling and Marketing Mix Decision for Industrial Products," *Management Science*, Vol. 25 (February 1979), pp. 191–204.

McGuire, Timothy W. and Richard Staelin, "An Industry Equilibrium Analysis of Downstream Vertical Integration," *Marketing Science*, Vol. 2, No. 2 (1983), pp. 161–192.

Williamson, Oliver E., *Markets and Heirarchies: Analysis and Antitrust Implications*, (New York: The Free Press, 1975).

Williamson, Oliver E., "Transaction Cost Economics: The Governance of Contractual Relations," *Journal of Law and Economics*, Vol. 22 (October 1979), pp. 233–262.

Williamson, Oliver E., "The Modern Corporation: Origins, Evolution, Attributes," *Journal of Economic Literature*, Vol. 19 (December 1981), pp. 1537–1568.

28

Diffusion of Franchise System Use in International Operations*

LAWRENCE S. WELCH

Although franchising has had a long history, its first significant penetration took place at the end of the nineteenth century in the form of so-called "product and tradename franchising" (U.S. Department of Commerce 1987). This development began in the U.S. and was followed in other Western countries, although concentrated in three main areas: motor vehicle dealerships, service stations and soft drink bottlers—of which Coca Cola is perhaps the best known example.

A new wave of franchising has occurred in the post-World War II period which has been distinguished from the "first generation" by its concern with the transfer of a more complete business system. Often called "business format franchising," it has been defined as being "characterized by an ongoing business relationship between franchisor and franchisee that includes not only the product, service and trademark but the entire business format itself . . . a marketing strategy and plan, operating manuals and standards, quality control and continuing two way communications" (U.S. Department of Commerce 1987, p. 3).

The growth of business format franchising in the post-War period has been particularly rapid, across an ever-broadening front (U.S. Department of Commerce 1987). As a mode of international operations it is being seriously considered by more and more companies in diverse locations as an alternative to the more traditional forms of foreign operations.

In this article the process of global development in franchise system use will be examined, with particular reference to recent Australian

* Adapted with permission from *International Marketing Review*, Vol. 6, No. 5 (1989), pp. 7–19.

experience of companies moving quickly from domestic operations to international franchising.

Development Pattern

The postwar development of franchise system use has tended to follow a path not dissimilar to that argued in the international product life-cycle concept. Initially, the business format franchising system was pre-eminently developed in the U.S. and grew rapidly there in the 1950s and 1960s. Although the focus of growth at the outset was domestic, with successful domestic expansion the attraction of foreign markets became more valid. Research indicates that perceived foreign market potential and foreign franchisee interest were far more important in stimulating the move into foreign markets than any immediate concern about domestic saturation. Nevertheless, the experience, confidence and raised horizons flowing from domestic expansion provided the basic springboard for foreign activity in a manner similar to pre-export patterns.

Thus, in the late 1960s and early 1970s the process of international expansion by U.S. franchisors began in earnest. As Table 28.1 indicates there has been a steady growth since 1971. Between 1971 and 1985 the numbers of franchisors operating abroad more than doubled while there was a much larger increase in the number of outlets actually established by these companies in foreign markets. Some of the outlets were set up as company-owned units, but primarily they represented a franchise sale to an individual franchisee or to a master licensee with responsibility for a region or country.

Because of its proximity and low cultural distance, Canada was of course the primary initial target for U.S. franchisors. Although there has been a drop from 1971 when 46% of U.S. franchisors' foreign outlets were located in Canada, in 1985 the corresponding figure was still 30%—making it by far the most important foreign market for U.S. companies (U.S. Department of Commerce 1987). Proximity was stressed in explaining the early move into Canada, but this factor was clearly not of sufficient strength to bring about a similar shift into Mexico. Other important factors undoubtedly come into play. Market potential has already been stressed. There is also the question of how readily an existing franchise format can be applied in a foreign market without major adaptation. Ready transfer is most likely to similarly advanced Western economies with comparable cultural characteristics. The desire to go with an unaltered proven package is strong. In Hackett's survey, 41.2% of companies had reported "no major changes in their franchise marketing package for overseas ventures" (1976, p. 71).

In a similar manner with respect to Canada, the bias towards other culturally similar, advanced countries such as the U.K. and Australia was a natural evolution, despite the proximity factor. The shift into Japan in some strength appears to argue against this trend, although the method of entry was important in supporting this development. The bulk of the penetration in Japan has been through master licensees, minimizing the demands of more direct involvement in developing operations in an alien culture (Grant 1985). As Table 28.1 indicates, Canada, Japan, Australia and the U.K. accounted for almost 70% of the foreign outlets of franchisors in 1985.

Beyond this core of countries there has been a gradual spread of U.S. franchisors to more and more diverse locations, some to be expected, such as the Scandinavian countries and the newly industrializing countries of Asia, while others have been somewhat surprising. For example, McDonald's is opening restaurants in Yugoslavia and Hungary, and Pizza Hut is negotiating to open 100 outlets in the Soviet Union. The growing importance of global markets to U.S. franchisors is perhaps best illustrated by the experience of McDonald's where its international segment has become the fastest growing part of the entire organization. Already operating in 44

TABLE 28.1 International Franchising by U.S. Companies*

Year	Growth Number of Companies	Total Foreign Outlets
1971	156	3,365
1974	217	9,663
1977	244	14,217
1980	279	20,428
1983	305	25,682
1985	342	30,188

Country or Region	Spread (1985) Number of Franchisors	Number of Outlets
Canada	239	9,054
Japan	66	7,124
Australia	75	2,511
United Kingdom	68	2,291 (69.5%)†
Continental Europe	73	4,398
Asia (less Japan and Middle East)	74	1,452
Caribbean	88	803
Mexico	36	542
South America	35	515

Notes: * Does not include automobile and truck dealers, gasoline service stations and soft drink bottlers; includes company and franchisee-owned outlets.
Notes: † Share of total outlets represented by first four countries.

countries, it has become more dependent on a wide diversity of foreign locations for continued growth.

The Australian Experience

Australia was one of the early favored locations for U.S. franchisors. Despite the adverse distance factor, cultural similarity, a high per capita income, a well developed service sector and a high level of penetration of U.S. firms in general made Australia a strong potental franchising recipient. At the forefront of the Australian invasion were those companies which had been very successful in the U.S., notably the fast food operators. One observer of the Australian franchising scene has commented "that it was the introduction of McDonald's into Australia in the early 1970s and McDonald's entry into franchising in the mid-1970s that gave franchising in Australia its real boost" (Bellin 1984, p. 27). Prior to this stage, as in the U.S. franchising had principally been of the "first generation" variety (product and trade name) in the same areas of motor vehicle dealerships, service stations and soft drink bottlers. Once the "second generation" versions began to spread into the 1970s, franchising's growth was extremely rapid, not only through the entry of foreign (mainly U.S.) franchisors, but also because of the rise of local imitators.

By its very nature franchising is a very open form of operations, offering typically a standardized format, although much of the complexity of the total business system involved remains obscured behind a seemingly simple facade. While a name can be protected, the type of product or service and general style of operation can be readily copied, as the McDonald's imitators in the U.S. and elsewhere have clearly demonstrated, however, not always successfully. In the Australian case the imitators have blossomed, covering a wide spectrum of products and services, including such areas as clothing, chocolates, soaps, tyres, financial services and fitness centers. They have followed very much the format established by the earlier U.S. franchising entrants. Even some well established manufacturing companies with retail outlets have sought to move from a company-owned to a franchised basis as a means of freeing tied up capital and providing a spur to motivation. One Australian bank, the Bank of Queensland, has been setting up new branches of franchised outlets while other banks are examining the possibilities of following suit.

As there are no general statistics maintained on the state of franchising in Australia it is not possible to give any precise figure to the extent of its development. Casual observation at the retail level very quickly indicates that the extent of franchising involvement, both foreign and local, is substantial. Using the broadest definition of franchising (both first, and second generation), the Bureau of Industry Economics (1981) found from a survey of small non-manufacturing firms in 1978 that 18.9% were engaged in franchising. More recently, franchising's share of retail sales is estimated to have reached at least 20% and may even be as high as 30%. Despite the limitations of such estimates it is clear that the franchising phenomenon has achieved a deep level of penetration in Australia, particularly in retailing activity, and has grown significantly beyond its U.S. inspired base.

The Outward Move

As a result of early imitation, many Australian companies have been applying the franchising system in a diversity of fields for some time. Inevitably, with their Australian expansion process, similar forces which eventually came into play in the U.S. and led U.S. operators to consider international activity have begun to take effect. The success of domestic expansion likewise pointed to wider possibilities, while these were often being exposed by foreign franchisee interest. In Australia's case, the smaller domestic market size quickly exposes the limits of domestic growth. Thus, as shown in Figure 28.1, we have begun to see a growing outward movement by Australian franchisors.

Included in the target market of interest has been the U.S. Not only is the market potential factor seen as strong but also as the home of franchising it is viewed as having a receptive environment for franchising operations. The Australian pattern is illustrative of a process which is also taking place at different rates in many other countries, so that ultimately the U.S. is likely to become an increasingly important recipient of global franchising activity, in much the same way as it has become the recipient of foreign direct investment operations. A prime example of this pattern is the Italian-based clothing store chain (mainly franchised), Benetton: "With limited room for expansion in Europe, Benetton has launched a major assault on the the U.S. market, where it has grown from zero to 650 shops in five years' (Bruce 1987, p. 28).

Paths to Foreign Franchising

As Figure 28.2 indicates, there are a number of feasible paths by which companies might enter foreign franchising operations, with some combination of prior franchising and foreign marketing experience. Although there has been no general empirical research to confirm the pattern, the general impression from reported experience in Australia, and from the particular cases examined in this article, would be that domestic franchising has preceded foreign involvement. This is in line with U.S. experience noted earlier.

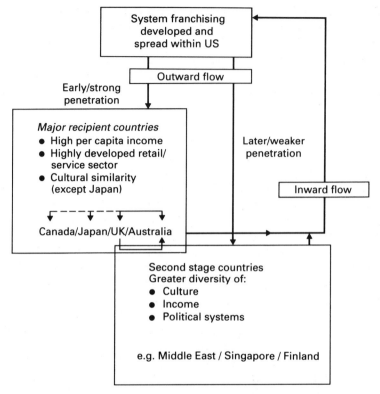

FIG. 28.1. International Spread of Franchising.

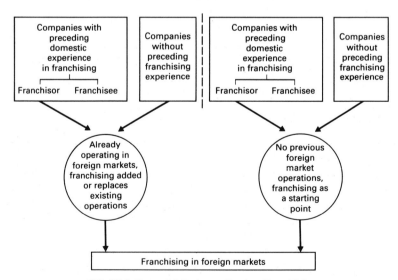

FIG. 28.2. Potential Paths to Foreign Franchising.

There are good reasons for expecting such an approach. The franchising development often begins as a response to a perceived local opportunity, perhaps as an adaptation of a franchising concept already operating in another foreign market. Either way, the market focus is clearly local to begin with. In addition, the local market provides a better environment for testing and developing the franchising format. Feedback from the marketplace and franchisees can be more readily obtained because of the ease of communication. Adjustments can be made more quickly because of the close local contact. A whole variety of minor changes in the format may be necessary as a result of early experience in areas such as training, franchisee choice, site selection, organization of suppliers, promotion and outlet decor. The early stages of franchise development represent a critical learning process for the franchisor, not just about how to adapt the total package to the market requirements but also regarding the nature of franchising method itself. Ultimately, with a proven package, and a better understanding of its operation, the franchisor is in a better position to attack foreign markets, and more confident about doing so with a background of domestic success.

The key franchising learning process can also readily develop on the franchisee side. Experience as a franchisee may be a prelude to the establishment of a different franchise chain, and ultimate internationalization. Alternatively, it may be that the company undertakes franchising in other countries on behalf of the international chain. For example, the partners who developed the Wendys Supa Sundaes (ice cream) franchising chain had been franchisees for five years before setting up their own chain; even as the first Wendys outlets were being established they still ran three Wimpy's hamburger restaurants. The transfer of knowledge and experience from franchisee activities parallels the pattern found for a number of Australian companies which switched from international licensee to licensor activities.

It can be expected too that there will be increasing numbers of master licensees for a given country which, having set up the chain locally, seek out the possibilities of expansion for the chain to another country. The master licensee is effectively operating as a franchisor within the country assigned, deriving the benefits of accumulated franchising experience and knowledge in much the same way as a franchisor of domestic origin. The loosely connected Australian end of the worldwide Budget car rental franchising chain moved from its Australian base (mixed company-owned and franchised outlets) to successfully develop South Pacific and then Asian operations, including Japan, under the Budget flag. In these moves the Australian company was the initiator having obtained rights to these areas from its licensor, Budget America. Originally though, the shift into franchising in domestic operations by Budget Australia, from a system of only company-owned outlets, was heavily based on know-how transferred from the U.S. company: "In large part the experience, assistance and encouragement of Budget U.S., made the franchising experiment work" (Layton 1981, p. 61).

While the most likely path into foreign franchising operations seems to be as an extension of a domestic franchising base, there is every reason to expect some cases whereby the shift is made from other, existing forms of foreign operations. In such cases there is an already established base of foreign experience and knowledge, and perhaps committed facilities, so it is not a blind leap into an unknown foreign environment. The conversion to franchising may be relatively simple, for example, if it is a matter of changing a chain of owned outlets into franchises. As licensing packages broaden and develop a stronger marketing component it can be expected that more will evolve towards a franchising system basis (Welch 1985). The motivation of the franchised owner-operator and the franchisee's capital contribution are strong incentives for the consideration of conversion possibilities. As well, the high international profile of franchising has brought it into stronger focus as a means of foreign operation.

Conversion of foreign operations to franchising in situations where the company also has some domestic franchising experience is a somewhat easier move because of the combination of both franchising and foreign marketing backgrounds. Of course, even for experienced international franchisors like McDonald's, the initial step into a foreign market will often be via a company-owned operation. By such means the company can ensure full control and is in a better position to make any required adaptations to portions of the total package, before rolling out on a franchising basis. In this case the alternative method is merely a prelude, or a sounding board, for the ultimate establishment of the franchise system. This process can be seen as part of an overall international franchising strategy.

Amongst the paths to foreign franchising shown in Figure 28.2, the least likely is that of the inexperienced franchisor starting into franchising first within a foreign market, but without any background of foreign marketing activity. It is possible that, for example, the new franchisor has work experience, lived in the foreign country previously, or is even a migrant from the country. Thus, there is not an unfamiliarity factor to contend with. However, the combination of previously unused techniques in an unfamiliar foreign environment, without previous foreign marketing experience, is a difficult one to contemplate let alone master successfully. The feasibility of such a path probably depends more heavily than in other situations on the ability of the foreign franchisee to develop the system.

Some Australian Cases

As noted already, the assimilation and imitation of franchise system use in Australia has proceeded rapidly since the early 1970s. This process has now led to a growing number of Australian franchisors which have established foreign operations or are seeking to do so. A case in point is the ice-cream franchising chain, Wendys Supa Sundaes. It opened its first outlet in 1979 as a company-owned operation. In fact, the initial intention was to establish just four outlets in the one city, Adelaide. At a very early stage though, outside interest in setting up an outlet in a new shopping complex in another city, Melbourne, was expressed—thereby stimulating an awareness of wider possibilities. The first franchised outlet was, however, not opened until 1981. Since then franchising has been the basis of growth throughout Australia: about ten outlets per year were opened up until 1987, during which a further 27 were added. Despite this rapid growth, by 1987 the company was beginning to feel the constraints imposed by the shopping center location of its outlets. Limits on the availability of good shopping center sites were expected to result in a lower rate of growth in the future. Inevitably then, international possibilities presented an alternative source of expansion. The foundation of its initial international interest was, however, laid in its domestic learning curve:

> Things for us on the local front are going extremely well . . . Overseas expansion seems to be the natural progression from here. We have learned a lot during the past eight years and I think we have ironed out most of the bugs in the system. (Burns 1987, p. 50).

The company's initial "pre-export" move was, however, stimulated by an unsolicited inquiry from an Australian with business connections in Hong Kong and South-East Asia. In response, a study tour of the region was undertaken in late 1986, but it was felt that the growth potential was insufficient to justify the set-up expenses. In the background was an interest in U.S. possibilities which had developed through frequent visits and contact with representatives of the U.S. company which supplies its machines–they had stressed the good U.S. market prospects for the concept. After meeting a U.S. franchising consultant at an international franchising conference in 1986, Wendys Supa Sundae has utilized the U.S. franchising consultant to advise on improvements to Australian operations and subsequently to assist in U.S. market entry. The intention has been to establish a joint venture as a basis for U.S. activities, although so far negotiations with potential partners have fallen through.

Dial-a-Dino's, a pizza delivery chain, began in a similar manner to Wendys, at the end of 1984, by establishing company-owned outlets. It was about one year and seven outlets later that the first franchise operation was established. Since then growth has proceeded rapidly throughout Australia via franchising. By late 1987 the company had an Australian chain of 83 outlets.

The founder of Dial-a-Dino's indicates that the intention to set up an international network was present at the outset, and was part of the driving force in the growth of the company. In late 1986 a tour of Asian countries was undertaken because of a perception that it would be easier to develop activities in Japan from an Australian base rather than in Europe or the U.S. As an outcome of the investigations, Japan was seen as a particularly viable market for entry. However, New Zealand was the first foreign market to be penetrated as a result of an unsolicited inquiry. The eventual New Zealand partner was interested in the pizza delivery business and had noticed Dial-a-Dino's operations on a visit to Sydney. The New Zealand entry was relatively straightforward with no capital contribution required: Dial-a-Dino's took a 33% equity in the New Zealand company in exchange for rights to the whole franchise system. From May, 1987 eight outlets had been established by late 1987: five franchised and three company-owned. New Zealand was viewed as an experimental market on which Dial-a-Dino's could cut its teeth before moving to larger and more demanding markets such as Japan.

Japanese market entry was likewise achieved via a joint venture arrangement, with equity exchanged for full access to the franchise system. This involvement was initiated by the Japanese in late 1986 as Dial-a-Dino's was investigating the Japanese market. The President of a Japanese company, (Ono Creative) had approached the Australian Trade Commission in Tokyo in search of a potential Australian partner with which to establish a pizza business in Japan, and was put in contact with Dial-a-Dino's. Despite some initial communications difficulties, the joint venture began operations in August, 1987. Some adjustments have been made for the Japanese market—for example, smaller pizzas, lighter dough and smaller delivery vehicles—but in general the franchised package is relatively unchanged.

The move into Japan has been followed quickly by the establishment of a similar joint venture arrangement in the U.K., with the first outlet opened in December, 1987. Such rapid expansion and international penetration are somewhat unusual but can perhaps be explained by a combination of the following factors:

(1) Successful franchising of the Australian network and the learning process therefrom;
(2) The international outlook of the founder;
(3) Fortuitous action by foreign companies interested in the pizza business;
(4) The type of entry mode: joint ventures without a capital contribu-

tion sharply diminished the financial demands of international expansion.

In another example of rapid expansion, Miniskips, which franchised a waste removal system, considered the possibility of international operations from the outset. Soon after the launch of the company's franchise chain its founders commented they "hope to launch Miniskips in New Zealand and are making inquiries in the U.S. and S.E. Asia, where Singapore and Hong Kong are considered the most likely targets" (Treadgold 1985, p. 113). Such early international interest to some extent runs counter to the earlier stress on expanding domestic operations first. McDonald's took about a decade from its early U.S. spread before initial flirtations with international markets began in the mid-1960s. It was not until the early 1970s that this became a serious international push.

The international interest at the outset by Miniskips can be partly explained by the background of the co-founders. Both were from England where the system for waste collection and disposal was first seen in operation. They were therefore clearly cognizant of the international possibilities of the business, and of the universality of the need they were serving.

Within 18 months of starting operations in 1985, a national chain of more than 80 franchisees had been established. Such rapid expansion placed a heavy strain on managerial time and resources. This strain was enhanced, since the company's base was in Perth whereas its major markets were on the other (Eastern) side of Australia. Thus, in carrying through its first international move in 1986, it merely sold the rights to the Miniskips package to a New Zealand company for a cash payment and a 14% equity interest, removing the need for direct involvement in establishing a New Zealand network. It had also begun investigations into the U.K. market.

Miniskips was taken over in early 1987 and subsequently went through a period of consolidation. By early 1988 all but 13 franchisees had been bought out. The aim was to establish the business on a sounder basis before resuming any outward push.

Cut-Price Deli is a retail chain of speciality food stores (delicatessens) which is perhaps illustrative of the rapid growth potential of franchising in comparison with company-owned operations. Its first store was acquired in 1974, and by 1982 it had established 16 company-owned stores. However, the company began experiencing significant staff and management problems. In attempting to resolve the situation, the partners who owned and ran the company decided to try franchising, the first franchise being sold in June 1982. Within 12 months, 25 additional franchises had been sold. At the same time the company refined its franchising system by a blending of existing elements (such as an established buying network) with franchising-specific components (for example, a training manual). Since then growth has continued throughout Australia and by early 1987, 110 outlets had been established.

Cut-Price Deli's first international move into New Zealand took place at the beginning of 1987—through a joint venture with a New Zealand investment company (Brierly Investments). A company-owned outlet represented the starting point of operations. The outlet was to function as a pilot store, demonstrating the concept and its viability before rolling out into the full New Zealand market on a franchising basis.

The interest in New Zealand had evolved out of a general recognition of the potential for applying its franchising system in international markets, as well as through direct connections with the New Zealand market via a previous supplier company (Huttons). Cut-Price Deli had used Huttons in Australia for some time until Huttons was taken over by Brierly Investments and withdrew to New Zealand. The move evoked an interest in New Zealand by Cut-Price Deli and eventually contact with Huttons led to the joint venture arrangement with Brierly Investments.

Cut-Price Deli has expressed an intention to ultimately enter the U.S. market although its next move was most likely to be into the U.K. However, the company has found that continuing rapid development in Australia has constrained its ability to take on international markets as rapidly as it would like.

Once again the four Australian franchising cases which have been examined illustrate the way in which the impetus of successful domestic expansion often leads to international interest. While domestic expansion inevitably ties up company commitment for some time, it provides the essential proving ground for the franchising system. The early interest in international possibilities may reflect a more positive environment for such moves in franchising in the 1980s as well as reflecting the nature of the expansion ethos of franchising itself. Success is demonstrated and judged by an ever-widening establishment of franchise outlets, and after initial domestic growth has been proven, the ultimate test is in the international arena.

Franchising from Developing Countries

The main focus of this article has been on the way franchising has spread from the U.S. to other advanced countries, and how these countries have absorbed and applied the technique, as illustrated in the Australian case, and have now begun to franchise internationally themselves. In the same way that the international product life-cycle model predicted the later development of exports of standardized products from the developing countries, it is relevant to ask whether such a pattern could evolve in the use of franchising. Given that the franchising operators have been moving into the developing countries (e.g., McDonald's in the Philippines and Venezuela), the pre-conditions for the type of demonstration effect which operated in the advanced countries are now being established. On that basis we should expect in the future to see the growth of diverse examples of home-grown franchising chains. Already many local versions have emerged in Malaysia (May, 1988). Ultimately, some of these are also likely to move to international operations. The limited scope of the tertiary/retail sector in some developing countries is of course bound to constrain the potential for such a process. Nevertheless franchising is such a well-tried and understood method in the advanced countries, with a developed infrastructure to support its use, that it represents a feasible path for companies from the developing area to consider in penetrating these markets. The ubiquitous franchised clothing chains, for example, in many advanced markets could be emulated, thereby providing a potential for adding value to clothing exports from the developing countries.

Conclusions

From a predominantly U.S. base, business format franchising has moved into global use in the 1980s. Those countries which began as recipients of the system have learned to use it successfully—as illustrated by the Australian experience. The end result of that success, in a growing number of cases, has been to also take its use into international operations, including to the U.S. It is possible to see this process continuing to the point where, like direct foreign investment, there is more balance in the global pattern of franchise system use, and that developing countries will become an identifiable part of this total picture.

Although still in the early stages of outward internationalization, the experience of the Australian franchisors indicates something of the power of franchising and its potential as a driving force in internationalization. The strong expansion ethos which seems to characterize franchising has important implications for the likelihood and speed of internationalization. That a small Australian company could within three years grow from nothing to a chain of 83 domestic outlets and operations in three countries with a "product" as seemingly simple and non-unique as a pizza delivery system is perhaps illustrative of franchising's potential.

However, the expansion ethos can lead to problems, as emerged in the Miniskips case, when companies become over-extended in the domestic expansion process, and then international possibilities emerge as well. There is a clear danger in attempting too much too early: international franchising, even via a master licensing system, is not as undemanding as, for example, filling a fortuitous export order. Given the demonstrated importance of the domestic learning curve as a prelude to international operations, it could be argued that franchisor strategy should be to establish a strong domestic base first. However, Australian and U.S. experience has shown just how important foreign franchise interest is in stimulating international involvement. If a franchisor does not respond there is the risk that other operators may be approached and ultimately the market is closed. Would a similar entry opportunity have been available in the New Zealand market to Dial-a-Dino's if it had waited until it was better established in Australia? Thus, the dictum of establishing at home first has to be balanced against the rapid changes in the international environment which are creating new opportunities and pressures for franchising and may require an earlier international responsiveness than was previously considered appropriate.

References

Bellin, H., "Franchising's Promising Future in Australia," *The Chartered Accountant in Australia*, Vol. 54, No. 8, (March 1984), pp. 26–8, 62.

Bruce, L. , "The Bright New Worlds of Benetton," *International Management*, No. 42, (November 1987), pp. 24–35.

Burns, W., "Wendys Supa Sundaes Eyes the Big U.S. Market," *Australian Financial Review*, 5 June, 1987, p. 50.

Grant, C., *Business Format Franchising*, (London: Economist Intelligence Unit, 1985).

Hackett, D. W., "The International Expansion of U.S. Franchise Systems," *Journal of International Business Studies*, Vol. 7 (Spring 1976), pp. 65–75.

International Trade Administration, U.S. Dept. of Commerce, *Franchising in the Economy*, 1985–87, (January 1987).

Layton, R. A. (ed.), *Australian Marketing Projects*, (Hoover Awards for Marketing 1980), (Sydney: Macarthur Press, 1981).

Treadgold, T., "Making a Name out of Muck," *Business Review Weekly*, 8 November, 1985, pp. 112–3.

Welch, L. S., "The International Marketing of Technology: An Interaction Perspective," *International Marketing Review*, Vol. 2 (1985), pp. 41–53.

29

The Bright Future of Service Exports*

RICHARD I. KIRKLAND JR.

Editors at the official Soviet news agency, Tass, eager to spread the *glasnost* gospel, now feed their articles into Nexis, the database run by the electronic information subsidiary of Ohio's Mead Corp. Subscribers from London to Lyon can punch up Communist copy on their personal computers—for a fee of course. Some 10,000 house-hungry Londoners have signed up for more than $500 million of mortgages since last May from a new subsidiary of Wall Street's Salomon Brothers. European executives, eager to get a package from, say, Amsterdam to Atlanta, are increasingly turning to Federal Express, the Memphis company whose international revenues have been doubling every year since it began operating overseas in 1984. Meanwhile, in Istanbul, tourists having a Big Mac attack can seek relief beneath the golden arches on Cumhuriyet Street—one of 209 McDonald's that opened abroad last year.

Across the globe, U.S. service companies are demonstrating some of the surprising ways that America can become competitive again. Last year they produced a world-beating $48 billion of service exports, according to the U.S. Commerce Department.

Those numbers almost certainly understate U.S. trade in what the British aptly call "invisibles." Because only a few services such as motion pictures, generate products that can be physically counted by customs officials, most estimates of service trade are based on extrapolations from industry surveys. Not only is the quality of such data inherently poor, but in many industries, such as computer and data processing services, the U.S. government does not even collect the numbers. Historically, record-keeping in services has been given a low

---

*Slightly abbreviated from *Fortune*, June 8, 1987, pp. 32–38, with permission.

priority. The U.S. tracks trade in roughly 10,000 categories of goods, but only about 40 categories of services. The best recent analysis, conducted by the U.S. Congress's Office of Technology Assessment, suggests that the true value of America's service exports may be twice as large as official statistics suggest.

Larger still, according to the O.T.A's estimates, are revenues of the overseas subsidiaries of U.S. advertising agencies, investment banks, insurers, consultants, and the like. If buyer and seller are in the same country, such revenues do not find their way directly into the U.S. balance of payments. But the unparalleled scale of those offshore sales—about $100 billion in 1983—offers yet another confirmation of America's historical hegemony in producing services and marketing them abroad.

New competitors have begun to chip away at the U.S. lead. The world's largest advertising conglomerate, for example, is now Saatchi & Saatchi of London. Tokyo giants dominate the latest lists of banks and brokerage houses, and the Japanese are moving aggressively in construction, hotels, and travel services. "Japan has launched a second export wave, this time in services," says Harry Freeman, an executive vice president at American Express. Last December the *Harvard Business Review*, ran a much noted article that asked, "Will Services Follow Manufacturing Into Decline?"

Happily, such fears are considerably exaggerated. Data Resources Inc. forecasts that between now and 1990, America's exports of services will rise by more than 60%. D.R.I. expects that the U.S. surplus on trade in the services this year will pass its previous postwar peak—$10.7 billion in 1982—and then keep on climbing, topping $38 billion by the end of the decade. Wharton estimates that by 1990 the U.S. service trade surplus will total $23 billion.

As used here, "services exports" refers to only one part of the service transactions that are included in the U.S. current account. These numbers measure what economists inelegantly call "nonfactor services"—mainly travel, tourism, fees and royalties, and business and professional services. Excluded are so-called factor service payments, which largely reflect income from holdings of stocks, bonds, and property abroad as well as profits from foreign direct investments by both manufacturing and service companies. In 1986 the U.S. claimed some $90 billion of such payments, of which no more than perhaps 15% reflects profits of the overseas subsidiaries of U.S. service companies.

Where is America's strength in selling services abroad? International transportation, which has made up about 30% of U.S. trade in services, will account for a big chunk of new service exports. According to the Commerce Department's definition, transportation exports occur when U.S. air or ocean carriers convey American goods abroad or sell tickets to foreign travelers. As U.S.-manufactured exports pick up, thanks to the weaker dollar, some portion of those goods will ride on American ships or in U.S. cargo planes, lifting transportation service exports. And America's battered international airlines are beginning to see a healthy increase in ticket sales to European travelers.

The lower dollar will also boost the international travel category, which constitutes about a fifth of service exports. Here again, it is important to understand the official definition. The Commerce Department defines travel "imports" as money Americans spend abroad on business and pleasure trips. "Exports" occur whenever foreigners pay for breakfasts in midtown Manhattan or zoom down Space Mountain at Disney World.

Most significantly, the U.S. should enjoy rapid expansion in overseas earnings from brainpower-driven services—the kind in which constant innovation, management skill, or heavy investment in technology are keys to success. One such sector is data processing and computer services. Last year, the international arm of Dallas-based Electronic Data Systems boosted revenues and earnings by nearly 90%—roughly triple the growth rate of E.D.S's domestic operations. Services billed to its General Motors parent accounted for a lot of that growth. But Gary Fernandes, chairman of E.D.S. International thinks that non-G.M. business will grow by at least 20% a year as foreign multinationals try to untangle and integrate their world-wide telecommunications and data processing networks.

Software producers, led by Ashton-Tate, Lotus Development, and Microsoft, already derive anywhere from 20% to more than 40% of their revenues from overseas sales. The U.S. Office of Technology Assessment estimated that the software trade surplus was around $3 billion in 1984, the most recent year for which data is available. "Software began as a very localized, nationally oriented industry," says Peter Cunningham, president of Input, a California consulting firm. "As the market becomes more global, the long-run trend favors companies that have a certain critical mass." Since 15 of the world's 20 biggest software companies are American, Cunningham thinks that the U.S. is in a strong position despite increasing competition from France's Cap Gemini Sogeti and Britain's Logica, among others.

U.S. databases like Nexis also have an edge, as do other kinds of electronic information firms. Now Connecticut-based Comp-U-Card International, an electronic shopping service whose revenues have soared from $4 million in 1983 to more than $140 million last year, gets about 15% of its profits from licensees in 28 countries. Says Walter Forbes, Comp-U-Card's chief executive: "I never gave a thought to licensing when we started this thing. But our system is so big, and so expensive to duplicate, that foreign entrepreneurs have decided it's cheaper to buy our expertise than build their own.''

Investments in technology can even give America's low-tech service champions a leg up overseas. International demand in the temporary-help market, for example, is increasingly driven by corporate customers seeking clerks who can handle the latest in word processing. "America has the highest degree of office automation in the world, and we pass that expertise on to our overseas offices," says Mitchell Fromstein, chief executive of Manpower, which get more than half its revenues from operations in 31 foreign countries. Manpower's fastest growth is in Japan and Britain.

Management skill is another big U.S. export. There is still not much respect abroad for managers of America's struggling smoke-stack industries, but it's a far different story in construction, health care, and business services. Says Ronald Marston, head of the international subsidiary of Nashville-based Hospital Corp. of America: "People everywhere are under pressure to control health costs, and they're turning to us for a transfer of technology from what they see as the best health care delivery system in the world.'' The biggest operator of private hospitals in the U.S., H.C.A. has acquired 28 hospitals abroad and signed contracts to operate nine others.

In Japan, ServiceMaster of Downers Grove, Illinois, is showing those masters of industrial quality control a few things about improving productivity and cutting costs when it comes to scrubbing floors and washing laundry. "The whole Japanese culture has been so oriented toward producing goods to export that they simply haven't developed the systems and expertise to compete in the kinds of services we provide," says Brian Oxley, 36, who grew up in Japan as the child of American missionaries and now runs ServiceMaster's international division. Working through joint ventures and licensees, ServiceMaster has in the past few years launched more than 500 home cleaning franchises in Japan and won contracts to do the housekeeping for 40 hospitals.

Having persuaded hundreds of local governments in the U.S. to contract out street cleaning and trash collection, $2-billion-a-year Waste Management Inc. of Oak Brook, Illinois, is cleaning up in Argentina, Saudi Arabia, and Australia. Fred Weinert, chief of the garbage king's international division, thinks revenues can grow 25% a year over the next five years. "Our main competitive advantage overseas is our experience," says Weinert. "Governments can check with their counterparts elsewhere and see how we've done. It becomes a small world.''

Rising anxiety over environmental hazards in the newly industrialized economies is also opening up new opportunities for U.S. service firms. "The masses in Asia are just beginning to revolt," says Charles Bruce, head of the international subsidiary of California-based U.R.S. Corp., a $116-million-a-year consulting firm that specializes in handling toxic wastes. By 1990, Bruce believes, U.R.S's international sales, which were minuscule six years ago, could account for 30% to 40% of the company's business.

As an exporter of pop culture, the U.S. enjoys an almost unassailable edge. Royalties from overseas rentals of films like *Rambo* or syndication of TV shows such as *Dallas* already produce a surplus of perhaps $1 billion on the U.S. trade balance. As governments in Europe loosen their regulatory grip on broadcasting, the surplus should grow rapidly. In addition, McDonald's and other U.S. franchisers can't seem to feed the global masses fast enough. In the last ten years the international portion of McDonald's annual sales has grown from 13% to 23%, and it shows no sign of slowing down.

Direct mail and telephone marketing, two well-developed—some might say overdeveloped—techniques in the U.S., are still in their infancy abroad. In the past few years, overseas expansion by the direct marketing subsidiaries of U.S. ad agencies has begun to produce annual billing increases in the 30% to 50% range. Headhunting is another made-in-the-U.S. service becoming popular in Europe. Los Angeles-based Korn/Ferry, the world's largest executive search firm, pulled in more than a third of its $70-million billings in 1986 from 21 overseas offices and expects the percentage to rise to 50% by the mid-1990s.

In Britain, property developers are calling in the Yanks to help cope with unprecedented demand for office space arising from deregulation of London's financial markets. Says Richard Halpern, president of Chicago-based Schal Associates, a construction management firm: "Because of our U.S. experience with big, computer-filled office buildings, we've been able to save our clients money by pointing out where projects were simply complex for complexity's sake."

Morgan Stanley and First Boston, along with Switzerland's Credit Suisse, are also helping finance a Rockefeller Center-size-office complex known as Canary Wharf in London's dock area. Architect is Skidmore Owings & Merrill of Chicago.

Nowhere has international growth been more explosive than in financial services. In the high-stakes struggle for dominance, Americans have no guaranteed advantage. Four of the world's five largest banks and four of the six largest securities houses are in Japan. So in financial markets where pure muscle counts, the Japanese will thrive.

Already Nomura Securities, Japan's biggest investment bank, has claimed the lead in the London-based business of underwriting so-called Eurobonds.

But U.S. companies hardly lack for capital clout. In the future the ranks of U.S. banking and investment giants—the likes of Citicorp, American Express, and Merrill Lynch—will be joined by industrial and insurance behemoths, including General Electric, General Motors, and Prudential. And as financial markets continue to deregulate in Tokyo, London, and New York, America's ever inventive investment bankers are confident that they will be able to transfer to the global arena their skill in pioneering and then dominating lucrative markets for new financial products, such as mortgage-backed securities and junk bonds. "There's just no way the Japanese are going to do to us in financial services what they did in automobiles," says the head of a major U.S. investment bank's London office.

Many U.S. service companies complain that their overseas expansion is stifled by numerous trade and investment barriers. For example, South Korea agreed to let a U.S. insurance company open an office there only after fierce arm-twisting by U.S. trade officials. In an elegant bit of diplomatic jujitsu, the Koreans granted the first license to Philadelphia-based Cigna, even though its New York rival A.I.G., America's biggest international insurer, had led the fight.

Some of those barriers may be coming down, though not right away. As a result of a six-year campaign by the Reagan Administration, 92 developed and developing countries that are part of the General Agreement on Tariffs and Trade (G.A.T.T.) agreed last fall to a round of global trade talks that for the first time will consider rules for trade in services. Though few American executives expect any payoff much before the next millennium, they hope that the global push for free service trade will at least discourage countries from setting up new barriers.

As total world trade in services expands, the U.S. may well find itself holding a somewhat smaller share of a much bigger pie. But such is the nature of free trade. On balance America's service industries exhibit few of the danger signs that signal decline.

30

Marketing to China: Still the Silk Road*

HANS B. THORELLI
JOSEPH Y. BATTAT

Ed. note: Clearly the 1989–90 turmoil in China has vastly increased the political risk perceived by executives in industrialized countries, who had been cuddled into the belief that gradual liberalization was to continue indefinitely. This could result in increasing reliance on trade and licensing rather than direct investment. We may also witness a polarization of commitments towards the extremes of very quick payoff and truly long-term perspectives.

The Silk Road

Views about the China market today are but a modern version of those held centuries ago. To most, China was that faraway, unreachable land inhabited by inscrutable people whose culture was fascinating yet strange. To others, China was the land of silk, tea, and other exotic products in demand in Europe and the rest of Asia. Like those who traveled the Silk Road in centuries past, modern traders in China know only too well the difficulties and dangers, but recognize the opportunities and potential of the China market.

A Door Ajar

It is only in the post-Mao era that trade opportunities have opened up to the West as the new leadership embarked on a programme of internal economic liberalization and instituted the so-called "Open Door" policy.

---

*Revised from *Euro-Asia Business Review*, Vol. 6, No. 2 (April 1987), pp. 22–26, with permission.

As a result of the Open Door policy, between 1978–1985 total foreign trade grew at a 19% compounded annual rate. Foreign trade in the Sixth Five-Year Plan (1981–1985) totalled U.S.$230 billion, double the amount of the fifth plan and the Seventh Five-Year Plan (1986–1990) forecasts annual growth rates of 7.5% for G.N.P. and 7% for foreign trade.

Unlike most other centrally planned economies, China expanded her foreign economic relations to include inward and outward foreign direct investments (F.D.I.): by the end of 1985, U.S.$5.85 billion of foreign direct investment had been contracted and U.S.$1.57 billion of F.D.I. actually spent in China. By 1989 total F.D.I. in China may well have exceeded U.S.$9 billion in value.

Priorities and Attractions

Notwithstanding the low income per capita, continuing rigidities in the socialist economic system and a host of problems resulting from China's semi-isolation from the international market in the last two decades, China offers attractive trade-opportunities in a number of areas:

1. the sheer size of her one billion-plus population which is enjoying a rapidly rising income (deflated per capita national income grew at 6.7% per annum between 1976 and 1984);
2. the reforms have created a large relatively open market sector (deflated sales of consumer goods grew by 9.8% per annum from 1976 to 1984, see *Zhongguo Tongji Nianjian*—1985);
3. the ability of her economic system to muster resources for large-scale projects; and
4. her leadership's commitment to an economy that is increasingly integrated within the community of nations (witness China's application for membership in G.A.T.T.).

There are four major ingredients that China has decided she needs from abroad for her modernization: advanced technology, enterprise management skills and knowhow, foreign capital, and experience in international markets. In the eyes of the Chinese leaders, F.D.I. in China constitutes an excellent vehicle to obtain all four of these ingredients. Since 1979, efforts have been made to attract multi-national corporations (M.N.C.) and, not least, overseas Chinese to invest in China.

The importation of foreign technology has greatly contributed to the rapid growth of foreign trade since the late 1970s and to a sizeable injection of advanced technology in a selective range of sectors. These include primarily energy and other natural resources, electronics, chemicals and petro-chemicals, transportation, communications and other infrastructure areas, machine tools and food processing.

Most of that technology was used to create new production facilities, although in recent years a growing emphasis is being put on transferring technology for the technical renovation of existing facilities, for import substitution in consumer goods, and to increase China's competitiveness in selected export-oriented industries. These trends are scheduled to continue, with some additional stress on the importation of soft technologies, such as computer software, management and marketing knowhow, banking, consulting and other services.

With the growing standard of living and the decentralization of foreign trade management, China's importation of durable consumer goods, such as cars and electronic appliances, soared in 1984 and 1985. The resulting "misallocation" of foreign exchange and a sizeable trade deficit in 1985 prompted the government to recentralize foreign trade management so as to avoid more "suboptimization" and scandals at the local levels, and to prohibit the import of cars in 1986.

Meanwhile, potential investors' enthusiasm has been dampened by factors such as the following:

- time lags and red tape in both negotiations and operations of their (joint) ventures;
- wide cultural and managerial differences;
- unexpected interventions in "managerial prerogatives" such as employee hiring and compensation;
- foreign exchange scarcity affecting operations and repatriation of profits;
- infrastructure deficiencies in such areas as communications and energy;
- labour problems resulting in low productivity;
- Chinese reluctance to allow a significant proportion of the output of foreign ventures to be sold domestically;
- a fairly substantial (1988 at least 20%) rate of inflation;
- An age-old and only gradually receding Chinese distrust of foreigners.

Marketing Culture Gap

One of the first things that strikes casual Western observers in China is the wide marketing culture gap that exists between their countries and China. Merchandise is poorly displayed and often inaccessible to customers, even in better shops such as the Friendship Stores that cater to foreigners. Few if any promotional activities take place. Sales clerks, rather than customers, are "kings" in the stores. A store that is known for its good customer services makes the news and is held up as a model for others to follow. At times, prices have little relation to the quality of goods and services.

Emerging from 20 years' quasi-isolation, experiencing an economy of scarcity, lacking a solid foundation for business laws, and operating under a highly-centralized socialist economic system, China has not developed much of what characterizes Western marketing culture. Indeed, in Leninist-Maoist socialism, marketing was a parasitical and exploitative activity.

The concepts of consumer sovereignty, protection and education are very weak. As long as sellers' markets prevail in China's economy of scarcity, weak market mechanisms will exist, and the system will be slow to respond to consumers' demands. Moreover, freedom of information and of movement of people, goods and services are quite limited by international comparison. Also, it is still unusual for foreign businessmen to have direct access to retail institutions, much less end consumers.

In the past, China's planned economy and its semi-autarchic state made the knowledge and application of many business theories and tools, such as the product life cycle, rather irrelevant. Enterprise managers felt little pressure to devise a marketing strategy, product line portfolio, or to allocate resources for product innovation and research and development. In sellers' markets the usefulness of market research to enterprise management was far from obvious. Even now, the conduct of market research is severely hindered by the lack of adequate and accurate databases, and the unfamiliarity with survey and other techniques.

The role of brand names is still weak in China. This does not mean there is no brand loyalty, or that buyers do not associate a product and its characteristics with a certain brand, but rather that there exist a number of factors that severely limit consumer choice. They include the lack of developed and stable channels of distribution, poor information and the prevailing sellers' markets, which mean there is little pressure on the manufacturer or the seller to establish brand names. Concepts of market segmentation and market differentiation are not consciously used. Enterprise managers are not familiar with them; furthermore the requisite data are not generally available.

Emergence of Marketing

An environment where marketing concepts can develop and be applicable is emerging in China thanks to recent economic policies and reforms. The substantial increase of supplies of consumer and light industrial products is creating consumer choice and with it the need for a producer marketing strategy to create and maintain a competitive advantage. Only recently, however, have basic concepts of marketing strategy and management been introduced among small, élite academic and business circles in China. The long process of establishing market channels and institutions has begun with the rural economy, which has experienced the highest growth rate of any economic sector in the last few years. The need for consumer protection laws is currently being debated, and the National People's Congress is drafting such laws.

An increasing number of enterprises have established a marketing department, as yet focused rather narrowly on sales management. In distribution and services there is increasing room for private initiatives alongside state and collective firms. Somewhat paradoxically, advertising seems to be the area of marketing which is developing the most rapidly in the P.R.C. All kinds of media (including TV and giant outdoor bill-boards) and ad agencies are available, and still often at surprisingly moderate rates. On the other hand, direct mail and catalogue sales are as yet practically unknown.

Always a challenge, pricing is a particularly vexing element of marketing strategy in China. Here is where the motto of all economic reform policies, "socialist planning with supplementary regulation by the market", will have to withstand its ultimate test. In many crucial sectors (such as housing and transport) prices are still vestiges of the totally planned era, when they were set on the basis of socio-political concerns rather than marketing factors (cost and demand).

However, in what may be the most vital area of all, i.e., foods, pricing is now practically free, given "normal" supply. In some cases, prices are "floating", that is, allowed to fluctuate between set limits. In other cases we find "double track" pricing, where the planned production quota of a food is subject to a fixed price, while above-quota output may be sold at market prices. Freeing up food prices has clearly taken political courage and the achievement here may bode well for the future. Meanwhile, China's politicians and economists agree with foreigners who find the pricing system irrational in several respects.

Middle Class Consumers

If present trends continue, foreign businesses are bound to get closer to the Chinese consumer markets (notably, when the firm has local production). Typically, the emerging middle class would be of primary interest. While data are poor, a rough estimate suggests that it may comprise some 200 million at this time. The proportion of middle-class households in rural areas is probably almost as great as in cities due to agriculture receiving first priority in the modernization effort.

A middle-class family would generally have a T.V., radio, camera, tape recorder and maybe a sewing machine and/or a fan, in addition to a suitable supply of bicycles (Li Xuezeng *et al.* 1986). On the other hand, only a small minority of families has refrigerators, clothes washers and other white goods, and our middle-class household may well share kitchen and/or bathroom facilities with a neighbor. Especially in urban areas housing is chronically scarce and crowded—rents are both controlled and heavily subsidized.

While consumer research is still all but non-existent, Thorelli made a pioneer survey of Chinese middle class-consumer attitudes, and behavior. Contrary to what might be expected, he found a highly "consumer-conscious" group, which enjoyed shopping, engaged in active information search, and was rather interested in fashion and style. They were willing to share their shopping experiences and advice with others, expressing more dissatisfaction than most other developing country consumers with both products and food sales-people (at least in state stores) and, not least, were more able to articulate what they thought the rights of modern consumers should be.

These vibrant consumers were also concerned about the lack of information. This may be due to poorly informed and, at least in the past, disinterested salespeople, and the fact that products generally come without much in the way of labels, manuals or informative brochures. Product quality of many P.R.C. consumer goods still needs a herculean boost.

Marketing Strategy

The burgeoning marketization of the economy introduced with the reforms, the rise of an increasingly sophisticated and discriminating urban consumer class and the results of this study present interesting marketing strategy implications.

- As brand loyalty is high, marketing strategy should aim at building such loyalty.
- As P.R.C. consumers are sensitive to social risk, promotion should emphasize the group rather than the individual (at the same time recognizing that individualism seems to be on the rise).
- Mass advertising is likely to have considerable potential in the P.R.C.
- International brands of demonstrably high quality have the potential of building high prestige in the P.R.C. Conversely, an initial bad image will be hard to overcome.
- Word of mouth is important in the P.R.C., suggesting a focus on opinion leaders.
- Store loyalty is likely to remain high in the P.R.C., even as markets become more open and competitive. Those gaining distributor

loyalty, therefore, are likely to hold a major differential advantage.

● Until now, price competition has been fairly nominal. Traditional emphasis on thrift should now encourage even more comparative shopping than in the past. (This observation is not necessarily inconsistent with store loyalty, see Thorelli 1982).

Considering China's current stage of economic and market development, multinational corporations wanting to include China in their global or East Asian business strategies face the following basic entry strategies: exporting to, investing in, and sourcing from China. Let us examine the implications of China's marketing culture and economic reforms on each of those strategies.

Selling to China

In contemplating their marketing strategies, sellers to China must operate on the following premises. As a planned economy, China, Inc., states its national and economic priorities in a variety of government documents, including her Five Year Plans and yearly National People's Congress economic reports. A careful study of stated priorities in the plans and recent business activities and trends will give potential sellers a fairly accurate reading of the likelihood that their products and services are on China's shopping list.

Dealing with a foreign trade bureaucracy in flux through waves of liberalization and restriction, centralization and decentralization, sellers face the challenge of ensuring that all bureaucratic grounds have been covered lest anyone of the many "mothers-in-law" jeopardizes the successful conclusion of the deal. (Chinese refer to the many organizations supervising an enterprise or a foreign trade corporation as "mothers-in-law" any of whom has a *de facto* veto power in a highly bureaucratic mode of operations.) These agencies may feel that to justify their existence it behoves them to extract additional concessions before approving a contract; a wise negotiator will keep this possibility in mind. In many cases, Chinese organizations involved in the negotiations are not entirely sure who all the "mothers-in-law" are or the extent of their jurisdiction. Foreign firms must be prepared to engage in barter, compensation trade, co-production and other forms of countertrade.

In the case of the supply of technology, at times costly promotion of the sellers' goods and services is required to remedy the incomplete knowledge of their technology, and to re-educate managers and technicians steeped in older ways of doing things. Such promotion may include business and technical seminars, the provision of promotional materials in Chinese, and affording prospective customers the opportunity to see the technology in operation, often outside China. Presence at some of the ubiquitous trade fairs is indispensable for personal contact, competitive intelligence, and market potential analysis. As personal contacts are crucial in the P.R.C., there is a great need for networking with the maximum feasible number of contact points in the relevant Chinese community of enterprises, institutions and authorities.

It is essential that technology suppliers assess carefully the environment where that technology will be used. Notwithstanding signs of a recent change of attitudes, Chinese have traditionally been unwilling to purchase adequate amounts of technical and managerial training and software, usually essential to its efficient use. At times the inefficient use or breakdown of a transferred technology due to its improper use is blamed on its quality or appropriateness.

Post-sale service is one of the weakest aspects of marketing in China. For all intents and purposes, suppliers of manufactured goods offer no warranty system, repair and maintenance service and spare parts. The poor service infrastructure is a reason for building high quality into the product from the outset. Foreign sellers desiring a deep penetration of the China market have been involved in the establishment of post-sales service in strategic locations. Training local personnel to provide an adequate level and quality of service to customers has been quite a challenge, as customer service was an unknown concept during the decades of total planning.

Investing in China

The lure of foreign exchange, technology, access to international markets and modern management has made many Chinese agencies and companies willing to negotiate joint ventures with foreign partners. In the important choice of a Chinese partner relevant considerations include the Chinese partners' access to sources of political and economic power, their business connections with potential domestic suppliers and distributors and indications of administrative support of the project at higher levels. At the end of the eighties there were well over a thousand J.V.s and a few score wholly-owned foreign ventures in the P.R.C. About one-half of the J.V. engagements are in the hands of Hong Kong and overseas Chinese. Japan comes next, and European and U.S. firms are partners in most of the remaining J.V.s.

Rarely will joint or foreign-owned ventures in China be permitted to dispose of all their output in the domestic market. Even if only a portion of the output is to be sold inside China, however, foreign investors are strongly advised to take full part in the formulation of marketing strategies. Their direct involvement in product design, product line strategy, establishment of distribution channels, a pre-

and post-sales service network and a promotion program would help complement their Chinese partners' comparative advantage.

Even without an equity position, a foreign corporation, a licensor for example, would often find it advantageous to work with its licensee to develop and implement a marketing program for the latter. By transferring its marketing knowhow to its licensee, a foreign corporation would help expand the market share of its products and make its licensing agreement more profitable. Of course, it may also foster a potential local (or even international) competitor in the process.

Sourcing from China

NIKE athletic shoes was one of the pioneer firms subcontracting production in China. In sourcing from China the selection of partners from among potential Chinese enterprises is again critical. An indication may be the benefits the potential partner gets as a supplier. Would he share the foreign exchange earned, or improve his prospects of obtaining foreign technology? Or is the price allocated to him by the state at least equal to, preferably higher than, the domestic price?

Product design and specifications and commercial issues follow next. Chinese familiarity with consumer or industrial end-user preference and taste in the West is rather superficial. It is imperative that a foreign buyer provides detailed product design and specifications and materials input if unavailable in China. In too many instances Chinese enterprises have not lived up to specifications and quality standards, or they have taken an unreasonable time to attain them. A prudent buyer would retain the right to engage in quality control in the supplier facility, phasing out only when the supplier meets the demands of international markets. At least, clauses that free buyers from accepting delivery of products not meeting product specifications and quality should be included in the contract.

The Chinese are not always aware of the seasonality of demand for many products in the world market, inventory carrying costs and other manifestations of the fact that "time is money". Differences in time concepts and weak awareness of marketing practices in the West give commercial issues more importance than foreigners may realize. Speedy, two-way communications and prompt responses to inquiries need to be stressed. Delivery schedules must be respected and sanctions imposed upon failure to do so. According to one estimate, some 30% of Chinese deliveries are late.

The Special Economic Zones

Facing an overall scarcity of development resources, the P.R.C. is manifestly prioritizing the coastal areas and the 14 Special Economic

Zones (S.E.Z.). The S.E.Z. generally involve more comprehensive and more variegated arrangements between host and investor companies than the free trade zones in many L.D.C.s (often merely involving tax rebates). This does not always mean that the non-Chinese partner is overwhelmed with the hospitality bestowed; frequently its autonomy in the selection of employees, sources of raw material, etc. is restricted in ways not encountered elsewhere. Typically, export requirements are substantial. The most recent, and largest, S.E.Z. is the island of Hainan ("the Hawaii of the P.R.C."), which was made a separate province in 1988. The planned focus of its development will be hi-tech and exotic agricultural exports as well as tourism.

Problems, Patience and Profit Potential

A basic problem in doing business with China is the analysis of market potential. Data sources are meager and marketing research facilities underdeveloped. Even when the international businessman thinks he has a fair idea of the local market potential there is the equally important question of just how much access to the market he will be permitted.

Other major problems abound. The prospects of direct contact with end-consumers are close to nil. Indeed, occasionally it presents problems to get in direct contact with prospective industrial customers. And when such contact is made be it with potential customers, suppliers or joint venture partners, it is often far from clear that they have the power to make the final decision. Moreover, channels are still rudimentary in many markets.

The Chinese are eager for technology transfer, but do not always appreciate its full value, notably of its "software" aspects. More serious obstacles are presented by the twin problems of foreign currency scarcity and the obsession with exports. The pressure to increase exports results in demands for various forms of countertrade. Even though a joint venture be a major exporter, it will not automatically retain the right to dispose of all foreign currency earned. Hard currency scarcity and a modest but tangible rate of inflation has resulted in a number of devaluations of China's currency in recent years—which remains a possibility, at least in the near term. The concern with exports notwithstanding, Chinese firms are often naive about what their products are worth in world markets, and not always appreciative of their partners' need for quality standards.

While the Open Door is still the official doctrine and an overall trend towards liberalization may be discerned, the fact remains that there have been significant variations in implementation of both domestic and especially international economic policy in recent years.

Unable to meet fully the expectations it has raised with foreign businesses, the P.R.C. has a credibility problem. Despite these problems there can be no doubt that China has significant market potential (and increasing competitiveness in world markets), and that future prospects—given a successive opening of domestic markets—are nothing but vast.

The keys to penetrating that market are personal presence, patience and an incremental approach. Personal presence is necessary to analyze the market, to decide on a suitable entry strategy and, of course, to negotiate the necessary deals. In addition, the Chinese treasure personal contact and trust. The need for adaptability is obvious, especially in extending services of various kinds, including training of both technical and marketing personnel. Whenever feasible, it is advisable to start with smaller, quick-return projects and increase their scope over time. This incremental approach establishes a presence in China and allows the parties time to build the mutual trust necessary for large-scale ventures.

Above all, patience is called for, and a willingness to gamble on the long-term—a characteristic more prevalent among European than American executives, and of course, a prominent strategy among Japanese companies. As the evening lovers stroll along the Bund in Shanghai, they cannot fail to see the huge blue moon on the other embankment—the SANYO neon sign. While waiting for the consumer electronics market to really open up to foreign producers Sanyo is marketing, yes, Coca-Cola vending machines!

References

Li Xuezeng, Yan Shenming, He Juhuang, and Jacques van der Gagg, *The Structure of China's Domestic Consumption*, Staff Working Paper 755, (Washington, D.C.: The World Bank, 1986).

Thorelli, Hans B., "Chinese Middle-Class Consumers Look at Marketing Issues," in *Proceedings of the Academy of International Business*, (1982) pp. 743–756.

Zhongguo Tongji Nianjian—1985 (China Statistics Yearbook—1985), (Beijing: China Statistical Yearbook, 1985), pp. 17, 33 and 466.

31

How Caterpillar China Coped with Key Obstacles in Major Licensing Deal*

BUSINESS INTERNATIONAL

According to James Martin, Caterpillar's manager of product source planning, Caterpillar started selling equipment to China in 1975 and began receiving requests for technology transfers in the late 1970s. In 1980, Caterpillar management developed a China strategy including sales, product support and technology transfer. It began implementation in 1982 with the establishment of Caterpillar China Ltd in Beijing. Martin notes, "We decided in 1980 that we had to take preemptive action to build a long-term position ahead of other competitors."

At that point in time, Caterpillar opted for licensing because it offered more freedom and control—and simultaneously assured hard currency income—than did joint ventures in China. (Caterpillar frequently relies on licensing to gain or maintain access to markets, but usually only when actions by local governments or competitors create barriers to further direct sales.) In its licensing program, Martin explains that the company decided to focus on *high-volume, medium-sized machinery* (such as tractors, wheel-loaders and diesel engines), which China urgently needed for construction projects in agriculture and industrial infrastructure.

China Knocks on the Door

In 1984, Caterpillar signed its first technical license in China for power-shift transmissions with the Ministry of Machine Building

---

* Reprinted from *Business International*, Vol. 34, No. 28 (July 13, 1987), pp. 217–219, with permission.

Industry (MMBI), the China Machine Building International Corp—the MMBI's trading arm—and two factories in Sichuan. In early 1985, the MMBI suggested that Caterpillar bid for a more comprehensive program covering 10 factories to produce components and complete machinery. The competition quickly narrowed down to Caterpillar and long-time Japanese rival, Komatsu Ltd. According to Martin, Caterpillar secured the contract over Komatsu's lower bid owing primarily to factors other than price. Besides product quality and strong track record in technology transfer, Caterpillar's sales campaign dealt directly with two critical bottlenecks in contract negotiation:

- *China's chronic foreign exchange shortage.* Caterpillar offered a countertrade program through the Hong Kong office of Caterpillar World Trade (CWT). CWT will buy manufactured goods from factories under the wing of the State Commission of Machinery Industry (SCMI)—which has superseded the MMBI—and turn the forex from overseas sales over to the factories in order to pay for Caterpillar semi-knock-down kits, components and equipment.
- *Contending bureaucratic interests.* Thanks to hints from MMBI officials, Martin was alerted to the increasing role that factory end-users are playing in contract decisions. "At first, we believed that the definite decision-making point was in Beijing with the SCMI. However, it soon became clear that the factories had a strong vote. Chinese officials we knew urged us to visit and try to win over some units that may have been leaning toward our competitor. Eventually, we were able to gain support from all 12 factories."

How the Agreement is Structured

Effective in April 1987, the package includes five technology transfer contracts, a countertrade pact and a used equipment sales agreement. The licensing pacts were signed with China Machine Building and the China National Technical Import Corp and cover supply to 10 Chinese factories in nine provinces of the designs and production expertise for specific models of Caterpillar track-type tractors, wheel-loaders, skidders, diesel engines and undercarriages. The package (to which has been added the 1984 power transmission deal) is being coordinated by SCMI.

Scope of the transfer. The know-how and countertrade agreements will last for eight years. Although Caterpillar generally prefers longer-term relationships with its licensees, renewal is unlikely as the Chinese prefer to buy, not lease, technology.

Know-how currently used in Caterpillar factories world-wide for these specific models will be featured and updated simultaneously with other Caterpillar plants; any improvements made in China will also be transferred to Caterpillar. The cost for such updating is incorporated into the fees and royalties of the six agreements. The program will include over 100 man-months of training in the U.S. besides on-site assistance from Caterpillar engineers to get the various factories on line.

Structure of compensation. As with most Chinese licensing pacts, direct compensation is divided into an up-front fee and royalties over the contract's eight-year term—all in U.S. dollars. Although Caterpillar officials declined to disclose the amount, it was probably well over the $5 million limit that requires high-level government approval.

Unusual pricing formula. A real concern in structuring the deal was obtaining sufficient and appropriate compensation for its expertise given China's preference for royalties based on net sales or net value-added. The U.S. firm gained a key concession by securing Chinese agreement to use a royalty schedule based on per unit output. Martin tells *BI* that the Chinese side went along with Caterpillar's request partly because this procedure would simplify reporting: Instead of needing to calculate costs and sales prices in China's complex and often irrational pricing system, the royalties would be directly proportional to output figures.

Royalties will thus be calculated based on the product of an average percentage of local content over the contract period, the unit output value, the (undisclosed) royalty percentage and total plant output. The critical figures for unit output value were negotiated between Caterpillar and the Chinese side. Caterpillar based its proposal on in-house sales price and production cost data. Tough bargaining with the Chinese and pressure from Komatsu dropped the actual figures below these benchmarks: "Since many companies are willing to cut prices to get their foot in the door, the Chinese agencies enjoy a strong bargaining position." However, Martin adds that "the compensation was within our parameters. We look to obtain other benefits beyond licensing fees and up-front payment." Each plant will incur obligations for royalties, but payment to Caterpillar will ultimately be channeled through China Machine Building or China National Technical Import.

Technology and market protection. Caterpillar's designs, factory production and management techniques are protected by confidentiality clauses for the term of the contract. While acknowledging that "protection is based mostly on trust," Martin believes that "it would not be easy in any case for the Chinese factories—which are at best 10 years behind most Western manufacturers—to replicate the sophisticated know-how we are providing in the short term."

A more pressing issue was discouraging reexports of Caterpillar-designed equipment, especially since Beijing's technology transfer rules prohibit any clauses "unreasonably" restricting such exports. Martin admits that this issue was extensively discussed, but contends Caterpillar will not be threatened. "It will take some time before Chinese factories attain the quality demanded by overseas markets. Moreover, there is a tremendous need in China for this equipment. We will also ease the forex needs through our CT program." Another important point is that the training program contained in this package is a great deal more extensive than those usually carried out by Caterpillar and will involve far more people than usual on the Caterpillar side.

32

MicroAge Targets Japan's Small Businesses in Franchising Venture*

BUSINESS INTERNATIONAL

The third-largest U.S. computer franchise chain, MicroAge Inc, will soon enter the highly competitive Japanese market through a licensing agreement with a major retailer, Nagoya-based U.N.Y. Co. In contrast with other international computer franchisors (*BI* '85 p. 294), MicroAge Japan (M.A.J.) is taking the "middle road," targeting small and medium-sized Japanese firms and cities. The case also demonstrates the utility of "marriage brokers" in Japan-U.S. linkups; the matchmaker here was the the Stamford-based International Management Technology Corp. (I.M.T.E.C.).

According to MicroAge officials, the firm, which franchises over 160 stores in the U.S. wanted to expand into Europe and Japan "for a long time." To oversee its international effort, the U.S. franchisor set up MicroAge International in June 1985. An agreement in January 1986 with Italy's Olivetti (which has had a 48% equity share in MicroAge Inc since 1982) paved the way to Europe. On February 28, MicroAge signed a licensing agreement with U.N.Y. to open computer stores throughout Japan under M.A.J., which will be 100% owned by U.N.Y.

A Fortuitous Encounter

I.M.T.E.C. President Joseph Lev tells *BI* that the pact came about partly through common business connections. In early 1985, after hearing of I.M.T.E.C.s success in negotiating arrangements between U.S. and Japanese firms, MicroAge International President William Ginalski enlisted Lev's aid. Says MicroAge's Linnea Maxwell: "Part

---

*Reprinted from *Business International*, Vol. 33, No. 16, (April 12, 1986), with permission.

of our strategy of going overseas is to find a local partner with the capability and resources to build up a network." I.M.T.E.C.s Lev went to Japan and brought three suitors back to MicroAge's headquarters near Phoenix.

MicroAge and I.M.T.E.C. officials say U.N.Y.s strong points include its retailing experience and moderate size—$2 billion in revenues against the other candidates (two $50 billion-plus trading companies). "MicroAge wanted a partner that would get personally involved," says Lev. Adds Maxwell, "A strong case for using U.N.Y. was its success in building networks for Circle K Corp." The Phoenix-based convenience store chain will soon open its 300th store in Japan under a licensing pact that I.M.T.E.C. helped negotiate five years ago with U.N.Y.

A possible problem lies in U.N.Y.'s focus on consumer markets: MicroAge's niche, small and medium-sized business, demands different selling skills and expertise. "It means you have to offer full service. Besides providing hardware and software, you must be able to offer maintenance: Business people need their equipment *today*," says Lev. Concerns were eased by the fact that U.N.Y. had developed a value-added reseller for the Japanese-language I.B.M. 5550 business computer system.

Lev adds that "U.N.Y., unlike the trading companies, did not have a strong association with any single computer hardware maker. We did not want our stores in Japan to market only one brand, but to offer solutions based on hardware from multiple manufacturers."

A Two-sided Market Niche

Says Lev: "What we're taking from the U.S. is the expertise on how to sell microcomputers to small businesses utilizing a vertical market concept." In the U.S., MicroAge sells package solutions for computerizing small business operations in defined business lines—e.g., construction firms and accountants—combining hardware and software from multiple manufacturers or vendors.

MicroAge and I.M.T.E.C. officials identify both sectoral and geographic aspects to the potential niche in Japan:

● *Small and medium-sized businesses:* While there are computer stores throughout Japan, computerization among small businesses and professionals in Japan has been slowed by lack of affordable systems. "The niche of the small company that is not yet automated will be our biggest opportunity," says Maxwell. She tells *BI* that U.N.Y.'s "market research revealed more vertical market software than we had thought available; but since it was not marketed well, awareness was not very high."

Lev says M.A.J. stores will sell Japanese hardware and software: "We are not looking to sell I.B.M. P.C.s to U.S. citizens living in Japan."

● *Medium-sized cities:* Outside of Japan's three premier metropolitan centers of Tokyo, Osaka and Nagoya are numerous cities with populations in the 100,000–700,000 range, where small businesses proliferate. "We think there is a tremendous opportunity to offer full service to customers in these second-tier cities," says Lev.

In September, M.A.J. will open its first company-owned store in Nagoya—U.N.Y.'s home turf. Initial sales strategies (based in part on market research commissioned by U.N.Y.) will be revised in light of performance. M.A.J. plans to open six more stores in 1987; despite its intent to focus on second-tier cities, these too will probably be in the Nagoya area. Plans call for about 80 stores to be opened by 1990, with a rising share of franchises.

Acclimatizing U.N.Y.'s management and staff to MicroAge's strategy will require considerable training and support and frequent travel between Phoenix and Nagoya. Says Maxwell: "So far, we've taught two bilingual courses (covering vertical market software, business plans and technical questions) to 12 U.N.Y. representatives conducted by our learning center for new franchisees." MicroAge staffers are being sent to Japan. Recent travelers include the firm's store development specialist to assist in store design and site selection and its vertical software marketing manager to identify market opportunities.

Licensing now—Equity later?

Although MicroAge's initial desire was to form a joint venture, M.A.J. will be 100%-owned by U.N.Y. and will have its own office. Lev called the pact a "knowledge licensing agreement," under which U.N.Y. will have the right to use MicroAge's trademarks, manuals, signs and other materials in exchange for an initial payment and royalties. The pact, according to Lev, is "of long duration with provisions for automatic renewal."

Lev says the licensing route was chosen because it was "simpler to negotiate. It's also easier from a tax standpoint for the company to get financial support from the Japanese parent, for which it's just a business expense."

Once M.A.J. gets on its feet, the door is apparently open for an equity holding. One indication of this was the decision by U.N.Y. President and M.A.J. Chairman Toshio Nishikawa to invite Micro-Age's Ginalski and I.M.T.E.C.'s Lev and Vice President Robert Hacker to join M.A.J.'s nine-member board of directors. Says Lev: "Nishikawa wants us to review M.A.J.'s plans and activities. If we object to something, our input can go directly into M.A.J."

33

How Japan Won a Contract to Build Turkey a Bridge*

LAWRENCE INGRASSIA

Istanbul, Turkey—Today, the 532nd anniversary of the conquest of Constantinople by the Ottoman Empire, Turkey's leaders will gather for a ceremony to mark a modern-day triumph of East over West.

This time, it is a victory of Japan over Britain and America. And the prize is a coveted contract to build a 3,576-foot suspension bridge—the fifth longest in the world—over the sparkling Bosporus Strait. As TV cameras watch, Turkish officials will lay the cornerstone for the half-billion dollar project, which also includes 130 miles of highway.

A Japanese-led consortium won the contract with a bargain-basement bid that startled even the Turks. The Japanese government also proffered subsidized, low interest financing—a crucial element in winning lucrative contracts nowadays. All told, the generous terms will save Turkey tens, and perhaps hundreds, of millions of dollars.

"It would be cheaper [for Japan] to go to the Turks and say, 'We'll give you the bridge,'" complains Crawford Watts, a blunt Scotsman who led the unsuccessful sales effort of Cleveland Bridge & Engineering, whose partners in the bidding included Bechtel Group Inc. of the U.S.

Cutthroat Competitors

Throughout the world, the competition among multinationals for such megaprojects is becoming increasingly cutthroat. The once-flourishing construction industry has fallen upon hard times. Business in the Arab

---

*Reprinted from *Wall Street Journal*, May 29, 1985, with permission.

world is drying up, as oil revenue dwindles, and debt-ridden African and Latin American nations are pinching pennies.

Competitors pulled out all the stops for the Bosporus bridge contract. As a crossroads linking Europe and Asia, it is an engineering showcase that could well lead to other big jobs for the builders. Behind the scenes lobbying featured everything from a visit to Turkey by the Duke of Kent, a cousin of Queen Elizabeth II, to a late-night hotel meeting in Washington between bidders and Turkish Prime Minister Turgut Ozal. Britain ultimately sweetened its own loan subsidy offer in a futile, last-ditch effort to avoid defeat.

The stunning victory of the Japanese–led group has left rivals grumbling about unfair competition from Japan Inc. It shows dramatically, the losers contend, how Japanese companies – with government help—go after conspicuous projects in order to get a foothold in international markets.

British Prime Minister Margaret Thatcher was among those who rebuked Japan: "It is very irritating, very irritating and deeply disappointing and a bitter blow when we keep our markets open to the Japanese, as a result of which they make very good profits, which enables them to give credit larger than we can give on projects."

Changing Times

To which the Japanese hardly deign to reply: "It is absurd to make comment on such rumors one by one," says a spokesman for Ishikawa-jima-Harima Heavy Industries Co., the leader of the winning group.

The outcome shows—painfully for the West—how times have changed. In the early 1970s, I.H.I. narrowly lost the contract to build the first Bosporus bridge, which spans the strait about two miles south of the second bridge site. British-owned Cleveland Bridge won that contract and seemed likely to win again.

Turkey has been planning a second bridge for nearly a decade. The first one, a majestic, 3,524-foot suspension bridge completed in 1973, at first was expected to meet traffic needs until the year 2000. But by 1976, the bridge had paid for itself in tolls, and commuter traffic and trucks hauling goods between Europe and the Mideast were backing up at the entrance.

Today, it can sometimes take 30 minutes to cross. The bridge is so important to commerce, and to troop movements in an emergency, that antiaircraft guns sit on the hills above it to fend off would-be attackers. Turks also take considerable pride in it. Post cards of the bridge—by night and by day, from up close and from afar—sell side by side with views of the Topkapi Palace, the erstwhile home of Ottoman sultans and their harems.

Just in Time

But plans for a second bridge gathered dust for several years. Turkey couldn't afford it. Finally, Turkey placed ads last summer seeking bids. And more than a little politics was involved. Prime Minister Ozal, in his 1983 election campaign, pledged to build a second bridge. Indeed, if the project is completed on schedule, it will be finished just in time for the 1988 election.

Turkey devised a clever strategy for awarding the contract. Many multinationals wanted to build the bridge, but few wanted to do the mundane highway work. So, officials decreed, preference would be given to groups bidding for both. Bidders also had to arrange financing—because Turkey, with $19.9 billion in foreign debt, probably couldn't do that on its own. "The bridge has great advertising value. You shouldn't blame us for taking advantage of that," says Atalay Coskunoglu, who directs Turkey's highways department.

From the start, there were two favorites: Cleveland Bridge, a subsidiary of Trafalgar House P.L.C., a diversified construction company that also owns ocean liners, including the Queen Elizabeth II; and I.H.I., an engineering concern that builds everything from power plants and oil refineries to bridges. In the end, there were six competing groups of more than 30 companies—including subsidiaries of Koppers Co. and I.T.T. Corp. as well as Japanese rivals of I.H.I.

Cleveland Bridge had an early edge. For its Turkish partner, it signed up the company everyone wanted—Enka Construction & Industry, the nation's largest contractor. Enka's political connections are legend. Not only is it believed to be a major contributor to Mr. Ozal's Motherland Party, but also several top government officials—including the Justice Minister—had been Enka executives. Other Enka managers have relatives in the Ozal government. "A local partner," Mr. Watts notes, "can handle the local difficulties."

The Japanese were disconsolate. "We thought we didn't stand a chance against Enka," recalls Kenji Kato, the manager of the Ankara office of Mitsubishi Corp. (which, with Nippon Kokan, K.K., is a member of the I.H.I. bidding group). Rather glumly, the I.H.I. group settled with its second choice, Sezai Turkes-Feyzi Akkaya. In fact, as it would turn out, this was a stroke of luck.

Cleveland Bridge also tried to outflank its rivals and end the competition before it started. Last October, it quietly made a preemptive offer for the bridge contract before it went to open bidding. Helping out was the Duke of Kent, vice chairman of the British Overseas Trade Board, who led a trade delegation to Turkey. The presence of the tall, debonair duke, a first cousin of the Queen, opens doors around the world.

John Fletcher, a Trafalgar House director, was among executives from various companies who went along. First in London and later on the flight to Istanbul, Mr. Fletcher briefed the duke about the bridge. The delegation initially met for an hour with the portly Mr. Ozal. Sitting around an oblong table, the group heard a speech by the prime minister on Turkey's economy. Afterward, when the duke had left, Mr. Fletcher met privately with Mr. Ozal for 20 minutes to discuss the bridge proposal.

For the hard sell, however, Mr. Fletcher saw Safa Giray, the public works minister. Don't waste time, Mr. Fletcher said, in effect. Give the contract to us. No thanks, the minister replied. We would rather see what others offer first.

Balky Bureaucrats

Meanwhile, Cleveland Bridge was pulling political strings back home. The obstacle it had to face was Britain's Export Credits Guarantee Department—which guarantees loans and sometimes subsidizes interest rates. Such financing is vital because commercial banks currently are reluctant to extend new loans to debtor countries like Turkey.

But the bureaucrats balked. The agency had nearly reached its ceiling on loans to Turkey and couldn't promise more.

Mr. Watts complained to Michael Fallon, a Conservative member of Parliament whose district includes the company's plant in England. He, in turn, enlisted the support of Richard Hickmet, another Tory M.P., whose district might make steel for the bridge. Together, they appealed for an urgent, private meeting with Mrs. Thatcher.

Over tea in her office at the House of Commons, the two M.P.s pleaded Cleveland Bridge's case for 45 minutes. Mr. Fallon—noting the 15% unemployment rate in his area—showed her photos of the first Bosporus bridge and of the Cleveland Bridge factory. The prime minister pledged her support. Shortly thereafter, she presided over a subcabinet meeting. Financing, Mrs. Thatcher decided, would be available. Letters bearing the good news were dispatched to Messrs. Fallon and Hickmet.

Still, Britain's $50 million loan package wouldn't be enough. So Cleveland Bridge went looking for partners who might get financing from *their* governments. Bechtel Group, the giant U.S. engineering company, and a West German contractor signed on.

I.H.I. was forging ahead, too. Unlike the British, the Japanese government didn't hesitate about a loan package. Last fall, Tokyo privately signaled that it would provide a low-interest yen loan equivalent to as much as $200 million.

Generally, Japan limits such financing to no more than $150 million. But the Bosporus Bridge was special. "The Japanese government likes big projects, display projects...not irrigation projects," Mr. Kato notes. Adnan Kahveci, an aide to Mr. Ozal, adds, "We knew they would bring a big cannon."

Italian Backing

But even Tokyo wasn't going to put up half a billion dollars. So the I.H.I. group brought in Impregilo S.p.A., an Italian construction company whose government also would oblige with subsidized loans in return for the business.

Though not given much of a chance against the front-runners, other groups were maneuvering, too. One long shot, led by the Nello L. Teer Co. subsidiary of Koppers Co. of Pittsburgh, even got a private meeting with Mr. Ozal in Washington in early April. Again, local connections paid off. The 11 p.m. hotel suite meeting was set up by Entes, a Turkish company in Nello Teer's bidding group. Wayne Greenlee, a Nello Teer executive, spoke to Mr. Ozal for half an hour.

But, to the dismay of Mr. Greenlee, his superiors at Nello Teer decided at the last minute not to bid because they felt financing was uncertain.

The moment of truth—the opening of bids—came April 17 in Ankara, where some 50 executives gathered in a highways department auditorium. The first bids were high: a group that included other British and Japanese companies as partners bid $929 million; a West German-led group offered to do the job for $1.1 billion. Then, officials opened the I.H.I. group's bid: $551 million.

A Big Letdown

Mr. Watts, of the Cleveland Bridge group, says his heart sank. "It was dreadful," he recalls. He knew that the Cleveland Bridge consortium's bid, opened last, would be $676 million.

Turkish officials were elated about Japan's low bid. "The amount was very surprising," says Yalcin Burcak, a Treasury official. Most officials had estimated a price of around $650 million, and no one seriously expected a bid below $600 million.

As if its huge price advantage weren't enough, the I.H.I. group's finance package clinched the deal. Its main feature: $205 million in Japanese government loans, at an interest rate of 5%, repayable over a 25 year period, with no payments for the first seven years. It also included Italian credits of at least $130 million at $2\frac{1}{2}\%$ to $7\frac{3}{4}\%$; and $231 million in commercial credits at higher rates.

Compare that with the Cleveland Bridge offer of $50 million in British government credits, including $37 million at 11.2% and repayable over 8½ years, plus a $13 million foreign-aid grant that wouldn't have to be repaid; some $250 million in loans from the U.S. Export-Import Bank, also at about 11%, and some $60 million from Brazil and $100 million from Yugoslavia at around 8% for any goods bought in those countries; plus commercial credits.

Too Little, Too Late

Cleveland Bridge nevertheless made a final pitch. With British government approval, it increased the foreign-aid part of its $50 million package to $18.6 million, and extended the repayment to 10 years; this reduced the effective interest rate to between 5% and 6%. The group also knocked $75 million off its price, lowering it to $601 million.

But it was too little, too late.

Ironically, the competing bids on the bridge alone were similar, at $110 million to $115 million. The I.H.I. group's overall price was lower largely because of low bids for the road work by I.H.I.'s partners, Sezai Turkes and Impregilo. The losers scoff at the bid price. "It's an unbelievable price, a crazy price. It's a question mark if they can get a profit," says Kafuzumi Noda, the Ankara agent of Nissho-Iwai Corp., a Japanese partner in a group that lost out to I.H.I.

Nonsense, the winners respond; they expect to make money. Of course, it is possible that the final price could end up higher. While the $551 million figure is guaranteed, design changes could increase costs—as they can in any such deal.

Hard Feelings

The Japanese loan has caused hard feelings in Britain. The British concede that it doesn't violate trade agreements that limit loan subsidies, because Tokyo calls its credit *foreign aid*, not a subsidy. But that is a technicality, the British argue. "If you want to buy a contract, and are willing to use enough aid, you can get it," says Richard Wilkinson, the first secretary of the commercial/economic section at the British embassy in Ankara. Despite such harsh words, Mrs. Thatcher and Cleveland Bridge have gone hat in hand to the Japanese, asking that Cleveland Bridge be allowed to do part of the work on the bridge as a subcontractor. A decision on the request is pending.

The Japanese insist they have nothing to apologize for. Japan made the loan to improve ties with Turkey. "In view of political and economic relations between Japan and Turkey, financial support for that extent is necessary," says an official at the Ministry of International Trade and Industry in Tokyo.

I.H.I.'s partner, Sezal Turkes, doesn't bother with such diplomatic niceties. Ayhan Sayrac, its marketing manager, says: "There's no such thing as fair or unfair."

34

Strategic Alliances — Guidelines for Success*

GODFREY DEVLIN
MARK BLEACKLEY

What is a Strategic Alliance?

Cooperative agreements have been common practice in the business community for a long time. Technology swaps; R & D exchanges; distribution, marketing and manufacturer–supplier relationships; and cross licences, to mention a few, are widely practised in most sectors of the economy.

Fundamentally many of these relationships are essentially casual in nature and are unlikely to dramatically change a company's competitive position. More recently a growing number do not conform to this pattern. These strategic alliances are specifically concerned with securing, maintaining or enhancing a company's competitive advantage. Unlike their predecessors they are a central aspect of a company's future direction and are a key strategic option.

Without a doubt they have enabled Glaxo to become one of the world's most successful companies and a leader in the pharmaceutical industry. The success of ranitidine, an H_2 blocker used in the treatment of ulcers, marketed internationally under the brand name Zantac, is largely responsible for this. Launched in Europe in 1981, the product's sales accounted for £829m in 1987, representing 48% of the Group's sales. This was achieved mainly through a network of alliances, the most successful being the co-marketing arrangement with Roche in the United States.

It is possible to distinguish this new breed of alliance from the old style of cooperative agreement. *Strategic alliances take place in the*

* Reprinted from *Long Range Planning*, Vol. 21, No. 5 (October 1988), pp. 18–23, with permission.

context of a company's long-term strategic plan and seek to improve or dramatically change a company's competitive position.

The concept of forming alliances, strategic or otherwise, is not new. Toshiba started doing this in 1906. The topic is in vogue and the number and scale of agreements being signed is growing rapidly. If you try to draw a map, you can easily see what a spider's web it has become. Figure 34.1 provides an illustrative network of alliances in the telecommunications industry.

Deals of every conceivable sort are being made. They do not appear to be specific to any particular country, industry or type of organization. They are occurring at all levels in corporations.

Some authors have attempted to put the subject into some form of strategic context (James 1985 and Perlmutter and Heenan 1986). For future success, senior management must ensure that this business route is viewed in a true strategic perspective rather than as an opportunistic "quick fix." Failure to do so may result in putting their organizations' growth, or even survival, at risk. Renault–AMC is a case in point. Prior to dissolving its arrangement with AMC, Renault invested $645m in AMC which nevertheless managed to incur losses of $750m over the period of the agreement. Such investment severely weakened Renault at a time when it was also facing problems in domestic markets.

The Driving Factors

Probably the greatest stimulus to alliance formation has been the emergence of global competitors and those corporations wishing to become global. This is particularly relevant in growth industries like telecommunications where corporations are making alliances in part to overcome *the national protection afforded to indigenous suppliers* or to share resources to further develop markets and products. Ericsson's strategic alliance with Telefonica (Spain) reaffirms this trend. The deal between Compagnie Générale d'Electricité (CGE), the French electrical group, and ITT produced a new manufacturing alliance capable of serving global markets and challenging its existing global competitors.

The rapid pace of technological development and innovation and the increasingly high costs of the associated research and development are also factors. Shorter product life cycles add momentum to the need to develop new and innovative products and exploit them widely. The Philips–Sony alliance for the joint product development of audio visual compact discs, the Olivetti–Canon arrangement to develop copiers and image processors, and the recent announcement by American Telephone and Telegraph that it was taking a 20% stake in

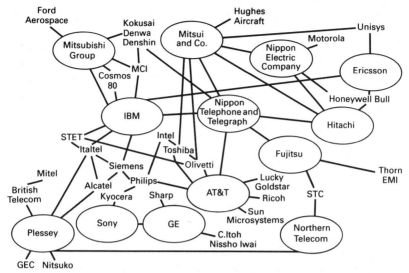

Source: SRI International

FIG. 34.1. Alliances in the telecommunications industry.

Sun Microsystems are characteristic. These trends are not endemic to the electronics industries. The American Cyanamid–Celltech collaborative arrangement centered on the latter's leading edge biotechnology development capability for "engineering" agents to attack cancer cells and the former's distribution and marketing capability.

The concentration of players in mature industries has encouraged those firms with access to capital to challenge traditional monopolies. Redland, the brick and roofing tile manufacturer, recently announced it had formed a strategic alliance with the Australian CRS building materials group in an attempt to challenge BPB Industries' monopoly of the U.K. plasterboard market. The company intends to take approximately 30% of the £250m market.

Governments have also been responsible for encouraging collaboration between companies on a wide scale. The most notable of these are the highly successful Euromissile and Airbus program and the much publicized European Strategic Program in Information Technologies (ESPRIT). This EEC sponsored program, whereby the EEC funds half the development costs, attempts to close the widening gap in information technology between Europe and the United States and Japan.

The objectives of the ESPRIT program are quite specific and highlight its strategic importance to Europe. These are to:

● provide European IT industry with the basic technologies it needs to meet the competitive requirements of the 1990s,

- promote European industrial cooperation in IT, and
- contribute to the development of internationally accepted standards. (Commission of the European Communities 1986)

The first phase of the work involved no fewer than 450 participating organizations at a total cost of £1bn. ESPRIT II will involve 28,000 person-years of work at a cost of approximately £2bn. A recent British Government White Paper (Department of Trade and Industry CM278) outlined by Lord Young, Trade and Industry Secretary, for instance, encourages collaborative research and the transfer of technology. The British Government wishes to foster longer-term research between companies and also between higher education institutions and companies.

The fashion and fear motives cannot be excluded as driving factors. As companies see more of their competitors being active in this regard, it is hardly surprising that they follow suit. Reputedly one of the motives given by Mitsubishi Motors (Japan) for its alliance with Hyundai Motors (S. Korea) covering the manufacture and distribution of a line of low price cars, was the *pre-emption of any potential alliance* between Hyundai and one of Mitsubishi's Japanese competitors.

Guidelines for Success

Senior management must be involved in all stages of the strategic alliance process but they should give particular attention to the following which will improve the chances of success:

- The decision to form a strategic alliance
- The choice of alliance partner
- The planned management of the alliance.

Decision to Form a Strategic Alliance

Alliances are just one of a range of business development routes which a firm may follow to improve or change its competitive position. It is essential that before choosing the alliance, it has been analyzed in the light of the company's overall corporate objectives and other strategic alternatives. The potential risks and benefits have to be identified and deemed acceptable. After careful consideration of the options available, Ford chose the strategic alliance route for its operations in Latin America. Mr Philip Benton Jr, Executive Vice-President in charge of Ford's non-North American operations has stated "when we decided we would stick around, we looked for the best way to stick around" (Gooding 1987). This resulted in the formation last year of Autolatina, a merger of Ford and Volkswagen's operations in Argentina and Brazil.

Senior management should therefore ask themselves the questions:

- Does an alliance improve our chances of success?
- Should it be part of our strategy?
- Or, is it only a stop-gap?

By its very nature, a "strategic" alliance, irrespective of type, warrants the attention of senior management within a company and, as such, the responsibility for it should not be delegated.

Choice of Alliance Partner

It cannot be over-stressed that, having identified the alliance route as being the best strategic business development route or *one* of the routes to follow, an in-depth search for the *right* partner must be undertaken. All too often senior executives have been heard to remark, in hindsight, that they were of the opinion that they should have been more rigorous in the search for, and the evaluation of, their prospective partners . . . divorces can be costly! There must be commitment to the strategic alliance from both sides. Carlo De Benedetti, Chairman of Olivetti has said "Is it easier to live with a girlfriend or a wife? It's much easier to live with a girlfriend. But normally in that relationship you don't have children; you don't create anything for the future. It's the same between companies engaged in joint ventures. It's much easier to have a simple arrangement by which you go to bed sometimes—say, twice a week or twice a month—with an ally, let us say in a supplier relationship. But, I believe an effective alliance must join the life of the two companies. That's the only way to create something for the future" (Kirkland 1987).

In choosing a company with which to form a strategic alliance, senior executives must be aware that what may seem to be a short-term operational benefit arising out of the alliance may, in fact, lead to the eventual loss of the company's strategic position, either to its alliance partner or to one of the company's competitors.

It is imperative that when choosing amongst potential partners the feasibility of the alliance must also be looked at from the perspective of the alliance partner. Senior management should ask themselves the following questions:

- What will the partner's strategic position be as a result of the alliance, both now and in the next few years?
- Why should the partner wish to enter into such an alliance?
- What weaknesses of the partner are likely to be strengthened by the alliance?

Similar questions relating to the management's own company should already have been asked at the earlier stage of deciding on a strategic alliance as the most suitable option to meet the company's objectives.

Management of the Alliance

Alliances do not manage themselves. They need to be managed just like any other business activity, or perhaps even more so. The management of the alliance needs to be planned. Unfortunately this may not be easy since it will normally bring two organizations together with different cultures, management styles and policies. Management incompatibility was one of the reasons given for the failure of the Dunlop–Pirelli alliance. An effective organization structure with supporting systems will greatly assist the task of management.

In order to increase the likelihood of gaining a competitive edge from the strategic alliance, senior management must ensure the following:

- *Maintaining a high profile*—The strategic alliance should be accorded high priority within the minds of the senior management. It is a weapon with which to gain a competitive edge and, as such, management should remain aware of its potential.

- *Monitoring the alliance*—Regular reporting on the performance and progress of the alliance against the objectives set for it by the company should be made available to senior management . . . like marriage, you have to work at it. In some cases, it is not possible at the outset to foresee the direction an alliance will ultimately take. It may be necessary to revise or amend the terms of the alliance agreement or even discontinue the alliance. In the recent merger of Uniroyal and BF Goodrich to form Uniroyal–Goodrich, the combined company did not perform according to BF Goodrich's expectations and so Goodrich sold out their share.

  The duration and termination of an alliance should be made part of negotiations with potential partners. They may be linked to the achievement or otherwise of the objectives set for the alliance. An orderly withdrawal from the alliance does, however, need to be managed. Unfortunately it is only at this stage that a company may realize it cannot afford to get out of the alliance and operate independently. In effect the company has become "alliance dependent," a situation which a more thorough monitoring could have avoided.

- *Accountability and responsibility*—The major barriers to effective decision-making within many organizations, and alliances are no exception, arise from problems associated with accountability and responsibility. It is essential that senior management establish an organization structure which has clear lines of accountability and responsibility. The role of the individual within the alliance must be defined and linked to a realistic set of objectives. Equally, the overall limits of power of the alliance need to be formalized.

- *Improve the "Information Retrieval" process*—The company's employees within the alliance are its "eyes and ears," their roles being to some extent to "learn" from the partner (particularly when the partner is also a competitor). Information channels should be established so that what is learnt is fed effectively into the relevant decision-making center of the parent company.

- *Bring sufficient resources to the alliance*—The company and its partner should contribute equally to the alliance (within the confines of the alliance agreement). In a recent alliance between a U.K. and a Japanese company, for every 20 Japanese employees sent to the United Kingdom for training, the U.K. company sent one employee to Japan. It is obvious that the potential for learning from the partner is dependent to a large extent on the size and quality of the resources devoted to the alliance.

- *"Fast Track" employees and positive personnel policy*—Only high quality staff should be recruited for the alliance. Depending on the type of alliance, such employees may need to operate in a mixed-nationality environment and have the necessary language skills. Being chosen to work for the alliance should be seen as enhancing a person's career prospects within the company, and not as a side-ways move. It will increase the motivation of the individual towards the alliance and should improve the likelihood of its success. To ease the eventual transfer back from the alliance, employees should be regularly informed of developments within the parent company.

- *Positive attitude*—The only attitude which can be adopted by senior management is one of "to win." Anything else should be considered unacceptable. This frame of mind needs to be instilled at all levels within the alliance.

- *Recognize the limits*—Alliances are not mergers. Nor are they joint ventures encapsulated as a free-standing entity. Therefore, the commitment to make them work at least needs a protocol and a top-level review structure. To keep them "live" they need clearly defined projects with finite goals and properly pooled resources. If you can't do this, messy attributions of blame soon replace goodwill and high expectations.

Success in the 1990s

The decision to enter into an alliance and the subsequent management of that alliance requires as much attention as, for example, acquiring another company or divesting a business unit . . . it is not something that can be entered into half-heartedly.

The prospects for a successful alliance can be improved by formalizing the various steps involved in choosing an alliance partner, negotiating the partnership agreement, and managing the alliance.

As the 1990s approach, the rate at which businesses form alliances or partnerships is expected to rise dramatically as firms strive to secure a competitive edge or "sandbag" a defensive shortcoming. If future collaborative ventures are to be successful, unlike many of their predecessors, senior management must ensure they are made in a strategic context and considered with other business development paths as a means to achieving particular corporate objectives. To improve the company's success rate, senior management must involve itself in all stages of the process. Neglect will ultimately weaken their company's competitive position and the bottom line.

References

Commission of the European Communities, *Directoriate General XIII: Telecommunication, Information Industries and Innovation*, 3rd Esprit Conference 1986, Brussels, September 29–October 1, 1986.

Department of Trade and Industry, *DTI—The Department of Enterprise*, CM278, (Her Majesty's Stationery Office, London).

Gooding, Kenneth, "Ford Profits from Forging Links with Competitors," *Financial Times*, September 22, 1987.

James, Barrie G., "Alliance: The New Strategic Focus," *Long Range Planning*, Vol. 18, No. 3 (June 1985), pp. 76–81.

Kirkland, Jr, Richard I., "Seven Wary Views from the Top," *Fortune*, February 2, 1987, pp. 51–52.

Perlmutter, Howard V. and David A. Heenan, "Co-operate to Compete Globally," *Harvard Business Review*, (March–April 1986).

35

International Barter and Counter-trade

SANDRA HUSZAGH
FREDRICK HUSZAGH

Managers can expect barter or countertrade demands if any one of three conditions exists: (1) the priority attached to the Western import is low; (2) the total value of the transaction is high; or (3) the trading country requires reciprocal purchases either to generate hard currencies needed for Western purchases or to service the foreign debt.

This reading (1) analyzes the marketing implications of barter and countertrade; (2) describes the basic forms of barter and countertrade, the typical products exchanged, markets served, and marketing objectives supported in each form; and (3) comments on the durability of these approaches through the 1990s.

Marketing Implications of Barter/Countertrade Mechanisms

Within academic publications and the trade press, considerable confusion exists about how the categories of barter and countertrade differ and which forms represent each category. At least four features distinguish barter from countertrade.

First, barter transactions are exchanges of goods or services without money, while countertrade includes partial or full compensation in money. Thus countertrade is still sensitive to currency swings in proportion to the monetary commitment. For example, in a countertrade transaction the Western supplier agrees to make reciprocal purchases from the foreign buyer which the supplier pays for in cash or credit.

Second, one contract formalizes a barter transaction while two or more contracts are generally required to consummate countertrade

439

transactions. Of the two contracts in countertrade deals, the first represents the initial sales agreement between the supplier and the foreign customer. The second contract details the supplier's commitment to purchase goods from either the foreign customer or a designated industry. Thus, the negotiation process leading up to the resulting contracts will demand greater outlays of time and talent by management. Third, compared to barter, countertrade requires a longer time for the completion of transactions and hence more risk to the firm. Barter's time frame of generally one year or less contrasts with the longer time span for countertrade. In some countertrade transactions, arrangements may extend over several years, with contract provisions allowing adjustment in the ratio of goods exchanged as market prices change.

Finally, compared to barter, countertrade requires a greater commitment and risk of the firm's resources. For example, some forms of countertrade require Western firms to provide licensing rights to technology and even capital investment in joint venture manufacturing. Thus barriers to successful countertrade activities are evident for small firms with low export volume and minimal experience in countertrade (Lecraw 1989).

The discussion of each transaction begins with the definition, followed by a review of each transaction in terms of the typical products exchanged, the foreign markets generally served, and the marketing objectives supported. Outside the scope of this treatment are other functional areas such as law, finance and accounting (Alexandrides and Bowers 1987; Korth 1987), and the detailed mechanics of these transactions.

Classic Barter

Also called straight, simple or pure barter, this transaction form is the simplest and oldest form of bilateral, nonmonetized trade. The two parties directly exchange goods or services; both parties function as buyers and sellers. Normally one contract formalizes the transaction, which typically spans less than one year. While no money changes hands, the parties construct an approximate shadow price for products flowing in each direction. When Western suppliers do not use the goods received, they may assign marketing responsibilities to third parties such as trading companies or other trading specialists. This delegation of marketing responsibilities occurs when managers are unaccustomed to dealing with goods received either in terms of their product characteristics, customer segment or distribution channels.

Classic barter offers outlets for the widest, most diversified array of export product lines compared to all other transaction forms. Products exported by Western suppliers include capital goods, commodities, and consumer goods and services. Typical imports range from manufactured goods to commodities.

Also leading all forms in the extent of market diversification, classic barter meets the needs of markets at all stages of economic development. Classic barter offers special utilities to Western firms in trading with commodity-based economies where currency volatilities are extreme.

Marketing objectives supported by classic barter center around developing new markets and further penetrating existing markets. These objectives typically require less corporate resources and are implemented in a shorter time frame compared to corporate objectives like product development, integrative growth and diversified growth.

Considering classic barter's support for product and market diversification and shorter-term corporate objectives, frequency of use and growth in volume might be expected through the 1990s. However, the problems of matching both parties' input needs with product outputs in an acceptable time period for deliveries may limit classic barter's future use.

To some extent the shortcomings of classic barter can be alleviated by closed-end barter, which involves finding a third party buyer for imported goods before the barter contract is signed. This reduces the risks associated with marketing unfamiliar products received and with the timing of deliveries, since such risks are assumed by the third party. Further, the marketing objective of diversified growth can be pursued efficiently if the Western barter partners establish trading company subsidiaries which manage marketing to third party buyers (Huszagh and Barksdale 1986).

Clearing Account Barter

In clearing account barter—also known as clearing agreements, bilateral clearing accounts, or simply bilateral clearing—the goal of trading parties is to exchange goods of equal value so that neither party has to acquire hard currency. Mainly practiced between Third World markets, and occasionally between such markets and Eastern European countries, bilateral agreements are set up between the trading entities' national governments.

The main intent of these agreements is to overcome foreign exchange controls and foreign currency shortages. Traded goods are valued in clearing account units rather than units of currency. These units effectively represent lines of credit in the central banks which are managed by the governments of trading countries. A balance sheet is maintained on goods exchanged, exporters are paid in domestic currencies, and importers credit the exporters' accounts in clearing units which can only be used to purchase goods in the importing country (Verzarui 1985). Each party commits in a single contract to purchase a specified, usually equal value of goods, typically over a one year period, although occasionally they extend over longer periods.

At the close of the contracted time period, one of several methods is used to handle trade imbalances: (1) settlement in a designated currency, (2) crediting imbalances against the next year, (3) paying a previously specified penalty, or (4) switching the rights to the trade surplus to trading specialists. These trading specialists "buy" surplus clearing units at a discount. However, to achieve hard currency sales, the trading specialists may have to reduce prices in the final transaction.

Products exchanged in clearing account barter typically include capital goods and basic commodities produced by industrializing or centrally planned economies. Since consumer goods and services are seldom offered, less opportunities for product diversification are presented than in classic barter. The unwieldy nature of the exchange process, the products offered and markets typically served suggest that Western firms will only reluctantly use this type of transaction over the next decade.

Counterpurchase

This form of countertrade, also called parallel trading or incorrectly labeled parallel barter, differs from other forms on several key features. First, each delivery is paid either partially or totally in cash or in bank credit. Second, products received are unrelated to the Western supplier's product lines, and typically cannot be used directly by that supplier. Therefore, products do not fit existing marketing expertise or distribution channels, and may involve considerable risks and costs in developing and executing unfamiliar marketing strategies (Bates 1986). Third, the Western firm is committed to accomplish or assist in accomplishing sales of products received to third parties. Western suppliers may receive imports either from the foreign customer or from an alternative source designed by the customer or his government. In centrally planned economies both the "customer" and the alternative source are state controlled.

Figure 35.1 illustrates counterpurchase arrangements. The Western supplier performs a "trade broker" role in-house or, given the demands of marketing unrelated goods, externalizes that role to trade specialists. In counterpurchase transactions, at least two contracts are signed, one in which the Western supplier's sale of products is formalized, the other in which that supplier agrees to purchase and

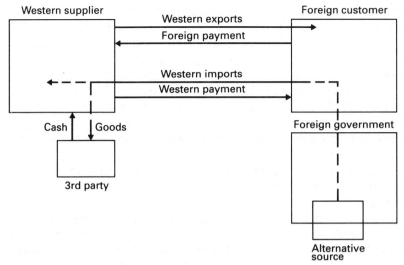

Note: Broken line represents optional transaction flows.

FIG 35.1. Counterpurchase.

market products from the foreign customer. The dollar amount that the Western firm agrees to purchase can be as much as the full value of the products originally sold. The period for taking back products from the foreign customer ranges from one to five years. When the Western supplier or a trade specialist designated by the supplier sells these goods, the trading cycle is complete.

The major advantage of these arrangements flows to the foreign customer since the net result is a committed market for their products. The foreign party gains a direct marketing effort, a worthy accomplishment considering the marketing expertise resident in successful Western firms.

Counterpurchase shares with classic barter opportunities for serving all types of markets with a wide range of products—capital goods, basic commodities, and consumer goods. The two transaction forms also offer options for commodity producers to unload discretely export surpluses without price disclosures (Cohen and Zysman 1986). Like classic barter, counterpurchase supports company objectives in both market development and market penetration.

However, when using counterpurchase arrangements several inherent problems must be resolved. The first problem is the synchronization of numerous transactions, since of all forms counterpurchase can represent the most extensive number of parties: (1) Western seller, (2) foreign buyer, (3) sources for Western imports in the foreign buyer's market, (4) third party customers for imports arranged by the Western seller, (5) trading specialists, and (6) banks.

Second, multiple transactions may be particularly aggravating given the issue of currency volatility in the foreign buyer's economy. Since trade imbalances, hard currency shortages, and extensive foreign debts often underlie governments' requirements for counterpurchase agreements, the probability of currency devaluations are high. Such devaluations will degrade the underlying goals of counterpurchase requirements, e.g., to replace hard currency used by the foreign party to acquire Western products.

Finally, for Western firms, successful counterpurchase arrangements require considerable trading experience not only in cushioning exchange rate risk, but also in protecting against nonperformance by parties involved, fluctuations in commodity values or other uncontrollable market conditions.

Compensation Trading

Also called buy-back, compensation trading differs from all other forms since it requires involvement in a foreign country's productive capacity. In place of direct investment, the Western firm exports process technology, managerial talent, capital, plant equipment or a complete turnkey facility.

Two separate, and parallel contracts generally are involved. In the first contract, the supplier agrees to build a plant or provide plant equipment which is typically accompanied by technology transfer. Upon delivery the foreign party usually makes a hard currency down payment for a portion of the contract's value. In the second contract, the supplier commits to take back as "payment" products resulting from the production facility for up to as many as 20 years. This essentially means that the balance due the supplier is paid for by future delivery of resulting products. These products are most often used directly by the Western firm.

The advantages to the host country are access to Western technology, equipment, and/or capital. The partial down payment also diminishes the drain on foreign currency reserves. When Western investment is part of the package, less capital is required from the foreign party while the production facility is developed.

For the Western firm, compensation trading offers the means to circumvent state ownership requirements in otherwise closed markets and regions, such as the U.S.S.R. and Eastern Europe. Compared to other forms, the firm achieves a better fit between its marketing expertise and imported products. Long-term arrangements can establish lower cost sources of finished goods or parts, providing essentially the same results without ownership of the means of production. However, firms must be cautious that the amount agreed upon does not exceed future demand or costs as alternative sources develop.

The major disadvantages to the Western supplier are those risks associated with conventional, long-term investments. These include political risk and the potential for creating eventual competitors which will cannibalize established markets. The challenge to Western supplier's competitiveness can be considerable when host country exports benefit from trade preferences, such as Most-Favored-Nation (M.F.N) or Generalized System of Preferences (G.S.P.), in the supplier's home market. A further consideration is the risk of disputes over product quality. This risk can be effectively managed if the Western supplier and the foreign partner agree to a system for monitoring output quality.

Company objectives supported by compensation trading are more extensive compared to other countertrade forms. In addition to developing new markets and further penetrating existing markets, integrative growth also results as Western firms guarantee long-term supplies for their own production facilities. The success of these arrangements rests on reduced cash outlays on the foreign party's side, and, on the Western firm's side, balancing supply against demand, maintaining cost efficiencies, and assuring product quality. If Western suppliers can implement these arrangements in industrializing markets, these factors for success may be more easily accomplished.

Offset

Another form of countertrade, offset is similar to compensation trading in that reciprocal purchases are for the Western supplier's direct use. As many as three contracts are negotiated to formalize (1) the Western firm's export sales, (2) the Western firm's import purchases from the foreign party, and (3) subcontracting by the foreign party when compensation trading is tied to the offset arrangement. Given the Western firm's direct consumption of imports, there is no trading specialist involved.

Typically, foreign buyers' offset requests range from 20–50% of the value of the supplier's products. In a highly competitive "buyers' market", demands for offset may climb to over 100%. In addition, the Western supplier may also have to commit to compensation trading which involves local manufacturing of parts incorporated into the finished products received by the foreign customer.

During the 1990s Western firms will continue to experience offset demands due to the benefits of (1) decreasing hard currency outlays by governments; (2) offering a financing alternative when interest rates and terms are exorbitant due to a lack of foreign customers' credit-worthiness; and (3) providing access to technology and generating local employment, when combined with compensation trading.

From the Western supplier's perspective, offset arrangements support company objectives in market penetration and market development. When joined with compensation trading, offsets also present opportunities for integrative growth. Western arms, aircraft and aerospace manufacturers have been active in utilizing offsets, particularly in military sales to developing and market-oriented developed countries as well (Cohen and Zysman 1986). A growing number of nations now require the use of offsets as preconditions for the sales of arms. The risks and costs of currency volatility are diminished by the proportion of the trade in products, an attractive factor for large sales.

Two major risks demand special attention by management. The first relates to the problem of non-performance by the foreign party, which requires rigorous qualification of potential foreign partners in advance. The second risk is whether by offset arrangements with rapidly industrializing nations Western firms may inadvertently create future competitors.

Cooperation Agreements

The major distinction between cooperation agreements and other forms of countertrade is that two Western parties are involved, with one Western firm specialized for the selling function and a second Western firm handling the buying function. Typically, a U.S. firm may deliver manufactured ("capital") goods to an Eastern European entity. In payment for these goods, the latter entity delivers raw materials to a Western European firm which in turn pays the U.S. firm. The value of the raw materials is equivalent to the value of manufactured goods originally sent to the Eastern European entity. Thus, the U.S. firm is removed from the obligation to buy unwanted goods, particularly those goods unsuited to the firm's marketing know-how. The Western European firm realizes a considerable reduction in transport costs from intracontinental trade. Advantages also relate to the lower probability of currency volatility since two Western currencies are generally involved in the cash transaction (from the Western European firm to the U.S. firm in the example discussed), although time delays can impose exchange rate losses. Problems associated with these arrangements include finding two Western firms with the appropriate supply/demand fit, and with the flexibilities to handle time delays in receipt of payment and/or in delivery of goods.

Compared to other forms of countertrade, Western firms can realize advantages in receiving only those goods needed, and product quality is usually assured since raw materials are generally received from the foreign principal. With uniform grading standards in place, raw materials are far more attractive to the Western party compared to manufactured goods where it is difficult to predetermine quality before goods arrive.

In terms of disadvantages, Western suppliers are presented with limited product and market opportunities. The burden of finding two Western firms with the appropriate supply-demand fit also impairs growth of this transaction form. However, smaller markets with mounting foreign debts may continue to demand cooperation agreements. Western capital goods manufacturers whose traditional markets both at home and abroad have reached saturation may willingly comply with such demands.

Conclusion

Major trading partners are not likely to coordinate tax and monetary policies throughout the 1990s. This lack of coordination and the dollar's pivotal role in international exchange set the stage for continued growth of barter and countertrade.

The distinctions between barter and countertrade demonstrate that countertrade requires more marketing effort by the Western firm and greater attention to legalities to protect the firm through multiple transactions. In addition, countertrade demands a higher level and longer time span of involvement in the foreign customer's business, particularly when technology transfer occurs. The cash component of countertrade transactions also raises the additional burden of currency volatility.

Compared to all forms, classic barter and counterpurchase offer firms opportunities for the most extensive degree of product and market diversification. Both forms also support firms in market development and market penetration. However, counterpurchase carries with it a longer time frame and trading experience is far more critical given multiple transactions and currency volatility.

Clearing account barter and cooperation agreements, while distinctively different regarding the degree of monetization and government involvement, are similar in their limited product and market diversification. Both forms also achieve only one marketing objective—market penetration. On the advantage side, both have some utilities in reducing currency volatility, since trade balances in clearing account barter are kept in clearing account units and currencies of Western parties are generally used in cooperation agreements. But, given the complexities of these two forms and their limited utilities in advancing marketing objectives, Western firms will likely focus on other transaction forms.

Compensation trading offers Western firms the best opportunities for integrative growth, since by the transfer of technology Western firms invest in a future source of products fitting their own production needs. Compensation trading is close to offsets in the structure of the transaction, however, only compensation trading involves direct technology transfer.

References

Alexandrides, Costas G. and Barbara L. Bowers, *Countertrade Practices, Strategies and Tactics*, (New York: John Wiley and Sons, Inc, 1987).

Bates, Constance, "Are Companies Ready for Countertrade?", *International Marketing Review*, Vol. 3 (Summer 1986), pp. 28–36.

Cohen, Stephen S. and John Zysman, "Countertrade, Offsets, Barter, and Buybacks", *California Management Review*, Vol. 28 (Winter 1986), pp. 41–56.

Huszagh, Sandra and Hiram Barksdale, "International Barter and Countertrade: An Exploratory Study", *Journal of the Academy of Marketing Science*, Vol. 17 (Spring 1986), pp. 21–28.

Korth, Christopher (ed.), *International Countertrade*, (Westport, Connecticut: Quorum Books, 1987).

Lecraw, Donald J., "The Management of Countertrade: Factors Influencing Success", *Journal of International Business Studies*, Vol. 20 (Spring 1989), pp. 41–59.

Verzariu, Pompiliu, *Countertrade, Barter, and Offsets*, (New York: McGraw-Hill Book Company, 1985).

36

Countertrade Suits Metallgesellschaft Fine*

GEORGE MELLOAN

Economists—especially free-market economists of the Austrian school—have for years been skeptical of countertrade, a form of barter much favored by cash-short Third World and socialist states. The critics argue that countertrade is inefficient and, more to the point, a means by which state enterprises can flood free markets with low-priced, state-subsidized products.

But there is at least one Austrian-born economist willing to defend countertrade. He is Heinz Schimmelbusch, 44-year-old deputy chairman of Metallgesellschaft A.G., a West German multinational that produces nonferrous metals and runs a global trading organization. "MG", as Mr. Schimmelbusch calls his company, also is the parent of Lurgi, S.A., a major industrial construction contractor.

With a world-wide distribution network and a factory-building subsidiary, MG is in an excellent position to conduct countertrade. It can sell new factories and at the same time contract to market the exports of those factories. So it has been developing that business in socialist countries with what it sees as mutual benefits. With metals smelting and other basic industries increasingly running afoul of environmental restrictions and high costs in North America, Western Europe and Japan, socialist nations may have happened upon a lucrative source of foreign exchange, which their otherwise backward economies have so much difficulty earning.

Mr. Schimmelbusch is something of a *Wunderkind* of West German industry. He was born in Vienna but earned his Ph.D. in economics at Tuebingen University in West Germany. After a brief hitch of

* Reprinted from *Wall Street Journal*, August 2, 1988, with permission.

teaching, he spent some time in New York honing financial skills at Morgan Stanley, Goldman Sachs and other firms and then joined MG in 1973. Last month, MG announced that he will become the company's chairman and chief executive officer when its current chairman, Dietrich Natus, retires next May. By German standards or almost any others, his has been a meteoric rise, no doubt owed mainly to the role he has played, through world-wide expansion of raw-materials operations, in restoring MG to health. It had suffered its first postwar loss in 1982 when deflation had depressed world prices of basic materials.

Mr. Schimmelbusch isn't betting the company's future on counter-trade. He expects that the developed world will continue to be the best source of growth and earnings. Lurgi, for example, is cashing in on the demands in the developed world for a clean environment by developing new technologies for recycling industrial materials, such as zinc residue contained in the dust from electrical arc steel furnaces. But countertrade is one of the most interesting lines of business, partly because of the earnings prospects it holds for the heavily indebted East-bloc nations and partly because of the controversy that surrounds it.

East-bloc countries, indeed, very often consider little else in a plant-construction project other than how much foreign exchange it will cost and how much foreign exchange it will earn. Sometimes that equation works out very well with the aid of countertrade. MG built a very large methanol plant in East Germany's huge Leuna chemical complex, which supplies about half of East Germany's chemicals. The East Germans needed methanol for their chemical industry and also had a cheap feedstock, natural gas piped in at concessionary prices by the Russians. They also needed foreign exchange.

So Lurgi built them a plant. Mr. Schimmelbusch explains how the deal is working: "It now produces 800,000 tons of methanol, of which 408,000 tons are going for export per year. We are buying 100%. The plant cost 400 million deutsche marks and the 408,000 tons of methanol, at 250 marks per ton, earn more than 100 million marks in foreign exchange a year. You invest 400 million marks and then deduct 250 million for capacity you needed anyway to supply national demand, and you have 150 million left. So you earn 100 million a year on a 150 million investment."

Obviously that's not a bad deal for the East Germans. How did it work out for MG? Well, the East German government paid cash for the plant. But MG suddenly had a very large supply of methanol to market. "That's about two to three trains a day into the whole logistics network of Western Europe into a market that doesn't need 408,000 tons of methanol. So outdated plants had to be closed, which took us three years to do. But now that is a *fait accompli*. That gave us a big boost in the methanol trade, in which we weren't a factor, but learned to be a factor over three years."

So it has. In April, MG made a deal with Tenneco Inc. under which Tenneco will recommission a methanol plant at Pasadena, Texas, that was shut down in 1983 due to low demand. MG financed the reopening and will market most of the plant's production which it figures will give it a strong position in the U.S. market as demand for methanol derivatives in gasoline rises.

Lurgi will make a big effort to sell a new gasoline additive process that it says further improves gasoline efficiency. "That will lead us to access to U.S. refineries and our oil trading subsidiary can provide other services to them."

But back to East Europe. Mr. Schimmelbusch thinks that the basic materials business, in depression in the early 1980s, now faces a bright future well into the 1990s. That's partly because of rising demand but also because so much capacity in the industrial world has been abandoned for environmental and economic reasons. It has become very difficult to find places to build new capacity.

"There has been a dramatic reduction in capacity in the United States, for instance, in copper refineries, copper smelters, the secondary lead industry, the zinc industry—almost an exodus. In Japan, the aluminum smelting industry vanished, from 1.6 million tons to zero. Please go to New Jersey or Texas or wherever and apply for permission to build a new metals smelter. Or go to Austria where there's a wonderful gold property and you say you will build a gold leaching operation in the next two years. Or go to a West German community and say: 'Guys, you have unemployment of 20%. I have the solution, a lead smelter.' It sounds like a joke. You don't even go there."

So socialist countries, seeking a scarcity of production locations in the West, are saying, "We have locations so why not use them?" It makes sense for them, it makes sense for MG and it is a natural outgrowth of environmental restrictions Western nations have placed on themselves. But that won't make Western economists and policy makers any happier about the growing in-roads of countertrade in world markets. Indeed, U.S. negotiators participating in the so-called "Uruguay" round of multilateral trade talks in May asked for a new set of ground rules under the General Agreement on Tariffs and Trade (GATT) to cover state enterprises. The U.S. complained specifically that countertrade can cause "serious trade distortions" inconsistent with "nondiscrimination and other GATT principles".

Mr. Schimmelbusch, for his part, thinks that countertrade is nothing more subversive than signing two deals at the same time. But—especially considering the political elements involved—this debate isn't over yet.

Further Reading — Part V

1. Cohen, Stephen S. and John Zysman, "Countertrade, Offsets, Barter, and Buybacks," *California Management Review*, Vol. 28 (Winter 1986), pp. 41–56.
2. Franko Lawrence G., "New Forms of Investment in Developing Countries by U.S. Companies: A Five Industry Comparison," *Columbia Journal of World Business*, (Summer 1987), pp. 39–56.
3. Harrigan, Kathryn Rudie, "Joint Ventures and Competitive Strategy," *Strategic Management Journal*, Vol. 9 (1988), pp. 141–158.
4. "LOF and Nippon Glass Enter Korean Auto Glass Market with Tripartite Venture," *Business International*, December 29, 1985, pp. 401–405.
5. "Mexico's In-Bond Industry Continues Its Dynamic Growth," *Business America*, November 26, 1984, pp. 26–28.
6. "Running a Licensing Department: The Critical Keys to Success," *Business International*, June 13, 1988, pp. 117–178.

VI
Developing, Implementing, and Controlling the International Marketing Mix

Introduction to Part VI

When designing a firm's international marketing strategy, one frequently faces the old problem of how to tackle the four instruments of the marketing mix: product, price, promotion and distribution. In Part VI the readers will find articles discussing the major international consideration within each of these marketing instruments.

Kreutzer offers an analytical framework for applying the concept of marketing-mix standardization. The first step in his analysis is concerned with whether such standardization is important for a branch or a market of the company in question. The aim of the second step is to find out ways in which marketing-mix standardization can be practiced. Kreutzer also explores the relation between segmentation and standardization.

Johansson and Thorelli concentrate on the issue of product positioning. The authors argue that many of the same considerations that go into the positioning strategy in the home country are directly relevant for international markets. However, there is an added element of complexity in that the country-of-origin of the imported product will often be a salient factor in the buyer evaluation process. The effect of country stereotype will be to shift the position of the product in the perceptual space and alter the overall evaluation of its merits.

Reading 39 by Beeth deals with problems of distribution. It is quite a lively piece on the do's and don'ts of finding and keeping good distributors in international marketing. The article is based on the author's many years of personal practical experience in American, Swedish and EEC firms. Beyond good distributor relationships, foreign marketing often succeeds simply because of entrepreneurial common sense, nimble responses to varied demands, and plain old courage.

Cavusgil in Reading 42 presents a framework to help managers handle the complex issue of export pricing. The complexity of export pricing lies in the large number of variables that affect international pricing decisions and the uncertainty surrounding them. The author classifies these variables as either internal or external to the organization. These variables include nature of the product, location of production, chosen system of distribution, government regulations, and management attitudes. After analyzing each factor, the author introduces three pricing strategies.

Becker follows up with the oft-encountered problem of price escalation in international marketing.

Trade fair is often an underrated marketing promotion tool. Reading 44 from *Business International* argues that this tool is rapidly gaining new cachet and participation as it is an essential component of any global marketing strategy. Experienced companies may find it to be one of the most cost-effective ways for a company to serve existing markets and expand into new areas.

37

Marketing-Mix Standardization: An Integrated Approach in Global Marketing*

RALF T. KREUTZER

Marketing-mix standardization is important when marketing is considered as a global concept. As an aid for enterprises taking the decision as to whether or not global marketing can support their company in working out competitive advantages, this article offers an analytical framework. The first step in the analysis is concerned with whether marketing-mix standardization is important for the branch or the market of the company in question. This step is oriented to strategic factors of success. The aim of the second step in the analysis is to find out the ways in which marketing-mix standardization can be practiced by one specific company. Segmentation as a concept is useful in this context when considered in relation to standardization (Keegan and MacMaster 1983).

Specification of a Global Marketing Concept

Philosophy and Features of Global Marketing

Global marketing is based on a specific marketing philosophy that seeks to overcome the individual approaches of single country points of view. To implement a "global approach," analysis evaluation and clustering of the global market take place primarily to elicit common points of interest of the markets, and of target groups in a way that reaches beyond national borders, instead of partially concentrating on existing differences. This integrative approach represents the basis for

* Adapted from Ralf Kreutzer, *European Journal of Marketing*, Vol. 22, No. 10 (1988), pp. 19–30, with permission.

a specific form of selection of markets as well as handling of markets, which aims at "standardization" as a fundamental strategy of marketing (Segler 1985).

At the same time, global marketing philosophy is not centered in an ill-balanced manner on the external sphere (the market). It also spills over into the internal sphere of the enterprise. Here, too, the question of mutualities is raised (e.g., relating to certain sets of problems, planning processes, processes of information research), which can be arranged in a homogeneous way and can thereby be standardized. Thus global marketing can be characterized by two different features:

(1) Standardization of marketing processes (process-oriented standardization);
(2) Standardization of marketing programs/marketing mix (program-oriented standardization).

Even if both types of standardization can be implemented independently of each other, attention should be drawn here to the positive interrelations. In many markets, process-oriented standardization and program-oriented standardization are not just complementary to one another; process standardization is often rather an instrument, partly even a precondition for the implementation of the standardization of marketing programs.

The standardization of marketing processes is primarily a question of standardizing the structures and processes for development, implementation and control of marketing concepts, as well as the information processes connected with them. By the standardization of sequences of work and problem-solving approaches (e.g., decision-making processes, staff-training programs, strategies for the launching of new products, controlling activities) a rationalization of marketing in general is sought (Kreutzer 1986).

Targets of Global Marketing

Connected with a standardization of marketing mix—which is of main interest here—are attempts which are being made to achieve cost reduction and an increased efficiency in the sphere of marketing by a standardization of marketing concepts. An essential aspect, from the German point of view, is not just the standardizing of advertising campaigns; global marketing is far more than global advertising. If you intend to make an overall use of the potential for cutting costs and increasing efficiency, it will be necessary to take a closer look at the marketing mix as a whole, with standardization in mind.

In the first place, cost-cutting potentials are central and should be translated into strategically important price advantages. Costs can be reduced by producing standardized products since large volumes are connected with "economies of scale." So-called "world-factories," which produce for worldwide demand, show how these cost-cutting potentials can be realized. An example of this is the Tesa production unit at Beiersdorf, Germany, where Scotch tapes are produced for the world market.

Possibilities of saving campaign-development costs can be achieved by concentration on one "unique selling proposition" of global communications. By identical positioning of products, for example, Europe-wide promotion campaigns become possible. Such a campaign was carried out by Levi-Strauss in 1985. Here it is only necessary to develop one promotion concept instead of a large number of different concepts. With such an approach, an additional reduction of expenditures on co-ordination can be achieved by one advertising agency tending one brand worldwide as a lead agency (which is, amongst others, the case of Toblerone with Saatchi & Saatchi Compton, as well as for Levi-Strauss with McCann-Erickson). Last, but not least, savings can be obtained on agency costs themselves (a decisive argument with Atari's step towards standardization).

After these examples of cost-cutting possibilities the question arises as to the ways in which marketing-mix standardization can lead to an increase in marketing efficiency. This aim can be achieved by using synergy potentials. Amongst other things this implies the use of spill-over effects in advertising in frontier-crossing media. If, for example, French TV programs with corresponding advertising are fed into the cable system of the Federal Republic of Germany intensification effects can occur with standardized advertising. Differential advertising, different product colors, incongruous positioning strategies or also distinct product names, result, on the other hand, in an irritation of consumers and thereby scatter part of the advertising impact to the winds. This is the case when, for example, the shampoo launched in Germany as Silkience is marketed in France by the name of Soyance and in Italy by the name of Sientel.

In the R&D branch, a globally integrated and standardized approach can widely control unproductive parallel work (i.e., a "re-invent the wheel" situation). Real effect increases however are not only rendered possible by the use of synergy effects between decentralized R&D departments, but also by multinational resource pooling. Many projects can thereby be implemented which hitherto have been held up on account of country-specific budget limitations.

A very important but also very difficult area of standardization is to lay down similar price strategies all over the world. If you see that, for example, the prices for Swiss watches are lower in Singapore or in Hong Kong than in Switzerland itself, you can imagine how difficult a similar price strategy is to execute. Such price differences are a big problem, especially when the countries concerned are close to one another. Here the phenomena of re-imports emerges. This is, for example, the case with therapeutical products within the European Community, where the price differences are extremely high. The solution to this problem may be that companies have to find out whether it is at least possible to fix a worldwide obligatory price range so as to reduce the attractiveness of re-importing their products.

Frame of Analysis for Marketing-Mix Standardization

To determine the branch/market-specific importance as well as the points of departure for an individual enterprise in standardizing its marketing mix, a two-stage process of analysis is appropriate. This can be carried out by the business enterprise's own employees, if need be supported by branch specialists. The following questions have to be answered:

(1) Can global marketing help with the achievement of branch or market-specific competitive advantages?
(2) If global marketing is suitable for the achievement of branch-specific competitive advantages, which possibilities specific to the enterprise exist to exhaust this potential of globalization?

Such a two-stage analysis is appropriate because if marketing-mix standardization is not of major importance for the whole branch or the market, then deeper considerations of standardization at company level are unnecessary. In such a case, the process of analysis ends after the first step.

Analysis of the Branch/Market -Oriented Importance of Marketing-Mix Standardization

The determination of the specific importance of market-mix standardization has to begin with the strategic factors of success of a branch or a market. With respect to these factors of success, the possibilities and consequences of a standardization strategy are to be analyzed and evaluated. In doing this, you have to be guided by those countries which are actually handled or are of potential interest. Depending on the results you obtain, you then have to decide whether marketing-mix standardization is important for the branch/market or not.

The basic branch/market definition must not be dealt with from a strictly product angle, but rather be in a wider sense demand-oriented (branch of soft drinks instead of branch of lemonades containing caffeine). Thus not only is dangerous marketing myopia avoided (Levitt 1960), but the wide perspective may often result in entire new spheres of standardization (e.g., the addressing of target groups for a whole range of soft drinks). The consequences of a standardization strategy are presented with regards to strategic factors of success which are valuable for several branches or markets; care must be taken to avoid pinpointing a frame relevant only to one branch or market which would be ill-balanced.

The possibility of exhausting the effects of experience curves by standardization represents a central point of departure for the determination of the specific importance of standardized working. If the cost situation becomes a central factor of success (in many cases due to missing purchasing power or due to a high intensity of competition), effects of experience curves in the product, R&D and marketing branches should be used. To effect this in production, a mass market or the possibility to build it has to exist. Only this offers the opportunity to exhaust advantages in volume. The use of the experience curves' effects is especially interesting for capital-intensive productions (as in the automotive or aircraft industries) because here the use of production processes favorable in cost brings significant cost reductions about (cf. VW's automated Golf-production for several European countries).

Cost advantages which are decisive for competition can also be a result of standardization in R&D. If the market situation doesn't force R&D activities to respond in an isolated way to single markets, "products for a global market" can be developed. The potential for reducing costs occurring here is especially important for the competitive strategy of branches with extremely high R&D costs, like the chemical industry (especially pharmaceuticals), the aircraft and automotive industries.

If the flexibility of production technology becomes a strategic factor of success, caused by country-specific necessities for adjustment, the employment of modular technology should be considered. Its use presupposes the possibility of using identical components (which can be standardized) in different product lines. Such a component standardization keeps production flexible, and scale effects can be used at the same time (Caterpillar built up a decisive barrier against its competitors during the Seventies by the use of such a modular technology).

Going beyond such experience-curve effects, the significance of the exhaustion of synergy potentials in the branch should be examined, i.e., whether global system efficiency can be called a critical factor of success. If this is the case, synergies in communication should be used. This becomes possible by standardized advertising (think of the worldwide "Shadow Campaign" of British Airways), and the use of global brand names (like Nivea, Lux, Marlboro, Pampers, Jack Daniels, Johnny Walker, etc.).

In some areas, e.g., in the spheres of fast food and soft drinks as well as in those of garment and accessories, purchase decisions are often "life-style oriented." We should strive for a marketing-political access to, or a build-up of such life-style oriented attitudes as an element in a trans-national orientation system of consumers. Only then can decisions for a product be disengaged from the network of national attitudes and thereby also from cultural constraints. Coca Cola and McDonalds, and also the Swiss watch brand Swatch, can be quoted here as models for the utilization of "life-style oriented attitudes" as a factor of success.

The consumers can even be forced into conformity by giving a leading character to prestige products, in order to build up a strong demand for imitation, i.e., establishing an imitative instinct. This is especially possible with "high-interest" products. These are products which attract keen interest from the consumer because of technical factors but also because of their status. An example, not noticeable only in the U.S.A., is the run on clothing after the fashion of Dallas and Denver stars; for many consumers the purchase of these clothes is connected with access to the "upper crust."

The internationality of the producers of a branch can also be a central strategic factor of success. This is the case if a global in-house service net is necessary for the purchase decision or if the image of a world brand, i.e., a global marketer, is of significance (this is right for automobiles and computers, but also for TV, disc-players, etc.; thus Philips is presently elaborating a global advertising concept for compact disc and video disc to answer the Japanese challenge). Marketing-mix standardization can also be an important element here.

The importance of standardization for a branch or market, determined in this way, gains entry to a branch-profile of standardization relevance (Figure 37.1).

If the relevance of standardization is not established or is not yet sufficient for a "global step" across national frontiers, the analysis process can be broken off here. As strategic factors of success are subject to certain dynamics in the passage of time, an examination of standardization relevance for a branch should be properly repeated, even if the result was negative, after about a year. If the branch profile on the other hand is found to be in a gray zone (between a clear positioning for or against standardization) additional branch/market-specific factors must be analyzed before making a decision.

If the presence of standardization relevance for one's own branch or market can be basically affirmed, it has to be examined in a second stage where the possibilities exist, specific to the business enterprise or product, for utilizing this potential to work out competitive advantages.

1. Step: Effects of a standardization strategy –
    in consideration of branch-oriented
    strategic success factors

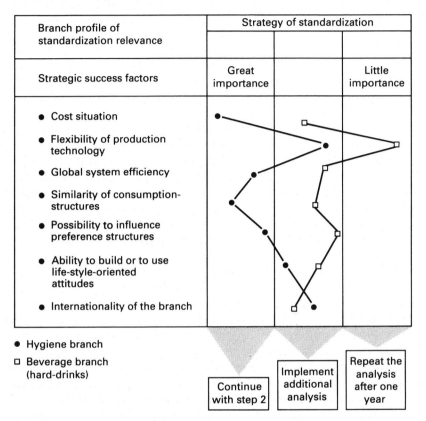

FIG. 37.1. Step 1: Standardization Relevance.

Analysis of the Company-Oriented Importance of Global Marketing

If the first stage showed that competitive advantages can be achieved by marketing-mix standardization in a specific branch or market, it is now necessary to find out about the potential of standardization of one's own company or of special products, as a second step. Before you can do this however a standardization-oriented segmentation has to be accomplished. This segmentation centers on the tracking down of the target group to be handled by standardized marketing. Segmentation has to answer the following questions:

(1) Which countries already handled and/or potentially interesting show the conditions necessary for global marketing?

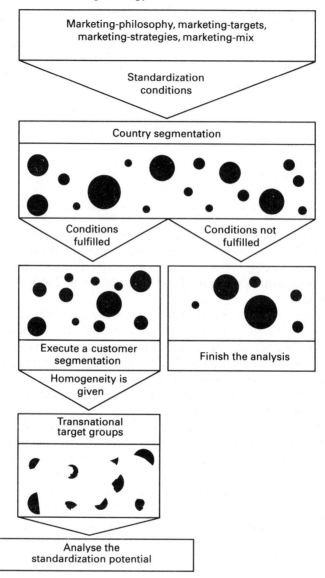

FIG. 37.2. Standardization-Oriented Segmentation.

(2) Of these, are there, trans-nationally, customers who are comparably structured with respect to their expectations of consumption and use and/or their habits?

We enter this two-stage segmentation (Figure 37.2) by starting with country segmentation. Here we have to divide relevant countries into

TABLE 37.1. Criteria for a Standardization-Oriented Country Segmentation

Technological criteria	*Economical criteria*
media scenery	market volume, market potential
distribution system	level of purchasing power
technological development	economical development
infrastructure	competitive situation
Ecological criteria	*Political-legal criteria*
provision of resources	legal restrictions
climatic conditions	law of competition
topography	commercial law
Socio-cultural criteria	
educational level	
linguistic habits	
religion	
culture	

two groups, depending on their appropriateness for standardized handling. For this reason the countries are grouped according to the presence of important conditions for standardization. To determine these requirement conditions the criteria shown in Table 37.1 must be considered.

With this country segmentation, it is of decisive importance to look at national differences in consideration of performance-specific (marketing) requirements; thus differences in the provision of mass media are irrelevant to standardization strategy, if those are —as often in capital goods industry—of no or only small importance for advertising a specific product, because of the dominance of personal communication (personal selling).

For those countries in which the "standardization conditions" are fulfilled, a second stage with customer segmentation follows; this can also be done by reference to a list of criteria (Table 37.2).

TABLE 37.2. Criteria for Consumer Segmentation

Orientation system	*Informational behavior*
religious, cultural background	habits of reading/watching TV
consumption trends, waves of fashion	position of opinion leaders
image leading countries,	demand for information
persons global open-mindedness	selectivity of perception
Purchase (decision) attitude	*Consumption pattern*
allocation of parts within collective	habits of utilization
purchasing patterns	service requirements, level of demand
frequency of purchases	demands to built-in-service
perceived risk at purchasing	household equipment
hierarchies of wants	*Waste disposal environment*
quality consciousness	pollution of environment
price consciousness; purchasing power	possibilities for recycling
brand name loyalty, shop loyalty	

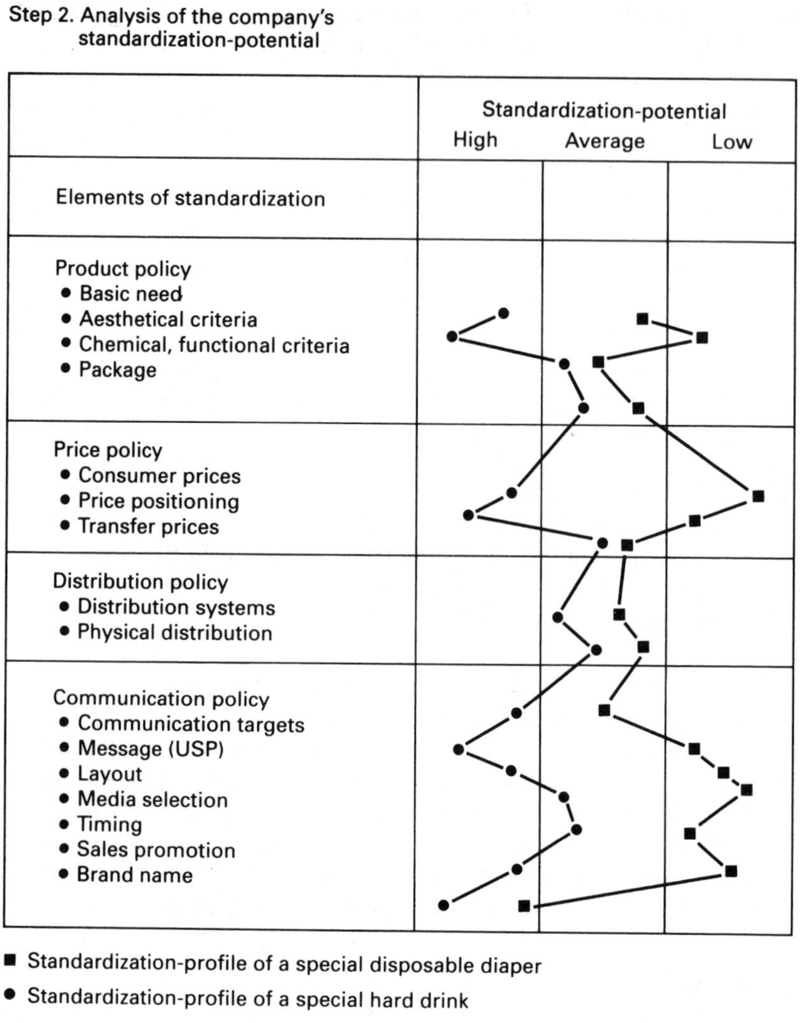

Step 2. Analysis of the company's
 standardization-potential

	Standardization-potential		
	High	Average	Low
Elements of standardization			
Product policy • Basic need • Aesthetical criteria • Chemical, functional criteria • Package			
Price policy • Consumer prices • Price positioning • Transfer prices			
Distribution policy • Distribution systems • Physical distribution			
Communication policy • Communication targets • Message (USP) • Layout • Media selection • Timing • Sales promotion • Brand name			

■ Standardization-profile of a special disposable diaper

● Standardization-profile of a special hard drink

FIG. 37.3. Step 2: Standardization Profile.

Trans-nationally homogeneous target groups are formed ("cross-cultural groups," e.g., music and motorbike fans, do-it-yourself workers, or teenagers with skin problems), to handle them trans-nationally with the same marketing concept. Trans-national does not necessarily mean global here, but rather the existing possibility of adjusting standardized marketing concepts to similar structured customer groups of a larger regional unit (keywords: regional marketing, Euro-marketing). In this way the possibilities for reducing costs and increasing efficiency can at least be used regionally.

If it is possible to identify trans-national target groups by this method, their characteristics together with the frame conditions of the incorporated countries, form the background for investigating the company's present performance especially the marketing mix—with regard to certain potentials of standardization. The approaches discovered for standardization can now be entered into a marketing-related standardization-potential profile to make them clearer (Figure 37.3). Such a profile-chart can essentially facilitate the comparison of the standardization potentials of different strategic business units, or even of single products and services.

In the chart the profiles of standardization potentials for two different product-classes are shown: The profile of special disposable diapers (e.g., Pampers) and the profile of a hard drink (Jack Daniels or Johnny Walker). These are the results of an analysis, which checks the possibilities of standardization within the marketing mix.

The results show that there are different ways of realizing a standardized concept within the marketing mix. In both cases it is possible to standardize the package at least on an average level. Difficulties arise as far as the price policy is concerned. Here it is only possible to reach a similar price positioning for disposable diapers. So Procter & Gamble selects only such markets as possess the necessary purchasing power to pay a price within the target price range. In the case of hard drinks, it is nearly impossible to gain a similar price positioning due to legal constraints. In Denmark, for example, you have to pay two or three times as much for the same Johnny Walker whisky as in Germany—this is due to tax regulations. In most cases it is possible to use one brand name on a worldwide basis. There are negative effects connected with particular names in only a few cases; you have to change brand names to avoid these unintentional images.

Conclusion

If you want to maximize use of a global marketing concept and to see the inevitable risks early enough, the concept should be subjected to a final stage of examination before it is implemented. The determination of the positive and negative effects of a standardization strategy on the countries and customers you have considered, and the possible consequences to your own company, are the issues at stake here. Only by evaluation of these effects, in the frame of a global marketing assessment, can the increasing importance of one-sided short-term advantages for the company be avoided. The possible long-lasting negative reactions from the countries or also from the consumers approached must not be neglected. But the opportunities which arise from a standardized approach only on a long-term basis, should also be considered here. Only such a complete evaluation—with corresponding consequences for the further development of the marketing concept—enables a well-balanced judgment to be made on the implementation of program-oriented global marketing.

References

Keegan, W. J. and N. A. MacMaster, "Global Strategic Marketing," in V. H. Kirpalani (ed.), *International Marketing: Managerial Issues, Research and Opportunities*, (Chicago, I11: American Marketing Association, 1983), pp. 94–105.

Kreutzer, R., *Standardization of Marketing Processes as a Strategic Point in Global Marketing*, Working Paper No. 41, Institute of Marketing, University of Mannheim, 1986.

Levitt, T., "Marketing Myopia," *Harvard Business Review*, Vol. 38 (July/August 1960), pp. 45–56.

Segler, K., *Strategische Analyse und Basisstrategien im internationalen Marketing*, PhD Dissertation, University of Mannheim, 1985.

38

International Product Positioning*

JOHNY K. JOHANSSON
HANS B. THORELLI

Introduction

This article presents a decision model for positioning products in markets abroad. It draws on empirical findings in the international marketing literature which show that a product's country-of-origin and associated stereotypes play an important role in buyer perceptions and evaluations (Bilkey and Nes 1982). Since perceptual influences from country stereotyping have the effect of introducing systematic shifts as well as random noise in individuals' beliefs about a product, the country-of-origin factors directly affect where a product is positioned in consumers' perceptual maps of the product space.

The international product positioning approach proposed here make it possible to evaluate explicitly how different countries' stereotyping affects a given position. The suggested procedure identifies the means by which the international marketer can measure the relative disadvantage or advantage a product possesses compared to those of competitors from other countries. In the proposed framework, overcoming a relative disadvantage requires a temporary price reduction or some other special inducement. Employing the concept of "efficient choices," the article shows how one can compute the amount by which price has to be reduced to overcome a deficient position.

* Slightly abbreviated from *Journal of International Business Studies*, (Fall 1985), pp. 57–75, with permission.

International Perceptual Maps

Product Positioning

The starting point behind the international positioning concept is the notion that an evoked set of products can be described as different bundles of attributes which are capable of generating a stream of benefits to the buyer and user. As part of the targeting of specific market segments the marketer will attempt to develop these attributes so that the benefits generated match the special requirements of that segment. This is a product design problem that involves not only the functional characteristics of the offering but also features such as the packaging, the brand name, and the styling. This design task is generally called "product positioning." Since in the final analysis what matters is the buyer's perception of the benefit-generating attributes, not the "actual" attributes scores (a "fast" car is one that is perceived to be fast, for example, not simply one that possesses good acceleration figures), product positioning is the activity by which a desirable "position in the mind of the customer" is created for the product.

Viewed in a multi-dimensional space (commonly denoted the "perceptual space" or "product space") a product can be graphically represented as a point defined by its attribute scores. Other products are represented by other points. If the points are close, the products have similar attribute scores and are thus fair substitutes. The further away a point is from another, the less the direct competition tends to be (since they differ considerably on the salient attributes). The location of a product's point in this product space is its "position." An example of a positioning map is given in Figure. 38.1.

The product space map of automobiles given in the figure is based on American respondents' perception of ten car makes. The positions shown in the map were derived using factor analysis to first reduce an original set of twelve attributes into a more manageable two dimensions and then plot the position using the factor scores of the cars on the two significant factors.

The figure also exhibits the overall rating vector for the automobiles in the U.S. market. This depicts the direction in which the desirability of a car increases, regardless of price. The vector was derived from the respondents' answers to an overall rating question for each car, regressing these on the cars' scores on the two dimensions across all respondents. By projecting each car's position on to the vector through a perpendicular line (such as the one from Audi) it is possible to identify the top choices in the market segment. Among these respondents, the most desirable cars are the BMW, the Audi and the Accord, while the Citation and the Mustang are tied for last place.

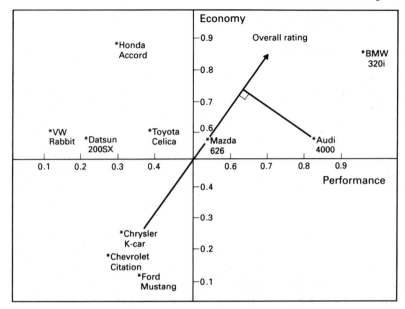

FIG. 38.1 Automobile Space Map with Preference Vector (United States).

The most advantageous position for the producer is one that yields the highest rating among the target segment. Whether this is a feasible position or not depends mainly on the company's specific production and marketing capabilities (whether customers can be convinced, for example). If the Ford company is able to manufacture the kind of car that can beat the BMW, it should at least consider this option since this particular group of people seems to favor that type of car. Alternatively, the Ford cars might be aimed at another target segment, or they will have to score better on attributes not accounted for in the product space map. Ford could offer superior service, bank credit, or other "augmenting" benefits which might be instrumental in making the customer buy its car.

The chief inducement to buy a "low-position" (in the sense that it does not represent a top choice in its market segment) product is the *price* paid. From a positioning viewpoint, a low price is the factor which allows less than top brands to be successful in a market. By the same token, the greater the differentials between a top choice like the BMW and its nearest competitor (the Audi 4000 in Figure 38.1), the greater the price premium that buyers are willing to pay for the BMW. The distance between the brands on the preference vector (where the perpendicular lines fall) is a measure of the degree of price discretion a company can exercise.

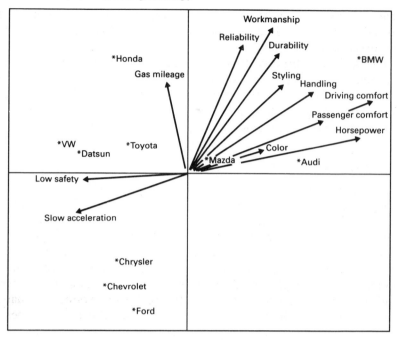

FIG. 38.2. Interpreting the Space Axes (United States)

The names of the axes, "Performance" and "Economy," are based on the underlying belief scores from the respondents across all the attributes. These are depicted in Figure 38.2 which is derived from the factor loadings employed in developing the product space. The direction of the vectors shows which of the two axes reflects more of each attribute (a car's score on an attribute vector can as before be identified by a perpendicular projection). The length of the vectors conveys the degree of importance that the attribute has in determining the space. For example, "Color" is not a very important attribute in this product space but "Driving Comfort" is, and for these cars the ratings of "Color" and of "Driving Comfort" follow the same pattern. For both attributes, BMW rates highest followed by the Audi, with VW Rabbit and Chevrolet Citation both showing low scores.

The twelve attributes as reflected in the vectors in Figure 38.2 make it possible to interpret what underlies the low ratings of the American cars. They are apparently seen as possessing no attractive features, scoring high only on undesirable attributes such as "Low Safety" and generally scoring low on desirable features (especially reliability, workmanship and durability). Re-positioning these cars to make them competitive with the Japanese models shown might involve more work than can be economically justified. It might simply be better to offer considerable price discounts; how large those discounts need to be is discussed in detail below.

Using the attribute vectors to give names to the two axes, it seemed reasonable to call the horizontal axis "Performance" and the vertical axis "Economy." The first dimension reflects the driving characteristics (including handling and acceleration) of the vehicle, the second the usage costs (gas mileage, repairs and depreciation) of the cars.

Country Stereotyping

There are numerous causes of misperceptions of a given product, many lodging in the unique perceptual biases and selectivity of each individual. There are also factors which create shared misperceptions among larger segments of a population. One such common source of misperception in international markets is country stereotyping. There is much evidence that people in one country tend to have common notions about people in other countries, and also that these stereotypical evaluations carry over into the realm of product evaluations (for a review, see Bilkey and Nes 1982). Since these stereotypes are shared among many people, the international marketer has to take them into account when positioning the product abroad.

What do we mean by "country stereotyping"? In the present context it can be interpreted as a way of thinking about people and products from a country which is "biased" and "colors" our beliefs about them. In the multi-attribute case, the biases show up in the belief ratings people give a foreign brand. Since automobiles represent one case where there are at least some attributes with objectively correct scores available (gas mileage, acceleration, repair records, etc.), some of the biases in the product space map of Figure 38.1 can be identified. The resulting map of misperceptions are shown in Figure 38.3. In calculating the "actual" positions, the completely subjective "styling" and "color" attributes were simply set at their means values for each model across all respondents, while the other true scores were assembled from consumer reports and auto magazines. Even though these "true" scores also suffer from subjectivity and potential country-of-origin bias, the extensive use of standardized tests and equipment makes CR ratings more objective than individual's own ratings (Maynes 1976, Chapter 5).

As can be seen from Figure 38.3, the misperceptions do not actually change the space map drastically, although most cars suffer from some degree of "incorrect" positioning. When interpreting the general tendency evidenced in the map it is necessary to keep in mind the fact that a position more to the Northeast is preferable, one towards the

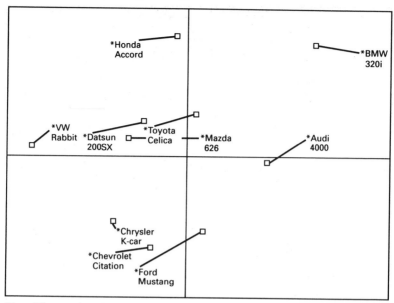

Note: The actual positions derived on the basis of auto magazines and *Consumers Report* ratings.

FIG. 38.3. Misperceptions: Actual Positions (Squares) Versus Perceived (United States).

Southwest leading to lower ratings. Thus, it is clear that these respondents tend to overrate the German cars (the BMW, the Audi, and even the U.S.-built V.W.) while under-rating the American and the Japanese cars (the one exception being the slightly overrated Mazda). Judging from the attributes depicted in Figure 38.2, the German cars are rated *too* high on driving comfort, handling and acceleration while the Japanese and American cars are rated *too* low on these factors.

Differences Across Countries

The stereotyping of products with a given country-of-origin is generally different across nations (see e.g. Bilkey and Nes 1982). To show how international differences in sterotyping affect the positioning of a product, it is instructive to look at the product space for the automobiles included in Figures 38.1–3, but for a set of Japanese respondents chosen to match the American cars sampled (see Appendix).

The product space among the Japanese differs to some extent from the one generated from the United States market (see Figure 38.4). The anchoring of the three American makes is similar to the early

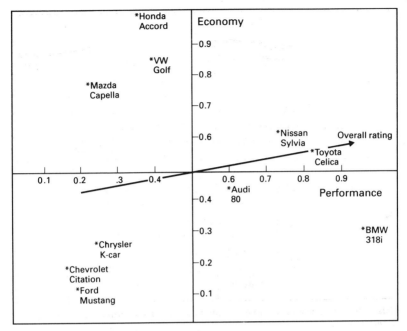

FIG. 38.4. Automobile Space Map with Preference Vector (Japan).

graph but the directions of the preference vectors has been changed and with them the position of the other makes. BMW is again the car most highly rated but now the Toyota and the Nissan Sylvia (as the Datsun 200SX is known in Japan) are close. Another noteworthy feature of the space map is the relatively large distance between the Toyota and Nissan makes on the one hand and the other two Japanese cars, Honda and Mazda, on the other.

To interpret the space axes we again turn to the vector projections of the attributes (Figure 38.5). A comparison with the corresponding figure for the U.S. sample (Figure 38.2) reveals that the space is largely a rotated version of the previous one. There are some minor differences in the exact attribute locations (the safety vector is here below the acceleration vector, for example) but otherwise the spaces have very similar interpretations. The horizontal axis can again be labeled "Performance" and the vertical "Economy." For the Japanese, however, the "Performance" and the "Economy" aspects of the cars seem to be closer together than the Americans. The attributes are clustered around the horizontal axis with gas mileage closest to the vertical axis.

"Misperceptions" among the Japanese are quite similar to the ones evinced by the respondents from the United States. The German cars

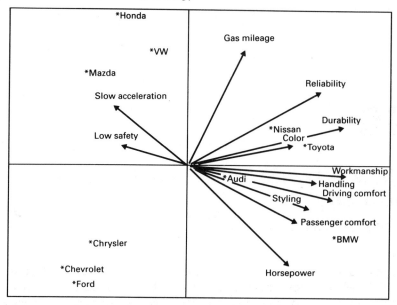

FIG. 38.5. Interpreting the Space Axes (Japan).

are overrated while the American cars are generally underrated (viewing a shift from West to East in the map as desirable because of the direction of the rating vector depicted in Figure 38.4).

Efficient Choices

The Efficient Frontier

One managerial issue in international positioning is the extent to which the misperceptions due to country stereotyping affect the chances that the product will be purchased. The direction of the biases has already been identified. But to see whether the effect is serious on the final purchases, it becomes necessary also to introduce the *prices* at which these alternatives are made available. An "inferior" (i.e., lowly evaluated) product might still be preferred if its price is very low.

The set of "efficient" choices comprises those evoked alternatives which provide a benefit per dollar others cannot match. These "dominant" choices are located on an "efficient frontier" in the space. They are identified by a calculation which divides each product's factor scores by the relevant price so as to arrive at a "benefit per dollar" figure. The new scores for the dimensions of the space are then used to develop a new space and position for each car. The relevant prices are

TABLE 38.1. Perceived and Actual Price

Car Model	Dollar Prices* U.S. Base Price Actual	Perceived		Japanese Base Price Actual	Perceived
Honda Accord	8085	7620		5280	5215
Datsun 200SX	7839	7674	Nissan Sylvia	6520	7513
Mazda 626	8245	8394	Mazda Capella	4600	5751
Toyota Celica	8244	8711		6560	7959
Ford Mustang	7153	7016		15640	11874
Chevrolet Citation	6650	6859		13120	11721
Plymouth K-Car	6858	7555		15400	12536
VW Rabbit	6849	7269	VW Golf	8280	8140
Audi 4000	11065	9411	Audi 80	16200	11331
BMW 320i	13290	11620	BMW 318i	15680	13414

Notes: * The Japanese yen has been converted at 250 to the dollar. The *actual* prices reflect the "Blue book" prices in the two countries in the Spring of 1982. There are of course various levels of discounts offered from these prices, so the *perceived* prices are not neccessarily "incorrect." In particular, the lower prices perceived for foreign cars in Japan (although still high) are probably due to a "gray market" in unauthorized imports.

given in Table 39.1, from which the perceived prices (multiplied by 0.0001 for scaling purposes) were used to compute the efficient choices for the American respondents (Figure 38.6) and those of the Japanese respondents (Figure 38.7).

In the figures the choices positioned in the Upper Northeast corner generally dominate those in the lower part of the quadrant (because of the way the preference vectors were projected in Figures 38.1 and 38.4). For example, in Figure 38.6, the Honda Accord provides more benefit per dollar than the VW Rabbit both in terms of "Performance/ $" and "Economy/$." The VW is "dominated" by Accord. The other (less efficient) cars do not offer sufficient benefits per dollar to be competitive with any brand positioned to the northeast of it.

As can be seen from the figures, most of the choices included are dominated by a minority of the cars at this aggregate level. The efficient cars for the Americans, for example, consist of the Honda Accord, the BMW, and the Audi. The other cars cannot offer sufficient benefits per dollar to be competitive in the aggregate, although there may well be niches of customers who perceive the cars different from the average depicted in the figure.

The Role of Price Reduction

The proposed framework can be used to compute how much of an added inducement is necessary for a product to become "efficient." Take, for example, the K-Car in Figure 38.6. In order for it to "beat"

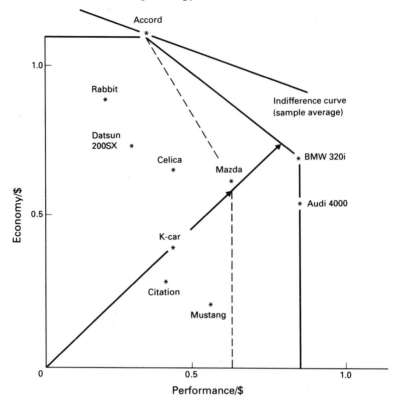

FIG. 38.6. Efficient Choice (U.S.).

the Mazda, its closest competitor on the constrained frontier, the K-Car needs a shift in position in a northeasterly direction. This shift can be accomplished by a reduction in the price of the K-Car of slightly more than $2000.

The computations required to arrive at this figure are carried out under the assumption that a price reduction will not change the perceptions of the product (e.g., there should be no adverse quality impact). Such an assumption is usually tenable only to the extent that the price reduction is temporary.

If a price decrease involves no perceptual change, its mix of attribute scores will stay the same. A decrease in price will simply shift the car outwards from the origin; an increase will move it towards the origin. This "fixed proportions" case is graphically represented in the efficient space by a vector projected from the origin through the car's present position.

The vector of the K-Car is indicated in Figure 38.6 for the

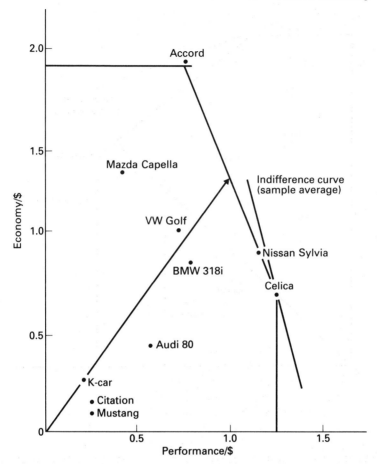

FIG. 38.7. Efficient Choices (Japan).

American sub-sample. As can be seen, the vector intersects the constrained efficient frontier just to the south of the Mazda car. This means that a price decrease that makes the K-Car competitive in the market will generally position it against the Mazda (although one could expect that also potential buyers of the Toyota and the BMW might be tempted judging from Figure 38.6).

The last step in the analysis is then to compute the required price discount that will move the K-Car onto the frontier. Projecting the vector out until the frontier is reached, it is easy to read the point of intersection off from the graph. Using the "Economy" dimension, we see that the K-Car has to reach a value of approximately .50 to be competitive with the Mazda. (Only one dimension needs to be used, since the other is given by the fixed proportionately requirement.) Since the K-Car's existing "Economy" score from the perceptual space (Figure 38.1) is about .26, the requisite new price X is generated by the following equation:

$$.26/X = .50, \text{ or } X = .52$$

Re-scaling to actual dollars, the selling price of the K-Car needs to be $5200 to make it efficient. The perceived price at the time of the study was $7555. The required discount is therefore

$$\$7555 - \$5200 = \$2355$$

It is, of course, also possible to carry out the same calculations for the Japanese sample. Using the graphs in Figures 38.4 and 39.7 to do just that, the requisite new price is much lower (about $2400, a stark contrast to the actual price of $15,400—see Table 38.1). This extreme value, based on the preceptions of these particular Japanese respondents, reflects the kind of competitive disadvantage the U.S. cars suffer in the Japanese market. Remember again, however, that there might well be some individuals within the market with different ratings for the cars than the average ones employed here—and that also there might be omitted attributes which affect the attractiveness of the U.S. cars particularly strongly (one example would be "Status"). Also, the relatively large differences between the actual prices in Table 38.1 and the perceived prices (used here) would lead one to suspect that the actual size of required discount could vary a great deal among individuals.

Summary Discussion

Competitive (Dis)Advantages

The framework of international product positioning presented in this paper bears a direct relationship to the identification of the firm-specific and country-specific advantages of the firm as discussed in the theory of the multinational enterprise. Quite generally, the position differences in the perceptual maps represent firm-specific advantages (FSAs) as perceived by the consumers in the market place. The differences can be related directly to the required price premiums or discounts necessary to make two alternative products of equal value to the buyer. This price differential will be reflected in actual prices, especially when the market is reasonably efficient so that competing alternatives are well known to the buyers.

Whether the individual firm will be able to provide the requisite price discounts over an extended period of time hinges directly on its cost situation and the possibly negative effects a low price might have on the brand image. Where the FSAs are lodged in factors which generate low cost per unit, a less desirable product from a positioning viewpoint might still be on the efficient frontier because of its lower price. The product is a best seller simply because of superior cost figures enabling the price to be kept low (a "low-cost" strategy). Alternatively, the particular attribute mix provided through a given offering might be such as to place the alternative on the efficient frontier of at least some segment (a "niche" in the market).

The misperceptions evidenced in these perceptual maps are generally due to image factors such as brand name and country-of-origin stereotypes and are thus examples of both firm-specific and country-specific advantages. This means that country stereotyping can at times represent quite a considerable price disadvantage in a market. Because of this, the multinational marketer might well consider the possibility of shifting production in such a fashion as to exploit the existence of country-specific advantages. The current vogue of establishing joint-ventures with the Japanese automakers can be viewed as one such attempt, where a positive country-of-origin association is substituted for a negative one.

Since country stereotypes can change considerably over time (*vide* the Japanese example), such "tricks" can be expected to work only in the short run. In the long run, the international marketer needs to offer a product which exhibits sufficiently strong FSAs to place it on the efficient frontier of at least some segment of the market. The viable options are those where either the product attributes are superior and present an opportunity for a premium price, or where the firm has a low-cost advantage and can push its product onto the efficient frontier by way of a lower price. The low price option suffers from the threat of low-cost producers starting elsewhere (the product life cycle argument), and also from the difficulty of maintaining a desirable positioning with high customer loyalty. For many companies the option of developing a superior product priced so as to be one of the efficient choices and targeted so as to become the preferred choice among at least a niche in the market will be the most viable alternative in the longer term. It is in this strategic decision process that the international positioning framework presented will be most useful.

When applying the international positioning framework it becomes important not only to identify the products in the evoked set and the preferences, but also what purchases are feasible under the customer's budget constraints.

Appendix: Data Collection

The illustration of the proposed method draws on a comparative study of American and Japanese respondents' evaluation of automobiles.

Cars were a natural choice since in both countries there is a large number of foreign makes available, and although specifications differ from country to country, many of the makes are quite similar in different countries.

The sampling was guided by the fact that students at several Japanese universities could be accessed. To ensure comparability this sampling frame was matched with a corresponding group in the U.S. The number of respondents on the U.S. side amounted to 70 graduate students at a West Coast university. The Japanese sample comprised a total of 82 usable returns, from 6 different universities in Japan (around Tokyo and Kobe). These students were both graduate and undergraduate, and belonged in the majority of cases to the motor clubs so common at Japanese universities. This strategem proved necessary to eliminate the relatively large number of students without driver's licences. (For further information concerning sample characteristics the reader is referred to Johansson, Douglas and Nonaka 1985.)

The ten car models and twelve attributes selected (after two pilot-studies) were the following (Japanese names in parenthesis where different):

CAR MODELS	ATTRIBUTES
Honda Accord	
Datsun 200SX (Nissan	
Sylvia)	Handling
Mazda 626 (Mazda	
Capella)	Horsepower
Toyota Celica	Acceleration
	Gas Mileage
	Safety
Ford Mustang	Driving Comfort
Chevrolet Citation	Passenger Comfort
Plymouth K-Car	Reliability
	Durability
VW Rabbit (VW Golf)	Workmanship
Audi 4000 (Audi 80)	Styling
BMW 320i (BMW 318i)	Color Selection

The "true" attribute values were collected from secondary sources (car magazines and Consumer Reports) and supplemented by base price figures collected from each country.

The layout of the questionnaire followed the standard multi-attribute format, with questions of belief ratings for the ten cars on each attribute followed by a rating of the importance of the attributes. The overall ratings then followed, after which familiarity with each model was assessed. The questionnaire ended with a few questions concerning background variables.

References

Bilkey, W. J. and E. Nes, "Country-of-Origin Effects on Product Evaluations," *Journal of International Business Studies*, Vol. 1 (Spring/Summer 1982), pp. 89–99.

Johansson, J. K., S. P. Douglas and I. Nonaka, "Assessing the Impact of Country-of-Origin on Product Evaluations: A New Methodological Perspective," *Journal of Marketing Research*, XXII (November 1985).

Maynes, E. Scott, *Decisionmaking for Consumers: An Introduction to Consumer Economics*, (New York: Macmillan, 1976).

Nag, Amal, "Chrysler Tests Consumer Reaction to Mexican-Made Cars Sold in U.S.," *Wall Street Journal*, July 23, 1984, Section 2.

Nagashima, A., "A Comparison of Japanese and U.S. Attitudes Toward Foreign Products," *Journal of Marketing*, Vol. 34 (January 1970), pp. 68–74.

39

Distributors — Finding and Keeping the Good Ones*

GUNNAR BEETH

This article is mainly concerned with distributors (including agents) of industrial equipment. Thus, not all of the conclusions are applicable to distributors in other fields. Generally, we have in mind "sole" distributors, that is, an exclusive distributor for each country.

The Importance of Having the Right Distributor

Most international companies looking at the actual range of performance of their foreign distributors find that it does not fall within, say, 80 to 120% of what they would expect from carefully determined market potential figures. Instead, performance varies from zero to over 200% of the expected, and the difference in performance between distributors is enormous. Finding excellent distributors is therefore all-important.

But even with your best efforts, you will never have a group of only excellent distributors. With careful and hard work, you can have a few excellent, many medium, and some mediocre distributors . . . and a few worthless ones whom you are always trying to replace. There is no way to hit 100%.

We many take as a rule of thumb, that in most countries with only *small* markets, there are in each field: zero or one excellent distributors, zero or one medium distributors, one or two mediocre distributors, and the remaining distributors are worthless to you.

* Adapted, by permission of the publisher, from *International Management Practice: An Insiders View*, Gunnar Beeth, copyright 1973 by AMACOM, a division of American Management Associations. All rights reserved.

In most countries with *bigger* markets, yet no markets so big that they warrant a subsidiary, there often are in an industrial equipment field: one or two excellent distributors, two or three medium distributors, several mediocre distributors, and the remaining distributors are worthless.

Finding the Good Ones

Lists of distributors broken down by fields of activity are available for each country from the U.S. Department of Commerce (good), from local chambers of commerce (usually not good), from local classified directories of various kinds (often too all-inclusive), and from other sources. But you don't want a list, you want the name of one distributor—the best one.

One or two firms may have contacted you, but the probability that they are the best is small. Don't waste your time contacting them all by mail and sending them forms to complete. Instead, follow these three steps toward finding a good distributor:

1. Go personally to the country, allowing ample time. Talk to the ultimate users of the equipment to find out from which distributors they prefer to buy and why. Two or three names will keep popping up in the replies you get.
2. Then go to those two or three distributors and see which one or ones you would be able to sign up.
3. But, before making the final choice, look for the distributor who has the key man for your line—as explained below.

Long ago, we used to travel around with a list on which we rated each distributor on a scale one to ten in each of twenty-four different activities and abilities. Then we weighed these different matters in accordance with the importance of each one and arrived arithmetically at a single over-all rating for each distributor. This was done by taking into account his sales force, his coverage of the market, management ability, service personnel's capability, financial strength, connections, warehouse and service facilities, spare parts stocks, performance in related lines, technical ability to understand the equipment, and several other items.

Unfortunately, the final rating figure for the distributors we were supervising showed no correlation at all to their actual performance.

Then we threw away the list and looked for what was common to the few excellent distributors with which we had the privilege to be working. In this way, we discovered a single new factor which replaced the 24-point list and this new factor bore considerable correlation to success. We started to look for a distributor who had one capable man who would take the new line of equipment to his heart and make it his personal objective to make the sale of that line a success in his country. In some small distributorships, this key man was the owner. In others, he was the sales manager or a salesman. In one company, he was the service manager. In one case, there were two such men instead of one, but that was a rare distributor who somehow did three times what we considered to be the possible volume for his country.

In actual fact, it is not as easy to find a good distributor in some countries, especially in very small, less industrialized nations where you might find that there are: zero excellent distributors; zero medium distributors; one or two mediocre distributors firmly tied to your competitors, and the remaining distributors are worthless to you.

Suppose none of them shows any sign of having or getting the key man you are looking for. What do you do?

First, you can try to find a local businessman in a different field—one who wants to fill the obvious need for a good distributor in your field. If that doesn't work, you can try to get one of the mediocre distributors to switch from the competitor to you. Occasionally you might get to him just when he has become angry at your competitor for some reason or another.

But failing that, you had better forget about appointing any distributor at all in that country—because having a worthless one will cost you time and money every year and possibly prevent a good newcomer in that country from asking for your line.

If everything else has failed, you may want to consider attending a local industrial exhibition in that country to ask further advice from the local prospective end users of your products. If there should be a nearby U.S. trade center, it can help you mount a small exhibition of your products for the specific purpose of finding a distributor.

When you interview distributors, what they tell you is often revealing about them in ways they do not realize. Here is an example. We used to sell compressors and call on distributors in the heavy construction field. For some of them, their prime line was Caterpillar tractors, and for others International Harvester tractors. When asked how their business was, some would answer "great" while others would say that it was impossible to compete against International Harvester or Caterpillar—whichever line they did not have.

Those who said it was impossible to compete raised one warning signal. Is this distributor going downhill? What has happened to him? Why can he not compete?

But those who said that the tractor business was great raised another equally important warning signal. Do they concentrate all of their efforts on their tractor line? Are they great in selling tractors and poor in selling everything else? Signing on distributors who are excellent for another manufacturer in an allied field does not always produce excellent results.

Keeping the Good Ones

The only way to keep a good distributor is to work closely and well with him, so that he can make money with your line.

View your business from the distributor's side. First of all, he must make money for himself. If that automatically makes him earn money for you, too, then fine. But if he does not make money with it for himself, any good distributor will quickly drop your line.

Even worse, he may put your line away and make it available only if one of his customers insists on getting some of your equipment—but otherwise do nothing for your line.

Thus, you must not only keep the good distributor but also keep the distributor good. And the last part is not always easy because there are many demands on his time from other lines of equipment and from customers with interests and problems outside your field. Somehow, you must arrange through direct mail and visits to keep your line constantly in front of your distributor and among his daily duties and thoughts.

It is best, of course, if you can require that he have one or more full-time persons handling your line. But if the potential sales volume is not high enough to warrant this effort, do not ask for it. If you cause the distributor losses through excessive demands on him, it will backfire on you.

Above all, you must not be stingy in matters such as paying for the training of his men and going beyond your legal warranty obligations to your distributor. He goes beyond his legal warranty toward his customers, and he expects the same from you.

It is important that the rules be spelled out in advance concerning payment of commissions to the distributor or agent. Especially the conditions relating to nonpayment of commissions must be clear. Nevertheless, when an unclear borderline case comes up, you should always rule in favor of your distributor. In the long run, the distributor's goodwill toward your company is more valuable than the commissions paid in borderline cases. The quickest way to destroy a distributor's goodwill is to make him feel cheated—even on a small matter.

Unless your sales volume with each distributor is very large, you cannot afford to run his business or remake a mediocre distributor into a good one.

One American company has an outstanding record of going against the above rule: Caterpillar. They will work so effectively with a distributor that they can make him good in many cases; but for most other companies, this method is too costly.

Instead, if a good distributor changes into a mediocre or bad one, the sooner you can replace him with an excellent alternative, the better. Of course, whether or not the new one will be excellent, you never know in advance. If the new distributor also turns out to be mediocre or worse, then you had better switch again as soon as you have found a third seemingly excellent prospect.

Some people argue that this switching shows a lack of stability and seriousness toward the ultimate users. Don't worry; the ultimate users are probably better aware of the shortcomings of your former distributor than you are. They appreciate your trying to find a good one and your sales figures show it quickly when you succeed. Any good list of distributors is in constant change because the distributors themselves quickly change. It might be that the key man for your line has left his distributor-employer, and your sales drop forthwith to 10% of what they previously were in that country. Unless you can get the distributor to replace the departed man with another excellent key man, or switch responsibility for your line to another one of his best men, don't keep that distributor—just hoping that things will improve.

Getting Rid of the Mediocre Distributors

When you do change, do it totally, quickly, cleanly, and thoroughly, without worrying about being called ruthless by your old distributor. He will always feel that your cancellation is an affront to him personally, anyway. He will say that you are not loyal. Forget it. An active, aggressive, changing distributor list produces more sales. In addition, your aggressive policies tend to keep the medium distributors on their toes and doing their best.

The lengthy distributor contract has only one important clause: the cancellation clause. The remainder is mainly a listing of who does what, written in legalese. In most light industrial equipment businesses, it should be possible for either party to cancel any time after the first year, upon sixty days' notice to the other party.

What happens to the distributor's stock in case of cancellation by the manufacturer should be spelled out. It will vary considerably from country to country because of local laws, but in no case should the manufacturer be required to take back any obsolete or otherwise unsaleable inventory. If the manufacturer must agree to take back any other inventory, it should be at the net f.o.b., factory price, less a hefty restocking charge, unless local laws force him to do otherwise.

Prior to signing a distributorship contract, the cancellation clause should be checked by a local lawyer to minimize any local indemnification requirements to distributors upon cancellation.

Of course, some distributors may object to a strong cancellation clause, but it is well worth fighting for despite the natural hope that you will never need to use it.

In some countries, the indemnification to distributors upon cancellation depends on just how the business is conducted. In France, if the distributor has certain obligations to report names and addresses of purchasers to you, the indemnification risk increases to compensate the distributor for the market information. In Germany, there is no indemnification to a true distributor, "Eigenhandler," but there is to a commission agent if he has certain reporting obligations.

Since the laws governing a distributor contract vary widely from country to country, their impact on cancellation of distributor contracts must be taken into account when choosing the country from which you want to service and supervise distributors. In an area such as Europe, you may prefer a country with favorable laws which you can invoke for governing the distributorship contracts.

To illustrate the opposite situation, assume that an American subsidiary to France supervises and supplies a distributor for Italy. In this case, the contract must be written so that either French or Italian law applies. Neither is particularly favorable, but Italian law is somewhat better than French law in case the distributor contract has to be cancelled.

But if the same Italian distributor had been supplied from an American subsidiary in Denmark, the contractor should get Danish law to apply, instead, in order to lower the risk of indemnification upon cancellation.

The cancellation of a distributor or licensee agreement can be a somewhat delicate transaction, and it must be handled carefully. If the distributor who is dropped is no good, then the remaining distributors in neighboring countries will understand and support the cancellation. But if the matter is not clear cut (e.g., for some business reason it should become necessary to drop a medium distributor), then the action must be thoroughly explained to the remaining distributors, customers, and others. An excellent distributor is never dropped. Any cancellation must, of course, always be thoroughly prepared under the applicable law.

Contrary to what distributors seem to feel, there is nothing morally wrong in terminating a distributorship which doesn't work out. And in the long run the true interest of a poor distributor will not be served by his representing your business anyway. Typically, the only economical way to improve upon an ineffective independent distributor is to change over to an effective one. Had it been your subsidiary instead, you could have eliminated the specific cause for the "distributor's" ineffectiveness. Unfortunately, this is usually too difficult to do in an independent company.

40

Black & Decker's Turnaround Strategy*

BUSINESS INTERNATIONAL

Black & Decker's name is as old as the power tool industry. Beginning in 1917, when it got a patent on the world's first portable power drill with pistol grip and trigger switch, Black & Decker virtually invented the industry. Its name soon became synonymous with everything associated with power tools. In Britain, for example, do-it-yourself remodelers are said to be "Black & Deckering" their homes. In France, someone who is "plugged in" to the social scene is said to be "très Black et Decker". In the U.S. an overly serious college student, formerly a "grind" or a "tool", is now known as a "Black & Decker". In early 1980s, in spite of its strong name recognition, this U.S. multinational manufacturer of power tools suffered from sales decline and lost market shares to Makita of Japan, Bosch of West Germany, and its domestic competitor, Emerson Electric's Skil. In 1985, the company had to write off $215 million for restructuring.

However, Black & Decker has achieved a strong comeback. Since 1986, the company's sales and earnings have been climbing steadily. In 1988, the company reported a 75% increase in annual earnings on sales of $2.3 billion. Its power tool business is now the fastest-growing in the industry—up about 20% in the U.S., vs. overall market growth of around 9% a year.

Black & Decker's turnaround can be attributed to the global strategies it has employed over the last few years. These strategies include:

- Global product rationalization.
- Aggressive acquisition and partnership.
- Brand name transfer.

---

* Adapted by Tiger Li from "How Black & Decker forged a Winning Brand Transfer Strategy," *Business International*, July 20, 1987, pp. 225–227, with permission.

495

Global Product Rationalization

Before 1985, Black & Decker's corporate structure remained a confederation of nearly sovereign fieldoms. Each subsidiary made decisions solely based on its own interest. British managers developed and sold their own products in Britain, as did their French and German counterparts, without any regard of global strategy. As a result, the company's product lines were highly fragmented and few of its products were standardized. Taking motors—the most expensive component of power tools—as an example, the company had to produce 100 different motors worldwide. Consequently, Black & Decker had to bear tremendous overhead cost and could not enjoy any efficiency from economies of scale.

Starting from 1986, Black & Decker abolished the geographical fieldoms and called for developing products that could be sold the world over. Soon, its fragmented manufacturing, research and development were unified by a coherent global business plan. The product standardization greatly reduced the cost of production and allowed the company to compete more efficiently in the world market. Today, Black & Decker makes fewer than 20 types of motors and is aiming for five.

Confronting Competitors by Acquisition and Partnership

One of the reasons that Black & Decker was beaten by its competitors in the past is that it had always acted defensively. Learning from its past lessons, the company adopted a new strategy—entering competitor's turf to compete. First, Black & Decker established a partnership with Shin Daiwa Kogyo Co., a strong outdoor products and tool company, to distribute its products in the Japanese domestic market dominated by Hitachi and Makita. To challenge Makita's vastly superior reputation in fine woodworking tools as well as to enhance its presence in Europe, Black & Decker acquired Elu Machines, a Swedish company producing comparable products.

In the U.S., Black & Decker purchased General Electric's small-appliance division to consolidate its presence in the household appliance market.

Apart from equity acquisition, Black & Decker also endeavored to acquire the best possible talent, including those from its competition. Mr. Archibald, CEO of Black & Decker, spent weeks persuading George Sherman, to defect from his job as head of Emerson Electric's Skil division to direct Black & Decker's power tool business. Two years after he joined Black & Decker, Sherman introduced 60 new or redesigned products, most of them in the industry's fastest-growing segment, cordless tools.

Winning Brand Transfer

After acquiring General Electric's small-appliance division, Black & Decker developed a successful strategy for the largest renaming of a consumer brand in history.

Under the terms of the acquisition agreement, B&D had three years to eliminate the GE name from the product line. Replacing the GE name and establishing brand recognition for B&D without losing market share involved several problems. First, GE was an established leader in the fiercely competitive market for home appliances, both in the U.S. and abroad, whereas B&D was still a relative newcomer. Second, GE would maintain a strong presence in the markets contiguous to housewares, such as microwave ovens and audio products.

With these risks in mind, B&D developed a marketing strategy for a transition that spotlighted the B&D name to communicate the quality, technological edge and service standards of the products. Emphasis was placed on dramatic and extensive television advertising and trade promotions to deliver the message as quickly and directly as possible. The key elements of the strategy included:

A new name and logo. Changing the company's name and logo proved an effective way to announce B&D's new line to consumers and the trade. Management dropped the word "manufacturing" from the company's title to match the broadened scope of B&D's operations. A new logo, which retained the shape and color of the traditional B&D orange hexagon, was used for all B&D products. This new image was introduced with heavy promotion of "flagship" products from the power tool and houseware lines, as well as appliances bearing the B&D name for the first time.

Securing distributor support. To ensure that distributors would continue to carry both the B&D and GE lines while the transition was under-way, B&D developed a trade promotion campaign called "Basics Plus". Under this program, if a retailer maintained or increased inventory of B&D products, the company would run free television spots using the retailer's name. While some industry observers were predicting massive losses, retailers increased their stock of B&D products by 6%. Basics Plus also provided a vehicle to strengthen the B&D association with the housewares category through a media linkage with leading retailers.

Phasing in the transition. During the first two years of the transition, references to the GE brand were downplayed. In addition, rather than convert the entire GE line simultaneously, B&D started with high-end GE products that had a strong competitive advantage in the market and were loosely identified with GE name. Next, a set of high-quality household products developed by B&D was introduced. Again, aggressive advertising and public relations supported the effort. B&D even launched a trade magazine for retailers to showcase its wares.

However, once the B&D name could successfully stand alone in the market, the company sought a more direct transfer of the equity in the GE name to B&D. This was done via commercials that relayed the transition from GE to B&D, product innovation and broad selection.

During the first year of the program, brand recognition increased dramatically, from 15% to 57%. The success of the U.S. program made it a model for the same transition in other regional markets. B&D subsidiaries in Canada, Latin America and Australia took the U.S. strategy and tailored it to their own markets. In all countries, B&D was careful to make sure that it recognized the distinct nature of its markets. This meant modifying the program to reflect different consumer tastes and channels of distribution. The degree of recognition for the B&D name was another important factor shaping local strategies: In Mexico, the GE name was not as strong as B&D. This facilitated a quicker and easier brand transfer. But in Brazil, the reverse was true and a different approach was required. B&D's subsidiary in Brazil tended to delay the transition and use more advertising.

41

3M's Global Marketing Plan: How a New Package Helped its Worldwide Reorganization*

BUSINESS INTERNATIONAL

A global marketing strategy can be vital to a firm's ability to meet international competition. But getting such a strategy off the ground is difficult, if not impossible, without a global brand image and an organizational approach that allows worldwide marketing coordination. Below, *Business International* looks at the successful method used by 3M and how it has stood the test of time.

In the early 1980s, 3M's magnetic audio/video products division faced significant market share erosion in all major markets. The traditional leader in North America and Europe, 3M had slipped considerably and in Japan was lagging local competitors by a large margin. According to George Burr, the division's marketing operations manager, 3M management was surprised at "the number of countries that had major companies moving into what 3M considered its highly profitable, safe markets." When senior management looked closely at the markets for magnetic tape products on a global basis, it found there were similar features in all 3M markets, and thus realized that its segmented approach was inefficient. That realization, plus accelerating worldwide market penetration by major competitors, led management to make a commitment to the division to develop a global marketing strategy.

What's in the Package?

As the centerpiece of the new marketing program, in 1985 3M introduced a new global brand identity and packaging for the entire line of

---

* Reprinted from *Business International*, Vol. 34, No. 28 (July 13, 1987), with permission.

Scotch TM magnetic media products. Assisted by Landor Associates, a leading strategic design consultancy based in San Francisco, extensive predesign market research was conducted in five countries representing the company's key markets, the U.S., the U.K., France, Germany and Japan, and included the following:

- A retail audit to determine where 3M products were being sold and how they were being merchandised;
- A visual audit to evaluate competitors' packaging and marketing support materials; and
- An analysis of consumer preferences, which confirmed that trends in the marketplace were consistent across national boundaries, reinforcing the importance of developing a distinctive and consistent image for 3M products on a global basis.

The research also yielded some significant competitive intelligence. It showed that there was a proliferation of brands with homogenous packaging, which contributed to consumers' inability to distinguish one product from another and fostered stiff price competition. In addition, an impending shakeout in the marketplace for video cassettes was about to intensify the battle for market share. However, on the positive side, the research revealed that consumers strongly identified the Scotch TM brand name with quality.

Based on this assessment, Landor developed a package that was radically different from that of any competitors; it was designed primarily to communicate the Scotch TM brand quality to a variety of markets. (The new identity is highlighted by a multicolored spectrum sphere below a bold print of the Scotch TM brand name.) It was also fashioned so that it could be used for all the division's products (the firm's first uniform package) and in all markets (packaging had differed from country to country).

To communicate the design change to consumers, 3M launched a major global advertising campaign featuring the multicolored sphere. Both television and print advertisements heavily emphasized the logo, which made it easier to adapt the commercial to different country markets. Burr notes that in the U.K., 3M had already launched a successful television campaign; the new package design and accompanying visual elements were easily integrated into the existing commercial. Foreign language versions of the commercial were produced in Japanese, German, Spanish and Italian, and theme music was tailored to reflect national taste. The visual impact and global transferability of the packaging were equally evident at trade shows where similar displays and selling brochures could be used with minor changes in all countries.

Organizational Keys

According to Burr, "The Landor project was the leading edge of the whole effort to develop a global marketing program, with the parameters spelled out and agreed to by marketing executives and senior management worldwide." There were at least three critical steps following the research and image development: setting up the mechanisms to improve communication between the parent and foreign subsidiaries, selling the idea of a global strategy to local management (no easy task at the launch phase) and coordinating future marketing strategy.

Prior to the initiation of the global strategy, marketing personnel in foreign subsidiaries communicated only sporadically with the U.S. parent but were obliged to follow a U.S. directive in planning for local markets. Today, market forecasting, capacity planning, updates on competitors and other significant market information are routinely shared, and biannual meetings are held in the U.S. While all marketing personnel worldwide continue to report vertically to local management, a U.S. global marketing director coordinates the dialogue with foreign subs with the support of three international marketing executives.

3M has also developed a capacity planning model to forecast relevant market determinants such as household hardware penetration, consumption rates and price. Each subsidiary contributes its input to the model. Burr notes, however, that "there have been a lot of growing pains" in the collection and processing of the data, as well as in trying to agree on realistic goals for each market.

What the Program Achieved

Over the past five years, the impact of the global marketing initiative has been impressive. In terms of market share and distribution, Burr says 3M has reached its goals in all three major markets. In Europe and North America, 3M says it has recovered the lead in the market. In Japan, the gain in market share has been especially dramatic: 3M has moved from the number-five slot to third place. In addition to boosting volume and market share, the program has helped to reduce the cost of marketing through the use of a unified packaging system.

Global marketing has also made a marked difference in accelerating product launch on a global scale. The latest addition to the 3M line, a high-grade Super VHS videotape (codeveloped with the Japanese electronics firm JCV) was introduced in Japan in April, in the U.S. this past month and will appear in Europe early next year. "Within six months," says Burr, "you have a leading-edge media form that is getting press everywhere. Previously, it would not have been possible for the product to get that much recognition so quickly." More important, the product was developed on the premise that "3M would *have* to have it as a lead item in Japan and other key markets."

42

Unraveling the Mystique of Export Pricing*

S. TAMER CAVUSGIL

In recent years, hundreds of U.S. companies have become involved in international business. The initial foreign activity is typically exporting. Perhaps the most puzzling part of international business for these firms is making pricing decisions.

What role should pricing play in the exporting company's marketing efforts? Can pricing be used as an effective marketing tool? Or would that practice expose the firm to unnecessary risks? What considerations affect the choice between incremental and full-cost pricing strategies? What approach should management take when setting export prices? How can the firm cope with escalations in international prices? What strategies are appropriate when a strong currency impairs overseas competitiveness? These are only a few of the many questions international marketing managers must answer.

Export pricing is a complex issue, and simple decision rules are often inadequate. The complexity lies in the large number of variables that affect international pricing decisions and the uncertainty surrounding them. These variables can be classified as either internal or external to the organization. The internal group includes corporate goals, desire for control over prices, approach to costing, and degree of company internationalization. The external group includes competitive pressures, demand levels, legal and government regulations, general economic conditions, and exchange rates.

Despite export pricing's importance and complexity, very little empirical research has been conducted that might give managers norms to follow (Terpstra 1983). This article attempts to illuminate

---

* Reprinted from *Business Horizons*, Vol. 31, No. 3 (May—June 1988), pp. 54–63, with permission.

this important area of international marketing management. The overall purpose is to provide a better understanding of export pricing issues and to identify propositions that can be tested by more definitive, large-scale surveys, as well as to generate findings and implications useful to export managers.

Personal interviews, two to three hours in length, were conducted with one or more executives at each of 24 firms. Most of the firms studied were exporters of industrial or specialized products. The typical firm employed about 500 persons. Background information about each firm was collected with the use of a structured questionnaire either prior to or during the interview. All firms were located in the Midwestern United States.

Pricing Literature

Price is the only marketing variable that generates revenue. Top marketing executives call pricing the most critical pressure point of the 1980s (*Marketing News*, 1983). Recently, with accelerating technological advances, shorter product life cycles, and increasing input costs, price changes have become more common. Despite these developments, academic research on pricing has been modest at best (Rao 1984).

The neglect of international pricing is even more serious (Baker and Ryans 1973). Intracorporate (transfer) pricing issues received attention during the 1970s, when study of multinational corporations (MNCs) was intense, but other pricing topics remain relatively unexplored (Arpan 1973).

Other studies have focused on pricing practices under floating exchange rates (Clague and Grossfield 1974), location of pricing authority within MNCs (Baker and Ryans 1973), price leadership of MNCs (Lecraw 1984), multinational pricing in developing countries (Leff 1975), and uniform pricing (Kressler 1971). Several studies have had a regional/industry focus. One found a relatively high degree of export price discrimination among industrial firms in Northern England (Piercy 1981). Another compared the pricing practices of chemical and construction industries in South Africa (Abratt and Pitt). A third, on the other hand, studied price-setting processes among industrial firms in the French market (Farley *et al.*, 1980).

The discussion here focuses on three major issues. First, those factors which have a bearing on export pricing are examined, and each factor's relevance is illustrated with company examples. The next section reveals that companies appear to follow one of three export pricing strategies. Finally, a decision framework for export pricing is offered.

Factors in Export Pricing

Export pricing is not a topic that lends itself easily to generalization. As with domestic pricing, any consideration of policies for setting export prices must first address the unique nature of the individual firm. Company philosophy, corporate culture, product offerings, and operating environment all have a significant impact on the creation of pricing policy. In addition, export marketers face unique constraints in each market destination.

The interaction of the internal and external environments gives rise to distinct—yet predictable—pricing constraints in different markets. These to a large extent determine export price strategy. For example, negotiation is normally required in the Middle East, so Regal Ware, a producer of kitchen appliances and cookware, uses a higher list price in such markets to leave a margin for discretion. But D. W. Witter, a manufacturer of grain storage and handling equipment, doesn't make price concessions in the Middle East. Witter is convinced that once a price becomes negotiable, the Middle Eastern buyer will expect and demand future concessions, making future negotiations interminable.

In Algeria, the interest rate is limited by the government. To counter this one company, a manufacturer of mining and construction equipment, builds the additional cost of capital into the price.

Six variables have important influences on export pricing. They are:

1. Nature of the product/industry;
2. Location of the production facility;
3. Chosen system of distribution;
4. Location and environment of the foreign market;
5. U.S. government regulations; and
6. Attitude of the firm's management.

A brief discussion of each factor is presented below.

Nature of the Product/Industry

A specialized product, or one with a technological edge, gives the firm flexibility. There are few competitors in such cases. In many markets there is no local production of the product, government-imposed import barriers are minimal, and importing firms all face similar price-escalation factors. Under such circumstances, firms are able to remain competitive with little adjustment in price strategy. Firms with a technological edge, such as the Burdick Corporation (hospital equipment) and Nicolet Instruments (scientific instruments), enjoy similar advantages, but both experience greater service requirements and longer production and sales lead times.

A relatively low level of price competition usually leads to administered prices and a static role for pricing in the export marketing mix. Over the years, however, as price competition evolves and technological advantages shrink, specialized and highly technical firms must make more market-based exceptions to their uniform export pricing strategies.

Many firms' export pricing strategies are also influenced by industry-specific factors, such as dramatic fluctuations in the price of raw materials and predatory pricing practices by foreign competitors (most notably the Japanese). The presence of such factors demands greater flexibility in export pricing at some companies: Ray-O-Vac adjusts export prices frequently according to current silver prices. Other companies negotiate fixed-price agreements with suppliers prior to making a contract bid.

Location of Production Facility

Many U.S. companies produce exported products only in the United States. These U.S. exporters are unable to shift manufacturing to locations that make economic sense. Purely domestic companies are tied to conditions prevailing in the home market, in this case the U.S.

Those companies with production or assembly facilities abroad, often closer to foreign customers, have additional flexibility in overseas markets. These companies find it easier to respond to fluctuations in foreign exchange. Cummins Engine, for example, supplies Latin American customers with U.S. production when the U.S. dollar is weak. When the dollar is relatively strong, U.K. plants assume greater importance.

A number of factors may have impeded the global competitiveness of U.S. manufacturers in recent years. These include lagging productivity in many sectors of the economy and, until recently, reluctance to seek global sources of supply for materials, parts, and components. Also, strong unions and a high standard of living in the U.S. have contributed to higher labor costs. Naturally, these comparative disadvantages are reflected in the quotations submitted to overseas buyers.

Chosen System of Distribution

The channels of export distribution a company uses dictate much in export pricing. For example, subsidiary relationships offer greater control over final prices, first-hand knowledge of market conditions, and the ability to adjust prices rapidly. With independent distributors, control usually extends only to the landed price received by the exporter. As one might expect, many of the executives interviewed spoke of the difficulty of maintaining price levels. These firms report that distributors may mark up prices substantially—up to 200% in some cases.

When a firm initiates exporting through independent distributors, many new pricing considerations arise. Significant administrative costs stem from the selection of foreign distributors and the maintenance of harmonious relationships. Discount policies for intermediaries must be established. Also, the costs of exporting (promotion, freight service, and so forth) must be assigned to either the intermediaries or the manufacturer. To minimize the administrative, research, and travel expenses involved in switching to direct exporting, most firms use a relatively uniform export pricing strategy across different markets. Gross margins are then increased to account for additional levels of distribution. In other cases, companies establish prices on a case-by-case basis.

The use of manufacturers' representatives offers greater price control to the exporter, but this method is used less frequently. Finally, sales to end users may involve negotiation or, in the case of selling to governmental agencies, protracted purchasing decisions. List prices are not used in these circumstances.

Firms often attempt to establish more direct channels of distribution to reach their customers in overseas markets. By reducing the number of intermediaries between the manufacturer and the customer, they offset the adverse affects of *international price escalation*. Excessive escalation of prices is a problem encountered by most exporters. Aside from shorter distribution channels, the firms studied had developed other strategies to cope with price escalation. These alternatives are listed in Figure 42.1.

Location and Environment of the Foreign Market

The climatic conditions of a market may necessitate product modification. For example, a producer of soft-drink equipment must treat its products against rust corrosion in tropical markets. Another company, an agri-business concern, must take into account climate, soil conditions, and the country's infrastructure before making any bid. Economic factors, such as inflation, exchange-rate fluctuations, and price controls, may hinder market entry and effectiveness (Frank 1984). These factors, especially the value of U.S. currency in foreign markets, are a major concern to most of the firms interviewed. Consequently, several companies have introduced temporary compensating adjustments as part of their pricing strategies. The unusually

● Shortening channels of distribution by reducing number of intermediaries or engaging in company-sponsored distribution. Fewer intermediaries would also have the effect of minimizing value added taxes.

● Reducing cost to overseas customers by eliminating costly features from the product, lowering overall product quality, or offering a stripped-down model.

● Shipping and assembling components in foreign markets. Popularity of the Free Trade Zones in Hong Kong, Panama or the Caribbean Basin is due to companies' desire to minimize price escalation.

● Modifying the product to bring it into a different, lower-tariff classification. The Microbattery division of Ray-O-Vac Corporation, for example, ships bulk to foreign marketing companies who then repackage. Another company, through consultations with local distributors, places products in "proper" import classifications. Proper wording is used for initial import registration to qualify for lower duties.

● Lowering the new price (landed price) to reduce tariffs and other charges by the importing country. This can be accomplished through the application of marginal cost pricing or by allowing discounts to distributors. Nicolet Instruments, a producer of scientific instruments, for example, compensates its distributors for the cost of installation and service. Western Publishing Company compensates it distributors for the differences in import duties between book and nonbook exports.

● Going into overseas production and sourcing in order to remain competitive in the foreign markets. Dairy Equipment Company located in Wisconsin, for example, supplies the European market with bulk coolers made at its Danish plant as a way of reducing freight costs.

FIG. 42.1. Strategic Options to Deal with Price Escalation.

strong value of the U.S. dollar during the first half of the 1980s was a significant factor in pricing strategy.

Since currency fluctuations are cyclical, exporters who find themselves blessed with a price advantage when their currency is undervalued must carry an extra burden when their currency is overvalued. Committed exporters must be creative, pursuing different strategies during different periods. Appropriate strategies practiced by the firms studied are outlined in Figure 42.2.

It must be noted that, while exporters can implement some of these strategies quickly, others require a long-term response. For example, the decision to manufacture overseas is often a part of a deliberate and long-term plan for most companies. And while some strategies can be used by any exporter, others, such as countertrade and speculative currency trading, are limited to use by the larger, more experienced exporters. In fact, most managers interviewed said that high-risk propositions such as countertrade deals should be used only by multinational companies.

The cultural environment and business practices of the foreign market also play a large role in export pricing. Some countries abhor negotiation, others expect it. As previously noted, D. W. Witter has successfully overcome the expectation of price negotiation in the

When domestic currency is WEAK . . .	When domestic currency is STRONG . . .
● Stress price benefits	● Engage in nonprice competition by improving quality, delivery and aftersale service
● Expand product line and add more costly features	● Improve productivity and engage in vigorous cost reduction
● Shift sourcing and manufacturing to domestic market	● Shift sourcing and manufacturing overseas
● Exploit export opportunities in all markets	● Give priority to exports to relatively strong-currency countries
● Conduct conventional cash-for-goods trade	● Deal in countertrade with weak-currency countries
● Use full-costing approach, but use marginal-cost pricing to penetrate new/competitive markets	● Trim profit margins and use marginal-cost pricing
● Speed repatriation of foreign-earned income and collections	● Keep the foreign-earned income in host country, slow collections
● Minimize expenditures in local, host country currency	● Maximize expenditures in local, host country currency
● Buy needed services (advertising, insurance, transportation etc.) in domestic market	● Buy needed services abroad and pay for them in local currencies
● Minimize local borrowing	● Borrow money needed for expansion in local market
● Bill foreign customers in domestic currency	● Bill foreign customers in their own currency

FIG. 42.2. Exporter Strategies under Varying Currency Conditions.

Middle East market. In some markets, a subtle barrier to foreign imports is erected in the form of procurement practices which favor domestic companies.

U.S. Government Regulations

Government policy also affects export pricing strategy. While the majority of the firms interviewed are not directly affected by U.S. pricing regulations, they feel that U.S. regulations such as the Foreign Corrupt Practices Act put them at a significant competitive disadvantage. One company often receives "requests" by overseas customers to add over $100,000 to the contract price and make appropriate arrangements to transfer the money to private accounts abroad. Interestingly, such requests are sometimes openly made. Submission to demands for "grease payments" appears to be the only option if businesses want to compete in certain countries.

Attitude of the Firm's Management

Many U.S. firms still view exporting as an extension of the domestic sales effort, and export pricing policy is established accordingly. Smaller companies whose top management concerns itself mostly with domestic matters have major problems setting export prices. Price determination of export sales is often based on a full-costing approach. The preference for cost-based pricing over market-oriented pricing reflects the relative importance given to profits and market share. This is particularly notable with firms that are unconcerned with market share and require that every quote meet their profit expectations. Other companies are more concerned with selling one product line at any price even below cost, and reap longer-term benefits from the sale of follow-up consumables and spare parts. Producers of expensive industrial equipment, scientific instruments, and medical equipment fall into this category.

Alternative Approaches to Pricing

Firms typically choose one of three approaches to pricing. These can be called the rigid cost-plus, flexible cost-plus, and dynamic incremental pricing strategies.

Rigid Cost-Plus Strategy

The complexity of export pricing has caused many managers to cling to a rigid cost-plus pricing strategy in an effort to secure profitability. This strategy establishes the foreign list price by adding international customer costs and a gross margin to domestic manufacturing costs. The final cost to the customer includes administrative and R&D overhead costs, transportation, insurance, packaging, marketing, documentation, and customs charges, as well as the profit margins for both the distributor and the manufacturer. Although this type of pricing ensures margins, the final price may be so high that it keeps the firm from being competitive in major foreign markets.

Nevertheless, cost-plus pricing appears to be the most dominant strategy among American firms. Approximately 70% of the sampled firms used this strategy. Over half of the firms using a cost-plus strategy adhered to it rigidly, with no exceptions. This approach may be typical of other exporting firms in the U.S. The following company examples illustrate the popularity of the rigid cost-plus pricing approach.

Autotrol is a Wisconsin manufacturer of water treatment and control equipment. The firm employs about 80 people, and exports account for about 60% of its estimated $14 million annual sales. Principal markets include Western Europe, Japan, Australia, New Zealand, and Venezuela. Autotrol sets export prices 3% to 4% higher than domestic prices to cover the additional costs. Such costs include foreign advertising, foreign travel, and all costs incurred when shipping the product from the factory to the foreign distributor. The firm has successfully exported for the past 15 years by using a rigid cost-plus strategy.

Chillicothe Metal Co. is a solely owned manufacturer of generator sets, pump packages, engine enclosures, controls, and spare parts. The firm has recently lost a significant portion of its foreign business. Sales dropped from $5 million in 1982 to $3 million in 1984, and the current employment of 40 is down from its 1982 high of 100. The company had successfully exported for more than 15 years, but current exports are down 40% from the 1982 level. Principal foreign markets are the Middle East, North Africa, and the Far East. The company adheres to a rigid cost-plus pricing strategy that includes a built-in margin ranging from 5% to 15%. However, the president has recently taken efforts to control costs, extend credit, and reduce margins for cash-in-advance customers in an attempt to counter the effects of the slow business cycle.

Dairy Equipment Co. produces milk machines, bulk coolers, and other high-quality equipment for the dairy industry. The company's annual sales are about $40 million, with current employment at 400. Although the company has exported continuously over the past decade, export earnings have become negligible. This has been caused by a significant drop in sales in the company's primary foreign market—West Germany. Gross profit has remained the company's primary export goal, but the rigid cost-plus pricing strategy has not yet proved to be effective. The company has always sought equal profitability from foreign sales, although fierce competition in some markets has forced it to consider lower profit margins. The company's export pricing policy remains a static element of the marketing mix.

These examples demonstrate that a rigid cost-plus pricing strategy may or may not be effective. They also imply that just because a strategy has been successful in the past, there is no guarantee that it will be successful in the future. Competitive pressures often force firms to reevaluate their pricing decisions and consider new alternatives.

Flexible Cost-Plus Strategy

One such alternative is a flexible cost-plus strategy. This is also the most logical strategy for companies that are in the process of moving away from their traditionally rigid pricing policies.

Flexible cost-plus price strategy is identical to the rigid strategy in establishing list prices. Flexible strategy, however, allows for price variations in special circumstances. For example, discounts may be granted, depending on the customer, the size of the order, or the intensity of competition. Although discounts occasionally are granted on a case-by-case basis, the primary objective of flexible cost-plus pricing is profit. Thus, pricing is still a static element of the marketing mix. The following cases are good examples of companies that use a flexible cost-plus pricing strategy.

Baughman, a division of Fuqua Industries, manufactures steel grain-storage silos and related equipment. The company currently employs about 125 people, and annual sales are around $6 million. The company has traditionally exported about 30% of its sales over the past 10 years, but recently exports have grown to over 50% of annual sales. Baughman's products are of high quality, and pricing has not often been an active element in the marketing mix. The firm's export sales terms consist of an irrevocable confirmed letter of credit in U.S. currency with no provisions for fluctuating exchange rates. Export and domestic prices are identical before exporting costs are added. However, Baughman will make concessions to this policy to secure strategically important sales.

Nicolet Instrument Corporation designs, manufactures, and markets electronic instruments that are used in science, medicine, industry, and engineering. The firm employs more than 500 people and has annual sales of over $85 million. Exports account for about 42% of total sales, and the firm has been exporting for the past 10 years. Major foreign markets include Japan, West Germany, France, Canada, England, Mexico, Sweden, and the Netherlands. Foreign and domestic prices are calculated according to full cost. Since Nicolet has held a technological edge, it has not been affected by competition in foreign markets. However, the competitive gap has been slowly closing, and the company now varies from administered prices more frequently.

Badger Meter manufactures and sells industrial liquid meters. The company employs 700 people, and its annual sales are estimated at $60 million. The company has sold internationally for more than 50 years, but export sales only account for 9% of total sales. Major markets include Europe, Canada, Taiwan, and the Philippines. The company owns a production facility in Mexico and has licensees in Ecuador and Peru. Cost-based list prices are used for both domestic and foreign markets. Although prices usually remain fixed, the company has, at times, offered special discounts to regain market share or to offset unfavorable exchange rates.

Flexible pricing strategies are useful to counter competitive pressures or exchange-rate fluctuations. They help firms stay competitive in certain markets without disrupting the entire pricing strategy. However, if competitive pressures persist and technology gaps continue to close, the company could face losing its export market. This is when a company may consider the third alternative.

Dynamic Incremental Strategy

The dynamic incremental pricing strategy was used by approximately 30% of the firms studied. Most firms using this strategy had sales well over $50 million with exports ranging from 20 to 65% of total sales. In the dynamic incremental strategy, prices are set by subtracting fixed costs for plants, R&D, and domestic overhead from cost-plus figures. In addition, domestic marketing and promotion costs are also disregarded.

This strategy is based on the assumption that fixed and variable domestic costs are incurred regardless of export sales. Therefore, only variable and international customer costs need to be recovered on exported products. This makes it possible for a company to maintain profit margins while selling its exported products at prices below U.S. list. It is also assumed that unused production capacity exists and that the exported products could not be otherwise sold at full cost. Companies can thus lower their prices and be competitive in markets that may otherwise be prohibitive to enter or penetrate. The following examples illustrate this strategy.

Flo-Con Systems, a subsidiary of Masco Inc., manufactures high-quality and sophisticated flow-control valves for molten-steel-pouring applications. The company employs 500 people and has sales between $50 and $60 million, of which 25% result from exports. A plant located in Canada produces final products, and an additional plant in Mexico is being considered. Flo-Con finds the nature of its markets very competitive. The firm's export prices are based on competitive prices in the local market. Management is often forced to temporarily overlook costs and margins to remain competitive and secure orders.

Ray-O-Vac, a producer of batteries and other consumer goods, has been exporting successfully for over 30 years. Its Micro Power Division employs 250 and has estimated annual sales of $100 million. The major products in this division include batteries for hearing aids and watches. Exports account for 20% of total business, and major markets include Europe, Far East, and Japan. These markets are entered through wholly-owned subsidiaries strategically located around the world. Each subsidiary may be treated as a cost or profit center depending upon the market circumstances. Competitive pressures demand flexible pricing, and discounts are often granted to gain market share or secure OEM business. Branch managers may adjust prices on a day-to-day basis to counter exchange-rate fluctuations. Export pricing is a very active ingredient in the firm's marketing mix.

Econ-O-Cloth is an independent manufacturer of optical polishing cloths and a wholesaler of related goods. Although the company has traditionally exported around 25% of its sales volume, this figure has slipped to around 5% over the past five years. Major markets include Canada, Mexico, and Western Europe. Econ-O-Cloth reduced export margins to compensate for the strong dollar in the early 1980s, and it considers pricing an active instrument for achieving marketing objectives. The firm continually monitors the foreign environment and at times modifies its prices and products to blend with foreign consumer demands. Econ-O-Cloth has been squeezed hard by competition, and it is still waiting for its dynamic pricing strategy to pay off.

The above examples demonstrate that pricing strategies are complex and that no single strategy suits a firm at all times. There is no guarantee that pricing strategies that work successfully today will continue to do so in the future. Many traditionally successful exporters have recently experienced sales downturns in their foreign markets. One can only speculate on whether a change of pricing strategies could have prevented these downturns. Also, it is not known to what extent other factors (poor market intelligence, weak distribution networks, no product modifications when they were needed, slow delivery, or poor image) were responsible.

The uncertainties of international business make it difficult for executives to select the pricing strategy that is best for their firm. As a result, most firms use the rigid cost-plus strategy until external pressures force them to reconsider. This strategy makes managers feel secure, and it is frequently used when a firm enters the export market. As competition and other external variables grow more intense, however, the firm typically makes exceptions to its pricing policy, moving from rigid to flexible cost-plus pricing. Few firms have attempted to price their export products according to the dynamic conditions of the marketplace. For these firms, the dynamic incremental strategy is usually required, and prices may change frequently in response to competition, the prevailing exchange rate, and other variables.

Most exporting firms appear to establish their pricing policies reactively, changing only when external pressures force the issue. In working this way, however, these firms lose valuable sales and market share during the transition period. Although this strategy may be defensible, three types of lags may result in irreversible damage. The recognition lag is the amount of time between an actual change in the environment and a company's recognition of that change. Reaction lag is the amount of time between the company's recognition of the problem and its decision to react to it. Finally, effectiveness lag is the amount of time needed to implement the decision.

One might conclude that if executives were proactive in their pricing strategy, they might avoid many of the headaches associated with exporting. But how can executives be sure which pricing policy is best for their firms? Considering all the variables that affect price, it is reasonable to assume that different pricing policies should exist for different markets. Furthermore, considering the volatility of foreign markets, one would suspect that these policies should be continuously reviewed and updated. It is not surprising, then, that most executives resort to setting their pricing policies reactively.

A Decision Framework for Export Pricing

Most companies lack a systematic procedure for setting and revising export prices. The absence of a formal decision-making procedure that incorporates and weighs relevant variables has led to the development of the framework described here. It is not intended to replace management judgment, since the business executive is usually in the best position to assess the suitability of various strategies and policies, but simply to provide a systematic framework for arriving at export pricing decisions.

Figure 42.3 illustrates the steps involved in a formal export price determination process. A brief description of each step is presented below.

Verification of Market Potential

The first step in the analysis gives firm information on the market potential in specific countries. The company can identify market potential for its products by using both formal and informal sources. Formal sources include market-research firms, the U.S. Department of Commerce, banks, and other agencies that provide information on foreign countries. Informal sources include trade shows, local distributors, international trade journals, and business contacts. During this process, those countries that do not demonstrate adequate market potential are dropped from the list of possible markets.

Estimating Target Price Range

Once it is determined that a market has sufficient potential, the firm observes the price ranges of substitute or competitive products in the

Verify export market potential

↓

Estimate target price range:
floor, ceiling, and expected prices

↓

Determine company sales potential at given prices

↓

Analyze import, distribution and transaction barriers

↓

Examine corporate goals and preference for pricing strategy

↓

Select suitable pricing strategy:
    1. Rigid cost-plus
    2. Flexible cost-plus
    3. Dynamic incremental

↓

Check consistency with current price setting

↓

Implementation: Select tactics, distributor prices, and end user prices

↓

Monitor export market performance and make adjustments as necessary

FIG. 42.3 Decision Process For Export Price Determination

local market to find its target price range. This consists of three prices:
- The floor price, that price at which the firm breaks even;
- The ceiling price, the highest price the market is likely to bear for the product; and
- The expected price, the price at which the firm would most likely be competitive.

Estimating Sales Potential

Assuming that a high enough level of sales potential exists to warrant market entry, management then identifies the size and concentration of customer segments, projected consumption patterns, competitive pressures and the expectations of local distributors and agents. The landed cost and the cost of local distribution are estimated. The potential sales volume is assessed for each of the three price levels, taking into account the price elasticity of demand.

Analyze Special Import, Distribution, or Transaction Barriers

If adequate sales potential exists, management then assesses any special import barriers not accounted for in its earlier efforts. These barriers include quotas, tariffs and other taxes, anti-dumping, price-maintenance, currency-exchange, and other governmental regulations that affect the cost of doing business in that country. In addition, internal distribution barriers must also be assessed. Lengthy distribution channels, high margins, and inadequate dealer commitment may present difficulties for the exporter. Finally, currency supply, payment terms, and financing availability should be reviewed. Is it customary for prices to be negotiable? Do customers expect certain credit or payment terms? Once again, sales potential, market share, and profitability should be analyzed in light of the above information in order to confirm the desirability of market entry.

Corporate Goals and Preference for Pricing

After deciding on a target market, some companies may not wish to consider anything but full-cost pricing (either rigid or flexible cost-plus). If desired margins can be achieved, this pricing policy can be implemented. If, however, the desired margins cannot be achieved, the firm can either abort market entry or resort to some form of marginal costing approach. If the firm's management is willing to consider pricing strategies that focus on market rather than profit objectives, it may continue the analysis with a systematic identification of the optimal pricing strategy.

Systematic Selection of Appropriate Pricing Strategy

The company needs to arrive at a strategy choice by systematically considering all relevant variables. Management faces a basic choice between a dynamic incremental pricing strategy and a cost-plus pricing strategy (either rigid or flexible). Dynamic incremental pricing implies a marginal costing approach, while cost-plus pricing implies full costing.

Figure 42.4 identifies 15 criteria that help management make choices between the two pricing strategies. Some criteria are derived from the

Conditions favoring . . . Marginal Costing/ Aggressive Pricing	Criteria	Conditions favoring . . . Full Costing/ Passive Pricing
	(a) Firm-Specific Criteria	
Low	Extent of product differentiation	High
Committed	Corporate stance toward exporting	Half-hearted
Long term	Management desire for recovering export overhead	Short term
Sufficient	Company financial resources to sustain initial losses	Insufficient
Wide	Domestic gross margins	Narrow
High	Need for long-term capacity utilization	Low
High	Opportunity to benefit from economies of scale	Low
	(b) Situation-Specific Criteria	
Substantial	Growth potential of export market	Negligible
High	Potential for follow-up sales	Low
Continuous	Nature of export opportunity	One-time
High	End-user price sensitivity	Low
High	Competitive intensity	Low
Likely	Opportunity to drive out competition	Unlikely
Favorable	Terms of sale and financing	Unfavorable
Low	Exchange rate risk	High
Low	Cost of internal distribution, service and promotion	High

FIG. 42.4. Criteria Relevant to the Choice Between Full and Marginal Costing.

general environment of the firm, while others are unique to the specific export opportunity being considered. Management may choose to weigh each group, as well as individual criteria, in arriving at a choice. Figure 42.4 spells out the conditions that call for incremental pricing.

Checking Consistency with Current Pricing

If a firm is already in the targeted market, the recommended pricing strategy should be compared to the strategy currently in place. If deviations exist, they should be explained and justified. If they cannot be justified, the firm should seriously consider adopting the recommended pricing strategy in order to achieve marketing goals more effectively. It is also important to check for consistency of export pricing policies across export markets to minimize any conflicts (such as inter-market shipping by competing middlemen).

Implementation

The exporter will determine specific prices for distributors and end users, in accordance with the recommended pricing strategy, and decide on specific pricing tactics. A strategy may fail in a specific market if execution is not effective or if reaction to change is slow. For example, distributors may vary their margins as a response to price changes. Similarly, distributors may hold a large inventory of products at the old price, creating a lag before the new pricing policy actually becomes effective.

Monitoring

Exchange rates can be one of the more volatile variables in international business, especially in developing countries. These rates should be monitored continuously, and the effect of their changes on pricing policy should be evaluated. Variables such as competition, regulations, and price sensitivity can be monitored periodically. As these variables change, the firm can adjust its pricing strategy appropriately. The proposed decision process, therefore, provides a proactive means of establishing pricing policies.

A major implication of this analysis is that no export pricing strategy will fit all of a company's products and markets. International pricing issues are extremely complex, and pricing decisions are fueled by many variables. It is important that the company establish a systematic and periodic approach in selecting a pricing policy. The approach should account for both internal and external variables affecting the firm's export efforts. This framework for export pricing is one such approach. Executives may wish to modify the model in order to better blend it with their firms' perspectives.

A second implication is that many U.S. firms may be overlooking lucrative foreign markets because of their strict adherence to the full-cost pricing approach. Furthermore, this rigid practice may hinder effective market penetration in existing foreign markets. A complete reassessment of the firm's market-share objectives may be needed. Committed exporters will allocate the resources needed to accomplish this task if it becomes necessary.

Finally, there is no guarantee that those pricing policies that are suitable today will work in the future. Changing business trends, exchange rates, consumer preferences, and competition are only a few of the variables that have caught successful exporters off guard. Therefore, a method for monitoring changes in the pricing policy variables should be established. The most volatile variables, such as exchange rates and competitive transaction prices, should be monitored more frequently. Once again, committed exporters will recognize the need for this and allocate the appropriate resources to establish an adequate monitoring system.

Although no best pricing strategy exists, most American firms have adhered to a full-cost approach, often disregarding conditions that are particular to their targeted foreign market. Many companies have abandoned lucrative foreign markets because of seemingly unattractive potentials. Other firms have relinquished sales and market share to local or more aggressive foreign competitors. The full-cost approach is a major deterrent to improving the exports of American businesses.

The establishment of international pricing policies is a dynamic process. Success with one strategy does not guarantee that the same strategy will continue to work. Many companies react passively when global changes make their traditional pricing policies obsolete. Such companies are usually forced to either abandon the market or adapt their pricing strategy to the new conditions. The lag times associated with recognition, reaction, and effectiveness can cause an irreversible deterioration in a company's sales, profits, and market share in the foreign country.

A proactive stance on establishing pricing strategy can often reduce or eliminate these lags, enhancing the firm's flexibility and responsiveness to changing business conditions. To develop a proactive stance, businesses need to establish systematic methods to monitor and evaluate the variables associated with an international pricing policy. Firms that are committed to international business will quickly recognize this and allocate resources accordingly.

The guidelines and decision process discussed in this article have been derived from the experience of exporting firms. Such an empirically-based approach to developing managerial guidelines is appropriate, given the current dearth of export pricing literature. Insights obtained from the field can rip away the shroud of mystery that surrounds export pricing decisions. At the same time, it should be noted that the managerial guidelines offered here are appropriate for a given set of conditions. The seasoned executive will realize that these recommendations are not substitutes for good business judgment. The proposed strategies may need minor modifications to better reflect a company's perspectives and constraints on international pricing.

References

Abratt, Russell and Leyland F. Pitt, "Pricing Practices in Two Industries," *Industrial Marketing Management*, Vol. 14, pp. 301–306.

Arpan, Jeffrey S., "Multinational Firm Pricing in International Markets," *Sloan Management Review*, (Winter 1973), pp. 1–9.

Baker, James C. and John K. Ryans, Jr., "Some Aspects of International Pricing: A Neglected Area of Management Policy," *Management Decisions*, (Summer 1973), pp. 117–182.

Clague, Llewellyn and Rena Grossfield, "Exporting Pricing in a Floating Rate World," *Columbia Journal of World Business*, (Winter 1974), pp. 17–22.

Farley, John U., James M. Hulbert and David Weistein, "Price Setting and Volume Planning by Two European Industrial Companies: A Study and Comparison of Decision Processes," *Journal of Marketing*, (Winter 1980), pp. 46–54.

Frank, Jr., Victor, H., "Living with Price Controls Abroad," *Harvard Business Review*, (March—April 1984), pp. 137–142.

Kressler, Peter R., "Is Uniform Pricing Desirable in Multinational Markets?" *Akron Business and Economic Review*, (Winter 1971).

Lecraw, Donald J., "Pricing Strategies of Transnational Corporations," *Asia Pacific Journal of Management*," (January 1984), pp. 112–119.

Leff, Nathaniel H., "Multinational Corporate Pricing Strategy in Developing Countries," *Journal of International Business Studies*, (Fall 1975), pp. 55–64.

Marketing News, "Pricing Competition is Shaping Up as 84's Top Marketing Pressure Point," November 11, 1983, p. 1.

Piercy, Nigel, "British Export Market Selection and Pricing," *Industrial Marketing Management*, (October 1981), pp. 287–297.

Rao, Vithala R., "Pricing Research in Marketing: The State of the Art," *Journal of Business*, (January 1984), pp. 539–559.

Terpstra, Vern, "Suggestions for Research Themes and Publications," *Journal of International Business Studies*, (Spring/Summer 1983), pp. 9–10.

43

Price Escalation in International Marketing*

HELMUT BECKER

The oft-encountered price escalation phenomenon in international marketing is illustrated in Table 43.1. Four different foreign market cases are compared with a typical domestic pricing situation—say, in the United States—including applicable markups in the conventional manufacturer-wholesaler-retailer marketing channel. While the examples are hypothetical, they are realistic in demonstrating the price pyramiding effect that is frequently encountered in international marketing. The product might be a low-priced, simple consumer gadget (such as an inexpensive electronic watch or calculator) retailing domestically for as low as $12. In all the export cases c.i.f. charges of $2.50 and a 20% tariff on c.i.f. value are added, but wholesale and retail margins are assumed to remain unchanged from the domestic situation, so that the true escalation effect can be fully appreciated. It must be realized, however, that foreign distributor margins may well be higher, particularly where channels are more fragmented and less efficient.

The examples in Table 43.1 are arranged sequentially, each succeeding case incorporating an additional pyramiding factor. The first export case parallels the domestic pricing situation, except for the c.i.f. and tariff charges. As can be seen in the Table, the wholesale distributor is at the same time the importer, and the price rises by "only" 70%, to the equivalent of $20.40.

More typically, however, the product will be brought into the country via an import distributor. The insertion of the importer into

* Excerpt from Helmut Becker, "Pricing: An International Marketing Challenge." In Hans B. Thorelli and Helmut Becker, *International Marketing Strategy*, Rev. Ed. (Elmsford, NY: Pergamon Press, 1980), pp. 206—217.

TABLE 43.1 International Price Escalation Effects (in U.S. Dollars)

International Marketing Channel Elements and Cost Factors	Domestic wholesale-retail channel	EXPORT MARKET CASES			
		Case #1 same as domestic with direct wholesale import c.i.f./tariff	Case #2 same as #1 w/foreign importer added to channel	Case #3 same as #2 with V.A.T. added	Case #4 same as #3 w/local foreign jobber added to channel
Manufacturer's net price	6.00	6.00	6.00	6.00	6.00
+insurance and shipping cost (c.i.f)	*	2.50	2.50	2.50	2.50
= *Landed Cost* (c.i.f. value)	*	8.50	8.50	8.50	8.50
+tariff (20% on c.i.f. value)	*	1.70	1.70	1.70	1.70
= *Importer's Cost* (c.i.f. value + tariff)	*	10.20	10.20	10.20	10.20
+importer's margin (25% on cost)	*	*	2.55	2.55	2.55
+V.A.T. (16% on full cost plus margin)	*	*	*	2.04	2.04
= *Wholesaler's Cost* (= Importer's Price)	6.00	10.20	12.75	14.79	14.79
+wholesaler's margin (33⅓% on cost)	2.00	3.40	4.25	4.93	4.93
+V.A.T. (16% on margin)	*	*	*	.79	.79
= *Local Foreign Jobber's Cost* (= Wholesale Price)	*	*	*	*	20.51
+jobber's margin (33⅓% on cost)	*	*	*	*	6.84
+V.A.T. (16% on margin)	*	*	*	*	1.09
= *Retailer's Cost* (= Wholesale or Jobber Price)	8.00	13.60	17.00	20.51	28.44
+retailer's margin (50% on cost)	4.00	6.80	8.50	10.26	14.22
+V.A.T. (16% on margin)	*	*	*	1.64	2.28
= *Retail Price* (= what consumer pays)	12.00	20.40	25.50	32.42	44.94
Percent Price Escalation over: Domestic	----	70%	113%	170%	275%
Case #1			25%	59%	120%
Case #2				27%	76%
Case #3					39%

the international marketing channel, as this was done in the second case, has the effect of more than doubling the foreign retail price to $25.50, an increase of 113% over its domestic counterpart.

In the third case, the situation is similar to the second, but a "value added tax" (V.A.T.) of 16% (as for example in the E.E.C.) is added to the assumptions. V.A.T. is essentially a noncumulative turnover tax that is levied only against the difference between the middleman's selling price and cost. Please note, however, that in the importer's case (Case 3) the V.A.T. is imposed on the full export selling price as this represents the "value added" to or introduced into the country from abroad. The full taxing of imported products is often thought to discriminate unfairly against them. By the same token, the refunding of V.A.T. on exported goods, amounting to an export subsidy in fact, is often considered to allow the exporter an unfair competitive advantage in foreign markets. Such uses of turnover taxes have occasionally called for retaliatory action on the part of the affected countries in the form of higher tariffs and/or import quotas. The V.A.T. causes the export price to rise another 27% over case two to $32.41 or 170% above the domestic equivalent.

In the fourth case, finally, it is assumed that the distribution channel is lengthened, presumably because it is less efficient than that of other countries. The introduction of an additional channel member raises the price by 39% over the third export case or 275% over the domestic price to nearly $45. The sales volume is likely to be curtailed by such a high price, necessitating in turn lower ordering quantities and/or causing low stock turnovers. As a consequence, costs and foreign middlemen margins will probably be higher than the domestic margins as was originally assumed for the illustrations. The escalation problem is further aggravated as a result.

44

Taking Advantage of Trade Fairs for Maximum Sales Impact*

BUSINESS INTERNATIONAL

An often underrated marketing tool—the trade fair— is rapidly gaining new cachet. For competitive reasons alone, participation in such shows is becoming an essential component of any global marketing strategy. But the trade fair also makes excellent financial sense. Experienced companies find it is one of the most cost-effective ways for an MNC to serve existing markets and expand into new areas.

In Europe, trade fairs have long been major marketing events. According to Joachim Schafer, president of Hanover Trade Fair U.S.A., the Hanover Fair in Germany (an annual multi-industry fair) attracts about 450,000 visitors and 5,500 exhibitors from 120 countries. Today, however, trade shows are becoming an increasingly important marketing venue in other regions. According to a U.S. Trade Show Bureau forecast, buyer attendance and exhibitor participation in U.S. shows are growing at a rate of 6% p.a.

More importantly, fairs are opening new avenues in traditionally difficult-to-crack markets in Asia and Latin America. U.S. Commerce Department officials say that with a few exceptions, liberalized import restrictions in developing countries have expanded the horizon of trade fairs beyond local producers—attracting companies from all over the world. Taiwan, for example, last year opened the Taipei World Trade Center, built exclusively for trade exhibitions. Commerce officials say the quality of shows in Latin America may vary depending on local political and economic conditions, but the major national multi-industry shows are generally well attended.

---

* Reprinted from *Business International*, Vol. 34, No. 41 (Oct. 12, 1987), pp.321–323, with permission.

Advantages of Trade Show Marketing

Corporate exhibitors and international show consultants cite numerous benefits trade show participation can offer:

● *Targeted audience.* According to William Mee, president of the U.S. Trade Show Bureau, more than 86% of all attendees represent "buying influences" (managers with direct responsibility for purchasing products and services). Of equal significance is the fact that trade show visitors are there because they have a specific interest in the exhibits. And Trade Show Bureau research has shown that most participants interested in a particular product have not received a sales call for as long as a year prior to the show.

● *Cost effectiveness.* Marketing through trade shows offers major savings over direct selling. Surveys conducted by the McGraw-Hill Laboratory of Advertising Performance and the Trade Show Bureau show the average cost of a direct sales call to be $230, while similar contact made at a trade show costs only $107. The same surveys also report that up to five direct sales calls are required on average to close a sale—bringing the total cost to $1,265, versus a total of $290 for a sale developed through a trade show. For marketing in foreign countries, the savings from trade show participation can be even greater.

● *Enhanced corporate image.* Trade fairs afford a rare opportunity to promote the corporate name to a highly select audience—and savvy companies make a concerted effort to use trade fair participation as an intrinsic part of their image strategies. Whether a firm is seeking to sustain a "leadership" image or raise its profile in a new market, trade shows provide more direct visibility to potential customers than any other form of advertising.

Image considerations also work in the negative. "A company's absence from important industry trade shows is likely to raise questions concerning its commitment to the market and to providing customer support," says Jerry van Dijk, vice president of Cahners Exposition Group, a leading international trade fair consulting firm. "If IBM pulls out of the banking show, the perception could be that IBM has given up on that market."

● *New product testing.* Although not all companies contacted by *BI* use trade shows frequently to introduce new products, those that do say it has proven a faster way to reach key customers than other traditional marketing strategies. Respondents say the opportunity to display and demonstrate the physical product has a much greater impact than verbal or print promotion alone.

Trade shows also present an ideal forum to conduct market research on new products before a commitment to produce them is made. Using an exhibit to demonstrate prototypes of new products "can save millions of dollars if the interest turns out not to be so strong as anticipated," says van Dijk.

● *Competitive intelligence.* Visiting competitor exhibits at a trade fair provides one of the best ways to identify those product areas where a competitor may be emphasizing promotional efforts. It is also a good way to identify distinguishing features of a competitor's product— particularly when it is new to the market.

● *New market intelligence.* Participation in foreign fairs can offer excellent opportunities for gathering market intelligence on new or particularly difficult markets. For example, Benjamin Martin, a vice president in the international division of Anchor Hocking Corp, notes that in "using trade fairs, you really find out valuable cultural information that may prompt significant changes in features such as packaging and labeling, or even discovery of markets for products that are no longer selling domestically." Martin, along with marketing executives from several other companies, suggest that trade fairs are an effective way to establish or strengthen a distribution network abroad.

How to Make an Exhibit Pay

Recognizing the benefits of trade show participation is only the first step in making the most of what can be an expensive undertaking. Who represents the company and how they do it are the real keys to success. Unfortunately, the tendency in many companies is to view fairs as either a nuisance assignment or a junket; the quality of representation gets short shrift. Experienced executives suggest the following pointers to help ensure that a firm gets the best possible return on its trade show investment:

☐ *Support from top management is essential.* Corporate respondents unanimously agree that successful exhibitions depend on the support of senior management, right up to the CEO level. In some cases, senior executives can play an influential role at the show itself. This is particularly true in Europe, where it is established practice for top managers to appear on the trade show floor. For example, a company like Olivetti, says Joachim Schafer, "is likely to have the heads of its own foreign subsidiaries in the U.S., Asia and Latin America on hand to speak directly to potential buyers from those parts of the world."

☐ *Pre-show promotion helps.* Companies and consultants interviewed say direct mail, including premiums (depending on the industry), are a very effective way to attract the right audience.

☐ *Know your audience.* Before a company attends a show, management should have a good idea of who is going to be there, i.e., high-level executives, technical people, distributors. The selection of booth personnel, display techniques and promotional approaches should be tailored to audience demographics.

☐ *Set written objectives*. Regardless of whether the primary purpose of the exhibit is to capture sales at the show or after, corporate respondents say it is critical that expectations be well-established prior to the show and that these be clearly communicated to company representatives. Companies note that in Europe there tends to be a greater emphasis on booking orders on the spot. In the U.S., on the other hand, broader marketing goals such as image promotion tend to take precedence over floor sales.

☐ *Train booth personnel*. Although many companies say they often do not have the time or budget to provide extensive pre-show training, most say it can make a big difference in how well the show goes. At Minnesota Mining & Manufacturing Co (3M), corporate Manager of Meetings and Trade Shows Hugh Morrisey says that "the majority of the divisions do have a pre-show meeting where they talk to booth personnel both about show objectives and trade show selling techniques that differ from direct sales."

☐ *Follow up systematically*. Develop a system to evaluate post-show performance and to track qualified leads. Some companies use extensive quantitative tallying through computer transmission. For example, at 3M, trade show leads are transmitted directly from the trade show floor back to the home office.

45

How Multinationals Can Counter Gray Market Imports*

S. TAMER CAVUSGIL
ED SIKORA

Gray market activity—parallel distribution of genuine goods by intermediaries other than authorized channel members—has always
concerned companies. In the international context, gray marketing
refers to the legal importation of genuine goods into a country by
intermediaries other than the authorized distributors. Gray marketers
are typically brokers who buy goods overseas, either from maufac-
turers or authorized dealers at relatively low prices and import them
into a country where prevailing prices are higher. Because the activity
of gray marketers parallels authorized distributors, gray marketers are
said to be engaged in "parallel importation."

Gray marketers appeal to their customers with lower prices. For
example, if purchased on the gray market, a $54,000 Mercedes 500
SEL, which meets all the U.S. safety and pollution-control requirements, can be bought for about 20% less than the price charged by the
local authorized dealer. Although gray market goods look similar to
their domestic counterparts, they may not be identical and may not
carry full warranties. For these reasons, purchasers of gray market
goods accept higher risks that are often overlooked.

The volume of gray market activity is significant. This is especially
true in the case of premium brands of automobiles, cameras, watches,
computers, perfumes, wine, champagne, glassware, tires and construction equipment.

For example, industry sources estimate that about 10% of IBM's
PC sales and 20% of Sharp Electronics' copier sales are accounted for

* Slightly abbreviated from *The Columbia Journal of World Business*, Vol. 23, No. 4 (Winter
1988), with permission.

by unauthorized channels. Taking again the example of Mercedes-Benz, it is estimated that about 22% of the automobiles this German car maker sold in the U.S. in 1984 were supplied by gray marketers. Authorized dealers accounted for the remaining 78%. In 1986, the total value of products distributed in the U.S. through gray market channels was estimated to be $10 billion.

The Coalition to Preserve the Integrity of American Trademarks (COPIAT) has estimated that a typical member company lost more than $4 million in sales to the gray market in 1984. Average sales loss reached $7.4 million per company in the camera industry and $6.5 million in the watch industry.

What has been the response of multinational corporations to gray markets? Despite the widespread and persistent nature of the problem, companies have been slow to respond with innovative measures. Typical responses have included lobbying and court battles to seek U.S. Customs' protection from gray market imports. As the discussion later in this article will illustrate, such efforts have largely failed.

Yet, multinational companies are not helpless in combatting gray market imports. Indeed, a small number of companies are beginning to formulate and implement creative strategies that have proven to be effective. This article explores both reactive and proactive strategies managers can employ to combat the detrimental impact of the gray market. The underlying premise of the article is that deliberate and carefully designed responses can be more effective than protectionist trade measures.

Why Should Managers Care?

Multinational company executives have reason to be concerned. Growing gray markets complicate at least four aspects of their business operations.

Erosion of Trademark Image

Manufacturers whose products are sold on the gray market risk a tarnishing of brand image when customers realize that the product is sold at a lower price through alternate channels. This is especially true of products that have "prestige appeal"—established by a premium price and exclusive distribution channels (i.e. perfume, cosmetics, watches, etc.). Gray marketers, therefore, are getting a free ride on the brand image created by the manufacturer.

Strained Manufacturer-Dealer-Customer Relations

Furthermore, many manufacturers rely heavily on the expertise of their dealer network. A strong network is built on a track record of trusting relationships between top management of the dealerships and the manufacturer. Such is the case with Caterpillar Inc., whose 200-plus dealers constitute one of the strongest industrial distribution networks in the world. But even Caterpillar is not immune to the gray market. In 1984, an estimated $600 million of gray market construction equipment flooded U.S. borders. Many coastal dealers were losing sales to gray marketers who were buying European-built Caterpillar equipment at prices substantially below U.S. list price. Many became frustrated with this situation, and some dealers were considering entering the gray market unless some relief was provided.

The gray market, therefore, can strain manufacturer-dealer relations and threaten long-term relationships that support the foundation of a strong distribution system. Fortunately, Caterpillar acted quickly to assists its dealers and engaged in some long-term measures to combat gray market activity at its source.

On a similar note, dealer-customer relations became tarnished when the gray market gets out of control. As customers become more comfortable with gray market prices, their perception of authorized dealers may be one of skepticism and distrust. Dealers risk losing the respect of loyal customers and do not gain the needed trust to win new ones.

Legal Liabilities

Aside from tarnishing company image and relationships, the gray market may cause complications in the legal arena. When a foreign-built product is produced for a developing country, it may lack certain safety features required in the United States or Europe. If a fatal accident occurs in the United States, for example, with a piece of equipment that was built for another country, would the manufacturer be liable? Fortunately, such an incident has not yet happened.

Disruption of Marketing Strategy and Profits

Finally, a company's marketing strategy and overall profit performance can be adversely affected by gray market activities. Forecasting accuracy, pricing strategies, merchandising plans, and other marketing efforts can be disrupted by an unexpected expansion of gray market imports. Therefore, the movement of the gray market should be anticipated when the firm develops its marketing strategy. Indicators such as an increasing price differential between countries, growing inventories, sharp changes in exchange rates and slowing foreign economies are all signals of probable gray market expansion.

An important point to recognize is that gray markets can result from a multinational company's *deliberate* strategy to remain competitive in a particular market. This is often accomplished through aggressive pricing and by trading off market share for short-term profits. In this situation, the manufacturer may tolerate the existence of gray market activity as an outcome of a global marketing strategy.

How Gray Markets Develop

Gray markets, at the international level, develop when there are substantial differences in the prevailing prices of the same product between two national markets. As long as the price differential is wide enough to allow gray market brokers an attractive return, they are likely to respond to demand and supply imbalances between the two markets. Thus, the two fundamental factors motivating entrepreneurs to engage in parallel importation are:

- substantial price differences between national markets, and
- the opportunity to offset supply shortages in the importing country at below-market prices.

While these factors pave the way for gray market activity, the following conditions also encourage its presence:

- competitive pricing strategies by a multinational firm leading to differential prices for the same product in different markets (typically between home and host markets);
- substantial fluctuations in exchange rates which tend to widen profit margins for gray market brokers;
- inability of a multinational firm to synchronize demand and supply in various national markets (leading to relative shortages of a product in some markets);
- unavailability in a market of foreign-made products with desired exclusives (e.g., unavailability of certain Mercedes-Benz and Porsche models in the U.S.); and
- relative ease with which products can be moved across countries and adapted for local use. (Most consumer products present no special difficulties here, while some industrial equipment may not be sold in certain markets without meeting local requirements.)

Typically, a combination of these factors leads to the development of parallel import channels. Managers must monitor these conditions as "tell-tale" signs of gray market troubles.

When to Respond to Gray Market Problems

But how large can the gray market be allowed to grow before it poses a threat to manufacturer's profitability? Multinationals have a difficult time assessing this point, which we will call the threshold level of gray market activity. It is at this level that an incremental increase in gray market share will substantially reduce the company's overall profits.

Intuitively, we know that the threshold level of gray market activity is a function of: (1) gross margin differentials between two national markets, and (2) the relative distribution of company sales between the two markets.

To illustrate, let's assume that an American multinational corporation realizes far lower profit margins for its product in Europe as a result of an aggressive marketing strategy. However in the U.S., much higher margins are maintained due to greater demand and competitive considerations. From a strict profitability viewpoint, the multinational can overlook gray market imports of its European product into the U.S. as long as a substantial proportion of its total sales are generated from the more lucrative U.S. market. However, as gray market sales grow in the U.S., they will "choke off" the higher profit margins achieved from authorized-channel U.S. sales and jeopardize the company's global profits. At this point, the manufacturer will be forced to respond to the fundamental factor causing the gray market activity (i.e., substantial price differential between the two markets), or accept lower global profitability for the company.

Unfortunately, the recognition that the gray market has become a real problem for the company often comes too late—after it has reached intolerable levels for the company and its dealers. Thus, some managements will only have the opportunity to react to gray markets. Other forward-looking managers will implement strategies to prevent and minimize the adverse effects of gray market activity.

Tables 45.1 and 45.2 present reactive and proactive measures, respectively, that companies can employ to cope with gray market imports. As can be seen, many trade-offs exist among the strategies in terms of implementation costs, long-term effectiveness, legal risks and other relevant criteria. In the next two sections, we will elaborate on each strategy.

Reactive Strategies to Combat Gray Markets

Often gray market imports grow unexpectedly to levels that require immediate attention. In this situation, a company can choose from among seven creative strategies to reduce the adverse impact of gray market activity. These are: strategic confrontation, participation, price cutting, supply interference, promotional bursts, collaboration and acquisition.

Strategic Confrontation

Strategic confrontation requires the authorized dealer take on the gray market broker head-on. The manufacturer's role with this strategy is

TABLE 45.1. Reactive Strategies to Combat Gray Market Activity

Type of Strategy	Implemented by	Cost of Implementation	Difficulty of Implementation	Does It Curtail Gray Market Activity at Source?	Does it Provide Immediate Relief to Authorized Dealers?	Long-term Effectiveness	Legal Risks to Manufacturers or Dealers	Company Examples
Strategic Confrontation	Dealer with manufacturer support	Moderate	Requires planning	No	Relief in the medium term	Effective	Low risk	Creative merchandising by Caterpillar and auto dealers
Participation	Dealer	Low	Not difficult	No	Immediate relief	Potentially damaging reputation of manufacturer	Low risk	Dealers wishing to remain anonymous
Price Cutting	Jointly by manufacturer and dealer	Costly	Not difficult	No, if price cutting is temporary	Immediate relief	Effective	Moderate to high risk	Dealers and manufacturers remain anonymous

Supply Interference	Either party can engage	Moderate at the wholesale level; high at the retail level	Moderately difficult	No	Immediate relief or slightly delayed	Somewhat effective if at wholesale level; not effective at retail level	Moderate risk at wholesale level; low risk at retail	IBM, Hewlett-Packard, Lotus Corp., Swatch U.S.A., Charles of the Ritz Group Ltd., Leitz, Inc., NEC Electronics
Promotion of Gray Market Product Limitations	Jointly, with manufacturer leadership	Moderate	Not difficult	No	Slightly delayed relief	Somewhat effective	Low risk	Komatsu, Seiko, Rolex, Mercedes-Benz, IBM
Collaboration	Dealer	Low	Requires careful negotiations	No	Immediate relief	Somewhat effective	Very high risk	Dealers wishing to remain anonymous
Acquisition	Dealer	Very costly	Difficult	No	Immediate relief	Effective if other gray market brokers don't creep up	Moderate to high risk	No publicized cases

Note: Company strategies include, but are not limited to those mentioned here.

TABLE 45.2. Proactive Strategies to Combat Gray Market Activity

Type of Strategy	Implemented by	Cost of Implementation	Difficulty of Implementation	Does It Curtain Gray Market Activity at Source?	Does It Provide Immediate Relief to Authorized Dealers?	Long-term Effectiveness	Legal Risks to Manufacturers or Dealers	Company Examples
Product/ Service Differentiation and Availability	Jointly, with manufacturer leadership	Moderate to high	Not difficult	Yes	No; impact felt in medium to long term	Very effective	Very low risk	General Motors, Ford, Porsche, Kodak
Strategic Pricing	Manufacturer	Moderate to high	Complex; impact on overall profitability needs monitoring	Yes	Slightly delayed	Very effective	Low risk	Porsche
Dealer Development	Jointly, with manufacturer leadership	Moderate to high	Not difficult; requires close dealer participation	No	No; impact felt in the long term	Very effective	No risk	Caterpillar, Canon

Marketing Information Systems	Jointly, with manufacturer leadership	Moderate to high	Not difficult; requires dealer participation	No	No; impact felt after implementation	Effective	No risk	IBM, Caterpillar, Yamaha, Hitachi, Komatsu, Lotus Development, insurance companies
Long-term Image Reinforcement	Jointly	Moderate	Not difficult	No	No; impact felt in the long term	Effective	No risk	Most manufacturers with strong dealer networks
Establishing Legal Precedence	Manufacturer	High	Difficult	Yes, if fruitful	No	Uncertain	Low risk	COPIAT, Coleco, Charles of the Ritz Group, Ltd.
Lobbying	Jointly	Moderate	Difficult	Yes, if fruitful	No	Uncertain	Low risk	COPIAT, Duracell, Porsche

Note: Company strategies include, but are not limited to those mentioned here.

one of support. The degree and type of support depend upon the strengths and weaknesses of the victimized dealer. Strategic confrontation can be carried out in the following ways:

● *Dealer Education.* Many weaker, non-aggressive dealers are prime targets for a gray market attack. When under attack, their first reaction may be an outburst of anger toward the manufacturer for allowing the gray market to exist. They may cry out for lower prices and complain that the manufacturer's profit is being made at their expense.

Such dealers may benefit from a broad understanding of gray market dynamics, including why it exists, where it exists, and what they can do about it. They also need to understand that the potential for gray market activity has *always* existed in their territory.

Dealers that are more sophisticated may require only training on additional ways to counter expanding gray market activities. More-informed dealers have usually accepted the existence of this threat and focus their energies on keeping the activity down to tolerable levels.

● *Analysis of Strengths and Weaknesses.* Manufacturers can also help dealers identify their strengths and weaknesses. Strategies can be developed that identify what dealer strengths can best be used against the gray market brokers. The analysis includes both the tangible product and the intangible dealer support-type services. Both must be considered for the analysis to be complete.

● *Promotion of Dealer Strengths and Competitive Weaknesses.* Advertising, direct mail and telemarketing are effective ways to promote the selected dealer strengths against particular broker weaknesses. Advertising also can promote dealer strengths while, at the same time, build doubt in the customers' minds about broker warranties and guarantees. Manufacturers can support this effort by sharing in the dealer's expenses.

● *Creative Merchandising.* Plans that provide options to customers is another way to accent intangible product differentiation. Short-term rentals leases, special financing (skip or ballon payments), guaranteed service and maintenance contracts, guaranteed buy-backs, and guaranteed availability are only a few of the ways dealers can create a market niche in their territory. In addition, manufacturers can participate by providing either financial assistance or free training for dealers who are interested in offering various merchandising packages.

One East Coast Caterpillar dealer confronted the gray market importers by expanding its short-term rental fleet, keeping a close ear to the marketplace and by modifying certain products to differentiate them from their European counterparts. One example is the modification of a D6D Track-Type Tractor with higher horsepower and longer track. The modified tractor appealed to a certain market segment that could not be touched by gray market brokers.

Participation

This reactive strategy requires dealers to purchase machines on the gray market. A formal or informal understanding with the manufacturer is strongly recommended. This strategy is often used by smaller dealers who do not have the financial muscle to implement a confrontation strategy.

By participating in the gray market, dealers are able to selectively match broker prices and thus prevent a dilution in their market share. The dealers can maintain their normal transaction price with most customers but have the flexibility to provide preferential treatment to customers who are opinion leaders in their community.

Participation should only be used as a short-term strategy to "sting" the gray market brokers until a more comprehensive strategy can be developed. The primary risk in long-term participation is that the customer perceives this as an endorsement of the quality and reliability in gray market products. The dealer then would nullify any effort to create doubt or uncertainty about the broker and his products.

Aggressive Confrontation: Price Cutting

Aggressive confrontation is comprised of precise and deliberate maneuvers to quickly reduce local gray market activities through price adjustments. This approach is riskier than strategic confrontation, and specific actions should be carefully assessed to identify if they fall within the company's range of comfortable business practice.

A common mode of aggressive confrontation is selective temporary price cutting. A financially strong authorized dealer can identify those "bread-and-butter" models of the gray market broker and either match or beat the gray market price. The manufacturer may even participate by offering the dealer a one-time price discount on selected models. The key to a successful price-cutting strategy lies in the dealer's ability to sustain the low price long enough to effectively reduce gray market activity. This strategy may carry two primary dangers:

- Irreversible profit loss may result if the broker survives the attack or the attack lasts so long that customers begin to perceive the low price as normal.

● Legal action may be taken by the broker if he can prove that the price cuts were designed and implemented for the sole purpose of eliminating competition.

This strategy was used successfully by some U.S. equipment manufacturers in early 1985, and in less than twelve months the first gray market brokers started trading foreign-manufactured equipment with higher price differentials. Other brokers shifted their trading focus to less competitive industries. As one distributor's sales manager said, "When we were certain that we would lose the deal, we would pull out a new, fully warranted "pool" machine priced 5% under the broker's price and pull the rug right out from underneath his feet." Such a strategy reflects the careful assessment of the manufacturer's strengths and weaknesses. In this case, a global manufacturing network provided a definite advantage.

Aggressive Confrontation: Supply Interference

A second aggressive confrontation technique is supply interference. If a financially strong dealer can identify the source of gray market importation, he may be able to bid up the price of these goods to a level where the gray market broker cannot sustain a profit.

Manufacturers also can participate in supply interference. Channels of supply can be interrupted at the wholesale or retail level with varying degrees of effectiveness. IBM used interference at the wholesale level in 1984 when it canceled several dozen of its 2,200 microcomputer dealers for participating in gray market activities.

Sometimes the mere threat of cancellation is enough to limit gray market activity. Hewlett-Packard, NEC Electronics, Leitz Inc., and Charles of the Ritz Group are among the companies that used announcements to discourage sales to unauthorized channels. On the domestic scene, Lotus Development Corporation stated that it intends to terminate anyone in its distribution network who was supplying its products to unauthorized dealers. The strategy was used to stop dealers from ordering large quantities of software at volume discounts and then selling the excess on the gray market.

Aggressive Confrontation: Promotion of Gray Market Product Limitations

A third example of aggressive confrontation, promotional bursts, have been a popular gray market strategy among manufacturers and authorized dealers. These bursts flood the media with messages that identify product differences and tactfully build doubt about gray market goods.

Although such efforts do not curtail gray market activity at its source, they may reduce the amount of gray market imports in targeted areas.

For example, some Komatsu dealers in U.S. territories advertised that they may not be able to supply parts for gray market construction equipment. Mercedes-Benz of North America mailed hundreds of letters to insurance companies, banks, and leasing companies warning them of the dangers and increased risks associated with gray market automobiles. Seiko and Rolex used radio and newspaper ads, respectively, to warn consumers that the manufacturer's warranty may not apply to products purchased through unauthorized channels.

Collaboration

This strategy can be summarized with "if you can't beat them, join them." Only a few authorized dealers have negotiated with their local gray market broker. Agreements usually require the dealer to purchase a fixed amount of gray market goods in exchange for the exclusive right to sell that particular brand in designated territories.

In one industry, a dealer initiated this strategy by default. In 1982 the manufacturer's product was in short supply. This was also a peak year for gray market activity, and the dealer risked losing his loyal customers to local brokers. To continue selling the manufacturer's brand, the dealer agreed to buy his brand from local gray market brokers in exchange for the exclusive right to sell it in his territory. As a result, the dealer kept his current customers, added some new business, and made a healthy profit off the low-cost foreign product.

Collaboration, although effective, does carry some legal risk. The primary concern is restraint of trade or collusion. In the above example, the dealer could not get the product through the manufacturer so it was doubtful that trade was restrained. On the other hand, when two retailers agree to sell only to designated customers, they effectively agree not to compete, which may violate antitrust laws.

Acquisition

A final reactive strategy against a threatening gray market importer is acquisition. Such a strategy can be seriously considered when the broker operations are located in a high-opportunity area where the authorized dealer has limited operations.

Before deciding on acquisition, several factors should be considered:

● The financial ability and potential likelihood of the broker to reopen under a different name after the acquisition is completed;
● effect of the acquisition on the dealer's image; and
● cost of the acquisition versus the cost of other alternatives.

Acquisition is probably the most expensive strategy and is seldom used. Its large initial cost must be weighed carefully against long-run benefits. From a legal standpoint, acquisitions are safe as long as they are not associated with attempts to monopolize. Nevertheless, the financial demands often make other strategies more attractive.

Proactive Strategies to Prevent Gray Markets

While reactive responses may provide relief from parallel imports, none are designed to address the fundamental causes of gray markets. Therefore, multinational companies must develop and implement proactive strategies to protect themselves and their authorized dealers from the harmful effects of gray market activity and these must be included in developing strategic marketing plans.

Proactive strategies to prevent gray market imports include product service differentiation and availability, strategic pricing, dealer development, marketing information systems, long-term image reinforcement, establishing of legal precedence, and lobbying. Table 45.2 provides additional comments about each proactive strategy.

Product/Service Differentiation and Availability

Product/service differentiation can be a very effective method of stifling the gray market. By designing products with exclusive features that have strong appeal to a certain market, manufacturers can reduce gray market activity.

Product differentiation may include safety, luxury, and functional features. These exclusive features can then be used to create brand preference over gray market imports. For example, a Canadian contractor might be reluctant to purchase gray market tractors from South America because they may not have been designed to operate in extremely cold weather (functional feature).

Ford and General Motors, on the other hand, by simply discontinuing the placement of EPA certification stickers on their Canadian-built cars, made it more difficult to import gray market autos through U.S. Customs (labeling feature).

Service differentiation can be just as effective. Through extended warranties or improved parts and service availability, a manufacturer can make its product more appealing than the gray market counterpart. Implementation of such strategies may warrant long-term decisions on product quality and parts and service requirements.

Strategic Pricing

As a multinational marketer develops competitive pricing strategies in various national markets, large price differentials should be expected to trigger the gray market. Management may move away from uniform pricing in global markets for a number of reasons: to penetrate a foreign market with high sales potentials, to ward off a competitive attack on a particular market, or to lower inventory levels of its foreign-manufactured products. Whatever the case may be, the larger the price differential, the higher will be the probability of gray market expansion.

Firms, therefore, should carefully consider the gray market implications of their pricing strategies. Although differential pricing may improve profitability, increased gray market activity "chokes off" some of this additional profit. Beyond the threshold level of gray market activity, any additional price differential will only result in decreased global profits for the company.

Porsche has apparently accommodated for the gray market in its U.S. pricing strategy. By "holding the line" on U.S. prices, Porsche hopes that customers will prefer to go through authorized channels rather than risk the uncertainty of purchasing on the gray market.

Dealer Development

If manufacturers expect to enjoy high profitability through differential pricing, they can reduce resulting gray market complications by paying attention to their dealers' long-term development needs. Strong dealers who aggressively and creatively market their goods have a much higher probability of warding off a gray market attack in their territory.

Therefore, it pays for manufacturers to invest time with their dealers to develop a strong distribution network. Caterpillar Inc. has extensive dealer development programs to improve dealer skills and expertise in marketing, finance, service, parts, data processing and other areas. Human resource development consultants of the company provide specialized training on effective management techniques, situational leadership and organizational development. Furthermore, a team of experienced Caterpillar representatives and managers are available through decentralized district offices around the world. These district teams provide continuous support and guidance to the dealer and valuable marketing information to the manufacturer.

Marketing Information Systems

Marketing information systems are a "must" in tracking gray market movements in the global arena. The most common method of tracking gray market goods is with warranty registration cards that are secretly coded to identify the original dealers who purchased the product. With this information, companies can identify where distribution system leakages are occurring and take the necessary corrective action.

Caterpillar's Service Information-Management System (SIMS) provides its dealers with worldwide access to warranty and service information on a particular machine through the machine's serial number. With a little ingenuity, Cat dealers can find out if their local brokers are selling used machines as new ones or painting a rosy picture about the machine's service history. Furthermore, Caterpillar can use this information to identify those dealers who are sourcing the gray market products to brokers.

Similar information systems have been implemented by Lotus Development Corporation and Yamaha to identify the source of leakage from their distribution channels.

Manufacturers can gather a significant amount of information through their distribution networks. Many dealers have extensive information systems on their territory activity and their customers. In addition, a large amount of information is passed by word of mouth. Manufacturers should not overlook this source.

An information system should be designed to monitor the following critical factors:

- price differentials between authorized distributor and gray market channels;
- threatening levels of gray market activity in sales territories;
- sources of leakages in distribution system;
- specific product models that become the target of gray market importers; and
- profile of gray market customers.

Building a reliable information system may take time, planning and coordination. However, the pay-off lies in knowing when to react, where to react and how to react to the gray marketers before they cause irreversible damage to company profits.

Long-Term Image Reinforcement

Long-term image building may be the most overlooked proactive strategy. Repetitive messages that promote the dealer's image and intangible services may discourage would-be gray market buyers. Promotion also can be used to reassure current customers that they made the right choice by buying from a particular distributor. A targeted direct mail program to existing customers is one way a dealer can reinforce customer loyalty. After a dealer has established a strong image, promotion can be used to create anxiety about doing business with other dealers or brokers.

Image building can also revolve around symbolic intangibles that appeal to the customer's need for prestige and/or power. A manufacturer or a dealer with a strong image may appeal to customers who have a need to affiliate with that image. These customers usually build a strong loyalty to a particular distributor or manufacturer. This loyalty may go undisturbed by low gray market prices. Therefore, it makes sense for manufacturers and dealers to invest in image building.

Establishing Legal Precedence

The legality of parallel imports has not been clear. As a result, some manufacturers have attempted to establish legal precedence by filing multiple suits against small brokers who cannot afford a costly defense. Such action was taken by Coleco Industries Inc. in an action to stop the parallel importation of Cabbage Patch Kids. Other companies have filed suits against gray market importers of such goods as toothbrushes, pain killers and apparel. In settling cases, importers have agreed to pay some of their profits, to re-export goods, to sell them to the trademark owners or to label them as gray market goods.

Lobbying

Lobbying can be thought of as a type of political advertising that promotes company's viewpoints and improves the changes that favorable legislation will be passed. With regard to gray market imports, lobbists can work on three fronts: influencing exchange rate policy; seeking protectionism against parallel imports; and increasing non-tariff barriers through regulatory agencies.

American multinationals have resorted to all of these actions with relatively little success. While most efforts focused on exchange-rate stabilization during the first half of the 1980s, recent attempts have been in favor of protectionist legislation and non-tariff barriers. Recently, for example, a proposal has been made for mandatory theft-marking of luxury gray market autos.

Much of the lobbying effort against the unauthorized importers by U.S. trademark owners has been assumed by the Coalition to Preserve the Integrity of American Trademarks (COPIAT). Formed in 1983, COPIAT is now made up of more than 40 companies that suffered the erosion of product image and marketing investment.

A long-awaited Supreme Court ruling on the legality of gray market imports, released on May 31, 1988, came as a major disappointment to COPIAT members and other manufacturers of trademark goods. COPIAT had sued to obtain an order directing the Customs Service to exclude the importation of gray market goods. COPIAT contended that the regulations (19 CFR 133.21 (c)(1)-(3)) that permit entry of such goods if the U.S. and foreign trademarks are owned by the same or affiliated entities or if the American trademark owner has authorized the foreign entity to use the mark are inconsistent with 19 USC 526. Although the District Court ruled against COPIAT, the D.C. Circuit Court reversed the ruling on May 6, 1986, claiming that the exclusions were unreasonable and therefore invalid because they conflict with the statute.

When the COPIAT case reached the U.S. Supreme Court's consideration early in 1988, a five-justice majority ruled that subsection (1) and (2) of the regulation are consistent with the statute. That is, when there is common ownership or control of the trademark in issue (which represents the greatest portion of gray market imports), the U.S. Customs Service will continue to allow importation of gray market goods. The Court ruled, however, that allowing imports under the "authorized use" exception (sub-section 3) was inconsistent with the law.

Conclusion: Management Action is Needed

The Supreme Court decision sends a clear message to trademark owners that they cannot rely on existing legislation to prevent parallel importation. A better strategy is to pursue efforts to combat gray market activity at its source. As the discussion in this article clearly demonstrates, managers have a variety of strategy options to effectively deal with gray market imports. Rather than brushing aside the problem as a temporary phenomenon or hoping for governmental help, multinational companies are better off implementing their own measures, which should prove more promising.

Managers should examine each of the proposed strategies carefully for potential implementation. The measures offered differ in terms of cost and difficulty of implementation, relief provided to authorized channel members, long-term effectiveness and legal implications. Some require close participation of dealers for successful implementation. Consequently, the most appropriate strategy response will vary. It is also important to note the complementary nature of the proposed strategies; simultaneous implementation of several strategies is often needed. Efforts in the area of dealer development or marketing information systems, for example, will prove effective when used in conjunction with other strategies.

In conclusion, multinational manufacturers and their authorized dealers have good reasons to be concerned about the gray market. Failure to respond with creative company strategies to expanding parallel imports can result in a tarnished trademark image, injured relations with dealers and customers, increased legal problems and impaired implementation of marketing strategies. The best solution is prevention, a strong proactive strategy. If, however, gray market activity approaches critical levels, there will be no choice but to react quickly. Afterward, when the gray market falls back to tolerable levels, manufacturers and dealers should continue to monitor this activity and acknowledge its existence in their long-term strategies.

Further Reading — Part VI

Christopher, Martin, Richard Lancioni and John Gattorna, "Managing International Customer Service," *International Marketing Review*, (Spring 1985), pp. 65–70.

"Factors that Influence Pricing Decisions," *International Management*, (June 1981), p. 3.

Hill, John S. and Richard R. Still, "Adapting Products to LDC Tastes," *Harvard Business Review*, (March—April 1984), pp. 92–101.

"Marketing Strategies: Adapting a U.S. Sales Approach to Penetrate the U.K. Market," *Business International*, September 14, 1985, pp. 289–291.

Martenson, Rita, "Is Standardization of Marketing Feasible in Culture-Bound Industries? A European Case study," *International Marketing Review*, Vol. 4, No. 3 (Autumn 1987) pp. 7–17.

McNally, George J., "Global Marketing: It's Not Just Possible, It's imperative," *Business Marketing*, April 1986, pp. 64–70.

Peebles, D. M. and J. K. Ryans, Jr., *Management of Internatioanl Advertising*, (Boston: Allyn & Bacon, 1984).

"Product Development: Companies Try New Approaches to Maximize Payoff from R&D," *Business International*, January 25, 1988, pp. 17–21.

VII
Integrated Marketing Planning and Action

Introduction to Part VII

In previous sections, selections covered marketing mix instruments, market entry strategies, and global market structures. Articles in this section will deliberate on how to harmonize marketing strategies with market structures in integrated marketing plans and how to carry out these plans in integrated actions.

Thorelli and Becker in the first selection discuss the issue of marketing planning by applying the ecologic view to the task of strategic as well as tactical planning in international marketing. A step-by-step procedure is sketched out, comprising the original commitment decision as well as an initial plan of operations. The authors stress that planning is an interactive process that requires constant monitoring, redefinition, adaptation, and re-evaluation of objectives and strategy, implementation and control in an effort to obtain maximum payoff from ever-changing marketing opportunities.

Chakravarthy and Perlmutter review four generic planning systems that are available to MNC: top-down planning, bottom-up planning, portfolio planning and dual structure planning. The ability of each of these systems to balance viability and legitimacy in the distinct business contexts is also discussed.

Johansson and Nonaka in Reading 48 reveal the factors behind Japanese export marketing performance. Based on a combination of secondary and primary data, the structures within which Japanese export companies operate are spelled out and integrated. The integration is shown to lead naturally to a particular strategic posture dominated by a long-run perspective and a high quality/price ratio in products meticulously adapted for very specific market segments.

The relationships of multinational corporations and less-developed host countries are always a burning issue. They are analyzed in the last reading by Thorelli.

46

Strategic Planning in International Marketing*

HANS B. THORELLI
HELMUT BECKER

In the orderly pursuit of any worthwhile endeavor, one requires a plan. While planning involves some inherent risks (one could be proven wrong by subsequent events), it is surely more risky not to plan; a plan forces one to focus on tomorrow. It provides the guideposts for future action toward one's goals, and it serves as a benchmark for evaluating performance. Indeed, without a plan that specifies *objectives* and provides for the *means of getting there*, an activity loses much of its purposefulness and direction. One is reminded of the meanderings of *Alice in Wonderland*, who was advised by the rabbit upon reaching a cross-roads, "If you don't know where you want to go, it really doesn't matter which way you turn."

Few marketing managers would compare themselves with *Alice*, though some may be "wandering" just as aimlessly. Business firms can be found at any position on the planning continuum, from simply "muddling through," to highly formalized planning, from relying on intuition to utilizing sophisticated simulation models, from "seats-of-the-pants" judgments to detailed tactical and strategic projections for the short and long term.

Not to underestimate its complexity, the planning *process* in international marketing is nevertheless rather similar to its domestic counterpart. A course of action is drawn up which incorporates all the aspects of deploying the instruments connected with the marketing of a product or service. The typical marketing plan has these elements:

---

* Revised from Hans B. Thorelli and Helmut Becker, "Strategic Planning in International Marketing", *International Marketing Strategy* Revised Edition, 1980 pp. 367–377.

557

1. Description of the situation: where are we? (diagnosis).
2. Identification of own strengths and weaknesses and opportunities and threats in the environment ("SWOT" analysis).
3. Definition of objectives of the plan: where do we want to be?
4. Forecasting sales, cost and profit contribution (prognosis).
5. Designing the marketing program based on 3 and 4 (strategic planning).
6. Estimating the necessary appropriations (budgeting).

While some may consider the determination of objectives as the first step and perhaps at the heart of the planning process, as in "management by objectives," others believe that strategy aspects are the most important. Regardless of which has the greater appeal, the important point to remember is that planning is an *iterative* process that requires constant monitoring, redefinition, adaptation, and re-evaluation of objectives *and* strategy, implementation *and* control in an effort to obtain maximum payoff from ever-changing marketing opportunities.

Despite the parallels to domestic marketing, planning in the international sphere is both more difficult and indispensable. For effective marketing there is a need for organizational coordination between all the firm functions. Though this may sound like a trifling truism at home, coordination is an absolute *must* in international marketing that can only be achieved through a well-thought-out plan. This is so because international markets are a lot more heterogeneous, and they contain far more unknowns. Only at the risk of courting disaster would the international marketer enter a foreign country without a well-laid plan. While the plan does not guarantee anything, it does increase the likelihood of success and it does help pinpoint pitfalls to avoid in the future.

This is not a Reading on "how" to plan. Rather, the approach taken here is to condense a large number of writings into summary matrix and checklist form. This is done to assist the busy executive in deciding "what" to plan for when entering international markets. There are five international marketing decisions that must be made and planned for:

1. *The commitment decision*: Given the firm's home market position and resource base, are foreign market opportunities attractive enough to mobilize an international marketing effort?
2. *The country-selection decision*: Which of several country alternatives is (or are) most attractive for selection as potential international target markets?
3. *Mode of entry and operations*: Which is the best way of entering the foreign market(s) chosen and conducting the firm's operations in them?

4. *Marketing mix decision*: Which of the various marketing instruments are most effective in the foreign market environment and in which combination?
5. *Marketing organization decision*: What is the best way for coordinating multinational marketing decisions, to retain centralized control with maximum local flexibility?

Strategic planning in international marketing comprises these five decision areas. As in marketing in general, international marketing planning is an iterative process. That is, the commitment decision cannot be made in isolation without reference to the possible target countries and the mode of entry, and vice versa. The specific combination of marketing tools being planned for, in turn, depends on the mode of entry and operations, as well as on the country or countries involved. The appropriate marketing organization to coordinate international decisions is greatly influenced by and interactive with all the other planning steps. In each case the major requirement is that objectives and strategy are fused with market structure in the local environment, all the while being coordinated globally.

The way in which the international marketing plan is approached in this reading is by combining the general planning steps with the major international decisions that must be made. This has been done in the international marketing planning matrix in Figure 46.1. Each cell in the matrix represents a step in the overall planning process. While some of the planning steps or cells may seem redundant, they in fact should be looked at as being part of the iterative review process between all the planning stages that should be continued until the final planning document is completed. The matrix, then, is designed to provide the planning framework for international marketing strategy. The detailed planning variables for each international marketing

International decisions	Marketing planning variables					
	Diagnosis of situation	SWOT analysis	Objectives	Sales vol. cost/profit forecasts	Marketing program	Marketing budgets
A. Commitment decision						
B. Country selection						
C. Mode of entry						
D. Marketing strategy						
E. Marketing organization						

FIG. 46.1. International marketing planning matrix.

decision are listed in Checklists A through E constituting the balance of this Reading.

Besides offering a planning framework, the Reading serves the dual purpose of integrating the materials in this volume. Thus it is natural that we shall apply the ecologic view in presenting our checklists. For a detailed restatement of the ecologic concept of marketing the reader is referred to Reading 1. Ecology implies that to avoid being at the mercy of the environment we have to plan for survival and growth. Briefly, it admonishes the planner to look at the firm's resources ("what are we good at?") and objectives ("what do we want to become?") and to analyze the environment for opportunities and restrictions ("what current or potential customer needs could our firm most effectively satisfy?"). The means of relating the environment (and in it notably the market structure) to the firm's objectives and resources is marketing strategy. Along with this volume's central theme, the key challenge in business planning is to harmonize market structure and marketing strategy—thus matching capability and opportunity.

It should be clear against this background that the checklists are illustrative, not normative. They make no pretense of restating "principles of international marketing management," but they should serve well as bases of reference to practical decision-makers. In any given business situation some of the factors referred to will almost surely seem irrelevant, and some variables not even mentioned here may be highly important. The checklists are not substitutes for executive judgment and experience.

Three comments about the checklists are in order. First, while there is hopefully a logical ordering among the various steps indicated on the lists we are not implying that they should necessarily be handled in numerical order. For example, in a given case it may be preferable to begin by an examination of objectives rather than of resources. Second, while the order between the steps is not so important it is indeed vital that there is feedback among all of them. For instance, it would clearly be suicidal to define a set of objectives without any reference to the operating environment. Third, it will be desirable at many junctures in the planning process—especially if it relates to an LDC—to include an estimate of the reliability and likely error margins of data employed.

Of the five checklists presented, Checklist A relates to the international commitment decision. Before a serious planning effort for an operation in any given country can be undertaken it seems logical to assume that a commitment decision of some kind has to be made, based on a preliminary analysis of various candidate countries. Assuming this has been done, Checklist B provides guidelines for selection of target markets among several alternative countries. Given the commitment to enter one of several specific countries, Checklist C helps specify the mode of market entry and operations. Checklist D details the instruments that comprise the initial marketing program. The marketing strategy must obviously be tailored to a chosen country and the mode of local market entry. Checklist E, finally, summarizes some of the aspects of organization and coordination that are so important to success in international marketing. Important ingredients of an effective performance audit are included as well.

The first-time marketing program that evolves should be flexible and regarded as preliminary. Due to the rapidity of change in international markets, an opportunity today may quickly turn into a problem or liability tomorrow. The appropriate time horizon will depend, of course, on such additional factors as the type of product, extent of commitment, the country involved, the financial strength of the firm, predictability of the local markets environment, and other variables.

Checklist A: The International Commitment Decision

This Checklist summarizes the factors to be considered when making the international commitment decision. The decision should be based on sound *reasons* for entering foreign markets. The firm's own *resource* base needs to be examined as do the company's *objectives* and philosophy. A preliminary analysis of various candidate countries and the type and extent of the commitment round out this decision area.

A.1. Reasons to enter markets abroad
   11. Enquiries received from abroad
   12. Domestic market saturation
       (follow international product life cycle)
   13. Greater profitability
       (margin greater and/or strong demand)
   14. Preempt competition
   15. Excess liquidity
   16. Going international as means of growth preferable to product diversification, acquisitions, market expansion, etc., at home
   17. Better utilization of current resources and differential advantage (capitalizing of synergy)
   18. Temporary overcapacity or excess or obsolescent inventory
   19. Opportunity for barter (see Reading 35)
   20. Securing sources of supply
   21. Pursue buyer companies moving operations abroad.

A.2. Own resources (strengths and weaknesses)
   22. Domestic operations "under control" (going international rarely a good escape from domestic problems)

23. Sources of differential advantage
    231. High quality image
    232. Cost leadership
    233. Manpower skills
    234. Patents
    235. High liquidity
    236. Marketing know-how
24. Sources of differential disadvantage
    (Often the obverse of advantages)

A.3. Own objectives and philosophy (see also Reading 1)
   31. Growth rate
   32. Means of growth (growth in current products vs. unrelated products, finance growth from within, attitude toward acquisitions and mergers)
   33. Desirability sources of differential advantage
   34. Profitability, return on investment required
   35. Risk preferences
   36. Liquidity preferences
   37. Market share desired, etc.

A.4. Type of country preferred
   41. Industrialized West, Japan
   42. LDC
   43. East Bloc

A.5. Type and extent of commitment

As to the type of country preferred, predictability, relatively low risk, excellent infrastructure, firm-to-firm transactions, relative absence of government intervention in individual transactions, stiff competition and moderate to good profits are signposts of the industrialized democracies. The LDCs typically evidence predictability; fairly high risk, poor infrastructure, high rates of inflation, a dual economy (large primitive, small modern sector), frequent government intervention in individual transactions, an environment of regulations which is somewhat flexible (negotiated concessions, tariff exemptions, etc.), modest competition, good to excellent profit perspectives to firms really understanding local conditions, and the challenge of contributing to human welfare more than elsewhere. East Bloc countries are highly unpredictable until a contract is signed but thereafter traditionally very reliable trading partners; they offer low after-sales risk, poor infrastructure (but distribution is the buyer's problem), firm-to-state transactions, little or no contact with end consumers, great demands for credit, a highly legalistic bureaucracy, typically either very heavy or almost no competition (you are the chosen instrument), somewhat unpredictable profitability (especially due to impossibility of predicting pre-contract selling costs), at least in the past high risks of piracy or grossly insufficient compensation for patents, designs, and other industrial property rights, interest thus far essentially in industrial products, and technical know-how. Both East Bloc and LDC suffer from hard currency deficits. This often leads to import restrictions on consumer goods and a tendency to use barter and countertrade.

Some firms prefer to limit their initial search to countries where English or some other world language is widely spoken in business circles. Regional approaches are getting increasingly popular, involving such areas as the European Community and Latin America.

Checklist B: The Country (Region) Selection Decision

Assuming the commitment to go international has been made and the preferred type of country has been identified, specific *country analyses* must be performed. Unless there are special reasons or circumstances pointing to a given country, several candidate countries of the favored type should be separately examined by means of a comparative framework that comprises both the *international* and *local* environments. At the local level the country analysis includes the government, business culture, marketing infrastructure, and demand analysis. Finally, the country-specific *financial requirements* and *time dimensions* must be considered.

B.1. International environment
    11. Relationships between home office country and country X
    12. Tariffs in country X
    13. Nontariff barriers in country X
    14. Currency stability and currency controls
    15. Transportation costs
    16. Barter and countertrade requirements

B.2. Local marketing environment
    21. Government stability
    22. Predictability of public policy
    23. Economic development, growth rate, development policies
    24. Sensitivity to business cycles, rate of inflation
    25. Government controls and regulations
        251. Regulation in competitive practices, antitrust enforcement
        252. State marketing bodies
        253. Health and safety
        254. Product labeling, standardization, consumer information, and disclosure requirements
        255. Public procurement practices

26. Local business culture
    261. Philosophy of competition and cooperation
    262. Extent of cartelization
    263. Respect for contracts
    264. Business ethics
    265. Social factors in business, "networking"
27. Marketing infrastructure
    271. Data availability and reliability
    272. Marketing research agencies
    273. Literacy
    274. Advertising media
    275. Advertising agencies
    276. Public warehousing facilities
    277. Extent and reliability of postal and telephone systems
    278. Transportation facilities and costs

B.3. Market structure and demand analysis (for additional details see Reading 1 and Part IV Readings)
    31. Consumer behavior (buying and usage patterns and patterns of symbolic significance, life styles, distribution of household expenditures, attitudes to foreign products)
    32. Distributors and margins
    33. Price range
    34. Product variations, quality criteria
    35. Competitors by size and type
    36. Competitive strategies
    37. Potential competition
    38. Local stage of product life cycle
    39. Market potential, short and long term

B.4. Financial estimates
    41. Short term
        411. Investment need
        412. Sales volume forecast
        413. Profitability estimate, return on investment
    42. Long term
        421. Taxation
        422. Currency stability and convertibility
        423. Profitability remittance and repatriation prospects

B.5. Overall suitability
    51. Country X fit in a regional approach
    52. Country X as part of a global market portfolio

Checklist C: Market Entry and Operations

This checklist helps determine the appropriate mode of market entry, the first part of the international operations plan. It is essential that the plan incorporate the general assumptions and specific forecasts on which it is based and that it be prepared in written form, especially if it is a first or "initial" plan. Without these essentials there is no built-in signal system for if and when the plan needs to be revised, nor can a plan lacking in these prerequisites rationally be used as an instrument of delegation, coordination, and evaluation of managerial performance.

If there is anything behavioral science has proven it is that, in Western cultures at least, enthusiastic execution of decisions presupposes some degree of involvement in the preceding decision-making process. Thus, planning cannot be simply delegated to a staff specialist in an obscure corner of the organization. Line executives will rarely have the time to do much of the data-gathering job; however, it is essential that they regularly partake in the actual shaping of the plan.

For the sake of simplicity we shall assume that the decision has been made to begin marketing operations in an LDC on a modest scale (no local production). Once an ongoing operation has been established the preparation of a marketing plan would be similar to that of making a domestic marketing plan; the main difference would be the incorporation of matters involving relationships with headquarters and any operations in third countries.

C.1. Objectives
    11. Sales volume expected during initial period; market share
    12. Profitability, return on investment (note: the larger the scale of operations, the more likely negative profits during a build-up period.)
    13. Permissible risk exposure
    14. Going in for a fast profit and then leave vs. aiming for a lasting commitment
    15. Philosophy of ownership vs. joint ventures, etc.
    16. Complete adaptation vs. acting as local change agent
    17. Data feedback for future decisions:
    Test marketing or other marketing research, acquisition of data to determine desirability and form of long-term commitment—all the while keeping costs of data generation and analysis in mind.
    18. Justification of local objectives in terms of overall company objectives (e.g., role in "portfolio" of business)

C.2. International environment
See *Checklist B*, item B.1.

C.3. Local marketing environment
    31. See *Checklist B*, item B.2.
    32. Local government view of our kind of product
    33. Could we—and should we—obtain favored treatment from government?

C.4. Market structure and demand analysis

    41. See *Checklist B*, item B.3. (see also Reading 1)

    42. Detailed industry and company sales forecast

C.5. Resources

    51. Expected sources of differential advantage (see *Checklist A*, item A.2.22)

    52. Local validity of own patents and trademarks

    53. Availability of company personnel with prior local experience

    54. Tasks to be performed by company, tasks to be contracted out: marketing research, advertising, distribution may all be contracted out, if desired, given sufficient local infrastructure

    55. Available sources of supply relative to expected sales volume. Supply from headquarters or from other subsidiaries or from outside firms. Adequacy of sources and their ability to adjust to possible fluctuations in demand

C.6. Mode of market entry

    61. Direct exports from home base

    62. Indirect exports through home country channels

    63. Direct exports through outside distribution channels

    64. Direct exports and sales through local sales branch

    65. Licensing, franchising, technology transfer

    66. Foreign direct investment (FDI) in joint venture

    67. FDI in wholly-owned assembly or integrated production facilities

Checklist D: Marketing Strategy and Program

Assuming the international commitment decision has been made, the country or countries selected, and the most likely mode of entry determined, this checklist numerates the *strategic* aspects in the overall marketing plan. These include the underlying strategic concept, rationale, general thrust, and consideration of appropriate and matching marketing mix variables.

D.1. Strategy

    11. Overall concept (Gesalt) of our international marketing strategy. Strategy should be explicitly related to local objectives and to our notion of differential advantage. Include definition of market niche, if nichemanship is sought. Deluxe image vs. mass marketer; low profile vs. beating the drum, etc.

    12. Rationale for contemplated differentiation from domestic strategy, if any. Such deviations are often desirable or even

inevitable. As they do lessen synergy their justification should, however, be made explicit.

13. Homogenization or segmentation of local demand

D.2. Marketing mix implications of strategy

21. Product: options, models to be marketed, modifications for local market, if any. Product simplification, invention

22. Price: skimming vs. penetration. Price relative to current and potential competition; price relative to our policies elsewhere. If price very high compared to domestic due to tariffs, freight, high distributor margins, etc., justify belief that it will be accepted locally. If planned local price is very low, contemplate side-effects on company operations elsewhere

23. Promotion and intelligence: budget, theme, media, timing. If major resources to be committed, include plan for measurement of promotional effectiveness. Labeling, consumer information. Feedback from the marketplace, marketing research

24. Distribution channels
    241. Mode of market entry, see *Checklist C*, item C.6.
    242. Functions to be performed by channel members or distributors. Exclusive vs. selective distribution
    243. Margins, promotional allowances (if any)
    244. Short term vs. long-term commitments. Note possible need for future flexibility

25. Post-transaction service
    251. Service and warranty system
    252. Spare parts: locally manufactured or procured vs. imported from home country or subsidiary
    253. Handling of customer complaints

26. Networking and trust: plan for the build-up of goodwill and customer confidence. The larger the operation and the longer its time perspective the more important is trust (see also Readings 1 and 6)

Checklist E: International Marketing Organization

To bring the plan into fruition requires adequate marketing organization. Checklist E includes among organizational factors the type and nature of *coordination* between headquarters and international units, scheduling, performance evaluation (audit), and preview of subsequent planning periods.

E.1. Headquarters services and coordination

11. Manpower allocation at headquarters (HQ) and overseas

12. Organizational adjustments at HQ, if any
13. Identification of areas of HQ direction, assistance and consultation. Areas of local autonomy
14. Reporting arrangements
15. Pricing and other policies for intra-company transfers

E.2. Schedules

21. Step-by-step timing of activities and the attainment of subtargets. PERT or flow diagram techniques may be helpful here.
22. Budgeting
   221. Master budget
   222. Projected profit and loss statements for each reporting period
   223. Proforma balance sheets for each reporting period
   224. Cash flow projections in each reporting period

E.3. Action potential at the end of the planning period

This is an advance audit of operational performance, assuming full realization of the plan. At the end of the period a post-audit should be undertaken, including re-evaluation of the commitment decision and its future implications. These management audits should comprise items of the type indicated below:

31. Resource profile, including personnel skills
32. Differential advantage
33. Data about the market structure and demand
34. Trust and goodwill
35. Patents and trademarks
36. Standing arrangements with local suppliers and customers
37. Competitive position
38. Performance relative to budget
39. Performance relative to other aspects of objectives and plan
40. Impact on host country

E.4. Contingency plan: contingency planning is the standby plan for emergencies. It may be a strike, an import prohibition, a currency devaluation, failure to obtain local financing if planned for, or simply the fact that some vital assumption about the future might be mistaken. Take a cue from the military and put down some ideas on how to meet likely contingencies.

E.5. Long-term plan: assuming that the substance of the initial plan will be realized, the long-term plan should at least present a sketch of the next three to five years. In abbreviated form the framework suggested above would be equally suited to the long term plan.

47

Strategic Planning for a Global Business*

BALAJI S. CHAKRAVARTHY
HOWARD V. PERLMUTTER

Two recent trends have made strategic planning more complex in a multinational corporation (MNC): globalization of several industries and increased activism of its stakeholders. Until a decade ago, most multinational corporations did not seriously deal with either global integration or stakeholder activism.

A globally focused firm uses its world-wide system of resources to compete in national markets. Various country subsidiaries consequently become highly interdependent in their operational strategies, since the minimum volume necessary to exploit scale economies and experience effects is unavailable within a single national market. In order to be a viable competitor in a global business, an MNC must ensure tight integration of its worldwide operations.

Concurrent with the above trend has been the increasing pressure on MNCs from host governments. These stakeholders are forcing MNCs to concern themselves more with issues of legitimacy, i.e., whether the actions of MNCs are consonant with the interests of the host country.

The fundamental planning challenge for an MNC is one of balancing the economic imperative of global integration with the political imperative of prudent stakeholder management. In an extreme case, the two can pull in opposite directions. Giving the subsidiary autonomy to pursue a strategy responsive to host government needs can nurture legitimacy, but it must be balanced with suitable controls to ensure proper integration of the subsidiary's

---

* Reprinted from *Columbia Journal of World Business*, (Summer 1985), pp. 3–10, with permission.

569

strategy with that of other subsidiaries. This paper focuses on the role of strategic planning systems in bringing about such a balance.

The paper is divided into two main sections. The first section elaborates the planning challenge. The second section describes briefly the choice of strategic planning systems currently available to an MNC and assesses their relevance for a global business.

The Challenges for Strategic Planning

Three important contextual factors define the business planning challenge faced by an MNC:

- the *economic imperative* that determines where the MNC should locate various elements of the value chain for a given business;
- the *political imperative* as shaped by the demands of host countries in which the MNC operates; and,
- the MNC's own *strategic predisposition.*

The Economic Imperative

Based on the economic forces operating in an industry, Porter (1984) offers two distinct strategic options for an MNC: a global strategy (cost leadership, differentiation, and segmentation) and a country-centered strategy (national responsiveness, or protected markets). Each of these strategies is distinguished by two criteria: (1) extent of global centralization/coordination, and (2) breadth of target segments within the industry (see Figure 47.1).

A primary determinant of whether a firm should pursue a global or country-centered strategy is the proportion of value added in the upstream activities of the industry's value chain. In industries such as automobiles, motorcycles, chemicals, steel, and heavy electrical systems, where significant value is added in upstream activities (i.e., R&D and manufacturing), MNCs have found it advantageous to pursue a global strategy. On the other hand, in industries such as insurance and consumer packaged goods, where a substantial proportion of value is added in downstream activities (i.e., marketing, sales and service), a country-centered stratgey has been more viable.

However, even within an industry, the choice of strategy depends on the segments of the value chain that a firm competes in. For example, if a firm in the aircraft industry merely sells and services aircrafts worldwide, a country-centered strategy may be appropriate to it. Similarly, if there are global customers for an insurance company's product (e.g., marine insurance), the company may have to pick a global strategy. As a corollary, a vertically integrated firm can choose

Extent of global centralization coordination

	Global cost leadership	Global differentiation	Protected markets
Broad			
Narrow	Global segmentation		National responsiveness

Breadth of
target segments
within the
industry

Global strategy   Country-centered strategy

Source: Porter (1984)

FIG. 47.1. Strategic Alternatives in a Global Industry.

to pursue different strategies for different segments of the industry's value chain.

Globalization of industries is on the rise because of the increasing potential for centralization and coordination of business activities (Porter 1984). The move towards centralization is helped by the continuing homogenization of product needs among countries and the marketing systems and business infrastructure through which these needs are served. Cheaper and more reliable transportation has also contributed to centralization. (The lack of such transportation was a major deterrent to inter-country shipments in the past.) Greater coordination is being facilitated primarily by the international communications revolution. Integrated transmission of voice, data, and video signals worldwide is projected to become a reality in the near future. The emergence of global buyers and suppliers also calls for greater coordination between the various subsidiaries of an MNC.

The above analysis of the economic imperatives confronting an MNC would suggest that global strategies (both cost leadership and differentiation) will displace country-centered strategies in several industries. However, the new political imperatives faced by an MNC represent a countertrend towards national responsiveness. These will be examined next.

The Political Imperative

Doz and Prahalad (1980) offer a useful framework for understanding the political imperatives that drive the business strategies of an MNC. They define two important determinants of business context: (1) the bargaining power of the MNC, and (2) the bargaining power of the host government. The bargaining power of the MNC is based on three sources: proprietary technology, worldwide market share (economies of scale), and product differentiation. The bargaining power of the host government is derived from its desire and ability to control market access, and the size and attractiveness of the national market that it controls.

In situations where the MNC is a technology or market leader and where the bargaining power of the host government is weak a global integration strategy is appropriate. For example, Boeing could choose a global integration strategy in Europe because of its relative power over host governments (Doz and Prahalad 1980). Boeing is a technology leader with a dominant share of the world market. Consequently, the host governments could not force it to adopt a more country-centered strategy.

On the other hand, in situations where the power balance is skewed in favor of the host government, a country-centered strategy is more appropriate. Examples of such an approach are provided by Honeywell in France and Chrysler in the U.K. (Doz and Prahalad 1980).

The push towards country-centered strategies comes from the growing number of powerful external stakeholders. Management must not only worry about an MNC's viability (i.e., meeting its profit objectives), but also about its legitimacy (i.e., stakeholder perceptions as to whether the firm's activities are consonant with the values of the host country).

Home and host governments are key external stakeholders and both have begun to regulate MNC activities with increasing sophistication. In addition to its role as a regulator, the host government can engage in other relationships with an MNC: as a co-negotiator (along with unions in labor relations), as a supplier (where public utilities and raw material industries may be state owned), as a competitor (through its public sector corporations), or even as a distributor (where channels are state owned). In coping with powerful external stakeholders such as the host government, the MNC requires strategies that are tailored to each national context.

Strategic Predisposition

The strategic predisposition of a firm is shaped by a number of factors: the circumstances of its birth, the leadership style of its CEOs, its past administrative practices, the myths and folklore that have endured in the organization, etc. Heenan and Perlmutter (1979) describe four distinct predispositions in an MNC:

- *Ethnocentrism* is a predisposition where all strategic decisions are guided by the values and interests of the parent. Such a firm is predominantly concerned with its viability worldwide and legitimacy only in its home country.
- *Polycentrism* is a predisposition where strategic decisions are tailored to suit the cultures of the various countries in which the MNC competes. A polycentric multinational is primarily concerned with legitimacy in every country that it operates in, even if that means some loss of profits.
- *Regiocentrism* is a predisposition that tries to blend the interests of the parent with that of the subsidiaries at least on a limited regional basis. A regiocentric multinational tries to balance viability and legitimacy at the regional level.
- *Geocentrism* is a predisposition that seeks to integrate diverse subsidiaries through a global systems approach to decision-making. A geocentric firm tries to balance viability and legitimacy through a global networking of its businesses. On occasion, these networks may even include the firm's stakeholders and competitors. Geocentrism can be further classified as enclave or integrative geocentrism. The former deals with high priority problems of host countries in a marginal fashion; the latter recognizes that the MNC's key decisions must be separately assessed for their impact on each country.

The above predispositions are seldom found in their pure form. An MNC's predominant predisposition is called its EPRG profile. An ethnocentric or polycentric EPRG profile is very common, while a

TABLE 47.1. Orientation of the Firm under Different EPRG Profiles

ORIENTATION OF THE FIRM	EPRG PROFILE:				
	ETHNOCENTRIC	POLYCENTRIC	REGIOCENTRIC	GEOCENTRIC	
1. MISSION	Profitability (viability)	Public acceptance (legitimacy)	Both profitability and public acceptance (viability and legitimacy)		
2. GOVERNANCE ● Direction of goal setting	Top down	Bottom up (each subsidiary decides upon local objectives)	Mutually negotiated between region and its subsidiaries	Mutually negotiated at all levels of the corporation	
● Communication	Hierarchical, with headquarters giving high volume of orders, commands and advice	Little communication to and from headquarters and between subsidiaries	Both vertical and lateral communication within region	Both vertical and lateral communication within the company	
● Allocation of resources	Investment opportunities decided at headquarters	Self-supporting subsidiaries, no cross-subsidies	Regions allocate resources, under guidelines from headquarters	World wide projects, allocation influenced by local and headquarters' managers	
3. STRATEGY	Global integrative	National responsiveness	Regional integrative and national responsiveness	Global integrative and national responsiveness	
4. STRUCTURE	Hierarchical product divisions	Hierarchical area divisions, with autonomous national units	Product and regional organizations tied through a matrix	A network of organizations, (including some stakeholders and competitor organizations)	
5. CULTURE	Home country	Host country	Regional	Global	

Source: 1. Perlmutter (1984)
2. Heenan and Perlmutter (1979)

TABLE 47.2. EPRG Profile in Different Functional Areas

EPRG PROFILE:

FUNCTIONAL AREA	ETHNOCENTRIC	POLYCENTRIC	REGIOCENTRIC	GEOCENTRIC
TECHNOLOGY Production technology	Mass production	Batch production	Flexible manufacturing	Flexible manufacturing
MARKETING Product planning	Product development determined primarily by the needs of home country customers	Local product development based on local needs	Standardize within region, but not across	Global product, with local variations
Marketing mix decisions	Made at headquarters	Made in each country	Made regionally	Made jointly with mutual consultation
FINANCE Objective	Repatriation of profits to home country	Retention of profits in host country	Redistribution within region	Redistribution globally
Financing relations	Home country institutions	Host country institutions	Regional institutions	Other global institutions
PERSONNEL PRACTICES Perpetuation	People of home country developed for key positions everywhere in the world	People of local nationality developed for key positions in their own country	Regional people developed for key positions anywhere in the region	Best people everywhere in the world developed for key position everywhere in the world
Evaluation and control	Home standards applied for persons and performance	Determined locally	Determined regionally	Standards which are universal, weighted to suit local conditions

Source: Heenan & Perlmutter (1979)
Perlmutter (1984)

regiocentric or geocentric EPRG profile is relatively new among MNCs. Each EPRG profile is associated with a distinct social architecture. The mission, governance structure, strategy, organization structure, and culture associated with the four EPRG profiles are described in Table 47.1.

The administrative systems associated with each EPRG profile reinforce one another and over a period of time define the distinct mode in which an MNC adapts to its environment. In a sense, the profile gets institutionalized and dictates the firm's behavior in a variety of functions (Table 47.2). In an ethnocentric multinational, for example, marketing, manufacturing, finance, and personnel decisions are typically made at headquarters with very little input from country managers.

The predisposition of an MNC can be at odds with the strategy appropriate to its economic or political imperatives. For example, an ethnocentric firm may find it difficult to adopt a nationally responsive strategy, or a polycentric firm may not be successful in implementing a global integration strategy.

Strategic Planning Systems: Choices and Limitations

The three forces described in the previous section can and often do pull in different directions. In fact, the planning challenge is to reconcile their differences. For ease of exposition, we will represent the various business contexts that an MNC can experience in a two dimensional framework (Figure 47.2).

The strategic planning systems that have been used in the past by large diversified corporations fall under four distinct categories: Model I, or top-down planning; Model II, or bottom-up planning; Model III, or portfolio planning; and Model IV, or dual structure planning (Chakravarthy and Lorange 1984). The ability of each of these systems to balance viability and legitimacy in the distinct business contexts defined by Figure 47.2 are discussed below.

Model I: Planning for Cell 4

Model I, a top down approach to planning, seeks to provide the MNC with a global competitive advantage through tight integration of its worldwide activities.

A Model I company is typically organized into several product groups worldwide. It is the responsibility of each product group manager to ensure the needed global integration through an elaborate formal plan that is monitored for progress each month at all levels of management. This planning system is associated with a large and

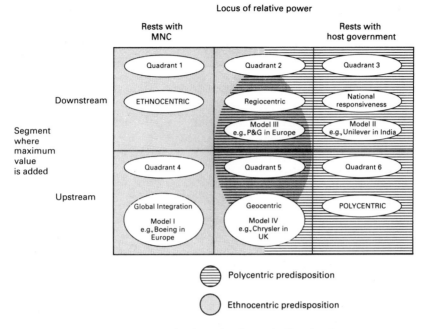

FIG. 47.2. A Framework for Choosing Strategic Planning Systems.

powerful planning staff at the headquarters, who carefully scrutinize and independently double check all strategic plans proposed by the national unit managers.

The legitimacy issue is dealt with in such a system through additional "citizenship costs" incurred by each subsidiary. In other words, the MNC using a Model I planning system chooses to pay the penalty for non-conformance with the host government's demands in the form of higher import duties and taxes. For a period under Harold Geneen, ITT was a company that followed such a system of planning.

The business context to which this system is best suited is cell 4. Cell 4 represents a business context where global integration is desirable and possible. The relatively high value that is added upstream suggests that the pooling of R&D and manufacturing activities among the MNC's various subsidiaries can result in important cost savings. A centrally coordinated strategic plan can facilitate the proper scheduling of these activities. Moreover, given that the locus of relative power rests with the MNC, it will face few obstacles from the host government for such an integration. Boeing's aircraft business in Europe falls in this cell. Other examples are IBM or AT&T (eventually) in world markets. This is not to suggest that these companies are restricted only to a Model I planning system, but to point out that given their contexts, they can use such a system.

It must be noted, however, that the locus of relative power can shift back to the host government if there are other eager competitors who are willing to collaborate with it. In fact, like in the case of Honeywell in France, the host government can provide suitable incentives to attract a "weak" MNC. This can mean loss of market for a Model I MNC. A Model I planning approach must be tempered, therefore, with some sensitivity to the needs of the host country.

Model II: Planning for Cell 3

A firm using a Model II planning system is typically organized by geographic areas (as opposed to product groups as in Model I). The smallest geographic unit is a national unit. Each national unit is delegated the responsibility for balancing its legitimacy and viability goals within broad guidelines issued by headquarters. The subsidiaries behave as if they are national companies. There are very few functional interdependencies across national units, and headquarters seldom resort to cross-subsidies. Typically, monitoring and control are financially oriented in a Model II planning system. The headquarters has a very thin corporate planning staff who act primarily as consolidators of national unit business plans.

Theoretically, a Model II planning system can be very responsive to the needs of the host government, but at cost in duplication of resources and limits to the economic advantages of multinationality. A Model II firm has competitive advantages over a national firm only in a few domains: pooling of financial risks, sharing of R&D costs, coordination of export marketing, and some skill transfers among subsidiaries. If Model I was overly focused on the economic imperative, Model II is especially partial to the political imperative.

Model II is best suited to a cell 3 business. Cell 3 represents a business where the economic imperative (high value added downstream) and the political imperative both point to a national responsiveness strategy. Unilever's operations in India are a case in point. The subsidiary sells consumer products, toiletries and animal feed, none of which lies in the core of essential industrial sectors as defined by the Indian government. Consequently, Unilever can operate in India only on the government's terms. In such a setting, a Model II planning process is quite appropriate. The parent exercises largely financial control and provides the subsidiary with technical and managerial assistance and with help in its export efforts when sought.

Model III: Portfolio Planning

Models I and II are suitable only for select business segments of a MNC and cannot be used consistently throughout the firm. Model I presumes that national stakeholders can be appeased by paying suitable citizenship costs. As the recent woes of Union Carbide in Bhopal, India, would point out, citizenship costs currently are being measured by more exacting world standards. Consequently, a planning orientation like Model I that completely ignores legitimacy issues can eventually hurt even the firm's viability.

On the other hand, a planning orientation that is predominantly responsive to national interests ignores the many advantages of multinationality. Given the trend towards globalization in many industries, a Model II planning orientation can hurt the competitive position of an MNC in world markets.

Instead of selecting one of the two pure archetypes discussed above, a diversified MNC can use both planning systems to suit its different business contexts. This approach is also called portfolio planning. An MNC using a Model III planning system is typically organized in global product divisions like a Model I firm. However, unlike a Model I firm, it uses a top-down or bottom-up planning process, depending on the context of each of its businesses. This is a popular approach among MNCs. According to a recent survey, over 50% of all U.S.-based diversified MNCs use this system of planning.

The attractiveness of an industry environment and the competitive strengths of the firm in that industry are normally the two determinants of whether the business will be subjected to a Model I or Model II planning system. A business in a growing national market where the company is trying to build market share will typically employ Model II planning, while a business in a maturing or mature national market where the company has a strong competitive position will generally use a Model I planning process. This is consistent with the emphasis on marketing (country-centered strategy) in the first business as the MNC tries to build market share, and on manufacturing and distribution (global integration strategy) in the second business as it seeks to improve operational efficiency.

Portfolio planning is best suited to a cell 1 or cell 2 business context. In either case, given the MNC's relative power over its host countries, it is free to attempt at least limited coordination among groups of countries in a region. Each such region is treated as a planning unit in a Model III system.

The Model III planning approach is most effective only when the planning challenge can be neatly compartmentalized as either integrative (regional integration) or adaptive (national responsiveness). This is indeed possible in several business contexts. The economic forces faced by a firm need not always be in conflict with the political forces. As Porter (1984) points out:

> Some economic forces favor standardization (e.g., scale economies) but others favor country-centered strategies (e.g., product heterogeneity and transport costs). Similarly, there are political forces working towards a country-centered strategy (e.g., local content rules and local ownership laws) and political forces favoring global strategies (export subsidies, R&D support for targeted industries), (1984, p. 30).

Designing a planning system that simultaneously encourages adaptation and integration within a region is, however, difficult. For example, in industries like telecommunications, a global integration strategy can optimally exploit special upstream resources like R&D and manufacturing; however, given the salience of this industry to national economies, host governments are likely to insist on a country-centered strategy.

Moreover, the assumption of Model III that a country unit can be initially subjected to a country-centered strategy (Model II) and then switched to a regional integration strategy (Model I), may be untenable in countries where such integration implies retrenchment in investment. This is especially true in countries where the MNC has several business interests. The host country can use its leverage in one business to extract concessions in another, where the MNC supposedly has more power over the host country. A sequential attention to the legitimacy and viability needs of a business, as proposed in Model III, needs to be replaced therefore with a system that can ensure simultaneous attention to these needs. Model IV on Dual Structure Planning is such a system.

Model IV: Dual Structure Planning

A cell 5 or cell 6 business context is the most difficult since it simultaneously requires a global integration and national responsiveness orientation. For example, Chrysler's operations in the U.K. should be responsive to the host government, while at the same time derive global integrative advantages to compete successfully with other international auto manufacturers.

In order to use a dual structure planning system, the MNC must be organized in a matrix structure, with product and area as its two dimensions. A planning system can then be designed to stress adaptation along one dimension and integration along the other. If, for example, the corporation wants the subsidiary to be country-centered, it should use an adaptive orientation for strategies formulated by the business side of the matrix, and use the area dimension of the matrix for integration. In other words, while national unit managers have leeway in adapting the company's business to their local environments, they would still be answerable for profit performance set through the budgeting process. Conversely, to implement a global business strategy, the MNC should allow adaptation on the area dimension at the national unit level while ensuring integration through the product dimension of the matrix. Thus, the integrative side of the matrix becomes in effect the operating structure, while the adaptive dimension becomes the strategic structure.

The relative emphasis on adaptation or integration within a national market can be altered by moving key managers to the appropriate side of the matrix, and by altering the planning, control, and reward systems used in that country. The planning system acts like a lens to focus the matrix structure toward a national responsive or global integrative orientation as required from country to country. It also leads to a more balanced orientation within each country than that provided by a Model III, especially if the MNC's culture encourages healthy confrontation between the two sides of the matrix. An example of a company that uses a dual structure planning is IBM. It is most useful to firms that are not widely diversified and that derive their competitive advantage from a common product-market, technology, or operation base.

A Model IV planning system can theoretically provide the simultaneous balance required between legitimacy and viability. The relative power difference between the two dimensions of the global matrix can be set at different equilibrium levels to suit each business context. However, fine tuning a global matrix structure through a Model IV planning system requires the simultaneous support of several other administrative systems including staffing, control, and reward systems. The orchestration of all of these systems can easily become an administrative nightmare. A recent survey showed that less than 5% of all MNCs attempted such a planning system.

Conclusions

The discussion in the previous sections showed how currently available planning systems are not quite suited to the needs of a global business. One way of dealing with this problem would be for the MNC to position itself in quadrants where the economic and political pressures are not conflicting. It can also attempt to rectify power imbalances with the host government by manipulating the resource dependencies of the subsidiary. However, as was pointed out earlier, current trends suggest that increasing numbers of global businesses will face the simultaneous challenge of global integration and national responsiveness. A hybrid of Model III and Model IV will be the best initial option for meeting this twin challenge.

A Hybrid Planning System

The Model IV planning system proposed in the previous section can theoretically help balance the visibility and legitimacy goals of an MNC. However, as mentioned earlier, dual structure planning is relatively new. Instead of attempting a company wide Model IV planning approach, it is perhaps more prudent to first attempt Model IV planning only within select regions where there are strong pressures for both legitimacy and viability (Chakravarthy 1984). Other regions can be managed using a Model III planning system.

In such a system, the headquarters must help balance the region's orientation towards integration and national responsiveness by maintaining a counterbalancing functional and administrative view. In other words, if the region seems to be veering off to a nationally responsive orientation, staff advisors at the headquarters must be managers who are biased towards global integration. Finally, the monitoring, control, and reward systems must acknowledge performance towards the goals of all major stakeholders of the firm, and not merely those of the stockholders of the parent company. The proposed hybrid system is discussed at length in a follow-up paper.

Strategic Predisposition

The major bottleneck we anticipate in implementing the hybrid planning system discussed above is the predominant ethnocentric predisposition exhibited by most MNCs. An enthnocentric firm essentially focuses on bottom line profits, and treats all political imperatives as unnecessary constraints. Even a polycentric firm pursues a country-centered strategy vigorously only when it is dictated by an economic imperative (cell 3 in Figure 47.2), and not as enthusiastically when imposed by a political imperative (cells 1 and 2 in Figure 47.2). The governing management paradigm in most MNCs seem to be overly biased towards viability.

On the other hand, most host governments expect the MNC to treat political imperatives as goals and economic imperatives (reasonable profits) as constraints. The mindsets of the MNC managers and their international stakeholders would seem to be irreconcilably different. Unless an MNC begins to change its predisposition, it is headed on a collision course with its stakeholders, regardless of the planning system that it uses.

The real challenge for an MNC is then to alter its predisposition to a more regiocentric or geocentric orientation. On occasion, the MNC may have to seek the cooperation of select competitors and important stakeholders in order to proactively simplify the environment in which it competes. Cooperation and competition are both accepted strategies under a geocentric predisposition.

The most important instrument available for changing the predisposition of an MNC is human resource management. Very few managers have personally internalized and resolved the tension between maximizing the firm's profit goals and emphasizing the needs of the host government. It is important, therefore, that the personnel policies of an MNC ensure: (1) that the proper mix of attitudes is nurtured through job rotation, promotion, and placement; and (2) that job assignments are carefully made in keeping with the manager's attitudes. The critical determinant of an MNC's successful adaptation to its environment is its ability to nurture relevant attitudes in its managerial work force.

References

Chakravarthy, B. S. and P. Lorange, "Managing Strategic Adaptation: Options in Administrative Systems Design," *Interfaces*, Vol. 14, No. 1 (1984), pp. 34–46.

Doz, Y. L. and C. K. Prahalad, "Headquarters Influence and Strategic Control in NMNCs," *Sloan Management Review*, (Fall 1981), pp. 15–29.

Heenan, D. A. and H. V. Perlmutter, *Multinational Organizational Development: A Social Architecture Perspective*, (Reading, Mass: Addison-Wesley, 1979).

Porter, M. E., "Competition in Global Industries: A Conceptual Framework," Paper presented at the Prince Bertil Symposium on Strategies for Global Competition, Stockholm School of Economics, November 7–9, 1984.

48

Japanese Export Marketing: Structures, Strategies, Counterstrategies*

JOHNY K. JOHANSSON
IKUJIRO NONAKA

Introduction

There is no need to argue any longer for the case that Japanese exporting companies have been singularly successful in penetrating foreign markets (although there have been failures, particularly in the earlier years.) The record, well documented elsewhere speaks for itself. Similarly, some of the factors which underlie this performance have been thoroughly discussed in various trade and related publications, both in the U.S. and Western Europe. The explanations, although partial in many cases, serve rather well as a guide to understanding the Japanese exporting prowess. Yet there is a need to place the various factors in a cohesive framework, in particular with respect to the role that marketing factors play in the overall picture, and also for the purpose of identifying what possible counterstrategies could be contemplated by Western firms. This integration is the basic purpose of the present paper.

The framework developed here draws on published secondary material as well as primary data collected through personal interviews in some of the larger exporting companies. In what follows, some of the basic environmental factors will first be briefly sketched. The article then discusses the intra-company factors in production and management systems which recently have been given so much attention by business scholars and practitioners. There follows a section on

* Reprinted from *International Marketing Review*, (Winter 1983), pp. 12–24, with permission.

585

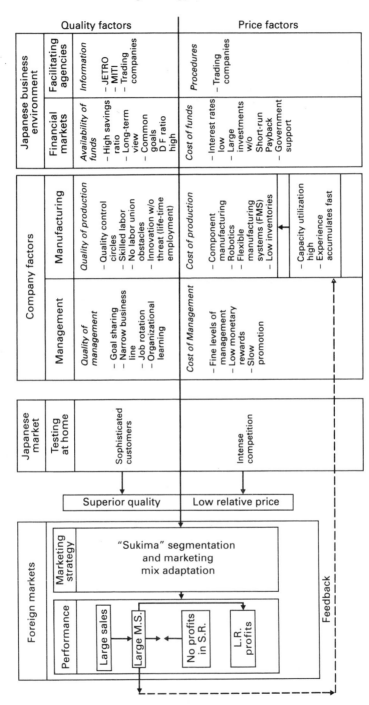

FIG. 48.1. Japanese Export Marketing: How a Superior Quality/Price Ratio is Achieved

marketing factors based on the primary data collected. Next the basic components of the Japanese marketing strategies abroad are reported. An integrative framework which summarizes the interdependence between the factors is then presented and discussed (for a capsule presentation of this part of the paper, see Figure 48.1).

In the last section of the article several alternative counterstrategies against the Japanese are discussed and evaluated.

Business Environment

One might well ask how such a "separate" people as the Japanese have been able to penetrate foreign markets so successfully. Part of the reason lies in the institutions created in Japan for the purpose of facilitating exports.

The trading company role is well known and requires little extended discussion here. It requires naturally only limited "export conscious-ness" to explore overseas markets if the company has easily available an external export division. Although trading company activities are largely concentrated in the staple commodity areas, the simple avail-ability of a world-wide network of contacts makes exporting a much less hazardous marketing task.

Other facilitating agencies include JETRO, the semi-public infor-mation organization which originally started out as an export promoter, changed its name to an *external* trade promoter, and recently (1982) began actively soliciting foreign suppliers to Japan. There is of course also considerable government support for the prioritized export industries, particularly through the MITI and Ministry of Finance, although direct subsidies are no longer common. An important factor relating to government and various bank activities concern the operations of the capital markets, with Japanese com-panies able to borrow considerable amounts of low-interest funds for overseas business (partly a function of the high savings ratio among Japanese households). Coupled with the strong long-term support from related companies with common goals in the so-called Zaibatsus, the financial constraints that so often operate upon Western companies abroad are much less binding for the Japanese firms.

Company Factors

Lately there has also been much attention paid to the internal factors of the organization, namely production and management systems, and how they impact on the Japanese company performance. Here, it is necessary to emphasize that the discussion concentrates on the larger Japanese firms. There are some exports also by small firms, but in contrast to, say, Italy, by far the greatest proportion of exports is accounted for by very large companies.

Production Systems

As is well known, it is in the large companies that the practice of life-long employment is most common. It is also in these companies that the individual rewards to the workers are the highest, both in terms of pay, bonuses, and status. This means in turn that these companies are seen as the most attractive employers for young workers and college students, and the most successful of the companies (often measured in terms of their domestic market share, i.e., size) can count on access to the cream of the crop of new employees.

By linking the semi-annual bonuses to company performance, the loyalty and life-long commitment to the company on the part of the employees are translated into strong incentives for hard work. In addition, the use of up-to-date technical production processes (robotics and flexible manufacturing systems) and quality control circles is fostered by the capability of the employees, and by the lack of industry-wide labor unions. Rather than building solidarity with workers in competing companies, the employees of a firm view them as competitors, and there is no necessary correlation between pay for a particular skill level between a high share company and a low share firm in the same industry.

The large company in Japan provides also the focus for a host of small component sub-contractors which in many cases are directly controlled by their single customer, either via financial and personnel policies, or simply as a matter of tacit understanding. An oft-quoted example of this is the "Kanban" system developed by Toyota and the low inventories such an arrangement makes possible. By "leaning on" these suppliers in times of reduced sales the large company is often able to sustain quite drastic shortfalls without necessarily damaging their worker morale or their financial viability. It goes without saying that for employees in these smaller companies the vision of a secure, life-long attachment to a company "provider" represents more of a "pipedream" than a real possibility.

Management Systems

The recent interest in Japanese management techniques represents another attempt to ferret out the intra-company factors which are decisive in the Japanese success. What is emerging is a picture of the organization as a "clan" or "family" with goal sharing, consensus, and mutual support taking precedence over confrontations, initiative and ambition. It is hard to assess the relative contribution that these new structures make to the successful performance observed, and the new writings tend to address this issue quite obliquely. But a couple of observations can be made.

First, it is clear that the relative looseness of position descriptions and lack of professional management training in the Japanese companies do make it possible to interact quite easily laterally, i.e., across organizational chains of command. Most of the managers have spent their whole working life in the company and are quite familiar with its operations, in particular since job rotation is enforced. By virtue of the fact that the companies tend to be much more industry-specific, i.e., operate within a relatively narrow line of industry, the amount of shared knowledge among managers in finance, marketing, production and personnel is generally very high. This by itself would tend to enhance their ability to make sound decisions with respect to foreign markets, and an ability to "pool" easily a large amount of information.

This latter point is emphasized in recent studies. In these analyses the Japanese organization is viewed as an "information processing unit" which is shown to perform very well in terms of organizational learning, i.e., developing the organizational skills to adapt to new contingencies. Since studies of the difficulties of breaking into foreign markets have demonstrated the importance of informational and learning factors (Johanson and Vahlne 1977) this provides support for the argument that management factors do indeed affect export performance.

Marketing Factors

The issue of information processing naturally leads into the question of marketing factors and their role in the successful Japanese performance. To what extent does the existence of government information agencies and worldwide trading companies contribute to the marketing research activities of these firms and their ultimate success in the marketplace? What is the role of marketing strategy variables such as segmentation and positioning, and the deployment of tactical measures comprising the marketing mix?

To find out the answers to some of these questions informal personal interviews were carried out with the export managers of 12 of the largest Japanese firms involved in exporting. The firms were selected on the basis of their performance abroad over the last decade and covered the three industries shown in Table 48.1.

Initially, two trading companies (Mitsubishi and C. Itoh) were interviewed to generate some background information and to develop the questionnaire.

TABLE 48.1. The Companies Interviewed

Electronics	Autos	Steel
Sony	Toyota	Japan Steel
Matsushita	Nissan	Nippon Kokan
Mitsubishi	Toyo Kogyo	Kawasaki
Denki	(Mazda)	
Hitachi	Honda	

The interviews all took place in the Japanese headquarters of the companies (in Tokyo, except for Matsushita—outside Osaka—and Toyo Kogyo—in Hiroshima). They were organized with the assistance of the Jetro headquarters in Tokyo, and involved an initial preparatory contact during which the questions were distributed, and a second meeting (usually a few days later) during which the actual interviews took place. The questions centered around two main themes, one concerned with the global expansion of the company (timing and selection of country markets, development of overseas manufacturing and sales offices) and a second theme dealing with the entry strategies and marketing decisions in selected countries. The interviews were held in English and were rather informal by necessity (partly to allow further probing of key topics). In several cases these probes necessitated the use of an interpreter, sometimes provided by the respondent himself. The interviews took an average of one hour and a half to complete, but allowed follow-up to be carried out later to clarify key points.

The reporting of the findings will first deal with informational factors, then cover the entry strategies employed. The discussion will then turn to promotion and price policies, the product/market interface, and finally report on the importance of the quality/price ratio.

Informational Factors

In terms of utilization of trading company information for foreign markets, the usage varies a great deal. Steel companies employ sogo shoshas for about 80% of their information needs, while electronics companies and autos average about 10 to 15%, some as high as 40% and some, like Sony, close to 0%. The government sources are used very rarely (Jetro seems to be more important for smaller companies), and the remaining percentage of market information is generated from company operations abroad and at home. The degree of importance of sources from abroad varies directly with the level of export and direct foreign investment.

There are other sources of information utilized by most of these companies. Many employ students and other expatriates abroad on an informal basis, encouraging and rewarding their search for information of interest. Also, the type of information gathered tends to be more varied than one would expect necessary on a pure marketing basis. Cultural, political and social events and developments are covered and serve to set the stage for more in-depth analysis contracted out to local research consultants. With the group consensus decision-making process it becomes natural to attempt to set specific research findings against the context of the country culture spelled out by other relatively loose data. Where one pressured decision maker easily can be overwhelmed by information overload, a group sifting through and evaluating the evidence without the necessity for individual responsibility for specific decision can be quite effective (although perhaps not as efficient) in arriving at a sound solution.

Without making too much of this aspect of the marketing process, it is clear that the emphasis by Western companies upon "scientific" research will not be sufficient when it comes to penetrating foreign markets. On the other hand, the Japanese approach can be time-consuming and irritating to the decision oriented executive in the Western company, where efficiency tends to be emphasized and relevancy demanded. An illustration of this dilemma was provided by one frustrated executive in the Japanese subsidiary of a Swedish multinational who wanted to copy the Japanese approach, and assigned his Japanese assistant to cover relevant newspaper articles about the Japanese market. When asked why he spent so much time on each of the dailies, the assistant answered simply "I think it is all relevant."

Entry Strategies

When asked about mode of entry, a similar pattern as for information sources emerged. The Japanese companies in autos and electronics tend to rely on wholly or partly owned subsidiary distributors, who then sell to retailers (dealers). There are exceptions. For example, Toyota did not find the market for trucks in Algeria to be large enough for full-fledged introduction and instead licensed one of the trading companies to undertake the marketing. The steel companies utilize trading companies almost exclusively. These matters are already well known, and of greater interest is perhaps the question of selection of countries (and timing).

Among the auto and electronics manufacturers, there was almost a complete convergence in their export expansion paths. The initial markets tended to be in South East Asia—another example of the "cultural distance" theory propounded by Johanson and Vahlne (1977). Before entering European markets, and, in particular, before entering the U.S. market, considerable experience in exporting had been built up in these original target markets. Furthermore, before entering the all-important Western markets, an attempt was made to enter another market with similar characteristics. The most common choice at this stage was Australia, which was viewed quite often as a "dress rehearsal" entry before approaching Western markets. What clearly emerged was a sense that these companies wanted to develop some exporting skills before taking on the major market countries—a type of "export experience curve" rationale.

Promotion and Price

There was a general consensus among the people interviewed that promotional efforts must be tailored to each country specifically, a "poly-centric" approach. There was no belief that the advertising successful in Japan could be used in other countries, for example. On the contrary, most of the firms hired local agencies to do their advertising, although in some cases branch offices of the large Japanese agencies (Dentsu, Hakuhodo), where local staffing existed, were used. Even though most of the sales offices established in the market countries had a fair number of Japanese expatriates, their functions were mainly confined to coordination and communication with the home office. There seemed to be no feeling that promotional know-how generated in the home market could be used to advantage abroad, a stark contrast to the "Put a Tiger in your Tank" standardization sometimes advocated by U.S. multinationals.

The respondents were generally unwilling to disclose much of the pricing schemes used for foreign markets. The general theme was one of seeing the entry into a market as a long-term "investment" and market penetration was accordingly a much more important pricing objective rather than quick profit-taking with a skimming approach. Several of the firms employed a version of the "experience curve pricing strategy" where a relatively low price was expected to lead to large volume and future cost savings. It became rather clear that individual markets were not seen as "profit centers" but rather as pieces in one large global puzzle. By generating sufficient funds at home and in some selected country markets where the share positions were strong, the lower returns emanating from a low price penetration strategy in newer markets could be sustained over a relatively long period of time.

Product/Market Policies

Speaking about product development, one recurrent theme emerging from the interviews was the dominant role of the home market. In a sense many of the managers interviewed saw success at home as the most difficult and the most important test of their products. The reason was the intense competition coupled with very sophisticated and demanding customers. If a reasonable success (i.e., market share) in the Japanese market could be attained, success abroad would come easy, relatively speaking. But at the same time, there was no question about the level of product adaptation which these companies were willing to pursue. In an attempt to corner the tradeoffs between adaptation and other market factors such as growth, size, probable share, and quick payout period, an informal attempt was made at a conjoint analysis. It failed, for the simple reason that the managers could not visualize "trading off" adaptation of the product against the quick profits that simple exporting of an unadapted product might have yielded.

There was no necessary agreement that the exported versions of the products would be of higher value or higher quality than domestic ones, if anything the opposite. But there was agreement on the fact that the products marketed abroad must show definite differential advantages over competitive alternatives. One standard example cited was Toyota's analysis of the VW Beetle before designing their own competing alternative. This line of attack was emphasized most by Sony, whose "innovativeness" has produced new features and products which set the norms for other products in the market, both in Japan and abroad.

Talking about market segmentation and product positioning, these project factors again came to the fore. Because of the reliance on the home market at the early stages of the product life cycle, the natural approach seemed for many to be one of identifying special segments where their particularly strong features would be an asset. This "niche" approach, as it has become called in the U.S., was usually likened to a "sukima" strategy, referring to the small opening that remains when a sliding door does not quite fit its frame. The general idea was that by entering through a "chink in the armour," existing competitors would not take notice and defend their product line strongly. From this "foot-in-the-door" entry further inroads would come naturally.

Most of the managers emphasized the "marketing concept" and their desire and intent to make sure that the foreign markets were supplied with products' they wanted. At Sony, in particular, and in a few other instances, more emphasis was placed on the notion that many products will create their own markets, and thus that the marketing concept was only partially valid. In these cases the role of formal marketing research was naturally seen as limited—as is well known, Sony does much less marketing research than most of its competitors in Japan and abroad (cf Levitt 1983, p. 99).

Quality/Price Ratio

One of the continuous re-iterations in these interviews was the desire to provide the customer with "good value," a high quality/price ratio. This was seen as the competitive edge provided by many Japanese products. The context in which they were speaking was of course somewhat different from Western companies: they were people who had been with these companies when "Japanese products" stood for shoddy quality sold at cut-rate prices. They did not view the approach as being "low-priced," even though initial entry in a new market might be accompanied by lower prices than standard for the quality offered. By obtaining a large market share, perhaps after some initial losses and only after several years in some cases (Honda's motorcycle plant in Belguim was one example, turning into the black only after about 10 years), the experience curve effect would serve to reduce costs sufficiently to justify the lower prices.

This emphasis upon a high quality/price ratio was coupled with a firm belief in the "rationality" of the buyer. They paid short shrift to the notion that people are willing to buy a particular product simply because it comes from a certain country (the "country-of-origin" bias). It might happen in a few cases, and in the short run. But over the longer run, no customers will continue to purchase an inferior alternative. Marketing to these managers was accordingly seen as a means by which "an offer that cannot be refused" is presented to the potential buyer.

An Integrated Framework

The way in which the various forces affect the strategy and performance of the Japanese exporting company can best be seen with reference to the scheme presented in Figure 48.1. To start unraveling the picture the point of departure might best be the competitive edge in markets abroad, the high quality/price ratio. How is such a high ratio achieved?

On the product quality side, the factors discussed above include the precise definition of narrow "sukima" segments to be used as "beach-heads" in the entry phase, and a fastidious adaptation of the product and other elements of the marketing mix to local conditions. These strategies are developed on the basis of a wide information and marketing research coverage of conditions in the targeted markets, and a deliberateness in the attack predicated upon the long-term view taken of an entry as an investment. The willingness to adapt and the care of the analysis is partially a natural consequence of the separateness that the Japanese feel with the rest of the world. There is no illusion that other peoples will like a product because the Japanese customers do.

The products marketed abroad have first shown their mettle in the competitive home market and tend to be the "winners" of that competitive struggle (there are exceptions: Sanyo is not a highly regarded competition in Japan, but does very well abroad. Sony is highly regarded, but nevertheless does not capture the major shares in the Japanese markets —see Kotler and Fahey 1982, p. 5). This competitive situation relates directly to the lack of industry solidarity among firms in the same markets, and the consequences in terms of manpower attractiveness, pay, and status that a high market share confers. It also is predicated on the sophisticated buyers in the Japanese markets in the areas where Japanese exports excel.

But to have good products to market, manufacturing must be attended to. Here, as we have seen, the Japanese companies have done very well. In terms of labor skills, production process technology, management on the shop floor and with innovations such as the quality control circles, the Japanese company might well be the world leader. As for the financial side of operations, the long-term, low-interest loans (which create the high debt/equity ratio so well known among Japanese companies) provide a setting where a long-term investment view of marketing abroad is made possible. Since some of the Japanese products are sufficiently new that education of the buyer and the creation of new markets are prerequisites for success, this financial base, plus the support of the government and other companies within the Zaibatsus, allows exactly the kind of strategic posture with a long-term view so necessary for successful performance.

On the pricing side, similar factors are at work. The focus on market share, which comes naturally after the experiences in the home market, predates the famous BCG demonstration that share and profitability go hand in hand. Specifically, the high market share goal naturally involves an experience-curve pricing strategy, with low prices leading the attainment of lower costs. But to properly capitalize on these experience effects a constant eye has to be kept on possibilities for improving and streamlining operations. The lack of union obstacles and the fact that building anew is quite natural among the Japanese with their post-World War memories intact (a point surprisingly often stressed in our interviews) have served well in allowing cost-cutting automation and robotization to take place.

For such plant investments to be justified, capacity utilization rates must be high—and the emphasis upon increased sales and market share has matched this criterion very well. One may of course question what will happen when these growth conditions slack off, and there is evidence that the companies are worried about these developments. But judging from the efforts of the steel companies, where a saturated world market has already been encountered, the Japanese companies will find a way to cope.

These investments in manufacturing and marketing are, again, made possible by the relatively accommodating financial support provided in the Japanese capital markets. For the low-cost operations the level of interest rates, in particular, has been instrumental. In this regard alone, the Western companies' recent attempts to counter the Japanese on-slaught have been severely hampered from the start.

In conclusion, the integrative framework provided by Figure 48.1 depicts a phenomenon that has been very hard to compete against in the world markets. Next, let us turn to the identification of some possible counterstrategies in the marketing domain that might prove worthwhile to explore.

Counterstrategies

To combat the success of the Japanese companies a number of counterstrategies can be (and have been) suggested. They range from government imposition of quotas, to easing the restrictions of the Japanese capital markets, to exhortations to "Buy domestic products." Here the focus will be on marketing counterstrategies, starting with existing strategies, then covering some emerging concepts and finally drawing upon some military analogies.

Existing Strategies

There are some possible counterstrategies which might be called traditional strategies. These include "aggressive" pricing, identification and filling of those product gaps that attracted the Japanese in the first place, and the pursuance of R & D leadership in hi-tech industries. Other suggestions can be derived from textbook principles, including the identification and targeting of unfilled market "niches" and the intense pursuit of new markets where the Japanese are not yet dominant.

More promising are perhaps the propositions by Porter (1980) concerning product differentiation, low-cost leadership (an "experience curve" strategy) and the explicit definition of company skills in filling the needs of small segments with special requirements. There are companies which have already "streamlined" their operations so as to make this last option natural. Having well defined product/market subsets coupled with a definition of skills in a relatively narrow sense has made it possible to increase cost efficiencies and also focus more attention on customer demands—in a sense this concentration of effort mirrors that of the more successful Japanese companies.

Emerging Strategies

These existing strategies will have to be abetted by more innovative new strategies to be successful against the Japanese. There are some new alternatives in the gestation stage and these emerging strategies might well serve their purpose and at the same time rewrite some of the traditional marketing principles.

The strong integration between marketing and production functions made possible by the flexible manufacturing systems in Japanese companies is one of the driving forces behind the new concepts. In the divisionalized, multi-product corporation close interaction between production and marketing staff is not easy. Marketing managers might have little or no knowledge of the basic production questions in their particular division, having been recruited from other divisions in the company. So is the case for the general manager. The streamlining of operations into more narrowly defined skill areas should serve by itself to make the lateral communications between marketing and production feasible and more fruitful. If in addition the organizational structure is augmented so as to make direct, face-to-face interactions between the functional managers a natural part of management activities, the Japanese advantages on this score might well be eliminated.

This development is behind what Kotler-Fahey identify as the emergence of a new function, the "management of product-market evolution" (p. 23). They see the tasks of the marketing manager to include the identification of new market segments, the development of products for these segments, and, most significantly, the continuous "management" of the development of these segments. The concept is dynamic, with marketing and products following closely the evolution of markets over time. As was mentioned previously, some Japanese do not view their marketing to be simply reactive to customer desires at any one given point in time. Rather, they readily acknowledge the possibility that their new products will by themselves change existing preferences, sometimes radically. As a consequence, it becomes important to anticipate customer reactions in the future as new products enter the market. And since some of the firm's own product and marketing policies will affect where the market will head, a natural conclusion is to help the movement in a direction where the firm's differential advantage is the greatest. The product/market management task discussed by Kotler-Fahey can thus be translated into a "pro-active" strategic posture.

This new thrust is also echoed in the new thinking about the marketing concept exemplified by Levitt (1977) and Thorelli (1983). These authors recognize explicitly that the role of the marketing orientation of firms in the past has been too "reactive," simply seen as a philosophy of satisfying the customers whatever their expressed desires tend to be. From this perspective both authors tend to fault modern marketing research techniques for being too "mechanistic," too concerned with method rather than content (Thorelli, p. 14). Their de-emphasis upon formal methods of marketing research is perhaps a natural outgrowth of the new orientation towards the dynamics of evolving markets. It can be reconciled with the existing know-how, however, if it is recognized that new product research has always been chancy at best. What seems to be emerging is a consensus that the Japanese invasion has made mature markets behave as new product markets, thus invalidating "tried-and-true" analytical methods.

"Military" Strategies

Some of these emerging strategies draw quite directly upon the structures and strategies employed by the Japanese. It is possible, perhaps, to extend this borrowing even further.

As was argued earlier, the Japanese in-roads have usually started with a "sukima" approach, avoiding direct confrontation where the "enemy" strength was greatest. Pushing the military analogy further, it is clear that an element of surprise is important and useful. A "surprise" strategy can be translated into an avoidance of doing "the usual thing." It mandates the kind of "new mind-set" requested by Kotler and Fahey (p. 25) and also the imaginative analysis of possibly "loose" market data demanded by Levitt and Thorelli. But it also involves keeping the enemy in the dark about intentions for the future—Chrysler's early announcement about auto models for 1985 would not be very sound according to this thinking.

Second, the military analogy suggests that the strategic analysis needs to pinpoint not only weaknesses but also possibilities of maneuvers which exploit these weaknesses through a surprise attack. To accomplish this, the "beachheads" selected should be such that there is relatively low involvement by the Japanese in the markets and the line of attack should be oblique rather than a direct frontal assault. This suggests a choice of several segments away from Japanese strongholds and a marketing strategy which offers little incentive and room for counterattacks. The basic aim would be to create a strong fortification in terms of product and service values which could withstand a possible counterattack and at the same time lessen the incentive for undertaking it.

Some of the new thinking about global strategies fits in well here. As Hout, Porter and Rudden point out, for certain companies in "global" industries (as opposed to "multi-domestic" industries) it becomes natural to mobilize the total company forces in combating the enemy. This mobilization involves making explicit trade-offs between market positions in different countries, allowing prices and revenues in some countries to remain low in order to constrain the mobility of competitors, and then collect on the firm's strength in other country markets.

Third, the military analogy serves to point to the possibility of "preemptive" strikes behind enemy lines. There is no doubt that the relatively protected home market has played a great part in allowing the Japanese firms to expand abroad. Judging from the moves into the Japanese markets by firms such as IBM and the recent liberalization of entry restrictions aggressive market campaigns towards selected segments in the Japanese home market are now quite feasible. In this context the possibility of using local forces, i.e. competing Japanese companies, as deterrents to a counterattack cannot be ignored. The recent tie-ups in joint ventures between Western and Japanese firms (Nissan and Volkswagen in Japan, GM and Toyota in the U.S., for example) in fact represents this type of strategy. By marshalling "guerilla" forces in the form of Japanese companies, including the trading companies, a radically different strategic situation is created. The Japanese companies have to carry part of the competitive fight among themselves, and if the fierce competition discussed earlier with reference to the domestic market is any indication, the results might be very interesting.

Summary and Conclusion

This paper has provided an integrated summary of the factors that lie behind the success of Japanese exporting companies abroad and how these factors interrelate to produce a high-level performance. As some of these "country-specific" and "firm-specific" advantages are being duplicated elsewhere (an effort which is rapidly underway in many countries and companies) one can expect the Japanese advantages to lessen. Even so, it is clear that they have a head start and that they are not sitting idly on their conquests. What emerges, therefore, is a clear possibility of ever more intensive competition on a global scale in the future. Whether or not the counterstrategies proposed in the latter part of the paper will prove sufficient and decisive is of course too early to tell, but there are reasons to expect that the "military" type of strategic thinking will be quite appropriate in this competitive "warfare."

A synthesis can be achieved centering on a "pro-active" marketing strategy. Marketing needs to be adapted to the idea that new markets and segments can be created by the company, that moves by competitors can and should be anticipated (see Porter's 1980 discussion), and that the entry, positioning and defense of the firm's products involves more than just the marketing function. Furthermore, this new synthesis involves close scrutiny of existing and potential customers to make sure that needs are anticipated and changes are made easier. The stance of the successful marketer resembles more that of a problem-solver, in the tradition often associated with companies like IBM. With more narrowly defined sets of specific company skills and more direct tie-ins with customers such a development would seem natural and should develop quite organically.

None of the strategic pointers presented are particularly new of themselves, but their combined impact could have radical consequences for the approach taken by marketers in the future. Most Western firms would seem *a priori* capable of the suggested reorientation, and several firms have, as already noted, pursued this type of strategy for some time. There is perhaps one potential problem down the road: The "professionalism" ascribed to by many individual organizational members in Western corporations might have to be erased. No longer will the marketing manager be "the marketer" in the company but everybody will have to do their share. Perhaps the functional manager will become an outmoded conception as the "professional man" again yields to Whyte's "organizational man." In this development the role of the professional business schools might well prove to be a reactionary one; but there is perhaps reason to expect that the "market mechanism" will assert itself in such a way that functional separation also in these institutions becomes a thing of the past.

References

Johanson, J. and J. Vahlne, "The Internationalization Process of the Firm—A Model of Knowledge Development and Increasing Foreign Market Commitments," *Journal of International Business Studies*, (Spring/Summer 1977), pp. 23–32.

Kotler, P. and R. Singh, "Marketing Warfare in the 1980s," *Journal of Business Strategy*, Vol. 1, No. 3 (Winter 1981).

Kotler, P. and L. Fahey, "The World's Champion Marketers: The Japanese?" Paper presented at the AMA Conference, Chicago, Ill., (August 1982).

Levitt, T., "Marketing When Things Change," *Harvard Business Review*, (November–December 1977).

Levitt, T., "The Globalization of Markets," *Harvard Business Review*, (May–June 1983), pp. 92–102.

Porter, M. E., *Competitive Strategy*, (New York: The Free Press, 1980).

Thorelli, H. B., "Concepts of Marketing: A Review, Preview and Paradigm," Keynote address at AMA Workshop on the Marketing Concept, February 1983.

49

Kodak's Matrix System Focuses on Product Business Units*

BUSINESS INTERNATIONAL

In 1985, after several years of lackluster financial performance, Eastman Kodak Co. began a total worldwide reorganization—emphasizing product management—in response to important changes in its business. Among the factors that influenced these changes were the strong dollar and growing pressure from tough foreign competitors. Although the restructuring is still going on, the major pieces are now in place and have helped Kodak triple 1987 earnings (to $1.18 billion) over 1986's. Internationally, the new system, though complex, is, according to Kodak's vice-chairman, "working surprisingly well."

The key change Kodak made was to shift from an essentially functional organization to a matrix-system based on business units. For years, the corporation had operated through huge manufacturing, marketing and R&D divisions, which had become slow-moving, entrenched bureaucracies. These have been replaced by 19 product-based business units, which are closer to their markets, more flexible and better able to respond quickly to new threats and opportunities. Each business unit is headed by a general manager, based at Kodak's Rochester, N.Y., headquarters.

J. Philip Samper, Kodak's vice-chairman, is in charge of making the reorganization work in the international sphere. A 27-year Kodak employee who spent much of his career abroad, Samper summarizes the new approach this way: "What we've done is establish the business unit manager's position as a truly global one. That individual is responsible for the bottom-line performance of his product area. We have designed a process whereby the business is driven by a worldwide business unit and implemented by a geographic unit."

---

* Reprinted from *Business International*, Vol. 35, No. 28 (July 18, 1988), with permission

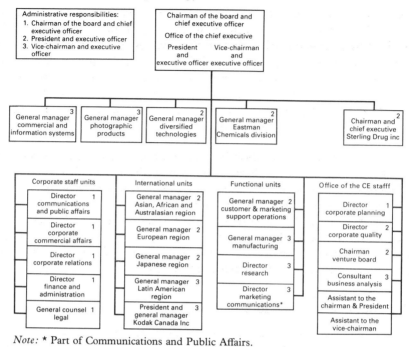

Note: * Part of Communications and Public Affairs.

FIG. 49.1. Eastman Kodak Organization.

The geographic units he refers to are Kodak's five regional organizations: Latin America (headquartered at the parent company in Rochester); Asia, Africa and Australia (Rochester); Europe (London); Canada (Toronto); and Japan (Tokyo). These regional units, as well as their country subsidiaries, serve as the "glue" between autonomous product operations.

How the matrix works

Using the European region as an example, Kodak's new reporting relationships can be sketched as follows: Each of 10 London-based European business unit managers reports directly to his worldwide business unit general manager. These individuals also report indirectly to Kodak's European general manager, also located in London. He provides the geographic, or market, interface for each business unit operating in Europe.

At the country level, the reporting relationships are different. Kodak's business unit managers report directly to the country general manager with the regional business unit managers coordinating their operational activities. The country general managers—most of whom are local nationals—function much like CEOs in the U.S. They spend much of their time ensuring that all the business units operating in the country work smoothly together. They constantly touch base with manufacturing, research, marketing and product people in their own companies and at the regional level. They are also responsible for personnel, finance, labor relations, government and all other "non-product" issues associated with running a large business in any country.

Kodak's matrix organization has yet another dimension, which takes the form of two key global function units—manufacturing and R&D—based in Rochester. The manager of worldwide manufacturing has a strong relationship with country factory managers, and the head of corporate R&D has a similarly strong connection to Kodak's lab chiefs around the world. For instance, the factory manager in France reports to both the general business unit manager for France and the worldwide manufacturing manager in Rochester.

The importance of coaching

Samper attributes the success of the matrix system overseas partly to the use of seasoned international executives in key business unit positions as "coaches" at both the country and regional levels. For example, several regional business unit managers in Europe are individuals who have worked abroad for a number of years and are particularly sensitive to the issues and conditions in countries other than the U.S. These individuals serve as role models for the less internationally oriented or less experienced regional and country business unit managers.

Cooperation and compensation

Decision-making in a matrix organization is almost always collaborative because of the dual (or three-way) reporting relationships and power sharing inherent in this approach. At Kodak, decision by negotiation and consultation is virtually forced upon executives because authority is split all the way up the line to the vice-chairman. There is no one who can serve as a tiebreaker if impasses develop. So, by necessity, most disputes are resolved lower down in the hierarchy.

To foster a cooperative, rather than a competitive, environment, Kodak has established a compensation process that encourages working for the common good. The pay of all key managers—the country general manager, the country business unit manager, the regional general manager, the regional business unit manager and the worldwide business unit manager—is based on the same numbers. If the annual operating plan for Germany says that X amount of a particular product will be produced and sold and Y amount of profit will be earned, those are everyone's goals. This approach makes the European and German general managers just as responsible for delivering performance on that product as is the business unit manager who "owns" it.

50

Performance Audits:
The MNC through the Glasses of
the LDC*

HANS B. THORELLI

The multinational corporation, MNC as we know it today, is essentially a product of the twentieth century. Young as MNCs are, many of them have had time to experience an entire life cycle from birth to death in one of several less developed countries (LDC), a drama proceeding from princely welcome to ignominious expulsion—with or without reasonable compensation (Table 50.1). It should be clear that nobody really "wins" from this outcome of the contest. The mutual interests of the participants call for not a drama but a partnership.

It has become customary to talk about the desirability of such a partnership in the last two decades. Yet it must be stated frankly that during that same period the ante has been "upped" considerably on the MNC wishing to operate in the spirit of partnership. The prime factor has been the proliferation of nations (from about 100 in 1945 to about 150 today) and the concomitant intensification of nationalism, especially (and perhaps inevitably) in the new nations. Today more than ever before in modern times the world political scene reminds us of medieval Europe. A second factor has been the proliferation of MNCs themselves, a factor which has enhanced competition and further reduced the bargaining position of the individual MNC relative to any given host country. Naturally, the competition within its borders of scores of MNC subsidiaries is generally highly beneficial to an LDC, a fact completely forgotten in contemporary discussions in United Nation circles. It may be that recognition of the contributions

* Revised from Hans B. Thorelli and Helmut Becker, *International Marketing Strategy* Revised Edition, (Elmsford, NY: Pergamon Press, 1980).

TABLE 50.1. Classical Drama of Multinational Business

Country Measures	Role of Country	Role of Company
Tax lures, concessions	Supplicant	Dictator
Import privileges on machinery, import restrictions on competitive goods	Junior partner	Master
"Strict" law enforcement	Arms-length	Arms-length
Discriminatory law enforcement, changes in concession contracts in favor of government	Master	Junior partner
Regulation, restrictions on remittance of profits or capital	Dictator	Supplicant

Note: The final state might be expulsion—with or without reasonable compensation.
Source: Hans B. Thorelli, "The multinational corporation as a change agent," *Southern Journal of Business* (July 1966), pp. 1–9.

of the multinationals will come only with the recent emergence of LDC-based MNCs.

Whatever the nature of the partnership or accommodation of the future, a periodic reevaluation of the relationship is most likely to become a standard operating procedure. Cummins Engine Company, Inc., is one of the concerns which conducts an annual internal corporate responsibility audit for each overseas operation.

This paper will deal with the evaluation of the MNC from the viewpoint of the LDC. It almost goes without saying that the MNC would be remiss if it did not also evaluate the LDC. Naturally, there are also many other stakeholders interested in evaluating the MNC, such as third-party LDCs, the home country, stockholders, customers, employees, creditors in various countries, competitors, and so forth. The discussion will be directed first to economic performance and practices, the area of almost exclusive interest in classic evaluation of managerial prowess. The "social indicators movement" suggests that the idea of a management audit must not be thus narrowly confined. This is certainly true in the LDCs. Thus, a second part of the paper is devoted to externalities and social performance.

Economic Performance and Practices

Earnings and Remittances

Consolidated earnings per share or a statement of consolidated return on investment (ROI) as a measure of performance might satisfy a Milton Friedman but almost certainly not an LDC. Its authorities would naturally like to know about the profitability of operations of the local subsidiary stated in accordance with local accounting practice. But this is not nearly enough. First, it might look askance at very high rates of profit as presumed evidence of undue exploitation rather than of superior performance, especially so if most of the surplus has been remitted to the home country. Admittedly, nowadays this kind of a showing would be confined largely to companies using the strategy of FIFO—that is, "Fast In, Fast Out!" For better or worse, such firms literally may be able "to get away with it" before the ex-host country even becomes aware of what went on, much like some fly-by-night operators do inside every country.

Second, the LDC is apt to be more impressed by a stable than by a great growth in earnings. In this respect they are more like Europeans than Americans. Clearly, such an attribute may have implications as to inventory evaluation and the creation of hidden reserves of a distinctly un-American character. Third, the LDC will tend to evaluate earnings data relative to the extent of local participation in ownership of the MNC subsidiary. Too, remittances to the home country tend to be a good deal more palatable if local owners are also getting a share of profits.

Minimum Performance Specified by Host Country

In most industrialized nations there are few, if any, minimum requirements as to economic performance imposed by government on the great majority of companies operating in the "private" sector. Many LDCs, on the other hand, take the view that companies—or, at least, companies of foreign origin—should meet certain minimum performance requirements in areas of special interest to the host country in return for local operating privileges. As is typical of LDC approaches to regulation, such requirements usually are not applied in a uniform manner, the prescriptions varying not only on an industry-by-industry but also on a company-by-company basis.

Requirements of this kind involve such matters as minimum (occasionally maximum) level of physical output, minimum quotient of exports of processed goods, maximum quotient or quantity of exports of non-processed raw materials, and minimum percentages of local materials, labor or value added embodied in end products. The host country is increasingly concerned also with some of the multinational business practices which in large measure influence the result of the local subsidiary. We are thinking primarily of a variety of corporate tax, currency translation, transfer, and pricing policies. Taken together, these are some of the principal everyday means by which the MNC tries to apply a global perspective of coordination in order to avoid country-by-country sub-optimization in its far-flung operations.

These are areas where the interests (at least, short-term) of the MNC and any single host country could be—and frequently are—at odds. The practices involved are sufficiently important to warrant separate comment.

Taxes

Barring undue political risks and constraints on remittances the natural preference of the MNC is to so regulate its internal relations and transactions that it shows high profits in countries with low tax rates and vice versa. This is a frequent empirical observation. Indeed in our own International Operations Simulation—a sophisticated MNC strategy exercise in the management game form—the attention of participating student teams is generally quickly drawn to the possibilities inherent in the differences in local tax rates, loss carryover provisions, and so forth, without any prodding from the administrator of the simulation.

Be it in practice or in the context of a strategy exercise, what seems to the MNC like conservative management of resources, to an LDC with a relatively high tax rate may appear as tax evasion. Clearly, there is room for legitimate differences of opinion as to what are reasonable tax behaviors and policies. The point is that the MNC is well advised not to take undue advantage of the possible naivete of the tax people in an LDC host country. Sooner or later the truth will come out, at which time it is only too easy—in the world in which we find ourselves—for the government to exercise its wrath.

Exchange Rates

European as well as American MNCs have had ample experience of the hazards of exchange rate fluctuations. To take but one European example, the Ericsson Telephone Corporation of Sweden in 1974 reported $29 million and in 1975 some $18 million "exchange losses charged to operations," principally to the Brazilian subsidiary. These large figures should be seen in relation to consolidated earnings before taxes for this MNC, which in each of these years hovered around $100 million. Clearly, the LDC will have an interest in how the MNC deals with currency fluctuations.

Let us first recognize the distinction between translation and conversion. Translation refers to the process of restating financial accounts from one currency to another. Conversion is the actual sale of one currency for another. Being simulated rather than actual exchange of currency, translation is inherently a matter of judgment. Several conventions exist as to how translation may be executed, each with its set of advantages and disadvantages. Of special concern to the LDC should be the fact that unfavorable translation rates may impede the ability of the local subsidiary to obtain future allocations of MNC resources, at least in the short term.

Involving actual exchange, conversion may be less controversial. However, when conversion has taken place at black market rates—typically with the implicit acquiescence of the local government—the LDC may have an interest in the actual rate not being disclosed.

Intracompany Transfers

The conditions surrounding the transfer of materials, components, and finished products across national borders between various units of the MNC are in principle—though often not in practice—a matter of internal discretion, whether it be exercised centrally or locally. Too often we tend to think of absolute price as the only relevant variable here. But as in all other marketing activity—and this is what we are talking about in such transfers—there are other considerations. Income, value added and sales taxes, and tariff duties are examples.

The price of materials relative to components and final products, and of components relative to final products, is another important variable affecting local performance as well as the balance between global optimization and local suboptimization. However irrational it may be from a global or even long-term local viewpoint, the pressure from LDCs is invariably in the direction of maximum local processing. MNCs in the future may expect increasingly to have to back up demonstrations of the reasonableness of relative prices with formal and sophisticated make-or-buy analyses in cases of imports of less than finally processed goods. Even so, we all know that strictly economic concerns will not always prevail.

Related to price is the use of accounts receivable (or, conversely, of prepayments) as means of extending intracompany credit, or to delay or advance international remittances and conversion of currencies. Here again, a strategy prompted by global considerations may not be viewed by an individual LDC as in its best interest.

Another aspect of intracompany marketing involves applications engineering, installation work, and the provision of patents and know-how. Such transfer of technology may obviously be of great value to the LDC. Sometimes the services involved constitute part of the purchase of goods; sometimes, they are paid for separately. This brings us to the general area of services payments.

Beyond the examples just mentioned payments are often made between units of an MNC (as indeed between units of many large domestic companies) for general management services, for marketing research, for executive development programs, for intracompany loans, and other services. Many an LDC may wish to establish whether such payments really are for bona fide sevices, or merely represent means of withdrawing funds and/or avoiding local taxes.

Accounting and Financial Reporting Systems

The financial reporting systems of the MNC must respond to at least three related but distinct sets of needs. There are the needs of conforming to the accounting practices and the reporting expectations of host countries. There are the needs of the MNC headquarters for standardization in reporting systems in order to "really" know what is going on and to ensure comparability between subsidiaries. Finally, there are the needs of the MNC for its own sake and for that of tax authorities in the home country to issue consolidated reports.

Without for a moment questioning the need for the development of international accounting standards one may safely predict that for the foreseeable future the variegated needs and stages of economic development among nations will mitigate against any single-system approach to financial reporting in MNCs. Multiple systems are here to stay, although perhaps not for as long as death and taxes! Yet, in any given case, outside parties have a legitimate claim to know just *what* system has been used. For instance, if there be hidden reserves, we want to know the why and how.

Externalities and Social Indicators

We now turn to social indicators and externalities, that is, areas of social costs and benefits occasioned by corporate action. The last 20 years have witnessed a lively discussion of social indicators, externalities, the quality of life, and the associated "social responsibilities of business." The intensity of the debate has been directly correlated with the industrialization and per capita wealth of individual nations.

Beyond a few United Nations documents, surprisingly little of tangible import has been written about social indicators relevant to the LDCs in general and to locally harbored subsidiaries of MNCs in particular. Yet there is a virtually endless range of possible "social performances" of business from the macro to the micro level, from social aspects of the very core of business operations to the grant-in-aid of an art exhibit. Although some issues have been clarified by legislation, there are generally no hard and fast rules regarding accountability and responsibility here. Neither is there any consensus as to what ought to be. Short term, at least, management is typically at liberty to lead or to lag relative to the actual or perceived needs of host countries in many of these areas.

We have chosen two such areas for discussion, both of which are relatively close to the "core" of business operations. One of them may be labeled loosely as "corporate citizenship" (or the MNC as resource transformer and employer) and the other "the MNC as a change agent." It almost goes without saying that there are no distinct borderlines between them.

Corporate Citizenship

Communications

The provision of information to local stakeholder groups is an important means of the MNC to build *trust* among these publics. In addition to annual reports, governments increasingly require confidential data from all areas of corporate activity. It is a miracle that Washington has not disappeared under the thousands of tons of forms it has commandeered from business. Even so, under the partnership concept it is often a good idea in the LDC voluntarily to furnish the government data that go beyond the requisite minimum. This is especially true in the area of future plans. Voluntary information programs should be directed also to stockholders, employees, the plant community, the press, and so on. Indeed, the more authoritarian and/or unstable the local government the greater the desirability of building rapport with other groups in society. The prudent MNC will increasingly undertake attitude surveys on a regular basis as a means of gauging how well it stays in tune with various publics.

Value Added

Conventionally, the value added is reflected in the difference between the value of the company's sales and that of its purchased inputs on the income statement. This is definitely of interest to the LDC. However, the host country also might well take an interest in how much of all purchases were local in origin. A Nestlé Alimentana S.A. publication provides an example, as indicated in Table 50.2. This kind of tabulation could easily be broken down further by categories of expenses (and sales) and by individual countries.

Employer Practices

The creation of employment opportunities is vital in literally every LDC. Number, compensation, training, promotion, and stability of

TABLE 50.2. Nestlé's Contribution to the Local Economy 1974 (in percentages and millions of Swiss francs, SF)

	Latin America	Africa	Asia	Total
Local expenses				
Purchases (goods and services)	59.3%	38.0%	31.0%	53.1%
Salaries and labor (including social charges)	11.2%	4.2%	4.4%	9.5%
Taxes	10.7%	7.5%	8.5%	10.1%
Total Local Expenses	81.2%	49.7%	43.9%	72.7%
External expenses				
Imports	15.1%	46.6%	51.5%	23.4%
Dividends, interests, and royalties	3.7%	3.7%	4.6%	3.9%
Total External Expenses	18.8%	50.3%	56.1%	27.3%
Grand Total Expenses, SF (100%)	2303.8	212.1	508.9	3024.9
Exports, SF	49.7	81.8	16.4	147.9

Source: Nestlé in the Developing Countries (Vevey, Switzerland: Nestlé Alimentana S.A., 1975), p. 14.

employment are matters of concern, as is the proportion of local relative to foreign management and professional personnel. Beyond working conditions and health and safety provisions many companies, notably in the extractive industries, face the challenge of providing schools, hospitals, stores, housing, and transportation facilities. In some of these areas the MNC must tread gently in order to avoid charges of paternalism.

It is also important not to forget the employment multiplier effect of many overseas operations. In 1976 Ford España had 244 Spanish suppliers, who had hired 11,000 new workers to handle the Ford business.

Ownership

To some companies, such as Caterpillar and Ford Motor Company, control associated with full ownership of overseas subsidiaries appears as a practical necessity. It well may be. In such instances, local participation in ownership may be stimulated by offering for sale shares in the MNC itself, rather than in the subsidiary. Verily, this is in the spirit of a truly global enterprise. Realistically, however, most MNCs encounter strong pressure to provide local capital an opportunity to participate in ownership of local operations. This may take the form of shares in the local subsidiary but also in joint ventures of different types.

Pollution

At the United Nations Conference on the Environment in Stockholm in 1972 many spokesmen for the LDC—warmly applauded by Communist delegates—declared that environmental protection was for the rich and filthy (not necessarily the filthy rich), while development must have priority in the LDC. To the jester this would suggest that the MNC subsidiary generate as much smoke and effluent as convenient, as tangible indicators of industrial progress. Seriously, social responsibility involves the selection of raw materials and manufacturing processes that have minimum polluting effects, the control of materials and processes to see that prescribed standards are met, and the installation of pollution abatement equipment. It also involves prompt action to rectify damage inflicted, as in the Union Carbide Bhopal incident.

It must be clear, nevertheless, that the constellation of tradeoffs between economy and environmental protection may be different in an already highly industrialized country and in an LDC. Differences in climate, flora, and fauna may also well justify the use of more potent herbicides and pesticides in some LDCs than in the home countries of MNCs. In situations like this the challenge to the MNC is to overcome by educational programs local suspicions that the pursuit of profits is more important to it than the welfare of host countries.

The MNC as a Change Agent

Value Structure

The cosmopolitan corporation should view itself as an agent of change, an agent of progress in LDC host countries. If it fails in this regard, it is likely to become the victim of nationalism. Yet to become an effective change agent the MNC must be a learner as well as a teacher, able to strike the delicate balance of constructive interaction.

By far the most important contribution the MNC can render to the host country is to contribute to a change in attitudes, a change in value structure among all the interest groups it encounters in the course of doing business. This is particularly true as regards consumers. Nothing could be more vital than introducing, and reinforcing, *a customer oriented marketing concept*. A basic prerequisite to economic development, at least in non-dictatorial nations, is a strengthened *individual need to achieve*. Modern marketing and merchandizing, by stimulating the individual to set *specific* goals in the area of property accumulation, and by dramatizing the relationship between effort, savings, and consumption, is a powerful vehicle in the creation of a climate of values conducive to growth. This fundamental insight is the basis of recent economic reforms in China.

Local stockholders frequently have to be educated to see the merit of long term corporate perspectives and of some sacrifice in payout for corporate citizenship measures. Employees must be induced to learn new skills, respect the discipline of industry, be concerned with quality as well as quantity of output, respond to economic incentives, and so on. To object that this is the "imperialism of values" is utter nonsense: as all LDCs want economic development they had better adopt some of the values which have proven conducive to such growth.

Corruption

A perennial issue in MNC-LDC relations is corruption. There is no way this huge topic can be given adequate treatment within the confines of this paper. What follows is a brief review of arguments pro and con and a tentative conclusion as regards subsidiaries of MNC operating in the LDC.

Arguments in favor of accepting the practice of corruption:

1. "When in Rome do as the Romans." This implies an abdication of the role of the MNC as a change agent insofar as ethics are concerned.
2. We should not practice "ethical imperialism," not "shove 'our' values down other people's throats." This argument is based on the questionable assumption that a majority of the population in the host country are in favor of corruption. Not only that: the argument also conveniently overlooks the fact that—for better or worse—the MNC brings pervasive changes in values in many other areas of life in the LDC.
3. We should simply be "neutral" relative to local values. Unfortunately, this argument is untenable. The average MNC subsidiary is a sufficiently major factor on the local scene that a neutral "going along" with the bribery system in effect means actively reinforcing it.
4. Corruption can play a positive role by building an invisible "web of trust" among participants. Maybe so. But the question is whether this is preferable to a visible web of trust based on functional merit.
5. Corruption can play a positive role as the "grease that lubricates" (German *Schmiergeld*) the local Establishment. Again we have the question whether a bureaucracy cannot be made to run along functional lines.
6. We can not afford to walk the straight and narrow as long as competitors bribe their way through the local bureaucracy. At the

level of everyday realities this is probably the strongest reason in favor of accepting corruption as "a fact of life." (A feature article in the *Wall Street Journal* (February 28, 1977) does suggest, however, that at least in the short run American MNCs have not suffered by discontinuing corrupt practices.) Of course, it does have a little of the flavor of the argumentation of several cadets in the recent West Point scandal: "You cannot get through here unless you cheat," or "Why should I be Simon pure when lots of my buddies are cheating?"

Arguments against corruption:

1. Corruption removes the causal relationship between honest effort and due reward. Thus the system is fundamentally counterproductive.
2. Corruption reinforces fatalism among the "little people" outside the bribery network.
3. Corruption reinforces existing inequalities and by definition involves discrimination. Thus, it tramples equal rights and is antidemocratic.
4. Corruption is a serious block against consumer emancipation in the LDC, as long as bribes can let you get away with selling imitation or fraudulent products, forget about quality control and the health and safety of your products, pollute the environment, use false weights and measures, and neglect warranties and consumer complaints.

Our own view is that while rich countries such as the United States can possibly absorb corruption as just another questionable business practice (and, indeed, we seem to have plenty of it), the LDC can ill afford the luxury. The dysfunctional effects of bribery are simply too great relative to the objective of economic development. There is plenty of room for both individual and, not least, collective initiatives among the MNCs active in a given host country to contribute to the gradual eradication of corruption.

Technology Transfer

The emphasis on transfer of product and production technology (patents and technical know-how) has been dangerously one-sided. From the viewpoint of balanced development, the transfer of marketing, accounting, and general management technology is at least as important. High time it is that the MNC and the business professions make use of every opportunity offered by the LDC to get on with the enormous task of technical assistance in these fields.

Building Infrastructure

A great challenge of the local MNC is to foster the development of indigenous business infrastructure, such as marketing research and advertising agencies, freight handlers, suppliers, and distributors. Clearly, this may also be viewed as an aspect of technology transfer. We have referred to Ford stimulating local sources of supply in Spain. Twenty years earlier Sears, Roebuck and Company did a truly pioneering job in Latin America by developing, training, and, frequently, financing hundreds of local suppliers and by introducing consumer credit on equitable terms. Unilever in Africa has provided booklets and advisors to local businessmen, showing them how to improve their operations in the key areas of marketing, finance and accounting.

Reducing Dualism

Nowhere is the coexistence of a metropolitan growth sector and a rural stagnation sector as prevalent as in the LDCs. A striking and unfortunate fact of life is that typically both the government and the business community of the LDC pay little more than lip service to the crying need for integration of the rural population into the general thrust of development. Yet, sustained growth of the national economy usually calls for heroic effort to develop agriculture and associated processing activities as well as rural trading and small local manufacturing establishments. Unilever in Africa is representative of MNCs which have accepted the need to bring the two halves of the dual economy together. The LDCs would be well served by many more examples of this kind.

Consumer Protection, Education, and Information

Paradoxically, consumerism is strictly an affluent-country phenomenon. You will not find a Ralph Nader in the Third World. Yet the average consumer is the true underdog of the LDC. Shoddy locally made goods are the order of the day in every nation where sellers' markets, import substitution, and producer unconcern with quality prevail. Unconscionable interest rates and credit arrangements frequently create a buyer dependency that is more like serfdom than consumer sovereignty. Imitation, fraudulent, and unsafe products galore permeate the marketplace. Their minds set on cement plants and heavy industry, LDC governments generally have no interest in consumers. The key to consumer emancipation is consumer protection, education, and information (in that order).

The infant milk formula case provides an unfortunate but telling example of the unhappy consequences of deficient (or outright misleading) consumer communication and information.

As consumer emancipation is as much a cause as an effect of economic development, and as substandard competition is clearly not compatible with the modern MNC, it is difficult to imagine an area where the long term interest of the MNC and that of the local population are more closely united. What we have here is the ideal area for voluntary action by such corporations, proceeding singly or in unison.

The Challenge of the MNC in the LDC

Our thesis is that the mutual interests of the LDC and the MNC call for a partnership or entente. The keystone of such an alliance is mutual trust and respect. One means of assuring that local operations are conducive to trust is a management audit ranging over the wide territory of managerial performance illustrated by our discussion. This audit may be an internal one, as is the case in Cummings Engine, or it may be carried out by consultants. The time may come also when host countries wish to undertake such audits under their own auspices although this may be less likely where MNCs are already doing it on a voluntary basis.

In some instances it may be in the best interest of the parties to spell out the performance expected by the MNC in some detail in what might appropriately be called *a social contact*. This may, for example, be desirable when an MNC becomes engaged in a socialist country in a major way. It is true that the overall objectives of growth do not differ much between free enterprise and socialist countries. However, they frequently differ as to the *means* appropriate to reaching the ends. This implies that an MNC going into a socialist country had better bargain for maximum acceptable discretion and other rules of conduct at as early a stage as possible. Once the ground rules are spelled out it may be easier in some respects to operate in a socialist country, as the authoritarian power of the state will be behind you.

But when all has been said and done at the local level, it is the mission of the MNC to retain and extend the global perspective. Never should we lose sight of the fact that it represents a more successful instance of international cooperation and a closer approach to global thinking than we have thus far encountered among governments. The MNC is the torchbearer of One World, and here in the end lies its lasting service to humanity.

Further Reading — Part VII

Bartlett, Christopher A. and Sumantra Ghoshal, "Tap Your Subsidiaries for Global Reach," *Harvard Business Review*, (November–December 1986), pp. 87–94.

Cavusgil, S. Tamer and Michael R. Czinkota, (eds.), *International Perspectives on Trade Promotion and Assistance*, (Westport, Connecticut: Quorum Press, 1990).

Hamel, Gary and C. K. Prahalad, "Do You Really Have a Global Strategy?" *Harvard Business Review*, (July–August 1985), pp. 139–148.

Popoff, Frank P., "Planning the Multinational's Future," *Business Horizons*, (March–April 1984), pp. 64–68.

Quelch, John A. and Edward J. Hoff, "Customizing Global Marketing," *Harvard Business Review*, (May–June 1986), pp. 59–68.

Wind, Yoram and Susan Douglas, "International Portfolio Analysis and Strategy: the Challenge of the 80's," *Journal of International Business Studies*, (Fall 1981), pp. 69–82.

General Readings in International Marketing

The journals and books from which our Readings were selected and the works referenced in them are recommended to gain further insights into the growing field of international business and marketing. The sources listed at the end of each Part are provided for the reader who wishes more in-depth coverage of various aspects of international marketing. The writings listed below are suggested as reference material for the reader desiring to broaden general understanding of international business.

Cateora, Philip, *International Marketing* 6th Edition, (Homewood, Ill: R. D. Irvine, 1987).

Cavusgil, S. Tamer and John R. Nevin, "State-of-the-Art in International Marketing: An Assessment," *Review of Marketing 1981*, Ben Enis and Kenneth J. Roering (eds), (Chicago, Ill: American Marketing Association), pp. 195–216 (Chapter 1 in Jain-Tucker reader).

Cavusgil, S. Tamer and John R. Nevin, *International Marketing: An Annotated Bibliography*, (Chicago, Ill: American Marketing Association, 1983).

Cavusgil, S. Tamer, *Advances in International Marketing*, (Greenwich, Co: JAI Press, annual volume since 1986).

Czinkota, Michael R. and Ilkka A. Ronkainen, *International Marketing*, (New York: Dryden Press, 1988).

Douglas, Susan P. and C. Samuel Craig, *International Marketing Research*, (Englewood Cliffs, NJ: Prentice-Hall, 1983).

Jain, Subhash C., *International Marketing Management* 2nd Edition (Boston, Mass: Kent Publishing Co, 1987)

Jain, Subhash C. and Lewis R. Tucker, *International Marketing: Managerial Perspectives*, (Boston, Mass: Houghton-Mifflin, 1988).

Keegan, Warren J., *Multinational Marketing Management*, (Englewood Cliffs, NJ: Prentice-Hall, 1984).

Majaro, Simon, *International Marketing: A Strategic Approach to World Markets* Revised Edition, (London: George Allen & Unwin, 1982).

Terpstra, Vern, *International Marketing* 4th Edition, (Hinsdale, Ill: Dryden Press 1987).

Toyne, Brian and P. G. P. Walters, *Global Marketing Management: A Strategic Perspective*, (Boston, Mass: Allyn and Bacon, 1989).

Much additional practical information for more specific purposes is available that should be consulted for individual international marketing problems: *Business International* is a high-quality source of many publications. Excellent surveys of international markets are continually prepared by the *Economist Intelligence Unit*. Such organizations as the UNCTAD/GATT, ITC, IMF, OECD, EEC, EFTA have a great variety of useful publications, most of them for the asking. The ministries of commerce and the embassies or consular services of most countries furnish advice about governmental services and information sources and may also help in handling particular trade enquiries. International organizations such as ESOMAR (European Society for Opinion and Marketing Research) provide information on marketing consultants and research agencies or firms available in different countries. Though no complete list appears to be in existence at this time, the annually published ESOMAR Handbook does contain information on facilities and organizations in numerous countries.

The reader who is interested in assembling a still greater variety and specificity of international market and marketing information resources should refer to the "International Marketing" section in Robert Ferber, ed., *Handbook of Marketing Research* (New York: McGraw-Hill, 1974). He or she will find source listing on individual countries or regions, industries, companies, products, organizations, international surveys and directories, and so forth. It should be remembered also that for major transactions and commitments even seasoned executives request the advice of commercial banks and international consulting or accounting firms.

Finally, the following periodicals can be consulted for current articles on international marketing. Please note that this not a comprehensive list.

Business International (as well as *Business Europe, Business Latin America,* etc.)
Business Horizons (Indiana University)
California Management Review (University of California)
Columbia Journal of World Business (Columbia University)
European Journal of Marketing
Harvard Business Review (Harvard University)
The International Executive (American Management Association & American Graduate School of International Management)
International Marketing Review (Michigan State University)
International Journal of Advertising
International Management (U.K.)
International Trade Forum (ITC, UNCTAD/GATT)
Journal of International Business Studies (Academy of International Business)
Management International Review (West Germany)
Marketing and Research Today (Formerly European Research)

Glossary

A-E	Architect-Engineering
AC	Average Consumer
ATC	Administrative Terms and Conditions
BI	*Business International*
CAD	Computer-Aided Design
CEO	Chief Executive Officer
CORE	COmpany Readiness to Export
CTC	Commodity Trading Company
CTV	Color Television
CV	Commercial Vehicle
DC	Developing Country
DIC	Differences In Conditions
DMU	Decision Making Unit
DOC	Department Of Commerce
EC	European Community
ECU	European Currency Unit
EMC	Export Management Company
ESPRIT	European Strategic Programme in Information Technologies
ETC	Export Trading Company
FDI	Foreign Direct Investment
FIFO	Fast In Fast Out
FMG	Federated Marketing Group
FOB	Free On Board
FSA	Firm-Specific Advantage
GATT	General Agreement on Tariffs and Trade
GNP	Gross National Product
GSP	Generalized System of Preferences
GTC	General Trading Company
HQ	Headquarters
ICC	International Chamber of Commerce
IM	Internal Market
IM	International Marketing
IS	Information Seeker
JV	Joint Venture
LDC	Less Developed Countries
M-S	Manufacturer-Supplier
MFN	Most Favored Nation
MNC	Multinational Corporation
MSU	Marketing Services Unit
NCR	National Cash Register
NIC	Newly Industrialized Countries
OECD	Organization for Economic Co-operation and Development

OEM	Original Equipment Manufacturer
OPEC	Organization of Petroleum Exporting Countries
OTA	Office of Technology Assessment
QRS	Quantitative Trade Restrictions
R&D	Research and Development
RAM	Random Access Memory
ROI	Return On Investment
SEE	State Economic Enterprise
SEZ	Special Economic Zone
SIC	Standard Industrial Code
SIMS	Service Information Management System
UNCTAD	United Nations Conference on Trade And Development
VAT	Value Added Tax

Country Index

Africa   112
Algeria   232, 311
Argentina   400, 505
Asia   58, 156, 527
Australia   148, 173, 383

Bangladesh   204
Brazil   67, 106, 113, 263, 498

Canada   113, 173
China   45, 403, 415, 221, 249

Denmark   64

East Asia   262
Eastern Bloc   449
Egypt   230, 233
England, *see* United Kingdom
Ethiopia   204
Europe   45, 57, 58, 61, 213

Federal Republic of Germany   57,
    64, 107, 165, 179, 215, 449, 461,
    500
France   14, 57, 214, 461

Greece   216

Holland   274
Hong Kong   35, 120, 186, 221, 391,
    461
Hungary   385

India   43, 263

Indonesia   190, 221
Israel   233

Japan   57, 61, 64, 67, 71, 113, 161,
    185, 213, 297, 430

Kuwait   233

Latin America   58, 107, 112, 262,
    527
Lebanon   230, 233
Libya   233

Malaysia   383
Mexico   384, 498
Middle East   107, 112, 229, 262, 307,
    383
Morocco   107, 230, 232, 305

North Africa   229, 307
Norway   173

Pakistan   361
Peru   17
Philippines   221, 395
Portugal   233

Saudi Arabia   230, 233, 274, 400
Singapore   35, 120, 221, 383, 461
South Africa   300
South Asia   58, 262
South Korea   25, 106, 120, 190, 221
Spain   233
Sweden   148, 173
Switzerland   217, 461

Taiwan   35, 120, 186, 221, 527
Thailand   106, 221
Tunisia   230, 232, 311
Turkey   120, 230, 306

U.S.S.R   108, 179, 385, 397
United Kingdom   18, 26, 57, 90, 113,
   217, 385, 500
United States   13, 26, 43, 57, 61, 72,
   161, 186, 213, 413

Venezuela   17, 395
Vietnam   221

Western Europe   57
West Germany *see* Federal Republic
   of Germany

Yugoslavia   385

Company Index

3M, USA   68, 499, 530
Allegheny International, USA   165
AMC, USA   432
Apple, USA   223
Arden Group, USA   63
Ashton-Tate, USA   399
AT&T, USA   432, 577

BASF, West Germany   67
Bell Laboratories, USA   63
Black & Decker, USA   331, 495
Boeing, USA   577
Bosch, West Germany   495
Brasil S. A., Brazil   114
British Steel, UK   331
Burdick Corporation, USA   505

Canon, Japan   57, 64, 432
Casio, Japan   57, 64
Caterpillar, USA   68, 235, 415, 489,
   546
Chillicothe Metal Co., USA   511
China Machine Building International
   Corp., China   415
Chrysler, USA   480
Circle K Corp., USA   420
Coca-Cola, USA   22, 39, 341, 383
Coleco Industries, USA   547
Colgate-Palmolive, USA   161

Daewoo, Korea   112
Davy Engineering, UK   331
Defibrator, Sweden   359
Dentsu, Japan   592
Dial-a-Dino's, Australia   391

East Asiatic Company,
   Denmark   106

Electronic Data Systems, USA   399
Emerson Electric, USA   495
Enzed, New Zealand   383
Ericsson Telephone Corporation,
   Sweden   27

Ford, USA   22, 311, 434
Fuji, Japan   68
Fujitsu, Japan   60, 63

General Electric, USA   68, 304
General Motors, USA   58, 92, 497
Gillette, USA   58, 165
GM, USA   185, 223
Goldman Sachs, USA   450

Hewlett-Packard, USA   63
Hindustan Paper Corporation,
   India   359
Hitachi, Japan   63, 490
Honda, Japan   57, 64, 69, 162, 302,
   464, 594
Honeywell, USA   68
Hyundai, Korea   111, 434, 222

IBM, USA   58, 63, 185, 531, 577
IKEA, Sweden   173-177
IMTEC, USA   4, 9
International Nickel, Canada   17
International Telephone & Telegraph,
   Europe   58

Jergens, USA   161

Kao Corporation, Japan   161, 300
Kodak, USA   601

627

Komatsu Ltd., Japan   416

Landor Associates, USA   500
Levi-Strauss, USA   461
Leyland, UK   69, 331
Lotus Development Corporation,
   USA   399
Lucas, UK   331
Lucky-Gold Star, Korea   112

Makita, Japan   496
Matsushita, Japan   57, 64, 297
Maxitrade, Brazil   114
McDonald, USA   39, 57, 397, 464
Mead Corp., USA   397
Mercedes-Benz, Germany   532
Metallgesellschaft A.G.,
   Germany   449
MicroAge, USA   419
Microsoft, USA   399
Midland Bank, UK   218
Miniskips, Australia   394
Mitsubishi Corp., Japan   108, 424,
   589
Mitsui, Japan   108
Morgan Stanley, USA   401, 450
Multitrade, Brazil   114

NEC, Japan   218
Nestlé, Switzerland   18, 217, 311
Nichimen, Japan   109
Nicolet Instruments, USA   285, 505
Nike, USA   411
Nippon Steel, Japan   59
Nippon Electric Company, Japan   63
Nippon Kokan KK, Japan   59
Nippon Telegraph and Telephone,
   Japan   62
Nissan, Japan   59, 70, 162, 477

Olivetti, Italy   62, 217, 419, 432

Pepsi Cola, USA   181
Petrobras, Brazil   114
Philips, Netherlands   62, 432
Proctor & Gamble, USA   301, 311

Proletarian Victory, USSR   179

Ray-O-Vac, USA   513
Renault, France   432
Roche, USA   431

Salamander AG, West Germany   179
Salomon Brothers, USA   161, 397
Samsung, Korea   111
Sanyo, Japan   413, 595
Seiko, Japan   57, 64
Sharp Electronics, Japan   531
Shin Daiwa Kogyo Co., Japan   496
Shiseido, Japan   301
Siemens, West Germany   17
Singapore Technology Corp.,
   Singapore   223
Sony, Japan   39, 57, 64, 432
Sumitomo, Japan   72

Texas Instruments, USA   58, 63
Tokyo Electric Company, Japan   66
Toshiba, Japan   63
Toyota, Japan   17, 59, 162, 297, 477,
   588
Turbo Tek, USA   185

Unilever, UK   17, 578
Union Carbide, USA   579
UNY Co., Japan   419

Volkswagen, West Germany   18, 27,
   70, 298, 434

Warner Communications, USA   301
Wendys Supa Sundaes,
   Australia   391
Wilkinson Sword Deutschland,
   Germany   165

Xerox, USA   57, 66, 68

Yasuda, Japan   68

Name Index

Almaney, Adnan J. 232
Amine, Lyn S. 103, 229, 308
Anderson, Erin 373
Atac, Osman A. 261

Battat, Joseph Y. 403
Becker, Helmut 523, 557
Beeth, Gunnar 487
Bellin, H. 386
Bilkey, Warren J. 148, 471
Bleakley, Mark 431
Bruce, L. 387
Burns, W. 391

Campbell, N. C. G. 327
Cavusgil, S. Tamer 104, 129, 147,
    201, 229, 261, 305, 503, 531
Chakravarthy, Balaji S. 569
Chiang Ching-kuo 224
Chiang Kai-shek 224
Coughlan, Anne T. 373
Cunningham, M. T. 327

Davidson, William 376
Delors, Jacques 216
Deng Xiaoping 258
Devlin, Godfrey 431
Doz, Y. L. 572

Eilts, Hermann F. 235
Erickson, G. M. 471

Fillmore, Millard 185

Ghauri, Pervez N. 353
Goldman, Arieh 244

Hackett, D. W. 384
Håkansson, H. 87, 328
Hauser, J. R. 480
Heenan, D. A. 583
Huszagh, Frederick 439
Huszagh, Sandra 439

Johansson, Johny K. 297, 471, 585

Kanabayashi, Masayoshi 161
Kotler, Philip 595
Kraar, Louis 221
Kreutzer, Ralf Thomas 459

Layton, R. A. 390
Lee, Woo Young 149
Levitt, Theodore 39, 593

Mark, Jeremy 161
McCall, J. B. 360
McGuire, Timothy W. 376
Melloan, George 449
Morita, Akio 297

Naisbitt, John 42
Nason, Robert W. 129
Nonaka, Ikujiro 297, 585

O'Boyle, Thomas F. 179
Ohmae, Kenichi 57

Parkinson, S. T. 330
Perlmutter, Howard V. 569
Perry, Commodore 185
Porter, Michael 328, 570, 595

629

Reinstein, Fred   185
Robinson, Richard D.   39

Sawyer, H. C.   329
Schypek, Joachim   165
Sikora, Ed   531
Steed, Judy   173

Thorelli, Hans B.   13, 73, 249, 341,
   377, 403, 471, 557, 597, 605

Toffler, Alvin   42

Urban, G. L.   48

Welch, Lawrence S.   383, 389
Williamson, Oliver   382

Subject Index

Accounting standard   610
Acquisition   162, 217, 495, 543
Adaptation   341
Advertising   189, 245, 293
  spill-over   461
  standardized   461
Agriculture   252
Alliances   218, 431
Allocation of resources   327
Antitrust   214
Artificial intelligence   129-139
Asian exports   221
Asian markets   221
Automated operations   601

Barriers   213, 517
  customs duties   214
  distribution   517
  import   517
  nontariff   547
  trade   214
  transaction   517
Barter   75, 439
Bidding
  close   289
  open   289
Blade industry   185
Brand identity   499
Brand loyalty   23, 408
Brand transfer   495
Bribery   256
Business culture   564
Business International   201
Buyer   272, 327, 357, 471
Buyer/supplier relationship   328

Capital intensity   58
Centralized economic planning   263
Chain ratio   309
Channel members   294

Clearing agreement   445
Clustering   201, 229
  climber   209
  dependent   204
  luxury   210
  rocking chair   210
  seeker   208
Commitment decision   559, 581
Commodity traders   53
Commodity trading company   108
Communications   349, 611
Compensation   417, 603
Compensation trading   440
Competitive clusters   119
Competitive intelligence   528
Competitive strength   431
Competitor   333
Consortium   69-70
Consumer   341, 407
  behavior   242, 318
  buying criteria   348
  education   616
  evaluation   471
  information   616
  perception   471
  protection   616
  satisfaction   348
  stereotyping   471
Consumer emancipation   257
Consumer goods   253
Consumer reports   344
Consumer surveys   297
Contract   174, 491
CORE software   129-139
Corporate citizenship   611
Corporate image   528
Corruption   267, 614
Cost   28, 513
  labor   58, 60
  R&D   60-61
Counterpurchase   442
Countertrade   439, 449

Country analysis 562
Country selection 558
Cross-licensing 62
Cultural distance 59, 153
Cultural revolution 250
Culture 41, 190, 358, 508
Culture gap 405
Currency transfer 607
Currency translation 607
Customer analysis 21, 327
Customer oriented 13
Customer satisfaction 15, 19

Data collection 312
Data feedback 20
Data processing 399
Dealer 350, 536
Dealer network 299, 521
Decentralization 253
Developing countries 262, 394
Differentiation 80
Direct investment 410
Distribution 162, 263, 531
  agent 373
  channels 22, 297, 319
  independent channel 373, 507
  integrated channel 373
  managerial implications 379
  subsidiary 373, 506
Distribution system
  Japan 187
Distributor 21, 293, 59
  commission 490
  contract 491
  evaluation 284
  indemnification 492
  performance 488
  sales force 488
Distributor support 497
Diversification 78
Dualism 616

Eastern bloc 181
EC 213, 329
EC Commission 213
Ecologic view 13-30
Economic imperative 570
Economic integration 215
Economic performance 606
Economic policies 31
Economic zones 411

Economies of scale 13, 40, 79, 230, 375
Efficient frontier 478
Employer practice 611
Entrepreneur 246
Entry mode 558
Entry strategy 174, 591
Environment 20, 94, 229-232
  business culture 358, 564
  demographic 287
  economic 287
  infrastructure 564
  international 563
  local market 507, 563
  market structure 564
  mixed-nationality 437
  political 287
  social 288
Environmental structure 23
Ethnocentrism 573
Europe 1992 213-219
European court 214
Exchange rate 507, 534, 607
Experience-curve 463
Export 262
  readiness 129
  steps 130
  variables 129
Export commitment 189
Export management company 117
Export marketing 147
  Japanese 585
  structures 585
Export pricing 503
  constraints 504
  decision framework 515
  factors 505
  literature 504
  target price range 515
  variables 503
Export trading company 103-127
External transactions 49

Feasibility report 267
Financial exchange 91
Financial operation 610
Financial services 214
First mover advantage 267
Fixed cost 513
Foreign Corrupt Practices Act,
  USA 509
Foreign exchange 255, 416, 507

Four tigers 221
Franchising 383, 419
  chains 395
  franchisee 383
  franchisor 383
Furniture chain 173

GATT 26, 216, 402
General trading company 105-106
Geocentrism 573
Global corporation 39
Global marketing 40
  clustering 459
  concept 459
  integrated approach 459
  targets 460
Global strategy 204, 495
Globalization 245, 509
Government Regulations, USA 509
Gray market 531
Grease payment 272, 509

Headquarters 17, 71
Heterogenization 341
Homogeneous product 334
Homogenization 40, 204, 229, 239, 341
Host country 607
Host government 573

Import 262
Import substitution 31
Income distribution 313
Independent intermediaries 374
Industrial equipment 487
Industrial goods 87, 262
Industrial market 327, 341
Industrial marketing 87
Inequality 256
Inflation 255
Information 90
Information gap 342
Information retrieval 437
Information seekers 341
Infrastructure 208
Innovation 79
Integration 61
Intellectual property 215
Interaction approach 87, 329
Internal transactions 49

International alliances 63
International competitiveness 129
International environment 25
International marketing
  customer-oriented 13
  production-oriented 13
  theories 13-14
International transportation 398
Internationalization 76
Internationalization process 147
  characteristics 148
  determinants 154
  external stimuli 150
  implications 157
  internal stimuli 150
  stages 148-152, 285
Intracompany transfer 609

Joint venture 67-69, 76, 161, 179, 221, 393
  problems 181
  quality 184
  raw material 183

Labor intensity 59
Language barrier 361
LDC 214, 305–324, 605
  demand estimation 305
  environment 305, 307
  market 18
  marketing research 306
Leadership 19
Learning curve 391
Legal liabilities 533
Letter of award/intent 357
Licensing 415
Licensing agreement 419, 492
Life cycle 27
Lobbying 547

Macro survey 309
Management 20, 99, 261, 238, 576
Management system 588
Market
  access 288
  automobile 59, 472
  contracting 375
  entry 391, 564
  growth 201
  homogeneous 248

imperfection 263
intensity 201
Japan 393
niche 420
operation 584
penetration 592
potential 204, 288, 313
protection 417
segment 262, 334
segmentation 27, 43, 201, 341, 593
share 20, 334
structure 21, 23
Market research 283
approaches 292
desk research 290
hard data 297
Japanese way 297
process 286
soft data 297
source of information 283, 290
Marketing
approach 262
concept 406
decision making 297, 302
environment 229
information system 545
infrastructure 25
intelligence system 264
management 407
mix 21, 155, 459, 559
opportunities 247
philosophy 459
plan 286
process 264
Marketing research 13, 157
approach 306
developing country 306
Marketing strategy 16, 21, 204, 229,
    262, 408, 533, 566
Mass media 240
Material business 451
Merger 217
Method of analogy 308
Military strategy 598
MNC 58, 67, 246, 569, 605
Modular technology 463
Motivation 250, 390
Multinational corporation 39
Multiple factor indices 309

Negotiation 182, 191, 353
bargaining power 270

contract 270
decision maker 270
financing 271
implementation 354
informal meeting 354-355
offer 354
strategy 191
third world 270
Negotiator 182, 363
Networks 73
Nichemanship 27
Nondifferentiated products 376

Objective 19, 560
Open door 254
Open market 251
Opinion leader 344
Organization 93, 587
alliance 436
centralized 53
headquarters 587
matrix system 601
structure 18, 50, 51, 218
Outsourcing 174
Outward-oriented 34

Pacific rim 221
Packaging 499
Parallel importation 534
Partnerships 186
Patent 75, 189, 377
Performance audit 605
Planned economy 409
Planning 190
framework 558
process 558
Political imperative 590
Polycentrism 573
Portfolio 335, 576
Preference vector 413
Price escalation 507, 523
Price 25
cutting 541
differential 473, 533
discretion 473
strategies 461
Pricing 21, 188, 318, 349, 417
Pricing strategies 510, 534
dynamic incremental 513
flexible cost-plus 511
rigid cost-plus 510

Private property 251
Procurement 214, 269
Product 21, 90
 adaptation 593
 category 375
 country of origin 415
 design 471-472, 500
 development 593
 differentiation 376, 544, 596
 evaluation 475
 homogenization 334
 life cycle 330, 384, 432
 management 601
 mix 349
 portfolio 327
 positioning 327, 471-472, 592
 rationalization 495
 specialized 505
 standardized 22, 386, 496
 testing 528
Production facility 506
Production system 588
Profit potential 412
Promotion 22, 162, 240, 529, 540, 592
Provincialism 304
Proxy indicators 310
Public ownership 251
Public sector 359
Purchase decision 464
Purchasing 87, 100
Purchasing power 464

Quality 199, 594

R&D 46, 57, 161, 217
Railroad 14
Regiocentrism 573
Relationships 91
Representative
 exclusive 266
 non-exclusive 266
Resources 566
Responsibility system 252
Retail 242, 300
Retail audit 500
Retailer 263, 376
Risks 78

Sales force 169

Sales potential 275
Screening 132
Segmentation 236, 466
Seller's market 262, 406
Service 28, 376, 386
Service differentiation 544
Service export 397
Service trade 397
Silk Road 403
Small business 419
Social exchange 91
Social indicators 610
Sogo Shosha 108, 590
Specialty searcher 343
Standardization 214, 229, 239
 component 463, 496
 marketing process 460
 marketing program 460
Strategic alliance 431
 advantage 431
 concept 432
 formation 434
 guidelines 434
 limit 438
 partner 435
 termination 436
Strategic planning 22, 557, 509
Strategic resources 330
Strategy 341, 390
 global marketing 499
 market entry 267
 negotiation 358
 reactive 535
Subsidiary 67
Supermarket 244
Supplier 294, 327, 357
Supply interference 542
Synergy 27, 78

Target groups 467
 cross-cultural 468
 homogeneous 467
 trans-national 469
Targeted audience 528
Tariff 26, 32
Tax 608
Technological diffusion 63
Technological infrastructure 64
Technology 93
 supply 409
 transfer 79, 409-410, 415, 615
Telephone marketing 401

Third world   449
   characteristics   262
   market   261
Trade audit   294, 310
Trade balance   401
Trade fair   293, 527
Trade opportunities   403
Trademark   189, 532
Trading companies   52
   Japanese   587
Transaction   48, 75
Transaction cost   375
Transferability   258
Triad power   57, 61-64
Trust   81
Turnkey agreement   274

Turnkey contract   75

U.S. Department of Commerce   487
Unemployment   187, 256

Value structure   613
Value-added chain   45, 611
Variable cost   513
Vertical integration   74

Warranty   490
Wholesale   263, 300
World Bank   262

Appendix

New Techniques for Executive Development and Training in International Business/Marketing

International business is literally a world of excitement. These days there are also new and exciting tools for executive development and self-assessment. The Cavusgil computer program (CORE) discussed in Reading 8 permits an executive or entrepreneur to make a self-assessment of his/her company's readiness to engage in export. Other decision support tools for international marketers are being developed by an Expert Systems Development team at Michigan State University under the leadership of Professor Cavusgil. In addition, an export trading company computer tutorial under the name of GETI ONE was developed by B. Davis, M. Czinkota and P. Bastok at Georgetown University.

There are also a handful of international business/strategy exercises in the computerized management game form. The most well known is the International Operations Simulation (INTOP) developed by Hans B. Thorelli, Robert L. Graves, and Lloyd T. Howells at the University of Chicago some 25 years ago. Having been used in its original mainframe version by over 100 institutions (Hitachi, Ltd. alone has had literally thousands of executives go through the exercise over a period of 15 years), INTOP is now enjoying a new burst of popularity in its participant-oriented, easily administered new PC version.

By late 1992 a turn-of-the-century International Operations Simulation Mach 2000 (INTOPIA) should make its appearance. It is being designed by Dr. Hans B. Thorelli (E. W. Kelly, Professor of Business Administration, Indiana University), Dr. Robert L. Graves (Associate Provost-Computing, University of Chicago) and Professor Juan-Claudio Lopez (Universidad Catolica de Chile). Simulating two hi-tech industries, electronic components and personal computers, the simulation involves several different world areas. INTOPIA permits virtually any types of transaction *between* companies (sales, loans, licenses, hedging, intra-company transfers, joint ventures, etc.)—still a unique feature in the world of management games. This kind of networking and strategic alliances permit a realistic division of labor between companies, and present them with the major challenge of planning objectives and strategy. International vendor and consumer markets are appropriately differentiated, four different currencies originating in different capital markets, and different public policies and environmental developments all present the opportunities and constraints met by executives in multinational/global operations. In addition, INTOPIA has an extraordinary degree of flexibility and adaptability to the management development purposes at hand in any given situation. INTOPIA uses an IBM-compatible PC with at least 640K RAM and a fixed disk.

Two other international business simulations worthy of mention are:

William R. Hoskins, *The Multinational Business Game* (1987)

This model is also designed for PC operation. For further information contact the author at American Graduate School for International Management, Glendale, AZ 85306 U.S.A.

Alfred G. Edge, Bernard Keys and Wm. E. Remus, *The Multinational Management Game* (privately published)

For further information contact Dr. Bernard Keys, Georgia Southern College, Statesboro, GA 30460-8152 U.S.A.

We believe that INTOPIA represents the current frontier in the development of international business simulations. Further information about both INTOP and INTOPIA may be obtained by contacting Dr. Hans B. Thorelli, School of Business, Indiana University, Bloomington, IN 47405 U.S.A.

Although these two simulations have marked differences, their administration is sufficiently similar for INTOP to provide an ideal training ground for administrators hesitant about making the time commitment required to make full use of the capabilities of INTOPIA.

About the Editors

HANS B. THORELLI is the E. W. Kelley Professor of Business Administration of Indiana University. He has published over sixty articles in professional journals. The books he authored or co-authored include *Strategy + Structure = Performance: The Strategic Planning Imperative*, *Consumer Emancipation and Economic Development: The Case of Thailand*, *Consumer Information System and Consumer Policy*, *The Information Seekers*, *Consumer Information Handbook: Europe and North America*, *International Operations Simulation*, and *The Federal Antitrust Policy*. His current research efforts are concentrated in the area of strategic planning and structure-strategy-performance relationships.

Dr. Thorelli has been a member of the Consumer Advisory Council for the President of the U.S., and of the National Advisory Council of the U.S. Small Business Administration. He is a former Vice-President—Public Policy of the American Marketing Association and a consultant to major U.S. and European multinational corporations and the Swedish government. He holds a Ph.D. and a LL.B. degree from the University of Stockholm.

S. TAMER CAVUSGIL is Professor of Marketing and International Business at Michigan State University where he also serves as the Director of the Michigan International Business Development Center. He is the author or co-author of several books in marketing and international business, and over seventy articles that have appeared in such journals as *Journal of Marketing Research*, *Journal of the Market Research Society*, *Business Horizons*, *European Journal of Marketing*, *European Research*, and *Journal of Business Research*. Currently, Cavusgil is the Editor of *International Marketing Review*, a professional journal with worldwide readership of practitioners and scholars in international marketing, and the Editor of the JAI Press Annual, *Advances in International Marketing*.

Dr. Cavusgil's eductional background includes MBA and Ph.D. degrees in business from the University of Wisconsin. Previously, he taught at Bradley University, the University of Wisconsin-

Whitewater, and the Middle East Technical University in Turkey. Cavusgil's research on the export marketing behavior of firms is widely recognized and his microcomputer software, CORE (COmpany Readiness to Export) is adopted by many firms in designing their export strategies. He frequently advises business, public sector agencies and developing country governments.